CHRONOLOGY
OF THE GREAT

CHRONOLOGY
OF THE GREAT WAR, 1914–1918

Edited by Lord Edward Gleichen

Greenhill Books, London
Stackpole Books, Pennsylvania

This edition of *Chronology of the Great War, 1914–1918*
first published 2000 by Greenhill Books, Lionel Leventhal Limited, Park House,
1 Russell Gardens, London NW11 9NN
and
Stackpole Books, 5067 Ritter Road, Mechanicsburg, PA 17055, USA

This edition © Lionel Leventhal Limited, 2000

British Library Cataloguing in Publication Data
Chronology of the Great War, 1914–1918. – (Greenhill military paperback)
1. World War, 1914–1918 – Chronology 2. World War, 1914–1918 – Campaigns
I. Gleichen, Edward Gleichen, Lord, 1863–1937
940.4

ISBN 1-85367-428-1

Library of Congress Cataloging-in-Publication Data available

Publishing History

Chronology of the Great War was originally published as *Chronology of the War* and was issued in three volumes: *Volume I, 1914–1915* was published in 1918; *Volume II, 1916–1917* was published in 1919; and *Volume III, 1918–1919* appeared in 1920 (all Constable, London). In 1988 the three volumes were brought together and published by Greenhill Books, retaining, however, the original pagination. Now the first Greenhill edition is reproduced, complete and unabridged, in paperback.

Printed and bound in Great Britain

TABLE OF CONTENTS

PART III

PREFACE

This *Chronology* is divided into three parts in order to present it as it was originally published under the auspices of the Ministry of Information. Compilation of the *Chronology* was supervised by Major-General Lord Gleichen, K.C.V.O., C.B., C.M.G., D.S.O., Director of the Intelligence Bureau 1917–18, who was the work's original editor-in-chief.

The three parts of the volume are:

> Part I   1914–15
>
> Part II   1916–17
>
> Part III   1918–19

In each part the material is presented thus:

(I)   **Tables** of contemporaneous events (preceded in the first part by a short chapter on events anterior to the outbreak of war), followed by a short résumé of the year's events.

(II)   **Appendices** explaining and enlarging on certain important events.

(III)   A voluminous **Index**, which also gives a record of a good many minor events which are not found in the Tables, and short abstracts of events in different theatres.

The work's main basis was *The Times* newspaper, corrected, checked and amplified by various histories and records, the chief ones of which were:

Nelson's *History of the War* by John Buchan.
The Times's History of the War.
Blue Books, White (Germany), Yellow (France), Orange (Russia), Grey (Belgium) and Red (Austria-Hungary) Books and Papers.
Various diaries of the war in different periodicals, notably in *Whitaker's Almanack*, the *Journal of the Royal United Service Institution*, the *Fortnightly Review* and, since 1917, *The New Europe*.
The Annual Register.
Chronologie de la Guerre (Berger-Levrault, Paris).
Tablettes Chronologiques (Larousse).
Kriegsdepeschen (official, Boll u. Pickardt, Berlin).
Kriegschronik (Münchner Neueste Nachrichten).
Chronik des deutschen Krieges (Beck, Munich).
Various newspapers and official records, English and foreign, besides other works.
(For the pre-Great War part, acknowledgment is also due to Mr. J. W. Headlam and his book *The History of Twelve Days*, and to Mr. W. Archer's *The Thirteen Days*.)

1988

NOTES

The *Chronology* has been compiled with the greatest care from the most reliable authorities – English, French and German – and where these give different dates for the same event every effort has been made to arrive at the right one. At the same time, it cannot be denied that where equally good authorities (even official ones in some cases) differ, it is more than possible that some errors may have crept in.

The Editors do not, however, wish to overburden the text by giving the various authorities for conflicting dates; they must therefore content themselves with appealing to their readers to assist them in discovering any errors, fixing the correct dates, and notifying them for correction in a subsequent issue.

Major-General Lord Gleichen's best thanks are due to Professor F. J. C. Hearnshaw (of King's College, London University) for his valuable assistance in the early stages as well as for compiling the Tables and Index and the Pre-War portion (up to July 21) of the 1914 part; also to the twelve or more ladies and gentlemen who acted as compilers, and particularly to the Assistant-Editor, Mr. L. C. Jane (of the War Trade Intelligence Department). Mr. J. W. Headlam-Morley and Mr. H. C. O'Neill (of the Department of Information) also assisted with advice in the early stages.

The date of an event should first be looked out in the Index; additional information is sometimes given in the Tables or Appendices.

In the Pre-War and Tabular Parts, Sundays are marked by the day of the month being in heavy type, thus: Oct. **24**. The more important events are also given in heavy type.

The figures in brackets in the Tabular part refer to the Appendices.

Spelling of Place-names: This very thorny subject has been settled by using the 1:1,000,000 Map (Royal Geographical Society and General Staff) as the main authority, whilst spelling the better-known places in the ordinary English way.

Columns:

"Western Front"	Comprises the Franco-German-Belgian front and any military action in Great Britain, Switzerland, Scandinavia and Holland.
"Eastern Front"	Comprises the German-Russian, Austro-Russian and Austro-Rumanian fronts.
"Southern Front"	Comprises the Austro-Italian and Balkan (including Bulgaro-Rumanian) fronts, and Dardanelles.
"Asiatic and Egyptian Theatres"	Comprises Egypt, Tripoli, the Sudan, Asia Minor (including Transcaucasia), Arabia, Mesopotamia, Syria, Persia, Afghanistan, Turkestan, China, India, etc.

| "Naval and Overseas Operations" | Comprises operations on the seas* and in Colonial and Overseas theatres, America, etc. |
| "Political, etc." | Comprises political and internal events in all countries, including Notes, speeches, diplomatic, financial, economic and domestic matters. (These include mobilisations, declarations of war and similar semi-military matters. Diplomatic documents or despatches referring to definite active operations come under the column concerned, e.g., a Note on the sinking of the "Lusitania" would come under "Naval", but a Note on submarine warfare in general would come under "Political"). |

On all the fronts, unfamiliar localities are generally defined by the name of some well-known district or place being given in brackets alongside; but when this is difficult on the Eastern or Western Front, the letters N., C. or S. (Northern, Centre or Southern) are given. On the Western Front the "Centre" includes all ground between lines running East and West through Compiègne and through Nancy (inclusive), and on the Eastern Front through Grodno and through Kolomea (inclusive).

1920

---

* Except where carried out in combination with troops on land; in this case the event comes under the Front concerned. (E.g., a combined bombardment of the Belgian coast from sea and land would fall under "Western Front".)

INTRODUCTION

The value of a detailed chronology to the student of history cannot be underestimated. This is particularly true when one is studying the First World War because of the complexity and extent of the events that occurred during a relatively short period of time. Researchers seeking guidance about the availability of a good chronology devoted to the First World War could consult A. G. Enser's *A Subject Bibliography of the First World War: Books in English 1914–1978* (London: Deutsch, 1979) and be referred to only two works, both produced "under official auspices". The first, compiled by the Committee of Imperial Defence, was entitled simply *Principal Events 1914–1918* and was issued back in 1922 by Her Majesty's Stationery Office. The second, compiled by the Ministry of Information originally entitled *Chronology of the War*, was published commercially by Constable between 1918 and 1920 in three parts and supplemented by a separate map volume. There were, of course, other contemporary chronological records produced including, most notably, *The Times Diary* and *Index of the War* (London: Hodder and Stoughton, 1921). However, it remains unfortunately true that no new chronology devoted specifically to the Great War has appeared over the last sixty years. Now that the First World War has become an essential element of any modern history course, be it at G.C.S.E. or University level, the reprinting of the Ministry of Information's *Chronology* is most timely.

This work is particularly useful since it not only contains detailed annual indexes but also a valuable commentary on the major events listed. The editorial team, led by Lord Gleichen, clearly sought to do justice to all theatres of operations and did not concentrate purely on the Western Front. By consulting German language sources, they also attempted to avoid too excessive a British bias in their presentation of events. As a reference librarian, I welcome its re-appearance in print.

Gwyn Bayliss
1988

ABBREVIATIONS

Have sometimes been made use of in order to save space, e.g.:—

Brit.	for	British.	Jul.	for	Julian Front.
Fr.	„	French.	Carn.	„	Carnic Alps.
Germ.	„	German, s.	Maced.	„	Macedonia.
Russ.	„	Russian, s.	Armen.	„	Armenia.
Austr.	„	Austrian, s.	Arg.	„	Argonne.
Gal.	„	Galicia.		etc.	etc.
Gall.	„	Gallipoli.	cr.	„	cruiser.
Eg.	„	Egypt.	subm.	„	submarine.
Transc.	„	Transcaucasia	T.B.D.	„	destroyer.
As. Mr.	„	Asia Minor.	cav.	„	cavalry.
Trent.	„	Trentino.		etc.	etc.

PART I
1914–1915

CORRIGENDA

EVENTS PRECEDING THE BRITISH DECLARATION OF WAR.

JUNE 23rd to AUGUST 4th (inclusive), 1914.

(Figures in brackets refer to Appendices.)

1914.
June

23-25 Kiel Canal reopened (owing to its having been deepened) by the Kaiser: Visit of the British Fleet under Sir G. Warrender : Kaiser inspects the Dreadnought H.M.S. " King George V."

28 Assassination at Serajevo of the Archduke Franz Ferdinand and his wife the Duchess of Hohenberg ([1]).

29 Austria-Hungary.—Secretary of the Legation at Belgrade sends despatch to Vienna suggesting Serbian complicity in the crime of Serajevo.

,, Anti-Serb riots in Serajevo and throughout Bosnia generally.

30 Great Britain.—Addresses in Parliament on the murdered Archduke: Lords Crewe and Lansdowne in House of Lords ; Messrs. Asquith and Law in Commons.

July

2 Announcement that the Kaiser will not attend the Archduke's funeral.

4 Austria-Hungary.—Funeral of the Archduke at Artstetten (50 m. W. of Vienna).

5 Council at Potsdam.

6 Kaiser leaves Kiel for a cruise in Northern waters.

7 Austria-Hungary.—Council of Ministers, including Ministers for Foreign Affairs and War, Chief of General Staff and Naval Commander-in-Chief : Council lasts from 11.30 a.m. to 6.15 p.m.

8 Count Tisza makes grave statement in Hungarian Chamber concerning the murder of the Archduke.

9 Austria-Hungary.—Emperor receives report of Austro-Hungarian investigation into the Serajevo crime.

,, The *Times* publishes account of Austro-Hungarian press campaign against the Serbians (who are described as " pestilent rats ").

,, **Scheme for Provisional Government in Ireland ([2]).**

10 M. Hartwig, Russian Minister to Serbia, dies suddenly at Austrian Legation in Belgrade.

12 Demonstrations in Ulster suggesting Civil War.

13 Reports of a projected Serbian attack upon the Austro-Hungarian Legation at Belgrade.

,, Grave article in *Times* on " Failure of Recruiting."

,, France.—Revelations in Senate (continued on Tuesday, 14th) of deficiencies in French military equipment ([3]).

,, Heavy selling of Canadian Pacific Railway shares in Berlin (continued to Thursday, 16th).

14 Government of Ireland Amending Bill passed by House of Lords.

1914.
July

15 **Count Tisza** makes statement in Hungarian Chamber concerning relations with Serbia : they " must be cleared up " (⁴).

17 **Austria-Hungary.**—Report that Serbia has called up 70,000 reservists and is preparing for war.

„ President Poincaré leaves Paris on a visit to the Tsar.

18-20 British Fleet at Spithead : reviewed by the King (⁵).

19 **Austria-Hungary.**—Press scare concerning alleged " Greater Serbia " conspiracy.

„ The King summons a **Conference to discuss the Home Rule Problem.**

20 President Poincaré reaches Kronstadt and is welcomed by the Tsar. Commencement of the trial of Madame Caillaux for the murder of M. Calmette on March 16 (⁶).

„ **Austria-Hungary.**—Preparations on Serbian frontier.

21 **Austria-Hungary.**—Conferences held at Ischl and Budapest concerning Serbia.

„ **Germany.**—French Ambassador informs Paris of first steps towards German mobilisation.

„ **Russia.**—Beginning of great Revolutionary Strike.

23 **Presentation of Austrian Ultimatum to Serbia** at Belgrade at 6 p.m., demanding answer within 48 hours (⁷). Publication in Vienna shortly afterwards. Bethmann-Hollweg writes circular to German Ambassadors saying " action and demands of Austria-Hungary fully justified." [Moment of presentation well-chosen : following absent from their posts : Serbian Prime Minister (Pashich), Kaiser (Norway), Franz Josef (Ischl), Poincaré and Viviani (Russia), Shebeko (Russian Ambassador in Vienna), Goschen (British Ambassador in Berlin]. German officers' leave stopped.

24 Serbia appeals to Tsar. Russian Cabinet Council meets. Sir E. Grey says :— " . . . never before seen one State address to another independent State a document of so formidable a character." He at once proposes four-Power (Great Britain, Germany, France, Italy) mediation.

„ Revolutionary movements in St. Petersburg.

„ Failure of Home Rule Conference announced : Irish deadlock.

25 Austria refuses Russian request for extension of time-limit.

„ Germany thinks crisis could be localised, but inclined to fall in with idea of mediation.

„ **Serbia orders mobilisation ;** order signed by Crown Prince at 3 p.m.

„ Russia conciliatory, but arranges for mobilisation of 13 corps on Russo-Austrian frontier if latter brings armed pressure to bear on Serbia.

„ **Serbian Government** leaves for Nish. **Hands in most conciliatory** and almost humiliating **answer** 5.58 p.m.(⁸). **Austrian Minister at Belgrade leaves** for Vienna at 6.30 p.m. Serbian General Putnik (Chief of Staff) arrested near Buda-Pest.

26 Germany thinks Russia will not fight, but threatens mobilisation, i.e., war, if Russia does not stop her preparations, and asks Entente States to keep Russia quiet. Kaiser and German Fleet return from Norway.

„ **Austria begins to mobilise** 8 corps on Russian frontier.

„ Sir E. Grey suggests Conference of Ambassadors in London.

„ Russia declares she will mobilise on Austrian frontier if Austria crosses Serbian frontier. General Putnik released with apologies.

„ **Montenegro orders mobilisation.**

„ Gun-running riot in Dublin : apparent approach of civil war (⁹).

27 Tsar wires to Belgrade that Russia cannot be indifferent to fate of Serbia : Russia still conciliatory : proposes to Vienna conversations *re* Serbia.

1914
July

27 Germany says she knows nothing of proposed Conference, but has taken mediatory steps. (No record of these.)

,, **Dispersal of British Fleet countermanded** at instance of Admiral Prince Louis of Battenberg. Statement by Sir E. Grey in House of Commons ([10]). Austria says proposals of mediation or Conference too late.

28 **Austria** issues manifesto and **declares war on Serbia** at noon : refuses proposals of mediation or Conference : has no quarrel with Russia.

,, Russia says mobilisation of Southern Corps will be announced to-morrow, but she has no aggressive intentions against Germany.

,, Russian Ambassador at Vienna wires to M. Sazonov that **Austrian general mobilisation order** has been signed.

,, Kaiser wires to Tsar he will use his influence with Austria.

,, Germany conciliatory, but throws responsibility of possible war on Russia.

,, End of Caillaux trial : Madame Caillaux acquitted.

29 Russia says as Austria will not consent to interchange of views, Gt. Britain must take initiative ; but she cannot let Austria get ahead of her, and has decided therefore to mobilise Southern Corps on Austrian frontier.

,, Russia officially informed by Germany (but not as a threat) that partial (Russian) mobilisation must be followed by war with Germany. **Russia** therefore **decides on general mobilisation.** (See Appendix ([11]) on " Sukhomlinov Revelations.")

,, Gt. Britain presses Germany again *re* mediation, but warns her that she (Gt. Britain) could not stand aside in all circumstances.

,, Council at Potsdam.

,, Germany makes out that she may not be able to prevent Austria going too far ; makes " infamous offer " that if Gt. Britain would remain neutral Germany would annex no French territory ([12]).

,, **Austrians bombard Belgrade** in afternoon.

,, Unsuccessful Austrian attempt to cross Danube between Belgrade and Gradishte (the first of 18 vain efforts prior to August 12).

,, MM. Poincaré and Viviani reach Paris.

,, German patrols cross French frontier. Extensive German and Austrian preparations.

,, Tsar tries to stop general Russian mobilisation 11 p.m.

30 Russia proposes to Germany at 2 a.m. to stop mobilising if Austria would eliminate clauses in ultimatum damaging Serbian sovereignty. Last chance of peace.

,, *Lokal Anzeiger* **announces German mobilisation.** Contradicted officially after time allowed for Russian Ambassador to wire it to St. Petersburg. Germany wires temporisingly to Vienna, but does not forward Russia's " last chance " proposal.

,, Russia learns of general Austrian mobilisation.

,, Prince Henry of Prussia wires to King George asking him to secure neutrality of France and Russia. The King says he is trying to persuade them to cease preparations, if Austria will not go beyond Belgrade. Hopes Kaiser will influence Austria.

,, Austria a little nervous, but refuses to alter the Note.

,, **Russia decides** definitely **on general mobilisation.**

,, German troops close to French frontier : French troops kept 10 km. behind it.

,, Sir E. Grey repudiates Bethmann-Hollweg's " infamous proposal " with scorn, but holds out olive-branch. No notice taken by Germany.

,, Mr. Asquith's speech in House of Commons ([13]).

31 **Russia** still complaisant, but as Austria is not responsive she **announces her general mobilisation.**

1914.

July

31 **Austria also announces general mobilisation.**

" **Germany declares Kriegsgefahrzustand***, and tells Russia (definite threat not delivered till midnight) that she proposes to mobilise unless Russia stops all military measures within 12 hours ([14]). She also informs France of her intention towards Russia, and **demands to know within 18 hours whether France will remain neutral** ([15]). (In that case she would have demanded the temporary cession of Toul and Verdun. M. Viviani, however, merely replied that France would act according to her interests.)

" France notifies her Ambassadors that Germany, whilst protesting peaceful intentions, has throughout by her dilatory or negative attitude caused all attempts at agreement to fail.

" Sir E. Grey goes to the furthest possible limit in endeavouring to persuade Germany to assist him in squaring matters between Austria and Serbia. Asks France and Germany whether they intend to respect Belgian neutrality; France says, " Certainly," Germany refuses to reply. British Cabinet not yet prepared to give France definite pledge of assistance.

" Financial crisis in London. Stock Exchange closed.

" **Belgian mobilisation decreed** for following day.

" M. Jaurès (Socialist leader) assassinated in Paris.

" **Mobilisation commenced in Turkey.**

August.

1 King George wires to Tsar that Germany recommended British proposals to Austria on 30th, but that Russian mobilisation was reported during Austrian cabinet meeting.

" Russia does not reply to German ultimatum expiring at noon.

" **French mobilisation ordered 3.40 p.m.**

" **Germany, having ostensibly ordered general mobilisation 5 p.m., declares war on Russia** 7.10 p.m.; makes out that Russians had crossed frontier in afternoon and begun war. (Declaration drafted before noon.)

" Tsar wires to King that he had to mobilise on account of Serbia; but that though he had promised Kaiser he would not move troops during negotiations, Germany had suddenly declared war.

" Austria at last moment appears accommodating to England.

" Italy declines to take part in war, as being an aggressive one.

" Sir E. Grey protests against detention of British ships in Hamburg.

" Belgium announces her intention of upholding her neutrality ([16]).

2 **German troops invade Luxemburg** very early. **France entered at four points** ([17]) Patrols kill French soldiers 10 km. over frontier near Belfort.

" **Poland invaded by Germans,** who occupy Kalish, Chenstokhov and Bendzin.

" **East Prussia entered by Russian raiders** near Schwidden.

" Libau bombarded by German light cruiser "Augsburg."

" **German Note to Belgium,** 7 p.m., alleging that Germany must violate her soil in order to "anticipate" the French attack in Belgium; demands that latter should remain passive; answer required in 12 hours.

" England assures France that British fleet will stop German fleet if latter attacks French shipping in Channel.

" **Moratorium proclaimed in England** ([18]).

3 **Belgian answer** to German Note, refusing demands, 7 a.m. King of Belgians appeals to King George for diplomatic intervention to safeguard Belgian integrity.

---

* *i.e.* Imminent-danger-of-war situation.

1914.
August

3 Lunéville bombed by German airmen.

,, Skirmish between outposts near Libau.

,, Grand Duke Nicholas proclaimed Generalissimo of Russian forces.

,, German reports—proved untrue—as to French officers in Belgium and French aviators over Karlsruhe, Nürnberg, etc.

,, **Germany declares war on France.**

,, **Order for British Mobilisation.**

.. Sir E. Grey speaks in House of Commons ([19]).

4 **Gt. Britain protests in Berlin** against German violation of Belgian treaty. Germany says French meant to invade Belgian territory, and she must take measures of defence. Violates Belgium at Gemmenich, early morning ; burns Visé and attacks Liége. **Germany declares war on Belgium.**

,, Bona and Philippeville (Algeria) bombarded by German cruisers " Goeben " and " Breslau."

,, Trieux, near Briey (France), taken by Germans. Speech by M. Viviani.

,, Chancellor's speech in Reichstag, acknowledging they are doing wrong ([20]).

,, Sir E. Grey wires to Sir E. Goschen telling him that unless satisfactory German assurances *re* Belgian neutrality are forthcoming, he is to ask for his passports.

,, **British mobilisation orders issued.**

,, Sir John Jellicoe takes command of British Fleet.

,, Sir E. Goschen's interview (" scrap of paper ") with Chancellor in evening ([21]) : **British ultimatum ([22]) and state of war at 11 p.m.**

1914. Aug.	WESTERN FRONT.	EASTERN FRONT.	SOUTHERN FRONT.
5	Liége: Fort Fléron silenced.	.. .. ..	.. ..
6	Liége: Forts Barchon, Chaudefontaine and Evêquée silenced. Longwy invested by the Germans.	.. .. ..	Obrenovats (Serbia) vainly attacked by Austrians, who lose guns in the retreat.
7	Liége: German infantry penetrate the city. Alsace invaded by the French. B.E.F. begins to land in France.	E. Prussia: First Russian Army, under Rennenkampf, crosses the frontier in force [26].	Bosnia entered by the Serbians.
8	Belgium: Main army falls back towards the Dyle. Alsace: French occupy Altkirch and Mülhausen.	.. ..	.. .. ..
9	Belgium: French cavalry in Belgium.	E. Prussia: Russian First Army advancing.	.. ..
10	Liége: the Germans occupy the city. Alsace: French fall back; Mülhausen evacuated. Lorraine: French advance in force under Gen. de Castelnau.	E. Prussia: Russians reach Tilsit. Poland: Austrian First Army, under Dankl, enters Poland and advances towards Lyublin and Kyeltsi.	.. .. ..
11	Belgium: battles near Tirlemont, St. Trond, and Diest. Lorraine: German counter offensive from Metz; vain attacks at Spincourt and Blamont.	.. .. ..	.. ..
12	Belgium: Germans seize Huy (Meuse), but are checked at Haelen and Dinant.	.. .. ..	Bosnia: Serbians and Montenegrins vainly attack Vishegrad.
13	Belgium: German check at Eghezee; Neufchâteau occupied by Crown Prince. France: Germans seize La Garde.	.. .. ..	First Austrian invasion of Serbia begun: Austrians force passage of the R. Drina.

Asiatic and Egyptian Theatres.	Naval and Overseas Operations.	Political, &c.	1914. Aug.
.. .. ..	" Königin Luise," German mine-layer, destroyed. " Goeben " and " Breslau " reach Messina ([23]).	**Austria-Hungary declares war on Russia. Great Britain mobilises ;** Lord Kitchener made War Secretary.	5
.. .. ..	H. M. S. " Amphion," British cruiser, sunk by German mine in North Sea. " Goeben " and " Breslau " escape.	Great Britain : Mr. Asquith speaks in Commons on the War ; Parliament votes £100,000,000 ([24]).	6
.. ..		Germany : Kaiser issues proclamation to his people ([25]). Great Britain : Prince of Wales inaugurates National Relief Fund	7
.. .. ..	Antivari (Montenegro) bombarded by Austrian fleet. Togoland entered by combined French and British force.	Russia : Tsar addresses the Duma. Switzerland mobilises and proclaims state of siege. U.S.A. offers its good services.	8
.. .. ..	H.M.S. " Birmingham," cruiser, sinks German submarine U15.	Germany, by means of Holland, offers terms of peace to Belgium ; they are rejected.	9
.. .. ..	S. Africa : Germans raid Cape Colony (from S.W. Africa), but abandon Swakopmund and Lüderitz Bay.	**France declares war on Austria-Hungary.**	10
.. .. ..	" Goeben " and " Breslau " enter Dardanelles.	Great Britain : The Press Bureau constituted.	11
.. ..		**Great Britain declares war on Austria - Hungary.** Turkey : Reported purchase of " Goeben " and " Breslau."	12
.. .. ..	E. Africa : British naval forces bombard and raid Dar-es-Salaam.	.. .. ..	13

1914. Aug.	WESTERN FRONT.	EASTERN FRONT.	SOUTHERN FRONT.
14	Belgium : French at Charleroi ; French push back Germans in N. Alsace and bomb German airsheds at Metz. Sir John French lands at Boulogne.	Galicia : Russians defeat Austrians at Sokal.	Serbia : Austrians driv Serbians back and oc cupy Loznitsa.
15	Belgium : Reduction of forts at Liége completed ; Germans checked at Dinant by the French. Alsace-Lorraine : Passes of the Vosges in French hands.	.. ..	.. .
16	Belgium : Indecisive action at Wavre. B.E.F. first contingent completes its landing. French successful in N. Alsace (Schirmeck, etc.).	East Prussia : General advance of Russian armies.	Austrians capture Sha batz (N.W. Serbia), bu Serbians check Austria advance between Loz nitsa and Shabats.
17	Alsace : Renewed French advance, take Marsal and Château-Salins. Sir John French takes up his headquarters at Le Cateau.	East Prussia : Russians defeat Germans at Stallupönen : Germans fall back on Gumbinnen.	**Battle of the Jadar** (be tween Shabats and Loz nitsa) continued.
18	Belgium : Germans occupy Tirlemont. Lorraine : French advance and cut line between Metz and Strasburg at Saarburg.	**Galicia: Russian invasion** from the East under Brusilov and Russki **begun** ([20]).	Austrians defeated a Shabats.
19	Belgium : Germans reach Dinant - Neufchâteau line and occupy Louvain ; Belgians, defeated at Aerschot, fall back towards Antwerp. Alsace : French re-enter Mülhausen and push on in Lorraine.	Poland : Austrians' advance checked near Kyeltsi.	End of Battle of the Jadar defeat of Austrians.
20	**Brussels evacuated** by Belgians and **occupied by Germans.** Namur bombarded. Lorraine : Powerful German counterattack near Saarburg and Morhange drives French back. British concentration Avesnes-Le Cateau completed.	East Prussia : **Battle of Gumbinnen.** Russian victory followed by occupation of the town, Goldap and Lyck.	Serbia : Disorderly flight of Austrians towards the frontier.

ASIATIC AND EGYPTIAN THEATRES.	NAVAL AND OVERSEAS OPERATIONS.	POLITICAL, &c.	1914. Aug.
.. ..	.. .. ..	**Russia** : Proclamation **promising** reconstruction and **autonomy of the** " **Kingdom of Poland.**"	14
.. .. ..	S. Africa : Meeting of disaffected Boers : Address by General Delarey ([27]).	**Japan** : **Ultimatum to Germany** demanding evacuation of Tsing-tau (Kiao-Chau) ([28]).	15
.. .. ..	Franco-British squadron enters the Adriatic.	.. .. ..	16
.. ..	Adriatic : Austrian cruiser sunk near Antivari.	Belgium : Government transferred from Brussels to Antwerp. Great Britain : Enrolment of Special Constables begins.	17
.. .. ..	.. .. ..	.. .. ..	18
.. ..	.. .. ..	Kaiser's alleged order for the destruction of " General French's contemptible little army " ([30]).	19
.. ..	E. Africa : Taveta occupied by the Germans : Uganda Railway attacked.	Rome : **Death of Pope Pius X.**	20

1914. Aug.	WESTERN FRONT.	EASTERN FRONT.	SOUTHERN FRONT.
21	Belgians forced to abandon their trenches at Namur. **Battle of Charleroi**, between Mons and the Meuse, between French and Germans begins. British move towards Mons.	East Prussia : Advance of Second Army under Samsonov ; occupation (Aug. 21-23) of Allenstein, Neidenburg, Soldau, Johannisburg, etc.	.. .. .
22	Belgium : Evacuation of Namur begun ; French defeated at Charleroi. Alsace-Lorraine : French defeat, Lunéville lost ; General withdrawal,	Poland : Russians evacuate Kyeltsi.	Shabats and Loznitza recovered by Serbians ; Austrians defeated on Drina.
23	**Namur falls. Battle of Mons** begins([81]): general German attack on the French from Charleroi to Dinant. French begin to fall back from Sambre and Meuse ; also in N. Alsace.	East Prussia : Germans evacuate Insterburg ; at the **Battle of Frankenau,** Germans driven back. Galicia : Russians take Brody and Tarnopol.	.. .. ..
24	**General Retreat from the Line of the Sambre and the Meuse ;** British fall back from Mons ; Germans massacre civilians at Dinant and occupy Tournai, but driven from Malines ; French offensive N. of Nancy.	Russians advancing in E. Prussia. Austrians advance in Poland beyond Kyeltsi.	.. .. ..
25	Retreat from Mons ; rearguard action at Landrecies ; Line of Le Cateau-Esnes occupied. Germans take Sedan ; Maubeuge invested ; Mülhausen again evacuated by the French. Last Namur fort silenced.	Poland : Austrian First Army defeats Russians at Krasnik and advances towards Lyublin.	Serbia : End of First Austrian invasion ; complete defeat of the Austrians with heavy losses.
26	**Battle of Le Cateau** ([33]) : British forced to retreat : Louvain destroyed by the Germans. End of French attempt to recover Alsace-Lorraine : French fall back in St. Dié region.	East Prussia : Soldau retaken by the Germans : Samsonov's communications cut : beginning of the Russian débâcle known as **Battle of Tannenberg** (25 m. S.W. of Allenstein). Galicia : Beginning of operations against Lemberg.	Novi Bazar evacuated by the Austrians.

ASIATIC AND EGYPTIAN THEATRES.	NAVAL AND OVERSEAS OPERATIONS.	POLITICAL, &c.	1914. Aug.
.. .. ..	South Africa invaded by German troops.	.. .. ..	21
.. .. ..	.. .. ..	Brussels : Germans levy £8,000,000.	22
Tsing-tau blockaded and bombarded by the Japanese.	.. .. ..	**Japan declares war on Germany.** Germany : Hindenburg receives command in East Prussia.	23
.. .. ..	Cattaro, Austrian Adriatic port, bombarded by Franco-British fleet.	.. .. ..	24
.. .. ..	Cameroons : Tepe occupied by the Allies.	**Austria-Hungary declares war on Japan.** Lord Kitchener's first speech as Secretary of State for War ([32]).	25
.. .. ..	**Togoland conquered** by the Allies : town of Atakpame occupied.	.. .. ..	26

B

1914. Aug.	Western Front.	Eastern Front.	Southern Front.
27	British fall back from St. Quentin. **Lille and Mézières occupied by the Germans.** Namur: Last of the forts reduced. Ostend occupied by mixed British force (Marines, etc.).	Galicia: Russians capture Halicz and Tarnopol.	.. ..
28	Germans capture Fort Manonviller (Avricourt). British on line Noyon-Chauny-La Fère: British cavalry successful near latter. **Fall of Longwy.**	Russians beat Austrians at Lützow (Gal.). E. Prussia: Russians approach Königsberg in the North: but in the south the Battle of Tannenberg continues against them.	.. ..
29	Stiff French rearguard fights. British retire to line Compiègne-Soissons. Germans occupy La Fère, Rethel, Amiens, etc.	E. Prussia: Battle of Tannenberg ends in the rout of Samsonov's Second Army.	.. ..
30	Laon occupied by the Germans. Paris bombed for the first time by German airmen.	East Prussia: Rout of Samsonov's army continues: Germans capture many prisoners.	Serbia: **Austrians recover from repulse of first invasion and prepare for second.**
31	Germans reach Givet. French Army holds the line Aisne-La Vesle-Reims-Verdun. **Battle of the Grande Couronne of Nancy (31st-11th Sept.).**	E. Prussia: Samsonov taken prisoner during Russian rout: Rennenkampf forced to begin a retreat to the frontier. Galicia: Austrian line broken near Halicz.	.. ..
Sept. 1	Action at Villers-Cotterets: 4th (Guards) Brigade checks German advance. Soissons bombarded and occupied by Germans.	E. Prussia: General Russian withdrawal towards the Bug. Galicia: **Battle of Lemberg** goes against the Austrians.	.. ..
2	British forces withdraw to Chantilly-Nanteuil. Malines bombarded by the Germans.	Galicia: Battle of Lemberg ends: rout of Austrians, who lose 130,000 men. Poland: Austrian advance checked at Lyublin.	.. ..
3	Germans reach and begin to cross the Marne: they occupy line Ville sur Tourbe - River Suippe - Château Thierry. Germans evacuate Lille.	**Lemberg,** capital of Galicia, **occupied by the Russians,** who capture much booty.	.. ..

Asiatic and Egyptian Theatres.	Naval and Overseas Operations.	Political, &c.	1914. Aug.
.. .. ..	" Kaiser Wilhelm der Grosse" sunk by H.M.S. "Highflyer." " Magdeburg," German cruiser, destroyed in Gulf of Finland.	France : M. Viviani's Ministry reconstructed : entry of MM. Millerand (War) and Delcassé (Foreign Affairs).	27
.. .. ..	Battle of Bight of Heligoland : the German cruisers " Mainz," " Köln," and "Ariadne" sunk ([34]).	.. .. ..	28
.. .. ..	Cameroons : British reverse at Garua. Samoa : German portion occupied by New Zealand troops.	.. .. ..	29
.. .. ..	Cameroons : British occupy Nsanakong.	.. .. ..	30
.. .. ..	.. .. ..	.. ..	31
			Sept.
.. .. ..	.. .. ..	Russia : St. Petersburg renamed " Petrograd."	1
Tsing-tau : J a p a n e s e troops landed for the attack on the fortress.	.. .. ..	France : The Government leaves Paris for Bordeaux.	2
.. ..	H.M.S. " Speedy " destroyed by a mine.	Rome : Election of Pope Benedict XV. Albania : Prince Wilhelm of Wied leaves.	3

1914 Sept.	WESTERN FRONT.	EASTERN FRONT.	SOUTHERN FRONT.
4	Advance of German First Army towards Paris diverted in a south-easterly direction. Belgians open dykes and stop a German advance on Antwerp.	Galicia : The Russians organise a government for the conquered regions.	.. .. ..
5	Retirement of British and French forces ceases. **Battle of the Ourcq** (Maunoury's 6th Army) **begins at mid-day.** Reims and Pont-à-Mousson occupied by the Germans.	Poland : Austrians defeated by Russians at Tomashov.	.. .. ..
6	**Battle of the Marne begins** ([37]). General offensive by French and British. German advance also checked at Beauzec, near Verdun, and at Jezanville, near Pont - à - Mousson. **Germans reach Provins, the most southerly point of their advance.**	Poland : The centre of Dankl's (Austrian) army broken at Krasnostav. Galicia : Beginning of **Battle of Grodek** (S. West of Lemberg) (continued till 12th).	Serbian Invasion of Syrmia* begun : the Save crossed at Novoselo : Obres occupied : failure to take Mitrovitsa.
7	**Battle of the Marne** (cont.) struggle on the Ourcq and Petit-Morin. Maubeuge captured by the Germans with many prisoners and guns. Sir John French's first despatch (published on 9th) ([38]).	Galicia : Fresh struggle round Grodek : Russian cavalry reach the Carpathians.	Second Austrian invasion of Serbia begins : the Drina crossed in force.
8	**Battle of the Marne** (cont.) Germans forced back over the river. General Foch's decisive move. Nancy vainly attacked. Troyon bombarded.	Galicia : Fierce battle round Rava Russka. Mikolajow (Carpathians) captured by Brusilov's Army.	.. .. ..
9	**Battle of the Marne** (cont.) British cross the river in pursuit of Germans : French carry the Ourcq. Battle of Fère Champenoise.	.. .. ..	Syrmia : Servians occupy D e c h. Montenegrins invade Bosnia.
10	**Battle of the Marne** ended. Germans retreat on west and centre. Pont-à-Mousson evacuated by Germans.	Poland : Dankl defeated in second **Battle of Krasnik**, Archduke Joseph defeated at Opole.	Syrmia : Serbians occupy Semlin.

* A district of Austrian Slavonia

Asiatic and Egyptian Theatres.	Naval and Overseas Operations.	Political, &c.	1914. Sept.
.. .. ..	.. .. ..	Great Britain : Mr. Asquith at Guildhall ([35]) justifies Britain's entry into the war.	4
.. .. ..	E. Africa : Germans attack Abercorn. H.M.S. " Pathfinder " sunk by German submarine. Wilson liner " Runo " blown up by a mine.	**Agreement of London :** Great Britain, France, and Russia pledge themselves to make no separate peace ([36]).	5
.. .. ..	Cameroons : British reverse near Nsanakong.	Great Britain : The Admiralty announce organisation of a Royal Naval Division.	6
.. .. ..	E. Africa : German reverse near Tsavo. Pacific Cable cut between Banfield and Fanning Island by " Nürnberg."	.. ..	7
.. .. ..	The " Oceanic " wrecked off north coast of Scotland.	Mr. Lloyd George : Speech on the need for economy ([39]).	8
.. ..	.. .. ..	Turkey : Announcement of **abolition of the Capitulations** after Oct. 1 ([40]).	9
.. .. ..	E. Africa : Germans occupy Kisi. **" Emden "** makes first appearance in Bay of Bengal ([41]).	.. .. ..	10

to 40 miles N.W. of Belgrade.

1914. Sept.	WESTERN FRONT.	EASTERN FRONT.	SOUTHERN FRONT.
11	Pursuit of the Germans from the Marne : the French recover Epernay, Châlons, etc.	Galicia : Russians close in on Grodek.	Serbia : Fierce battle with Austrian invaders at Krupani.
12	Troyon : Germans compelled to raise siege. Lunéville reoccupied by the French. Belgian sortie from Antwerp threatens German communications.	Galicia : End of Battle of Grodek and Rava Russka : total defeat of Austrians ; Grodek captured. Poland : Austrians try to cross the San under heavy fire.	Syrmia : Serbians occupy Jarak.
13	Allies recover Soissons and force the passage of the Aisne there. Amiens recovered by the French. Germans begin to drive the Belgians back into Antwerp : Battles along line Aerschot-Malines.	E. Prussia : Russians turn on their pursuers and defeat them at Sredniki near the Niemen.	Serbians and Austrians fighting in both Serbia and Syrmia.
14	**Battle of the Aisne** begins (continued till Sept. 28). Germans halt on the Aisne and N. of Reims. Heavy fighting round Missy and Vailly.	Poland : Russians force the passage of the San in pursuit of Dankl's beaten army	Bosnia : Vishegrad taken by Serbians and Montenegrins.
15	The Aisne : Heavy German counter-attacks : Soissons shelled. The Argonne : Germans begin slow advance, continued to Oct. 21. Arras occupied by Germans.	E. Prussia : Russians prepared to resist German pursuit on the Niemen. Bukovina : Russians occupy Czernowitz.	Serbia : Austrians pushed back across the Drina save at a few points : their second invasion of Serbia suspended.
16	The Aisne : Gen. Joffre abandons frontal attacks and forms plan to turn the German right. Germans enter Valenciennes.	Galicia : Russians advance towards Przemysl.	.. .. ..
17	The Aisne : Heavy fighting round Soissons. Sir John French's second despatch ([42]) (published Oct. 19).	.. .. ..	Syrmia : Serbians evacuate Semlin.
18	The Aisne : Heavy fighting round Noyon and Reims.	Poland : Russians take Sandomierz.	.. .. ..
19	The Aisne : Strong general German attacks : also on the Meuse forts (Verdun).	.. .. ..	..

Asiatic and Egyptian Theatres.	Naval and Overseas Operations.	Political, &c.	1914. Sept.
.. ..	Bismarck Archipelago : Australian expedition captures Herbertshöhe.	.. .. ..	11
.. ..	E. Africa : Germans defeated near Kisi.	.. .. ..	12
sing-tau : Japanese capture the railway at Kiao-chau town.	Solomon Islands : Australian troops capture Bougainville. "Hela," German cruiser, sunk by British submarine E.9.	Germany : Herr v. Bethmann Hollweg's reply to Mr. Asquith's Guildhall speech of Sept. 4 published.	13
.. ..	S. Africa : Union forces surprise and defeat Germans at Raman's Drift. "Cap Trafalgar" sunk by H.M.S. "Carmania" (E. coast S. America).	.. .. ..	14
.. ..	S. Africa : Meeting of rebels at Potchefstroom. D e l a r e y accidentally shot on his way thither with Beyers.	.. .. ..	15
.. ..	.. ..	..	16
.. ..	S. Africa : German raid near N a k o b. Gen. Beyers dismissed from his command.	.. ..	17
.. ..	S.W. Africa : British occupy Lüderitz Bay (which Germans had evacuated militarily on Aug. 10).	Great Britain : Parliament prorogued : King George's speech ([43]). Mr. Asquith's Edinburgh speech.	18
.. ..	Admiral Troubridge recalled for enquiry into escape of "Goeben" and "Breslau."	Mr. Lloyd George's speech to Welshmen on German barbarities ([44]).	19

1914. Sept.	Western Front.	Eastern Front.	Southern Front.
20	The Aisne : Bombardment of Reims Cathedral.	E. Prussian Frontier : Russians abandon Augustovo : Germans lay siege to Osovyets.	Quietude in the Balkan theatre of war.
21	The Aisne : French recover Noyon and advance to Lassigny in effort to turn the German right wing. Troyon again attacked.	E. Prussian Frontier : Germans reach the Niemen. Galicia : Russians take Jaroslau.	.. ..
22	The Aisne : A day of comparative calm. Düsseldorf: sheds raided by British airmen.	Galicia : Russians approach Przemysl.	.. .. ..
23	The Aisne : The battle extends northward along the R. Oise.	.. .. ..	Bosnia : Serbians and Montenegrins make progress towards Serajevo.
24	The Aisne : The battle tends to stalemate. Péronne occupied by the Germans.	Galicia : Przemysl invested by the Russians	.. .. ..
25	The Aisne : Reims again bombarded. **Battle of Albert** begun by the Germans to prevent encirclement. Noyon and Lassigny taken from the French. Camp-des-Romains and St. Mihiel on the Meuse taken by the Germans.	E. Prussian Frontier : Russians driven across the Niemen, which they proceed to defend.	.. .. ..
26	The Aisne : Local combats only. Battle of Albert : Fierce fight from Oise to Somme. St. Mihiel : Vain German efforts to cross the Meuse at. Siege of Antwerp begun by the Germans. **Indian troops land at Marseilles.**	E. Prussian Frontier : **Battle of the Niemen** (Sept. 26-28) : Vain German efforts to cross. Siege of Osovyets : Vain German assaults. Galicia : Russians occupy Rzeszov.	.. .. ..
27	The Aisne : Battle dying down. Battle of Albert : Heavy fighting continued. Malines occupied by the Germans.	Galicia : Russians press on towards Cracow and the Carpathian Passes.	.. .. ..

Asiatic and Egyptian Theatres.	Naval and Overseas Operations.	Political, &c.	1914. Sept.
.. ..	H.M.S. " Pegasus " disabled by German cruiser " Königsberg " at Zanzibar.	.. .. ..	20
.. .. ..	.. .. ..	Mr. Winston Churchill's Liverpool speech ([45])	21
.. ..	S. Africa : Botha assumes command in place of Beyers. " Emden " bombards Madras. " Scharnhorst " and " Gneisenau " bombard Papeete (French Tahiti). H.M.S's. " Aboukir," "Hogue" and " Cressy " sunk by submarine.	.. .. ..	22
.. .. ..	.. .. ..	Great Britain : Impending end of Moratorium announced.	23
sing-tau : British force arrives at Laoshun to assist the Japanese.	Kaiser Wilhelm's Land (New Guinea) : Australians occupy town of Friedrich Wilhelm.	.. .. ..	24
.. .. ..	.. .. ..	Germany : Hindenburg placed in command of combined Austro-German offensive in Poland and Galicia. Great Britain : Mr. Asquith's Dublin speech : appeal to Volunteers.	25
sing-tau : German outposts driven in.	S. Africa : British reverse at Sandfontein.	.. .. ..	26
.. .. ..	.. .. ..	.. .. ..	27

1914. Sept.	Western Front.	Eastern Front.	Southern Front.
28	Battle of the Aisne ends. Battle of Albert continued with great fury. Antwerp: Bombardment of forts Waelhem, Wavre, St. Catherine.	Galicia: **Russians in possession of** Krosno, and also of **Dukla Pass.** Hungary raided by Russian cavalry (**46**).	.. ..
29	Battle of Albert ends in repulse of the Germans. Antwerp: Fort Wavre Ste. Catherine silenced. French lose Lassigny.	E. Prussian Frontier: **Germans withdraw from the Niemen** and raise the siege of Osovyets.	.. ..
30	Battle extends northwards round Roye and Arras. New French army concentrated round Amiens and Lens. French occupy Lille. Antwerp: Waterworks destroyed.	Germans entrench S. of Kyeltsi (S.W. Poland).	.. ..
Oct. 1	Battle round Roye: Vain German efforts to break French line. St. Mihiel: French destroy bridge made over Meuse. Antwerp: Fort Waelhem silenced. B.E.F. begins to leave the Aisne and move west and then north.	E. Prussian Frontier: Russians recover Augustovo and begin a nine-days' attack (**Battle of Augustovo**) on the retreating Germans.	.. ..
2	**Battle round Arras:** French hard pressed. Antwerp: Belgians retire across the Nethe: Germans occupy Termonde.	E. Prussian Frontier: Russians recover Mariampol.	Bosnia: Serbians and Montenegrins renew their advance toward Serajevo.
3	Ypres occupied by the Germans. Antwerp: Fall of outer defences: Legations leaving.	**Beginning of First Austro-German invasion in force for capture of Warsaw.** Germans take over command of Austrians.	.. ..
4	**Rapid German advance towards the Coast:** Germans occupy Lens, Comines, Poperinghe, Bailleul, etc. Lille bombarded by Germans.	Poland: Rapid Austro-German advance against Russian centre.	Bosnia: Serbians and Montenegrins driven back from the Serajevo region.
5	Antwerp: Germans force the line of the Nethe at Duffel. 3 British Naval Brigades reach Antwerp.	.. ..	.. ..

Asiatic and Egyptian Theatres.	Naval and Overseas Operations.	Political, &c.	1914. Sept.
.. ..	.. .. ..	.. .. ..	28
apanese bombard Tsing-tau.	" Emden " : Second haul of captures announced. (See above, Sept. 10.)	Great Britain : East coast ports closed to foreign trawlers.	29
sing-tau : German destroyer sunk in the harbour.	.. .. ..	Great Britain : Reply of British theologians to German published.	30
.. .. ..	.. .. ..	Italy : Protest against Austrian mine - laying. Turkey : Closing of the Dardanelles.	Oct. 1
.. ..	E. Africa : British victory at Gazi. H.M.S. " Cumberland " captures 9 German liners, etc. in Cameroon River.	Great Britain : Mr. Asquith's speech at Cardiff disclosing German proposals to Britain in 1912.	2
.. ..	North Sea : British Admiralty notifies the laying down of a defensive mine-field.	.. .. ..	3
.. .. ..	.. .. ..	German Professors' manifesto issued.	4
.. .. ..	.. .. ..	Albania : Essad Pasha nominated head of a Provisional Government.	5

1914. Oct.	WESTERN FRONT.	EASTERN FRONT.	SOUTHERN FRONT.
6	Arras heavily bombarded by the Germans. British troops disembark at Ostend and Zeebrugge. Antwerp: Germans capture Lierre.	Poland and Galicia: **Russians fall back along the whole front** in face of German advance.	..
7	**Antwerp: Evacuation begun:** Germans force the passage of the Scheldt and threaten the retreat of the Allies.	Galicia: Russians forced back to the San. Hungary: Withdrawal of Russian raiders ([45]).	..
8	General Foch takes supreme command of the Allied armies defending the Coast. Fighting at Roye. Antwerp: The city bombarded: Belgians and Naval Brigades leave (being cut off and losing 2,000 interned in Holland). Sir John French's third despatch ([47]) (published Oct. 19).	East Prussia: Russians take Lyck.	..
9	**Antwerp occupied by Germans.** Düsseldorf: Zeppelin sheds raided by Allied airmen.	East Prussia: End of **Battle of Augustovo:** Germans defeated. Poland: Austro-Germans approach Ivangorod: beginning of a twenty-days' struggle.	..
10	Antwerp: the last forts surrender. Belgians check German pursuit at Melle. Lille again bombarded by the Germans.	Poland: Germans occupy Lodz. Hungary again raided by Russians ([48])	..
11	**Battle of Flanders begins,** a desperate struggle for the coast lasting for some six weeks and including (a) Battle of the Yser, Oct. 16, *seq.* (b) Battle of Ypres, Oct. 19, *seq.* Paris heavily bombed. Cavalry fighting near Hazebrouck.	Poland: Germans take Sochaczew. Galicia: Russians forced to raise the siege of Przemysl, which is reprovisioned from Cracow. Austrians recover Jaroslau.	..
12	**Ostend** and Zeebrugge **evacuated** by the Allies. Reims evacuated by Germans (*circa*).	..	..

ASIATIC AND EGYPTIAN THEATRES.	NAVAL AND OVERSEAS OPERATIONS.	POLITICAL, &c.	1914. Oct.
.. .. ..	.. .. ..	.. .. ..	6
.. .. ..	Marshall Islands in Pacific Ocean occupied by Japanese.	Belgium : Seat of Government moved from Antwerp to Ostend.	7
sing-tau : Japanese capture " Prince Heinrich " hill.	British Submarine E.9 sinks German destroyer S.126 at mouth of Ems.	.. .. ..	8
.. .. ..	.. .. ..	Italy : Cabinet crisis : resignation of General Grandi, Minister for War.	9
.. .. ..	.. .. ..	**Rumania : Death of King Carel.** Succeeded by his nephew Ferdinand.	10
.. .. ..	Russian cruiser " Pallada " sunk by German submarine in Baltic.	.. .. ..	11
.. .. ..	S. Africa : Martial law proclaimed throughout the Union.	.. .. ..	12

1914. Oct.	WESTERN FRONT.	EASTERN FRONT.	SOUTHERN FRONT.
13	Ypres occupied by the Allies, who attempt an offensive. **Lille** and Ghent **occupied by the Germans.** Heavy fighting between Bethune and La Bassée.	E. Prussia: Germans recover Lyck.	.. ..
14	Bailleul occupied by the Allies. Bruges occupied by the Germans.	E. Prussian Front: Germans take Mlava. Poland: Germans announce occupation of all the country up to the line of the Vistula.	.. ..
15	Ostend and Zeebrugge occupied by the Germans. The Allied lines extended to the Coast.	Poland: **First Battle for Warsaw** begins along all the line of the Vistula (till 23rd).	.. ..
16	Aubers, Armentières, Neuve Chapelle and Warneton occupied by the Allies. Fighting round Lille. Belgians driven out of Forest of Houthulst. **Battle of the Yser** begins with German attack on Dixmude.	Poland: Germans within seven miles of Warsaw, which the Russians prepare to evacuate.	.. ..
17	Herlies captured by the Allies: **End of the offensive of the Allies.** Heavy German counter-attacks impose a strenuous defensive for a period extending to Nov. 17.	Poland: Crisis of Battle of Warsaw: Russian reinforcements reach the city and save it from capture.	.. ..
18	The Yser held by the Belgians against the Germans: struggle from Lombartzyde to Keyem. Roulers occupied by the Germans after fierce 3-days' battle.	Galicia: Beginning of a desperate but vain effort of the Austrians to cross the San.	.. ..
19	The Yser: German attacks on Lombartzyde repulsed. B.E.F.: Transfer from Aisne to Flanders completed. **First Battle of Ypres** begins: Sir H. Rawlinson unable to occupy Menin. Sir John French's despatches of Sept. 17 and Oct. 8 published.	Poland: Germans cross the Vistula at Josefov, etc.	.. ..

Asiatic and Egyptian Theatres.	Naval and Overseas Operations.	Political, &c.	1914. Oct.
.. .. ..	S. Africa : Open rebellion of Lt.-Col. Maritz.	Belgium : the Government established at Havre in France. Antwerp mulcted of £20,000,000.	13
.. .. ..	... .	.. .. ..	14
Tsing-tau : The beginning of the end. Non-combatants allowed to leave.	S. Africa : Rebels routed at Ratedraai. North Sea : H.M.S. " Hawke " sunk by German submarine.	.. .. ..	15
Tsing-tau : General attack begins (⁴⁸)	H.M.S. " Yarmouth " sinks the " Emden's " collier," Markomannia." Cattaro bombarded by the Allied fleets.	Italy : Death of Marquis di San Giuliano, Minister for Foreign Affairs. Canadian troops arrive in England.	16
.. .. ..	H.M.S. " Undaunted " with accompanying destroyers sink four German destroyers off Dutch coast.	.. .. ..	17
.. .. ..	Belgian Coast : British monitors under Adm. Hood aid the Belgians in the Battle of the Yser. Loss of Brit. Submarine E.3 announced by German wireless.	.. .. ..	18
.. .. ..	.. .. ..	New Naval Decoration, the Distinguished Service Medal, established.	19

1914. Oct.	WESTERN FRONT.	EASTERN FRONT.	SOUTHERN FRONT.
20	Battle round Arras : fierce German attack repulsed. Poelcapelle captured by the Germans. Indian Exped. Force (Cavalry, Meerut and Lahore Division) reaches the front. Heavy fighting near La Bassée.	Poland : German attacks in front of Warsaw weakening : Russians begin to take the offensive.	..
21	The Yser : Critical day : Dixmude heavily bombarded and assaulted. Arras also heavily bombarded and attacked. The Argonne : French recovery begins.	Poland : **Germans begin retreat from Warsaw** : Battle of Kasimiryev : Russki annihilates the Germans who had crossed the Vistula.	..
22	The Yser : Struggle for Dixmude continued. Battle of Ypres : Germans capture Langemarck. **Battle round La Bassée** : Beginning of a severe 10-days' effort of the Germans to break through.	..	..
23	The Yser : Germans take Lombartzyde, but are again repulsed from Dixmude. Allies lose ground near La Bassée. Battle of Ypres : Furious attacks near Langemarck.	Poland : Germans abandon siege of Ivangorod : Russians everywhere advance and harass the retreat. They retake Jaroslau.	..
24	The Yser : The French recover Lombartzyde. Indian troops arrive near Bethune. Battle of Ypres : Germans occupy Polygon Wood, but fail at Gheluvelt. Battle round Arras at its height.	..	..
25	Vain German efforts to break through the Allied lines at Dixmude, Ypres, La Bassée and Arras. Vermelles re-occupied by the Germans.	Germans in full retreat in Poland.	..
26	Yser : German progress stopped : attack on Pervyse repulsed. Heavy fighting round Ypres, La Bassée, and Arras.	..	..

ASIATIC AND EGYPTIAN THEATRES.	NAVAL AND OVERSEAS OPERATIONS.	POLITICAL, &c.	1914. Oct.
.. .. ..	.. .. ..	Germans report 149,000 French, 107,000 Russian, 32,000 Belgian, and 9,000 British prisoners. British losses to date 57,000, including sick.	20
.. .. ..	.. .. ..	Russia : State sale of alcohol abolished. Great Britain : Reply to manifesto of German professors published.	21
.. .. ..	S. Africa : Rebels routed at Keimoes. " Emden's " third list of captures announced.	.. .. ..	22
.. .. ..	.. .. ..	.. .. ..	23
.. .. ..	S. Africa : Overt rebellion of Beyers and De Wet.	Great Britain : Importation of sugar prohibited.	24
.. .. ..	S. Africa : Rebels routed at Calvinia. Destruction of German submarine by H.M.S. " Badger " announced.	Great Britain : Death of Sir Charles Douglas, Chief of Gen. Staff. Germany : Gen. von Moltke, C.G.G.S., " unwell," his duties undertaken by Gen. von Falkenhayn.	25
.. .. ..	S. Africa : Maritz driven into German territory. Cameroons : Allies occupy Duala.	.. .. ..	26

c

1914. Oct.	WESTERN FRONT.	EASTERN FRONT.	SOUTHERN FRONT.
27	Yser: Belgians, with French aid, maintain unbroken the front Nieuport-Dixmude. Neuve-Chapelle taken by the Germans. Germans pushed back E. of Nancy.	Poland: Russian victory along the line Petrokov-Radom.	.. .. ..
28	Yser: Germans retake Lombartzyde. Neuve-Chapelle retaken by the British.	Poland: Russians recover Lodz. Galicia: Austrians defeated at Sambor.	.. .. ..
29	Yser: Germans take Ramscapelle. The Belgians open the sluices of the canal. Heavy fighting round Festubert (La Bassée).	.. .. ..	.. .. ..
30	Yser: Germans forced by floods to retreat. Ypres closely pressed by the Germans. Germans press back French along the Aisne.	Poland: Russians defeat Germans at Bakalaryevo.	.. .. ..
31	Yser: French recover Ramscapelle. Ypres: Crisis of the great battle. Germans take Gheluvelt and break the British line. The Worcesters save the situation and recover Gheluvelt.	Bukovina: Russians reoccupy Czernowitz.	.. .. ..
Nov. 1	Battle of Ypres continued with great violence: Germans capture Messines, Hollebeke and Wytschaete.	Poland: German retreat continued.	.. .. ..
2	Germans withdraw from nearly the whole of the left bank of the Yser, and concentrate for attack on Ypres. British lines pierced at Neuve Chapelle, which the Germans reoccupy.	East Prussia re-entered by Russian forces.	.. .. ..

ASIATIC AND EGYPTIAN THEATRES.	NAVAL AND OVERSEAS OPERATIONS.	POLITICAL, &C.	1914. Oct.
.. .. ..	S. Africa: Beyers defeated by Botha at Commissie Drift, near Rustenburg. H.M.S. "Audacious" sunk by mine off the N. Irish Coast. French liner "Amiral Ganteaume" sunk. "Emden" captures Japanese ship "Kamasaka Maru."	Portugal: Naval Reserves called up.	27
.. .. ..	"Emden" appears at Penang and destroys Russian cruiser "Zhemchug," etc.	Great Britain: Resignation of Prince Louis of Battenberg from office of First Sea Lord ([49]). Trial of Archduke's murderers at Serajevo.	28
Egypt: Beduin tribes raid the frontier.	Turkish Fleet attacks Odessa, Novorossisk, and Theodosia, and sinks Russian destroyer, etc.	Great Britain: Lord Fisher appointed First Sea Lord. **Turkey enters the war** on the German side ([50]).	29
.. .. ..	S. Africa: Rebels routed at Schuit Drift. "Königsberg" discovered hiding in Rufiji River (E. Africa).	Great Britain: Trial of the German spy Karl Lody begins. Turkey: Allies' Ambassadors ask for passports.	30
Tsing-tau: Final intense bombardment begins.	H. M. S. "Hermes" (cruiser) sunk in Straits of Dover.	Italy: Resignation of Salandra Cabinet. Occupation of Saseno (Albania).	31
			Nov 1
Tsing-tau: The "Bismarck" forts silenced, H.M.S. "Triumph" assisting the Japanese.	**Battle of Coronel** (Pacific): H.M.Ss. "Monmouth" and "Good Hope" lost in fight with Von Spee's German squadron ([51]).	Turkey: British Ambassador leaves Constantinople.	
.. .. ..	North Sea proclaimed by the British Admiralty to be wholly a military area as from Nov. 5.	Turkey: Russian and French Ambassadors leave Constantinople. Great Britain publishes an account of Turkish provocations.	2

1914. Nov.	Western Front.	Eastern Front.	Southern Front.
3	Allies occupy positions on the Yser, abandoned by the Germans. Fighting on the Aisne (Vailly, Chavonne, etc.).	Poland : Russians defeat Austro - Germans at Kyeltsi, which they recover.	Dardanelles Forts bombarded by British and French fleets. Cattaro bombarded by Montenegrins.
4	Lombartzyde recovered by the Allies. Battle of Ypres continues.	Galicia : Austrians defeated at Jaroslau ; loss of 19,000 prisoners and 40 guns in 12 days.	.. .. ..
5	Germans repulsed at Le Quesnoy - en - Santerre (Roye).	Poland : Germans in retreat move their headquarters back to Chenstokhov.	Montenegro : Invasion by Albanians checked.
6	Ypres : Fierce German attacks repelled : heavy fighting round Klein-Zillebeke.	Galicia : Line of the San once more in Russian hands : Austrians in retreat towards Cracow.	.. .. ..
7	Lombartzyde again captured by Germans. Heavy German attacks on the Allies at Givenchy (La Bassée) and Arras. German attacks near Roye and Vimy repulsed.	.. .. ..	Russians bombard Turkish ports in the Black Sea.
8	Battle along line Dixmude-Ypres - La Bassée - Arras continued : German attacks repulsed. French continue to advance in the Argonne, and occupy Vregny (Aisne).	E. Prussia : Russians re-enter Eydtkuhnen and Stallupönen : they advance into the Imperial forest of Rominten.	**Serbia : Third Austrian invasion begun :** advances on three lines, viz., towards (i) Nish, (ii) Shabats, (iii) Valyevo.
9	Ypres : Violent German attacks : British position again in danger.	Poland : Germans evacuate Kalish and Chenstokhov, etc. Silesia entered by Russian cavalry, Rail cut at Pleschen.	.. .. ..
10	Yser : Germans take Dixmude. Ypres : Germans take St. Eloi.	E. Prussia : Russians re-enter Goldap.	.. .. ..
11	Ypres : Some British trenches penetrated by the Prussian Guard, but recovered	.. .. ..	Serbia : The Serbians in retreat ; their headquarters moved from Valyevo to Kraguyevats.

Asiatic and Egyptian Theatres.	Naval and Overseas Operations.	Political, &c.	1914. Nov.
Armenia: Bayazid occupied by Russians. Arabia: Akaba on Red Sea bombarded and occupied by British.	**Yarmouth bombarded** by German cruisers. British submarine D.5 sunk by a mine in fight with cruisers.	**Serbia breaks off relations with Turkey.** Bulgaria declares intention to remain neutral.	3
Armenia: Russian advance from Caucasus; Diadin occupied.	E. Africa: **British reverse at Tanga** (⁵²). German cruiser "Yorck" destroyed by a mine near Wilhelmshaven.	Persia refuses to join Turkey in war against the Entente.	4
.. ..	.. .. ..	**Great Britain declares war on Turkey and annexes Cyprus.** Kaiser removed from Navy List. Italy: Salandra Cabinet reconstructed (⁵³).	5
Tsing-tau: Central fort stormed and 200 prisoners taken.	.. .. ..	Great Britain: The spy Lody shot at the Tower.	6
Capture of Tsing-tau: Japanese take 2,300 prisoners. **Mesopotamia: British force lands** in Persian Gulf.	S. Africa: Union troops defeated by De Wet at Doornberg.	.. .. ..	7
Mesopotamia: Fao on Persian Gulf occupied by British.	S. Africa: Rebels routed at Sandfontein. Russians sink 4 Turkish transports in Black Sea.	.. .. ..	8
Armenia: Battle of Koprukeui.	**"Emden" destroyed** at Cocos Island by H.M.A.S. "Sydney" (⁵⁴). "Geier," German cruiser interned by U.S.A. at Honolulu.	Mr. Asquith's Guildhall speech setting forth the aims of the Allies: "We shall never sheathe the sword," etc.	9
.. .. ..	"Königsberg" blocked up in Rufiji River.	.. .. ..	10
Mesopotamia: British outposts attacked at Saniya.	H.M.S. "Niger" sunk by German submarine.	Great Britain: Parliament opened; the King's Speech.	11

1914. Nov.	WESTERN FRONT.	EASTERN FRONT.	SOUTHERN FRONT.
12	Ypres again fiercely attacked by the Germans ; latter take Lombartzyde.	Galicia : Przemysl again invested by the Russians. Miechow, near Cracow, occupied. E. Prussia : Russians again enter Johannisburg.	Montenegrins defeated Grahovo (Bosnian frontier).
13	The French recover Tracy-le-Val.	E. Prussia : Russian advance threatens Thorn. Galicia : Russians occupy line of Dunayetz and threaten Cracow.	.. ..
14	The Battles round the Yser and Ypres dying down.	E. Prussia : Russian advance checked. **Poland : Beginning of a new** and powerful **German invasion** along the Vistula from Thorn as base.	.. ..
15	Battle of Ypres : Last serious attack of the Germans (made by the Prussian Guards) beaten off.	Poland : Russians retreating b e f o r e the strong German advance from Thorn, take up the line Gombin-Lodz.	Serbia : Austrians continue to advance : the Serbians fall back south eastwards.
16	Rains and floods put a term to the struggles on the Yser : Fighting dying down round Ypres. Germans fail to cross the Aisne at Vailly.	Poland : Russian rearguards defeated at Vlotslavek and Kutno.	.. ..
17	**End of the first Battle of Ypres ; stationary warfare now the rule.**	Poland : Violent conflicts round Plotsk. Galicia : Russians begin to recover Carpathian Passes.	.. ..
18	Fighting limited to artillery duels and local skirmishes.	E. Prussia : Russians defeated at Soldau. Poland : Russians in retreat towards Lovich. Galicia : Austro-German offensive from Cracow.	.. ..
19	.. .. ..	Poland : Mackensen captures Piontek and opens the way to Lodz.	Serbia : Austrians take Valyevo : Serbians retreat.
20	Sir John French's 4th despatch published dealing with Battle of Ypres ([57]).	Poland : German attacks on Russian line from Lovich to Skiernievitse.	.. ..

Asiatic and Egyptian Theatres.	Naval and Overseas Operations.	Political, &c.	1914. Nov.
.. .. ..	S. Africa : De Wet defeated at Mushroom Valley.	Turkey : Formal declaration of war against the Triple Entente.	12
.. .. ..	.. .. ..	.. .. ..	13
.. .. ..	S. Africa : Rebels routed at Bultfontein.	Death of F.M. Earl Roberts in France.	14
Mesopotamia : Skirmish between Turks and British at Sahain.	.. .. ..	.. .. ..	15
.. .. ..	" Berlin," German auxiliary cruiser, interned at Trondhjem.	Turkey : Sultan, at German instigation, proclaims the " Holy War " ([55]). Great Britain : Mr. Asquith moves War Credit for £225,000,000.	16
Mesopotamia : Turks decisively routed at Sahil.	.. .. ..	Great Britain : Mr. Lloyd George introduces his first War Budget ([56]).	17
Armenia : Turkish offensive compels Russians to retreat.	Libau on Baltic shelled by German squadron. " Goeben " and " Breslau " engaged by a Russian squadron in Black Sea ; the " Goeben " damaged.	.. .. ..	18
.. .. ..	.. .. ..	.. .. ..	19
Egypt : The Bikanir Camel Corps beats off the Turks on the coast towards Port Said.	Admiralty announces extension of mine-field in North Sea.	.. .. ..	20

1914. Nov	WESTERN FRONT.	EASTERN FRONT.	SOUTHERN FRONT.
21	British airmen raid Zeppelin factory at Friedrichshafen (L. of Constance).	Poland : Germans attack Russians at Lovich.	.. ..
22	Trench warfare established along the whole front; artillery duels and, later, local raids.	Poland : Germans approach Lodz; heavy fighting begins. Galicia : Russians defeat Austrians (6,000 prisoners) on front Cracow-Chenstokhov,	Serbia : Austrians pressing on from Valyevo Serbians in retreat towards south-east.
23	Ypres heavily bombarded by the Germans, much damage done to the Cathedral and Cloth Hall. British trenches near Festubert attacked; some lost, but recovered.	Poland : Russian line shattered by Mackensen between Rzgov and Kolyushki, S.E. of Lodz: critical situation.	.. .. .
24	.. .. ..	Poland : Arrival of Russian reinforcements saves situation ; heavy fighting round Strykov and Lodz.	.. .. .
25	Arras bombarded by the Germans.	Poland : Three German divisions nearly encircled at Lodz, escape through delay of Rennenkampf. Hungary raided by Russian cavalry.	.. .. .
26	German attacks on Missysur-Aisne and along the Yser Canal repulsed.	Bukovina : Austrians again evacuate Czernowitz.	.. .. .
27	Reims town and cathedral again bombarded.	.. .. ..	.. .. .
28	Germans concentrate large forces for attacks on Arras.	Poland : Germans severely defeated near Brzezany. Galicia : Russians once more secure Carpathian Passes.	Serbia : Battle between Austrians and Serbians at Lazarevats.
29	Ypres : Strong German attack repulsed. Argonne : French complete recovery of nearly all territory taken by the Germans Sept. 15–Oct. 21.	Poland : Germans bombard Lodz.	Serbia : Evacuation of Belgrade by the Serbian begins.

ASIATIC AND EGYPTIAN THEATRES.	NAVAL AND OVERSEAS OPERATIONS.	POLITICAL, &C.	1914. Nov.
Egypt : Skirmish at Katiya, near Suez Canal. Mesopotamia : **Basra occupied by British** forces from India.	.. .. ..	.. .. ..	21
Armenia : Russians occupy Koprukeui.	.. .. ..	.. .. ..	22
Mesopotamia : B r i t i s h troops make formal entry into Basra.	Zeebrugge bombarded by British squadron. German submarine U.18 rammed and sunk; its crew saved.	Portugal : Congress authorises the Government to intervene on side of Allies when and how it deems proper.	23
.. .. ..	.. .. ..	Great Britain : Royal Warrant increasing pay of subordinate Army officers.	24
.. .. ..	.. .. ..	Poland : Polish National Council issues in Warsaw a manifesto emphasising necessity of a thorough defeat of the Germans.	25
.. .. ..	H.M.S. " Bulwark " blown up in the Medway (foul play suspected—loss of 800).	.. .. ..	26
.. .. ..	.. .. ..	U.S.A. : President Wilson condemns bombardment of unfortified towns.	27
Egypt : Turkish advance in force towards Suez Canal announced.	.. .. ..	.. .. ..	28
.. .. ..	German submarines appear about Havre, etc.	The King leaves England on a visit to the Army in France.	29

1914. Nov.	WESTERN FRONT.	EASTERN FRONT.	SOUTHERN FRONT
30	King George visits British Front. Artillery duels round Dixmude, Ypres, and Arras.	**Battle of Lodz** increasing in intensity.	.. .. ..
Dec. 1	Vermelles, near Bethune, recovered by the French. King George visits Indian troops ; confers G.C.B. on Gen. Joffre.	Fierce fighting in the suburbs of Lodz.	.. .. ..
2	Germans try to cross Yser on rafts, south of Dixmude ; decisively repulsed. French occupy Lesménils (Moselle) and Burnhaupt (Alsace).	Hungary : Russians occupy Bartfeld.	Serbia : Austrians occupy Belgrade ; Serbians begin counter-offensive in Suvobor region.
3	French progress towards Altkirch (Alsace).	.. .. ..	Serbia : **Battle of the Ridges** (Rudnik Malyen) begins.
4	French strengthen hold on Vermelles, and capture Langemarck in Belgium.	Galicia : Russians, advancing once more on Cracow, occupy Vieliczka.	.. .. ..
5	Reims once again bombarded. French airmen bomb air sheds at Freiburg-in-Breisgau.	.. .. ..	Serbia : Austrians defeated on the Ridges with loss of 15,000 prisoners and 19 guns.
6	Long-distance (22 miles ?) bombardment of Dunkirk by the Germans.	Poland : Russians evacuate Lodz and withdraw towards the Bzura-Ravka lines.	Serbia : Austrians in disorderly flight from the Ridges towards the frontier.
7	Vain German efforts to cross the Yser near Pervyse. Indian Exped. Force completed by arrival of Sirhind Brigade from Egypt.	**Second Battle for Warsaw** begun by the Germans. Russian attacks in E. Prussia. Galicia : Northern sector of the forts of Cracow bombarded by the Russians.	.. .. ..
8	Long-distance bombardment of Furnes by the Germans.	.. .. ..	Serbia : Austrians completely defeated south of Belgrade (**Battle of Rudnik Ridges**).
9	.. .. ..	Battle for Warsaw ; heavy fighting round Mlava and Petrokov.	Serbians reoccupy Valyevo.

Asiatic and Egyptian Theatres.	Naval and Overseas Operations.	Political, &c.	1914. Nov.
.. .. ..	.. .. ..	France: The "Yellow Book" published. Pacific statements by Crown Prince.	30
			Dec.
Armenia: Russians capture Sarai and Bashkal.	S. Africa: Surrender of De Wet.	.. .. ..	1
.. .. ..	.. .. ..	Speech by Herr v. Bethmann-Hollweg in Reichstag blaming Britain for the war. Ireland: Seditious paper seized in Dublin.	2
.. .. ..	.. .. ..	Italy: Prime Minister defines attitude towards the war.	3
.. .. ..	S. Africa: Rebels heavily defeated near Reitz by Botha.	Belgium: King George visits Belgian headquarters and confers K.G. on King Albert.	4
.. .. ..	S. Africa: Rebels offer to negotiate; Botha demands unconditional surrender.	.. .. ..	5
.. .. ..	Damaged German submarine U.16 enters Esbjerg Harbour (Denmark).	The Pope tries to bring about a Christmas truce.	6
Mesopotamia: British success at Mezera. Turks driven back S. of Batoum (Transcauc.).	S. Africa: Rebel General Beyers defeated at Bothaville and drowned on his flight in the Vaal River.	French Bourse re-opens.	7
.. .. ..	S. Africa: Collapse of rebellion; 1,200 rebels surrender. Battle of Falkland Islands, Adm. Sturdee sinks most of German squadron ([59]).	Great Britain: Trial of Ahlers for high-treason commenced.	8
Mesopotamia: Turks evacuate Kurna.	.. .. ..	Ahlers convicted.	9

1914. Dec.	WESTERN FRONT.	EASTERN FRONT.	SOUTHERN FRONT.
10	Ypres once again attacked fiercely, but vainly, by Germans.	Austrians defeated near Cracow with loss of 4,000 prisoners.	.. .. ..
11	.. .. ..	Poland : Russians repel German attacks north of Lovich.	.. .. ..
12	.. .. ..	Galicia : Austro-German counter-offensive from Hungary begins ; the Dukla Pass carried and the Russians at Cracow threatened.	Serbia : Austrians utterly defeated, re-cross the Drina. Bosnia : Vishegrad taken by Montenegrins.
13	Germans withdraw from the Yser Canal.	Battle for Warsaw raging. Galicia : Battle for Cracow ending owing to Austro-German offensive from Hungary.	Serbia : **Rout of the Austrians completed.**
14	Ypres again attacked by Germans.	.. .. ..	..
15	Allies cross Yser Canal and advance from Nieuport towards Lombartzyde.	Poland : Heavy fighting round Sokhachev.	Serbia : Austrians evacuate Belgrade, recross Save, and bring their third invasion to an end, after loss of 28,000 prisoners, 70 guns, etc.
16	.. .. ..	Russians end their retreat and make stand on Bzura-Ravka-Pilitza line (30 miles S.W. of Warsaw).	.. .. ..
17	Armentières bombarded by Germans.	Poland : The Germans occupy Petrokov.	.. .. ..
18	Indian troops begin an attack on the Germans round Givenchy (La Bassée) ; a five days' battle commenced. French pressure towards Péronne.	Galicia : Austrians recover the Lupkow Pass over the Carpathians.	.. .. ..

Asiatic and Egyptian Theatres.	Naval and Overseas Operations.	Political, &c.	1914. Dec.
.. .. ..	German submarines attack Dover. "Nürnberg" sunk by Sturdee's squadron.	France: Government returns to Paris from Bordeaux. Germany: v. Falkenhayn definitely supersedes v. Moltke.	10
.. .. ..	"Goeben" having been repaired after damage of Nov. 18, bombards Batoum.	Rumania forbids export of metals and textile material.	11
.. .. ..	.. .. ..	.. .. ..	12
.. .. ..	British subm. B11 enters the Dardanelles and sinks Turkish battleship "Messudiya."	.. .. ..	13
.. .. ..	.. .. ..	Publication of Mr. Bonar Law's letter to Mr. Asquith on Aug. 2 ([59]).	14
Syria: Alexandretta bombarded by H.M.S. "Doris."	Westeinde bombarded by British fleet. Result of enquiry into loss of H.M.S. "Bulwark" ([60]).	.. .. ..	15
.. .. ..	Hartlepool, Whitby and Scarborough bombarded by German warships ([61])	.. .. ..	16
Armenia: The Turks recover Koprukeui and begin to force the Russians back.	.. .. ..	Egypt: British Protectorate proclaimed. Italy: Prince Bülow reaches Rome as German ambassador extraordinary.	17
.. .. ..	German cruiser "Friedrich Karl" reported lost in Baltic.	Egypt: Hussein I. proclaimed Sultan ([62]). Meeting of three Scandinavian Kings at Malmö. Great Britain: Conviction of Ahlers quashed ([63]).	18

1914. Dec.	WESTERN FRONT.	EASTERN FRONT.	SOUTHERN FRONT.
19	Allied airmen bomb German airsheds at Brussels. Germans counter-attack at Givenchy and Festubert.	Galicia : Desperate sortie by Austrian garrison of Przemysl repelled by Russians.	.. .. ..
20	**Battle of Givenchy** continued. Furious German attacks on Indian troops.	Poland : Russians holding the Bzura against heavy German assaults. Galicia : Russians begin to counter-attack and to recover the Carpathian Passes.	.. .. ..
21	British troops aid the Indians at Givenchy to repel the Germans.	Poland : Vain German efforts to cross the Bzura.	.. .. ..
22	Battle of Givenchy begins to die down ; British positions held. French make progress towards Noyon.	Fresh sortie from Przemysl repulsed by Russians.	.. .. ..
23	Belgians cross the Yser and establish themselves on R. bank South of Dixmude.	Poland : Germans succeed in crossing the Bzura at two points. Galicia : Russians compelled to raise the siege of Cracow.	.. .. ..
24	British bomb German airsheds at Brussels. Dover bombed by German aeroplane. French successes at Perthes - les - Hurlus (Champ.) and Consenvoye (Meuse).	Reported rising of Rumanians in Transylvania.	.. .. ..
25	.. .. ..	Poland : Germans driven back beyond the Bzura. Galicia : Austrians defeated at Tarnow ; the **Austro-German offensive at an end.**	Italy : **Valona in Albania** occupied.
26	French airmen bomb German airsheds at Frescati, near Metz. French progress in Alsace, above Cernay.	Poland : Germans abandon attempt to capture Warsaw by direct attack across the Bzura.	.. .. ..

Asiatic and Egyptian Theatres.	Naval and Overseas Operations	Political, &c.	1914. Dec.
.. .. ..	S. Africa: Capt. Fourie and Lieut. Fourie condemned for high treason.	.. .. ..	19
Armenia: Russians defeat the Turks near Lake Van.	S. Africa: Capt. Fourie shot; his brother's sentence commuted.	.. .. ..	20
.. .. ..	.. .. ..	.. .. ..	21
.. .. ..	Raid by rebels under Maritz: loyal Boers defeated.	France: Meeting of the Chambers; M. Viviani makes statement concerning the war. Great Britain: Adm. Sir G. A. Callaghan appointed to the Nore.	22
Egypt: Arrival of Australian and New Zealand troops at Cairo.	.. .. ..	Germany: Captain of the "Yorck" sentenced to two years' detention for loss of ship.	23
.. .. ..	Portuguese Colony of Angola (S.W. Africa) invaded by Germans.	**Marocco: Great Britain recognises French Protectorate.** 134,000 German and 225,000 Austrian prisoners claimed by Russia to date.	24
Armenia: **Battle of Sarikamish:** Turkish counter invasion against the Caucasus reaches its limit.	German warships off Cuxhaven bombed by British naval airmen supported by H.M.Ss. "Arethusa" and "Undaunted."	.. .. ..	25
.. .. ..	.. .. ..	.. .. ..	26

1914. Dec.	WESTERN FRONT.	EASTERN FRONT.	SOUTHERN FRONT.
27	Germans bombard St. Dié (N. Vosges), Belgians take German trenches and prisoners E. of Lombartzyde.	Poland: Germans defeated by Russians at Skiernevitse. Russians occupy Carpathian passes again.	.. .. ..
28	Village of St. Georges, near Nieuport, recovered by the Belgians and French.	Poland: Germans in retreat; entrench W. of Bzura.	Montenegrins repel Austrians at Grahovo.
29	French beat off German attempts to recover St. Georges. Success at Apremont (Arg.).	Galicia: Austrians in retreat; hard pressed by Russians.	Albanians, incited by Austrians, attack Montenegrin posts and are repulsed.
30	Dunkirk attacked by German aeroplanes.	Poland: Germans fight violent rearguard actions at Bolimov and Inovlodz.	.. .. ..
31	Artillery duels on the whole front; especially round St. Georges, La Bassée, Roye and Verdun. French recover part of Steinbach (Als.).	Poland and Galicia; Austro-German retreat. Hungary: Once more raided over the Passes.	Serbia: Preparations to meet new Austrian invasion.

Asiatic and Egyptian Theatres.	Naval and Overseas Operations.	Political, &c.	1914. Dec.
.. .. ..	.. .. ..	.. .. ..	27
Armenia : Turks repulsed from Sarikamish ; they begin a disastrous retreat.	North Sea : Drifting German mines destroy eight vessels.	.. .. ..	28
.. .. ..	British squadron active on Belgian coast.	U.S.A. : Note presented to Great Britain concerning treatment of American commerce ([64]).	29
British Consul at Hodeida (Red Sea) not yet released by Turks.	.. .. ..	.. .. ..	30
Egypt : Preparations to meet expected Turkish attack complete.	.. .. ..	Prussian losses to date, 753,000.	31

RÉSUMÉ OF MAIN EVENTS IN 1914.

June 28	.. ..	Assassination of Archduke Franz Ferdinand.
July 23	.. ..	Austrian ultimatum to Serbia, and answer July 25.
,, 28	.. ..	Austria declares war on Serbia.
Aug. 1	.. ..	Germany declares war on Russia.
,, 2	.. ..	German troops invade Luxemburg and France.
,, 3	.. ..	Germany declares war on France.
·, 4	.. ..	Germany violates and declares war on Belgium ; Gt. Britain declares war on Germany.
·· 4 to 20	..	Germany strikes at Belgium (captures Liége, 7.**8**, and Brussels 20.**8**).
,, 5	..	Austria declares war on Russia.
,, 7 to Sept. 1	..	Russian invasion of Prussia (R. beat Germans at Gumbinnen, 20.**8**, and Frankenau, 23.**8** ; are beaten at Tannenberg, 26-29.**8**).
,, 10 to Sept. 20	..	Austrian invasion of Poland (A. beat Russians at Krasnik, 25.**8** ; are beaten at Tomashov, 5.**9** ; Krasnostav, 6.**9** ; and Krasnik, 10.**9**).
,, 10 and 12	..	France and Gt. Britain declare war on Austria-Hungary.
,, 13 to 25	..	First Austrian invasion of Serbia (A. beaten at Jadar, 17-19.**8**).
,, 18 to Sept. 28	..	Russian invasion of Galicia (R. beat Austrians at Lemberg, 1-3.**9**, and invest Przemysl).
,, 20 to Sept. 5	..	German thrust at Paris (G. beat French at Charleroi, 21.**8**, and Namur, 23.**8** ; and British at Mons, 23.**8**, and Le Cateau, 26.**8**).
,, 23	.. ..	Japan declares war on Germany.
,, 28	.. ..	Battle of the Bight of Heligoland.
Sept. 6 to Oct. 17	..	Franco-British offensive (beat Germans on the Marne, 6-10.**9** ; Aisne, 14-28.**9** ; Albert, 25-29.**9** ; Arras, 1-2.**10** ; and Battle of Flanders).
·, 7 to 17	..	Second Austrian invasion of Serbia (A. beaten on Drina, 15.**9**).
,, 13 to 25	..	Russians fall back to the Niemen.
,, 26 to Oct. 9	..	Russians repulse Germans on the Niemen and press them at Augustovo, 1-9.**10**.
Oct. 3 to Nov. 1	..	Austro-German invasion of Poland and thrust at Warsaw (Russians fall back and raise siege of Przemysl, 6-11.**10** ; First battle for Warsaw, 15-20.**10** ; Germans retreat, pursued by R. in Poland and Galicia).
,, 4 to 15	..	Germans advance towards the Franco-Belgian coast.
·, 9	.. ..	Fall of Antwerp.
,, 11 to Nov. 20	..	Battle of Flanders (La Bassée, 12.**10**-8.**11** ; Yser, 16.**10**-14.**11** ; Ypres, 19.**10**-20.**11**).
,, 29	.. ..	Turkey enters the War.
Nov. 1	.. ..	Battle of Coronel (off Chile).
,, 2 to 13	..	Second Russian invasion of Prussia.
,, 3 and *sqq.*	..	Russian campaign in Armenia begins (R. beat Turks at Sari-kamish, 25.**12**).
,, 5	.. ..	Gt. Britain declares war on Turkey.
,, 7	.. ..	Capture of Tsingtau.
,, 8 to Dec. 15	..	Third Austrian invasion of Serbia (A. occupy Belgrade, 2.**12** ; routed at Rudnik, 3-8.**12**).
,, 14 to Dec. 31	..	German invasion of Poland from Thorn ; second thrust for Warsaw (second battle for Warsaw, 7-26.**12**) ; Austro-German retreat.
,, 21	.. ..	British occupy Basra.
,, 22 to Dec. 13	..	Russian successes in Galicia ; Przemysl reinvested.
Dec. 8	.. ..	Battle of Falkland Islands.
,, 17	.. ..	British Protectorate over Egypt ; Prince Hussein Kamel appointed Sultan.

APPENDICES, 1914.

([1]) *June* 28.—Heir to Austro-Hungarian throne, together with his wife, murdered whilst driving in the streets of Serajevo, by Princip, a young Bosnian member of the Greater Serbian Party, who shot them with a Browning pistol : the bombs for an immediately previous attempt by one Chabrinovich on the same day (resulting only in wounding an officer) were identical with some from the Serbian arsenal at Kraguyevats.

([2]) *July* 9.—The House of Lords completed the recasting of the Amendment Bill (Ireland). Among the Amendments adopted was one excluding the Unionists of the West and South (as well as Ulster) from the jurisdiction of the judiciary appointed by the Home Rule Government ; and another withdrawing the administration of the Land Purchase Acts from the control of the Irish Parliament.

([3]) *July* 13.—M. Humbert's indictment of Army Administration in the Senate ; debate continued the following day revealing serious deficiency in guns, matériel, etc. Army Committee formed to report in October.

([4]) *July* 15.—Tisza, Count : Extreme caution and reserve employed. Foreshadowing of the War. Relations with Serbia "must be cleared up," though manner not indicated. Police régime at fault in Bosnia. Regarding "Greater Serbia" propaganda, complete solidarity between himself and the Ban of Croatia. Agitation to be combated, though avoiding unnecessary panic and alarm.

([5]) *July* 18.—The King, accompanied by the Prince of Wales, arrived at Portsmouth for the Naval Review. Great display of naval power ; over 200 ships assembled, also seaplanes, aeroplanes and dirigibles. Visit curtailed by political crisis. Next day the King made a tour of the lines, and paid informal visits to some ships. On the Monday, great Naval Review : 22 miles of warships passed in procession before Royal Yacht. Evolutions by naval aircraft, Royal inspection of patrol flotillas and tactical exercises between 1st and 2nd Fleets.

([6]) *July* 20.—Trial of Madame Caillaux, wife of former Minister of Finance, for murder of M. Gaston Calmette, editor of the *Figaro*, perpetrated in order to prevent the publication in the *Figaro* of certain documents written by M. Caillaux.

([7]) *July* 23.—Austrian Note demanded formal declaration from Serbian Government condemning anti-Austrian propaganda and promising rigorous punishment of all officials and officers participating in it ; the suppression of all societies and propaganda directed against Austria-Hungary and the elimination of all teachers and methods of education tending to produce anti-Austrian feeling ; the dismissal of all officers and officials reported to be connected with such propaganda, evidence to be furnished by Austria ; Austrian representatives to assist Serbia in repressing the anti-Austrian movement and to take part in the judicial proceedings (on Serbian territory) against all persons connected with the Serajevo tragedy. The Serbian reply to be made by 6 o'clock on July 25.

([8]) *July* 25.—Reply to Austro-Hungarian Ultimatum delivered shortly before 6 p.m. by Premier, M. Pashich, to Austro-Hungarian Minister. Serbian Government denies responsibility for articles in Press and emphasises peaceful work of Societies. Agrees to hand over all and sundry, regardless of rank and situation, proved guilty of complicity in Serajevo tragedy. Will issue any order on the subject. Of the eleven chief points in Ultimatum, eight are accepted, one accepted subject to proof, one rejected conditionally, and one accepted conditionally. If the reply is deemed unsatisfactory, arbitration and mediation is proposed.

([9]) *July* 26.—Dublin : Grave encounter between 2nd K.O.S.B.'s and civilians owing to stoning of former by mob. Four civilians killed—one a woman. Sequel to gun-running by Nationalist Volunteers, Hill of Howth. Lord Mayor demands authority on which troops fired.

([10]) *July* 27.—Sir E. Grey makes statement in Parliament, July 27, announcing attempt to induce the Great Powers not immediately concerned in the Austro-Serbian conflict (Germany, France, Italy, Britain) to meet in conference at London. Russia and Austria to be asked to suspend military operations while the four Powers endeavour to arrange a settlement.

([11]) *The Russian mobilisation of July 29th and 30th as evidenced by the " Sukhomlinov Revelations " (Sept., 1917)*.*—The action of the German Government who, whilst they supported Austria in her attack on Serbia, refused the right to Russia to make any military preparations, inevitably drove Russia to mobilise against Germany as well as against Austria.

July 29.—Russian mobilisation against Austria (*i.e.*, in four Southern districts only) definitely determined on in the morning, and German Ambassador informed between 12 noon and 1 p.m. Order signed by the Tsar and confirmed later by counter-signatures of three Ministers at evening Council. Bombardment of Belgrade became known at St. Petersburg during late afternoon. Pourtalès, German Ambassador, announced at 7 p.m. that Germany must mobilise if Russia does not stop all military preparations. About the same time the Tsar received a telegram from the Kaiser pressing him not to allow things to go as far as war. The Tsar, annoyed at contradictory messages, consulted Council, and they ordered complete mobilisation, *i.e.*, German frontier (three Northern Districts) as well. Another telegram from Kaiser received by Tsar at Tsarskoe Seloe at 10 p.m., more conciliatory : Kaiser gives his word of honour that Germany would take no steps if Russian mobilisation cancelled. Thereupon Tsar telephoned to Sukhomlinov (Minister of War) to cancel the mobilisation in the three Northern districts. Sukhomlinov said he was sorry, but it was a physical impossibility, and pooh-poohed the Kaiser's telegram. Tsar thereupon telephoned to Yanushkevich (Chief of General Staff) at 11 p.m. Latter said he could not stop mobilisation, especially as 400,000 Russian reservists had already been called up. The Tsar, only half convinced, gave absolute order for *partial* mobilisation only. Yanushkevich went to Sazonov (Foreign Affairs) and showed him the impossibility of stopping it. Sazonov settled to speak to Tsar in the morning. Then Yanushkevich rang up Sukhomlinov 11.30 p.m. Sukhomlinov agreed it was too late to stop mobilisation, and told him to do nothing.

July 30.—Partial mobilisation (*i.e.*, four Southern districts) announced ; but mobilisation was really also proceeding in Northern districts. (This the Tsar did not know.) Sukhomlinov went with Sazonov to the Tsar and told him an untruth, *i.e.*, that only partial mobilisation was taking place. Sazonov had very early this morning made a fresh and final proposal to Germany for a formula on which negotiations could be based, but Germany rejected it without even referring it to Austria. Sverbeyev (Russian Ambassador at Berlin) had also telegraphed, on the strength of the false declaration in the *Lokal Anzeiger*, that German mobilisation had been ordered (announcement probably put in by the War Party in Berlin in order to force the hands of their own Government). Consequently, at a Council held at St. Petersburg at 4.30 p.m., general mobilisation was at once (in ten minutes) definitely settled on. Tsar grateful to Sukhomlinov for his determination. Latter much relieved.

It is very clear that responsibility for general Russian mobilisation rested entirely with Germany, who had throughout acted so as to force this course of action on Russia.

([12]) *July* 29.—British Government was offered assurances by Germany that, provided British neutrality was certain, no territorial acquisitions would be taken from France (in the event of a victorious war), but no undertaking could be given with regard to the French Colonies. Dutch neutrality to be recognised, Belgian to be conditional on military necessity, but after the war, if Belgium did not side against Germany, her integrity would be respected.

([13]) *July* 30.—Prime Minister moves postponement of the consideration of the second reading of the Amendment Bill (Government of Ireland). At the moment when the " issues of peace and war are hanging in the balance it is in the interests of the whole world " that Great Britain " should present a united front and be able to speak and act with the authority of an undivided nation."

([14]) *July* 31.—German ultimatum to Russia (midnight, July 31-August 1) that if within 12 hours she did not demobilise, Germany would mobilise. No answer being received, Germany declared war (" accepts the challenge ") at 5 p.m., August 1.

([15]) *July* 31.—German ultimatum to France (July 31) demanding to know within 18 hours her attitude in the event of a Russo-German War.

([16]) *Aug.* 1.—Note presented to the various European Governments stating that Belgium proposed to carry out strictly her obligations under the Treaty of London, and had mobilised her army to defend her neutrality and her international obligations.

---

* Acknowledgments to Mr. J. W. Headlam's articles in *Westminster Gazette*, October 2, 3, and 5, 1917.

(17) *Aug.* 2.—French frontier crossed by German troops at four points (Cirey, Longlaville, Petite-Croix, etc.), regardless of fact that war had not been declared nor had the German Ambassador left Paris. French orders given not to fire on German scouting parties, unless they attacked.

(18) *Aug.* 2.—Proclamation in *London Gazette* of partial moratorium (postponement for one month of payment on bills of exchange, other than cheques).

(19) *Aug.* 3.—Sir E. Grey announces in Parliament the attitude which the Government had adopted towards the European crisis and the active steps taken. Assurance had been given to France of the protection of our Fleet should the German Fleet attack the French Coast or the French shipping ; no engagement had as yet been made to send an expeditionary force out of the country. Germany was prepared if we would pledge ourselves to neutrality to agree that her fleet would not attack the northern coast of France. " This is too narrow an engagement for us ; we cannot issue a declaration of unconditional neutrality."

(20) *Aug.* 4.—" . . . A French inroad on our flank on the Lower Rhine would have been fatal to us. So we were forced to set aside the just protests of the Luxemburg and Belgian Governments. The wrong—I speak openly—the wrong that we now do we will try to make good again as soon as our military ends have been reached. When one is threatened as we are, and all is at stake, one can only think of how one can hack one's way out . . . "

(21) *Aug.* 4.—Sir E. Goschen's final interview with German Chancellor, Herr von Bethmann-Hollweg, after the British ultimatum with regard to Belgium had been rejected. Chancellor deprecated going to war for the sake of " neutrality," for " a scrap of paper." Had British Government considered price at which compact would have been kept ?

(22) *Aug.* 4.—Great Britain presents ultimatum to Germany. Ultimatum required that Germany should give unequivocal assurances that she would respect the neutral territory of Belgium guaranteed by her in 1839 and endorsed by her (in writing) in 1870. Failing this assurance, Great Britain would " take all steps " to uphold the neutrality of Belgium and the observance of the treaty.

(23) *Aug.* 5.—" Breslau " chased into Messina harbour by British cruisers. Owing to misunderstanding she escapes with " Goeben," August 6.

(24) *Aug.* 5.—Speech in House of Commons outlining " infamous proposal " (*v.* Appendix (12)) made by Germany with regard to Belgium, and defining our object : (1) To fulfil solemn international obligations, (2) to vindicate the rights of small nationalities against the aggression of larger Powers.

(25) *Aug.* 7.—General Rennenkampf's main army crosses the frontier at Suwalki, and commences the invasion of East Prussia.

(26) *Aug.* 7.—Kaiser issues proclamation to the German people stating that since the foundation of the Empire he and his ancestors had laboured for peace, but " in the midst of perfect peace, enemies surprise us." " We shall resist to the last breath of man and horse."

(27) *Aug.* 15.—Meeting at Treuerfontein (Western Transvaal) of Dutch Burghers, convened at instigation of rebel and German plotters. Address by General Delarey, who possessed unrivalled influence in Western Transvaal, to about 800 burghers. Situation in Europe explained and exhortation to keep cool and await events.

(28) *Aug.* 15.—Ultimatum regarding the evacuation of Tsing-tau (the naval port of Kiao-chau, the German Protectorate in China) presented to Germany by Japan.

(29) *Aug.* 18.—Southern Russian army enters Galicia in three columns, following three separate railways converging on Lemberg. Second Russian Army (General Russky) crossing frontier 14.8.14 captures town of Sokal. Third Russian Army (General Brusilov) moving westward menaces Second Austrian Army by way of Tarnopol and valley of Sereth.

(30) *Aug.* 19.—Extract from Order reported issued by Emperor, 19.8.14, H.Q., Aix-la-Chapelle :—" It is my Royal and Imperial Command that you concentrate your energies, etc., etc. . . . to exterminate first the treacherous English, and to walk over General French's contemptible little army."

(31) *Aug.* 23.—*Mons, Battle of.*—The British Force, consisting of the 1st and 2nd Corps (1st and 2nd, 3rd and 5th Divisions) and Cavalry Division (four Brigades) holding a front of over twenty miles along the line Binche-Mons-Pommeroeul, violently attacked by von Kluck's Army of at least four Corps besides cavalry. The Force was isolated through the 5th French Army (Lanrezac) on the right falling back during the afternoon, and its left flank was being threatened by the German 2nd Corps from the

N.W. Consequently, after heavy losses had been inflicted on the enemy, a retirement was ordered for the next day and was successfully carried out by alternate Corps, the Germans being kept off by severe rearguard actions.

([32]) *Aug.* 25.—*Kitchener, Lord : First Speech as War Minister.*—Troops for past 36 hours in contact with superior German forces, maintained all traditions of British soldiery. Estimated casualties so far over 2,000. 69 Territorial Battalions volunteer for service abroad. 100,000 recruits practically secured. Principle to observe, maximum forces of enemy Empires constantly diminish, our reinforcements steadily increase, army worthy of British Empire results. New Field Army in six or seven months may total 30 divisions continually maintained in field. If war prolonged and future adverse, greater sacrifices required from Empire and nation.

([33]) *Aug.* 26.—*Le Cateau, Battle of.*—The close pursuit by von Kluck's 1st Army caused the British 2nd Corps (3rd and 5th Divisions) to halt in its retirement from Mons and give battle on the high ground west of Le Cateau. Strengthened by most of the 4th Division on its left and 19th Brigade on its right, the 2nd Corps (Sir H. Smith-Dorrien) withstood terrific artillery fire and violent attacks by the enemy till about 3 p.m., when, its right being penetrated and rolled up, it continued the retirement on St. Quentin in good spirits, the Germans being too exhausted by their losses to pursue in force. Sordet's French Cavalry Corps came up during the battle and assisted on the left.

([34]) *Aug.* 28.—*Bight of Heligoland, Battle in.*—1st Battle-cruiser Squadron, under Rear-Admiral Beatty, 1st Light Cruiser Squadron, under Commodore Goodenough, and a strong force of destroyers sink 3 German cruisers and 2 destroyers, and damage many others.

([35]) *Sept.* 4.—Patriotic appeal to the citizens of London, emphasising the efforts made to preserve peace and paying tribute to the splendid response of the British Empire to the call to arms.

([36]) *Sept.* 5.—*No Separate Peace.*—Agreement signed on behalf of England, France and Russia by Sir E. Grey, M. Cambon, and Count Benckendorff respectively. All parties mutually engage not to conclude peace separately during present war, and when peace terms are discussed, no one of the Allies will demand peace without previous agreement of each of the other two.

([37]) *Sept.* 6.—*The Marne, Battle of.*—On September 5, Joffre decided on counter-offensive, and on following day retirement turned into advance. Order of battle from East to West :—

    Allies : Army of Lorraine and 2nd Army (Castelnau and Dubail) beyond the
             Meuse ; 3rd Army (Sarrail) ; 4th Army (Langle de Cary) ; Cavalry ;
             9th Army (Foch) ; 5th Army (Fauchet de l'Espérey) ; Conneau's Cavalry
             Corps ; British Force (French) ; 6th Army (Maunoury). Total (W. of
             Meuse) about 47 infantry and 9 cavalry divisions.
    Germans : 6th Army (Cr. Prince Rupprecht) and 7th Army (v. Heeringen) beyond
             the Meuse ; 5th Army (Crown Prince) ; 4th Army (Duke A. of Württem-
             berg) ; 3rd Army (v. Hausen) ; 2nd Army (v. Bülow) ; 1st Army (v.
             Kluck). Total (W. of Meuse) about 46 infantry and 7 cavalry divisions.

The German right was swung back along the Ourcq, and the French 6th Army, which conformed, attacked, as well as some of the Allied Forces, on the 5th Sept. Kluck's plan was to disregard British (who were believed disorganised), to move across their front and attack the left of the 5th Army ; but being, during the next two days, tackled on his extreme right by the 6th Army, and the British unexpectedly attacking his forces moving against de l'Espérey's left, he found his right centre driven in, and began to fall back by the 8th. The German retreat was also largely caused by the 5th and 9th French Armies, after magnificent fighting (especially on the part of the latter at Fère Champenoise), penetrating the German centre on the 9th and 10th September. Further east desperate fighting took place, where violent attacks by the 4th and 5th German Armies were repulsed with some difficulty by the French. (East of the Meuse, Castelnau before Nancy, and Dubail, after severe fighting, drove the enemy out of Lunéville and St. Dié.) By September 12, the Germans (W. of the Meuse) had fallen back, pursued by the Allies, to the strongly fortified line of the Aisne.

([38]) *Sept.* 7.—Sir J. French's first despatch covers the period since the landing of British troops (1st Corps, 1st and 2nd Divisions; 2nd Corps, 3rd and 5th Divisions and 1st Cavalry Division) in France up to their retirement to the Oise (August 28) on the line Noyon-Chaulny-La Fère. It describes the battles of Mons (23rd), Landrecies (25th), Le Cateau (26th), together with the arrival of the 4th Division on the 25th.

and the general retreat necessitated by the overwhelming German forces, and the movements of the French troops who assisted in this theatre. Sir H. Smith-Dorrien and the R.F.C. specially singled out for distinction.

(39) *Sept.* 8.—" Silver Bullet " speech at Local Government Board to Deputation from the Association of Municipal Corporations. Points out necessity for curtailing expenditure and foretells heavy outgoings.

(40) *Sept.* 9.—The Capitulations were treaties which conferred on the nation concerned the privilege of governing its own subjects within the Ottoman Empire. This led to endless complications and troubles, especially in Egypt. In the case of England and France the capitulations dated from the 16th century. See *Times*, September 12, 1914. *Enc. Brit.*, ed. 1910, s.v.

(41) *Sept.* 10.—The " Emden " appears in the Bay of Bengal (after having been " lost " since the outbreak of war) and captures six British vessels—5 sunk and the 6th sent into Calcutta with the crews.

(42) *Sept.* 17.—Sir J. French's second despatch of September 17 covers the period from August 28 to September 10. It describes the continuation of the retreat, change of base from Havre to St. Nazaire, arrival on line south of the Marne, Joffre's determination to counter-advance, movements of French and British armies, and their advance on September 6, and the battle of the Marne (September 6 to 10), and mentions the beginning of the battle of the Aisne (September 12).

(43) *Sept.* 18.—The King's Speech at the Prorogation of Parliament roused remarkable enthusiasm, members rising in their places and singing the National Anthem. " We are fighting for a worthy purpose, and shall not lay down our arms until that purpose has been fully achieved."

(44) *Sept.* 19.—Historic recruiting speech to the London Welsh at the Queen's Hall. " Scrap of paper " theory of treaties ; " treaties are the currency of international statesmanship."

(45) *Sept.* 21.—Confident recruiting speech at Liverpool. German Navy to be dug out " like rats in a hole."

(46) *Sept.* 28.—Dukla and Uzsok Passes seized by Russians and raids by cavalry ensued. These movements not only of strategic but of economic and political importance ; Germans drew on horse supplies of Hungary to recoup their losses, and this trade would be affected by hostile incursions. Politically, hopes were based on the hatred of the Slav mountaineers and Hungarian plainsmen being aroused against Germany on account of troops being used for German purposes and country left defenceless.

(47) *Oct.* 8.—Sir J. French's third despatch of October 8 covers the period from September 11 to the end of September. It describes the crossing of the Ourcq, arrival at the Aisne and crossing of this river by most of our forces, together with the severe fighting involved; arrival of the 6th Division on the 16th ; necessity for more and heavier guns ; German counter-attacks perpetually defeated up to the 28th, when they died away. Our total losses during this period 561 officers and 12,980 men.

(48) *Oct.* 16.—General bombardment of Tsing-tau from the sea by combined British and Japanese forces, assisted by aeroplanes. " Iltis " and " Kaiser " Forts considerably damaged. Casualties to Allied forces, 3 only, all British.

(49) *Oct.* 28.—Admiral Prince Louis of Battenberg, owing to totally unfounded suspicions regarding his nationality and loyalty, resigns office as First Sea Lord, and is succeeded by Lord Fisher.

(50) *Oct.* 29.—Turkey enters war on the side of Central Empires. Telegram from Petrograd states that German-Turkish warships " Breslau " and " Hamidia " bombarded simultaneously and unexpectedly unfortified seaside towns of Theodosia (Crimea) and Novorossisk respectively.

(51) *Nov.* 1.—Rear-Admiral Sir Christopher Cradock's squadron, consisting of " Good Hope " (flag) 14,100 t., " Monmouth " 9,800 t., and " Glasgow " 4,800 t., engaged by " Gneisenau " 11,400 t., " Scharnhorst " 11,400 t., " Dresden " 3,540 t., " Leipzig " 3,200 t., " Nürnberg " 3,350 t., under Admiral Count von Spee off Coronel (the coast of Chili) ; " Good Hope " and " Monmouth " sunk.

(52) *Nov.* 4.—Tanga, German port on the Moschi Railway, (E. Africa), attacked unsuccessfully by an Indian Expeditionary Force with one British battalion. 1st Loyal North Lancashire Regt., 101st Grenadiers, I.A., and 1st Kashmir Rifles suffered heavily during the engagement in the town, and forced to retreat to coast and re-embark. Casualties nearly 800, including 141 British officers and men. Germans displayed great cunning in defence of town, also employing native *ruses de guerre*.

(⁵³) *Nov.* 5.—Baron Sonnino made Minister of Foreign Affairs. General approval. Hopes entertained Minister will bring about reconstruction of Balkan League for protection of Italian interests. Salandra, Premier ; Carcano, Treasury ; Daneo, Public Works.

(⁵⁴) *Nov.* 9.—German cruiser "Emden" (4.1 in. guns, Capt. von Müller) run down and forced to fight by H.M.A.S. "Sydney" (6 in. guns, Capt. J. C. T. Glossop, R.N.) at Cocos (Keeling) Islands, Indian Ocean, where former ship had landed armed party to destroy wireless and cut cable. German ship driven ashore and burnt—230 casualties. "Sydney" losses totalled 18. Damage caused to British commerce by "Emden" estimated at £2,211,000.

(⁵⁵) *Nov.* 16.—"Jehad" proclaimed with much pomp at Constantinople by the Sheikh-ul-Islam, under German influence. Kaiser represented as convert to Islam. Moslem subjects of France, Russia and England alleged to be ripe for revolt.

(⁵⁶) *Nov.* 17.—First War Budget.—Chief points : War Loan of 350 millions at 3½ per cent., issued at 95, redeemable at par from 10-14 years. Income Tax and Super-tax doubled (2s. 6d. earned, 1s. 6d. unearned), a third extra only charged this year. Beer to cost consumer ½d. per half-pint extra ; Tea tax raised 3d. per lb., making it 8d. ; Reduction of licence duty for publicans according to curtailment of business hours.

(⁵⁷) *Nov.* 20.—Sir J. French's despatch (fourth) of November 20, covers the period from the beginning of October to November 19 (12th the last date mentioned), including the Givenchy-Armentières-Wytschaete fighting, and the first battle of Ypres. It describes the transfer of the British army from the Aisne to the North-west, and its swing round to the East, arrival of the 4th Corps (7th and 8th Divisions) and 2nd Cavalry Division in Flanders, fighting of the 2nd Corps near La Bassée, 3rd Corps near Armentières, and 1st and 4th Corps, etc., round Ypres.

(⁵⁸) *Dec.* 8.—"Leipzig," "Nürnberg," "Scharnhorst," and "Gneisenau" sunk by Rear-Admiral Sir F. Sturdee's squadron "Invincible," "Irresistible," "Kent," "Cornwall," "Glasgow," off the Falkland Islands.

"Invincible"	...	17,250 t.	"Gneisenau" ...	11,400 t.
"Irresistible"	...	17,250 t.	"Scharnhorst" ...	11,400 t.
"Kent"	... ...	9,800 t.	"Dresden" (sunk	3,540 t.
"Cornwall"	...	9,800 t.	later)	
"Glasgow"	...	4,800 t.	"Leipzig" ...	3,200 t.
			"Nürnberg" ...	3,350 t.

(⁵⁹) *Dec.* 14.—At informal meeting of Unionist Chairman and Parliamentary Agents, contents of letter sent by him and Lord Lansdowne to Mr. Asquith, Sunday 2.8.14, divulged. In their opinion and that of colleagues consulted, security and honour of United Kingdom jeopardised if Government hesitated to support France and Russia. Offer support of Opposition to any measure deemed necessary for that object.

(⁶⁰) *Dec.* 15.—Report of enquiry shows that the explosion which caused the loss of the ship was due to the accidental ignition of ammunition on board. No evidence to support suggestion that explosion was due to treachery.

(⁶¹) *Dec.* 16.—Scarborough : enemy cruisers attacked town about 8 a.m. Entered S. Bay under cover of dawn and mist. Bombardment lasted half-hour, 18 people killed, 100 wounded. Whitby : bombarded same day about 9 a.m. for half-hour. Abbey and private property slightly damaged. No damage of military importance.

(⁶²) *Dec.* 18.—British Protectorate declared in Egypt ; abolition of Turkish suzerainty. Deposition of Khedive Abbas Hilmi owing to anti-British intrigues ; Khedivate with title of Sultan of Egypt offered to, and accepted by, his uncle, Prince Hussein Kamel, second son of Ismail Pasha.

(⁶³) *Dec.* 18.—Adolf Ahlers, naturalised British subject and lately German Consul at Sunderland, had been sentenced to death for high treason for having incited and assisted German reservists to return to Germany.

(⁶⁴) *Dec.* 29.—U.S.A. protests against detention of ships and unwarrantable interference with U.S. foreign trade ; objects to British treatment of conditional contraband. Friendly, but rather sharply worded.

INDEX.

Figures in black type represent the month : *e.g.*, 4.**1** = 4th Jan. ; 24.**11**, 24th Nov. ; etc.

N.B.—In the following index a number of items are included which, by reason of their uncertainty or for some other cause, it has not been found easy or convenient to place in the Chronological Tables. Dates which can at present be only approximately given are indicated thus :—" *c.* 25.**8**."

" AUDACIOUS," H.M.S. (battleship).
Sunk by a mine, 27.**10**.

AUGUSTOVO (N. Poland).
Abandoned by Russians, 20.**9**; Recovered, 1.**10**; Battle near, 1-9.**10**.

AUSTRIA-HUNGARY.
Councils regarding Serbia, 7.**7**, 21.**7**; Ultimatum to Serbia, 23.**7**; Minister leaves Belgrade, 25.**7**; Partial mobilisation, 26.**7**; Declaration of war on Serbia, 28.**7**; General mobilisation, 1.**8**; Declaration of War on Russia, 5.**8**; Declaration of War on Japan, 25.**8**.

" BADGER," H.M.S.
Destroys German submarine, 25.**10**.

BAILLEUL (France).
Occupied by British, 14.**10**.

BAKALARYEVO (N. Poland).
Russian victory at, 30.**10**.

BARTFELD (Hungary).
Occupied by Russians, 2.**12**.

BASRA (Mesopotamia).
Evacuated by Turks, 21.**11**; Occupied by British, 21-23.**11**.

BATOUM (Black Sea).
Bombarded by "Goeben," 11.**12**.

BATTENBERG, PRINCE LOUIS OF
(now Marquis of Milford Haven).
Resigned office of First Sea Lord, 28.**10**.

BAYAZID (Armenia).
Occupied by Russians, 3.**11**; Evacuated by Russians, c.17.**11**.

BEAUZEC (near Verdun, France).
German advance checked at, 6.**9**.

BELGIUM
Decides to defend neutrality, 1.**8**; Receives German ultimatum, 2.**8**; Appeals to Britain for aid, 3.**8**; Invaded by Germans, 4.**8**; Receives offer of German peace, 9.**8**; Declines offer of German peace, 12.**8**; Government moved to Antwerp, 17.**8**; Government moved to Ostend, 7.**10**; Government moved to Havre, 13.**10**.

BELGRADE (Serbia).
Bombarded by Austrians, 28.**7**. *sq.*; Evacuated by Serbians, 29.**11**; Entered by Austr., 2.**12**; Austr. expelled, 15.**12**.

" BERLIN " (German armed Cruiser).
Interned at Trondhjem, 16.**11**.

BETHMANN-HOLLWEG, HERR V. (German Chancellor).
Interview with Sir E. Goschen, 4.**8**; Speech in Reichstag, 4.**8**; Reply to Mr. Asquith, 13.**9**; Speech in Reichstag, 2.**12**.

BEYERS, GENERAL (South Africa).
Dismissed from his command, 17.**9**; Revolted, c.24.**10**; Drowned in Vaal River, 7.**12**.

" BIRMINGHAM," H.M.S.
Sinks German submarine, 9.**8**.

BISMARCK ARCHIPELAGO.
Occupied by Australian troops, 11.**9**.

BLAMONT (Lorraine).
Attacked by Germans, 11.**8**.

BONA (Algeria).
Bombarded by " Goeben " and " Breslau," 4.**8**.

BOTHA, GENERAL (South Africa).
Assumes command of Union forces, 22.**9**; Crushes the rebellion by 8.**12**.

BOTHAVILLE (South Africa).
Beyers defeated, 7.**12**.

BOUGAINVILLE (Solomon Islands).
Captured by Australian troops, 13.**9**.

" BRESLAU " (German cruiser).
Bombards Bona and Philippeville, 4.**8**; At Messina, 5-6.**8**; Enters Dardanelles, 11.**8**; Reported purchase by Turkey, 12.**8**; Engaged with Russian squadron, 18.**11**.

BRITISH EAST AFRICA.
(See East Africa).

BRITISH EXPEDITIONARY FORCE.
Begins to land in France, 7.**8**; landing completed, 16.**8**; Concentration effected, 21.**8**; Removal from the Aisne begun, 3.**10** Established in Flanders complete, 19.**10**.

BRODY (East Galicia).
Taken by Russians, 23.**8**.

BRUGES (Belgium).
Occupied by Germans, 14.**10**.

BRUSSELS.
Occupied by Germans, 20.**8**; Levy of £8,000,000 demanded, 22.**8**; German airsheds bombed, 19 and 24.**12**.

BRZEZANY (E. Galicia).
German advance upon, 19.**11**; Heavy German defeat near, c.28.**11**.

BUDGET (British).
First introduced during the war, 17.**11**.

BULGARIA.
Proclaims neutrality, 3.**11**.

BÜLOW, PRINCE (German Ambassador).
Reaches Rome on special mission, 17.**12**

BULTFONTEIN (South Africa).
Rebels routed at, 14.**11**.

" BULWARK," H.M.S.
Blown up in Medway, 26.**11**; Report of enquiry issued, 15.**12**.

BZURA, RIVER (Poland).
Russ. retreat to, 16.**12**; Germ. try to cross, 21.**12**; Germ. cross, 23.**12**; Germ. driven back, 25.**12**; Germ. abandon, 26.**12**.

CAILLAUX, MADAME (France).
Trial of, begun, 20.**7**; Trial of, ended, 28.**7**.

CALLAGHAN, ADMIRAL SIR G. A.
Resigns command to Jellicoe, 4.**8**; Appointed to the Nore, 22.**12**.

CALVINIA (South Africa).
Rebels routed at, 25.**10**.

EAST PRUSSIA.
Entered by Russ., 2.8 and 7.8 ; General Russ. advance, 16.8 ; Evacuated by Russ., 16.9 ; Re-entered by Russ., 2.11 ; Advance by Russ. checked, 14.11.

EGHEZEE (Belgium).
Belgian success at, 13.8.

EGYPT. ⁹
Violation of frontier by Beduins, 31.10 ; Skirmish near Port Said, 20.11 ; British Protectorate proclaimed, 17.12 ; Sultan Hussein I. proclaimed, 18.12 ; Australian and New Zealand troops arrive at Cairo, 23.12.

" EMDEN " (German commerce raider).
First appearance, Bay of Bengal, 10.9 ; Bombards Madras, 22.9 ; Lists of captures announced, 29.9 and 22.10 ; Sinks " Kamasaka Maru," 27.10 ; Sinks " Zhemchug," 28.10 ; Destroyed by H.M.A.S." Sydney," 9.11.

ÉPERNAY (Reims).
Occupied by the Germans 4.9 ; Recovered by the French, 11.9.

EYDTKUHNEN (East Prussia).
Russ. victory announced, 19.8 ; Germ. recover, c.16.9 ; Russ. re-enter, 8.11.

FALKENHAYN (German General).
Becomes Acting Chief-of-Staff, 25.10 ; Definitely supersedes Moltke, 10.12.

FALKLAND ISLANDS (Naval Battle of).
Admiral Sturdee defeats Admiral Count Spee, 8.12.

FAO (Persian Gulf).
Occupied by the British, 8.11.

FÈRE CHAMPENOISE (Battle of) (*v.* La Fère).

FESTUBERT (Bethune).
Battles at, 13.10 ; 29.10 ; 23.11 ; 19.12.

FISHER, LORD.
Becomes First Sea Lord, 29.10.

FLANDERS (Battle of).
(Including battles of Yser and Ypres) 11.10 to 20.11.

FOCH (French General).
Brilliant move at the Marne, 8.9 ; Takes command of the Allies in view of the impending Flanders battle, 8.10.

FOURIE (Capt. and Lieut.) (South Africa).
Trial and condemnation, 19-20.12.

FRANCE :
Revelation of military unreadiness, 13-14.7 ; Order for mobilisation, 1.8 ; Entered by German troops, 2.8 ; Declares war on Austria, 10.8 ; Government moved to Bordeaux, 2.9 ; " Yellow Book " published, 30.11 ; Government returns to Paris, 10.12.

FRANKENAU (East Prussia).
Germans defeated at, 23-24.8.

FRANZ FERDINAND (*v.* Archduke).

FREIBURG - IN - BREISGAU (Baden).
Airsheds bombed by Fr. airmen, 5.12.

FRENCH, SIR JOHN (now Viscount).
Lands at Boulogne, 14.8 ; Visits the President and General Joffre, 15.8 ; Takes up Headquarters at Le Cateau, 17.8 ; Sends first despatch, 7.9 ; Sends second despatch, 17.9 ; Sends third despatch, 8.10 ; Sends fourth despatch, 20.11 ; Invested with O.M., 3.12.

FRESCATI (W. of Metz).
Airsheds bombed by French airmen, 26.12.

FRIEDRICHSHAFEN (Württemberg).
Zeppelin factory raided by airmen, 21.11.

GALICIA (Austria).
Russian invasion begins, 18.8 ; Eastern portion conquered, 16.9 ; Western portion nearly conquered, 28.9 ; Austrian recovery begins, 3.10 ; Russians check Austrians, 18.10 ; New Austro-German advance, 18.11.

" GEIER " (German cruiser).
Interned at Honolulu, 9.11.

GEORGE V., KING.
Calls conference *re* Home Rule, 19.7 ; " King's Speech " *re* the war, 18.9 & 11.11 ; Visit to Army in France, 29.11 and 5.12.

GEORGE, RT. HON. D. LLOYD.
Speech at Local Government Board, 8.9 ; Speech at Queen's Hall, 19.9 ; Introduces first War Budget, 17.11.

GERMANY.
News of preparation for mobilisation, 21.7 ; " Infamous Offer " to Britain, 29.7 ; " State of War " proclaimed, 31.7 ; Ultimatum to Russia and France, 31.7 ; General mobilisation announced, 1.8 ; Declaration of War on Russia, 1.8 ; Ultimatum to Belgium, 2.8 ; Declaration of War on France, 3.8 ; Declaration of War on Belgium, 4.8.

GHELUVELT (near Ypres. Belgium).
Heavy German attacks, 24-31.10.

GHENT (Belgium).
Occupied by the Germans, 13.10.

GIVENCHY (Bethune).
Heavy German attacks, 13.10 ; 7.11 and 18-23.12.

" GNEISENAU " (German cruiser).
Bombards Papeete, 22.9 ; In battle of Coronel, 1.11 ; Sunk off Falkland Is. 8.12.

" GOEBEN " (German cruiser).
Bombards Bona and Philippeville, 4.8 ; At Messina, 5-6.8 ; Enters Dardanelles, 11.8 ; Reported purchase by Turkey, 12.8 ; Damaged in Black Sea fight, 18.11 ; Bombards Batoum, 11.12.

" GOOD HOPE," H.M.S.
Sunk in Battle of Coronel, 1.11.

clamation, 7.8; Alleged message *re* Brit. army, 19.8; Adorns himself with Iron Cross, 1.11; Removed from Brit. Navy List, 5.11.

" KAISER WILHELM DER GROSSE."
Sunk by H.M.S. " Highflyer," 27.8.

KAISER WILHELM'S LAND.
Occupied by Australian troops, 24.9.

KALISH (Poland).
Occupied by Germans, 2.8; Evacuated by Germans, *c.*9.11.

KASIMIRYEV (Poland).
German defeat at, 21.10.

KATIYA (near Suez Canal).
Skirmish with Turks, 21.11.

KEIMOES (South Africa).
Rebels routed at, 22.10.

KIAO-CHAU.
(See Tsing-Tau).

KIEL CANAL (re-opening of).
British naval visit, 23-25.6.

KISI (British East Africa).
Occupied by Germans, 10.9; German reverse near, 12.9.

KITCHENER, LORD.
Appointed Secretary of State for War, 5.8; First speech in Parliament, 25.8.

KLEIN ZILLEBEKE (near Ypres, Belgium).
Battle of, Germans repulsed, 6.11.

" KÖLN " (German cruiser).
Sunk in Battle of the Bight, 28.8.

" KÖNIGIN LUISE " (German minelayer).
Destroyed by British scouts, 5.8.

" KÖNIGSBERG " (German cruiser).
Disables H.M.S. " Pegasus," 20.9; Discovered in Rufiji River, 30.10; blockaded, 10.11.

KOPRUKEUI (Armenia).
Battle at, 9.11; Occupied by Russians, 22.11; Recovered by Turks, 17.12.

KRASNIK (S. Poland).
Austrians defeat Russians, 25.8; Russians defeat Austrians, 10.9.

KRASNOSTAV (S. Poland).
Austrians defeated, 6.9.

KROSNO (Galicia).
In possession of the Russians, 28.9.

KRUPANI (Serbia).
Austrian advance checked, 11.9.

KRZESZOV (Galicia).
Russians seize bridge over San, 14.9.

KURNA (Mesopotamia).
Evacuated by the Turks, 9.12.

KUTNO (Poland).
Russians defeated by Germans, 16.11.

KYELTSI (Poland).
Evacuated by the Russians, 22.8; Re-occupied by the Russians, *c.*6.9; Again evacuated by the Russians, *c.*6.10; Again recovered by the Russians, 3.11; Austrians defeated near, 20.11.

LA BASSÉE (Bethune).
Severe fighting round, 13.10, *sq.*; Critical battle near, 22.10 and 2.11.

LA FÈRE (W. of Laon).
Victory of British cavalry near, 28.8; Occupied by the Germans, 29.8.

LA GARDE (France).
Occupied by the Germans, 13.8.

LANDRÉCIES (La Cateau).
Battle of, 25.8.

LANGEMARCK (Belgium).
Occupied by the Germans, 22.10.; Recovered by the French, 4.12.

LAON (France).
Occupied by the Germans, 30.8.

LASSIGNY (Noyon).
Allies lines extended to, 21.9; captured by the Germans, 25.9.

LAW, RT. HON. BONAR.
Letter of 2.8 to Mr. Asquith published, 14.12.

LAZAREVATS (Serbia).
Battle of, 28.11.

LE CATEAU.
G.H.Q. at, 17.8; Lines occupied by the British, 25.8; Battle of, 26.8.

" LEIPZIG " (German cruiser).
Sunk in Battle of Falkland Islands, 8.12.

LEMBERG (Lvov) (Galicia).
Battle of, 1.9-2.9; Occupied by Russians, 4.9.

LENS (France).
Occupied by Germans, 3.10.

LE QUESNOY-EN-SANTERRE (Chaulnes).
Germans defeated at, 5.11.

LIBAU (Baltic Provinces).
Shelled by German ships, 2.8 and 18.11; Skirmish near, 3.8.

LIÉGE (Belgium).
Attacked by Germans, 4.8; Fort Fléron silenced, 5.8; Three other forts silenced, 6.8; The city occupied, 10.8; Last forts reduced, 15.8.

LIERRE (Belgium).
Taken by the Germans, 6.10.

LILLE (France).
Surrendered to Germans, *c.*27.8; Evacuated by Germans, *c.*3.9; occupied by French troops, 30.9; Bombarded by Germ., 4-10.10; Occupied by Germ., 13.10.

LODY, KARL HANS (German spy).
Trial commenced, 30.10; Execution, 6.11.

LODZ (Poland).
Evacuated by Russians, 10.10; Recovered by Russians, 28.10; Fierce battle for, 22.11, *sq.*; Germans re-occupy, 6.12.

LOMBARTZYDE (Belgium).
Captured by Germans, 23.10; Recovered by French, 24.10; Re-captured by Germans, 28.10; Retaken by French, 4.11; Finally secured by Germans, 7.11.

by the Fr., 10.8 ; Recovered by the Fr.,
19.8 ; Again evacuated by the Fr., 25.8.
MUSHROOM VALLEY (South Africa).
Defeat of De Wet, 12.11.
NAMUR (Belgian Fortress).
Bombarded by the Germans, 20.8 ;
Trenches evacuated by Belgians, 21.8, *sq.*;
Evacuation of the city begins, 22.8 ;
Germans capture the city, 23.8 ; Last of
the forts reduced, 27.8.
NANCY (France).
Violent German efforts to take the
place defeated on 25.8 ; 8.9 and 27.10,
Battle of Grande Couronne, 31.8-11.9.
NATIONAL RELIEF FUND.
Inaugurated by Prince of Wales, 7.8.
NEUVE CHAPELLE (France).
Occupied by the British, 16.10 ; taken
by the Germans, 27.10 ; Recovered by the
Brit., 28.10 ; Retaken by the Germ., 2.11.
NEW GUINEA (German).
Town of Friedrich Wilhelm occupied,
24.9.
NICHOLAS, GRAND DUKE (Russia).
Placed in command of Russian armies,
3.8 ; Issues Proclamation to Poles, 14.8.
NIEMEN, RIVER (East Prussian frontier).
Russians driven to, 15.9 ; Vain German
efforts to cross, 26-28.9 ; Germans retire
from, 29.9.
NIEUPORT (Belgium).
Violent German attacks repelled, 27.10;
Allies advance from, 15.12.
" NIGER," H.M.S.
Sunk by German submarine, 11.11.
" NO SEPARATE PEACE."
Agreement signed in London, 5.9.
NORTH SEA.
Proclaimed a military area, 2.11 ;
(see also s.v. Mine-Fields).
NOVI BAZAR (Serbia).
Evacuated by the Austrians, 26.8.
NOVOROSSISK (on Black Sea).
Bombarded by Turkish fleet, 29.10.
NOYON (13 m. N.E. of Compiègne).
Occupied by the French, 21.9 ; cap-
tured by the Germans, 25.9.
NSANAKONG (Cameroons).
Occupied by Brit., 30.8 ; Brit. reverse
near, 6.9.
" NÜRNBERG " (German cruiser).
Sunk off Falkland Islands, 10.12.
NYASSALAND (South Africa).
Repulse of Ger. invasion announced, 10.9.

OBRENOVATS (Serbia).
Vainly attacked by the Austrians, 6.8.
OBRES (Syrmia).
Occupied by the Serbians, 6.9 ; evacu-
ated by the Serbians, 12.9.
" OCEANIC," H.M.S. (auxiliary cruiser).
Wrecked, 8.9.

ODESSA (South Russia).
Bombarded by Turkish warships, 29.10
OPOLE (Poland).
Battle of, 10.9
OSOVYETS (Poland-Russian frontier fort).
Attacked by Germans, 20.9 ; Siege
abandoned by Germans, 29.9.
OSTEND (Belgium).
Occupied by British force, 27.8 ; Belg.
Govt. removes to, 7.10 ; Evacuated by
Allies, 12.10 ; Occupied by the Germans,
15.10.
OSTERODE (Battle of).
s.v. Battle of Tannenberg.
OURCQ, RIVER.
Battle of, 6, 7.9 ; French repulse
Germ., 9.9 ; Brit. cross in pursuit, 11.9.

PACIFIC CABLE.
Cut by German Cruiser " Nürnberg,"
7.9.
" PALLADA " (Russian cruiser).
Sunk in Baltic by submarine, 11.10.
PAPEETE (Tahiti).
Bombarded by " Scharnhorst," etc.,
22.9.
PARIS.
Bombed by Ger. airmen, 30.8 and 11.10.
" PATHFINDER," H.M.S.
Sunk by German submarine, 5.9.
" PEGASUS," H.M.S.
Destroyed by " Königsberg," 20.9.
PÉRONNE (France).
Temporarily occupied by Germ., 26.8 ;
Permanently occupied by Germ., 24.9.
PERSIA.
Declines to join Turkey in war, 4.11.
PERSIAN GULF.
s.v. Mésopotamia.
PERVYSE (Belgium).
German attacks repulsed, 26.10, 7.11.
PETIT-MORIN, RIVER (France).
Combat on line of, 7.9 ; Allies force
passage of, 8.9.
PETROKOV (Poland).
Russian victory at, 27.10 ; Occupied
by Germans, 17.12.
PHILIPPEVILLE (Algeria).
Bombarded by the "Goeben" etc., 4.8.
PIONTEK (Poland).
Captured by the Germans, 19.11.
PLESCHEN (Silesia).
Russians cut railway at, 9.11.
POELCAPELLE (Belgium).
Germans secure possession of, 20.10.
POINCARÉ, PRESIDENT (France).
Leaves Paris on visit to Tsar, 17.7 ;
Reaches Kronstadt, 20.7 ; Returns to
Paris, arrives, 29.7.
POLAND.
Russia's promise of autonomy, 14.8 ;
Proclamation by National Council, 25.11.

E

SASENO (Albanian island).
Occupied by the Italians, 31.**10**.

SCARBOROUGH.
Bombarded by German fleet, 16.**12**.

" SCHARNHORST " (German cruiser).
Bombards Papeete, 22.**9**; At Battle of Coronel, 1.**11**; Sunk off Falkland Islands, 8.**12**.

SCHUIT DRIFT (S. Africa).
Rebels routed at, 30.**10**.

SCHWIDDEN (E. Prussia).
Occupied by Russians, 2.**8**.

SEDAN (France).
Taken by the Germans, 25.**8**.

SEMLIN (Syrmia).
Occupied by the Serbians, 10.**9**; Evacuated by the Serbians, 17.**9**.

SENLIS (17 m. S.W. of Compiègne).
Occupied by the Germans,. 4.**9**.

SERAJEVO (Bosnia).
Archduke Franz Ferdinand murdered, 28.**6**; Anti-Serbian riots, 29.**6**; Serbians and Montenegrins approach, 2.**10**; Serbians and Montenegrins driven back, 4.**10**.

SERBIA.
Receipt of Austrian note, 23.**7**; Serbian answer received: Austrian Minister leaves, 25.**7**; Mobilisation, 26.**7**; Austrian efforts to invade, 29.**7**–12.**8**; First Austrian invasion, 13.**8**–25.**8**; Second Austrian invasion, 7.**9**–15.**9**; Third Austrian invasion, 8.**11**–15.**12**.

SHABATS (Serbian frontier town).
Occupied by Austrians, 16.**8**; Austrians defeated near, 18.**8**; Evacuated by Austrians, 22.**8**.

SILESIA.
Raided by Russians, 9.**11**.

SKIERNIEVITSE (Poland).
Battles at, 20.**11** and 27.**12**.

SOISSONS (France).
Bombarded and taken by Germans, 1.**9**; Evacuated by Germans, c. 12.**9**; Allies force Aisne at, 13.**9**; The town shelled, 15.**9** *sqq*.

SOKAL (N. Galicia).
Austrians defeated by Russians, 14.**8**.

SOKHACHEV (Poland).
Occupied by Germans, 11.**10**; Evacuated by Germans, c. 23.**10**; Heavy fighting round, 15-16.**12**.

SOLDAU (E. Prussia).
Occupied by Russians, 21.**8**; Recovered by Germans, 26.**8**; Re-occupied by Russians, 9.**11**; Once more recovered, 18.**11**.

SOLOMON ISLANDS.
Annexed by Australian troops, 13.**9**.

SOUTH AFRICA.
First seditious meeting, 15.**8**; Second seditious meeting, 15.**9**; Raided by Germans, 10.**8**; Invaded by Germans, 21.**8**;

Lüderitz Bay occupied by British, 18.**9**; Martial law proclaimed, 12.**10**; Revolt of Beyers and De Wet, 24.**10**; Collapse of Rebellion, 8.**12**.

SPECIAL CONSTABLES (Great Britain).
Enrolment begins, 17.**8**.

" SPEEDY," H.M.S.
Destroyed by a mine, 3.**9**.

SPINCOURT (Lorraine).
Battles at, 11.**8** and16.**8**.

SPITHEAD (England).
Naval Review at, 18-20.**7**.

SREDNIKI (Poland).
Germans defeated by Russians, 13.**9**.

STALLUPÖNEN (E. Prussia).
Russ. occupy, 17.**8**; Russ. evacuate, c., 12.**9**; Russ. re-occupy, 8.**11**.

STRYKOV (Poland).
German advance upon, 19.**11**; Fierce battle at, 24.**11**.

SUBMARINES.
B11 torpedoes "Messudiya," 13.**12**; D5 sunk by mine, 3.**11**; E3 announced sunk, 18.**10**; E9 sinks German destroyer, 8.**10**; U15 sunk by "Birmingham," 9.**8**; U16 interned, 6.**12**; U18 rammed and sunk, 23.**11**.

SUEZ CANAL.
Skirmish near, 21.**11**; Turkish advance towards, 28.**11**.

SUVALKI (N. Poland).
Occupied by . Germans, 15.**9**; Recovered by Russians, c., 9.**10**.

SUVOBOR (Serbia).
Serbian attack on Austrians, 2.**12**.

" SYDNEY," H.M.A.S.
Destroys the "Emden," 9.**11**.

SYRMIA.
Serbian invasion of, 6-12.**9**.

TANNENBERG (E. Prussia).
Battle begins, 26.**8**; Defeat of Russians complete, 29.**8**; Utter rout, 31.**8**.

TANGA (E. Africa).
Severe British reverse, 4.**11**.

TARNOPOL (Galicia).
Russians occupy, 23.**8**.

TARNOW (Galicia).
Russians defeat Austrians, 25.**12**.

TAVETA (East Africa).
Germans occupy, 20.**8**.

TERMONDE (Belgium).
German check at, 8.**9**; Occupied by the Germans, 2.**10**.

THEODOSIA (Black Sea).
Bombarded by Turkish fleet, 29.**10**.

THORN (W. Prussia).
Threatened by Russian advance, 13.**11**; Basis of German counter-attack, 14.**11**; German advance in force from, 16.**11**.

TIRLEMONT (Belgium).
Battle between Belgians and Germans,

1915

1915. Jan.	WESTERN FRONT.	EASTERN FRONT.	SOUTHERN FRONT.
1	French take a wood near Mesnil-les-Hurlus, Champagne.	Russians advance at the Uzsok Pass and in the Bukovina.	.. .. ..
2	.. .. ..	Russian successes on the Bzura and Ravka. Hard fighting near Gorlitse. Russian progress near the Uzsok and Rostoka Passes.	.. .. ..
3	French fail in attack on Boureuilles (Argonne), but carry a height near Cernay (Alsace).	Russians occupy Suczava (Bukovina).	Austrians occupy AdaTsiganlia, an island near Belgrade.
4	French advance near St. Georges (Flanders), and complete capture of Steinbach (Alsace) after several days' fighting.	.. .. ..	.. .. ..
5	French blow up half-a-mile of German trenches in the Argonne.	.. .. ..	.. .. ..
6	French occupy woods north of Altkirch (Alsace).	Russians occupy Kimpolung (Bukovina) and reach Hungarian frontier.	.. .. ..
7	French occupy Burnhauptle-Haut (Alsace).	Heavy German attacks on lower Ravka repulsed.	.. .. ..
8	French carry Hill 132, N. of Soissons, and capture Perthes (Champagne). Germans retake Burnhaupt-le-Haut.	.. .. ..	.. .. ..
9	German counter-attacks near Soissons and at Perthes repulsed.	.. .. ..	.. .. ..
10	French make further progress at Hill 132 and N. of Perthes. 16 German aeroplanes attempt to cross Channel, but, foiled by the weather, bomb Dunkirk.	.. .. ..	.. .. ..

Asiatic and Egyptian Theatres.	Naval and Overseas Operations.	Political, &c.	1915. Jan.
Heavy fighting at Sarikamish (Russ. Armen.).	H. M. S. "Formidable" torpedoed in the Channel	Institution of the Military Cross announced (Warrant of 28/12/14.)	1
Battle of Sarikamish continues.	H.M.Ss. "Fox" and "Goliath" bombard Dar-es-Salaam.	..	2
Very heavy fighting at Sarikamish, and at Ardahan (Transcauc).	..	Arrest of Cardinal Mercier (Belgium) for Pastoral Letter.	3
Russian victories at Sarikamish and Ardahan; Turkish army corps destroyed at the former.	..	..	4
..	Union forces occupy Schuit Drift on the Orange River.	..	5
..	..	Lord Kitchener reviews the military situation in the House of Lords.	6
..	..	British Note with "preliminary observations" in reply to American Note of 29/12/14 on interference with neutral trade(¹).	7
..	..	..	8
..	Capture of the last rebels in the Transvaal announced.	British answer to U.S. Note of 29/12/14 published.	9
Turks reported advancing on Suez Canal.	..	..	10

1915. Jan.	WESTERN FRONT.	EASTERN FRONT.	SOUTHERN FRONT.
11	German counter - attacks repulsed and fresh progress made by French N. of Soissons. Fierce fighting at Beauséjour Farm (Champagne).	.. .. ..	.. .. ..
12	Germans recapture eastern slopes of Hill 132 (Soissons).	Russians capture several villages near Rosog (E. Prussia).	.. .. ..
13	Germans recover all Hill 132, and take the heights of Vregny.	Russians advance on Lower Vistula and occupy Serpets N. of Plotsk.	.. .. ..
14	French withdraw to S. bank of Aisne opposite Missy and Crouy. Germans claim 5,200 prisoners and 14 guns in the fighting near Soissons.	.. .. ..	.. .. ..
15	German advance near Soissons checked.	.. .. ..	.. .. ..
16	French artillery drives Germans from trenches near Nieuport. French successes in engagements at Blangy, near Arras, and in Champagne.	Russians continue to advance on Lower Vistula, repulse heavy attacks near Bolimov (on Ravka), and occupy the Kirlibaba Pass (Bukovina).	.. ..
17	German attacks near Autrêches, N.W. of Soissons, repulsed. German works in the Bois-le-Prêtre (near Pont-à-Mousson) captured	.. .. ..	.. ..
18	Further French progress in the Bois-le-Prêtre.	.. .. ..	.. ..
19	Zeppelin drops bombs on Yarmouth and on King's Lynn and neighbourhood.	.. .. ..	.. ..
20	French progress in the Bois-le-Prêtre. Fierce fighting at the Hartmannsweilerkopf (Alsace.).	Russians take Skempe (N.W. Poland), advance in the Bukovina, and repulse Austrian attack on the Kirlibaba Pass.	.. ..

Asiatic and Egyptian Theatres.	Naval and Overseas Operations.	Political, &c.	1915. Jan.
.. .. ..	.. .. ..	.. .. ..	11
.. .. ..	Union forces occupy Raman's Drift (Orange River).	German use of poison shells reported from Paris.	12
Battle of Kara Urgan (Armenia), which has lasted several days, continues desperately. Turks occupy Tabriz (Persia).	Germans attack Jasin (German E. Africa).	Resignation of Count Berchtold, Austro-Hungarian Minister of Foreign Affairs. He is succeeded by Baron Stephen Burian.	13
.. .. ..	Union forces occupy Swakopmund, German S.W. Africa.	.. .. ..	14
Russians take 4,000 prisoners near Kara Urgan.	.. .. ..	.. .. ..	15
Russian victory at Kara Urgan, Turkish corps routed.	.. .. ..	.. .. ..	16
.. .. ..	French submarine "Saphir" sunk in the Dardanelles.	.. .. ..	17
Turks driven back W. of Chorok river (Armenia).	.. .. ..	.. .. ..	18
.. .. ..	Surrender of British force at Jasin (except 40 Kashmiris—ammunition finished).	.. .. ..	19
.. .. ..	.. .. ..	.. .. ..	20

1915. Jan.	WESTERN FRONT.	EASTERN FRONT.	SOUTHERN FRONT.
21	French take woods near the farm of Beauséjour, but lose ground in the Bois-le-Prêtre.	Further Austrian attack at the Kirlibaba Pass repulsed.	.. .. ..
22	Heavy fighting at Fontaine Madame and St. Hubert (Argonne) and at the Hartmannsweilerkopf. Aeroplane raid by the Germans on Dunkirk, and by the British on Zeebrugge.	Austrians, having been strongly reinforced, recapture Kirlibaba.	.. ..
23	Continued heavy fighting in the Argonne and Alsace.	.. .. ..	.. .. ..
24	.. .. ..	.. .. ..	.. .. ..
25	German attacks repulsed by French near Ypres and by British W. of La Bassée. Ground lost by French near Craonne.	Zeppelin brought down by Libau forts. Russian advance in Pillkallen district (E. Prussia). Hard fighting in Carpathians.	.. ..
26	Continued fighting near Craonne; successful French counter-attacks.	Russian success near the Dukla Pass.	.. .. ..
27	Germans repulsed in the Argonne. French progress in the Vosges, especially near Senones.	.. .. ..	.. .. ..
28	German aeroplane raid by night on Dunkirk.	Russians driven back near Beskid Pass.	.. ..
29	British repulse German attack at Cuinchy (S.W. of La Bassée). Failure of German attempts to cross the Aisne near Soissons.	Continued heavy fighting between Dukla and Wyszkov Passes; Russians losing ground. Russians advance towards Tilsit.	.. ..
30	French lose ground and 700 prisoners in Western Argonne.	German offensive near Lipno (N.W. Poland) driven back.	.. ..

Asiatic and Egyptian Theatres.	Naval and Overseas Operations.	Political, &c.	1915. Jan.
.. .. ..	British s.s. "Durward" sunk by submarine near Maas lightship.	H.M. Ambassador at Washington announces that s.s. "Dacia," if captured, will be placed in a Prize Court ([2]).	21
.. .. ..	.. .. ..	.. .. ..	22
Two Turkish divisions defeated at Khorsan (Armenia).	.. .. ..	.. .. ..	23
.. .. ..	**Battle of the Dogger Bank** ([3]). Maritz and Kemp repulsed at Upington.	Publication of letter by Mr. Bryan refuting charge that U.S.A. Government had shown partiality to the Entente.	**24**
British raid on Alexandretta; telegraph wires cut.	German light cruiser "Gazelle" torpedoed by Russian submarine off Rügen, but towed to harbour.	German Government issues decree seizing all stocks of grain and flour as from Feb. 1.	25
Turks renew their attacks in Armenia. Patrol engagement near El Kántara (Suez Canal).	Loss of H.M.S. "Viknor," auxiliary cruiser, announced.	.. .. ..	26
Russians take Gorness (Armenia), capturing staff of a Turkish division.	.. .. ..	Britain arranges a loan of 5 millions to Rumania.	27
.. .. ..	Russian torpedo-boat bombards Trebizond and Rize.	.. .. ..	28
.. .. ..	German torpedo-boat sunk by Russian submarine off Cape Moen, Denmark. French take Bertua (Cameroons).	.. .. ..	29
Russians defeat Turks at Sufian, and drive them from Tabriz.	German submarine sinks four British merchant vessels off Lancashire coast.	.. .. ..	30

1915. Jan.	WESTERN FRONT.	EASTERN FRONT.	SOUTHERN FRONT.
31	.. .. ..	Determined German attacks in region of Bolimov gain a little ground.	.. .. ..
Feb. 1	German attack W. of La Bassée repulsed by French and British. French progress near Perthes.	Continued fighting near Bolimov, Russians regaining ground. Russians advance in Carpathians from Dukla Pass to the Upper San.	.. .. ..
2	.. .. ..	Russians storm Skempe (N.W. of Poland). Continued desperate fighting on Ravka near Bolimov.	Austrians repulsed by Montenegrins in Herzegovina.
3	German attacks in Champagne repulsed.	Russians recover Gumin, near Bolimov, and other ground in the sector. They withdraw from the Tucholka and Beskid Passes, but advance near the Uzsok Pass.	.. .. ..
4	British casualties on Western front to this date approximately 104,000.	Continued heavy fighting on Bzura-Ravka front; Russians cross Bzura and take positions near Dachova. Russians falling back in Bukovina.	.. .. ..
5	.. .. ..	Russian successes on Bzura and Ravka. Continuous fighting in the Carpathians; enemy attacks repulsed.	.. .. ..
6	British capture brickfield E. of Cuinchy.	Austrians recapture Kimpolung.	.. .. ..
7	Heavy German attack at Bagatelle (Argonne).	Germans take offensive on S. wing of E. Prussian front, and advance 40 kilometres towards Johannisburg. Very heavy fighting at Kosziowa, N.E. of Tucholka Pass: enemy finally checked. Austrians reach Upper Suczava valley, Bukovina.	..

ASIATIC AND EGYPTIAN THEATRES.	NAVAL AND OVERSEAS OPERATIONS.	POLITICAL, &c.	1915. Jan.
.. .. ..	.. .. ..	.. .. ..	31
			Feb.
Turks (estimated at 12,000) advance towards Suez Canal.	Hospital ship "Asturias" attacked by German submarine off Havre.	Bread and flour rations introduced in Germany.	1
.. .. ..	.. .. ..	German Loan of £3,000,000 to Bulgaria.	2
Turkish attempts to cross Suez Canal at Tussum, Serapeum, and El Kántara, repulsed by Indian troops and Egyptian Artillery, 600 prisoners.	Kemp and 500 rebels surrender at Upington.	.. .. ..	3
.. .. ..	German attack on Kakamas (N.W. Cape Colony) repulsed.	Germans declare waters round the United Kingdom a " war region " as from Feb. 18 (⁴).	4
.. .. ..	.. .. ..	Army Estimates provide for 3 million men.	5
.. .. ..	The " Lusitania " arrives at Liverpool under the American flag.	Mr. Lloyd George returns from a conference at Paris with the French and Russian finance ministers.	6
.. .. ..	.. .. ..	British Foreign Office issues statement justifying use of neutral flag " for the purpose of evading capture at sea." Allied financial resources to be united.	7

1915. Feb.	WESTERN FRONT.	EASTERN FRONT.	SOUTHERN FRONT.
8	Continued fighting at Bagatelle ; no change of front.	Germans take Johannisburg. Austrians continue to advance in Bukovina.	.. .. ..
9	.. .. ..	Germans take Biala and turn Russian right flank near Pillkallen. Russians withdraw beyond the Suczava.	.. .. ..
10	German attacks at Marie Thérèse work (Argonne) and at the Ban-de-Sapt (Alsace).	German left reaches line Pillkallen - Vladislavov, and, advancing, captures Eydtkuhnen and Wirballen. Germans repulsed at Kosziowa.	.. .. ..
11	Further repulse of Germans at Marie Thérèse work.	Germans take Serpets (N. W. Poland), but are repulsed at Kosziowa. Austrians reach line of Sereth.	.. .. ..
12	.. .. ..	Germans occupy Mariampol, Kalvaria, &c., in Poland ; their centre makes progress towards Lyck (E. Prussia). Austrians having forced the Jablonitsa Pass, advance rapidly in E. Galicia.	.. .. ..
13	French take, but fail to hold, a wood near Souain (Champagne). Germans take Xon signal station and village of Norroy, near Pont - à - Mousson. German attack in Lauch valley (Alsace).	Germans take Russian positions before Lyck. Fierce fluctuating struggle in Carpathians.	.. .. ..
14	Germans take British trenches near St. Eloi ; French regain some ground near Norroy. Germans take Sengern and Remsbach, in Lauch valley.	Germans take Lyck ; whole of E. Prussia clear of Russians. Russians hold their ground in W. Carpathians, but Austrians take Nadworna (E. Galicia).	.. .. ..
15	British recapture trenches near St. Eloi.	Germans occupy Plotsk.	Advance of Albanians into Serbia reported.

Asiatic and Egyptian Theatres.	Naval and Overseas Operations.	Political, &c.	1915. Feb.
Turks officially stated to be in full retreat E. of Suez Canal.	"Breslau" bombards Yalta (Crimea), and Russian cruisers bombard Trebizond.	.. .. ..	8
Heavy dust storms interfere with pursuit of Turks.	S.s. "Wilhelmina" arrives at Falmouth ([6]).	.. .. ..	9
.. .. ..	.. .. ..	British Note in reply to U.S.A. Note of 29/12/14 on interference with neutral shipping ([6]).	10
.. .. ..	Cargo of s.s. "Wilhelmina" seized and placed in Prize Court.	U.S.A. Notes to the United Kingdom on the use of neutral flag ([7]) and to Germany on the conditions of the submarine "blockade" ([8]).	11
.. .. ..	Raid by 34 British Naval aeroplanes on Ostend, Zeebrugge, and other points in Belgium.	Welsh Guards Battalion formed.	12
British surprise Turks at Tor (Gulf of Suez), killing 60; 102 prisoners.	.. .. ..	.. .. ..	13
.. .. ..	.. .. ..	.. .. ..	14
.. .. ..	.. .. ..	Government answer to German blockade.	15

1915. Feb.	WESTERN FRONT.	EASTERN FRONT.	SOUTHERN FRONT.
16	Sharp infantry actions in Champagne and the Argonne. French counter-attack at Norroy repulsed.	Continued fighting on E. Prussian front, Russians falling back on the Niemen. Further German reverse at Kosziowa. Austrians take Kolomea (Bukovina).	Albanians driven over Serbian frontier.
17	Small French advances near Roclincourt (N. of Arras), near Perthes, and N.W. of Verdun. Two Zeppelins wrecked off N.W. Denmark.	Russians defeated on line Plotsk-Ratsionj (N.W. Poland). Great battle near Nadworna and Kolomea. Austrians take Czernowitz.	.. .. ..
18	Sharp fighting near Arras, in Champagne, near Verdun, and in Alsace. French recover the Xon signal station and Norroy.	Germans take Tauroggen (N.E. of Tilsit). Austrian offensive on the Dunajec near Tarnow.	.. .. ..
19	French make a little progress at Les Eparges (E. of Verdun). Heavy fighting in the Vosges; Germans take the Reichsackerkopf and occupy Metzeral and Sondernach.	Russian counter-offensive on E. Prussian frontier. Sorties at Przemysl repulsed. Austrian offensive on Dunajec checked after slight advance. Russian retreat near Nadworna.	Bombardment of forts at entrance to Dardanelles by 5 British and 3 French battleships and battle-cruisers.
20	Germans gain a little ground near Ypres. French take wood N. of Perthes, and progress near Les Eparges. German advance S.E. of Sulzern (Alsace).	German attacks at Kosziowa repulsed.	Bombardment of Dardanelles forts continued.
21	German aeroplane drops bombs at Colchester and other places in Essex; no damage. French progress N. of Perthes. Germans take Hochrod and Stossweiler (Alsace).	Successful Russian counter-attacks near Lomja and Plotsk. Russians carry heights near Lupkow and Wyzskow Passes, and make successful attack on Austrians S.E. of Stanislau.	.. .. ..
22	Zeppelin bombs Calais. Heavy bombardment of Reims; cathedral vault broken. French capture trenches and two woods on the line Souain-Beauséjour.	Germans report that "the pursuit of the Russians is now finished," and claim over 100,000 prisoners in E. Prussian offensive. Heavy fighting at many points in N. Poland, especially near Przasnysz, where strong German attacks are repulsed. Big battle begins south of the line Dolina-Stanislau.	.. .. ..

Asiatic and Egyptian Theatres.	Naval and Overseas Operations.	Political, &c.	1915. Feb.
.. .. ..	Renewed Franco-British air-raid on Ostend, Zeebrugge, and other points in Belgium.	German reply to U.S.A. Note about submarine "blockade." U.S.A. Note to United Kingdom about seizure of cargo of "Wilhelmina."	16
.. .. ..	.. .. ..	.. .. ..	17
.. .. ..	German submarine "blockade" begins.	.. .. ..	18
.. .. ..	Norwegian s.s. "Belridge" torpedoed in Channel, but not sunk.	Memoranda published by British Government in reply to U.S.A. Notes about the neutral flag ([9]) and s.s. "Wilhelmina." ([10]).	19
.. .. ..	.. .. ..	.. .. ..	20
Turks driven across River Ichkalen (Armenia).	.. .. ..	.. .. ..	21
.. .. ..	Occupation of Garub (German S.W. Africa) by Union forces.	.. .. ..	22

1915. Feb.	WESTERN FRONT.	EASTERN FRONT.	SOUTHERN FRONT.
23	.. .. ..	Russians advance across the Bobr, S.E. of Augustovo. Germans report capture of 300 guns in recent offensive.	.. .. ..
24	French progress N. of Mesnil (Champagne).	Germans cross Niemen near Sventsiansk, and take Przasnysz, with 10,000 prisoners and 20 guns. Russians take Mozely, near Bolimov.	.. .. ..
25	Small British advance near La Bassée. Further French progress near Mesnil. Heavy bombing of German rear in Champagne.	Continued heavy fighting near Przasnysz; Russians take 2,600 prisoners. Russians retake Stanislau. Germans bombard Osovyets.	Bombardment resumed at Dardanelles; outer forts reduced.
26	French take two lines of German trenches N. of Mesnil.	Russians report German retirement near Przasnysz.	Dardanelles: Straits swept clear for 4 miles.
27	French take part of Beauséjour, near Perthes (Champ.).	Russians retake Przasnysz. 5,400 prisoners reported. Russians report capture of 4,000 prisoners near Dolina (S. Gal.).	Dardanelles operations hindered by bad weather.
28	French make progress near Perthes. Germans bombard Soissons and Reims Cathedral.	.. .. ..	.. .. ..
March 1	French establish a new line two kilometres in front of old positions between Perthes and Beauséjour.	Niemen River front: Collapse of German offensive; signs of a general retreat ([11]). Heavy fighting near Grodno and Osovyets. Austrian attacks repulsed in the Carpathians ([12]).	.. .. ..
2	German counter-attacks repulsed near Perthes.	Niemen River front: Continued Russian offensive, prisoners reported to number over 10,000. Continued heavy fighting near Grodno and Osovyets. Russians bombard Czernowitz. Austrian attacks repulsed at Lupkow Pass.	Dardanelles: Naval bombardment resumed ([13]).

Asiatic and Egyptian Theatres.	Naval and Overseas Operations.	Political, &c.	1915. Feb.
.. .. ..	Entrance to the North Channel, except S. of Rathlin Island, closed by British Government. Occupation of Nonidas and Goanikas (German S.W. Africa.).	.. .. ..	23
.. .. ..	Loss of H.M.S. "Clan McNaughton," auxiliary cruiser, announced.	.. .. ..	24
.. .. ..	Seven British merchantmen sunk by submarines in first week of "blockade." Arrivals and sailings, 1,381.	.. .. ..	25
.. .. ..	.. ..	.. .. ..	26
.. .. ..	"Dacia" intercepted in Channel by French and taken into Brest. Admiralty proclaim blockade of German E. Africa.	.. .. ..	27
.. .. ..	.. ..	.. .. ..	28
			March
.. .. ..	.. .. ..	Premier announces presumed "enemy destination" ships will be detained if necessary. £187,000,000 asked for.	1
.. .. ..	.. .. ..	Anglo-French note to Germany declares policy of reprisals in retaliation for submarine blockade; neutrals protest ([14]). S. African Government issues White Book on the rebellion. Austria declares a Metal Week, steel being excepted.	2

1915. March.	WESTERN FRONT.	EASTERN FRONT.	SOUTHERN FRONT.
3	French repulse attacks by German Guards N.E. of Mesnil (Champagne). Germans again bombard Reims.	Russians retake Stanislau and village of Krasna; over 6,000 prisoners. Austrian attacks repulsed in the Carpathians.	..
4	..	Prisoners taken by Russians round Stanislau increased to 19,000. Continued fierce Austrian attacks in the Carpathians.	Dardanelles: Bombardment of the inner forts continued.
5	French attack on German positions at Hartmannsweilerkopf. Zeppelin wrecked near Tirlemont.	Germans concentrate strong forces between Thorn and Mlava. Russians cross the Bistritza (E. Carpathians) and threaten Austrian flank.	Dardanelles: Narrows forts bombarded by "Queen Elizabeth" from Gulf of Saros; fort L blown up and others damaged.
6	..	Austrian attacks in the Carpathians again repulsed. They retreat in the Bukovina.	Dardanelles: Bombardment continued by "Queen Elizabeth" and 7 other warships.
7	Ostend bombed by six British aviators.	Russians pursue retreating Germans in Augustovo Woods (N. Poland). Heavy fighting at Osovyets. Further Austrian attacks repulsed at Baligrod (Carpathians).	Dardanelles: "Queen Elizabeth," "Ocean" and "Agamemnon" continue bombardment from Gulf of Saros. Fort Dardanos batteries silenced.
8	Local attack by Germans, after heavy bombardment, fails at Dixmude.	Severe fighting on whole front north of Vistula. Fighting goes in favour of Russians round Osovyets. Despite heavy losses, Austrians continue to attack at Baligrod. Russians checked at Kosziowa (S. Carpathians), but retain positions by a counterattack.	Dardanelles: Operations hindered by bad weather.
9	French gain ground in the Perthes-Mesnil district. Heavy fighting between Four-de-Paris and Bolante.	New German offensive near Przasnysz. Russian advance N. of Osovyets. Heavy artillery firing along the river Narev. Austrian attacks fail in the Carpathians.	..

ASIATIC AND EGYPTIAN THEATRES.	NAVAL AND OVERSEAS OPERATIONS.	POLITICAL, &c.	1915. March.
hwaz (Persian Gulf): Turks located in strength at Ghadir, W. of Ahwaz; heavy Turkish attack forces retirement, but is repulsed.	Vice-Adm. Sir Doveton Sturdee's despatches on Falkland Isles battle published. Adm. Sir David Beatty's despatches on Dogger Bank (24.1.) engagement published.	South Africa: Debate on the Rebellion in the Union Parliament.	3
.. ..	Submarine U8 sunk by destroyers in the Channel; crew taken prisoner. s.s. " Thordis " rammed and sank a German submarine.	Admiralty decides enemy submarine prisoners cannot be afforded " honourable treatment."	4
.. ..	British warships bombard Smyrna.	German Note issued in answer to attempt of United States to mitigate rigours of war zone. Issue of £50,000,000 3% Exchequer Bonds announced.	5
.. ..	.. .. ..	Greece: King Constantine forces the resignation of Venizelos cabinet.	6
.. ..	Several coast batteries silenced at Smyrna.	.. .. ..	7
.. ..	Heraclea (Eregli) (Asia Minor) and neighbouring coast bombarded by Russian Black Sea fleet. Ostend bombed.	Greece. M. Zaimis having refused to form a ministry, King Constantine summons M. Gounaris, who forms a cabinet. In a council at Vienna, the Emperor Francis Joseph accepts the principle of a rectification of frontiers in favour of Italy.	8
.. ..	Submarine U12 rammed and sunk by H.M.S. " Ariel."	Bill introduced to give Government powers over Munition Works.	9

1915. March.	WESTERN FRONT.	EASTERN FRONT.	SOUTHERN FRONT.
10	**Battle of Neuve Chapelle begins ([16]).**	Russians repulse renewed German attacks on the Niemen and W. of Grodno.	Dardanelles : R e n e w e d bombardment.
11	British make progress near Neuve Chapelle, occupying village of l'Epinette.	**New German offensive near Przasnysz develops.**	.. .. .
12	German counter-attacks repulsed at Neuve Chapelle.	Russians repulse German attacks near Augustovo Woods and N. of Przasnysz.	French force for Dardanelles collecting in N. Africa.
13	German attacks fail, and French gain ground, in counter - attacks in Champagne. Belgians gain ground on the Yser. Germans bombard Ypres.	German offensive checked near the Augustovo Woods and Przasnysz. Austrian attacks fail in the Carpathians and E. Galicia.	.. ..
14	**Battle of St. Eloi begins ;** ([18]) Germans attack S. of Ypres. Belgians make progress in the bend of the Yser and S. of Dixmude. Violent German attacks fail between Four-de-Paris and Bolante.	Continued Russian success in the district of Przasnysz.	.. ..
15	Battle of St. Eloi continues ; British regain the village. French make new progress in Champagne and the Argonne ([20]).	Russian counter offensive along both banks of the Orzec (N. Poland). Austrian centre broken by Russian counter offensive near Smolnik (Carpathians).	H.M.S. " A m e t h y s t " dashes into Straits and is damaged.
16	French gain an important crest and repulse strong counter attacks N. of Mesnil.	.. .. :.	.. ..
17	.. ..	Austrians, reinforced, try to cross the river Pruth in Bukovina.	.. ..

ASIATIC AND EGYPTIAN THEATRES.	NAVAL AND OVERSEAS OPERATIONS.	POLITICAL, &C.	1915. March
.. ..	German armed auxiliary cruiser "Prinz Eitel Friedrich" puts into Newport News (U.S.A.) for repairs.([17])	Greece : Gounaris ministry sworn in. ([18]). Further report on German treatment of civilians in occupied territory issued by the French Government. A new Note on the Anglo-French naval blockade presented by the United States.	10
Cavalry reconnaissance to N a k a i l a (W. of Basra).	British auxiliary cruiser "Bayona" torpedoed and sunk close to coast of Scotland.	.. .. ..	11
.. .. ..	.. .. ..	.. .. ..	12
.. .. ..	.. .. ..	.. .. ..	13
.. .. ..	German cruiser "Dresden" sunk by British warships off Juan Fernandez ([19]).	.. .. ..	14
.. ..	.. .. ..	British reply to the German Submarine Blockade issued. Germany compensates the United States for the sinking of the "W. P. Frye."	15
.. ..	.. ..	.. .. ..	16
.. .. ..	.. .. ..	.. .. ..	17

1915. March.	Western Front.	Eastern Front.	Southern Front.
18	Violent indecisive fighting between Four-de-Paris and Bolante.	Russians occupy Memel (E. Prussia). Continued Austrian attacks repulsed in the Carpathians and Bukovina.	Dardanelles : Attack o the Narrows ; two fort destroyed. H.M.S "Ocean," H.M.S. "Irre sistible," and French warship "Bouvet" sunk French warship "Gau lois" damaged.
19	Germans attack heavily in the Vosges.	Austrian sortie from Przemysl fails.	Dardanelles : Ba weather stops opera tions.
20	Germans regain some trench elements near Notre Dame de Lorette.	Russians attack, taking 2,400 prisoners, near Smolnik.	Dardanelles : Violen storm.
21	French regain lost trench elements near Notre Dame de Lorette. Severe fighting at Bagatelle (the Argonne).	Germans reoccupy Memel. Germans abandon attack on Osovyets and withdraw their artillery.	.. ..
22	Two Zeppelins attack Paris.	**Capitulation of Przemysl to the Russians ;** 126,000 prisoners and 700 big guns ([21]).	.. ..
23	Germans bombard Reims and Soissons ; French silence the German guns at Soissons.	.. .. ..	Dardanelles : Bombard ment resumed.
24	.. .. ..	.. .. ..	.. .. ..
25	.. .. ..	Russian counter-offensive makes progress in the Carpathians ; 5,700 prisoners taken.	.. .. ..
26	French gain summit of Hartmannsweilerkopf. 6 French airmen bomb Metz.	Continued Russian advance in the Carpathians, 2,500 prisoners reported. Lupkow Pass taken.	.. .. ..
27	French make progress at Les Eparges.	Russians repulse German attacks in the Niemen district.	.. .. ..

Asiatic and Egyptian Theatres.	Naval and Overseas Operations.	Political, &c.	1915. March.
.. ..	.. .. ..	Rumania calls up seven classes (1909–1915).	18
.. ..	.. .. ..	Thirty-four Trade Unions agree to expedite munitions output.	19
.. ..	German S.W. Africa : General Botha defeats German force at Riet, on the Swakop.	.. .. ..	20
.. ..	.. .. ..	Italian military attaché leaves Vienna.	**21**
urkish raiding forces discovered near El Kubri (Suez).	.. .. ..	.. .. ..	22
urkish raiding forces routed by British near El Kubri.	.. .. ..	Seizure of " Dacia " declared valid by French Courts.	23
.. ..	British Naval airmen raid Hoboken (near Antwerp).	Chile protests against violation of her territorial waters by the British at the battle of Juan Fernandez.	24
. .. ..	Submarine U29 sunk. German submarine sinks Dutch s.s. " Medea."	.. ..	25
. .. ..	.. .. ..	.. .. ..	26
. .. ..	.. .. ..	.. .. ..	27

1915. March.	WESTERN FRONT.	EASTERN FRONT.	SOUTHERN FRONT.
28	French repulse all counter-attacks at Les Eparges.	Attempted renewal of offensive by Germans in N. Poland. Failure of Austrian attacks and progress by Russians in the Carpathians.	..
29	..	Germans take Tauroggen (N.E. of Tilsit). Further Russian advance in the Carpathians; 5,600 prisoners.	..
30	Germans bombard Reims Cathedral.	..	..
31	..	Germans bombard Libau. Severe fighting in the Carpathians.	..
April 1	British air raid on Zeebrugge and Hoboken. Germans occupy Cloister Hoek (near Dixmude).	Russian advance checked in W. Poland. Russians make progress in the Carpathians.	Bulgarian *Komitadjis* attack the Serbs at Valandovo.
2	German attack stopped at Bagatelle (A r g o n n e). French air raids on German aviation camps in Belgium and Lorraine.	Russian cavalry defeat German cavalry in N. Poland. Russians take Cigielka (Carp.).	..
3	French take Regniéville (Woevre).	Russian attacks repulsed in the Carpathians. Severe fighting north of Czernowitz.	..
4	French make progress S. of St. Mihiel (Meuse) and in the Woevre district. Germans take Driegrachten.	Russian hospital bombed at Radom (Poland). Russians occupy Cisna and reach Sztropko (Carp.). Fierce battle at Okna (near Czernowitz).	..

ASIATIC AND EGYPTIAN THEATRES.	NAVAL AND OVERSEAS OPERATIONS.	POLITICAL, &c.	1915. March.
.. ..	German submarine torpedoes and sinks s.s. "Falaba." ([22]). Russian Black Sea fleet bombards the forts on the Bosporus. Smyrna forts shelled.	.. .. ..	28
.. .. ..	.. .. ..	Holland protests against the sinking of one ship, the shelling of another, and the detention of two more, by the Germans.	29
.. .. ..	.. .. ..	.. .. ..	30
.. .. ..	.. .. ..	Home Secretary appoints a Committee of enquiry into the recruiting of men from retail trades.	31
			April
ussians occupy Tsria (Transc.).	South African forces occupy Hasuur (Germ. S. W. Africa). British s.s. "Seven Seas" torpedoed off Beachy Head.	Bismarck centenary celebrations. Herr Dernburg, interviewed by New York Times, justifies sinking of s.s. "Falaba" ([23]). Scheme for a Dockers' Battalion at Liverpool published.	1
.. ..	Trawlers "Jason," "Gloxinia" and "Nellie" sunk in North Sea by submarine U10	American note to Great Britain on the blockade ([24]). Correspondence between Gt. Britain and Germany as to submarine crews taken prisoner by former, published ([25]). Austria offers Italy a rectification of frontier in the Trentino ([26]).	2
rench expeditionary force begins to land at Alexandria.	Turkish cruiser "Medjidia" sunk by a mine off Odessa ; Russian Black Sea fleet engages the "Goeben" and "Breslau." South African forces occupy Warmbad (Germ. S.W. Africa).	Greece : Publication of a memorandum of 24.1.15 by M. Venizelos to King Constantine on Greek foreign policy ([27]). American military mission, attached to the German Staff, recalled.	3
ussians defeat Turks at Olty (Armen.).	"Goeben" and "Breslau" withdraw to Bosporus.	Greece : Publication of a further memorandum by M. Venizelos, dated 30.1.15, on Greek foreign policy ([29]).	4

1915. April.	WESTERN FRONT.	EASTERN FRONT.	SOUTHERN FRONT.
5	Belgians repulsed at Drie-grachten. French make progress E. of Verdun, but are repulsed in the Argonne.	Russians make further progress in the Carpathians.	..
6	French make progress E. of Verdun and in Alsace. Indecisive fighting on the Meuse front.	Russian advance in the Niemen district.	Serbian artillery silence bombardment of Belgrade.
7	Indecisive fighting near St. Mihiel.	Further Russian advance in Carpathians.	.. ..
8	French attacks in the Woevre district repulsed.	Indecisive fighting in the Carpathians.	.. ..
9	French complete the capture of Les Eparges. Germans bombard Reims. Indecisive fighting on the Meuse.	Russians make progress near Suvalki. Continued indecisive fighting in the Carpathians.	.. ..
10	French success in the Bois de Montmare (Woevre).	Severe fighting for the Uzsok Pass (Carp.).	Austrian gunboat shell Belgrade. Albanian bombard Durazzo.

Asiatic and Egyptian Theatres.	Naval and Overseas Operations.	Political, &c.	1915. April.
..	Union forces occupy Kalk-fontein and Kamus (Germ. S.W. Africa). United States demands £46,000 for the sinking of " W. P. Frye."	King George V. prohibits use of alcoholic drinks in any of the royal house-holds. Mr. John Red-mond addresses the Na-tional Volunteer Con-vention at Dublin.	5
Russians enter Artvin (Armen.).	Battleships and aeroplanes bombard Smyrna. Ger-mans defeated at Kar-unga (Germ. E. Africa). Warmbad taken.	Greek note to Bulgaria and Bulgarian note to Serbia on the *Komitadji* out-rages. British Govern-ment appoint a com-mittee on munitions of war.	6
Skirmish between Turks and British N.E. of El Kántara (Egypt).	..	German Minority Socialists publish a manifesto against the war. Appeal by the Churches for re-straint in use of alcohol is followed by a memorial by business men to the same effect.	7
Deportation and massacre of Armenians in the Otto-man Empire begins ([29]).	" Prinz Eitel Friedrich " interned at Newport News.	Attempted assassination of Hussein Kamel, Sultan of Egypt. Italian note to Austria, demanding terri-torial concessions in re-turn for neutrality ([30]).	8
..	..	Greece: M. Venizelos temporarily retires from public life.	9
..	Belgian relief ship " Har-palyce " torpedoed.	White Book published, con-taining correspondence between the British Gov-ernment and the U.S. Ambassador on German treatment of prisoners of war and interned civilians. ([31]). German note to U.S.A. protesting against the unneutral conduct of America ([32]). Pope Bene-dict XV. orders prayers for peace.	10

1915. April.	WESTERN FRONT.	EASTERN FRONT.	SOUTHERN FRONT.
11	Germans repulsed at Les Eparges. Severe fighting near Albert.	Germans bombard Osovyets. Russians capture Wysocko Nizhne, near the Uzsok Pass.	.. ..
12	Failure of French attack S.E. of Hartmannsweilerkopf. French consolidate their positions at Les Eparges. German airship bombs Nancy.	Russians checked E. of the Uzsok Pass.	.. ..
13	French progress near Berry-au-Bac. Failure of French attacks near Maizeray.	Russians capture heights near the Uzsok Pass.	.. ..
14	Germans accuse the French of using poison gas near Verdun. Zeppelin raid on Tyneside.	Germans repulsed before Osovyets. Indecisive fighting at the Uzsok Pass. Russians make progress E. of Czernowitz.	.. ..
15	Ostend bombed by 15 Allied aeroplanes. French airship bombs Freiburg. Severe fighting off Ostend. Sir John French's despatch on operations from Feb. 2 to March 20 published.	.. .. ..	.. ..

Asiatic and Egyptian Theatres.	Naval and Overseas Operations.	Political, &c.	1915. April.
Turks attack British at Kurna (Mesop.) and Ahwaz (Persian Gulf).	Harrison liner "Wayfarer" torpedoed. "Kronprinz Wilhelm" arrives at Newport News.	Count Bernstorff publishes the German note to U.S.A. German reprisals announced *re* British treatment of captured submarine crews : 39 British officer prisoners under arrest. Bulgaria agrees to mixed Serbian and Bulgarian commission on frontier incidents in Macedonia.	11
Indecisive fighting at Kurna and Ahwaz. Turks attack Basra from W. and S.	French cruiser "St. Louis" bombards Gaza.	Papal Note to President Wilson declaring the readiness of the Pope to co-operate for the restoration of peace.	12
Turks beaten N. of Basra and retreat from Shaiba (S.W. of Basra).	Publication of Rear-Adm. Hon. H. Hood's despatch on patrol action on Belgian coast, Oct. 17–Nov. 9, 1914.	M. Radoslavov, Bulgarian premier, orders disarmament of Turco-Bulgarians on Serbian frontier. Italy presses Austria for an answer to the Note of April 8. Munitions Committee meets under the chairmanship of Mr. Lloyd George.	13
British offensive S. of Shaiba routs Turks.	.. .. ..	Mr. Fisher states in Australian Parliament that the Government will send every available man to the war. Mr. Harcourt states that the Dominions will be consulted as to peace terms. General von Bissing suppresses the Belgian Red Cross.	14
Russian Black Sea fleet bombards Ergeti and other places on the coast of Anatolia.	.. .. ..	.. .. ..	15

1915. April.	WESTERN FRONT.	EASTERN FRONT.	SOUTHERN FRONT.
16	German attacks repulsed at Notre Dame de Lorette. French airships bomb Strassburg and other German towns. Zeppelin raid on East. Anglia ; aeroplane bombs Faversham and Sittingbourne.	Russians capture two heights S.W. of Rosztoki Pass (Carp.).	Allied fleets bombard Enos. Albanian rebels bombard Durazzo.
17	British take Hill 60 (St. Eloi)	Austrian offensive towards Stryj (E. Gal.).	.. .. .
18	German attacks repulsed at Hill 60.	Russians repulse attacks in the Carpathians.	.. .. .
19	German retirement in Alsace. Fighting for Hill 60. Sir John French denies that the British have made use of poison gas.	.. .. ..	Austrians bombard Se (near the Iron Gates).
20	Germans bombard Reims and Ypres. Germans retake Emberménil (Lorr.).	Austrians repulsed near Gorlitse.	.. .. .
21	Continued fighting for Hill 60. French take " the Cow's Head," two lines of trenches, near St. Mihiel.	Russians take Hill 1002, N.E. of Lubonia (Carp.).	Affair between frontie guards on the Austro Italian frontier.
22	**Second battle of Ypres begins ;** town of Ypres largely destroyed ; German advance checked by Canadians, after French retreat before **poisonous gas** attack. Progress by the French near St. Mihiel.	Russian attacks repulsed on both sides of the Uzsok Pass. Austrian attack towards Stryj fails.	Anglo-French force lande at Enos.

Asiatic and Egyptian Theatres.	Naval and Overseas Operations.	Political, &c.	1915. April.
Turks reach Urumia (N. W. Persia).	French cruiser bombards El Arish. British transport "Manitou" sunk by Turkish torpedo-boat destroyer. 51 lost.	British apology to Chile for sinking the "Dresden" in Chilean waters published. Austria declares that the Italian proposals are in the main unacceptable. Sinking of "Katwyk" by German submarine causes excitement in Holland.	16
Anglo-Indian cavalry occupy Nakaila.	French cruiser bombards Turkish camp S. of Gaza. British submarine E15 runs ashore near Kephez Point. Turkish t.b. "Demir Hissar" forced by H.M.S. "Minerva" to run ashore at Chios.	Herr Dernburg conducts a peace campaign in U.S.A.	17
.. .. ..	Union forces occupy Seeheim (Germ. S.W. Africa). Frontier raid repulsed on the N. border of Peshawar valley.	.. .. ..	18
.. .. ..	Germans evacuate Keetmanshoop (Germ. S.W. Africa).	Germany expresses regret for sinking of "Katwyk."	19
Turks lay siege to Van (Armen.).	Union forces defeat the Germans at Kebus (N. of Keetmanshoop). Anglo-French troops take Mandera (Cameroons).	Mr. Asquith at Newcastle denies that military operations have been hampered by lack of munitions. Correspondence between Great Britain and U.S.A. on the "Peklat" case published ([33]). President Wilson announces that U.S.A. hopes to share in restoration of peace ([34]).	20
.. .. ..	.. .. ..	Mr. Lloyd George delivers a speech on the capacity of the country for producing munitions.	21
.. .. ..	Resumed bombardment of the forts at Smyrna.	British Admiralty suspends passenger traffic between England and Holland.	22

1915. April.	Western Front.	Eastern Front.	Southern Front.
23	Second battle of Ypres: German attack east and west of St. Julien repulsed by Canadians; Germans take several hamlets.	.. .. ..	Turkish coast bombarded by Allied fleet in the Gulf of Saros.
24	Second battle of Ypres: Germans take St. Julien; French and Belgians recover Lizerne; 3rd Canadian brigade withdrawn.	Austrians capture Ostaij, height S.E. of Kosziowa.	.. .. ..
25	Second battle of Ypres: Germans retake Lizerne; British repulsed at St. Julien. Germans capture and lose summit of Hartmannsweilerkopf (Alsace).	Severe fighting near Stryj.	**Dardanelles: Anglo - French forces land on both shores of the Straits.**
26	Second battle of Ypres: Germans pierce British line at Broodseinde; French recover Het Sas; British fail to recover St. Julien. British airmen bomb Courtrai and various neighbouring places.	.. .. ..	Dardanelles: Hill 141 stormed and V Beach secured.
27	Second battle of Ypres: Allied attack N. of Ypres checked by use of gas.	German advance towards Shavli (Baltic Provinces)	Dardanelles: Allies establish themselves across the Gallipoli Peninsula.
28	Second battle of Ypres: German offensive definitely stopped. Germans bomb Dunkirk, Pervyse and Nancy; French bomb Friedrichshafen. Germans storm French position at Les Mesnils.	Very **powerful Austro-German offensive** under Von Mackensen begins between the Dunajec and Biala Rivers (W. Galicia). Russians driven back.	Dardanelles: Allied forces, aided by "Queen Elizabeth," advance on Krithia.
29	Second battle of Ypres: Artillery duels north of Ypres; Canadians withdrawn from the Ypres salient. Germans bombard Reims and Dunkirk.	Continued German advance in Galicia; also in the Baltic Provinces; Libau-Dvinsk railway reached. Russians repulse Austrian attacks in the Uzsok Pass.	.. .. ..

Asiatic and Egyptian Theatres.	Naval and Overseas Operations.	Political, &c.	1915. April.
.. ..	British Government declares a blockade of the Cameroons. White book on military operations in Togoland published.	Sir E. Grey presides over a conference of the French, Russian, Italian and Serbian ministers.	23
.. ..	Fighting round Kilimanjaro (Germ. E. Africa).	.. .. ..	24
.. ..	Russian Black Sea fleet shells the forts of the Bosporus.	Herr Dernburg in U.S.A. outlines unofficial German peace terms.	**25**
Russian advance on Olty (Armenia).	" Kronprinz Wilhelm "interned. Germans repulsed at Trekopjes, N.E. of Swakopmund (Germ. S.W. Africa.).	Lord Kitchener and Mr. Asquith on German barbarity ([35]).	26
Russians expel the Turks from Kutur (Persia). Baghdad railway bridge over Euphrates at Jerablus stated to be open for traffic.	French armoured cruiser " Léon Gambetta " sunk by an Austrian submarine in the Adriatic. " Queen Elizabeth " sinks a Turkish t.b. off Maidos. Submarine E14 sinks a Turkish gunboat in the Sea of Marmora.	Mr. Churchill announces that 29 prisoners from German submarines are separately confined and specially treated as a reprisal against the German submarine campaign.	27
Skirmishes E. of the Suez Canal.	Germans defeated at Gibeon (Germ. S.W. Africa). South African Government publishes a Blue Book on the rebellion.	.. .. ..	28
Turks retreat from neighbourhood of the Suez Canal.	Submarine E14 sinks a Turkish transport in the Sea of Marmora.	Mr. Lloyd George announces the Government scheme with regard to alcoholic drinks.	29

G

1915. April.	WESTERN FRONT.	EASTERN FRONT.	SOUTHERN FRONT.
30	Second battle of Ypres: Attempted German advance from St. Julien repulsed. Zeppelin raid on East Anglia.	Germans reach the railway stations of Muravievo and Radziviliski (Prov. of Kovno, Baltic Provinces).	.. .. ..
May 1	Second battle of Ypres: Repulse of German attack on Hill 60; British ordered to withdraw to new line.	Germans occupy Shavli and approach Libau (Baltic Provinces). Austro-German offensive towards the Uzsok Pass.	Dardanelles: Turks attack the Allied line at Gallipoli.
2	Second battle of Ypres: German attack repulsed near St. Julien.	Austro-Germans take Gorlitse and Ciezkowica and cross the Biala (Galicia). Russians take Mt. Makovka (near Stryj), but lose it again.	Dardanelles: Turkish attack and Franco-British counter-attack; British fail at Gaba Tepe.
3	Second battle of Ypres: Withdrawal to new British line completed. Germans again driven back.	Germans continue to advance towards Mitau (Baltic Provinces); 8,200 prisoners reported. Austro-Germans make progress in Galicia and the Carpathians.	Dardanelles: Turks unsuccessfully attack the French lines at Gallipoli.
4	Second battle of Ypres: French advance between Lizerne and Het Sas; Germans capture Zonnebeke, Westhoek and Zevenkote.	Severe fighting in Galicia: Russians stand on the Visloka R.	Dardanelles: British failure at Gaba Tepe.
5	Second battle of Ypres: Germans gain a foothold on Hill 60.	Germans bombard Grodno; are checked south of Mitau.	.. .. ..
6	Second battle of Ypres: British recover some trenches on Hill 60.	Austrians occupy Tarnow (Galicia).	Dardanelles: Second battle of Krithia begins.
7	.. .. ..	Russians fall back to the Vistok, and retreat in the Carpathians.	
8	Second battle of Ypres: British lose Frezenberg Ridge under terrific shelling.	Germans take Libau. Further Russian retreat in Galicia.	.. .. ..

Asiatic and Egyptian Theatres.	Naval and Overseas Operations.	Political, &c.	1915. April.
.. .. ..	Australian submarine AE2 sunk by Turkish warship in the Sea of Marmora.	German warning in U.S. newspapers *re* sailing in " Lusitania."	30
.. .. ..	Two German t.b.'s sunk by British destroyer in North Sea. Union forces occupy Kubas (Germ. S.W. Africa). " Gulflight,"American oil tank vessel, torpedoed by German submarine.	Navigation resumed between England and Holland. Chinese Note to Japan requiring the restoration of Kiao-chau, and making other demands.	**May** 1
.. .. ..	Russian Black Sea fleet shells the forts on the Bosporus. Union forces occupy Otjimbingwe (Germ. S.W. Africa).	Turkish Minister of War sends British and French subjects into the danger zone at Gallipoli.	2
.. .. ..	Submarine E14 sinks a Turkish gunboat in the Sea of Marmora.	**Italy denounces the Triple Alliance** ([36]). Advertisement in American papers states that ships flying the British flag are liable to destruction in the war zone.	
.. ..	.. .. ..	Budget, estimated expenditure £1,632,654,000 introduced by Mr. Lloyd George ([37]).	4
Turks reported severely beaten by Russians in Armenia.	Union forces occupy Karibib (Germ. S.W. Africa).	.. .. ..	5
.. .. ..	Mr. Harcourt makes a statement as to poisoning of wells by Germans in S.W. Africa ([38]).	.. .. ..	6
Massacres of Christians in Ottoman Empire.	" Lusitania " torpedoed off S.W. coast of Ireland ; 1,198 men, women, and children drowned, including 124 U.S. citizens.	Japan presents an ultimatum to China ([40]). Sir E. Grey sends a message to the Ottoman Government as to the placing of allied civilians in the danger zone ([39]).	7
.. .. ..	.. .. ..	.. .. ..	8

1915. May.	WESTERN FRONT.	EASTERN FRONT.	SOUTHERN FRONT.
9	Second battle of Ypres: British retake Wieltje. They fail in an attack on Aubers ridge (N. Chapelle).	Germans defeated at Krakinow (Baltic Provinces).	.. ..
10	French take cemetery of Neuville St. Vaast and part of Carency (N. of Arras). British repulsed on Aubers ridge.	German retreat in Baltic Provinces.	.. ..
11	Second battle of Ypres: Germans bombard Ypres-Menin road. French take fort and chapel of Notre Dame de Lorette.	Germans evacuate Shavli. Austro-German advance in Galicia. Russians fall back to the San R.	.. ..
12	French capture Carency.	Germans occupy Kyeltsi (Poland). Austro-German advance in Galicia and N. of Uzsok Pass. Austrian retreat S. of Pruth.	Dardanelles: Cape Tekeh ("Gurka Bluff") captured by Gurkas; H.M.S. "Goliath" torpedoed.
13	Second battle of Ypres: Very severe German bombardment. Cavalry, etc., hold on. French complete conquest of Bois le Prêtre.	Russian retreat in Galicia. Russians occupy Sniatyn (R. Pruth).	.. .. ..
14	Second battle of Ypres: French and Belgians advance near Het Sas and Steenstraate.	Battle of the San: Austro-Germans take Jaroslav. Russians take Kolomea.	.. .. ..
15	**Battle of Festubert:** Successful British attack. French occupy Het Sas.	Russian left drives back Austrians on the Dniester.	.. .. ..
16	Battle of Festubert: British advance continued. Zeppelin raid on Calais.	Severe Austrian defeat between Kyeltsi and Ostrovyets (S. Poland).	.. .. ..
17	Battle of Festubert: Ground consolidated. Zeppelin raids on Dunkirk and Ramsgate.	Austro-Germans cross the San.	.. .. ..
18	Battle of Festubert: British advance to La Quinque Rue-Bethune road.	Austrians drive Russians from Sieniawa (San).	Dardanelles: Turks attack at Gaba Tepe.

ASIATIC AND EGYPTIAN THEATRES.	NAVAL AND OVERSEAS OPERATIONS.	POLITICAL, &c.	1915. May.
.. .. ..	..	.. ..	9
.. .. ..	Sinking of "Lusitania" causes anti-German demonstrations in London and Liverpool. Submarine E14 sinks a transport in the Sea of Marmora.	President Wilson on the "Lusitania." "There is such a thing as a man being too proud to fight," &c.	10
Russian progress in the district of Tabriz.	French take Eseka (Cameroons).	.. .. ..	11
.. .. ..	**Union forces occupy Windhoek** (Germ. S.W. Africa).	**Report of Bryce Committee** published ([41]). Anti-German riots in England.	12
.. .. ..	.. .. ..	Italy : Signor Salandra resigns. German Sovereigns struck off the Garter roll.	13
.. .. ..	U.S.A. note to Germany on the "Lusitania" question ([12]).	**Article in the "Times" on the shortage of munitions.** Internment of enemy aliens in Great Britain begins.	14
.. .. ..	.. .. ..	Insurrection in Portugal.	15
.. .. ..	.. .. ..	Italy : King Victor Emmanuel refuses to accept Signor Salandra's resignation. Baron Burian states the concessions offered by Austria to Italy.	16
Russians occupy Ardjiche on Lake Van (Armenia).	..	Signor Giolitti leaves Rome.	17
.. .. ..	.. .. ..	Lord Kitchener in the Lords insists on the importance of an adequate supply of munitions.	18

1915. May.	WESTERN FRONT.	EASTERN FRONT.	SOUTHERN FRONT.
19	.. .. ..	Germans take Lutkow (Gal.).	Dardanelles : Turks repulsed at Gaba Tepe.
20	Battle of Festubert continues : slight British advance.	Von Mackensen bombards Przemysl.	.. .. ..
21	French capture White Road near Souchez.	Beginning of Russian counter - offensive to cover evacuation of Przemysl.	.. .. ..
22	Battle of Festubert : British advance S. of Quinque Rue. German air raid on Paris.	.. .. ..	.. .. ..
23	Battle of Festubert : German attack repulsed.	.. .. ..	Austrians attack in the Carnic Alps.
24	Final German attack E. of Ypres repulsed Ground E. of Festubert made good. French take Les Corneilles (N.W. of Angres).	Austro-Germans occupy Radyno (Gal.).	Italians advance on the Trentino and Carnic fronts, and occupy Caporetto and Cormons on the Isonzo front.
25	Close of the battle of Festubert.	Austro - Germans take bridgehead of Zagrody on the San.	Italians capture Monte Altinino (Trentino).
26	Zeppelin raid on Southend.	Austro-Germans gain successes in severe fighting round Przemysl.	.. .. ..
27	French take Les Quatre Bouquetaux (near Souchez). Severe fighting in Bois-le-Prêtre.	Russians take Sieniawa (N.W. of Jaroslau) and Kindowary (Shavli district).	Italians occupy Grado and Ala (Trentino).
28	French advance in the "Labyrinth" (N. of Arras.)	Russians take Bubie (Baltic Provinces). Austro-German advance on Przemysl continues.	.. .. ..

Asiatic and Egyptian Theatres.	Naval and Overseas Operations.	Political, &c.	1915. May.
Russians take Van.	.. .. ..	Mr. Asquith announces impending reconstruction of the Ministry. Age limit for recruits fixed at 40.	19
.. .. ..	.. .. ..	Extraordinary p o w e r s granted to Italian Government. Italian Green Book on negotiations with Austria published ([43]).	20
Turks retreat on Bitlis (Kurdistan)	.. .. ..	Austrian note to Italy ([44]). U.S.A. postpones note to Great Britain on the blockade.	21
.. .. ..	Russian battleship " Penteleimon," torpedoed in the Black Sea.	Italian mobilisation ordered	22
.. .. ..	Submarine E11 sinks a gunboat in the Sea of Marmora.	**Italy declares war against Austria.** Italian note to the ministers of Italy in foreign countries on the denunciation of the Triple Alliance. Allies warn Turkey on question of Armenian massacres ([45]).	23
.. .. ..	Austrian naval raid on Italian Adriatic coast, and first air raid on Venice.	.. .. ..	24
Russians occupy Miandob (Persia).	H.M.S. " Triumph " torpedoed off Gallipoli. American s.s. " Nebraskan " torpedoed.	**Formation of Coalition Ministry** ([46]); Nationalists approve refusal of Mr. John Redmond to take office. Treaty between China and Japan ([47]).	25
.. .. ..	.. .. ..	Unionist party meeting at Carlton Club decides in favour of the Coalition.	26
.. .. ..	H.M.S. " Majestic " torpedoed off Gallipoli. H.M.S. " Princess Irene," auxiliary ship, blown up in Sheerness harbour.	Admiral Sir H. Jackson appointed First Sea Lord. Portugal : President Arriaga resigns.	27
Russians occupy Vastan (on Lake Van).	.. .. ..	Dr. Bethmann-Hollweg denounces Italy in the Reichstag ; Statement *re* vodka ([48]).	28

1915. May.	WESTERN FRONT.	EASTERN FRONT.	SOUTHERN FRONT.
29	French take Ablain (Souchez).	Russian counter-offensive forces Austrians to retreat in E. Galicia.	Dardanelles : Turkish success at Gaba Tepe. Italians occupy Valona.
30	Germans attack at Hooge. French success near Souchez.	Austro-Germans attack forts of Przemysl. Russian success on the San.	Dardanelles : British repulsed at Quinn's Post. Italians make progress in Trentino. Italian air raid on Pola.
31	Fighting at Hooge. French take Souchez refinery, and advance in the " Labyrinth." Zeppelin raid on London.	Austro-Germans capture Stryj and the three N. forts of Przemysl.	.. .. ..
June. 1	Continued fighting in the " Labyrinth " (N. of Arras). French capture trenches at Souchez.	Unsuccessful German gas attack W. of Warsaw.	Austrian aircraft bomb Bari and Brindisi. Italians hold slopes of Monte Nero (across Isonzo), and advance in Adige Valley.
2	.. .. ..	Austro-German attack on Przemysl. Austrians beaten on the Dniester at Mikolajow.	.. ..
3	British take trenches at Givenchy.	**Austro - Germans retake Przemysl.**	Dardanelles : Turkish attack repulsed at Gallipoli.
4	Zeppelin raid on E. Coast.	.. .. ..	Dardanelles : French and British make a general attack at Gallipoli.
5	Fighting continues N. of Arras. German counter-attacks on French E. of Lorette Ridge repulsed.	.. .. ..	..
6	Zeppelin raid on E. Coast. (24 killed, 30 injured.)	Enemy cross the Dniester at Zurawno, and continue their advance E. of Przemsyl.	.. ..
7	Flight Sub-Lieut. Warneford destroys a Zeppelin between Ghent and Brussels. French offensive near Hébuterne. French progress N. of Arras. Repeated German counter-attacks repulsed N. of the Aisne.	.. .. ..	.. ..

Asiatic and Egyptian Theatres.	Naval and Overseas Operations.	Political, &c.	1915. May.
.. .. ..	Anglo-French take Njok (Cameroons).	Dr. Braga elected President of Portugal.	29
.. .. ..	Severe fighting in Cameroons. British take Sphinxhaven (on Lake Nyassa, Germ. E. Africa). German note to U.S.A. on the " Lusitania " ([49]).	.. .. ..	30
British defeat Turks at Kurna (Tigris).	Germans capitulate to Anglo-French at Monso (Cameroons). Italians attack Pola.	Dissatisfaction in U.S.A. at German note on the " Lusitania." Riots in Ceylon.	31
Turkish retreat on the Tigris, pursued by naval flotilla.	.. .. ..	Lord Kitchener made a K.G.	June 1
.. .. ..	British submarine sinks a German transport in Sea of Marmora.	.. .. ..	2
Capitulation of Amara (Mesop.) to the British.	.. .. ..	Bill to create Ministry of Munitions introduced.	3
.. .. ..	.. .. ..	Mr. Lloyd George speaks at Liverpool on the output of munitions ([50]).	4
.. .. ..	Italian fleet bombards lighthouses and stations on the islands of the Dalmatian Archipelago, and Monfalcone.	Mr. Winston Churchill speaks at Dundee on the Dardanelles expedition.	5
.. .. ..	.. .. ..	.. .. ..	6
.. .. ..	.. .. ..	.. .. ..	7

1915. June.	WESTERN FRONT.	EASTERN FRONT.	SOUTHERN FRONT.
8	French hold all Neuville St. Vaast, and make progress in the " Labyrinth " and at Hébuterne.	.. .. ..	.. ..
9	.. .. ..	German attacks repulsed in the Shavli district. Austro-Germans pressed back to right bank of the Dniester.	Italians occupy Monfalcone (Isonzo front).
10	.. .. ..	Austro-Germans driven back near the Dniester at Zurawno.	.. ..
11	French advance five furlongs on a front of 1¼ miles and repulse a strong counter-attack S. of Hébuterne (S. of Arras).	Austrians lose 16 000 prisoners at Zurawno.	.. ..
12	.. .. ..	Austro-Germans cross the Dniester at Kolomea. Germans attack N. of Shavli, N. of Przasnysz, on the Bzura and at Mosciska (Gal.).	Italians make progress in the Carnic Alps. Malborghetto bombarded.
13	French repulsed at Souchez. Success of the French S.E. of Hébuterne.	Austro-Germans attack successfully from the San to Mosciska. Russian counter-attack on the Styr and Tysmienice.	.. .. ..
14	.. .. ..	Russians fall back towards Grodek line (Lemberg).	.. .. ..
15	French airmen bomb Karlsruhe. British take, but fail to hold, German front line trench E. of Festubert. Zeppelin raid on N.E. Coast.	German advance on right bank of San.	.. ..
16	British advance N. of Hooge, and E. of Festubert. French gain ground in severe fighting N. of Arras. French advance in the Vosges.	Continued fighting E. of the San.	.. .. ..
17	French carry Buval Bottom (N. of Arras). Germans set fire to and evacuate Metzeral (Alsace).	Russians announce enemy loss of 120,000 on Dniester during the last month.	Italians complete capture of heights on left bank of the Isonzo, dominating Plava.

Asiatic and Egyptian Theatre	Naval and Overseas Operations.	Political, &c.	1915. June.
.. .. ..	.. .. ..	Ministry of Munitions Bill amended ([51]). Mr. Bryan U.S. State Secretary resigns ([52]). Mr. Lansing succeeds.	8
.. .. ..	Second American note on the "Lusitania" despatched. German submarine sinks two British t.b.'s. A U-boat sunk.	Canada announces intention to raise a further 35,000 men.	9
.. .. ..	Anglo-French take Garua (Cameroons).	.. .. ..	10
.. .. ..	Second American note on the "Lusitania" published.	Mr. Lloyd George speaks at Bristol on munitions.	11
.. .. ..	.. .. ..	Great Britain informs Germany through the U.S. Ambassador that submarine prisoners are now treated as ordinary prisoners ([53]).	12
.. .. ..	.. .. ..	Greece : General election ; Venizelists win 193 out of 316 seats.	13
.. .. ..	.. .. ..	Second reading of the Finance Bill.	14
.. .. ..	Germans lose submarine U. 14.	Vote of credit for £250,000,000 ([54]).	15
.. .. ..	.. .. ..	Mr. Lloyd George takes the oath as Minister of Munitions.	16
.. .. ..	.. .. ..	.. .. ..	17

1915. June.	WESTERN FRONT.	EASTERN FRONT.	SOUTHERN FRONT.
18	..	Official report issued on the Russian operations during the past month on the Dniester ([55]).	..
19	French gain ground near Souchez. French bombard Münster (Alsace).	Austro-Germans attack the Grodek line (Gal.) ; Russians retreat.	..
20	Further French advance near Souchez. German counter-attacks on the heights of the Meuse repulsed.	..	Italians consolidate their positions in the Monte Nero region.
21	French repulse German counter-attacks N. of Arras. French gain ground in Lorraine.	Austro-Germans take Zolkiew and Rawa Ruska. Austrians repulsed at Nizniow (Dniester).	Dardanelles : French advance.
22	German gains recovered by French on the heights of the Meuse. French occupy Sondernach (Lorraine).	**Austrians retake Lemberg.**	Italians repulse Austrian attacks at Freikofel (Trentino).
23	..	Austro-Germans checked on the Zurawno-Demeszkowiec line (Dniester front).	..
24	Germans repulsed in an attack on the heights of the Meuse.	..	..
25	Continued fighting N. of Arras and on the heights of the Meuse. French airmen bomb railway station at Douai.	Russians fight a rearguard action at Bobrka.	Austrians repulsed in the Carnic Alps.
26	**Battle of the Argonne** begins ; Crown Prince attacks.	Russians repulse heavy German attacks on Bukaczowce-Halicz front (E. Galicia), but retreat.	..

Asiatic and Egyptian Theatres.		Naval and Overseas Operations.			Political, &c.	1915. June.
..	..	Austrian warships raid the Adriatic coast of Italy.			..	18
..	..	..	..	..	Conference at Boulogne between Mr. Lloyd George and M. Albert Thomas, French Under-Secretary for War.	19
..	..	H.M.S. "Roxburgh" cr,,damaged by torpedo.			..	20
..	..	..	..	..	Christian De Wet found guilty of treason (6 yrs. and £2,000). Mr. McKenna announces Government proposals for a 4½% War Loan.	21
..	..	German submarine sunk at Borkum.			..	22
..	..	..	..	..	Munitions Bill introduced by Mr. Lloyd George.	23
..	..	..	..	..	British memorandum on neutral commerce handed to U.S. Ambassador. Mr. Asquith announces forthcoming bill on the registration and organisation of national resources ([56]).	24
..	..	Bukoba (Germ. port on L. Vict. Nyanza), destroyed by British column.			..	25
..	..	..	..	..	General Sukhomlinov, Russian Minister for War, resigns ; General Polivanov succeeds him.	26

1915. June.	WESTERN FRONT.	EASTERN FRONT.	SOUTHERN FRONT.
27	French repulse German attacks on the heights of the Meuse and at Metzeral.	Germans occupy Halicz, and advance to the Bug. Russians retreat from the line of the Dniester to Gnila-Lipa line. Russian attacks break down N. of Przasnysz.	Dardanelles: British carry four Turkish lines near Krithia. Serbians capture island of Michaiska (Danube).
28	French advance at Souchez.	Continued Russian retreat in Galicia.	Dardanelles: British attack Achi Baba.
29	.. .. ..	**Austro-Germans advance towards the Vistula and the Bug.** Russians repulse an attack near Halicz.	Dardanelles: Turkish counter-attacks repulsed with heavy loss.
30	Failure of German attacks at Bagatelle (Argonne) and Metzeral.	Germans cross Gnila Lipa line. Austro-German advance from Tomashov. Germans claim 150,650 prisoners in June.	Dardanelles: French take six lines of Turkish trenches. Gen. Gouraud wounded, succeeded by Gen. Bailloud.
July 1	.. .. ..	Germans (Mackensen) occupy Zamosc (near Upper Bug). Germans (Linsingen) cross Gnila Lipa S. of Rohatyn (Galicia). Russians evacuate bridgehead near Tarlov (Vistula).	.. .. ..
2	German success near Four de Paris (Argonne); severe fighting; enemy repulsed near Blanleuil.	Austrians (Archd. Jos. Ferd.) occupy Krasnik; heavy Austro-Russian engagements between Vistula and Bug.	Great **battle for Carso Plateau** begins. Italians nearing Tolmino (Jul.).
3	.. .. ..	Russians leave Gnila Lipa for Zlota Lipa (Galicia).	Dardanelles: Turks lose 5,150 k. and 15,000 pris. in last 5 days.
4	Battle of the Argonne dies down; Crown Prince fails to break French line.	Austro-Germans reach the Zlota Lipa.	Heavy attack by Turks against Naval and 29th Divisions repulsed (Gall.) Serbians enter Durazzo (Albania).

Asiatic and Egyptian Theatres.	Naval and Overseas Operations.	Political, &c.	1915. June.
.. .. ..	Coast of Asia Minor opposite Chios bombarded by H.M.S. " Hussar."	.. .. ..	27
.. .. ..	German warships bombard Windau (Baltic).	.. .. ..	28
.. .. ..	.. .. ..	National Registration Bill introduced by Mr. Walter Long ([57]).	29
.. .. ..	.. .. ..	Welsh miners' dispute settled. Changes in Russian Cabinet ([58]).	30
			July 1
.. .. ..	Leyland liner " Armenian " torpedoed off Cornish coast. Otavi (S.W. Africa) occupied by Gen. Botha. H.M.S. " Lightning " damaged by mine or torpedo.	British Commission on trade with Sweden arrives Stockholm. Total German casualties to date, reckoned at 1,700,000, of which 306,000 killed, and 500,000 permanently disabled.	
.. .. ..	German cruiser " Pommern " sunk by British Subm. in Danzig Bay. Russian warships sink the " Albatross " off Gothland.	Munitions Bill sent to House of Lords after 3rd reading.	2
.. .. ..	S. Africa's offer of volunteer contingent announced by Gen. Smuts.	.. .. ..	3
Lahej (near Aden) attacked by Turks.	" Königsberg " (cruiser) partially destroyed by monitors in Rufiji river (Germ. E. Africa). French liner " Carthage " torpedoed and sunk off Cape Hellas.	.. .. ..	4

1915. July.	WESTERN FRONT.	EASTERN FRONT.	SOUTHERN FRONT.
5	Fierce fighting at Souchez, Arras, and on Meuse.	Severe enemy defeat between Vistula and Bug, and their offensive between Veprj and Bug repulsed. **Northern movement of Austro-Germans from Galicia towards Kholm-Lyublin line suspended.**	Sir I. Hamilton's despatch issued describing Turkish counter attacks beaten off June 30 to July 2. Turkish attempt to dislodge British from Gallipoli Peninsula defeated.
6	German success at Vaux Féry (Meuse). French recapture position on heights of the Meuse. British capture trenches near Pilkem.	Archduke Josef Ferdinand beaten near Krasnik. Russians take 15,000 prisoners between Krasnik and Lyublin.	Battle for Carso plateau developing.
7	..	Von Mackensen held up near Krasnostav.	Italians attack bridgehead at Gorizia and are repulsed. Despatches published from Sir I. Hamilton dated May 20, covering period March 13-May 5 ([59]).
8	French success at Fontenelle (Vosges). British repulse German attack S.W. of Pilkem.	Austrian troops withdraw to heights N. of Krasnik after defeat on Urzedowka.	Monticello taken by Italians (Trent.)
9	..	Austrian offensive on Zlota Lipa repulsed.	Italians capture Malga Sarta and Costa Bella (Trentino).
10	..	Austrians counter-attack on Bistritza (Krasnik). Gen, Russki, C.-in-C. Northern front.	..

ASIATIC AND EGYPTIAN THEATRES.	NAVAL AND OVERSEAS OPERATIONS.	POLITICAL, &c.	1915. July.
British evacuate Lahej and retire to Bir Nasr, then to Aden, after attack by Turks.	.. .. ..	Statement concerning German violation of neutral mails on Swedish mail steamers. Lord Fisher appointed Chairman, Inventions Board.	5
.. .. ..	S. Africa's offer of Imperial Contingent gratefully accepted by Government.	Anglo-French Conference at Calais.	6
.. .. ..	.. .. ..	.. .. ..	7
.. .. ..	Union troops reach Tsumeb (Germ. S.W. Africa), releasing all prisoners captured by enemy. German reply to "Lusitania" Note ([60]). Italian cruiser "Amalfi" torpedoed and sunk by Austrians in Mediterranean.	Third reading of National Registration Bill. Order in Council passed to increase Canadian Exp. Force to 150,000 men. Austrian Note to Rumania.	8
Bomb thrown at Sultan of Egypt.	**S.W. Africa conquered ; German troops surrender unconditionally to Gen. Botha.** Attempted torpedo attack on Cunarder "Orduna."	Anglo - Portuguese Treaty of Commerce ratified at Lisbon. Lord Kitchener appeals for more recruits at Guildhall. Mr. Walter Long makes statement on conscription ([61]). Export of gold prohibited in France.	9
Turks attack Russians near Karaderbent (Transc.).	Gen. Botha makes known terms of surrender in S.W. Africa. Lord Kitchener cables congratulations and invites him to England.	German reply to American Note published ([62]).	10

1915. July.	WESTERN FRONT.	EASTERN FRONT.	SOUTHERN FRONT.
11	Despatch dated June 15 from Sir J. French published, covering operations from April 5 to May 30 (⁶³).	Fighting on Lyublin front continues; Austrians lose nearly all ground gained in past week. Enemy attacks on Zlota Lipa and Dniester repulsed. Russians withdraw to R. bank of Urzedowka.	Successful Italian offensive in Carnia region. Venice bombed by Austrian aeroplanes for fourth time.
12	Crown Prince checked in Argonne, after vigorous offensive. German advance round Souchez and capture cemetery. German attack in "The Labyrinth" (N. of Arras) repulsed.	Enemy offensive on the Bobr and Narev fronts (N.E. of Warsaw).	Turkish trenches before Achi Baba captured. Italian air raid on Pola.
13	New German offensive in Argonne. They capture French line at Vienne-le-Château and the height of La Fille Morte.	Austrian advance across Dniester in Bukovina; German attack on Narev.	French advance to the Kereves Dere stream (Gallipoli).
14	Germans attack Belgians on Yser canal and are repulsed.	**Russians fall back towards Narev. Great Austro-German offensive from Baltic to Bukovina begins.** Enemy capture Przasnysz (Narev).	Montenegrins repulse Austrian attack at Grahovo (Montenegro).
15	Failure of Germans in attempt to reach L. bank of Yser results in heavy losses.	New German offensive towards Riga develops. Germans storm line S. of Zielovna (near Przasnysz), and force Russians to retreat towards the Narev.	Italian offensive in Upper Cadore develops (Dolomites).
16	German attack in Lorraine (forest of Parroy) and in sector of Fontenoy (W. of Soissons).	Between Vistula and Bug Germans attack Russians on the Wolitsa, and Russians repulse Archduke N. of Krasnik. Russians defeat Austrians on E. bank of Dniester and capture 2,000 prisoners.	.. .. ..
17	.. .. ..	Heavy fighting between Vistula and Bug. Mackensen continues offensive on the Wolitsa.	Serbians evacuate Durazzo (Alb.), at request of Italians, but keep neighbouring strategical points.

Asiatic and Egyptian Theatres.	Naval and Overseas Operations.	Political, &c.	1915. July.
..	Destruction of "Königsberg" completed on Rufiji River (German E. Africa).	..	11
..	Engagements reported between British - Belgian force and Germans on N. Rhodesian frontier.	State control of coal industry announced in Germany. S. Wales miners conference rejects Government proposals.	12
Death of Sultan of Lahej from wound received during Turkish attack.	..	£570,000,000 (besides £15,000,000 through the P.O.) subscribed to War Loan. Strikes proclaimed an offence.	13
Turks driven from Nasriya (Euphrates) by British force from Kurna.	..	**National Registration Bill passes** House of Lords.	14
..	..	Strike of Welsh miners begins.	15
..	..	..	16
..	"Lusitania" report issued by Lord Mersey.	Two spies condemned to death at Westminster Guildhall. **Signing of secret treaty between Turco-German Allies and Bulgaria.**	17

1915 July.	WESTERN FRONT.	EASTERN FRONT.	SOUTHERN FRONT.
18	German attack at Souchez repulsed.	Mackensen captures Krasnostav. Windau (Courland coast) captured. Russians retreat from N. and W. of Warsaw and on entire front of Vistula and Bug.	Italian success on Isonzo, 2,000 prisoners.
19	German attack near Les Eparges (Verdun), repulsed with heavy losses, also W. and S.W. of Souchez.	Russians concentrating on Narev. Germans attacking N. and S. of Warsaw. Fiercest fighting on Lyublin-Kholm line.	Italian success on Carso plateau after two days' fighting : capture of M. San Michele. Total casualties in Dardanelles to June 30, 42,434, announced in House of Commons.
20	French advance up valley of the Fecht towards Münster (Alsace).	Stubborn Russian defence of Lyublin-Kholm railway. Heavy fighting S. of Ivangorod. Russians evacuate positions W. of Groitsi and retreat N. of Novogorod (Warsaw region). Germans break through Russian line on the Bubissa (N).	Italians attack round Gorizia and capture of 500 prisoners on Carso.
21	.. .. ..	Ivangorod fortress invested. Russian offensive round Sokal expels enemy from R. bank of Upper Bug.	Italian advance at Plava (Julian).
22	French positions E. of Metzeral (Alsace) attacked, captured, and finally evacuated by enemy. French gain near Bagatelle (Argonne).	Russians cleared from L. bank of Vistula above Ivangorod. Enemy storms Miluny (Warsaw) and attacks Narev bridge-head at Rojan.	Austrians hold bridgehead of Gorizia against fierce attacks. Italians capture 1,500 prisoners on Carso.
23	.. .. ..	Fortresses of Rojan and Pultusk stormed and river Narev crossed by Germans. Russians overtaken and defeated near Shavli (Courland).	Italians advance along Luznica Ridge (Julian). Innsbruck bombed.
24	German attack near Hooge repulsed. Dunkirk bombarded. French capture positions in Ban de Sapt (Vosges).	.. .. ..	Austrian attacks on Luznica Ridge (Julian) repulsed.

Asiatic and Egyptian Theatres.	Naval and Overseas Operations.	Political, &c.	1915. July.
Turks reported to have ordered Greeks to evacuate Aivali (N. of Smyrna).	Italian cruiser " Giuseppe Garibaldi " torpedoed.	Prince Hohenlohe-Langenburg, German ambassador at Constantinople, received by King Ferdinand at Sofia.	18
.. .. ..	.. .. ..	Venizelist movement gains ground as opposed to Germanophil policy ot Gounaris. Bulgaria again declares neutrality.	19
.. .. ..	.. .. ..	Welsh miners strike settled (⁶⁴).	20
British force reaches Euphrates from Kurna and captures Turkish troops. British reoccupy Sheikh Othman (Aden).	.. .. ..	.. .. ..	21
Announced that 30 Turkish officers with arms cargo sailed for Tripoli ; Italians demand war on Turkey.	.. .. ..	Mr. Roosevelt denounces his countrymen as accessories after the fact to Germany's crimes in Belgium. Turkish portion of Dedeagach railway ceded to Bulgaria with territory (600 sq. miles) between river Maritza and frontier.	22
Italian garrisons massacred in revolt of Senussites in Tripoli, German and Turkish officers in command.	Austrian warships bombard Ortona and the Tremiti Islands(Adriatic). Third American Note to Germany re "Lusitania" published (⁶⁵).	.. .. ..	23
Turks defeated outside Nasriya (Euphrates).	.. .. ..	Strikes and German outrages in munition factories irritate public opinion in U.S.A.	24

1915. July.	WESTERN FRONT.	EASTERN FRONT.	SOUTHERN FRONT.
25	.. .. ..	Enemy reaches Posvol and Poneviezh district on the Dvina. Russian Government evacuates factories at Riga and Warsaw. Enemy troops cross Narev above Ostrolenka.	Italians progress on Lower Isonzo. Barracks at Verona bombed.
26	Attacks by Crown Prince in Argonne checked. French success on Lingekopf (Alsace)	Enemy held on Narev line, fierce fighting E. of Rojan; Zeppelin captured by Russians. Germans repulsed at Shlok (Riga), warships co-operating.	Italians occupy crests on Julian front and capture Monte Sei Busi; and attack Plateau of Doberdo. Great fire in Constantinople.
27	French capture position above Lingekopf. Soissons and Reims bombarded.	Enemy captures Goworowo (E. of Rojan). Warsaw attacked on three sides. Austrians lose heavily in attack near Majdan-Ostrowski and on front Terriatin-Annopol (Cholm region). Fighting for the Pruth S.E. of Poltusk proceeding.	.. .. ..
28	Air-raid on St. Omer.	Germans cross Vistula between Warsaw and Ivangorod. Russians repulsed S.W. of Gora Kalvariya (S. of Warsaw). Austrians repulsed beyond the Kamienka (Upper Vistula).	Austrians repulsed in Carnia. Italian offensive in Cordevole Valley (Venetian Alps) progressing. Italians evacuate positions just W. of Gorizia.
29	Artillery action Souchez and Soissons sectors, around Arras, etc. Nancy bombed.	Line of Lyublin-Kholm railway cut by enemy. German troops break through Russians positions W. of the Veprj. Unsuccessful enemy attempt to advance between Narev and the Orz.	Strong Italian offensive in Cordevole valley.

Asiatic and Egyptian Theatres.	Naval and Overseas Operations.	Political, &c.	1915. July.
Kasriya shelled, attacked and occupied by British troops under Gen. Gorringe.	U.S.A. steamer "Leelanaw" torpedoed. French occupy Lomie in Cameroons; rising in Zemen district, Germans retreat.	.. .. ..	25
Announced that Nejd (N.E. Arabia) has proclaimed its independence and put Turkish garrisons to flight.	French operate against Lagosta (Adriatic) destroying Austrian submarine supply station, etc. Italians land and capture Pelagosa Island (centre of Adriatic), German destroyer sunk by British submarine in North Sea.	Great Britain's reply to American Note of March 30 received in Washington ([66]). Canada's recruits up to date, 140,000.	26
Russians forced back by Turks near Mush (Asia Minor).	3 Danish schooners torpedoed by German submarine. Railway from Ancona to Pesaro bombarded from sea.	Mr. Asquith announces total military casualties to July 18, 830,995; naval 9,106. French Chamber agrees to necessity of Parliamentary control for army.	27
.. ..	.. .. ..	Final debate on Compulsory Service; Mr. Asquith reviews situation. Mr. Lloyd George speaks on munitions ([67]).	28
.. ..	Loss of French submarine "Mariotte" in Dardanelles. Austrians attempt to recapture Pelagosa. American Note to Germany concerning the "Leelanaw" reported.	Mr. Lloyd George speaks at conference of mining industry ([68]).	29

1915. July.	WESTERN FRONT.	EASTERN FRONT.	SOUTHERN FRONT.
30	British line pierced at Hooge by enemy using "flame - throwers." 45 French aeroplanes bomb Freiburg (Baden), Pfalzburg (Lorraine), and petrol factories at Pechelbronn, &c.	**Russians fall back along entire line,** only resisting N. of Grusbieszow (lower Bug). Evacuation of Warsaw continues. Austrians occupy Lyublin.	Italian offensive in Trentino resumed. Italian bombard forts in and around the Cadore valley and Sexten (Carn.).
31	End of big movement. lasting ten days, of German troops from Eastern to Western front.	Germans cross the Aa (Riga), after two days' fighting. Desperate fighting and German advance on Kamienka front (Vistula). Russians ejected from positions near Kurow (Lyublin). Kholm occupied by Germans.	Riva (and Garda) bombarded by seaplanes Austrian positions there taken.
Aug 1	Artillery duels in Artois, valley of the Aisne, N.W. of Reims, and in Western Argonne ; enemy attacks repulsed here. British retake some trenches at Hooge.	Mitau (Riga) evacuated, and captured by Germans. Latter held on Blonie line, W. of Warsaw ; they progress on the Narev. Austrians capture Novo Alexandria station (Ivangorod).	Enemy counter - attack on Mt. Medetta (Carn. and is repulsed.
2	Fighting in the St. Hubert region (Argonne). Les Eparges (Verdun) bombarded. Enemy attacks position on the Linge and Barrenkopf ridge(Vosges). German success at Hill 213 (Argonne).	Russians retreat E. of Ponevyej (Dvinsk). Germans claim 9,000 prisoners taken near Lomja (E. bank of Vistula), and at Ivangorod. On the Leczna-Kholm line (C) Russians lose 2,000 prisoners and evacuate their positions.	Italian offensive near M Sei Busi (Carso) progresses : beaten back o Polazzo plateau.
3	German night attacks in Argonne repulsed.	Russians retire N. of Lomja ; Germans cross Narev. Mackensen victorious near Kholm.	.. ..

Asiatic and Egyptian Theatres.	Naval and Overseas Operations.	Political, &c	1915. July.
Turkish success reported in Grsbudo Hills(Armen.) Cholera among Turkish troops at Constantinople.	Leyland liner "Iberian" torpedoed.	United States protests against fraudulent use of passports by German spies. Political crisis and resignation of Japanese cabinet. Pope addresses letter to heads of belligerent States([69]). £7,500,000 voted for new Dutch naval programme. Australian Federal Government proposes War Tax.	30
.. ..	.. .. ..	French Note on German outrages at Roubaix published. M. Radoslavov declares Bulgaria has no intention of joining Central Powers or of attacking Serbia.	31
			Aug 1
.. .. ..	Galata bridge (Constantinople) blown up by British submarines.	Kaiser and Tsar each issue manifesto on first anniversary of war. Former swears that his conscience is clear. Great Britain orders motor-boats in U.S.A.	
.. .. ..	British submarine sinks German transport in Baltic with troops of von Below's army.	£200,000 subscribed in Canada for machine-guns. Full correspondence concerning Prize Courts, between Sir E. Grey and the American Ambassador, published by Foreign Office ([70]). German Note regarding the "William P. Frye" received by U.S.A. ([71]). Third report of French Commission on atrocities published.	2
Turks claim Alashgerd (Armen.) retaken from Russians.	French battleships bombard Sighadjik (Smyrna). Russians sink number small vessels in raid on Anatolian coast.	Reply of Entente Powers to Bulgarian Note of June 14 (text secret). Parliamentary control for French army established.	3

1915. Aug.	WESTERN FRONT.	EASTERN FRONT.	SOUTHERN FRONT.
4	.. .. ..	Germans threaten Warsaw ; civilians evacuate ; Blonie-Nadarzyn line (15 m. W. of Warsaw) abandoned by Russians. Latter evacuate Ivangorod.	Castle of Lizzana (Rovereto) destroyed by Austrians. Italians occupy Col di Lana (Cordevole, Ven. Alps).
5	Heavy fighting in the Vosges and at Hill 213 (Arg.).	**Capture of Ivangorod** by Austrians. **Germans enter Warsaw.**	Italian airship captured at Pola. Progress on the Carso by Italians. Gen. Sàrrail succeeds Gen. Gouraud as C. in Chief in Near East.
6	.. .. ..	Germans repulsed at Osovyets (N.C.). Archd. Jos. Fred. enters Lyublin.	Two divisions effect surprise landing at Suvla Bay and attack, with Anzacs on R. and S. force on Achi Baba.
7	German attacks in Argonne and Vosges repulsed with heavy losses (est. 4,000).	Russians repulse Germans near Riga. Enemy attacks Kovna ; Russian retreat behind Jara. Enemy attacks with gas near Osovyets. Sierok (N. Georgievsk) occupied. Enemy reaches Vistula near Pienkow.	Gallipoli : Very heavy fighting and losses ; little progress; frightfully hot. Italian artillery reaches Ercavallo Peak (Trentino).
8	.. .. ..	Germans attack Kovna, repulsed with heavy losses. Novo Georgievsk cut off in the East. Praga (Warsaw) occupied. Mackensen forces Russians back across the Veprj.	Monfalcone dockyard (N. Adriatic) bombed. Night raid by Austrians into Italian positions in Trentino. British attack on Anafarta (Gall.) repulsed.
9	Zeppelin raid on East Coast; one airship destroyed at Dunkirk. British recapture trenches at Hooge. French air-raid on Saarbrücken.	Osovyets evacuated and destroyed by Russians. Night attack on Kovna fortress ; Germans lose three battalions in Russian counter - attack. Germans advance E. of Warsaw.	Heavy Anzac losses ; Turks getting stronger.

ASIATIC AND EGYPTIAN THEATRES.	NAVAL AND OVERSEAS OPERATIONS.	POLITICAL, &c.	1915. Aug.
.. .. ..	French battleships bombard Spelia and Scalanova (opp. Samos).	Anniversary Service at St. Paul's ([72]). Losses announced ([73]). French Chamber renews "Union sacrée." Mr. Tribich Lincoln, spy and ex-M.P., arrested in New York. Rumania votes £4,000,000 for military purposes. National Cabinet for New Zealand decided on.	4
Russians capture Turkish positions near Olti and Sarikamish (Transc.) and repel counter-attacks.	.. .. ..	Strike in Belgian coal district. Germans fire on strikers. Russian Ministry of Munitions proposed. Duma votes 35 million roubles for refugees.	5
.. .. ..	.. .. ..	345 British establishments declared "Controlled" under Munitions of War Act. Combined Entente Note to Balkan States ([74]).	6
.. .. ..	.. .. ..	Rumania mobilises 10 classes reservists. National Relief Fund totals £5,431,671 in one year.	7
Bushire (Pers. Gulf) occupied by British as reprisal for 2 officers killed there on July 12.	German Fleet attacks Riga and is repulsed. H.M.S. "Ramsay" sunk by German steamer "Meteor" (blown up to avoid capture). H.M.S. "India" auxiliary cruiser, torpedoed off Norway	German unsuccessful peace tentatives to Russia through Denmark. Naval General Service Medal instituted.	8
Jerusalem - Beersheba railway opened. Turkish attacks at Olti and Passin (Armen.) repulsed. 255,000 Armenians from Van migrate into Transcaucasia.	Gadji (Cameroons) reported evacuated by Germans after French operations. H.M.S. "Lynx," dest., mined and sunk. Turkish battleship "Kheir-ed-Din Barbarossa" torpedoed by British submarine	Italian Consuls throughout Turkey preparing to leave.	9

1915. Aug.	WESTERN FRONT.	EASTERN FRONT.	SOUTHERN FRONT.
10	Gains at Hooge consolidated. British artillery and aircraft active on Belgian Coast.	Vilna and Kovna being evacuated. Novo Georgievsk and Brest Litovsk bombarded. Germans reach Kaluszyn (E. of Warsaw). Russians dislodged N.W. of Kock (Veprj); Lomja and Ostrov (Bug) in enemy hands	Vigorous Italian offensive on Isonzo. Italian advance in Ortler range (Upper Adige). Feint landing at Karachali (Gulf of Saros, Gall.) Turkish counter attack on Chunuk Bair nearly succeeds.
11	German attacks in Argonne and Vosges repulsed.	Dvinsk evacuated.	British attack in Gallipoli dies away. Powerful Austro-German concentration announced in S. Hungary.
12	Zeppelin raid on East Coast; 29 victims.	Russians evacuate Sokolov, Syedlets, Lukow (E. of Warsaw); material evacuated from Riga. Austro-German armies in touch W. of Brest-Litovsk and form unbroken line. Germans driven back beyond Aa, S.W. of Mitau. Russians capture Kovarsk and Toviamy (W.S.W. of Dvinsk).	Italians leaving Turkey. Serbians retaliate for Austrian bombardment of Belgrade by bombarding Semlin and Panchev
13	German attacks in Argonne repulsed. Germans bombard Raon l'Étape (Argonne).	Germans thrust back after three days' fighting from Vlodava (on the Upper Bug).	Italian progress on the Carso and advance Sexten valley (Carn.).
14	10 French aeroplanes bombard Valley of Spada (St. Mihiel, Meuse).	Russian sortie from Kovna repulsed. Enemy force Nurzec (C.) crossing. Russians attack near Czernowitz (Bukovina).	.. ..
15	Violent bombardment on Yser front.	1,730 Russians taken prisoners outside Kovna. Losice, Biala, and Mezyrecze (W. of Brest) captured; enemy crosses Bug E. of Droghiczyn. Russian line broken at Bransk (on Nurzec), 5,000 prisoners taken.	Venice bombarded by sea plane.

ASIATIC AND EGYPTIAN THEATRES.	NAVAL AND OVERSEAS OPERATIONS.	POLITICAL, &c.	1915. Aug.
Russians pursue Turks on Upper Euphrates and capture important height in valley of Passin.	German fleet bombards Riga and is again driven off.	New Japanese cabinet formed ([75]). America's reply to Germany regarding " William P. Frye " despatched ([76]). Duma decides on enquiry into abuses connected with munitions. Bucharest refuses to authorise transport of German munitions to Turkey.	10
.. .. ..	.. .. ..	Paris " Temps " publishes text of secret memorandum to German Chancellor from six leading economic organisations in Germany ([77]).	11
Russian left wing reoccupies Alashgerd (Armen.).	Naval engagement between German and Russian fleets near Oesel (Riga). French cruiser shells and destroys German munition factory at Jaffa.	10,000,000 francs in gold deposited in one week in Banque de France. U.S.A. reply to Austria affirms export of munitions of war not against laws of neutrality. King Albert made Col.-in-Chief of 5th Dragoon Guards.	12
.. .. ..	French t.b.d. sinks Austr. subm. in Adriatic.	Bulgarian Premier, M. Radoslavov, explains Bulgaria's aims, etc., to American press ([78]).	13
.. .. ..	Transport " Royal Edward " sunk in Aegean ; 600 out of 1,400 saved.	.. .. ..	14
.. .. ..	.. .. ..	National Register taken. Cholera in Hungary. Striking exposure of German intrigues in *New York World.*	15

1915. Aug.	WESTERN FRONT.	EASTERN FRONT.	SOUTHERN FRONT.
16	.. .. ..	Russian army withdrawn to Brest - Osovyets - Kovna line. Byelostok (Grodno) partially evacuated. Kovna bombarded ; breach made in defences. Austrians cross Krzna (Brest). Germans repulsed from Mitau (Riga).	Montenegrin success on border against Austrians. Adm. de Robeck's despatch of 1.7.15 on Dardanelles landing 25/26.4.15 received (v. 24.8.).
17	Zeppelin raid on E. Coast. French gain footing on ridge in Vosges (Sondernach crest). Night attack on Sondernach by Germans.	Novo-Georgievsk furiously attacked and outlying forts captured. Austrians approach Brest-Litovsk. Russians driven across Bug at Konstantinov. **Fall of Kovna.** Enemy approaches Byelostok-Byelsk railway and cuts Kholm - Brest - Litovsk railway.	Italian advance on Bacher valley (Dol.), Vrsik crest, Sta Maria and Sta Lucia hills (Jul.),
18	French capture position on Ablain - Angres road (Vimy), and trench on Schratzmännele crest (Vosges).	.. .. ..	Italian progress towards Tolmino and in Upper Rienz (Julian).
19	Germans retake trenches on Ablain-Angres road.	**Fall of Novo Georgievsk.** Russians driven back between Augustovo and Osovyets (N. Centre). German progress beyond Niemen E. of Tykocin. Mackensen reaches Piszcza and gains ground towards Brest-Litovsk.	.. .. ..
20	.. .. ..	Russians evacuate Byelostok ; enemy occupies Byelsk (N. of Brest).	Topkhaneh (Arsenal at Constantinople) bombed by Russian aviators.
21	.. .. ..	.. .. ..	Second British Suvla attack (Gall.) on Anafarta fails.

Asiatic and Egyptian Theatres.	Naval and Overseas Operations.	Political, &c.	1915. Aug.
Russians enter Van (Armenia). Russian communiqué announces defeat of Turks and occupation of Kep (Euph). ; Turks driven back near Olti (Transc.).	Cumberland coast towns shelled by German submarine. German fleet attacks at entrance of Gulf of Riga.	**Manifesto on National Service** signed by notable men of all parties in England. Venizelist candidate elected President of Chamber ; Greek Government resigns.	16
1,200 Bunerwal rebels attack camp at Rustam (Peshawar) ; one officer killed.	Austrians attack Pelagosa Island (Centre Adriatic).	Germans claim two million prisoners to date : 330,000 British, French and Belgian ; rest Russian. Proposals of Entente examined by Serbian cabinet. Italian war loan totals 4 millions.	17
.. .. ..	Russian naval success in Gulf of Riga. German Fleet retires losing two cruisers (including "Moltke") and eight torpedo boats. Russian gunboat "Sivuch" sunk.	Offices of "Labour Leader" raided.	18
Turks prevent Italians leaving Smyrna.	Liner "Arabic" (White Star) torpedoed and sunk. Americans on board. German force landing at Pernau (Riga) destroyed by Russians. Norwegian mail steamer "Haakon VII." stopped by Germans and mails seized. Norwegian Government protests. British subm., "E 13," shelled when aground at Saltholm in neutral Danish waters.	Reichstag opened ; speech by Chancellor ([79]). Bulgarian Foreign Minister resigns. British forces total 3,825,000, including Colonial troops.	19
.. .. ..	Naval battle of Riga continues. German Fleet penetrates Gulf.	**Italy declares war on Turkey.** Second reading of War Loan Bill in Reichstag. 1,000,000,000 marks voted.	20
.. .. .	German Fleet retires from Riga, disembarkation having failed.	British Government declares **cotton absolute contraband.**	21

1915. Aug.	WESTERN FRONT.	EASTERN FRONT.	SOUTHERN FRONT.
22	French occupy Schratzmännele crest (Vosges).	Russians fall back from the Bobr and Niemen ; **fall of Osovyets.**	.. .. ..
23	Week of air raids begins. French bomb Tergnier and Noyon (c). British bomb Lens, Henin Liètard and Loos and German camps in Belgium.	Stubborn fighting round Kleszczeli (S. of Byelsk) ; Russians hold their own.	Italians attack bridgehead at Tolmino (Jul.).
24	French air raid into S. Baden (Lörrach).	Enemy breaks through advanced position near Dobrynka (S.W. of Brest).	Austrians, reinforced, resume offensive along Italian front. Naval despatch on Gallipoli published ([82]).
25	British line extended : French positions taken over. French bomb Dillingen iron works ; air raids in Woevre, Argonne and Artois.	**Storming and fall of Brest-Litovsk.**	Brescia bombed by Austrians. Account published of operations in Gallipoli since Aug. 6 ([83]). Fighting at Cattaro between Austrians and Montenegrins.
26	French bomb poison-gas factory Dornach.	Germans occupy fort of Olita on Niemen and advance S.E. and N.E. of Brest-Litovsk.	Italian progress in Val Sugana (Trent.).
27	German trenches captured between Sondernach and Landersbach (Alsace). French bomb Mülheim (Baden) and Châtel station (Argonne).	Russian line on Zlota Lipa broken near · Brzezany (E. Galicia). German troops massing on N.W. frontier of Rumania.	Italians storming Monte Rombon (Plezzo, Jul.). Austrians attack Montenegrins at Grahovo (Mont), and are repulsed.

Asiatic and Egyptian Theatres.	Naval and Overseas Operations.	Political, &c.	1915. Aug.
.. .. ..	German destroyer sunk by two French torpedo boat destroyers near Ostend.	M. Venizelos accepts Premiership.	22
.. .. ..	British warships bombard Zeebrugge and Knocke. British submarine torpedoes Turkish supply ship " Isfahan" opposite Constantinople.	Greek Cabinet formed ([80]). Serbian Parliament adopts order of the day ([81]).	23
.. .. ..	.. .. ..	Germany expresses regret to Denmark for bombardment of British submarine in Danish waters.	24
Coast of Asia Minor and Syria declared in state of blockade. Horrible Armenian massacres reported.	.. .. ..	.. .. ..	25
Rustam (N.W. India) column defeats Bunerwals at Surkhabi.	German submarine sunk by British airman off Ostend.	Letter published from Sir E. Grey in answer to German Chancellor's speech. ([84]). Speech by M. Viviani in French Chamber, followed by vote of confidence ([85]). Lord Selborne addresses agricultural representatives ([86]).	26
Attack reported on British and Russian Consuls at Kengaver (Persia) by band of ruffians under German Vice-Consul.	.. .. ..	South Wales Miners' Federation refuse Mr. Runciman's award ; Government refuses to meet them in further conference. Count Bernstorff notifies Mr. Lansing " full satisfaction " will be given U.S. for sinking "Arabic." German submarines now forbidden to attack merchantmen without warning.	27

1915. Aug.	WESTERN FRONT.	EASTERN FRONT.	SOUTHERN FRONT.
28	Air raid on Compiègne..	.. .. ..	Italians carry and hold Monte Cista (Val Sugana, Trent.).
29	Violent artillery duel in Argonne.	Enemy nears Grodno and Vilna. Lipsk (Grodno) stormed, Sidra section evacuated. Germans attack bridgehead of Dvina at Friedrichstadt (N.).	.. .. ..
30	.. .. ..	Russian victory on Strypa. (S. Galicia), taking 4,000 prisoners and 30 guns.	Italians eject Austrians from Monte Maronia (Jul.). French aeroplanes bomb Akbachi Sliman and Chanak (Gallipoli).
31	Germans claim successes in the Vosges.	Russians beat Germans near Lutsk (Upper Styr River). 7,000 prisoners.	Serbian troops at Durazzo.
Sept. 1	.. .. ..	Germans storm Grodno ; Austrians enter Brody ; Russians concentrate round Vilna.	.. .. ..
2	.. .. ..	**Fall of Grodno ;** Boehm-Ermolli advances E. of Brody ; Russians retreat to the Sereth ; fierce fighting near Vilna.	Unsuccessful assault by Italians on bridgehead of Tolmino. British submarines sink 4 Turkish transports off Akbachi Sliman and Nagara (Gall.).

Asiatic and Egyptian Theatres.	Naval and Overseas Operations.	Political, &c.	1915. Aug.
Bunerwals again defeated, Malandri Pass (N.W. India).	.. .. ..	Messages from M. Sazonov and Gen. Polivanov ([87]).	28
Swat natives repulsed at Sandaki (N.W. India).	.. .. ..	.. .. ..	**29**
.. .. ..	.. .. ..	German Ambassador's account of his last interview with Sir E. Grey republished from German press. Great Britain makes concessions to American trade with regard to blockade. Letter from Mr. Balfour gives total deaths from Zepp. raids as 89—all civilians.	30
Rustam column again drives Bunerwals back.	.. .. ..	Dispute in S. Wales Coalfield officially ended ([88]).	31
			Sept. 1
Island of Ruad (between Latakia and Tripoli, Syria) occupied by French.	.. .. ..	Serbia replies to communication of Entente Powers, *re* settlement of Balkan question. German acceptance of American demands *re* submarine warfare communicated by Count Bernstorff ([89]).	
German intrigues in Persia; Mr. T. G. Graham, British Consul-Gen. at Ispahan, attacked and wounded. Final scattering of Bunerwals on N.W. Frontier (India).	British transport "Southland" torpedoed in Aegean.	Gen. Polivanov appointed Prime Minister in Russia. American press publishes peace terms now being propagated by Germany ([90]). Scandinavian groups of Inter-parliamentary Union meet at Copenhagen ([91]).	2

1915. Sept.	WESTERN FRONT.	EASTERN FRONT.	SOUTHERN FRONT.
3	.. .. ..	Germans force Russians at Friedrichstadt to E. bank of Dvina; Russians re-enter Grodno and hold line between Dniester and Pripet marshes. Austrians reach R. bank of Sereth. Grand Duke Nicholas appointed Viceroy of Caucasus. Gen. von Beseler appointed Governor General of Russian Poland.	.. .. ..
4	Artillery actions round Arras, and N. of Châlons.	Enemy offensive on Dubno-Kovna road developing; Russians retire slowly in centre.	Successful Italian actions in Trentino and in Plezzo basin (Julian).
5	Heavy bombardments continue along Belgium and French fronts, especially in Arras region. This completes 13th day of incessant artillery duel on Western front. French aircraft bomb barracks at Dieuze and Mörchingen.	Tsar takes supreme command ([92]), with Gen. Alexeiev as C. of S., Gen. Russki succeeding latter as G.O.C.i.C. Northern Army ([93]); fighting on Styr and Sereth.	Night attack at Dardanelles by Turks repulsed by Australians.
6	French squadron of 40 aeroplanes bombs Saarbrücken.	Russians pressed back in centre by Germans and over E. Galician border by Austrians; heavy fighting near Brody.	Austrians active on Italian fronts.
7	Belgian coast (Westeinde and Ostend) bombarded by British and French fleets. French aeroplane squadron bombs Freiburg, Lens, Saarburg, etc.; Zeppelin raid on East Coast of England, 50 casualties, 7 killed.	Austrians enter Dubno([94]); successful Russian counter-offensive on Sereth at Tarnopol and Trembovla.	Serbians drive enemy from works on Danube and Drina fronts.

Asiatic and Egyptian Theatres.	Naval and Overseas Operations.	Political, &c.	1915. Sept.
.. .. ..	British mounted infantry cause severe loss to enemy near Maktan (German E. Africa).	Rumania forbids export of cereals.	3
.. .. ..	Allan liner " Hesperian " torpedoed off Irish coast, W. of Queenstown ; sinks later with loss of 32 lives.	.. .. ..	4
Defeat of Mohmands on Indian frontier by Gen. Campbell at Hafiz Khor (Gundao Valley).	Mine explosions on Uganda railway. Trains derailed, no casualties.	.. .. ..	5
Reports received of appalling condition of Armenians in Asia Minor ; Germany and Austria refuse to interfere.	Turkish destroyer, " Yar Hissar " sunk by submarine in Sea of Marmora. Renewed activity in German E. Africa. Fighting on Rhodesian frontier near Saisa, between Germans and Belgians. Russian destroyers in Black Sea damage Turkish cruiser " Hamidiya " and sink four coal transports.	Turco-Bulgarian frontier convention signed at Dimotika. "Archibald" documents discovered in U.S.A., compromising Austrian Ambassador, Dr. Dumba.	6
Russians repulse Turks at River Arkhave and annihilate Turkish corps at Olti (Armen.).	Destruction of submarine U 27 ([95]).	German Note handed to U.S.A. Ambassador at Berlin justifying sinking of "Arabic"([96]). Exchange of cordial messages between Tsar and President Poincaré. Italy declares cotton absolute contraband of war. Unrest among railway workers in S. Wales.	7

1915. Sept.	WESTERN FRONT.	EASTERN FRONT.	SOUTHERN FRONT.
8	Renewed German offensive in Argonne ; Allies bomb Ostend, Nesle, Metz, etc. ; Zeppelin raid E. Counties and London, 20 killed, 86 wounded.	Great Russian victory at Tarnopol and Trembovla (Sereth), 8,000 prisoners. Battle of Vilna proceeding.	Italians assume offensive in Cadore (Dolom.), but are repulsed at Doberdo (Carso).
9	Heavy indecisive fighting in the Vosges.	Russians hold their own in N. ; return to their former positions on the Sereth (S.), 5,000 more prisoners ; give way slowly in the centre.	.. .. ..
10	Steenstraate and Ramscapelle heavily shelled by Germans.	Enemy attacks N. of Vilna, serious fighting in centre. Russian success continued in S. Galicia.	Greek officers summoned to Athens.
11	Zeppelin raid at night on E. Coast (Eng.) ; no casualties.	Russians take offensive on Dvina, but withdraw N.W. of Vilna. Enemy falls back towards line of Strypa (S. Galicia).	.. .. ..
12	Heavy bombardments at points along the French front. Zeppelin raid on E. coast ; no casualties.	Vilna-Dvinsk railway cut near Svyentsyani. Russians pressed back E. of Grodno.	Active fighting along Italian fronts.
13	Numerous French air raids in the South. Sir Percy Scott placed in command of aerial defences of London. Two Zeppelin raids on Kentish and Essex coasts ; 7 persons injured.	Desperate fighting from the Dvina to the Vilia, and vigorous enemy offensive towards Dvinsk (battle of Meiszagola). Rumania orders partial mobilisation.	Bulgarians and Macedonians called to the colours.
14	.. .. ..	Continued pressure by enemy on N. sector ; Russians successful in Rovno and Tarnopol (Gal.) districts.	Various small successes on either side on Italian front.
15	Lord Kitchener states 11 new Army Divisions sent to France ; 17 miles more French front taken over.	Fighting W. and S. of Dvinsk. Germans aim at dividing Russian Vilna and Dvinsk groups ; the enemy advances on Pinsk ; driven back across Strypa in the S.	Removal of Turkish heavy artillery from fortresses to Gallipoli.

Asiatic and Egyptian Theatres.	Naval and Overseas Operations.	Political, &c.	1915. Sept.
Situation at Ispahan reported threatening.	French auxiliary cruiser " Indien " torpedoed off Rhodes.	Secret Socialist Meeting at Berne ; French socialists refused participation. Admiralty Air Department re-organised.	8
Wounding and death of British Vice-Consul at Shiraz (Persia).	Monfalcone Dockyard shelled by Italians. Van Rensburg and forty-two rebels sentenced at Pretoria.	Turco-Bulgarian Convention confirmed [97]. United States Government demand recall of Dr. Dumba. Mr. Lloyd George stirs up Labour at Trade Unions Congress [98].	9
Disquieting news from Persia ; gendarmerie disaffected and German intrigue rife.	Skirmish S. of Songwe River (border of German E. Africa).	.. .. ..	10
Ispahan evacuated by European residents.	.. .. ..	.. .. ..	11
.. .. ..	Belgian Relief ship " Pomona " sunk.	.. .. ..	12
.. .. ..	.. .. ..	Relations of Rumania with Central Powers critical [99]. Further revelations by *New York World* of German intrigues.	13
Persian Government begins to deal with dangerous situation in Ispahan.	Small British success at Maktan (E. Africa).	Extensive contraband trade in Holland revealed. Entente l ers hand Note to Bulgaria. Parliament reassembles.	14
.. .. ..	.. .. ..	Agitation in Bulgaria against Germanophil policy. Lord Kitchener anxious about falling off of recruiting. Mr. Asquith on Vote of Credit [100].	15

1915. Sept.	WESTERN FRONT.	EASTERN FRONT.	SOUTHERN FRONT.
16	.. .. ..	Situation Vilna - Dvinsk critical, but Russians stubborn. Pinsk occupied by Germans.	.. .. ..
17	.. .. ..	Vilna and Dvinsk dangerously threatened ; Russians retire between Vilia and Pripet rivers, but check enemy about Rovno.	.. .. ..
18	Lively actions along French front. Belgian coast bombarded by French artillery and British fleet.	**Fall of Vilna ;** Russians retreat towards Minsk ; Germans retire in Rovno region.	Slight Italian successes along their whole front.
19	.. .. ..	Germans reach Smorgon and Molodechna (between Vilna and Minsk). Fine Russian stand on Upper Vilia.	Artillery engagement near O r s o v a and Tekia (Danube).
20	Lively artillery actions on French front.	Heavy fighting in Northern sector and near Riga.	Sir I. Hamilton's desp. of 26,8.15, covering operations in Gallipoli 5 May to 30 June, published. Artillery engagements on Drina & Danube fronts. Heavy fighting, Plezzo and Carso fronts. Serbian positions re-attacked at Orsova and Tekia.
21	French successes on Aisne-Marne Canal and at Hartmannsweilerkopf (Vosges)	Tough fighting in N. sector round Dvinsk, etc. ; Russians re-occupying Smorgon. A u s t r i a n s driven back in Rovno region.	**Mobilisation of Bulgarian army** ordered.
22	Fierce fighting Neuville sector (Arras) and Forest of Apremont(Vosges). Stuttgart bombed.	Successful Russian operations along whole line except in centre.	Australian casualties at Dardanelles to date, 19,183, including 4,604 killed.
23	Numerous artillery engagements along whole line ; successful French air-raids.	Russians recapture Vileika (Minsk). Germans driven back across Oginski Canal (Pinsk). Russians take Lutsk and capture nearly 12,000 prisoners.	General mobilisation of Hellenic forces as " measure of elementary prudence " in view of Bulgaria's attitude. Bulgaria issues decree of mobilisation ; Premier repeats declaration of " armed neutrality."

ASIATIC AND EGYPTIAN THEATRES.	NAVAL AND OVERSEAS OPERATIONS.	POLITICAL, &C.	1915. Sept.
.. .. ..	.. .. ..	Taff Vale Railway dispute ended. Prorogation of Russian Duma till Nov. 14th.	16
.. .. ..	Loss of submarine E.7 in Dardanelles announced.	Debate in House of Commons on National Service ([101]). Austria, much annoyed, recalls Dr. Dumba " for consultation."	17
Swedish gendarmerie in Persia disbanded.	.. .. ..	.. .. ..	18
Turks fortifying Mersina, deporting Armenians and recruiting at Adana (S. Asia Minor) in view of coming Egyptian campaign.	British transport " Ramazan " sunk by submarine in Aegean : 300 Indian troops lost.	Statement by Herr von Jagow re Germany's submarine policy ([102]).	19
.. .. ..	.. .. ..	Compulsory Service League formed in N.S. Wales. Bulgaro-Turkish Convention for " maintenance of armed neutrality " by former. Stimulating open letter from Mr. Lloyd George ([103]).	20
.. .. ..	.. .. ..	Budget introduced by Mr. McKenna ([104]). Opening of Dutch Chambers ; determination to preserve neutrality.	21
Extensive preparations in Syria for renewed Turkish attack on Egypt reported.	Dutch liner " Koningin Emma " mined ; towed up Thames. 250 passengers saved.	Third German War Loan closed ; reported amount £601,500,000. White paper (Cd. 8012) issued concerning the " Archibald " papers ([105]).	22
.. .. ..	.. .. ..	Conciliatory German Note to U.S.A. in the " William P. Frye " case. U.S. refuse safe conduct to Dr. Dumba unless officially recalled. Meeting of S. African Party at Johannesburg , organised attack on General Smuts.	23

1915. Sept.	WESTERN FRONT.	EASTERN FRONT.	SOUTHERN FRONT.
24	.. .. ..	Varying encounters all along Russian front.	Austrian aeroplanes bomb Pozharevats ; enemy attempts to cross the Drina frustrated. Bulgarian Premier states mobilisation not directed against Serbia.
25	**Great Allied offensive begins (Battle of Loos and in Champagne).** the British fleet co-operating on Belgian coast. British attack S. of La Basseé Canal, 5 miles of enemy trenches captured, including Hohenzollern Redoubt stormed with partial success. French attack N. of Arras gains footing. In Champagne French assault between Suippe and Aisne, driving enemy from front positions. Other positions won include ground at Souchez.	Germans attacking Dvinsk from the S. are driven back with severe losses. Varying fortunes on rest of front.	.. .. ..
26	Stubborn British defence against counter - attacks round Loos ; French progress in Champagne, taking 16,000 prisoners. British bag 2,600 prisoners, 9 guns, etc.	Fighting round Dvinsk continues ; Germans driven back S. of Pinsk.	.. .. ..
27	Brilliant attack by Guards on Hill 70 (Loos) ; severe fighting continue there and in Champagne ; German offensive in Argonne (Fille Morte, etc.) driven back.	Germans attacks at Eckau (Riga), Dvinsk and on Vilia and Niemen repulsed.	.. .. ..
28	Severe fighting round and N. of Loos ; ground recaptured N. of Hill 70. British capture altogether 3,000 men and 21 guns. French continue to gain ground E. of Souchez and progress in Champagne.	Russians abandon Lutsk. Enemy presses Russians back in Pripet district, N. and S., but loses heavily in marshes.	.. .. ..

Asiatic and Egyptian Theatres.	Naval and Overseas Operations.	Political, &c.	1915 Sept.
.. .. ..	.. .. ..	Liquor Control Regulations applied to the area of " Greater London. " MM. Take Jonescu and Fili- pescu demand mobili- sation of Rumanian Army. National Registration Bill passed in New Zealand.	24
.. .. ..	Russian Fleet bombards enemy positions on Gulf of Riga ; enemy bat- teries silenced.	Turco-Bulgarian Agree- ment signed. King Con- stantine and M. Venizelos reported in perfect agree- ment.	25.
Reported expulsion of all Greeks from Smyrna.	.. .. ..	Bulgarian Premier assures no intention of attacking Greece. Rumania desires understanding with Bul- garia. Signor Barzilai's speech on German pre- meditation ([106]).	26.
Reports received de- scribing exterminating massacre of Armenians at instigation of Talaat Bey, abetted by Ger- mans (e.g. Baron Oppen- heim).	.. .. ..	.. .. ..	27
British victory at Kut-el- Amara (Tigris). British lose under 500 ; Turkish prisoners, 1,650. Enemy bolts towards Baghdad.	Fire and explosion on Italian battleship " Bene- detto Brin."	Allies victory in Cham- pagne confirms Greece in her antagonistic attitude to Central Powers. Dr. **Dumba recalled** uncon- ditionally from U.S.A. ; Trades Union and Labour bodies debate Compul- sory service. Plan settled for Anglo-French loan ([107]). Sir E. Grey defines policy as regards Balkan States ([108]).	28.

1915. Sept.	WESTERN FRONT.	EASTERN FRONT.	SOUTHERN FRONT.
29	**French capture Vimy crest** ; progress towards Tahure (Champagne); total French captures 23,000 prisoners and 79 guns. Heavy fighting Hohenzollern redoubt and Hulluch. British lose ground near Hooge (Ypres).	Severe fighting S.E. of Dvinsk and on Strypa (Gal.) ; Russians driven back in Pripet region.	.. .. ..
30	French gain more ground in Champagne; fighting round Loos continues. Special " Order of Day " by Sir J. French ([110]).	German advance comes to a standstill nearly all along line, though Russians still retiring slowly round Lutsk and in Southern Pripet marshes region. Russians still hold Dvinsk strongly.	Italian offensive continues amid ice and snow.
Oct. 1	Minor actions, Souchez and Lorraine.	German attacks on Dvinsk and Smorgon ; Linsingen gains ground 25 m. E. of Lutsk.	Unsuccessful Italian attacks on Tolmino ; **Concentration of Austro-German forces along Serbian frontier.**
2	British fleet and Belgian artillery bombard Westeinde.	.. .. ..	.. .. ..
3	Enemy capture part of Hohenzollern redoubt (Loos). French bomb Metz.	Desperate fighting in Lake region S. of Dvinsk ; Russian offensive Postavi-Smorgon collapses.	Germans checked on Serbian frontier. **Concentration of Bulgarian forces.**
4	.. .. ..	Russians take offensive between Drisviati Lake and Smorgon (N.E. of Vilna).	Artillery action along Belgrade-Save front.
5	British attack N. of Loos and French attack in Champagne indecisive.	Riga front active ; lively actions near Smorgon.	Italians progress towards Rovereto (Trent.). **Allied troops land Salonika** ([113]). Bulgarians moving under German officers.
6	French carry Tahure and the Butte (Hill 192) (Champagne).	Heavy fighting Dvina front and in Lakes district ; Rumanians fortifying Giurgevo (Ruschuk).	Austrians attack Belgrade forts.

Asiatic and Egyptian Theatres.	Naval and Overseas Operations.	Political, &c.	1915. Sept.
.. .. ..	.. .. ..	M. Venizelos speaks on relations between Greece and Bulgaria([109]). "Unionist Federation" party formed in Rumania under M. Filipescu.	29
.. .. ..	.. .. ..	Labour Meeting resolves that Voluntary System with special recruiting campaign sufficient. King George sends congratulatory message to Sir J. French. Labour Council, Sydney, Australia, opposes compulsory service unless wealth conscripted.	30
			Oct.
.. .. ..	British monitors bombard Lombaertzyde and Middelkerke.	.. .. ..	1
.. .. ..	.. .. ..	Balkans : " Situation one of utmost gravity " (Grey) ([111]). Agreement between Bulgaria and Central Powers to enter war on 15th.	2
.. .. ..	Zeebrugge bombarded from sea.	**Russian ultimatum to Bulgaria.**	3
.. .. ..	Two Russian squadrons off Varna.	Protests in Greek Chamber against Allies landing at Salonika. Allies' ultimatum to Bulgaria ([112]).	4
.. .. ..	.. .. ..	Dr. Dumba sails ; **M. Venizelos resigns ;** Lord Derby, Director of Recruiting ([114]). Entente Ministers at Sofia demand passports.	5
.. .. ..	Reports of valuable Belgian co-operation in Cameroons, beginning on Sanga in Oct., 1914.	Armenian massacres discussed, H. of Lords ; 800,000 reported killed since May, with German connivance.	6

1915. Oct.	WESTERN FRONT.	EASTERN FRONT	SOUTHERN FRONT.
7	Vigorous fighting in Champagne and Argonne, indecisive.	Continued fighting in Dvinsk region.	Austro - Germans across Drina, Save and Danube; total estimated 400,000. 20,000 Allied troops at Salonika.
8	Important German attack near Loos repulsed. Huge enemy losses.	Russians capture 1,000 prisoners, Novo Alexinatz (Gal. border, E. of Lemberg).	**Austrians enter Belgrade ;** Serbs evacuate it after checking advanced-guard. Sir I. Hamilton's despatch on Suvla Bay.
9	Severe fighting near Loos, held by French and British. Sir J. French's despatch on last 5 days.	Russians pressed back N.W. of Dvinsk and S.W. of Pinsk ; heavy losses in Volhynia.	Austrians attack Montenegrin frontier ; occupy Belgrade ; Gallwitz crosses below Semendria. Austrian attack on Isonzo front repulsed.
10	.. .. ..	Scattered fighting along most of line, except Dvinsk.	Enemy cross Danube in force at Semendria ; many civilians killed at Belgrade.
11	.. .. ..	Desperate fighting near Dvinsk ; Ivanov captures 2,000 Austrians on Strypa (Gal.).	**Bulgars attack Serbs** from Byelogradchik ; Belgrade partly destroyed.
12	.. .. ..	Fighting in Dvinsk region continues.	Bulgars driven off by Serbs S. of Zayechar (Bulgar-Serb. border).
13	Successful British attack S.W. of Hulluch. Zeppelin raid on London : 59 killed, 114 injured.	Russians hold their own at L. Drisviati (Dvinsk), but driven back across Strypa.	Serbs tenaciously hold country S. of Belgrade ; Sarrail arrives at Salonika.
14	.. .. ..	Violent fighting at Illukst (Dvina) ; enemy checked on Strypa.	Austro - Germans storm Pozharevats ; Bulgars attack on Nishava river.
15	Lively fighting along French front.	.. .. ..	Bulgarians bombard Valandova ; occupy Vranya. Italians occupy Pregasina (N. of Lake Garda).
16	.. .. ..	Heavy fighting along Russian front, specially near Mitau (Riga).	Austro-Germans storm Vranovo (Pozharevats), and Bulgars forts E. of Zayechar.

Asiatic and Egyptian Theatres.	Naval and Overseas Operations.	Political, &c.	1915. Oct.
.. .. ..	French transport sunk by Austrian submarine ; 2 Russian destroyers sink 19 Turkish supply ships, coast of Anatolia.	New Greek Cabinet under M. Zaimis ([115]) ; benevolent neutrality programme. British Labour Leaders appeal for volunteers for Army.	7
British force attacks 9,000 Mohmands (Ind. front.), scoring heavily.	British submarine destroys German transport in Baltic.	Anglo - French munitions agreement ; Miners' Federation " triple alliance."	8
.. .. ..	British capture Wumbiagas (Cameroons).	Bulgarian Cabinet reconstructed ([116]). U.S.A. naval programme issued.	9
.. .. ..	British submarine sinks " Lulea," German metal steamer.	Popular discontent in Bulgaria at Germanophil policy.	10
Turkish offensive at Ichkau (Transcauc.) repulsed.	Adm.D'Artiges du Fournet French naval C. in C., vice Boué de Lapeyrère in E. Mediterranean.	**Lord Derby produces recruiting scheme** ([117]). Prohibition of " treating."	11
Russians repel Turks in Van Pass and at Arkhava (Coast).	.. .. ..	**Greece refuses Serbia's appeal** ([118]). **Edith Cavell executed** at Brussels.	12
Renewed Armenian atrocities reported by U.S. Ambassador at Constantinople.	Action near Broën (Den.) between British subm. and German force. 1 T.B.D. sunk.	**M. Delcassé resigns.** Rumania declines to act. Viviani on Balkan situation ([119]).	13
.. .. ..	E.19 sinks German T.B.D. near Faxö.	U.S.A. Army increase approved. **Bulgaria declares war on Serbia.** British policy expounded by Sir E. Grey ([120]).	14
Germans evacuate Kermanshah (Pers.).	.. .. ..	**State of war between Great Britain and Bulgaria** from 10 p.m.	15
Termination of British occupation of Bushire (by agreement with Persia.).	British subm. sinks 5 German transports in Baltic. Blockade declared of Bulgarian (Aegean) Coast.	**State of war between France and Bulgaria from** 6 a.m.	16

1915. Oct.	WESTERN FRONT.	EASTERN FRONT.	SOUTHERN FRONT.
17	.. .. ..	Enemy active about Jakobstadt (R i g a); Russians successful on middle Styr (S. Polesia).	Bulgars force Timok valley and take Egri Palanka; Franco-Serbs defeat Bulgars at Strumitsa (S.W. Bulg.).
18	.. .. ..	Germans advance on the Dvina; Russians capture Chartorysk (Styr).	Austro-Germans and Bulgarians advancing in force (from N. and E. respectively).
19	Repulse of Germans near Hulluch. .	Heavy fighting round Mitau; Russians successful on Styr.	Italian offensive in Trentino continues.
20	German gas attack E. of Reims heavily repulsed.	Ivanov takes 7,500 prisoners near Tarnopol.	Serbians holding Orsova region bravely, but pushed back towards Shabats (in N.W.). Sir C. Monro C.-in-C. Mediterranean.
21	.. .. ..	Germans capture Dvina bank 10 m. E. of Riga. Fighting at Baranovichi (N. Polesia).	Germans advance W. of the Morava; Bulgars take Kumanovo; French take Robrovo.
22	.. .. ..	Germans advance W. of Chartorysk and capture Kolki.	Austrians take Shabats (N.W. Serbia), and Bulgars Üsküb (S. Serbia); former cross Drina (Herzegovina).
23	.. .. ..	Germans storm Illukst; hard fighting near Postavi (S. of Dvinsk) and on Oginski Canal (Polesia).	Heavy fighting Carso front. v. Gallwitz crosses at Orsova. Serbs beaten at Üsküb and Kladovo.
24	French capture " La Courtine," important German work (Champagne).	Germans repulsed on Lower Aa (Riga).	Fierce fighting E. of Knyajevats; Bulgars take Prahovo and Negotin (Danube). Aeroplanes bomb Venice.
25	.. .. ..	Furious fighting near Illukst, Üxküll, Lake district and Chartorysk.	Italian Trentino offensive successful; Serbs fighting Bulgars N. of Pirot; Serbs recapture Veles. Bulgars retire on Ishtip.
26	Fight for " La Courtine " continues; enemy attack fails.	Germans advance at Illukst.	Germans and Bulgars join at Lyubishevats (Danube); Serbs retire from Knyajevats. Enemy on wide front 25–40 m. S. of Belgrade.

ASIATIC AND EGYPTIAN THEATRES.	NAVAL AND OVERSEAS OPERATIONS.	POLITICAL, &c.	1915. Oct.
.. .. ..	Zeebrugge bombarded from the sea.	British Government offers Cyprus to Greece if she will fulfil her treaty obligations to Serbia.	17
.. .. ..	.. .. ..	Sir E. Carson resigns office of Attorney-General.	18
.. .. ..	.. .. ..	**Italy declares war against Bulgaria.**	19
.. .. ..	.. .. ..	Lord Derby explains his scheme : 46 groups.	20
.. .. ..	Allied squadrons bombard Dedeagach (Aegean), Varna and Burgas (Black Sea).	The King goes to France. Greece rejects offer of Cyprus.	21
.. .. ..	Russian landing party beats off Germans near Domesnes (G. of Riga) and captures stores.	M. Filipescu (Unionist leader, Rumania) states policy towards Balkans ([121]).	22
.. .. ..	British subm. sinks "Prinz Adalbert" (c r u i s e r) near Libau (Baltic). Germans seize Swedish steamer "Capella."	King George appeals for more men : " The end not yet in sight."	23
.. .. ..	.. .. ..	U.S.A. note *re* Blockade, etc. ([122]) ; U.S. Trust Co. formed ; R. Fay, German wrecker, arrested New York.	24
.. .. ..	French success at Sende (Cameroons).	Order in Council modifies Prize Law ([123]). Greece only " loosing her sword " (King C.).	25
Persian Cossacks sent to help British and Russian Consuls at Kengaver (Kermanshah).	British transport "Marquette " torpedoed in Aegean.	Mr. Fisher appointed Australian High Commissioner in London ; National Registration ordered in New Zealand.	26

K

1915. Oct.	WESTERN FRONT.	EASTERN FRONT.	SOUTHERN FRONT.
27	King George, after visit to French Armies, issues Order of the Day to them. Germans repulsed in Champagne.	Indecisive fighting on most of front; Russians driven back from the Styr.	Bulgars capture Zayechar, Knyajevats and heights N.W. of Pirot.
28	King George thrown with horse whilst inspecting, and somewhat seriously injured.	Enemy concentrating heavily near Riga; fierce fighting on Dvina river.	General Italian attack along coastal front, especially against Gorizia. Bulgars take Pirot and threaten railway communications.
29	.. .. ..	.. .. ..	Bulgars recapture Veles. French take Strumitsa Station.
30	Germans retake Butte de Tahure (Champagne).	Russian success near Tarnopol (Gal.); claim 8,000 prisoners; Germans claim 3,000.	Enemy takes Kraguyevats. British support French at Gevgeli. Latter repulse Bulgars at Krivolak (Vardar River).
31	Steel helmets being introduced on British front.	.. .. ..	British take part in action Gevgeli Doiran front (Mac.).
Nov. 1	Sir J. French's Despatch published, covering period 25.9.15 to 8.10.15 ([126]).	Food scarcity in Petrograd owing to lack of system.	Italian successes near Gorizia and Zagora (Jul.). Babuna Pass (between Üsküb and Prilep) held by 5,000 Serbians for more than a week against six divisions. Austro-German brutality ([127]).
2	General Maunoury succeeds Gen. Galliéni as Military Governor of Paris	German Press cheerful about prospect of Russian dissensions yielding profit to Central Powers.	.. .. ..
3	German attack in Champagne; French trenches penetrated, Hill 199.	Russian victory in Galicia (Siemikowice on Strypa) 5,000 prisoners; successful actions also in region of Dvinsk.	.. .. ..

Asiatic and Egyptian Theatres.	Naval and Overseas Operations.	Political, &c.	1915. Oct.
.. .. ..	British subm. sinks 4 more German steamers in Baltic. Russians bombard Varna.	M. Pashich (Serbian P.M.) wires urgently for help. Australian Cabinet changes ([124]). S. African elections (99 Botha-ists).	27
.. .. ..	H.M.S. "Argyll" wrecked off Scotland. H.M.S. "Hythe" sunk off Gallipoli.	**M. Briand succeeds M. Viviani** as French P.M. ([125]). Lt.-Gen. Sir B. Mahon to command on Salonika front.	28
.. .. ..	.. .. ..	Text published of agreement (5.9.14) of Allies not to conclude separate peace. Japan adheres. (19.10.15).	29
.. .. ..	Nigerian and Gold Coast troops under Col. Mayer successful in Cameroons.	Count W. Metternich appointed German Ambassador at Constantinople.	30
.. .. ..	.. .. ..	Japan warns China against monarchical movement.	31
			Nov.
.. .. ..	S.s. "Hocking," flying U.S. flag, but under German management, seized and taken to Halifax.	Return of the King from France after his accident. Agricultural Relief Committee visits France ([126]).	1
British and Russian Ministers at Teheran assured by Persian F.O. that report of agreement with Germany without foundation.	.. .. ..	Mr. Asquith's speech on a smaller Cabinet, a **War Committee,** and possible Compulsion ([127]). China declines Japan's advice on subject of monarchical movement.	2
.. .. ..	.. .. ..	Declaration of policy by M. Briand : closer co-operation with Allies. M. Thomas, Minister of Munitions.	3

1915 Nov.	WESTERN FRONT.	EASTERN FRONT	SOUTHERN FRONT.
4	Fierce fighting in Champagne.	.. .. ..	Turkish attacks at Anz[a] repulsed. Serbians che[ck] Bulgarians at Izv[o] (Macedonia).
5	Fighting continued N. of Massiges (Champagne).	Germans repulsed with heavy losses at Platonovka, S. of Lake Sventen (Dvinsk).	Fall of Nish, after 3 day[s] fighting. Germans g[ain] thereby Danube an[d] Ottoman railway rout[e] Main German-Bulgaria[n] forces join at Krivivi[r] 35 m. N. of Nish.
6	.. .. ..	.. .. ..	German munition co[n]voys arrive Ruschuk f[or] Bulgaria and Turkey.
7	.. .. ..	Gen. Alexeiev's estimate of German and Austro-Hungarian forces in field ([133]). Russians progress near Riga. Russian casualties over two millions to end September.	Austro - Germans reac[h] Krushevats and forc[e] Morava River at Kra[gu]yevo.
8	.. .. ..	Germans on defensive on Russian front. German fortified positions in region of Kolki (Chartorysk) occupied.	Italians carry Col di Lan[a] (Ven. Alps) by assaul[t] Skirmishes in Strum[m]itsa region. French tak[e] number Bulgar prisone[rs].
9	.. .. ..	Russian success on the Styr (N. of Kolki), 3,500 prisoners.	Bulgarians take Lesk[o]vats (on line to Salonika[)].

Asiatic and Egyptian Theatres.	Naval and Overseas Operations.	Political, &c.	1915. Nov.
.. .. ..	.. .. ..	Lord Lansdowne announces in H. of L. that Government would spare no pains to prevent General Election during the War. Greek Cabinet defeated after speech by M. Venizelos. M. Skouloudis appointed Premier ([130]).	4
.. .. ..	Mr. de Wet in election campaign in S. Africa and Generals Botha and Smuts declare identification of Union with British cause.	Committee appointed to facilitate trade of the country ([131]).	5
Ex-Khedive, Abbas-Hilmi sends resignation to Sultan of Turkey. His intrigues in Italy unsuccessful.	Dutch Government interns crew of German submarine U8. Success at Banyo mountain (Cameroons) by Gen. Cunliffe.	Suspension of *Globe* for publishing misleading statements about Lord Kitchener, etc. Latter is visiting near Eastern Theatre to report on situation.	6
.. .. ..	German cruiser "Undine" sunk by British submarine off S. Coast Sweden. Italian liner "Ancona" shelled and sunk by German submarine under Austrian flag; 25 Americans on board, many lives lost.	Text of American Note *re* British contraband and blockade policy published ([132]).	7
.. .. ..	.. .. ..	Drastic criticism in H. of Lords of Government's measures, especially the Press Censorship.	8
.. .. ..	German submarine sinks Japanese steamer off coast of Marocco. Protest against German detention of American ship "Pass of Tsalmaha," seized by German submarine.	Re-affirmation at Guildhall by Mr. Asquith of ends for which we are at war ([134]). U.S.A. announces that all non-contraband shipments consigned to Germany will be deemed immune.	9

1915. Nov.	WESTERN FRONT.	EASTERN FRONT.	SOUTHERN FRONT.
10	.. .. ..	German lines broken W. of Chartorysk; 2,050 prisoners.	Turkish reports of artillery duels in the Dardanelles.
11	.. .. ..	German retreat near Riga, Russian victory at Kemmern near Gulf of Riga, co-operation of fleet.	Serbians reconquer greater part of Kachanik Gorge. French victory over Bulgarians after 3 days' fighting from Gradsko to Veles.
12	French mining successes in Argonne.	Meeting between Kaiser and Hindenburg. Hindenburg threatens to resign if Kaiser insists on capture of Riga and Dvinsk.	Germans control railway from Belgrade to Constantinople.
13	.. .. ..	.. .. ..	Orderly retirement of Serbians to Mitrovitsa, new war capital. French progress towards Veles.
14	Violent German attacks in " Labyrinth " (Artois) repelled by French. Enemy losses very severe.	German retreat S.W. from Riga and the Shlok and Kemmern regions.	Austrian aircraft bomb Verona; 30 killed, 49 injured. Serbs evacuate Babuna positions E. of Prilep.
15	... .	.. .. ..	Very successful attack on Turkish trenches by 52nd Division at Gallipoli.
16	.. .. ..	.. .. ..	Bulgars take Prilep. Serious Serbian position. Monastir evacuated. Bulgars fall back from Cherna river after defeat by French.
17	French Army Committee of Senate insist on use of asphyxiating gas.	.. .. ..	.. .. ..
18	Canadians raid enemy trenches S.W. of Messines.	.. .. ..	Austro-German advance parallel to Kossovo plateau. Serbian army divided within 2 fronts— Mitrovitsa-Prishtina and Prilep-Monastir.

Asiatic and Egyptian Theatres.	Naval and Overseas Operations.	Political, &c.	1915. Nov.
Russians advance on Teheran. Persian gendarmerie, under foreign officers, revolts and imprisons British subjects. German intrigues in Persia.	Great fire at American munition works, Bethlehem Steel Co., German incendiaries suspected. Many guns destroyed.	Mr. Asquith announces strengthening of General Staff by more intercommunication with Allies ([135]). Speech by M. Sazonov on future policy.	10
.. .. ..	Transport " Mercian " attacked by submarine; 103 casualties.	German mission to Greece. Greek Chamber dissolved; new elections to be held. Lord Derby warns unmarried men of compulsion if fail to enlist voluntarily before Nov. 30 ([136]).	11
British force under Townshend advances to within 7 miles of Ctesiphon. Shah of Persia receives Allied Ministers and declares himself friendly.	.. .. ..	.. .. ..	12
.. .. ..	Conference at Pretoria on raising of E. African contingent by General Smuts.	.. .. ..	13
Turks and Germans defeated by Russians in Persia. Turkish Ambassador and Austro-German Ministers leave.	Loss of submarine E20 in Sea of Marmora.	.. .. ..	14
Publication by F.O. of attacks on British officers, etc., in Persia ([137]).	.. .. ..	Mr. Winston Churchill's speech re Antwerp and Dardanelles expeditions ([138]). Rejoins his regiment.	15
.. .. ..	.. .. ..	.. .. ..	16
.. .. ..	Hospital ship " Anglia " sunk by mine in Channel. 85 lost.	War Committee of Cabinet arrives Paris for War Conference.	17
.. .. ..	Unsatisfactory Austrian Note about "Ancona" to U.S. Government; not expected to go to extremes yet.	M. Cochin, French envoy, received by King Constantine.	18

1915. Nov.	WESTERN FRONT.	EASTERN FRONT.	SOUTHERN FRONT.
19	.. .. ..	.. .. ..	" Pacific Blockade " of Greece proclaimed by the Allies.
20	.. .. ..	.. .. ..	.. .. ..
21	.. .. ..	Great shortage of arms, munitions and uniforms in Russia.	Fall of Novi-Bazar. Serbians driven from last positions in Old Serbia.
22	.. .. ..	.. .. ..	.. .. ..
23	.. .. ..	Russians successful in struggle for Tsarzemunde (Riga front).	Fall of Mitrovitsa and Prishtina (keys of plain of Kossovo). Germans claim 17,000 prisoners and 35 guns. Serbians driven W. from Kossovo Plateau. French capture Brusnik and protect Krivolak from Bulgar bombardment. Austrians evacuate Mori and Rovereto (Trent.), and ask for German help on Isonzo.
24	.. .. ..	Russians turn German L. flank by capture of Yanopol, N. of Illukst (Dvina); Germans abandon salient.	Serbian Government moved to Skutari (Alb.).

ASIATIC AND EGYPTIAN THEATRES.	NAVAL AND OVERSEAS OPERATIONS.	POLITICAL, &c.	1915 Nov.
.. .. ..	More British submarines enter the Baltic.	Lord Derby's letter to Mr. Asquith defining recruiting position ([139]). German lies about India contradicted by India Office ([140]). German proclamations being sent to India through Shanghai, urging Moslems to Holy War.	19
.. .. ..	Germans in strong force in E. Africa ([141]).	Greek King and Government give Lord Kitchener assurances that Greece would never attack Allied troops.	20
Prince Firman Firma, Minister of Interior, takes measures to put end to German activities in Persia.	Tibati (Cameroons) occupied by Allies.	.. .. ..	21
Battle of Ctesiphon (25 m. S. of Baghdad). Turks beaten, not routed. 1,300 prisoners; our casualties one-third our force. Revolt of Persian Gendarmerie organised by German Minister.	Germany offers £1,000 for each of American passengers lost in "Lusitania." Offer refused by America.	.. .. ..	22
.. .. ..	Operations about Yaunde (Cameroons) by English and French contingents. Enemy losses heavy.	.. .. ..	23
Marshal von der Goltz takes command Mesopotamia.	.. .. ..	Permanent organisation of Allied countries for supply of munitions announced by M. Thomas. Conference in London.	24

1915. Nov.	Western Front.	Eastern Front.	Southern Front.
25	.. .. ..	.. .. ..	Salonika to be base of Allied operations. Reply of Greek Government concurred in Allied Note. British aircraft bomb Constantinople - Dedeagach railway. Turkish activity in Gallipoli.
26	Raid of 23 aeroplanes on German camp near Albert.	.. .. ..	Serbians refuse German Peace Offers; condition being that they allow Germans free passage.
27	German attack N. of " Labyrinth " (Artois) repulsed.	.. .. ..	Large supplies munitions arrive Ruschuk. 40,000 Austro-Germans expected. Rumanian precautionary mines laid in Danube.
28	.. ..	German 82nd Divisional Staff surprised and taken prisoner near Pinsk ; 2 generals captured.	Bulgarian and Austro-Germans advancing on Monastir. Successful Italian attacks on the Carso and slopes to the N.W. Lord Kitchener visits Greece, S.E. and Italian fronts. German H.Q. report main operations closed in Serbia.
29	.. .. ..	Successful Russian action at Illukst (Dvina).	Bulgars claim 17,000 prisoners at Prizrend.
30	Artillery activity along whole front.	.. .. ..	Italians progress towards Gorizia.
Dec. 1	.. .. ..	.. .. ..	.. .. ..
2	.. .. ..	Enemy driven back left bank Styr river (Gal.).	Invasion of N.W. Montenegro reported by German H.Q.

Asiatic and Egyptian Theatres.	Naval and Overseas Operations.	Political, &c.	1915. Nov.
British retirement from Ctesiphon to Kut *via* Azizia.	.. .. ..	New recruiting campaign in Australia. Mr. Hughes, the Premier, announces voluntary enlistment will be adhered to ; very successful results.	25
Russians defeat Turks and Kurds and occupy Karaj and Yengi Iman, 40 m. from Teheran.	.. .. ..	Mr. Stanton, Ind. Lab. candidate, stands as protest against pacifist and anti-recruiting policy of late Keir Hardie, and wins seat by 4,206.	26
Grand Sheikh of the Senussi maintains friendly attitude towards Egyptian Government.	.. .. ..	.. .. ..	27
.. .. ..	German subm. and aeroplane destroyed by British seaplanes off Belgium	Patriotic proclamation by King Nicholas of Montenegro. Greek Government replies to Allies.	28
.. .. ..	.. .. ..	Canadian output munitions largely increased.	29
Rearguard actions on Tigris ; Turks strongly reinforced. British casualties during retreat of 80 m., 4,567 men and two gunboats.	.. .. ..	King Nicholas appeals for help to Diplomatic Corps. Allied Gov'ts' Pact of London signed by Italy. Large German post-war copper order to U.S.A. German casualties to date. [143].	30
.. .. ..	German naval control over Swedish boats exposed [143].	Baron Sonnino's speech on Italian adhesion to Pact of London [144]. " Transito " Syndicate formed, to expedite goods *via* Sweden to Russia. Lord Lansdowne on the Declaration of London [145].	Dec. 1
.. .. ..	.. .. ..	Reasons for non-entry of U.S.A. into War [146].	2

1915. Dec.	WESTERN FRONT.	EASTERN FRONT.	SOUTHERN FRONT.
3	General Joffre appointed C. in C. of the French Armies.	Austrian offensive repulsed at several points in Galicia.	Defeat of Serbians by Bulgars on the White Drin river : much booty taken.
4	.. .. ..	.. .. ..	British land fresh forces at Salonika and quantities war material.
5	.. .. ..	Russian front at Dvinsk bombarded. Germans report collapse Russian attack near Lake Babit, W. of Riga.	Monastir evacuated by General Vassich. Bulgar attack on French bridgehead at Demir Kapu (Vardar river) repulsed.
6	First Meeting of Allied War Council in Paris.	.. .. ..	British force, Strumitsa, bombarded by the Bulgarians ; infantry attack repulsed. Essad Pasha declares himself pro-Ally ([150])
7	Yser inundations compel Germans to abandon advanced trenches.	.. .. ..	French evacuate Krivolak and retire to strong position in Demir Kapu Pass, 20 m. N. Greek frontier. Ipek taken by Austrians. British pressed back to valley of Vardar from Lake Doiran 1,300 casualties.
8	.. .. ..	.. .. ..	Evacuation of Gallipoli begins. French and British troops fall back towards Greek frontier.
9	Fighting in Champagne, initiative with Allies. General Castelnau appointed Chief of Staff and Commander French front.	Artillery activity on Riga front, gas attack by Germans.	Retreat of Allies from Vardar. British lose 8 m.g., 1,500 casualties

Asiatic and Egyptian Theatres.	Naval and Overseas Operations.	Political, &c.	1915. Dec.
British forces arrive Kut-el-Amara.	British submarine sinks Turkish T.B.D., Sea of Marmora, 2 officers and 40 men saved.	British casualties in all theatres of war given by Prime Minister ([147]). Recall of Captains Boy-Ed and von Papen requested by U.S.A. ([148]). Swedish shipping grievances against England.	3
.. .. ..	.. .. ..	War Conference at Calais, Lord Kitchener present. Mr. Ford's peace expedition starts from U.S.A. in the " Oscar II. " (v 28.12.)	4
Siege of Kut begins; 4 Turk divisions, under Nur - ed - Din, surround town.	French subm. " Fresnel " sunk by Austrian warship off Albania. U.S. ship " Petrolite " attacked by Austrian submarine.	King Constantine's statement to Times correspondent ([149]). 10,000 Mohammedans in India protest against demanding political concessions in hour of Empire's danger.	5
.. .. ..	Capture of Captain Stanley Wilson by Austrian subm. when carrying despatches in Greek steamer. Durazzo bombarded by Austrian squadron.	M. Venizelos's election manifesto ([151]). Terms of Pact of London published by F.O. ([152]).	6
.. ..	.. .. ..	Resolution passed in favour of re-nomination and election of President Wilson. President Wilson's war message to Congress denouncing pro-Germans in U.S.A.	7
Heavy Turkish bombardment Kut, attacks repulsed, heavy losses enemy, lasting till 11th.	Publication Admiralty despatch re destruction German cruiser " Königsberg " last July, German E. Africa ([153]).	2,026 State Munition works declared " controlled " between July 12 and Dec. 6, 1915.	8
Russians occupy Sultan Bulak Pass (Persia); Turco-German mercenaries routed. Persian rebels and mercenaries defeated by Russians in Hamadan.	.. .. ..	Herr Scheidemann declares in Reichstag Socialists refuse discuss cession Alsace Lorraine. M. Venizelos replies to King Constantine in Times.	9

1915. Dec.	WESTERN FRONT.	EASTERN FRONT	SOUTHERN FRONT.
10	German activity Ypres salient ; 3,000 shells on our position, little damage.	.. .. ..	Italians carry strong position above Bezzecca basin (Carn.). Austrian aeroplanes bombard Ancona
11	Belgian powder factory blown up near Havre, many lives lost.	.. .. ..	Publication of Gallipoli casualties up to Dec. 11 (154). Bulgarians attack Anglo-French front at Furka (Maced.) and lose 8,000 men.
12	British raid near Neuve Chapelle.	.. .. ..	Paris official report : Successful retreat in Macedonia. Agreement to withdraw Greek Division E. of Salonika.
13	Trench fighting near the Somme. French batteries destroy at St. Mihiel the only German bridge spared by the flooded Meuse. Anti-aircraft control in Gt. Britain transferred to W.O.	.. .. ..	Allied troops withdrawn across Greek frontier. Salonika to be fortified 80,000 enemy troops between Monastir and Greek frontier. Greek Government informed their ships at Malta now free to proceed. Bulgarians enter Doiran and Gevgeli.
14	.. .. ..	.. .. ..	.. .. ..
15	Resignation of Sir John French, succeeded by Sir Douglas Haig as C. in C., former being made a Viscount.	Germans report Russians penetrated positions N. of L. Drisviati, repulsed by counter attack. Russians repulsed near mouth of Beresina river.	.. .. ..
16	British raids near Armentières.	.. .. ..	Italian troops landed Avlona (Albania).

ASIATIC AND EGYPTIAN THEATRES.	NAVAL AND OVERSEAS OPERATIONS.	POLITICAL, &c.	1915. Dec.
.. .. ..	Half million bushels Canadian wheat for Allies burnt at Erie (Penn.) Naval action in Black Sea ; Russians sink 2 Turkish gun-boats.	War Council Allies, Paris, decides hold Salonika. Boy-Ed and von Papen recalled as requested by U.S.A.	10
300 hostile Arabs encountered by reconnoitring force near Mersa Matruh (W. Eg.) and driven W. with many casualties. Russians occupy Hamadan(Pers.); rebel strength 8,000 irregulars, 13,000 gendarmes, with rifles and machine guns.	.. .. ..	Great rush of recruits, last 2 days under the age group s y s t e m. Yuan Shih-kai accepts throne of China.	11
.. .. ..	.. .. ..	Lord Derby's recruiting campaign closed.	12
British force under Col. Gordon defeats 1,200 Senussites at Wadi Shaifa, near Mersa Matruh.	.. .. ..	All American and Canadian securities to be loaned or sold to the State. Supplementary German War Cred it Bill for £500,000,000.	13
.. .. ..	General Sir H. Smith-Dorrien to command in E. Africa.	M. Schroeder, pro-Ally ed. of the " Telegraaf " (Amsterdam) acquitted of charge of "imperilling Holland's neutrality." Premier refuses to reduce Ministerial salaries and intends to continue drawing his own.	14
.. .. ..	.. .. ..	.. .. ..	15
.. .. ..	.. .. ..	New 5% Exchequer Bonds issued at par.	16

1915. Dec.	WESTERN FRONT.	EASTERN FRONT.	SOUTHERN FRONT.
17	.. .. ..	Austrians repulsed on River Strypa (Gal.).	German threat to invade Greece. M. Skouloudis forbids Bulgarian troops to set foot on Greek soil.
18	.. .. ..	.. .. ..	.. .. ..
19	Intense artillery activity on whole French front. Heavy bombardment with gas near Ypres : line everywhere intact.	Enemy column dispersed with great losses N. of Lake Miadzol (Dvinsk).	British attack at Cape Helles (Gall.) won 200 yds. of trench.
20	Six German aeroplanes bomb La Panne, H.Q. of King and Queen of Belgians.	General Russki invalided and relieved of command.	Successful evacuation Anzac and Suvla [155]; Turks completely deceived. Bulgar-Greeks collision at Koritza (N. Epirus). Dip. discussions Turkish forces : Dardanelles, 15 Div. ; Constantinople, 3 ; Adrianople, 6. Italian troops at Durazzo, rallying point for Serbs.
21	French success Hartmannsweilerkopf, 1,300 prisoners.	.. .. ..	Turks claim evacuation of Gallipoli as "great Turkish victory, heavy British losses." Fact : 3 wounded.
22	Germans active on Yser and Ypres sectors ; positions wrecked by Allies. Enemy regained footing at Hartmannsweilerkopf.	.. .. ..	Bulgarians occupy strategic positions along Greek frontier ; strength about 120,000, with heavy guns from Varna.
23	French success at Hartmannsweilerkopf.	.. .. ..	.. .. ..

Asiatic and Egyptian Theatres.	Naval and Overseas Operations.	Political, &c.	1915. Dec
Russians drive hundreds of Kurds back to their mountains.	British advance in Cameroons. Jang Mangas taken after sharp fighting. Small German cr. "Bremen" and T.B. sunk by submarine in Baltic.	Debate on Anglo-Danish Agreement, signed 19.11.15, text not published.	17
Turks surprised in advanced trenches at Kut, about 30 killed and 11 prisoners.	.. .. ..	.. .. ..	18
.. .. ..	Naval simultaneous bombardment Turkish front Cape Helles.	.. .. ..	19
Russians take Kum (Pers.); German intrigue there stopped. Turkish forces: Armenia 11 Divs; Syria, 6 Divs.; Smyrna, 3 Divs.	.. .. ..	Derby groups of single men called up. German Government disavows its secret agents in U.S.A. Gounarist majority at Greek elections; Venizelists did not vote. Release of General de Wet (S.A.) on signing guarantee. Mr. Lloyd George's speech on work Ministry Munitions, inferior to Germans, skilled men wanted.	20
.. .. ..	Mangeles (Cameroons) taken by Col. Mayer, 3 days' fighting. Italian destroyer sinks large Austrian ship laden with arms, and rams attacking submarine.	Sir William Robertson appointed Chief of Imperial General Staff (succ. Sir Archd. Murray—to Eg.). Success French "Loan of Victory," £560,000,000 ; British soldiers encouraged to subscribe.	21
Sir Archd. Murray appointed to Egypt (vice Sir J. Maxwell) to command in the Mediterranean.	Loss of Japanese liner "Yasaka Maru."	2nd "Ancona" note to Vienna ; U.S.A prepared for a break.	22
Kut, violent attack by Turks : a number penetrated N.E. corner of fort, but ejected by Oxf. L.I., etc. ; afterwards, blockade only.	.. .. ..	Mr. Choate urges America to be prepared to "render whatever aid we can to our neighbour."	23

1915. Dec.	WESTERN FRONT.	EASTERN FRONT.	SOUTHERN FRONT.
24	.. .. ..	Heavy fighting on the River Strypa.	Salonika in state of defence; Germans disturbed at Allied occupation.
25	The King sends Christmas message to his troops, and thanks Indian troops, through the Prince of Wales, on their departure.	.. .. ..	.. .. ..
26	.. .. ..	.. .. ..	.. .. ..
27	.. .. ..	Attack by the Russians on the Austrians in N Bukovina, ranging from the Pruth river to N. of the Dniester river.	French occupy Castellorizzo, near Rhodes. Greek protest.
28	French carry trenches in the Vosges. Artillery activity on whole front. **Departure of Indian Corps** for another front.	Germans routed by Lettish detachment on Aa river (Courland).	.. .. ..
29	German post destroyed N. of La Fille Morte (Argonne).	.. .. ..	.. .. ..
30	Five German mines explode N. of Loos, causing some British casualties.	Heavy fighting in Bukovina continues.	Enemy airships drop bombs on Salonika, so Allies arrest the four enemy Consuls and send them to Toulon.
31	German attack on the Hirzstein (Vosges) repulsed. Small German success N.W. of Hulluch.	Strong Russian offensive across River Styr (Gal.) at Chartorysk.	.. .. ..

ASIATIC AND EGYPTIAN THEATRES.	NAVAL AND OVERSEAS OPERATIONS.	POLITICAL, &c.	1915. Dec.
.. .. ..	French liner " Ville de la Ciotat " torpedoed Mediterranean, 80 lives lost.	.. .. ..	24
Principal Arab force attacked and dispersed near Matruh. Rebel force routed near Teheran. Prince Firman Firma, pro-Ally, nominated Premier.	.. .. ..	Herr Ballin's definition of " Freedom of the Seas " published in " Vossische Zeitung " ([156]).	25
.. .. ..	German steamers sunk on Lake Tanganyika.	.. .. ..	26
.. .. ..	.. .. ..	.. .. ..	27
.. .. ..	4,000 lbs. rubber seized on the " Oscar II." (Swed.) ; was consigned to enemy agents.	Cabinet decides for Compulsion—single men before married ones.	28
.. .. ..	Sea fight off Cattaro ; Austrian scout and 5 destroyers driven off by Allied ships. French submarine " Monge " sunk and 2 Austrian destroyers.	.. .. ..	29
.. .. ..	S.S. " Persia " torpedoed off Crete, 333 lives lost, including U.S.A. Consul at Aden. H.M. cruiser " Natal " blown up in harbour, 304 lost.	.. .. ..	30
.. .. ..	.. .. ..	Prussian losses to date 2,536,000, of whom 600,000 killed, 356,000 missing. Austrian Note to U.S.A. re " Ancona."	31

RÉSUMÉ OF MAIN EVENTS IN 1915.

Jan. 1 to Feb. 4 ..	Third thrust for Warsaw; Russians hold up enemy on the Bzura-Ravka Rivers; Russian successes in Trans-Caucasia.
„ 1 to Apr. 17 ..	Russo-Austrian struggle in Galicia and the Carpathians; Russians eventually successful.
„ 3 *et sqq.* ..	Turks take and lose Tabriz to the Russians; enemy activity (*v.* Egypt) in Syria.
„ 14 to July ..	Campaign in German S.W. Africa,
„ 24	Battle of the Dogger Bank.
Feb. 3	12,000 Turks attack Suez Canal and are beaten off.
„ 6 to Mar. 21 ..	Russians, driven from E. Prussia, hold up Germans on the Niemen, Bobr and Narev rivers.
„ 18	German submarine " blockade " begins.
„ 19 to Apr. 6 ..	British naval attacks on the Dardanelles (entrance cleared 26.2; big attack on Narrows fails, 18.3).
Mar. ..	Fighting (British v. Turks) in Lower Mesopotamia.
„ 8 to 15 ..	Battle of Neuve Chapelle.
„ 22	Przemysl surrenders to the Russians.
Apr. 9 *et sqq.* ..	British and French military force (120,000 under Generals Sir I. Hamilton and d'Amade) concentrate outside Dardanelles.
„ to July	Appalling Armenian massacres (?800,000) by Turkish order.
„ 22 to May 24 ..	Second battle of Ypres. (British pressed back.)
„ 25 to 28 ..	Battle of the landings in Gallipoli (S.W. corner and Anzac Cove).
„ 28 to July 3 ..	Great Austro-German attack in Galicia (Russians driven back from the Dunajec to the San, 28.4 to 12.5; from the San to Lemberg, 15.5 to 20.6; fall of Przemysl, 3.6; of Lemberg, 22.6; Germans held on the Zlota Lipa, 28.6 to 3.7).
May 7	" Lusitania " torpedoed.
„ 15 to 25.. ..	Battle of Festubert.
May to July	Heavy and intermittent fighting in Gallipoli.
June	British take offensive E. of Suez Canal.
„ 26 to July 4 ..	Battle of the Argonne.
July 2 to 18 ..	Pressure on the Warsaw salient from N.W. and S.W. (fall of Przasnysz, 15.7).
„ 9	Surrender of German S.W. Africa.
„ 14	National Registration Bill passed.
July 15 to Sept. 30 ..	Russian retreat from Warsaw (fall of Ivangorod, 4.8, of Warsaw, 5.8, of Kovna, 17.8, of Novo Georgievsk, 19.8, of Osovyets, 23.8; battle of Meiszagola-Vilna, 2-12.9; fall of Pinsk, 16.9, of Vilna, 18.9; Germans checked, and Russian counterstrokes in Volhynia and Galicia, 18-30.9).

July 17   ..   ..   Secret treaty between Bulgaria and Central Powers; defeat of Allied diplomacy.

Aug. 6 to 10   ..   Landing and battle of Suvla Bay, etc.

,, 10 to 21   ..   Naval fighting in Baltic and Gulf of Riga; Germans repulsed.

Sept. 7 to 29   ..   British occupy Bushire.

,, 19 to Dec.   ..   Austro-German invasion of Serbia (Bulgaria mobilises, 21.9; Serbia discouraged by the Allies from attacking Bulgaria, 27.9; Belgrade occupied, 9.10; Bulgaria declares war on Serbia, 11.10 and attacks her in N.E. and S.E., 14.10; Serbia appeals in vain to Greece for help, 11 10; fall of Nish, 6.11; after gallant fighting, disastrous retreat of Serbian armies to Montenegro and Albania, 14.11 to 20.12; fall of Monastir, 5.12.)

,, 21 to Dec.   ..   Operations of Franco-British troops on Macedonian front (150,000 men granted, 21.9; begin landing at Salonika, 3-7.10; Allies' relations severed with Bulgaria, 5.10; fighting v. Bulgarians, 19-27.10; Allies driven back on defensive, 5.11 to 12.12; Salonika put in state of defence and Greek troops removed, Dec.).

,, 25 to Oct.   ..   Great Franco-British attack in Champagne and Artois; (Tahure, Lens, Loos, &c.; slight general advance, Vimy Ridge taken 29.9.)

,, 25 to Oct. 31   ..   German thrusts at Dvinsk and Riga repulsed.

,, 28   ..   ..   British take Kut-el-Amara.

Oct. 11   ..   ..   Lord Derby's Recruiting Scheme.

,, 12   ..   ..   Nurse Cavell murdered.

,, 14 to 19..   ..   Allies declare war on Bulgaria.

Autumn   ..   ..   Numerous risings in Persia against the British and Russians, and murders, engineered by Germans; enemy diplomats, threatened by Russian force, leave Teheran, 14.11; Irritation in U.S.A. v. Central Powers.

Nov.   ..   ..   Decision taken to evacuate Dardanelles; rising of Ali Dinar (Darfur); successful Russian counter-attack from Riga to Dvinsk; indecisive fighting in Volhynia; battle of Ctesiphon, 22.11.

Early Dec.   ..   ..   Gen. Townshend besieged in Kut, 5.12; Italians land two divisions in Avlona (Alb.).

Dec. 20   ..   ..   Anzac and Suvla evacuated.

,. 24   ..   ..   Russian offensive v. the Bukovina begins.

,, 13 to 25   ..   British beat the Senussi near Mersa Matruh (W. Egypt).

,, 28   ..   ..   Compulsory Service principle adopted in Great Britain.

Up to Dec. 9th, total British casualties, killed, wounded, and missing, since the beginning of the war, were :—

	Officers.	Other ranks.
Flanders and France	16,471 ..	387,988
Dardanelles	5,045 ..	109,510
Other theatres	1,665 ..	24,019
Total	23,181	521,517

(For Prussian casualties, v. Tables, Dec 31).

N.B.—Operations going on throughout the year in Armenia, the Cameroons, and East Africa.

APPENDICES, 1915.

(1) *Jan. 7.*—The Note admits that a belligerent Power should interfere with neutral trade only when its national safety demands it, but holds that this does not exclude the right to interfere with contraband destined for the enemy. It is further admitted that foodstuffs should not be detained without a presumption that they are intended for the armed forces of the enemy, but it is added that Britain can give no unconditional undertaking to observe this principle in view of the methods of warfare followed by the Central Powers. The Note insists on the necessity, under modern conditions, of bringing ships into port for examination. It is pointed out that Britain's policy has been forced upon her by the growing danger that neutral countries will become bases of military supplies for the enemy.

(2) *Jan. 21.*—The "Dacia," a vessel of the Hamburg-Amerika line, had been lying at Port Arthur, Texas, since the outbreak of war. With the permission of the United States Government, she was bought by an American citizen of German origin, Breitung by name, who purposed to send her to Bremen with a cargo of cotton shipped by American citizens. The destination, however, was afterwards changed to Rotterdam. The point at issue was the validity of the transference to neutrals of vessels belonging to a belligerent. Cotton not being treated as contraband at this time, the British Government offered, if the ship were seized, to purchase the cargo or have it forwarded without charge to Rotterdam.

(3) *Jan. 24.*—The German cruiser "Blücher" was sunk, and two battle-cruisers, with several smaller vessels, were damaged. No British ships were lost, but the battle-cruiser "Lion," Vice-Admiral Beatty's flagship, was put out of action and had to be towed to harbour.

(4) *Feb. 4.*—"The waters round Great Britain and Ireland . . . are herewith proclaimed a war region. On and after February 18, every enemy merchant vessel found in this region will be destroyed without its always being possible to warn the crew and passengers . . . Neutral ships will also incur danger in the war-region, since. . . it cannot be guaranteed that attacks intended for enemy ships will not affect neutral ships also. Vessels sailing to the north of the Shetlands, in the eastern part of the North Sea, and in a zone at least 30 knots wide along the Netherlands coast, are not menaced by any danger."

(5) *Feb. 9.*—The "Wilhelmina" carried a cargo of food shipped by an American firm to an American citizen in Germany.

(6) *Feb. 10.*—The following are the chief points of the Note : (a) Any modern war must result in the dislocation of the trade of neutrals. (b) Figures are quoted to show that the export trade of the United States has not been injured by British measures. (c) The doctrine of "continuous voyage" is defended and supported by precedents from the American Civil War. (d) The British procedure in dealing with neutral ships and cargoes is justified. (e) The British view regarding conditional contraband is explained, but it is added that the British Government are doubtful whether the existing rules are suited to existing conditions, it being impossible in a country like Germany to draw a clear line between the civil and the military population, especially as the German Government has taken control of foodstuffs. (f) The British Government will still endeavour to avoid injury to neutrals, but the German submarine policy has made it necessary for them to consider what measures they should adopt in protection of British interests. "It is impossible for one belligerent to depart from rules and precedents and for the other to remain bound by them."

(7) *Feb. 11.*—The United States Government, while not denying that a belligerent ship may lawfully use a neutral flag when in imminent danger of capture or destruction, states that it would view "with anxious solicitude" any general use of the United States flag by British vessels.

(⁸) *Feb.* 11.—The Note states that the possibilities arising out of the conditions of Germany's submarine policy are viewed by the United States Government " with such grave concern " that it feels compelled to request the German Government to consider " the critical situation . . . which might arise were German naval forces . . . to destroy any merchant vessel of the United States or to cause the death of American citizens . . . " The German Government is reminded that " the sole right of a belligerent dealing with neutral vessels on the high seas is limited to visit and search, unless a blockade is proclaimed and effectively maintained, which (the United States Government) does not understand to be proposed." If the commanders of German vessels of war should destroy American vessels or the lives of American citizens, " it would be difficult " for the U.S. Government to view the act as anything but " an indefensible violation of neutral rights." In such a case, it " would be constrained to hold the Imperial Government to a strict accountability . . . and to take any steps which might be necessary to safeguard American lives and property . . . "

(⁹) *Feb.* 19.—It is urged that the British Merchant Shipping Act allows the use of the British flag by ships of other nations for the purpose of evading capture, and no nation has forbidden such use of its flag. It is added, however, that the British Government has no intention of advising British merchant shipping to use foreign flags as a general practice or to resort to them except in order to escape capture or destruction. A belligerent vessel has the obligation of ascertaining the character of a ship before capturing it, and the British Government cannot assume responsibility for what may happen if this is disregarded.

(¹⁰) *Feb.* 19.—The memorandum states that when the " Wilhelmina's " cargo was seized, the British Government had before them the German decree of January 25, under an article of which imported grain and flour might be delivered only to certain organisations under Government control or to municipal authorities. It has since become known that on February 6 this article was repealed. The effect of this change must be decided in the Prize Court. The article in question, however, was not the only reason for the seizure of the cargo : the conduct of Germany was sufficient justification.

(¹¹) *March* 1.—German offensive against Russia began, 6.2.15, in N.W. Poland : was stopped on the line Plotsk-Raciaz after a severe battle, 16.2.15–18.2.15. The Germans began an offensive from E. Prussia, 20.2.15, which was stopped on the line Kovna-the Niemen-Przasnysz-Grodno-Osovyets. Germans took Przasnysz, 26.2.15, but the town after changing hands several times was finally secured by the Russians, 27.2.15. Hindenburg then attempted an offensive in the Kherjele-Przasnysz district, but was beaten back and retired to prepared positions, 14.3.15.

(¹²) *March* 1.—An Austrian offensive in the Carpathians in the region of the San River was checked, 1.3.15—4.3.15. A further offensive on a 90-mile front, between Gorlice and the Uzsok Pass, continued until 21.3.15, the aim being probably to relieve pressure on Przemysl. which the offensive failed to do.

(¹³) *March* 2.—The Dardanelles operations were hampered by bad weather. The outer forts were destroyed and the straits cleared of mines for four miles by 2.3.15. On the following days inner forts were destroyed and the straits cleared to the Narrows, which were bombarded from 7.3.15 to 16.3.15, H.M.S. " Queen Elizabeth " and other ships firing from the Gulf of Saros across the peninsula. H.M.S. " Irresistible " and " Ocean " and the French " Bouvet " were sunk by mines while attacking the Narrows at close quarters, and further operations were stopped by bad weather.

(¹⁴) *March* 2.—Anglo-French Note, 2.3.15, stated that in answer to the German submarine blockade all trade in and out of Germany would be stopped. U.S.A. protested, and suggested to both belligerents a mitigation of the rigours of the war zone. Other neutrals also protested. Germany answered by demanding free food supply through German and neutral ports ; free supply of raw materials for civilians ; British adoption of the Declaration of London ; British abandonment of the use of neutral flags, and the guarantee that British merchantmen should not be armed. Great Britain replied by an Order in Council, 19.3.15, forbidding all trade to and from Germany in enemy or neutral bottoms.

(¹⁵) *March* 10.—Gounaris cabinet included : M. Gounaris, Prime Minister and Minister of War ; M. Zographos, Foreign Affairs ; M. Protopapadakis, Finance ; M. Stratos, M. Tsaldaris, etc.

(¹⁶) *March* 10.—British first took the offensive at Neuve Chapelle, 10.3.15. Neuve Chapelle was taken on the first day, l'Epinette on the second, counter attacks beaten off on the third, and Aubers reached.　Prisoners amounted to 1,400 ; total enemy loss estimated at nearly 10,000.

(¹⁷) *March* 10.—German armed liner " Prinz Eitel Friedrich," which had sunk various ships, including the " William P. Frye," arrived at Newport News, U.S.A., 10.3.15, for repairs.　The question of interning the vessel was raised, but as a result of negotiations, Germany apologised and paid compensation for the sinking of the " William P. Frye."　The German ship was, however, not repaired within the time permitted by international law, and was interned on April 8.

(¹⁸) *March* 14.—German offensive at St. Eloi, 14.3.15, resulted in the capture of the village and part of the British front line system.　Counter attacks resulted in the recovery of the village and most of the lost ground.

(¹⁹) *March* 14.—The German cruiser " Dresden," which escaped from the battle of the Falkland Isles, was sunk by British warships off the island of Juan Fernandez in Chilean territorial waters, 14.3.15.

(²⁰) *March* 15.—French operations in Champagne during March resulted in the gain of important high ground near Perthes and Beauséjour, and of the commanding summit of the Hartmannsweilerkopf in Alsace.

(²¹) *March* 22.—The siege of Przemysl lasted continuously from 11.11.14 to 22.3.15.

(²²) *March* 28.—S.s. " Falaba," bound for South Africa, was torpedoed and sunk south of the St. George's Channel, 28.3.15, with a loss of 100 lives, including many women and children, the passengers being given only five minutes to take to the boats.

(²³) *April* 1.—Herr Dernburg declared Great Britain to be the cause of the prolongation of the war, and to have obstructed Germany in Marocco and Mesopotamia. Suggested freedom of the seas and the retention of Belgium as a basis on which Germany could make peace ; later offered evacuation of Belgium, if England would grant freedom of the seas and liberty for German expansion outside Europe.

(²⁴) *April* 2.—America asserted the right to carry innocent shipments through neutral countries ; declared the inclusion of neutral ports in the blockade to be novel and expected that England should respect the rights of neutrals.

(²⁵) *April* 2.—Germany declared that prisoners from submarines were not treated as prisoners of war.　Great Britain answered that their treatment was better than that of British prisoners of equal rank in Germany and that prisoners from submarines were not honourable opponents, having been engaged in killing non-combatants.

(²⁶) *April* 2.—Austria offered district of Rovereto, Riva, Tione, excluding Madonna di Campiglio, neighbourhood of Trento, and district of Borgo up to Lavis.

(²⁷) *April* 3.—Venizelos asserted that Greece was bound by treaty to help Serbia against a Bulgarian invasion ; suggested the cession of Kavalla to Bulgaria in the last resort in view of the danger to Hellenism in event of a German-Turkish victory.

(²⁸) *April* 4.—Venizelos explained the reason for the overture to Bulgaria and of its abandonment ; the offer of the Entente to send a division to Macedonia not regarded by Greek general staff as enabling Greece to go to help of Serbia.

(²⁹) *April* 8.—Deportation began at Zeitoun in Cilicia, and continued with massacres through 1915 from one Armenian centre to another all over the Ottoman Empire.

(³⁰) *April* 8.—Italy demanded cession of Trentino, Dalmatian Islands, Gorizia and Gradisca ; rectification of eastern frontier ; renunciation of Austrian interests in Albania ; recognition of Italian sovereignty over Valona ; Trieste to be an independent state ; amnesty to all military and political prisoners in the ceded districts.　Italy to pay Austria 200,000,000 lire and to remain neutral.

(³¹) *April* 10.—White Book containing correspondence between British Government and American Ambassador in London ; British treatment of German prisoners better than German treatment of British prisoners.

(³²) *April* 10.—Memorandum declared that U.S.A. was unneutral in allowing export of munitions to the Allies.

(³³) *April* 20.—Sir Edward Grey stated that the " Peklat " was conveying noncombatants from Tsing-tau when that place was about to be besieged and was thus increasing the strength of the fortress.　The non-combatants were sent to their destinations : a contrast to the German torpedoing of the " Amiral Ganteaume," which was conveying refugees to England.

(³⁴) *April* 20.—Mr. Bryan stated, in addition, that to prohibit supply of contraband to the Allies would be an unneutral act.

(³⁵) *April* 26.—Lord Kitchener stated that Germany had stooped to acts which vie with those of the Dervishes.　Mr. Asquith, in the Commons, stated that reparation would be exacted from all proved to have been guilty of such acts.

(³⁶) *May* 3.—Italian Note stated that the Triple Alliance had lost its value as a result of Austria's action in July, 1914, which was opposed to the spirit and letter of the treaty.

(³⁷) *May* 4. — Estimated revenue, £270,332,000; estimated expenditure, £1,132,654,000. Proposed drink taxes abandoned; no change in taxation beyond adjustment of income tax in case of endowment insurance.

(³⁸) *May* 6.—General Botha protested against the poisoning of wells; the German commander admitted the fact and gave as an excuse that the wells were marked poisoned.

(³⁹) *May* 7.—Members of the Ottoman Government would be held personally responsible for the safety of British and French civilians transported from Constantinople to Gallipoli.

(⁴⁰) *May* 7.—Japan demanded that China should grant in full her demands as to Shantung, Manchuria and Mongolia : should not alienate coasts and islands and the Han-Yeh-Ping Co. Other points to be discussed.

(⁴¹) *May* 12.—Bryce Committee on Belgium stated that " murder, lust and pillage prevailed on a scale unparalleled in any war between civilised nations during the last three centuries."

(⁴²) *May* 14.—Note stated that German methods were incompatible with the freedom of the seas : that the German government would be held accountable for infringement of American rights; that American citizens have the right to sail on legitimate business without being exposed to illegitimate dangers; that German use of submarines against commerce must infringe rules of justice; and that Germany must disavow guilty commanders, make reparation and prevent recurrence of such deeds.

(⁴³) *May* 20.—Austria offered concessions in S. Tyrol; the W. bank of the Isonzo as far as the population is Italian; Trieste to be a free imperial city with an Italian university; recognition of Italian sovereignty over Valona; Austria to be politically disinterested in Albania; amnesty for political and military prisoners and appointment of a mixed commission to settle details as to new boundaries.

(⁴⁴) *May* 21.—Austria regretted denunciation of Triple Alliance, justified her actions in 1914 against Serbia, professed willingness to consider concessions to Italy, and declined responsibility for Italy's repudiation of the alliance.

(⁴⁵) *May* 23.—Allies will hold members of the Ottoman Government personally responsible for the massacres of Armenians about the middle of April at Erzerum, Bitlis, etc., in Cilicia and near Van.

(⁴⁶) *May* 25.—Mr. Asquith, Prime Minister; Lord Lansdowne; Mr. Balfour, First Lord of the Admiralty; Sir E. Grey, Foreign Secretary; Mr. Bonar Law, Colonial Secretary; Lord Kitchener, War; Mr. Lloyd George, Munitions; Mr. Henderson, Education; Sir E. Carson, Attorney General; Mr. McKenna, Chancellor of the Exchequer. Ministry contained 12 Liberals, 8 Unionists, one Labour and one non-party member.

(⁴⁷) *May* 25.—China undertook not to alienate sea coasts and islands; to open new treaty ports in Shantung and E. Inner Mongolia; to lease Port Arthur, etc. for 99 years; not to convert Han Yeh-Ping Co., into a State concern without consent of Japanese capitalists; not to allow establishment of any shipyard, coaling, naval or military station under control of a foreign power or financed with foreign capital on the Fukien coast. Kiao-Chau to be restored to China on conditions at the end of war.

(⁴⁸) *May* 28.—Vodka : Statement in *Times* of May 28, that during period September, 1914-April, 1915, the States Savings Banks in Russia received deposits, the monthly totals of which showed average of £3,800,000, as compared with scarcely £100,000 for the respective months of 1913 and 1914. This is ascribed to total prohibition of sale of spirits.

(⁴⁹) *May* 30.—Germany ignored the demand for the cessation of submarine warfare against neutral shipping; laid the blame on Great Britain, and asserted that the " Lusitania " carried concealed mounted guns.

(⁵⁰) *June* 4.—Mr. Lloyd George addressed the Dockers' Battalion, and also a meeting of trade representatives at Liverpool on the question of munitions, and dealt especially with the effect of trade union restrictions upon output.

(⁵¹) *June* 8.—An amendment to the Ministry of Munitions Bill made it clear that the Minister had no new powers to coerce workmen.

(⁵²) *June* 8.—Mr. Bryan's resignation was thought to be due to the uncompromising character of the American Note, but the Note when published proved to be moderate in tone. The Note denies that the " Lusitania " was armed, carrying cargo forbidden by American law, conveying troops from Canada or supplied with trained gunners.

It adds that these allegations in no case affect the legality of the methods of the German naval authorities and invokes " principles of humanity which throw into the background any special circumstances of detail that may be thought to affect the case."

([53]) *June* 12.—The British Government announced that the German submarine prisoners had been released from naval custody, and that it is now expected that 39 British officers who had been the subject of reprisals should be returned to ordinary detention camps.

([54]) *June* 15.—Moving the vote of credit, Mr. Asquith stated that the daily cost of the war since 1.4.15 had been £2,666,000, and that future daily expenditure might be over £3,000,000.

([55]) *June* 18.—The Report reviewed operations from 15.5.17, when the Russians, retreating from the Carpathians, turned on their pursuers near Stryj and Bolechow. The Russian front was broken at Stryj, and it was decided to fall back on the Dniester, heavy losses having been inflicted on the Austrians, who suffered severely at Mikolajow (2.6.15), Zurawno (8-9.6.15), and between Zayechow and Zurawno (15.6.15). From 29.5.15 to 15.6.15, the Russians claimed 40,000 prisoners in this sector, and placed the total enemy loss at from 120,000 to 150,000 men.

([56]) *June* 24.—The memorandum insisted on the wish of Great Britain to minimise the inconvenience caused by the war to neutral trade. It states that the right of confiscation for breaches of the blockade has been waived and that neutrals have been given the right to institute proceedings in the Prize Court. It denies that there has been undue delay in dealing with detained goods, and describes the concessions granted as to cotton shipments.

([57]) *June* 29.—The National Registration Bill provided for the Registration of all people between 15 and 65 years of age in England, Scotland and Wales, Scilly Isles and (with reservations) Ireland.

([58]) *June* 30.—The Russian Ministry included M. Khvostov as Minister of Justice, M. Samarin as Procurator of the Holy Synod, and M. Krivoshein.

([59]) *July* 7.—The despatch covers the period March 13-May 5. Sir Ian Hamilton, after explaining the difficulties of the situation, describes the attempt by battleships to force the Narrows on March 18, and the military landing on April 25. He gives a detailed account of the fighting (paying tribute to the gallantry of all troops concerned), the attempt to capture Krithia, Achi Baba, and the Turkish methods of attack.

([60]) *July* 8.—The German attack is defended and proposal made that Americans should travel in their own or neutral ships with sailings notified in advance.

([61]) *July* 9.—Mr. Long declared to a deputation that though the National Registration Bill does not contemplate compulsory service, the Government have not tied their hands in the matter.

([62]) *July* 9.—Germany declares her campaign essential for combating the blockade. She undertakes to respect American vessels not carrying contraband and guaranteed by the U.S.A. to that effect, or neutral vessels under the American flag bearing the same guarantee.

([63]) *July* 11.—Sir J. French's seventh despatch, dated G.H.Q., 15.6.15, describes our capture of Hill 60, on April 17, and its loss on May 5. It records the first use of asphyxiating gas on April 22 at the second battle of Ypres, when the French Division abandoned its position from Steenstraate to the Poelcapelle road. Connection was re-established on the 23rd, between the left of the Canadian Division and the French right. The Canadian line was further forced back on the 25th, and the retirement to the new line was completed on May 4. Our line, after being re-organised, fell back on the 13th and 25th. The battle of Festubert, on May 9 and 16, gained for us ground on a front of four miles.

([64]) *July* 20.—New terms of compromise, drawn up by Mr. Lloyd George, were accepted by the Miners' Council.

([65]) *July* 23.—The Note, in acknowledging the German Note, dated July 8, rejects its proposal that certain designated vessels should be immune from attack. It reiterates the immutable principle of the right of neutrals to go unharmed, and intimates that any act in contravention of these rights will be regarded as deliberately unfriendly.

([66]) *July* 26.—The Note maintains that Great Britain has not departed from the main principles of international law, and gives precedents, during the blockade of Bermuda, for her action, suggesting that if a neutral country is aggrieved the remedy can be sought in courts or, eventually, in arbitration.

([67]) *July* 28.—Mr. Lloyd George said that through the Munitions Ministry and Labour Exchanges about 20,000 volunteer workers had become available. Highly skilled engineers were also being released from the colours for the work. Addressing himself to trade-leaders, he implored them to suspend trade union practices and announced a new and great programme which had been decided upon.

(⁶⁸) *July* 29.—Mr. Lloyd George reviewed the situation, forecast the difficulties and struggles ahead, and deprecated the "Business as usual" attitude.

(⁶⁹) *July* 30.—The Pope declares his intention of devoting all his energies to the re-establishment of peace, and suggests an interchange of views between the parties involved. He includes in his Apostolic Benediction those "not yet belonging to the Roman Church."

(⁷⁰) *Aug.* 2.—American Ambassador opens with statement that the U.S.A. Government insist on rights of their citizens under rules governing neutrals' trade in time of war. Sir E. Grey quotes in reply attitude of U.S. in Civil War, when these rules were modified to meet the circumstances, and points out that there are many ports which cannot be regarded as offering facilities only for the commerce of neutral country where they are situated.

(⁷¹) *Aug.* 2.—The Note reiterates the previous justification, agrees to pay damages or abide by arbitration. It asserts that, as the wheat on board the "W. P. Frye" was intended for England, and it was impossible to take the ship to Germany, her destruction was justified on general principles.

(⁷²) *Aug.* 4.—Resolution passed at London Opera House and at all War Anniversary meetings, ran as follows :—" That on the anniversary of the declaration of a righteous war this meeting declares its inflexible determination to continue to a victorious end the struggle in maintenance of those ideals of liberty and justice which are the common and sacred cause of the Allies."

(⁷³) *Aug.* 4.—British losses during the first year :—

$$76,000 \text{ killed}$$
$$252,000 \text{ wounded}$$
$$55,000 \text{ missing}$$

Total   ...   383,000

(⁷⁴) *Aug.* 6.—The Note, to Bucharest, Sofia, Nish, Athens and Cettinje, proposed settlement of differences caused by 1913 war, based on condition of joining the Entente.

(⁷⁵) *Aug.* 10.—Count Okuma, Prime Minister ; Dr. Ikki, Interior ; Mr. Taketomi, Finance ; Baron Ishii, Foreign Affairs ; V.-Admiral Tomoshburo, Navy.

(⁷⁶) *Aug.* 10.—While the U.S.A. re-affirm that Prussian-American treaty was violated, it agrees to accept payment for vessel, stipulating that no treaty rights are waived by acceptance of such payment.

(⁷⁷) *Aug.* 11.—The Memorandum defines Germany's aims (economic), which include an enduring peace and an extension of German power " with territorial gains, including the possession of seaports on the Franco-Belgian coast and the fortresses of Verdun and Belfort."

(⁷⁸) *Aug.* 13.—M. Radoslavov stated that Bulgaria is prepared to enter the war when she receives guarantees that in Serbia and Greek Macedonia her claims will be satisfied. She is negotiating with both groups of Powers.

(⁷⁹) *Aug.* 19.—Herr v. Bethmann-Hollweg accuses the Allies of having caused the war and of seeking to deceive the people as to the real situation.

(⁸⁰) *Aug.* 23.—M. Venizelos, Prime Minister and Foreign Affairs ; General Danglis, Minister of War ; M. Micailis, Minister of Marine ; M. Repauli, Minister of Finance.

(⁸¹) *Aug.* 23.—Order of the Day declared country's resolution to carry on struggle for Serb-Croatian-Slovene race by the side of the Allies, and expressed approval of Government policy.

(⁸²) *Aug.* 24.—The despatch describes the part played by the Navy in the landings at Gallipoli, and is followed in the *London Gazette* by the announcement of the award of six Naval V.C.'s.

(⁸³) *Aug.* 25.—At no point was real objective gained. The attack from Anzac Bay established troops just below the summit of Sari Bair and Chunuk Bair. The attack from Suvla was checked after an advance of 2¼ miles, and the two lines were connected along a front of 12 miles. Losses great on both sides, but "the ground gained and held is of great value."

(⁸⁴) *Aug.* 26.—After repudiating the accusation that Great Britain and Belgium were in league against Germany, and quoting the German Chancellor's offer to us to become a party to the violation of Belgian neutrality, the letter recapitulates the efforts of Great Britain to avert war, and concludes with a vehement declaration that a peace with Germany in supreme power on land and sea would be intolerable.

(⁸⁵) *Aug.* 26.—" France will not end the struggle until her righteous cause is victorious, until all chance of similar crimes has been removed, until the political and economic independence of Belgium is secured, and until we have again our Alsace and Lorraine."

(⁸⁶) *Aug.* 26.—The speech forecasts the grim struggle ahead, the demands for further man-power, and consequent shortage of labour. The recommendation of Lord Milner's Committee concerning wheat and the subsequent decision of the Government not to incur the financial risk involved is regretted, and the suggestion made that County Councils should serve as links between farmers and the Board of Agriculture.

(⁸⁷) *Aug.* 28.—M. Sazonov deals vigorously with German intrigue in Russia, and Germany's efforts to sow dissension among the Allies. He repeats Tsar's words that " Russia will never make peace with Germany as long as a hostile soldier remains on her soil." General Polivanov announces that Russia is raising another 2,000,000 men, and repudiates suggestion that Allies were not helping her to the full extent of their powers.

(⁸⁸) *Aug.* 31.—Proceedings at Board of Trade resulted in considerable concessions to the miners, an important one being the inclusion of the craftsmen in the benefit of the bonus turn.

(⁸⁹) *Sept.* 1.—Germany states :—" Liners will not be sunk by our submarines without warning and without ensuring the lives of non-combatants, provided that the liners do not try to escape or offer resistance." Question of reparation left for further discussion.

(⁹⁰) *Sept.* 2.—Include preposterous demands for the cession of the Belgian Congo and French African Colonies, as " compensation " for evacuation of Belgium and Northern France. Serbia to be divided up, Poland given independence as a " buffer " state. Stock item of " the freedom of the seas " not omitted.

(⁹¹) *Sept.* 2.—President stated Scandinavia united in keeping compact of an honourable neutrality, and had no ambitious plans.

(⁹²) *Sept.* 5.—Army Order signed by Tsar, issued September 5 :—" To-day I have taken supreme command of all the forces of the sea and land armies operating in the theatre of war. With firm faith in the clemency of God, with unshakable assurance in final victory, we shall fulfil our sacred duty to defend our country to the last. We will not dishonour the Russian land.—(signed) NICHOLAS, General Headquarters."

(⁹³) *Sept.* 5.—The Northern, Central and Southern fronts of the Russian Army are now respectively under Generals Russki, Evert, and Ivanov.

(⁹⁴) *Sept.* 7.—Chief objective of enemy to gain possession of railway system from Riga to Lemberg. To this end is swinging northwards with Grodno as the axis, and South on Kovna.

(⁹⁵) *Sept.* 7.—Sunk U boats reported as : Identified, 7 ; unidentified, believed or known to have been sunk, at least three ; besides losses claimed by French and British Navy and merchantmen.

(⁹⁶) *Sept.* 7.—Germany justifies as matter of self-defence ; willing to submit case to Hague Tribunal. Whole question of right of Americans to travel on belligerent passenger-ships re-opened.

(⁹⁷) *Sept.* 9.—New frontier line follows River Tonga to Kara-Agach, the railway station of Adrianople, which is given to Bulgaria, thence by course of the Maritza to the estuary. Definitive text of convention as yet unsigned.

(⁹⁸) *Sept.* 9.—" With you victory is assured, without you our cause is lost." " This is a war of material." " This country is not doing its best." Government was strictly keeping its bargain with Trade Unions ; he gave proof that labour was not ; unless necessary unskilled labour obtained, nation making straight for disaster. Not enough skilled labour to go round.

(⁹⁹) *Sept.* 13.—Germany demands passage of Austro-German troops through Rumanian territory, and fulfilment of Rumania's undertaking to supply £8,000,000 worth of benzine and other requisites.

(¹⁰⁰) *Sept.* 15.—Fourth vote of credit this year raises total voted 1915–16 to £900,000,000. Seven votes of credit since outbreak of war amount to £1,262,000,000. Number of men recruited for Army and Navy not far short of 3,000,000.

(¹⁰¹) *Sept.* 17.—Arguments for : Present one-seventh of Western front occupied by us not sufficient to ensure victory ; extravagance and injustice of present system ; moral effect in the field and on Allies' financial prospects. Certain opponents expressed same open mind as Labour member " prepared to be convinced by events." Mr. Thomas declared absolute opposition of Trade Unionists.

(¹⁰²) *Sept.* 19.—Submarine procedure restricted in case of passenger and neutral-owned ships ; opportunity given for safety of those aboard . . . Retaliatory measures confined to belligerents ; onus rests on opponents to avoid suspicion or hostile actions. Hoped agreement with America.

(¹⁰³) *Sept.* 20.—Give Government fair chance to decide ; cease clatter outside Council Chamber, and personal recrimination, "issue one of fact not principle," settle it in spirit worthy of its gravity. Facts warranted to sober most fatuous optimist ; land in jeopardy ; aroused in time " we shall win."

(¹⁰⁴) *Sept.* 21.—New taxes : 50 per cent. on excess profits and on certain imports on grounds of foreign exchange and luxuries. Raised taxes : by 40 per cent. on income tax ; postal charges ; imports of certain comestibles, tobacco, motor-spirit, patent medicines. Exemption from income-tax limited to £130 ; scale of abatements on larger incomes reduced. Revenue from new taxation : £30,924,000 ; from postal charges £1,980,000.

(¹⁰⁵) *Sept.* 22.—Dumba's papers prove his government less guiltless of nefarious " strike " schemes than Bernstorff asserts for his Government ; latter defends purchase of war material and factories as legitimate obstacle to supplying the Allies ; v. Papen's purchasing activities shown up in letter to wife, where he sneers at " idiotic Yankees."

(¹⁰⁶) *Sept.* 26.—Recent revelation of communication received by Italian Ambassador in Constantinople from German Ambassador, July 14, 1914, proved pre-meditation of Austro-German offensive. Italy thus given full liberty of action ; determined to secure natural boundaries of country.

(¹⁰⁷) *Sept.* 28.—Issue of £100,000,000 5 per cent. bonds at 98, repayable at end of five years, or convertible into 4½ per cent. bonds of the two Governments ; repayable not earlier than 15, not later than 25 years by two Governments jointly or severally.

(¹⁰⁸) *Sept.* 28.—No disturbance of friendly relations with Bulgaria, as long as attitude unaggressive ; otherwise prepared to help friends in Balkans ; British policy further-ance of Balkan States' aspirations, not sacrificing independence of any.

(¹⁰⁹) *Sept.* 29.—Bulgaria's mobilisation declared for "armed neutrality," similar interpretation to be given to Greece's ; situation grave. Bulgaria not hiding intention of ignoring treaties *re* territorial *status quo* between herself and neighbours. Greece will resist any attempt at predominance of a Balkan state. Glad if assurance could lead to simultaneous demobilisation. King, Government, and Opposition apparently at one.

(¹¹⁰) *Sept.* 30.—Sir J. French's special Order of the Day : 1st and 4th Corps carried first line ; 11th Corps and 3rd Cavalry Division subsequently thrown into fight. Third and Indian Corps and troops of 2nd Army assisted main operations S. of La Bassée. Great help rendered by operations of 5th Corps, S. of Ypres. Capture of over 3,000 prisoners ; some 25 guns.

(¹¹¹) *Oct.* 2.—Sir Edward Grey stated that German and Austrian officers were arriving in Bulgaria to take active direction of army ; similar to action taken in Turkey, when latter forced by German officers to make unprovoked attack on Russia. Allied Powers were bound to support States menaced by such proceedings.

(¹¹²) *Oct.* 4.—Russia's ultimatum said that presence of German and Austrian officers at Ministry of War, concentration of troops on Serbian frontier, extensive financial support from enemy leave no doubt as to Bulgaria's intentions. If her government does not within 24 hours break with enemies of Slav cause and Russia, Russian Minister will be recalled.

(¹¹³) *Oct.* 5.—Allied Governments had previously negotiated with Greek Govern-ment which, being, neutral, raised a protest. French officers, however, were allowed to prepare for landing. Greek Government informed of landing by letter from French Minister at Athens ; Allies sending help to Serbia ; rely upon Greece, equally allied to Serbia, not to oppose measures.

(¹¹⁴) *Oct.* 5.—Lord Derby's address to Recruiting Meeting at Waterfoot ; felt in posi-tion of receiver in bankrupt concern ; recruiting bad, too optimistic view taken of situation ; was himself for National Service ; Trade Union rally put each man on his mettle ; voluntary system depended on result. Mr. Thomas less pessimistic ; proud of what British had done ; only let Government speak out.

(¹¹⁵) *Oct.* 7.—New Greek Cabinet consists of : M. Zaimis, Premier and Foreign Affairs ; M. Gounaris, Interior ; General Yanakitsas, War ; Admiral Condouriotis, Marine ; M. Dragoumis, Finance, etc., etc.

([¹¹⁶]) *Oct.* 9.—M. Radoslavov, Prime Minister, relinquishes Interior and retains Foreign Affairs; M. Christo Popov, Interior; Major-General Naidenov, War, etc.

([¹¹⁷]) *Oct.* 11.—Lord Derby's Recruiting Scheme, produced on October 11, and explained in full on October 19, called on all fit men to enlist voluntarily; those wishing to join at once could do so, others to register and wait till called up. 46 groups, of which first 23 to be unmarried men, last 23 married men; to be called out successively as required, a fortnight's notice being given; 3s. per diem allowed to those ready to join at once.

([¹¹⁸]) *Oct.* 12.—Greeks stated that Greco-Serbian Treaty, 1913, purely Balkan in character; present attack on Serbia incident in European war; Treaty contemplates attack by third Power, Serbia attacked by two Powers as well as by Bulgaria; considers *casus foederis* not arisen. Further, Serbia unable to fulfil stipulation of furnishing Greece with 150,000 men.

([¹¹⁹]) *Oct.* 12, 13.—M. Viviani, on the diplomatic situation, said that the Allies realised danger of Bulgaria's resentment since treaty of Bucharest; endeavoured to make re-union of Balkan peoples; mutual, freely given sacrifices best guarantee for future peace; Rumania, Greece, Serbia, ready to help; Bulgaria's collaboration withheld, made claims upon her four frontiers at expense of four neighbours. Allies in complete agreement about assisting Serbia.

([¹²⁰]) *Oct.* 14.—Sir E. Grey and Lord Crewe stated that we wish to keep Balkans out of the war; effort towards Balkan agreement by mutual concessions; enemy, regardless of other States, offered Bulgaria more than the Allies; Greece and Serbia must now rise or fall as one; Russian co-operation assured. Lord Crewe emphasised aim of Central Powers to disunite Balkans; ours to unite; enumerated enormous obstacles to union.

([¹²¹]) *Oct.* 22.—M. Filipescu states Rumanian policy is favourable to Bulgaria, though conversant with treaty between latter and Germany; informed Serbia at beginning of war not to count on her assistance in case of infringement of Bucharest Treaty; same policy pursued with regard to Greece. His request to Premier to notify Sofia that Rumania would not allow Bulgaria to attack Greece, refused.

([¹²²]) *Oct.* 24.—America's Note *re* Blockade and seizure of American cargoes stated that British Orders in Council illegal under international law and void; also discriminatory in that Scandinavia able to ship to Germany, United States not; blockade not binding on neutrals unless actually accomplished; denies proof of shipments to Germany; in any event neutrals entitled to ship non-contraband.

([¹²³]) *Oct.* 25.—Order in Council (dated October 20) published, abolishing the Article 57 of Declaration of London, by which the character of a vessel was to be determined by the flag she was entitled to fly. This Order, therefore, re-enacted the old rule, by which a vessel if under an enemy flag was considered an enemy, but if under a neutral flag her character was to be investigated and she to be condemned or otherwise accordingly. (It had been found that ships under a neutral flag were often wholly or in part enemy's property.)

([¹²⁴]) *Oct.* 27.—Mr. Fisher, High Commissioner in London; Mr. Hughes, Prime Minister and Attorney-General; Mr. Pearce, Defence; Mr. Jensen, Navy; Mr. Mahon, External Affairs.

([¹²⁵]) *Oct.* 28.—M. Briand, Premier and Foreign Affairs; M. Jules Cambon, Secretary General at Foreign Office; Gen. Galliéni, War; Admiral Lacaze, Marine; M. Ribot, Finance; M. Malvy, Interior; M. Viviani, Justice.

([¹²⁶]) *Nov.* 1.—Sir J. French's despatch, dated 15.10.15, is chiefly concerned with the operations at Loos, and covers the period 25.9.15 to 8.10.15. Our own casualties were very heavy (officers, 2,958; other ranks, 45,288); those of the German 8,000 to 9,000 in dead alone. He justifies his resort to the gas attack methods of the Germans.

([¹²⁷]) *Nov.* 1.—The Austro-Germans in their progress distinguished themselves by their calculated brutality to the civilian population. It had the direct military object of causing a wholesale panic in order to encumber the few roads with fleeing households and thereby to impede the retreat of the Serbian army and guns. The two Serbian armies were hopelessly isolated by the Bulgarian advance from Usküb, northwards towards Prishtina. The first, or northern, retired towards Montenegro. The second, or southern, into the mountains of Central Albania.

([¹²⁸]) *Nov.* 1.—Ruthless destruction wrought by the invaders in the districts of Champagne and Lorraine; visited by the Agricultural Relief of Allies Committee (instituted by the Royal Agricultural Society). Sent several consignments of reapers and binders and other machinery in time for hay and corn harvests. Funds, animals and produce to be contributed. Work of the Society of Friends in the Sermoise district and elsewhere has been of the greatest importance in helping to replenish denuded homesteads.

(129) *Nov.* 2.—Mr. Asquith spoke of our achievements on land and sea, declared British policy with regard to the succour of Serbia, announced that there would be a War Committee of not less than three and not more than five members, and explained Lord Derby's recruiting scheme. Compulsion, if necessary, voluntary recruiting too haphazard. Unmarried men wanted first.

(130) *Nov.* 4.—M. Skouloudis announced that any Allied troops which might be driven across that frontier must be disarmed and interned, but he eventually gave in to the Allied demands, removed most of the Greek troops from Salonika, and handed over the whole " zone of manoeuvres " to the Allies, including all roads and railways.

(131) *Nov.* 5.—" The Prime Minister has appointed a Committee to inquire into difficulties and congestion arising from time to time at harbours, ports and docks in the United Kingdom." The most important work required of the Committee was to expedite the discharge and loading of vessels at all ports in the country, and thereby increase the supply of tonnage so greatly required at the present time.

(132) *Nov.* 7.—110 German divisions in the *West*. 50 German and 40 Austro-Hungarian divisions of Germany and Austria are on the *Russian* front, and 20 Austro-German divisions invading Serbia. More co-ordination of Allied armies demanded.

(133) *Nov.* 7.—The American Note as to the maritime policy of Great Britain was a strongly-worded protest against our construction of the law of contraband and blockade and repudiated our suggestion that Americans have sufficient redress through our Prize Courts.

(134) *Nov.* 9.—" Be the journey long or short, we shall not pause or falter till we have secured for the smaller States of Europe their charter of independence, and for Europe itself, for the world at large their final emancipation from the reign of force."

(135) *Nov.* 10.—" We must found the policy of this century on an Anglo-Franco-Russian alliance. Others nations will probably enter this alliance, but we must form the kernel of it. The future of European culture, as opposed to German *Kultur*, depends on the defeat of that Power, and on the means adopted by which to prevent her from developing her forces afresh."

(136) *Nov.* 11.—No marriage contracted after Registration day (August 15, 1915) will entitle any man to be relegated to the married groups. Whether a man is indispensable or not will be decided, not by the man or his employer, but by competent authorities and tribunals.

(137) *Nov.* 15.—Two British officers killed July 12 and the British Vice-Consul at Shiraz killed September 8 ; all at German instigation.

(138) *Nov.* 15.—Mr. Churchill maintained in the House of Commons that, with regard to the Antwerp and Dardanelles expeditions, he had not acted contrary to the advice of the professional experts. Emphasised the extensive gap which separated the naval from the military activities. Lord Fisher did not object at first.

(139) *Nov.* 19.—" Married men not to be called up till young unmarried men have been. If these young men do not come forward voluntarily, you will either release the married men from their pledge or introduce a Bill into Parliament to compel the young men to serve. If Parliament did not pass such a bill the married men would be automatically released from their engagement to serve." Confirmed by Mr. Asquith.

(140) *Nov.* 19.—The German Press announced that revolt has broken out everywhere in India ; that Brahmins, Buddhists and Mohammedans have united to make all difficulties for the detested English, etc., etc. The Secretary of State for India (Mr. Austen Chamberlain) announces that there is not a word of truth in these statements from beginning to end, neither is it true that the Nizam of Hyderabad had been deposed by his subjects.

(141) *Nov.* 20.—It is estimated that there are not less than 4,000 German officers and soldiers in the colony, and about 30,000 native troops. Included are the officers and crew of the German war-vessel " Königsberg," with the guns from that vessel.

(142) *Nov.* 30.—Official list of Prussian* military casualties published up to date :—

484,218 killed and died of wounds
384,198 severely wounded.
27,674 died of disease.
381,141 missing.

---

* Prussian includes all German except Bavaria, Saxony, and Navy.

(143) *Dec.* 1.--The Foreign Office published a statement sent to the Admiralty by a well-known firm of solicitors that the master of a Swedish steamship informed them that his clearance papers, certifying that his ship was carrying no contraband, were printed in German as well as in Swedish ; that the Swedish Custom Houses always telegraphed to Berlin informing them of the sailing of the vessel, and that she was not carrying contraband ; further, that all Swedish vessels were stopped at the South entrance of the Sound and carefully examined by German patrol-boats. The German idea of " freedom of the seas " for neutrals.

(144) *Dec.* 1.--Baron Sonnino, Minister of Foreign Affairs, announced in the Italian Chamber of Deputies that Italy had formally entered into the Agreement by which France, Russia, Great Britain, and later, Japan, would none of them conclude peace separately. The Government would give aid to Serbia by revictualling and supplying ammunition and facilitating concentration of the Serbian Army while awaiting the time of vengeance.

(145) *Dec.* 1.--Lord Portsmouth charged the "pundits of the Foreign Office," through their interpretation of the Declaration of London, with having harassed the British Fleet for the benefit of our enemies. Lord Lansdowne replied that the Declaration of London was dead as an instrument of national obligation, but with certain important modifications was valuable as a convenient principle for the guidance of our Prize Courts and the Prize Courts of our Allies. He said it was very different from the Declaration of 1911.

(146) *Dec.* 2.--" Perhaps at the end of the war combatant Europe will find that in the interest of those engaged the fact of the U.S.A. not having participated in the struggle will prove of the greatest benefit. At the return of peace at least one great nation will then be found financially and industrially capable of responding to the financial and industrial needs of the others, at the moment when Europe will be economically exhausted." (Quoted from the *New York Nation.*)

(147) *Dec.* 3.--Figures given by the Prime Minister to Mr. Molteno show that up to November 9, 1915, the British casualties in all the theatres of war amounted to :-- Officers, 22,119 ; other ranks, 488,111 ; total, 510,230.

(148) *Dec.* 3.--Mr. Lansing informed Count Bernstorff that Captain Boy-Ed, Naval Attaché at Washington, is a "*persona non grata*," owing to his connection with the conspiracy of Hamburg-Amerika Line to supply German warships from American ports. Revelations as to forging of passports. Captain von Papen (Military Attaché) engaged in conspiracy to disorganise American factories suspected of making munitions for Allies.

(149) *Dec.* 5.--King Constantine complained bitterly of the " unjust and cruel attacks that had been made upon him and the suspicions which existed as to his intentions and sentiments." He pledged the friendship of Greece towards the Allies, and especially towards England, and firmly denied the existence of any treaty with Bulgaria.

(150) *End of Nov.*--Essad Pasha, who had made for himself a little Albanian kingdom after the flight of the Prince of Wied, welcomed the Serbian fugitives in every way, while he expelled all Austrian and Bulgarian subjects from his territory and " gave Teutonic agents who appeared in December to stir up the northern tribes a taste of Albanian justice."

(151) *Dec.* 6.--" In view of the comedy of the forthcoming elections . . . This party cannot lend itself to this comedy unworthy of a free people and contrary to the national will. It will consequently not take part in the Elections, and will leave to the Government full and entire responsibility for its deviation from the political régime and for the disasters which the Government is preparing."

(152) *Dec.* 6.--" The British, French, Italian, Japanese and Russian Governments mutually engage not to conclude peace separately during the present war. The five Governments agree that when terms of peace come to be discussed no one of the Allies will demand conditions of peace without the previous agreement of the other Allies."

(153) *Dec.* 8.--Destruction of the last of the enemy's oversea raiders, the " Königsberg," when lying some distance up the Rufiji river, in July, 1915. Monitors--the " Severn " and the " Mersey," and two aeroplanes--made two attacks, July 5 and 11, the last being completely successful, and the work of the R.N.A.S. and high-angle fire of the monitors highly praised.

(154) *Dec.* 11.--" In seven months over 25,000 officers and men had perished ; over 75,000 were wounded, and over 12,000 missing--casualties nearly twice the number of the force which landed on April 25 . . . Over 96,000 cases had been admitted to hospital. The chief causes were dysentery and para-typhoid . . . An enterprise which had shown such unparalleled losses, and which, what with the proba-

bility of ill weather and the certainty of an increased enemy strength, boded so ill for the future, ought clearly to be relinquished, if relinquishment was possible."—(Nelson, " History of War," Vol. XII., p.55.)

(¹⁵⁵) *Dec.* 20.—Mr. Asquith, in communicating the information to the House of Commons, said the withdrawal of the troops was made in pursuance of a decision come to some time ago by the Cabinet. He added that the fact that the operations had been so successfully carried out reflected the utmost credit on the Generals on the spot, the Admiral and his staff, and all ranks of the Army and Navy. " Few more anxious decisions have ever fallen to the lot of a British Commander than that on which Sir Charles Monro was required to pronounce the final word. The problem fell into three parts : Suvla, Anzac, Cape Helles (the latter being evacuated January 8, 1916) . . . But in each zone there remained a matter of three or more divisions to be moved. The whole thing was a gigantic gamble with fate, but every precaution was taken to lessen the odds . . . success depended upon two things, mainly—fine weather and secrecy. The first was the gift of the gods, and the second was attained by sheer bluff. . . . Our lines lay to all appearances as they had been for the last four months, but they were only a blind. We kept up our usual fire and received the Turkish answer, but had any body of the enemy chosen to attack they would have found the trenches held by a handful . . . Before midnight the last guns had been got on board, and at 1.30 a.m. on Monday morning (20th) the final embarkation of the troops began. . . . The Highland Mounted Brigade acted as the rearguard (at Suvla) to fight the expected action that never came. . . . The operations at Anzac were conducted on the same lines . . . but the intricate Anzac lines and exceeding precariousness of many of the positions made the movements of guns and troops far more difficult . . . Half the guns and half the men of the N.Z. batteries disappeared in a single night. As at Suvla, only picked battalions were left to the end, and there was desperate rivalry as to who should be chosen to act as rearguard. On the Saturday night three-fifths of the entire force was got on board the transports. On Sunday night the rest left, with 2 men wounded as the total casualties. By 5.30 a.m. on Monday morning the last transports moved from the coast, leaving the warships to follow. . . ."—(Nelson, " History of the War," Vol. XII., pp. 57, etc.)

(¹⁵⁶) *Dec.* 25.—" In this connection the demand for the freedom of the seas comes once more into prominence. In peace time the seas were always free, but during the war we have found to our cost that it is the strongest fleet which rules the seas. Therefore, means must and will be found to guarantee freedom of traffic to mercantile fleets not only in peace-time but also in time of war."

INDEX.

Figures in black type represent the month :
e.g., 4.**1**=4th Jan. ; 24.**11**=24th Nov. ; etc.

casualties to date, 27.**7**; On Compulsory
Service, 28.**7**; On War Credit, 15.**9**;
Announces a War Committee, 2.**10**;
On Compulsory Service 2.**11**; At Guild-
hall, 9.**11**; On General Staff, 10.**11**;
On War Committee, 11.**11**; On Salaries
question, 14.**12**.

ASTICO, RIVER (Trentino).
Active fighting on, 12.**10**.

" ASTURIAS " (hospital ship).
Attacked by submarine, 1.**2**.

ATROCITIES, GERMAN.
Bryce's report published,   12.**5**;
French reports on, published, 2.**3**, 10.**3**,
31.**7**, 7.**8**.

AUBERIVE (Champagne).
Fighting at, 1, 15.**10**.

AUBERS RIDGE (Neuve Chapelle).
Unsuccessful British attack, 9.**5**.

AUGUSTOVO (North Poland).
Germans retreat through woods of, 7.**8**.

AUS (S.W. Africa).
Occupied by Union forces, 1.**4**.

AUSTRALIA.
War Tax proposed, 30.**7**; Labour
Council, Sydney, opposes compulsory
service, unless wealth conscripted, 30.**9**;
Cabinet changes reported, 21.**10**; New
recruiting arrangements, 25.**11**.

AUSTRIA.
Week declared for metal collection,
2.**3**; Changes in Ministry, 1.**12**.

AUSTRIA-HUNGARY.
Burian succeeds Berchtold as Foreign
Minister, 13.**1**; Proposals to Italy regard-
ing South Tyrol : Italy demurs, 16.**4**;
Italy denounces Triple Alliance, 3.**5**;
Presentation of Cessions proposed, 18.**5**;
Note to Italy regarding Triple Alliance,
21.**5**; Italy declares War on, 23.**5**.

AVIATION.
French appoint M. R. Besnard Under-
Secretary of State for, 14.**9**.

AVLONA (Valona, Albania).
Occupation by Italians, 29.**5**; More
Italian troops landed, 16.**12**.

BABUNA PASS (Central Serbia).
Taken by Bulgarians, after 16 days'
fighting, 17.**11**.

BADEN.
French air-raid into, 24.**8**.

BAGATELLE (Argonne).
Fighting at, 7-8.**2**; Heavy mining and
fighting, 21.**3**; German attacks stopped,
2, 15, 21.**4**; French advance, 4.**5**; German attacks repulsed, 6-8, 12.**5**; Heavy
fighting, 29.**6**.

BALFOUR, RT. HON. ARTHUR.
Letter on Germany's submarine policy,
6.**9**.

BALIGROD (Carpathians).
Fighting near, 4, 7, 8, 28.**3**.

BALKANS QUESTION.
Serbian reply to Entente *re* settlement of, 1.**9**; M. Molinov's (Bulgarian)
views, 4.**9**; Sir E. Grey defines British
policy, 28.**9**; M. Viviani on, 12.**10**; Sir E.
Grey and Lord Crewe on, 14.**10**.

BALLIN, HERR.
Imperial confidences, *Times* 15.**4**; Ex-
posure in the *Times* 23.**4**; Defines
" Freedom of Seas," 25.**12**.

BALTIC PROVINCES.
Germans begin advance into, 27.**4**;
Russian offensive, 8.**5**; German advance on
Riga, July; (v. Riga, Mitau, Shavli, Aa, etc.)

BALTIC, THE.
Russo-German naval engagements in,
10 to 21.**8**; British submarines sink enemy
vessels, especially 8-23.**10**.

BAN-DE-SAPT, THE (Vosges).
Severe fighting at, 10.**2**, 24.**7**.

BANYO, MOUNT (Cameroons).
Taken by British, 6.**11**.

BARANOVICHI (Vilna).
Enemy advances towards, 9.**9**; Continued fighting near, 22, 24, 27.**9**; Successful Russian fights, 8-9, 19, 21.**10**.

BARI.
Bombed by Austrian aircraft, 1.**6**.

BARTFELD (Hung. Carpathians).
Severe fighting to North of. 25.**3** to 3.**4**.

" BAYONA," H.M.S. (Brit. aux. cruiser).
Torpedoed, 11.**3**.

BEAUSÉJOUR (Mesnil, Champ.).
Fighting near, 21.**1**, 22.**2**; French take
fort, 27.**2**; Further severe fighting, 8, 9,
28.**4**., 4.**5**.

BEERSHEBA (Bir Saba).
Railway to, completed, 9.**8**.

BELFORT.
Bombed. 21.**4**. and 17.**10**.

BELGIAN COAST.
Despatch of Rear-Admiral Hood *re*
coast-patrol action (Oct. 17 to Nov. 9,
1914). issued 13.**4**; Especially bombarded
by Fleet, 7, 8, 25, 30.**9**., 2, 10, 22, 24,**10**.

BELGIAN RED CROSS.
Suppressed by von Bissing, 14.**4**.

BELGIUM.
Report of Lord Bryce's Committee
on German atrocities in, issued, 12.**5**;
Strike in, 5.**8**.

BELGRADE.
Bombarded, 6.**4**; Austrian gun boat
fires on, 10.**4**; Shelled by Austro-Germans,
4-6.**10**; Austrians cross Danube at. 8.**10**;
Enemy occupies, 9.**10**; Serbians driven
back from heights covering, 11-22.**10**.

**BELGRADE-CONSTANTINOPLE
RAILWAY.**
Controlled by Germans, 12.**11**

BOTHA, GENERAL.
Congratulated on South-West African work, and invited to Europe, 10.7 ; Resolution by House of Commons, 12.7.
BOULOGNE.
Conference on munitions, 19.6, &c.
BOUREUILLES (Argonne).
Attacked by French, 3.1 ; French attack fails, 5.4.
" BOUVET," LE (French battleship).
v. Dardanelles.
BOY-ED and VON PAPEN, CAPTAINS.
Recall requested, 3.12 ; Recalled, 10.12.
" BREMEN " (cruiser).
British submarine sinks in Baltic, 17.12.
BRENTA, RIVER (Trentino).
Italian success in Valley, 18.9.
BRESCIA.
Bombed, 25.8, &c.
" BRESLAU."
Bombards Yalta (Crimea), 8.2 ; Engages Russians in Black Sea, 3.4 ; Takes refuge in Bosporus, 4.4.
BREST LITOVSK.
Bombarded, 10.8 ; Enemy closing in on, 16-19.8 ; falls, 25.8.
BRIAND, M.
Premier *vice* Viviani, 28.10 ; Declaration of policy. 3.11.
BRIANSK (Poland).
Russian centre broken at, 15.8.
BRINDISI.
Bombed by Austrian aircraft, 1.6
BRODY (Galicia).
Fall of, 1.9 ; Advance of Boehm-Ermolli's forces east of 2.9 ; Austrians report successes N.E. and S.W. of, 6.9.
BROODSEINDE (Ypres).
German attack and success, 23-26.4
BROOKE (Rupert).
Poet's death at Lemnos, 23.4.
BRYAN, W. J.
U.S.A. State Secretary : Letter defending U.S.A. against charges of favouring Entente, 24.1 ; Disagrees with President Wilson's second Note on " Lusitania," and resigns, 8.6.
BRYCE, VISCOUNT, v. Atrocities.
BUCHAREST.
Ministers refuse transport of munitions through, 11.8 ; Anti-German demonstrations, 24.9.
BUDGETS.
Introduced by Mr. Lloyd-George, 4.5 ; introduced by Mr. McKenna, 21.9.
BUG, RIVER.
Germans advance to the, 27.6 ; Germans cross the, 18.7 ; Germans advance East of Drohiczyn, Russians retire, 15-18.8.
BUKOBA (L. Victoria Nyanza).
Destroyed by British column, 25.6.
BUKOVINA.
Russians conquer, 1, 3, 6, 16, 20.1 ;

Austrians recover, 22.1., 4, 6-9.2 ; Alexeiev loses Czernowitz, 18.2 ; Further Austrian successes, 17-18.3 ; Russians driven back, Russians advance again, 21.3 ; Russian success, 15.5 ; Russians fall back, June ; Austrians advance, 13.7 ; Big Russian attack, heavy fighting between Rivers Pruth and Dniester, 27 to 31.12
BULAIR (Gallipoli).
Bombardment by Allied Fleet, 8.5.
BULGARIA.
German Loan of 3 millions to, 2.2 ; Declines responsibility for *Komitadji* raid, 6.4 ; Commission *re* frontier incidents accepted, 11.4 ; Disarmament of Turko-Bulgarian population on Serbian frontier and internment suspected Bulgars, 13.4 ; Secret treaty with Central Powers, regarding cessions of territory to Bulgaria, 17.7 ; Again declares neutrality ; Prince Hohenlohe, Germ. Ambass., received at Sofia, 18.7 ; Reply to Bulgarian Note by Allies, 3.8 ; Foreign Minister resigns, 19.8 ; Bulgarian Aims explained by M. Radoslavov, 13.8 ; Circular Note defining attitude, 13.9 ; General mobilisation foreshadowed, 13.9. Agitation against Germanophil policy, 15.9 ; Opposition dissuades King against Germanophil policy, 17.9; Convention with Turkey for " Armed Neutrality," 20.9 ; Mobilisation of Army ordered, 21.9 ; Premier explains reason, 24.9 ; No intention of attacking Serbia or Greece, 26.9 ; Trouble with Agrarians (anti-war), 28.9 to 3.10 ; Begins concentration on Serbian frontier, 3.10 ; Order to civilians to evacuate Thracian coast, 5.10 ; Allies ultimatum, unsatisfactory reply received, 4, 5.10 ; Ruptures imminent, 7-18.10 ; Germany denies secret treaty at Athens, 10.10 ; British rupture, 13.10 ; Begins war on Serbia, 14.10 ; Gt. Britain and France declare war, 15, 16.10 ; Italy declares war, 18.10.
BULGARIAN COAST.
Four German submarines sent to protect, 1.10 ; Blockaded by Allies, 16.10 ; Allied squadron bombards, 21.10., and on other dates.
BUNERWALS.
Irruption into Peshawar district, 17.8 ; Defeated by Rustam Column at Sarkhabi, 26.8 ; Defeated near Malandri Pass, 28.8 ; Further defeat, 31.8 ; and final scattering, 2.9
BURGAS (Black Sea).
Russian Fleet bombards, 21, 27.10.
BURIAN, BARON STEPHEN.
Austro-Hungarian Minister of Foreign Affairs, 13.1.
BUSHIRE (Persia).
British occupy, 8.8 ; British occupation terminates, 16.10.

BZURA, RIVER (Warsaw).
Fighting on, 2.**1**., 4-5.**2** ; German massed attack, 12.**6**.

CADORE (Ven. Alps).
Occupation of passes by Italians,24.**5** ; Italian offensive in, 15.**7** ; Renewed offensive, 8.**9**.

CALAIS.
Zeppelin raids on 22.**2**., 16.**5** ; War Conference at, 4.**12**.

CAMEROONS (v. Garua, Yaunde, etc.)
Campaign begins, 29.**1** ; British blockade declared, 23.**4** ; Continued fighting throughout the year between Germans and Anglo-French force, especially 24-31.**5** ; Capture of Garua. 10.**6** ; Anglo-French successes in Southern, 25-30.**10** ; valuable co-operation of Belgians reported, 6.**10**.

CANADA.
Announced intention to raise a further force of 35,000 men, 9.**6** ; Expeditionary Force increased, 8.**7**.

" CAPELLA " (Swedish Steamer).
Seized by German torpedo boat, 23.**10**.

CAPORETTO (Julian).
Occupation by Italians. 24.**5**.

CARENCY (Vimy).
French attack and capture, 9-12.**5**.

CARLEUL, CHÂTEAU DE. (Vimy).
German trenches captured, 26.**5**.

CARNIC FRONTIER
Austrian artillery attack, 23.**5** ; Val, Inferno occupied by Italians, 24.**5** ; Repulse of Italians W. of Plöcken, 26.**5** ; Italians progress, two passes occupied, 12.**6** ; Austrian attacks repulsed, 26.**6** ; Italian offensive, 11.**7** ; Italians repeatedly repulse enemy, 23.**9**.

CARPATHIANS (v. Galicia).
Hard fighting in, in region S. and S.W. of Przemysl ; Eventual Russian successes, 27.**2** to 28.**3** ; Russians retreat in May; Further fighting in autumn.

CARSO (Plateau E. of Lower Isonzo River).
Battle for, begins, 2.**7** ; Successful Italian actions, 6-20.**7** ; 500 prisoners taken, 20.**7** ; Offensive continues, 31.**7** ; Italians progress, 6-13.**8** ; Repulsed at Doberdo, 8.**9** ; Seize Monte San Michele, 10.**9** ; Further successes, 14-20.**9** ; Heavy fighting 3-26.**10** ; Italians advance again, 1-3, and 21-28.**11**.

CARSON, SIR E.
Resigns office as Attorney-General, 18.**10**.

" CARTHAGE " (French liner).
Sunk, 7.**4**.

CASTELLORIZO (E. of Rhodes, S.W. Asia Minor).
Occupied by French, 27.**12**.

CASTELNAU, GENERAL DE
Appointed to command the French front, 9.**12**.

CASUALTIES.
Total military, to July 18, announced, 27.**7** ; total naval British, to July 20, announced, 27.**7** ; Number of British, during first year of war, stated to be 381,982, to Aug. 4 (announced) 14.**9** ; Casualties on Western Front since Sept. 25, published, 1.**11** ; Since war began, published, 3.**12**. (v. also Résumé.)

CASUALTIES (German).
To date, estimated, announced, 1.**7**, 2.**8**, 31.**12**.

CATTARO.
Fighting at, 25.**8** ; Two Austrian destroyers and one French submarine sunk off, 29.**12**.

CAUCASUS, THE.
Grand Duke Nicholas appointed Viceroy of, 5.**9**.

CAVELL, EDITH.
Executed at Brussels, 12.**10**.

CENSORSHIP (Press).
Letter from Home Secretary on (*Times*), 12.**10**.

CEYLON.
Riots caused by racial and commercial animosity ; much Moslem property destroyed, 31.**5**

CHÂLONS.
Continuous bombardment N. of, Sept. ; Zeppelin bombs, 3.**13**.

CHAMPAGNE.
Violent artillery fighting during September ; Great French offensive begins, Germans driven back between the Suippe and Aisne, 25.**9** ; French advance between Auberive and Ville-sur-Tourbe, 26.**9** ; German second lines attacked, 27.**9** ; Progress toward Hill 185, and N. of Massiges, 28.**9** ; Continued progress N. of Massiges, and Butte-de-Tahure, 29.**9** ; Fighting N. of Mesnil, 29.**9** ; French successes about Mesnil, 29-30.**9** ; Indecisive fighting about Navarin, 1-3.**10** ; Heavy fighting round Tahure, 9-12.**10** ; Enemy gain footing E. of Auberive, 15.**10** ; Continued artillery fighting throughout, 16-18.**10** ; German attacks E. of Reims defeated, 19-21.**10** ; French capture La Courtine, 24.**10** ; Stubborn fighting round La Courtine, 25-29.**10** ; Continuous artillery work round Tahure, 26-28.**10** ; German attack at Hill 199 and Chausson Farm, 3-4.**11** ; Hard fighting, ground regained by French, 9.**12**.

CHARTORYSK (Volhynia).
v. R. Styr, Sept.-Oct. ; German lines broken by Russians, 10.**11**.

CHICHKOVO (Dvinsk).
Russians repulse enemy near, 7.**10** ; Capture parts of enemy forces near, 16.**10**.

CHILE.
Protests against violation of her waters at battle of Juan Fernandez, 24.3. Receives British apologies, 16.4.

CHINA.
Japan's amended proposals to China, *re* Manchuria, etc., 26.4 ; Chinese Note to Japan, 1.5 ; Ultimatum from Japan, 7.5 ; Acceptance of ultimatum, 9.5 ; Treaty with Japan, 25.5 ; (see Chino-Jap Treaty, App.⁴⁷) ; Japan offers advice on internal situation, 30.10 ; Advice rejected, 2.11 ; Yuan Shi-Kai becomes Emperor, 11.12.

CHOLERA.
In Austria and Galicia, 29.6 ; Among Turkish troops, 30.7.

CHOLM (=Kholm, E. Poland).
Occupied by enemy, 31.7 ; Russians defeated N.E. of, 3.8.

CHOLM-BREST LITOVSK RAILWAY.
Enemy reaches line of, 17.8.

CHOLM-LYUBLIN LINE.
Enemy movement on, suspended, 5.7.

CHURCHILL, RT. HON. WINSTON.
Meets M. Augagneur *re* Dardanelles, 21.4 ; Speeches to munition workers, 17.9 ; resigns, 11.11 ; Speech on Antwerp and Dardanelles, 15.11.

CITÉ ST. ÉLIE (Loos).
Tactical point, beginning of British offensive, 25.9 ; Quarries west of, taken by British and lost, 25.9 ; Retaken by British, 26.9 ; British gain trenches W. of, 8.10 ; and S.W. of, 13.10.

CIVIDALE (Friuli).
Enemy reinforced, attack Italians near, 24.9 ; Fighting in zone continues, 26.9 ; Italian offensive, 30.9

" CLAN McNAUGHTON," H.M.S.
Lost, 24.2.

CLOISTER HOEK (Flanders).
Occupation by Germans, 1.4.

COALITION MINISTRY.
Formation of, 25.5 ; Ratified by Unionists, 27.5.

COCHIN, DENYS, M.
French envoy received by King of Greece, 18.11.

COLCHESTER.
Raided by German aeroplane, 21.2.

COL DI LANA (Upper Cordevole, Dolomites).
Occupied by Italians, 4.8 ; Italian successes on the, 22-28.10 ; Again taken by Italians, 8.11.

COLONIES, BRITISH.
To be consulted as to terms of peace (Colonial Secretary), 14.4.

COMPULSORY SERVICE.
Debate on, 28.7, 15, 17, 28, 30.9 ; Principle accepted by Cabinet, 28.12.

CONSTANTINOPLE.
Perturbed Turkish families leave for Asia Minor, 13.3 ; E.11 sinks ships at, 27.4 ; Deported British and French to be sent to danger zone, 2.5 ; Great fire in, 26.7 ; Galata bridge blown up, 1.8 ; Desolate condition and exodus of Armenians and Greeks, 3.9 ; Appointment of Commission on losses through Allied bombing, 18.9.

CONSTANTINOPLE-DEDEAGACH Railway.
British aircraft bomb, 25.11.

CORDEVOLE VALLEY (Upper, Dolom.)
Italian offensive in, 28-29.7 ; Italian success in, 14.9 ; Heavy artillery duel in, 30.9 ; Successful Italian operations in, 18-22.10.

CORMONS (Isonzo).
Occupation by Italians, 24.5.

CORTINA (Ven. Alps).
Capture by Italians, 30.5.

COTTON.
Dissatisfaction in U.S.A. *re* Britain's holding up of, at British ports, 19.5 ; Mr. Lloyd George says cotton is not reaching Germany, 19.5 ; Strike of cotton workers at Oldham, 26.5 ; Declared contraband, 21.8 ; Germany denies inconvenience resulting from above, 1.9 ; Italy declares absolute contraband, 7.9.

" COURTINE, LA " (Champagne).
French capture strong work known as, 24.10 ; Obstinate fighting at, 25-29.10.

COURTRAI.
Allied air raid on, 30.3 ; British air raid on, 26.4.

CRAONNE (Aisne River).
Heavy fighting near, 15, 26.1.

CREDIT, VOTES OF.
Supplementary (1914 - 15) for 37 millions, 1.3 ; Vote (1915-16), for 250 millions, 1.3 ; (Supplementary), for 250 millions, 15.6 ; for 150 millions, 20.7 ; for 250 millions, 15.9 ; for 400 millions, 12.11.

CTESIPHON (Mesopotamia).
Advance of British on, 12.11 ; Battle of, 22.11 ; British retire from, 29.11.

CUINCHY (La Bassée).
German attack repulsed, 29.1 ; British success near, 6.2.

CUMBERLAND COAST TOWNS.
Shelled by German submarine, 16.8.

CYPRUS.
British Government offers to Greece in return for help to Serbia, 17.10 ; Offer rejected, 21.10.

CZERNOWITZ (Bukovina).
Taken by Austrians, 17.2 ; Russians advance on and bombard, 28 ; Russian success E. of, 14.4 ; Russians attack near, 14.8 ; Bombed, 9.10 ; Russians threaten, 24.12.

DOBERDO PLATEAU. (Carso).
Italians attack, 26.**7**; Repulse of Italians at, 9.**9**; Failure of Italians to reach district of, 14.**9**; Minor fighting near, 8.**10**; Italians repulsed, 17.**10**.

DOBROMIL (Przemysl).
Capture by Austrians, 15.**5**.

DOCKERS' BATTALION.
Started, 1.**4**.

DOGGER BANK.
Battle of, 24.**1**; Despatch (Adm.Beatty) concerning, 3.**3**.

DOLINA (East Galicia).
Fighting near, 22.**2**; Russians take 4,000 Austrians, 27.**2**.

DOLOMITES, THE (v. also under localities)
General artillery fighting in region of, 7.**9**; Continued fighting in, 28.**10**.

DOMESNES (Gulf of Riga).
Russians land and drive off Germans, 22.**10**.

DONAJETZ, RIVER (West Galicia).
Austrian attack on, 18-19.**2**; Austro-German advance against Russia on, 28.**4**; Austro-German crossing, 1.**5**.

DONAUESCHINGEN.
Bombed by French, 13.**9**.

DORNACH (Alsace).
Air raid on, 26.**8**.

" DRESDEN " (German cruiser).
Sunk by three British warships off island of Juan Fernandez, 14.**3**; British apology for violation of Chilean waters, 16.**4**.

DRIEGRACHTEN (Flanders).
Capture by Germans, 4.**4**; Belgian attempt repulsed, 5.**4**; Belgian and German successes, 9.**4**.

DRINA, RIVER.
Fighting on Serbian front, 7-8.**9**; Serbians frustrate enemy crossing, 24-25.**9**; Austro-Germans cross, 7.**10**; Serbians hold enemy up on, 9.**10**; Battles developing on, 11.**10**; Enemy crosses at Vishegrad, 22.**10**.

DRINK RESTRICTIONS.
v. Alcoholic Drinks.

DRISVIATI, LAKE (Dvinsk).
Russians drive enemy from villages, 25.**9**; Continual fighting near during struggle for Dvinsk, October ; Russians penetrate enemy line near, 14.**10**; Russian success on, 16.**12**.

DROHICZYN (Poland).
Fighting in the district of, 5-6.**9**; Reached by von Mackensen, 7.**9**.

DROHOBYCZ (Przemysl).
Austrian attacks repulsed, 18.**5**; Russian line broken to south-east, 26.**5**.

DUBISSA, RIVER (Kovna).
Russians cross, 16.**5**; Russians and Germans claim success, 23.**5**; Russian line broken, 20.**7**.

DUBNO (Volhynia).
German offensive develops towards Rovno, 4.**9**; Fighting begins north of, on River Styr, 5.**9**; Entry of, by Austrians, 7.**9**; Fighting north,west of, 22.**9**; Russians in region of, retire to River Ikva, 25.**9**; Russian retirement north of, 28.**9**.

DUKLA PASS (Carpathians).
Fighting at, 26-29.**1**, 1.**2**; Austrians enter, 5.**5**; Retreat of Russians from, 8.**5**.

DUMA votes grant for refugees, 5.**8**; Enquiry *re* munition supply, 10.**8**.

DUMBA, DR. K. T. (Austro-Hungarian Ambassador to U.S.A.).
Compromised by " Archibald " documents, 6.**9**; Interview with Mr. Lansing, 8.**9**: Recall demanded by U.S.A. Govt, 9.**9**; Recalled by Austrian Govt, " for consultation," 17.**9**; Letter of protest to Mr. Lansing, 7.**9**; Refused safe conduct by U.S.A. State Department, 23.**9**; United States not satisfied with recall " on leave," 27.**9**; Recalled unconditionally ; Departure settled, 28.**9**; Sails for home, 5.**10**.

DUNAJEC, RIVER. (v. Donajetz River).

DUNKIRK.
Raided by German aeroplanes, 10, 22, 28.**1**; 28, 29, 30.**4**, 10.**5**, and at other times ; Zeppelin raid, 17.**5**.

DURAZZO (Albania).
Bombarded by Albanians, 10, 16, 28.**4**; Serbians enter, 4.**7**; Serbians evacuate, 17.**7**; Shelled by Austrian squadron, 6.**12**; Italians meet Serbians ; Three Italian battalions occupy town, 21.**12**.

DUTCH.
Increase of Landstorm by, 30.**7**.

DVINA, RIVER (North Russia).
Crossing forced by Germans at Lennewaden and Friedrichstadt, 3.**9** : Success of Russians on, 21-22.**9**; Heavy fighting along, from Dvinsk to Friedrichstadt, 29.**9** to 25.**10**.

DVINSK.
Russian civilians evacuate, 11.**8**; Germans advancing on from three directions, 11.**9**; Vigorous German offensive towards, 13.**9**; Continued progress, 15.**9**; Enemy surround, 16.**9**; Struggle for bridgehead, 17.**9**; Further German attacks, 18.**9**; Desperate fighting near, 20-22.**9**; Fierce struggle round continues, 24.**9**; Germans launch big attack, 25.**9**; Russian position south-west captured, 26.**9**; Struggle round continues, 27.**9**; Stubborn fighting round north-west and south of, 29.**9** to end of October ; Especially in Lake district to south, 30.**9** to 11.**10**; Russians hold Germans on the whole; Russian successes, 3.**11**; Russian front again bombarded, 5.**12**

FOUR DE PARIS (Argonne).
Violent fighting between, and Bolante, 9, 14, 18.**3**; French attack to N. of, fails, 20.**4**.

FOURNET, DARTIGE DU, Vice-Admiral.
Appointed C.-in-C. French Naval Forces (Greek waters), 11.**10**.

FRANCE.
Minister of Aviation appointed,14.**9**; State of war between, and Bulgaria, 16.**10**; French Ministry (Viviani) resigns : M. Briand becomes Premier, 28.**10**.

FREIBURG-IM-BREISGAU (Baden).
Bombed by French, 15, 17.**4**, also 30.**7** and 7.**9**.

FRENCH CIVIL POPULATION.
Further report on treatment of French by Germans issued, 10.**3**.

FRENCH FRONT.
Intense artillery activity everywhere, 19.**12**.

FRENCH, SIR JOHN.
Fifth despatch (20.**11**-2.**2**), d. 2.**2**; 6th despatch (2.**2**-5.**4**, Neuve Chapelle), d. 5.**4**, pub. 15.**4**; 7th despatch (15.**4**-15.**6**, second battle of Ypres and Festubert), d. 15.**6**, pub. 11.**7**; 8th despatch (2.**6**-8.**10**, battle of Loos),d. 15.**10**, pub. 2.**11**.; Special order *re* Loos, 30.**9**; Resigns command in field, 15.**12**.

FREZENBERG (Ypres).
German attack, and British retreat, 8-9.**5**.

FRIEDRICHSHAFEN (Lake Constance).
French air raid, 28.**4**.

FRIEDRICHSTADT (Dvina River).
Bridgehead attacked, 29.**8**; Germans capture bridgehead, 3.**9**; Enemy advance S.E. of, 8.**9**.

FRIULI (N.E. Italy).
Italian advance continues over, 25.**5**.

" FRYE, WILLIAM P." s.s. (U.S.A.).
Destroyed by Germans, c.5.**3**; Germany apologizes, 15.**3**; U.S.A. Note demanding indemnity, 5.**4**; U.S.A. protest at German Prize Court decision, 28.**4**; Germany notifies U.S.A. of Prize Court decision, 18.**5**; British and German Notes received in U.S.A., 2.**8**; U.S.A. reply *re*, 10.**8**.

FURKA (Macedonia).
Bulgarians attack, lose 8,000 men, 11.**12**.

FURNES (Belgium).
Enemy bombards, 24-27.**10**.

GABA TEPE (Anzac; v. also Gallipoli).
Landing of Anzacs; fighting, 25.**4**; Heavy fighting at, 9-31.**5**, 30.**6**, 4.**7**; Attack and carry Lone Pine, 6-7.**8**; Severe fighting towards Khojah Chemen; repulsed, 7-9.**8**; Turkish counter-attack, 10.**8**; Anzac left takes part of Hill 60, 22.**8**; Consolidates it, with others, 27.**8**.

GALATA BRIDGE (Constantinople).
Blown up by British submarine, 1.**8**.

GALICIA.
Russians aligned along Donajetz River and Carpathians tb Bukovina, Jan.-Feb. ; Austrians attack in Carpathians, end of Jan. ; Held up at Kosziowa (Uzsok), end of Feb. ; Russians hold passes covering Przemysl, end of March ; Capture of Przemysl by Russians, 22.**3**; Mackensen. forces Donajetz and Biala lines, 28.**4**-2.**5**; and the Visloka, 7-8.**5**; Russians fall back behind the San, 12.**5**; Fall of Jaroslav, 16.**5**; Battle of the San, 15.**5**-2.**6**; Stryj lost, 1.**6**; Przemysl falls to the enemy, 2.**6**; Brusilov beats von Bothmer on the Dniester, 8-11.**6**; Russians fall back on Grodek position, 14.**6**; Russians beaten at Rava Russka, 20.**6**; Lemberg falls to the Austrians, 22.**6**; Russian retreat continues, 25.**6**; Lose Halicz, 28.**6**; Successful Russian counter-attack on the Strypa River, 30-31.**8**; Russian resistance in east, on Sereth River, 6.**9**; Strong Russian successful counter-attack : take 80,000 prisoners, 7.**9**-17.**9**; Austrians defeated near Tlusto, 22.**9**; Heavy fighting near Novo Alexinetz and Tarnopol, 29.**9**-9.**10**; Ivanov's victory on Strypa, 11-12.**10**; Further indecisive fighting, 13,21.**10**, and in Nov. ; Ivanov attacks enemy on the Strypa, 24-28.**12**, and pushes for Bukovina, Dec. ; Strong Russian offensive, 31.**12**.

GALLIPOLI (v. also Dardanelles).
Landing of British forces at Cape Helles, and of Australians and New Zealanders at Gaba Tepe, (Anzac Bay), severe fighting both places, 25.**4**; French on Southern shore, 25.**4**; Establishing French and British forces across peninsula (French back), 27-29.**4**; First battle of Krithia : Turkish attack repulsed, 1-4.**5**; Unsuccessful fighting at Gaba Tepe, 2-4.**5**; British and French civilians sent from Constantinople to —, 6.**5**, and back, 14.**5**; second battle of Krithia ; very heavy fighting ; advance 1,000 yds, 6-8.**5**; Heavy fighting at Anzac, 9, 10, 18, 19-5; Gen. Bridges, commanding Anzacs, killed, 15.**5**; Truce agreed on, 24.**5**; Capture of " Le Haricot " by French, 28.**5**; Turkish repulse 28.**5**, 3.**6**; Third battle of Krithia : severe fighting advance 500 yds, 4.**6**; Turkish attacks, 1, 5, 11, 16, 18.**6**; French attacks 21.**6**; British attacks, 28.**6**; Turkish attack on our right and at Anzac driven off, Gen. Gouraud wounded, 29-30.**6**, 1-2.**7**; General Turkish attacks repulsed, 4-5.**7**; Allies attack, little result, 14.**7**; Various attacks by both sides, 13, 21, 23, 28.**7**; Our losses nearly 50,000 to date ; Great British attack be-

GOLTZ, MARSHAL VON DER.
Commands Turks in Mesopotamia, 24.11.

GORIZIA (R. Isonzo).
Italians attack bridgehead, 9-22.7; Italians evacuate positions before, 28.7; Austrians regain bridgehead, 26.10; Incessant Italian bombardment, 28.10; Italian offensive, 1-3.30.11.

GORLICE (Carpath.).
Fighting near, 2.1; 9, 18, 28.3; Repulse of Austrians, 20.4; Capture by Austro-Germans, 2.5.

GOTHLAND.
Russo-German naval action off, 2.7.

GOUNARIS, M. (Athens).
Succeeds in forming Cabinet, 10.3; Secures majority at Greek elections, 19.12.

GRADO (N. Adriatic).
Austrian aeroplanes bomb, 9.9.

GRAFENSTAFEL (Ypres).
German gas attack and fierce fighting, 23-26.4.

GRAHOVO.
Montenegrins attacked at, 27.8.

GREAT BRITAIN.
British answer to U.S.A. Note on sea policy published, 9.1; Inter-Allied Financial Conference,6.2; German submarine blockade, 18.2; Industrial unrest, March, November; Budget for 1,132 millions (Lloyd George), 4.5; Bryce Report issued, 12.5; Defence of the Realm Bill, 12.5; Coalition Government and New Cabinet, 3.6; Ministry of Munitions Bill, 9.6; Second Finance Bill, 14.6; 4½ per cent. War Loan Bill, 21.6; Welsh Miners troubles, July to September; Munitions of War Bill, 2.7; War Loan reaches £585,000,000, 13.7; National Registration Bill passed, 14.7; Third War Budget of 1,590 millions (McKenna), 21.9; Declaration of War on Bulgaria, 15.10; Offers Cyprus to Greece, 17.10; Offer rejected, 21.10; Third Finance Bill, 21.10; Derby Scheme issued, 21.10; Blue Book re no separate peace issued, 29.10; Mr. Asquith's statement on situation, 2.11; Government buy or borrow all American and Canadian securities in Great Britain, 13.12; 5 per cent. Exchequer Bonds issued, 16.12; Compulsory service principle accepted by Cabinet, 28.12.

GREECE.
Gounaris Cabinet, 10.3; Note to Bulgaria pointing out danger of incursions, 6.4; M. Venizelos gains 193 seats out of 316 and forms Ministry, 13.6; M. Venizelos resigns, 16.8; New Cabinet under M. Zaimis, 23.8; Objection to Serbian cessions to Bulgaria, and condition of Greco-Serbian frontier, 10.9; King Constantine signs general mobilisation decree, 23.9;

Perfect agreement between King and M. Venizelos, reported, 25.9; Allied victory in Champagne increases enmity against Central Powers, 28.9; M. Zaimis declares neutral policy of, M. Venizelos exposes danger of, 11.10; Refuses Serbia's appeal for help against Bulgaria, 12.10; British Government offers Cyprus, 14.10; Offer rejected 21.10; King makes statement of his attitude towards the war, 25.10; M. Skouloudis, Prime Minister, 4.11; Promises of Government to Lord Kitchener 20.11; Answer to the Quadruple Note, 25.11; German mission, 11.11; Chamber dissolved, 12.11; Pacific blockade of, proclaimed, 19.11; M. Skouloudis refuses Bulgarian troops entry into, 17.12.

GREEK FRONTIER.
Franco-British troops withdraw towards, 13.12.

GRETNA GREEN.
Troop-train disaster at Quintonshill, 22.5.

GREY, SIR EDWARD.
Presides at Conference of Ambassadors in London, 23.4; Correspondence re. Prize Courts published, 3.8; Account of last interview with Prince Lichnowsky published,30.8; On Balkan situation, 2.10; On British policy in Near East, 14.10.

GRODEK (Gal.).
Russians occupy line, 14.5; Russians retreat from, to position in front of Lemberg, 19.6.

GRODNO (R. Niemen).
Continued German attacks on, 1-5.3; Germans bombard, 5.5; Enemy nears, 29.8; Outer forts captured by Germans, 1.9; Fall of, 2.9; Russian temporary re-entry, 3.9; Russian resistance N.E. of, 16.9.

"GULFLIGHT," S.S.
U.S. oil vessel torpedoed by German submarine. 1.5.

"HAAKON VII."
Norwegian mail-steamer stopped by Germans, 19.8.

HAFIZ KHOR (Indian frontier).
Mohmands defeated, 5.9.

HAIG, SIR DOUGLAS.
Succeeds Sir John French as C.-in-C., 15.12.

HAJVORUKA (Strypa).
Russians storm enemy position, 11.10; Capture village S. of, 12.10; Enemy recaptures, 13.10.

HALICZ (Gal.).
Occupied by Germans, 27.6; Germans repulsed near, 29.6.

HALICZ-BUKACZOWCE (Gal.).
Repulse of Germans on front of, followed by Russian retirement. 26.6.

HAMADAN (Persia).
Rebels defeated by Russians, 9.**12**; Occupied by Russians, 11.**12**.

HAMBURG.
Three British steamers detained at beginning of war, sunk in harbour, (Lloyd's), 23.**10**.

"HAMIDIA," THE (Turkish Cruiser).
Damaged by Russian torpedo boat in Black Sea, 6.**9**.

HAMILTON, SIR IAN.
Appointed to command Dardanelles Expeditionary Force, end of February ; First despatch of 20.**5** (13.**3** to 5.**5**), issued, 5.**7** ; Second despatch, 26.**8** (5.**5** to 30.**6**) ; Third despatch, 11.**12** (6.**5** to 17.**10**) ; Relieved by Gen. Monro, 16.**10**.

"HARICOT, LE," (Gall.).
Capture by French, 20.**5**.

"HARPALYCE "(Belgian Relief Ship).
Torpedoed, 10.**4**.

HARTMANNSWEILERKOPF (Alsace). (Vosges).
Fighting at, 20.**1**, 22.**1** ; French re-attack, 5.**3** ; Gain summit, 26.**3** ; Stubborn fighting for, 6-26.**4** ; Temporary German gain on, 9.**9** ; French progress reported, 21.**9** ; Heavy fighting for, 4-18.**10**, and 21-23.**12**.

HASUUR (S.W. Africa).
Occupied by Union forces, 1.**4**.

HÉBUTERNE.
French advance S. of, and German counter-attack repulsed, 7-12.**6**.

HEJAZ RAILWAY (v. Damascus).

HELLES, CAPE
British false attack, 19.**12**.

HERACLEA (v. Eregli).

HERZEGOVINA.
Austrians repulsed in, 2.**2**.

" HESPERIAN " (Allan Liner).
Torpedoed off Irish coast, 4.**9** ; Semi-official German denial of responsibility, 14.**9** ; Admiralty proof of enemy attack, 20.**9** ; Declaration by German Admiralty concerning, and Capt. Smellie's report, 24.**9**.

HET SAS (Ypres).
Fighting at, 23.**4** to 17.**5**.

HILL 60 (S. Ypres).
Capture by British, 17.**4** ; German attacks repulsed, 18-21.**4** and 1.**5** ; Success-ful German gas attack, 5.**5** ; Re-capture by British, 6.**5**.

HILL 70 (Loos).
Captured by British, 25.**9** ; Position N. of, lost, 26.**9** ; Brilliant attack by Guards on, 27.**9** ; Ground N. of, re-captured, 28.**9**.

HILL 140 (Vimy Ridge).
French capture, 29.**9**.

HOBOKEN (Antwerp).
Submarine works at, bombed, 24.**3** ; British air raid, 1.**4**.

HOCHROD (Alsace).
Occupied by Germans, 21.**2**.

HOHENZOLLERN REDOUBT (Loos).
Partially s t o r m e d, 25.**9** ; Fierce struggle round, 29.**9** ; Enemy retakes greater part of, 3.**10** ; Germans bomb S. portion of, 4.**10** ; British capture main trench of, 13.**10**.

HOLLAND.
Tension with Germany, 8.**4** ; Suspen-sion of sea traffic with the United King-dom, 22.**4** ; Navigation re-opened, 1.**5** ; New Naval programme, 30.**7** ; Queen Wilhelmina re-asserts neutrality, 21.**9** ; Proof of extensive contraband trade, 24.**9**.

HOOGE (Ypres).
Germans attack château, 9.**5** ; Fight-ing at, 30-31.**5** ; British advances N. of, 15.**6** ; German trenches near, captured, 19.**7** ; German counter-attacks repulsed, 24.**7** ; British lines at, pierced, 30.**7** ; Lost trenches at, re-captured, 9.**8** ; British lose Bellewarde Farm and Ridge, 25.**9** ; Enemy trench S.W. of, captured, 25.**9** ; Germans gain footing in British front line, 29.**9** ; lost trenches at, mostly recovered, 1.**10**.

HORODENKA (Dniester and Pruth area).
Defeat of Austrians, 11.**5**.

HOUTHULST (Ypres).
Forest of, fired by British artillery, 20.**9**.

HULLUCH (Loos).
British capture western outskirts of, 25.**9** ; German counter-attacks repulsed N.W. of, 27.**9** ; severe fighting N.W. of, Germans gain footing, 30.**9** ; British capture 1,000 yards near, but unable to hold, 13.**10** ; German attack repulsed, 19.**10** ; German success at, 31.**12**.

HUSSAKOW (Przemysl).
Heavy indecisive fighting, 16-27.**5**.

" HUSSAR," H.M.S.
Bombards coast opposite Chios, 27.**6**.

" HYTHE," H.M.S.
Sunk in collision off Gallipoli, 28.**10**.

" IBERIAN," S.S.
Torpedoed, 30.**7**.

IKVA, RIVER (Brody).
Voinitza captured by Russians, 22.**9** ; Violent encounters on, 24.**9** ; Russians retire towards, 25.**9**.

ILLORI (Libau).
Russian repulse by Germans, 30.**5**.

ILLUKST (Dvina R.).
Russians occupy heights N.W. of, 12.**10** ; Germans storm, 23.**10** ; Furious fighting E. of, 25-26.**10** ; Russian success at, 24 and 29.**11**.

" INDIA," H.M.S.
Torpedoed, 8.**8**.

INDIA.
Gift of guns by, 27.**4**.

INDIA (N.W. Frontier).
Raid repulsed, 18·**4**; Irruption of Bunerwals into Peshawar district, 17.**8**; Bunerwals successfully engaged by Rustam column, 26, 28, and 31.**8**; British position at Sandaki attacked; Defeat of Mohmands, 5.**9**; Defeat of native force at Kak Fort, 28-29.**9**; British force attacks and defeats Mohmands, 8.**10**.

INDIAN CORPS.
Leaves France for " another field of action," 28.**12**.

" INDIEN " (French Aux. Cr.).
Torpedoed off Rhodes, 8.**9**.

INNSBRUCK.
Bombed, 23.**7**.

IPEK (Serbia).
Captured by Austrians, 7.**12**.

ISHTIP (Serbia).
Occupied by Bulgarians, 25.**10**.

ISMAILÍA (Suez Canal).
Feint on, 2.**2**.

ISMID (Sea of Marmora).
Lt. D'Oyly Hughes tries to cut railway (single-handed) at, 21.**8**.

ISONZO, RIVER.
Italian advance hindered by floods, 9.**6**; Italians capture heights on left bank, dominating Plava, 17.**7**; Battle on, develops, 18-21.**7**; Italian progress, 25.**7**; Italian offensive resumed, 10.**8**; Fighting on upper, 4.**9**; Austrian artillery bombard towns on lower, 6.**9**; Austrian planes bomb Italian camp, 7.**9**; Austrians strongly reinforced on, 14.**9**; Italians repulse enemy at various points, 9.**10**; More fighting on, 20.**10**; Italians take many prisoners, 23.**10**; Fighting on, 2-3, 28.**11**.

ISPAHAN (Persia).
Russian vice-consul murdered, 7.**5**; Outrage on British Consul-General, 2.**9**; British and Russian Consuls and Bank managers threatened, 8.**9**; European residents evacuate, 11.**9**.

ITALIAN FRONTIER.
Austrian Emperor agrees to rectification of, if Italy neutral, 8.**3**.

ITALIAN MILITARY ATTACHÉ.
Leaves Vienna for Rome, 21.**3**.

ITALIAN NAVAL FEAT.
T.B.D. sinks Austrian munitions ship, and rams submarine, 21.**12**.

ITALY.
Sonnino's Note to Austria formulates demands, 8.**4**; Austrian answer, 25.**4**; Note to Austria, ending Triple Alliance, 3.**5**; Demonstrations in favour of war, 14.**5**; Extraordinary powers conferred on Government by Chamber and Senate, 20-21.**5**; Green Book on Austro-Italian negotiations issued, 20.**5**; Mobilisation ordered, 22.**5**; Declares war on Austria, 23.**5**; Note to Italian representatives and to foreign powers, 23.**5**; Declares blockade of Austro-Hungarian and Albanian coasts, 26.**5**; War on Turkey, 20.**8**.

ITALY, KING OF.
C.-in-C. Italian forces, 26.**5**.

IVANGOROD.
Invested, 21.**7**; Fall of, 5.**8**.

JABLONITZA PASS (E. Carp.).
Taken by Austrians, 12.**2**.

" J'ACCUSE ! " (by H. Fernau).
Seized in Switzerland, 15.**7**.

JACKSON, ADMIRAL SIR H.
First Sea Lord, 27.**5**.

JACOBSTADT (Dvina).
Russians take offensive in district of, 11.**9**; Fighting near, 6, 17, 27.**10**.

JAFFA.
Munition factory destroyed at, 12.**8**.

JAPAN.
Proposals to China *re* claims, 26.**4**; Note from China, 1.**5**; Ultimatum to China, 7.**5**; Acceptance by China, 8.**5**; Treaty with China, 25.**5**; Political crisis in, 30.**7**; New Cabinet formed, 10.**8**; Approval of compact between Allies, 31.**10**.

JAPANESE STEAMER.
Sunk by German submarine, 9.**11**.

JAROSLAV (Przemysl).
Occupation by Austro-Germans, 14.**5**.

JASIN (Germ. E. Africa).
Besieged by Germans, 13.**1**; Three companies British surrender (except 40), 19.**1**.

JERABLUS.
Railway bridge over Euphrates opened, 27.**4**.

JERUSALEM.
Railway from, to Beersheba, opened, 9.**8**.

JOFFRE, GENERAL.
Returns to French H.Q. after visiting Italian front; Message to General Cadorna 7.**9**; Order of the Day, before the assault of 25.**9**; Published in England, 1.**10**; C.-in-C. of all French armies, 3.**12**.

JOHANNISBURG (E. Prussia).
Re-taken by Germans, 8.**2**.

KABUS (S.W. Africa).
Defeat of Germans, 20.**4**.

KACHANIK PASS (Serbia).
Occupied by Bulgarians, 28.**10**; Partly recovered by Serbians, 11.**11**.

KAISER.
Manifesto by, 1.**8**.

N

KOVNA-OSOVYETS-BREST LITOVSK.
Russians withdraw to line of, 16.8.

KRAGUYEVATS.
Chief Serbian arsenal taken by Austro-Germans, 30.10.

KRALYEVO (Serbia).
Passage of W. Morava River forced by Austro-Germans, 7.11.

KRASNIK (S. Poland).
Occupied by Austrians, 7.1; Latter driven out in February; Archd. Josef Ferdinand occupies, 2.7; Badly beaten, 5-9.7.

KRASNOSTAV (Poland).
Germans checked at, 5.7; German success near, 18.7.

KREUZBERG RIDGE (Tyrolese frontier).
Fighting in district of, 5-7.9.

KRITHIA (Gall.).
Desperate fighting near, 28.4 to 8.5, 4.6; Attacks on, 30.6, 12.7.

KRIVOLAK (Serbia).
Evacuated by French, 7.12.

"KRONPRINZ WILHELM" (Armed N. German Lloyd).
Entered Newport News, U.S.A., 11.4; Interned at, 26.4.

KRUSHEVATS (Serbia).
Reached by Austro-Germans, 7.11.

KUBAS (S.W. Africa).
Occupation by Union Forces, 1.5.

KUM (Persia).
Taken by Russians, 20.12.

KUMANOVO (Serbia).
Bulgarians advancing towards from E., 17.10; Bulgarians capture, 21.10.

KUM KALE (Gall.).
French land and re-embark, 25, 26.4.

KURDS.
Driven back N.E. of Lake Van, Armenia, 17.12.

KURNA (Mesopotamia).
Turks attack British, 11-12.4; British victory, 31.5.

KÜSTENDIL (Bulg.).
Bulgarians advancing from, threatening Nish-Salonika Railway, 17.10.

KUT-EL-AMARA (Mesop.).
Defeat of Turks at, 28.9; Townshend's force falls back to, 3.12; Siege begins, 5.12; Turkish attacks repulsed, 8-11.12; British success, 17-18.12; Further Turkish attacks repulsed, 23-25.12.

KYELTSI (Poland).
Occupation by Germans, 12.5.

LA BASSÉE.
Repulse of German attacks near, 25.1, 29.1, 1.2; British gain near, 25.2; British advance in region of, 16, 24, 25.5; Heavy artillery action from, 9, 14-17, 24.10.

LA BASSÉE (Canal).
British deny German success S. of, 23.9; Enemy trenches captured S. of, 25.9.

LABOUR.
Labour ministry in South Australia, 1.4; Labour recruiting campaign meeting, 30.9; Sydney Labour Council opposes Compulsory Service, 30.9; M. Albert Thomas addresses Labour meeting, 6.10; Committee issues Manifesto, 6.10; Mr. Asquith and Lord Kitchener address Labour Conference on military situation, 7-8.9.

"LABOUR LEADER," THE.
Offices raided, 18.5.

"LABYRINTH," THE (N. Arras).
French progress, 28-31.5; Fighting at, 1.6; German attacks repulsed, 12.7; French take trenches N. of, 25.9; Severe fighting, 14.11; German attack repulsed, 27.11.

LA FILLE MORTE (Arg.).
Germans repulsed, 27.8; Heavy fighting at, 4, 7, 10.10.

LA FOLIE (Vimy).
French reach, 26.9; French progress on heights of, 1 and 11.10.

LAGARINA VALLEY (Trent.)
Fighting in, 18-19.10.

LAGOSTA ISLAND (Dalmatia).
French operations on, 26.7.

LAHEJ (Aden).
Attacked by Turks, 4.7; Evacuated by British, 5.7; Death of Sultan of, 13.1.

LANGEMARCK (Ypres).
Capture by Germans, 23.4; Bombed by British, 26.4.

LA PANNE (Belgium).
Bombed by 6 German aeroplanes, 20.12.

LATIN-AMERICAN ARBITRATION TREATY.
Between Argentine, Brazil and Chile, 25.5.

LAUCH VALLEY (Vosges).
German attacks in, 13-14.2.

LECZNA-KHOLM (Poland).
Line evacuated by Russians, 2.8.

LEDRO VALLEY (Trent.).
Italian surprise attack in, 5.9; Brilliant Italian success in, 22.10; Italians command, 25.10.

"LEELANAW," s.s. (American).
Torpedoed, 25.7; U.S.A. Note to Germany re, 29.7.

LEINTREY (Lorraine).
Heavy fighting, with severe French losses, 8-22.10.

LEMBERG.
Re-captured by Austrians, 22.6.

MACEDONIA.
Bulgarians bombard Valandova,15.**10**;
Bulgarians enter Ishtip and Radovishte,
19.**10**; Bulgarians capture Veles 20.**10**;
Bulgarians capture Üsküb, 22.**10**; French
occupy Strumitsa Station, 29.**10**; Fall of
Monastir, 5.**12**; Allies retreat in, 7 to 13.**12**.

MACHAK (Serbia).
Fierce fighting at, E. of Knyazhevats,
24.**10**.

MACKENSEN, GENERAL VON.
Commands powerful offensive in W.
Galicia, April; Held up at Krasnostav,
5.**5**; Advancing between Vistula and
Bug, 29.**6**. C.-in-C. invasion Serbia, Oct.

MAHON, Lieut.-Gen. SIR B.
Appointed C.-in-C. British troops
Salonika front, 28.**10**.

MAILS (Neutral).
Statement concerning, issued by British Government, 31.**7**.

MAISONS DE CHAMPAGNE.
French repulse Germans near, 1.**10**;
Hostile bombardment, 12, 28.**10**.

MAIZERAY (Woevre).
French advance towards, 5.**4**; Failure
of French attacks, 13.**4**.

" MAJESTIC," H.M.S.
Torpedoed off Gallipoli, 27.**5**.

MAKTAN (E. Africa).
Fighting 10 miles S. of, 3.**9**; British
success at, 14.**9**.

MALANDRI PASS (Indian Frontier).
Bunerwals engaged near, end of Aug.

MALBORGHETTO (Carn.).
Fortress of, bombarded, 12.**6**.

MANDARA (Cameroons).
German positions captured, 20.**4**.

MANGELES (Cameroons).
Taken after five days' fighting, 21.**12**.

**" MANITOU," ** Transport.
Sunk in Aegean, 16.**4**.

MARCO (Trent.).
Italian successes near, 4.**9**.

MARIAMPOL (Pol.).
Occupied by Germans, 12.**2**.

MARINE BLOCKADE.
U.S.A. objection to Anglo-French, 10.**3**.

MARITZ (S.A. rebel).
Attacks Upington, 24.**1**.

MARMORA (Sea of).
British submarine sinks German transport in, 2.**6**.

**" MARQUETTE " ** (British Transport).
Torpedoed in Aegean (announced),
26.**10**.

MASSIGES (Champ.).
French progress N. of, 28.**9**; Germans
surrender N. of, 29.**9**; French take Hill
191, 30.**9**; Germans bombard, 12.**10**;

French capture trench, 26.**10**; Severe
fighting at, 5.**11**.

MAUNOURY, GENERAL.
Military Governor of Paris, 2.**11**.

McKENNA, RT. HON. R.
Introduces Budget, 21.**9**.

MEDAL.
Naval General Service, instituted, 8.**8**.

**" MEDEA " ** (Dutch s.s.).
Torpedoed by German submarine, 25.**3**.

MEDINA (Arabia).
Railway from Damascus completed,
early 1915.

**" MEDJIDIA " ** (Turkish Cruiser).
Sunk by mine off Odessa, 3.**4**.

MEISZAGOLA (Vilna).
Battle of, near Vilna, begins, 2.**9**;
Desperate fighting; finishes with Russian
retreat, 16.**9**.

MELAZGERD (Armenia).
Re-occupied by Russians, 12.**8**.

MEMEL (E. Prussia).
Invaded by Russians, 18.**3**; Retaken
by Germans, 21.**3**.

MERCIER, CARDINAL.
Arrest of, for pastoral letter, 3.**1**.

MERCKEM (Flan.).
Retreat of Germans to, 6.**4**.

MERSA MATRUH (Egypt).
Arabs defeated near, 11-13 and 25.**12**.

MERSINA (S. Asia Minor).
Turks fortifying, and deporting Armenians from, 19.**9**.

MESNIL (Meuse).
Fighting near, 1.**1**; French progress
near, 24-26.**2**; French attack German line
N. of, and make progress despite counter-
attacks, 26.**2** to 16.**3**; Fighting at, 8, 28,
30.**4**; Fight for salient N. of, 29.**9**; Heavy
fighting at, 1-3.**10**; Enemy bombards
Butte de, 12.**10**.

MESOPOTAMIA.
Sir J. Nixon takes command, January;
British reconnaissance on Ahwaz (Kurun
River), driven back, 3.**3**; Cavalry at Nak-
haila, 11.**3**; British repel Turkish attack
on Basra (Shaiba), 13-17.**4**; British beat
Turks at Kurna, 31.**5**, Amara, 3.**6**, and
Nasriya (Euphr.), 25.**7**; Attack and
occupy Kut-el-Amara, 28, 29.**9**; Towns-
hend presses N. towards Baghdad, Oct-
ober; Battle of Ctesiphon, 22-22.**11**;
Retires, and reaches Kut, 3.**12**; Siege of
Kut begins, 5.**12**; Turkish assaults
repulsed, 24.**12** et seqq; Turks build
five lines of defence between Kut and main
British force, December.

METTERNICH, COUNT WOLFF.
Appointed German Ambassador Extraordinary in Constantinople, 30.**10**.

METZ (Germany).
Successfully bombed by French, 26.**3**;
French long range bombardment of Fort

Patriotic message of engineering and ship-building societies, 10.**4**; Mr. Lloyd George, Minister of Munitions, 25.**5**; Mr. Lloyd George speaks on, at Liverpool, 4.**6**, and Bristol, 11.**6**; Conditions for Anglo-French agreement, 8.**10**; Representatives present report from front, 11.**10**.

MUNITIONS (Ministry of).
Bill to create, introduced, 3.**6**; amended 8.**6**; passed, 15.**6**; Text published, 25.**6**.

MUNITIONS OF WAR ACT.
To House of Lords, 2.**7**; Government decides to apply to Welsh miners, 13.**7**; 345 establishments controlled under, 6.**8**; 714 establishments controlled under, 7.**9**.

MUNITION WORKS.
Bill for giving Government powers over, 9.**3**; Trade Unions agree to expedite, 19.**3**.

MUSH (Armenia).
Russians retire near, 27.**7**.

NAGARA (Dard.).
Bombardment by Allied Fleet, 9.**5**; Turkish transports sunk off, 29.**8**.

NAKHAILA (Mesop.).
Turks retreat to, 14.**4**; Occupation by Anglo-Indian cavalry, 17.**4**.

NANCY.
Bombed, 12, 28.**4**; 29, 31.**7**; 16.**10**.

NAREV, RIVER (Poland).
German offensive fails, 26.**2**; Heavy artillery fighting right bank, 9.**3**; Enemy offensive on, 12.**7**; Enemy advance checked, 14.**7**; Russians retire towards, 17.**7**; Russians concentrate on, 19.**7**; Germans cross, 23.**7**; Germans cross above Ostrolenka, 24-25.**7**; Germans held on, 26.**7**; Reached by enemy near Lomzha, 2.**8**; Lomzha occupied, 27.**8**.

NAROCH, LAKE (Vilna).
Desperate fighting, 3.**10**; Hotly contested during autumn.

NASRIYA (Mesop.).
Turks driven from, 14.**7**; Fight outside, 24.**7**; Occupied by British, 25.**7**.

"NATAL," H.M.S.
Sunk in harbour, internal explosion, 30.**12**.

NATIONAL REGISTRATION.
Mr. Asquith announces forthcoming Bill, 24.**6**; Bill introduced, 29.**6**; Third reading, 8.**7**; House of Lords, 14.**7**; Taken, 15.**8**.

NATIONAL SERVICE.
Register taken ,15.**8**; Manifesto on, 16.**8**; Women's meeting, Queens' Hall in support of, 3.**9**; Trade Union Congress debate on, 7.**9**; Second Women's meeting, 10.**9**; Mr. Lloyd George's letter on, 20.**9**.

NATIONAL VOLUNTEERS (Irish).
Review and Convention at Dublin, 4-5.**4**.

NAVARIN FARM (Champ).
French success, 29.**9**; Heavy fighting about, 1-9.**10**.

NAVY (U.S.A.)
New 5-years programme for increasing 14.**10**.

" NEBRASKAN " (U.S.A. s.s.)
Torpedoed off Coast of Ireland, 25.**5**.

NEGOTIN (Vardar River, Serb.).
Captured by Bulgars, 24.**10**; Serbs. driven beyond, 26.**10**.

NEJD (Arabia).
Declares its independence, 26.**7**.

NEPAL.
Gift of guns received from Maharaja, 27.**4**.

NEUTRAL COMMERCE.
British memorandum on, to U.S.A., 24.**6**.

NEUTRAL MAILS.
German violation of, 5.**7**.

NEUVE CHAPELLE.
British successful attack, 10-12.**3**; 1,400 prisoners taken.

NEUVILLE ST. VAAST (Vimy).
Heavy fighting; French progress, 10-26.**5**; Entirely in French hands, 8.**6**; Severe hand-to-hand fighting, 16-22.**9**; French progress beyond, 8.**10**; Heavy fighting at, 15, 27.**10**.

NEW SOUTH WALES.
Compulsory Service League formed; 20.**9**.

NEW ZEALAND.
National Cabinet for, 4.**8**; National Registration Bill passed, 24.**9**; ditto enforced, 26.**10**.

NICHOLAS II., EMPEROR.
Issues fine manifesto, 1.**8**; Speech, at first meeting of Special Conference of National Defence, 4.**9**; Takes supreme command of the Russian forces, 5.**9**; Exchanges messages with President Poincaré, 7.**9**.

NICHOLAS, GRAND DUKE.
Relieved of chief command and appointed Viceroy of the Caucasus, 3.**9**.

NIEMEN, RIVER.
Crossed by Germans, 24.**2**; Russians repulse German attacks, 1, 10, 27, 28.**3**; Russian positions on, abandoned, 22.**8**; Germans thrown back over, near Novo Grodek, 3.**10**.

NIEUPORT (Flan.).
Fighting near, 16.**1**; Reciprocal heavy bombardment near, 7.**10**.

NISH.
Communications with Belgrade cut, 11.**10**; and with Prahovo, 13.**10**; Taken by Bulgarians, 5.**11**.

NISHAVA VALLEY (Serb.).
Bulgarian offensive, 14.**10**; Serbians lose and re-capture positions, 24.**10**.

PACT OF LONDON.
Italy adheres, 1.12; Declaration published, 6.12.
PADON PASS (Tyrol).
Italians repulsed, 26.5.
"PAKLAT " (German steamer).
Correspondence published concerning seizure of the, 20.4.
PALANKA (Serbia).
Serbians defeated S.W. of, 25.10.
"PANTELEIMON " (Russian battleship).
Torpedoed in Black Sea, 22.5.
PAPEN, VON, v. **BOY-ED.**
PARIS.
German air raid, 22.5.
PARLIAMENTARY CONTROL.
French Chamber agrees to, of Army, 27.7.
PARROY (Lorraine).
Enemy repulsed S. of Forest of, 2.10; Fighting in Forest of, 8.10; Violent enemy bombardment, 29.10.
PASHILINA (Dvinsk).
Fierce fighting at, ending in check to enemy, 9.10.16.10.
PEACE.
Chicago Times reports that Germany would discuss terms, 9.4; Papal Note to President Wilson, 13.4; Herr Dernburg's peace campaign in U.S.A., 17.4 Conditions to be proposed by Kaiser (according to Dutch papers), 18.11.
PELAGOSA ISLAND (Mid-Adriatic).
Italians capture, 26.7; Austrians attack, 29.7; Austrians attack again, 17.8; Italians evacuate, 21.8.
PERNAU (Gulf of Riga).
, German attempt to land at, fails, 20.8.
PÉRONNE.
Infantry action S.W. of, 18.9; Mine warfare S.W. of, 20.9.
PERSIA.
Turks take Tabriz, beginning January; Russians beat Turks at Sufian and retake Tabriz, 30.1; Hostile Persian tribesmen appear at Bushire, 12.7; British occupation of Bushire. 7.9 to 29.10; Russians beat much superior force of Turks at Dilman (L. Urmia), beginning May; Numerous local risings against British and Russians, engineered by German Minister, Prince Henry XXXI. of Reuss, autumn; Attack on British and Russian Consuls reported, 27.8; British Consul-General at Ispahan attacked and wounded, 2.9; Disaffection of Gendarmerie and German intrigue, 10.9; British Vice-Consul at Shiraz killed, 9.9; European residents leave Ispahan, 11.9; Reported efforts of Government to deal with unrest in country, 14.9; Reported disbandment of Swedish Gendarmerie, 18.9; Rumour of Alliance with Germany denied, 2.11; Shah re-

ceives Allied Ministers, 12.11; Russians defeat Turks and Germans in, 12.11; Austrian, German and Turkish Ministers leave, Shah refuses to accompany them, 13-14.11; F.O. papers on attacks on Consuls published, 15.11; Prince Firman Firma, takes stern measures with pro-Germans, 21.11; Revolt of Gendarmerie, 22.11; Russians reach Teheran, end of November; Shah's Government defied by Germans, 30.11; Reuss, with 15,000 ruffians at Kum and Hamadan, beginning December; Russians take Hamadan, 11.12; and Kum, 20.12; Prince Firman Firma, Premier, friendly, 25.12.
"PERSIA," s.s. (P. & O.)
Torpedoed off Crete, 30.12.
PERTHES (Champ.).
Captured by French, 8.1; Fighting near, 9-10.1, 1.17.20-21.2 and in March; Heavy fighting N. and N.E. of, 25.9 to 3.10. (See also Mesnil).
PESHAWAR.
Revolt at, 17.8.
PETROGRAD.
Food scarcity begins, 1.11.
"PETROLITE,' s.s.
U.S. steamer attacked by Austrian submarine, 5.12.
PFALZBURG (Lorraine).
Bombed, 30.7.
PICARDY.
British line extended in, 25.8.
PILKEM (Ypres).
Taken by Germans, 23.4; French counter-attacks, 24-26.4; German attack near, repulsed, 8.7; British repulse attack near, 7.8.
PILLKALLEN (E. Prussia).
Russians advance near, 25.1; fall back, 9, 10.2.
PINSK (Polesia).
Mackensen progressing towards, 7.9 Fighting near, 8.9; Continued advance; of enemy on, 15.9; Germans capture, 16.9; Enemy moving eastward of, 17.9; German army corps forced to retreat for Logishin, N. of, 25.9; Heavy German losses in marshes, 28.9; Enemy successes S.W. of, 9.10; Fighting continues, S.W. of 12.10.
PIROT (Serb.).
Outer positions captured by Bulgarians, 18.10; Fighting continued, 25.10; Taken by Bulgarians, 28.10;.
PLAVA (Julian).
Italian advance at, 21.7; Attack by Austrians in zone of, 12.9; Austrians hold Isonzo from, to Tolmino, 19.9; Italians repulse enemy, 9.10; Strong enemy positions taken, 24-26.10.
PLEZZO (Julian).
Continued Italian bombardment, 2.9;

" QUARRIES," THE (Loos).
British take and lose, 25.**9**; British retake, 26.**9**; British repulse repeated attacks, 3.**10**; Capture trench, 13.**10**; Enemy repulsed, 18.**10**.

" QUEEN ELIZABETH," H.M.S.
Shells Narrows forts from Gulf of Saros, 6.**3**; Sinks transport off Maidos (9 miles off, in 3 shots), 27.**4**; at Gallipoli, 28.**4**; Returns to England, June.

QUINN'S POST (Gall.).
Severe fighting near, 9.**5**, 29-31.**5**; See Gaba Tepe.

RABROVO (S. of Strumitsa).
French drive back Bulgars, 21-22.**10**.

RACING (Horse).
Stopped in England, Newmarket excepted, 19.**5**.

RADOM.
Air raid on Russian Hospital, 4.**4**.

RADOM-IVANGOROD.
. Railway reached by Germans, 18.7

RAFALUKA (River Styr).
Important Russian successes near, 17, 19.**10**.

RAILWAY WORKERS.
Unrest in S. Wales and settlement, 5-17.**9**; Executive Council of National Union of, closing meeting and pledges, 17.**9**.

RAM (Danube).
Serbian positions at, shelled, 4.**10**; Austrians cross Danube at, 8.**10**; Repulse of enemy E. of, 9.**10**; Serbian position stormed, 11.**10**.

RAMAN'S DRIFT (S.W. Africa).
Occupied by South Africans, 12.**1**.

" RAMAZAN," H.M.S.
British transport sunk by subm., 19.**9**.

" RAMSAY," H.M.S.
Sunk, 8.**8**.

RAMSGATE.
Zeppelin raid, 17.**5**.

RAVA-RUSSKA (near Lemberg).
Captured by Austro-Germans, 20.**6**.

RAVKA RIVER (W. Poland).
Fighting on, 2, 7, 16, 31.**1**, 1-5, 24.**2**; Russians fail to cross, 1.**4**.

" RECRUIT," H.M.S. (destroyer).
Sunk by German submarine, 1.**5**.

RECRUITING.
Arrangements to secure "unstarred" men, 30.**9**; Urgent meetings, *re* 2.**10**; Lord Derby appointed Director of, 5.**10**; Lord Derby explains scheme, 11.**10**; Lord Derby defines recruiting position, 19.**11**.

RECRUITS.
Need of, stated by Lord Kitchener, 18.**5**; Age limit fixed at 40, 19.**5**; Lord K. states numbers falling off, 15.**9**; Mr. Asquith gives numbers since 1.**1**, 15.**9**.

REDMOND, JOHN.
Speech at the National Volunteer Convention at Dublin, 5.**4**.

REICHSACKERKOPF (Vosges).
. Captured by Germans, 19.**2**; Heavy fighting at, 19.**3**; Fighting to French advantage, 28.**10**.

REILLON (Lorraine).
Heavy fighting near, 8-17.**10**.

REIMS.
Town (and Cathedral occasionally) bombarded, 22, 28.**2**, 3, 23.**3**, 9, 20, 29.**4**, 19, 27.**7**, 9, 21.**8**; Repulse of German attacks E. of 19-27.**10**.

REVAL (Gulf of Finland).
Zeppelins bomb port near, 10.**9**.

RHODESIA.
Fighting on frontier at Saisa, 26.**6**, 6.**9**; Other engagements on border, 12.**7**.

RIGA (Town).
German offensive towards, 15.**7**; Factories evacuated, 25.**7**; Germans repulsed near, 7.**8**; Attacked from the sea, 8, 10.**8**; Evacuated by civilians, 12.**8**; Stripped by Russians early September, 1915; Action near, 20.**9**; Russian success at Stungen, S. of, 22.**9**; Violent cannonade near, 25.**9**; Growing activity on front near, 5.**10**; Fierce fighting on front of, near Mitau, Olai, Üxküll, etc., 19-27.**10**; Retreat of German left wing, 10-14.**11**; German artillery and gas attacks, 9.**12**.

RIGA, GULF OF.
German fleet at entrance of, 8, 12, 16.**8**; Russian naval success, 18.**8**; Naval battle continued, 20.**8**; Enemy positions on, shelled by Russian fleet, 25.**9**.

RIVA (L. Garda).
shelled by Italians, 31.**7**; Italians repulsed near, 25.**10**.

" RIVER CLYDE " (Gall.).
Landing of troops from collier, under terrific fire at Beach V. (Seddul Bahr), 25.**4**.

ROBERTSON, SIR WILLIAM.
Appointed Chief of Imperial Staff, 21.**12**.

ROMANONES, COUNT (Spanish Statesman).
Declared possession of Tangier to be the aspiration of all political parties, 18.**4**.

RONCEGNO (Trent.).
Destruction of by Austrians, 8.**9**.

ROOSEVELT, THEODORE.
Statement *re* Count Bernstorff's Note, 2.**9**.

ROSSKOFEL (Carnic).
Italians reach summit, 25.**10**.

ROSZTOKI PASS (Carpathians).
Russians advance S. of, 7.**4**; Austrians repulsed near, 9.**4** and 20.**4**.

ROUBAIX (Lille).
French Note *re* outrages on civilians at, 31.**7**.

sians, 30.5; Fierce battle of, Russian retreat, 15-16.6.

SANAGA RIVER (Cameroons).
Final success in operations along, helped by Belgian ship "Luxembourg," reported, 6.10.

SANDAKI (Indian frontier).
British attacked by natives, 28-29.8.

SANTA MARIA (Julian).
Italian attacks on, 17.8, 9.9; Counter attacks repulsed, 22.9.

"SAPHIR," French submarine.
Sunk, 17.1.

SAPIGNEUL (Reims).
Fighting at, 11, 15-20.9; Germans withdraw from, 21.9.

SARI BAIR (Gall.).
Crest partially occupied, 7.8.

SARIKAMISH (Transcauc.).
Battle of, Turks heavily defeated, 1-4.1.

SARNY (Polesia).
Severe fighting in zone of, 27-28.9; Enemy's advance checked, 4.10.

SAROS (GULF OF) (Gall.).
Bombardment of Narrows forts from, 6.3; Bombardment of the coast by Allied fleet, 23.4.

SARRAIL, GEN.
Appointed C.-in-C., Near East, 6.8; Arrives at Salonika, 13.10; Withdraws to Vardar River, 10.12.

SASENO, ISLE OF (Alb.).
Occupation by Italians, 30.5.

SAVE RIVER.
Fighting on Serbian front on, 8.9; Enemy movement on, checked by Serb. artillery, 3.10; Checked in some places, enemy crosses at others, 4-9.10; Serbs check crossing at Zabrezie and Jarak, 8-10.10; Fierce fighting at Shabats, 9.10.

SCALANOVA (opp. Samos).
French bombard, 4.8.

SCANDINAVIA.
Inter-parliamentary Union, meeting of Scandinavian groups, Copenhagen, 2-3.9

SCARPE RIVER (Arras).
Heavy reciprocal bombardment N. of, 4-10.10.

SCHEIDEMANN, HERR.
Socialist refusal to discuss cession of Alsace-Lorraine, 9.12.

SCHRATZMÄNNELE (Vosges).
Ridge claimed by both sides, 31.7; French occupy, 18-22.8; stubborn fighting, 12-18.10.

SCOTT, ADM. SIR P.
Appointed Commander London Anti-Aircraft defences, 13.9.

SEDDUL BAHR (Gall.).
Fight for, 26.4.

SEEHEIM (S.W. Africa).
Occupation by Union Forces, 18.4.

SELBORNE, LORD.
Important address to agricultural representatives, 26.8.

SEMENDRIA (Danube).
Serbs driven from positions, 20.9; After heavy fighting, v. Gallwitz crosses Danube, at and below, 9-10.10; Enemy captures town, 11.10; Serbians driven back, 17.10.

SEMLIN.
Bombarded by Serbs, 12.8.

SENDE (Cameroons).
French seize post on Yaunde railway, 25.10.

SENUSSI.
Unrest stirred up by Turks and Germans, July; Apparently friendly attitude towards Egyptian Government, 27.11; Hostilities begin at W. Shaifa, 13.12; Routed at W. Mergid, both near Mersa Matruh, 25.12.

SERAPEUM (Suez Canal).
Turks repulsed at, 3.2.

SERBIA.
Invaded by Albanians, 15-16.2; Government views on Balkan question, 1, 5.9; Enemy checked on Danube, Save, and Drina fronts, 7, 8.9; Fighting along Danube, 19, 20.9; Enemy attempts on Drina fail, 24, 25.9; Enemy air-raids, 29, 30.9; Large concentration of Austro-German troops on N. frontier, 1.10; German failure at Semendria, 3.10; Hostile incursions from Drina front, 5.10; Ultimatum from Bulgaria to, 6.10; Austro-German invasion begun, 7.10; Belgrade occupied by enemy, 9.10; Hostilities with Bulgaria begin, Bulgarians cross frontier at Kadibogas, 11.10; Greece refuses aid against Bulgaria, 12.10; Bulgaria declares war on, 14.10; M. Pashich, Premier, wires to England for help, 27.10; Over-running of, October, November, December; N. Army retreats into Albania and S. Army retreats South, November; Fall of Nish, 6.11; Refuses German peace offers, 26.11; Allies land at Salonika and support, October-December.

SERETH RIVER (Gal.).
Russians retreat towards, 2.9; Crossed by Austrians, 3.9; Russian successes on, 5-9.9; Russian retreat on, 18.9; Enemy captures heights near Tarnopol, 11.10.

SEXTEN VALLEY (Julian).
Italian advance in, 7-13.8.

SHABATS (Save).
Fierce fighting near, 9.10; Austrians advancing towards, 20.10; Matchva Plain cleared of Serbs, 22.10.

SHAIBA (Basra).
British force defeats Turks, 12-14.4.

Whole Colony surrendered, 9.**7**; Terms of surrender published, 10.**7**.

SPELIA (opp. Samos).
Bombarded by French, 4.**8**.

SPEYER, SIR E.
Resigns British honours, 18.**5**; King refuses to accept renunciation, 22.**5**.

SPHINXHAVEN (Lake Nyassa).
Captured by the British under Commander Dennistoun, R.N., 30.**5**.

STANISLAU (Gal.).
Fighting near, 21-22.**2**; Russians retake, 25.**2**; 6,000 Austrian prisoners taken near, '3.**3**; Russians advance continued near, 4.**3**.

STANTON, Mr. C. B.
(Pro-War candidate), elected for Merthyr Tydvil on death of Mr. Keir Hardie, 26.**11**.

STEEL HELMETS.
Introduction on Western front first mentioned, 8.**11**.

STEENSTRAATE (Flan.).
Capture of bridge by Germans, 22.**4**; Capture by Germans, 23.**4**; Destruction of bridge by Belgian artillery, 24.**4**; French advance, 4.**5**; Capture of part of Steenstraate and bridge by French and Belgians, 14.**5**; German counter-attacks repulsed, 15.**5**.

STEINBACH (Vosges).
Capture completed by French, 4.**1**.

STOKHOD, RIVER (Volhynia).
Desperate fighting for crossings, 27, 28.**9**; Russians repel enemy attacks on, 6.**10**.

STOSSWEILER (Vosges).
Occupied by Germans, 21.**2**.

STRASSBURG.
French air raid, 16.**4**.

STRIKES.
Proclaimed conditional offence, 13.**7**.

STRUMITSA REGION (S.W. Bulg.).
Franco-Serbians occupy, 17.**10**; Bulgarian attacks on French line, 8.**11**; Bulgar attacks repulsed by British, 6.**12**.

STRYJ RIVER AND TOWN (E. Gal.).
Russians advance between Stryj and Dolina, taking 7,000 prisoners, 29.**3**; Repulse by Russians of attacks towards, 14-17.**4**; Fierce fighting, 25.**4** to 29.**5**; Capture by Germans of town, 31.**5**.

STRYPA RIVER (Gal.).
Russian victory on, 30.**8**; Germans driven back across, 13-15.**9**; Desperate engagement, S.W. of Tarnopol, 29.**9**; Ivanov's victory on, 11.**10**; Further captures, 12.**10**; Russians driven back across, 13.**10**; Enemy's offensive checked, 14.**10**; Austrians repulsed, 17.**12**; Heavy fighting begins, 24.**12**; Russian success, 31.**12**.

STUTTGART.
Bombed by French, 22.**9**.

STYR RIVER (Volhynia).
Stubborn fighting on, 5, 6.**9**; Enemy crosses, 28.**9**; Russians driven over, at Chartorysk, 29, 30.**9**; Heavy fighting about Kolki and Chartorysk, 3-9.**10**; Enemy crosses and takes latter, 10.**10**; Stubborn Russian resistance, 11-13.**10**; Russians re-take Chartorysk, 18.**10**; Struggle continues, 19-27.**10**; Russians cross to L. bank, 31.**12**; Russian victory, 9.**11**; Enemy driven from left bank, 2.**12**.

SUBMARINES, ACTION BY.
H.M.S " Formidable " torpedoed, 1.**1**; German U8 sunk, 4.**3**; U12 sunk, 9.**3**; U29 sunk, 25.**3**; E15 run ashore off Kephez (Dard.), crew prisoners, 17.**4**; Torpedoed by 2 British boats under Lt.-Com. Robinson, 18.**4**; E14 (C. Boyle) enters Sea of Marmora and sinks Turkish gunboat, 27.**4**; E14 sinks another gunboat and 2 transports, 29.**4**, 13.**5**; AE2 (Austral.), sunk by Turks, 30.**4**; E11 (Naismith), after destroying 3 steamers, enters Constantinople and torpedoes transport and wharf, 23-25.**5**; 4 Turk. transports sunk by British, 29.**8**; Turk destroyer sunk by British, 6.**9**; E7 lost in Dardanelles, 4.**9**; U27 acknowledged sunk, 7.**9**; British destroy 18 enemy ships in Baltic, 8-18.**10**; Sink German cruiser near Libau, 23.**10**; U8 interned for violating Dutch neutrality, 6.**11**; E20 sunk in the Dardanelles announced, 14.**11**.

SUBMARINE WARFARE.
Government decides that S. prisoners cannot be given honourable treatment, 4.**1**; S. " Blockade " of Great Britain announced by Germany, 4.**2**; " Blockade " begins, 18.**2**; Attitude of U.S.A. towards " blockade " 11.**2**, 16.**2**; Anglo-French Note to Germany threatening reprisals, 2.**3**; British reply by prohibiting all trade with Germany, 15.**3**; Correspondence *re* treatment of S. prisoners, 2.**4**, 12.**6**; Acceptance by Germany of U.S.A. demands, 1.**9**; Statement by Herr v. Jagow concerning, 19.**9**; Count Bernstorff's letter to Mr. Lansing *re*, 5.**10**; 177 British ships sunk between 18.**2**, 20.**10**.

SUCZAVA (Bukovina).
Russians occupy, 3.**1**; Austrians reach, 7.**2**; Russians withdraw beyond, 9.**2**.

SUEZ CANAL.
Turks begin advance across desert, January; Turks reach Katiya, 29.**1**; Turks repulsed at Tussum, 2.**2**; Turks repulsed along Canal, from Bitter Lakes to Ismailïa, and at El Kántara (400 Turks killed and 600 prisoners), 3.**2**; Second attempted attack (near Suez) driven off, 22, 23.**3**; Patrols active in desert, 3 11-28.**4**.

TRADE.
Committee formed to facilitate work at the docks and transport, 6.11.

TRADE UNION CONGRESS.
Meeting at Bristol, 6.9 ; Conference *re* Conscription, 28.9.

TRANS-CAUCASIA (and Armenia).
Russians wipe out Turks at Sarikamish, 1.1 ; Turks driven out of Ardahan, 3.1 ; Another Russian victory at Kara Urgan, 17.1 ; Rout of Turkish force, January ; All quiet by March ; Russian victory at Dilman (L. Urmia), beginning of May ; 500,000 Armenians massacred by Turks, April, May ; Minor Russian successes, 5.8 ; Turks prepare again in September ; Grand Duke Nicholas takes command, September ; Fighting in coast region, Turks repulsed, 10-12.10.

"TRANSITO, LTD."
Syndicate for transit of goods *viâ* Sweden to Russia, 30.11.

TRAWLERS.
5 British, sunk by German subm., 2-22.4 ; 26 German, captured by British patrols, 4-19.10.

TREATY OF COMMERCE.
Anglo-Portuguese, ratified, 9.7.

TREBINJE (Herzeg.).
Austrians disperse Montenegrins, 30.4.

TREBIZOND.
Bombarded by Russians, 28.1, 8.2.

TREKOPJES (S.W. Africa).
Defeat of Germans by the Union Forces, 26.4.

TREMBOVLA (Gal.).
Russian success, 7, 8.9 ; Desperate engagement, W. of, 15.9 ; Enemy pursued by Russian cavalry, S.W. of, 25.9.

TRENTINO.
Frontier skirmishes, 21.4 ; Military preparations, 22.4 ; Repulse of Austrians at Tonale and Forcella, 24, 26.5 ; Italian offensive in, resumed, 30.7 ; Austrian raid into, 8.8 ; Fighting in the, 4-15.9 ; Italian success near Arsiero, 17, 18.8 ; Successful Italian offensive towards Tyrol, 18-25.10 ; Mori and Rovereto evacuated by Austrians, 23.11.

TREVES (Trier).
Bombed. by French, 13.9.

TRIESTE.
Anti-war demonstration at, 21.4 ; Italian airship raid, 26.5.

TRIPLE ALLIANCE.
Reported Franco-Italian agreement ending, 26.4 ; Denunciation of, by Italy, 3.5 ; Signor Barzilai explains Italy's position *re*, 26.9.

TRIPOLI.
Turkish officers sent to, 22.7 ; Revolt of Senussi, 23.7.

" TRIUMPH," H.M.S.
Torpedoed off Gallipoli, 25.5.

TSAR (v. Nicholas, Emperor).

TSUMEB (S.W. Africa).
Union troops reach, 8.7.

TURKEY.
Campaigns in Dardanelles, Egypt, Mesopotamia, and Transcaucasia, *q.v.* ; Decrees slaughter of Armenians, *q.v.* ; and *v.* " Breslau " ; Italians leaving, 12.8 ; Italy declares war on, 20.8 ; Turco-Bulgarian Convention *re* frontier, 6.9 ; Turco-Bulgarian Convention text sent to Constantinople, 15.9 ; Turco-Bulgarian Convention signed, 25.9 ; Arrangement with Bulgaria for exchange of troops for war material, 13.10.

TUSSUM (Suez Canal).
Turks repulsed at, 3.2.

TYNESIDE.
German airship raid, 14.4.

TYROL.
Fighting on Italian frontier, 1-14.9 ; Italian offensive towards, 18-25.10.

UDINE (Friuli).
Enemy tries to force Italians back on, 10.9 ;

UGANDA.
German attempt to destroy railway, 20.4 ; Further mine explosions on, 5, 9.9.

" UNDINE."
German cruiser sunk by British subm, 7.11.

" UNION SACRÉE."
Renewed by French Chamber, 5.8.

UNITED STATES OF AMERICA.
Policy defended by Mr. Bryan, 24.1 ; exchange of notes with Britain on interference with neutral trade, 7.1, 10.2, 16.2, 19.2 ; On use of neutral flag, 11.2, 19.2 ; attitude towards German subm. policy, 11.2, 16.2 ; Military Mission recalled from German Staff, 3.4 ; Note on British blockade, 2.4 ; Note to Germany *re* " W. P. Frye." 5.4 ; Note to Great Britain *re* reprisals against German trade, 6.4 ; Note to Germany *re* sinking of merchant and passenger vessels, 14.5 ; Dissatisfaction with Great Britain's treatment of commerce, 19.5 ; Decision to postpone protest to Great Britain, 21.5 ; Dissatisfaction over German Note, 31.5 ; Notes *re* " Lusitania," June, 23.7 ; German reply to Note, published, 10.7 ; Third Note (" Lusitania "), 24.7 ; British reply, 26.7 ; Protest *re* passports, 30.7 ; British correspondence with Ambassador *re* Prize Courts published, 3.8 ; Reply to Austrian Notes, 5, 12.8 ; Germany accepts demands *re* subm. warfare, 1.9 ; German propaganda in, against proposed Loan to Allies, September ; Mr. Lansing on

VIOLU (Vosges).
Enemy attack, 3.10; French guns wreck German works, 15, 19.10.

VIRAVA (Carp.).
Occupation by Russians, 1.4; Repulse of Russian attack, 3.4; Russian retreat, 7.5.

VISHEGRAD (Herzegovina).
Enemy crosses Drina into Serbia from, 22.10; Captures works on further bank, 25.10.

VISLOKA RIVER (Galicia).
Russians stand on the, till 8.5.

VISTOK RIVER (Galicia).
Retreat of Russians across, 10.5; Crossing by Austro-Germans, 7.11.

VISTULA RIVER.
Desperate fighting on right bank, 8.3; Engagements at various points, 2.7; Enemy driven off, 5.7; Heavy fighting, Russians retire, 17, 18. 22.7; Enemy crosses S. of Warsaw, 28, 29.7; Enemy reaches at other points, 7.8.

VIVIANI, M. (French Premier).
On diplomatic situation *re* Balkans, 12, 13.10; Resigns Premiership, 28.10.

VOLHYNIA (Russia).
Enemy retires from strong points in, 18.9; Much fighting in, in autumn.

VOLKOVYSK (Grodno).
Russians retire towards, 4.9; Enemy offensive, 5.9; Heavy fighting, 6.9; Fall of, 7.9; Enemy advance E. from, 9.9.

VOSGES MOUNTAINS.
Fighting in, 3, 4, 6-8, 20, 22-23, 27.1; 10, 13-14, 18-21.2, and throughout year; French advance in the, along heights commanding valley of the Fecht, Steinbruck taken, 16.6; Metzeral taken, 17.6.; German attacks in, repulsed, 7, 11.8; French attack in, 17.8; Heavy artillery fighting in, during September; Violent combats reported in, 3, 9, 10, 21.9; Heavy indecisive fighting in, at Hartmannsweilerkopf, Schratzmännele, Violu, Barrenkopf, etc., 3-28.10; Successful French assaults in, 28.12.

VOUZIERS (Aisne).
Bombed by French, 30.9 and 2.10.

VRANYA (Serbia).
Heavy fighting at, Bulgars in partial occupation, 15-20.10.

VREGNY (Aisne River).
Heights taken by Germans, 13.1.

WAR BONDS.
Proposed 22.11; Issued, 5%, tax-free, 16.12.

WAR COMMITTEE.
Composition announced by Mr. Asquith, 11.11.

WAR COUNCIL, ALLIED.
First meeting in Paris, 6.12.

WAR LOAN.
New, at 4½% announced, 21.6; £585,000,000 subscribed, 13.7; Indian, issued, 17.8.

WARMBAD (S.W. Africa).
Occupied by Union troops, 3.4.

WARSAW.
Russians retire round, 18.7; Factories evacuated, etc., 25-30.7; attacked on 3 sides, 27.7; Evacuation proceeding, town attacked, 4.8; Fall of, Germans enter, 5.8; Enemy advances E. of, 9.8; Reopening of schools and university, 1.9.

WAR ZONE.
Harsh German answer to U.S.A. *re* rigours in, 5.3.

WELSH GUARDS.
Formation of battalion sanctioned, 12.2.

WESTEINDE (Belgium).
Shelling of German batteries at, 7.9, 2.10.

WESTHOEK (Ypres).
Capture by Germans, 4.5.

WHITE DRIN RIVER (Albania).
Defeat of Serbians, 3.12.

WIELTJE (Ypres).
Capture by Germans, 8.5; Re-capture by British, 9.5.

WIEPRZ RIVER (Galicia).
Russian positions broken west of the, 29.7; Russians forced back across the, 8.8.

"WILHELMINA," s.s.
Arrives at Falmouth, 9.2; Cargo seized, 11.2; Case discussed by U.S.A. and Britain, 16.2, 19.2.

WILMINGTON (U.S.A.).
Big powder factory explosion, 30.11.

WILSON, PRESIDENT.
Speech, hoped U.S.A. would have share in restoration of peace, 20.4; Speech at Philadelphia, "too proud to fight," 10.5; Nominated for re-election, Message to Congress, 7.12.

WILSON, STANLEY. CAPT.
Captured by Austrian submarine, 6.12.

WINDAU (Baltic).
Captured by Germans, 18.7; Bombed by Russians, 2.8, 10.9.

WINDHOEK (S.W. Africa).
Occupation by Union Forces, 12.5.

WIRBALLEN (Russian frontier).
Taken by Germans, 10.2.

WOEVRE, THE.
Heavy artillery fighting in, September.

WOMEN.
30,000 presented themselves at Labour Exchanges for war work by 3.4; Conference on question of employment of women,

PART II
1916–1917

TABLE OF CONTENTS

CORRIGENDA

Page.
146 For " MORRONE " read " MORONE."
159 Under " WALLACE," for " Gen. Peyton " read " Major Gen. Peyton."
160 For " YUSUFIZZ- " read " YUSUF IZZ-."
311 Under " HAIG," add " created K.T., 14.7."
326 For " TÉTON " read " TETON."

1916. Jan.	Western Front.	Eastern Front.	Southern Front.
1	.. .. ..	**Russian Offensive on the Strypa and the Styr** (Gal.) ([1]). Indecisive fighting in N. throughout month ([2]).	King Peter of Serbia reaches Salonika.
2	Bombardment of Hartmannsweilerkopf (Als.).	Heavy fighting N.E. of Czernowitz.	.. .. ..
3	.. .. ..	Development of Russian offensive in Bukovina and E. Galicia and Poland.	.. .. ..
4	.. .. ..	.. .. ..	Artillery duel in S. Tyrol.
5	.. .. ..	.. .. ..	**Austrian offensive in Montenegro.**
6	.. .. ..	.. .. ..	.. .. ..
7	.. .. ..	Russians storm Chartorysk.	Sir Ian Hamilton's despatch on Suvla Bay published. Embarkation of French and English at Seddul-Bahr (Dardanelles) begins, after repulse of a Turkish attack.
8	.. .. ..	Severe fighting in Galicia.	**Evacuation of the Gallipoli Peninsula** completed one casualty. H.M.S " King Edward VII." sunk by striking a mine crew saved.
9	Slight German attack in Champagne.	Further Russian offensive in Bukovina.	Austrians assault Mt. Lovchen (Montenegro).
10	.. .. ..	.. .. ..	Austrians take Mt. Lovchen. Sir A. Murray succeeds Sir C. Monro in comd. of Med. Expdy Force.
11	Munition explosion at Lille.	.. .. ..	French land in Corfu ([7]) ; Greek protest.

Asiatic and Egyptian Theatres.	Naval and Overseas Operations.	Political, &c.	1916. Jan.
.. .. ..	British take Yaunde (Cameroons).	Canada increases her overseas force to 500,000. King Peter of Serbia reaches Salonika. Tsar appointed British Field Marshal.	1
Turks shell Kut-el-Amara.	P. & O. " Geelong " and " Glengyle " sunk in Mediterranean.	.. .. ..	2
.. .. ..	.. .. ..	Anti-Ally press campaign in Greece ; Greek Government protest against arrest of Consuls at Salonika.	3
Gen. Aylmer moves from Ali Gherbi to relieve Kut.	White paper on the " Baralong " case ([3]).	Lord Derby's report on recruiting published ([4]).	4
.. .. ..	.. .. ..	Military Service Bill introduced ([5]). British answer re " Baralong " case ([3]).	5
.. .. ..	British subm. sunk off Dutch coast.	Labour Congress opposes Military Service Bill .	6
Gen. Aylmer defeats Turks at Sheikh-Saad.	.. .. ..	Count Bernstorff presents a memorandum on submarine policy to U.S.A. Government. Great Britain arranges to ration Holland.	7
.. .. ..	.. .. ..	.. .. ..	8
Turks fall back to the Wadi.	.. .. ..	.. .. ..	9
Russian offensive in Armenia. Sir A. Murray's command in . Egypt limited to country E. of line 5 miles W. of Suez Canal.	.. .. ..	.. .. ..	10
Sir J. Maxwell commanding in remainder of Egypt.	German raider " Moewe " reported to be operating in Atlantic.	.. ..	11

1916. Jan.	WESTERN FRONT.	EASTERN FRONT.	SOUTHERN FRONT.
12	.. .. ..	Resumption of Russian offensive in Galicia.	Allies blow up bridges at Demirhissar and Kilindir. Armistice between Montenegro and Austria.
13	.. .. ..	.. .. ..	Austrians take Cettinje.
14	Severe bombardment of Givenchy.	.. .. ..	Heavy fighting near Gorizia.
15	.. .. ..	Russian progress on the Styr, S. of Pinsk.	Serbian troops land in Corfu.
16	Lille bombed.	.. .. ..	Gen. Sarrail takes command at Salonika. Gen. Mahon administratively under Sir A. Murray.
17	.. .. ..	Russian offensive dies down.	Austrians announce capitulation of Montenegro.
18	.. .. ..	Austrians claim complete victory in Galicia and Bukovina.	.. .. ..
19	.. .. ..	Renewed activity N.E. of Czernowitz.	.. .. .
20	.. .. ..	.. .. ..	Negotiations between Austria and Montenegro broken off.
21	.. .. ..	Renewed Russian attack in E. Poland.	.. .. ..
22	Aeroplane raid on Dover, 1 killed, 6 injured.	.. .. ..	Austrians occupy Antivari and Dulcigno (Montenegro). Austro-Bulgarians take Berat (Alb.)

Asiatic and Egyptian Theatres.	Naval and Overseas Operations.	Political, &c.	1916. Jan.
..	.. .. ..	Military Service Bill secures s e c o n d reading. Herr Liebknecht expelled from Socialist party in Reichstag.	12
Gen. Aylmer attacks the Wadi (Mesop.). Turks reported at Kermanshah (Persia).	.. .. ..	.. ..	13
Russians occupy Arkhava (on Black Sea). British take Wadi; Turks retreat to Um-el-Hanna	German reply on the " Baralong " case (³). Austrian cruiser sunk off Cattaro by " Foucault."	Lord Chelmsford appointed Viceroy of India.	14
Russians enter Kangavar (Persia)	" Moewe " captures s.s. " Appam " and sends her to Norfolk, Va. British monitors shell Westeinde (Belg.).	**Von Papen papers published in U.S.A. (²).**	15
Russians forced to evacuate Kangavar. **General Russian Offensive in Transcaucasia begins.**	Westeinde shelled by British monitor.	.. .. ..	16
Turks retreat towards Erzerum. Bad weather hampers the Kut relief force.	Russian torpedo boats sink 163 sailing ships in Black Sea.	.. ..	17
Turks repulse B r i t i s h column W. of Kurna (Mesop.). Russians take Hasan-Kala (Armenia).	Allied warships bombard Dedeagach (Bulg.) Germans evacuate S. Cameroons (retiring into Spanish territory).	.. .. ..	18
Gen. Aylmer resumes his advance up the Tigris. Gen. Sir P. Lake succeeds Sir J. Nixon in Mesopotamia command.	Allied warships bombard Porto Lagos (Bulg.). Anglo - French occupy Ebolowa (Cameroons).	War Council of Allied Ministers in London.	19
Russians take Sultanabad (Persia). Russian progress in Armenia.	British submarine in the Adriatic sinks an Austrian destroyer.	British Government buys 800,000 tons of wheat in Rumania.	20
Failure of attack on Turkish position at Um-el-Hanna, 23 miles from Kut; mud awful.	.. .. ..	.. .. ..	21
Armistice for 6 hours on Tigris ; relief force hampered by floods.	Russian torpedo boats sink a further 40 sailing vessels in Black Sea.	.. .. ..	22

1916. Jan.	WESTERN FRONT.	EASTERN FRONT.	SOUTHERN FRONT.
23	Air-raid on Kent; no damage. German offensive near Neuville - St. Vaast (Arras).	.. .. ..	Austrians take Nikshich and Skutari (Montenegro).
24	German offensive near Nieuport (Yser).	.. .. ..	Italians lose ground near Gorizia.
25	Severe fighting near Arras.	.. .. ..	**Montenegro accepts Austrian terms.**
26	.. .. ..	.. ..	.. .. ..
27	German attacks repulsed at Neuville and N.E. of Loos.	.. .. ..	Austrians repulsed on Upper Isonzo. Kaiser meets King Ferdinand (Bulg.) at Nish.
28	Germans take Frise (Somme) and trenches near Givenchy; repulsed at Carnoy (Mametz).	.. .. ..	Serbians move S. in Albania. Austrians occupy Alessio and San Giovanni di Medua (Alb.). Allies occupy Kara Burun (Salonika): Greek protest.
29	German offensive at Dompierre (S. of the Somme). Zeppelin raid on Paris.	Renewed fighting on the Strypa and in Bukovina; Austrians claim success.	.. .. ..
30	Germans repulsed by French at Dompierre. Zeppelin raid on Paris.	.. .. ..	.. .. ..
31	Six Zeppelins raid E. Anglia and Midlands; 70 killed and 113 injured.	.. .. ..	.. .. ..
Feb. 1	.. .. ..	Violent cannonade S.E. of Riga.	Zeppelin raid on Salonika. Serbians repulse Austrians near River Ishmi (N. Albania).
2	.. .. ..	.. .. ..	.. .. ..

ASIATIC AND EGYPTIAN THEATRES.	NAVAL AND OVERSEAS OPERATIONS.	POLITICAL, &c.	1916. Jan.
Dispersal of Senussi Camp at Halazin, 25 miles S.W. of Mersa Matruh (W. Egypt). Deep mud.	.. .. ..	King Nicholas of Montenegro arrives at Rome.	23
Russians advance on forts of Erzerum.	.. .. ..	Military Service Bill passed by Commons.	24
Gen. Aylmer encamped at El Owasa (Orah).	Gen. Smuts appointed to command in E. Africa.	Statement on contraband in parcel mails to neutral countries published by Press Bureau.	25
Sir Percy Lake joins the Kut relief force.	.. .. ..	Commons debate on the blockade. Austro-German protest to Rumania on sale of wheat to Great Britain.	26
Part of Turkish positions at Kut flooded; Turks fall back 2,000 yards.	British monitors bombard Westeinde. German camp at Nkan captured (German East Africa.)	Order in Council on control of shipping and a restriction of imports. Order in Council on the duties of the Chief of the Imperial General Staff (⁹).	27
.. .. ..	.. .. ..	American protest against British search of parcel mails and British reply published.	28
Russians bombard ridge protecting Erzerum.	.. .. ..	Protest against closing of London museums. Labour conference decides to allow its members to remain in the Cabinet.	29
.. .. ..	.. .. ..	.. .. ..	30
.. .. ..	.. .. ..	War Savings Committees inaugurated.	31
			Feb.
Russian progress in Armenia. Russians drive back Turks in Kermanshah district.	"Appam" brought to Norfolk, Va. by a German prize crew.	M. Goremykin, Russian Premier, resigns: M. Stuermer appointed. Prince Yussuf-Izz-ed-Din, Turkish heir-apparent, commits (?) suicide.	1
.. .. ..	Zeppelin "L. 19" lost in North Sea. (Admitted by Germany).	.. .. ..	2

1916. Feb.	WESTERN FRONT.	EASTERN FRONT.	SOUTHERN FRONT.
3	Germans shell Loos ..	Resumed Russian attack in Bukovina.	.. .. ..
4	.. .. ..	.. .. ..	Austrians occupy Kroja 25 miles N. of Durazzo.
5	.. .. ..	.. .. ..	.. .. ..
6	German Bombardment of Loos. Allies bombard Lille. German gas reservoirs at Navarin bombed by French.	.. .. ..	.. .. ..
7	.. .. ..	Heavy artillery duel round Riga.	.. .. ..
8	.. .. ..	Russians reach W. bank of Dniester.	.. .. ..
9	French regain part of trenches lost at Frise, and repulse Germans at Vimy Ridge. Air raid on Margate and Broadstairs, 3 injured. Germans' reserves estimated at 2,000,000 [10].	Severe fighting in Volhynia and Galicia.	Fortification of Monasti by Bulgaro-Germans reported. Germans reported at Gevgeli. Serbian Govt. set up a Corfu.
10	Germans repulsed S. of Frise.	.. .. ..	75,000 Serbian troop brought to Corfu.
11	French success near Mesnil (Champ.).	Russians repulsed S. of Dvinsk.	French reinforcement reach Salonika : righ bank of Vardar occupied
12	German offensive W. of Soissons and temporary success at Pilkem (N. of Ypres).	.. .. ..	Austrian air raid on Italian coast.

Asiatic and Egyptian Theatres.	Naval and Overseas Operations.	Political, &c.	1916. Feb.
.. ..	.. .. ..	Australian War Loan totals nearly £21,000,000. Rumanian cereal crop reported to be sold to an Austro-German syndicate.	3
.. ..	.. .. ..	.. .. ..	4
.. ..	Germans from Cameroons interned in Spanish Guinea.	.. .. ..	5
.. ..	Four Austrian destroyers driven to Cattaro by British cruiser and French torpedo boat covering retirement of Serbian army to Corfu.	.. .. ..	6
.. ..	.. .. ..	.. .. ..	7
.. ..	Turkish positions on Anatolian coast bombarded by Russian Fleet. "Amiral Charner," French cruiser, torpedoed off Syrian coast (374 drowned).	Von Papen papers published as a White Paper. Rumanian reservists recalled from Salonika.	8
Maj.-Gen. W. Peyton succeeds Maj.-Gen. A. Wallace in command of W. force, Egypt.	"Moewe" reported to have sunk 5 ships since January 16. Agreement between U.S.A. and Germany on the "Lusitania" case reported.	Military Service Act comes into operation. Extension of restrictions on lighting and on sale of sugar. Greek neutrality reaffirmed ([11]).	9
.. ..	Four mine-sweepers attacked by Germans off Dogger Bank ; one sunk.	Montenegrin Premier defines position of Montenegro ([12]). Mr. Garrison, U.S. War Secretary, resigns. German Note to U.S.A. on arming of merchantmen ([13])	10
ostile Arabs occupy Baharia Oasis (200 m. S.W. of Cairo).	H.M.S. "Arethusa" mined off E. coast.	.. .. ..	11
.. ..	Reconnaissance against Salaita (E. Africa). Gen. Smuts sails from S. Africa.	Franco-Italian conference decides for an Allied Conference at Paris.	12

1916. Feb.	WESTERN FRONT.	EASTERN FRONT.	SOUTHERN FRONT.
13	German attack W. of Soissons repulsed. Heavy fighting round Frise : French lose ground. Heavy bombardment by Germans of Hooge.	Russians take Garbonovka (Dvinsk region). Severe fighting in Galicia.	Bulgarians take Elbasan (Albania).
14	Germans take 600 yards of British front trench between Ypres-Comines railway and the Canal.	Continued Russian success round Dvinsk.	Austrian airmen bomb Milan, Treviglio, Bergamo and Monza.
15	French regain ground at Tahure (Champ.).	German attacks in Dvinsk district repulsed.	.. 　 .. 　 ..
16	.. 　 .. 　 ..	.. 　 .. 　 ..	Montenegrin troops land in Corfu. Bulgaro-Austrian advance on Durazzo.
17	.. 　 .. 　 ..	.. 　 .. 　 ..	.. 　 .. 　 ..
18	Artillery duel at Ypres.	.. 　 .. 　 ..	Italian advance in Collo zone.
19	.. 　 .. 　 ..	Gen. Kuropatkin appointed to command the Northern front.	.. 　 .. 　 ..
20	Germans attempt to cross Yser at Steenstraate, capture post at Boesinghe. Aeroplane raid on E. coast ; 1 killed, 1 injured.	Russian success on the Dniester in Bukovina.	Deportation of Greeks from Xanthi by Bulgarians.

Asiatic and Egyptian Theatres.	Naval and Overseas Operations.	Political, &c.	1916. Feb.
Russians take a fort at Erzerum. Russians occupy Khanys (Armen.). Russians occupy Daulatabad (Persia).	.. .. ..	Reported that 2,000 German periodicals have ceased publication owing to shortage of paper.	13
Russians take another fort at Erzerum.	.. .. ..	Remaining classes of single men called up in Great Britain. Declaration by Entente Ministers at Havre ([14]). Partial Rumanian mobilisation completed. Messrs. Rigden sentenced.	14
Agreement between Brit. Govt. and Bakhtiari (Persia).	.. .. ..	Parliament meets. M. Sazonov makes representations to Allied Conference Speeches on the war by Mr. Asquith and Lord Kitchener ([15]). Senator Root attacks U.S. foreign policy ([16]).	15
Russians take Erzerum; nearly 13,000 prisoners and 323 guns. Arabs desert from Turkish army in large numbers.	Conquest of Cameroons practically completed.	Air debate in Commons. U.S. refuses German proposals on the "Lusitania" question. Entente renews pledges to Belgium.	16
British land at Chios. Vurla bombarded.	.. .. ..	Republican party in U.S. Congress promises support to Administration in opposition to German sub marine policy.	17
Russians take Mush and Aklat (Armenia).	Surrender of Mora completes conquest of Cameroons by Anglo-French forces. German attack repulsed at Kachumbe (Uganda).	Debate in French Chamber on government control in army zone : Government secures vote of confidence.	18
. .. ..	Gen. Smuts arrives at Mombasa.	Letter from Prince Nicholas of Greece to " Le Temps " ([17]). Action begun in Admiralty Court to recover "Appam." Greek protest against Fr. action in Corfu. U.S. protest to Turkey on Armenian massacres.	19
British airmen destroy power station at El-Hassana (Sinai).	.. .. ..	.. .. ..	20

1916. Feb.	WESTERN FRONT.	EASTERN FRONT.	SOUTHERN FRONT.
21	**Battle of Verdun begins.** German successes. Zeppelin L. 77 brought down by French.	.. .. ..	Gen. Sarrail received by King of Greece ([18]).
22	Battle of Verdun : Germans fail at Brabant, but take Haumont Wood and the Beaumont salient.	.. .. ..	.. .. ..
23	Battle of Verdun : French evacuate Bois des Caures, Ornes and Samogneux. Germans claim 3,000 prisoners. French regain part of trenches at Givenchy.	.. .. ..	.. .. ..
24	Battle of Verdun : front extended from Malancourt to Fromezy : part of Bois des Fosses taken by Germans.	.. .. ..	Durazzo evacuated by Albanians : Essad Pasha goes to Italy.
25	Battle of Verdun : Germans claim 10,000 prisoners : Germans take heights of Louvemont : French organise line of Champneuville-Ornes and evacuate civil population of Verdun : Gen. Pétain arrives.	.. .. ..	.. .. ..
26	Battle of Verdun : Germans capture Fort Douaumont: French save the situation by a counter-attack and repulse Germans at Poivre Hill.	.. .. ..	Activity on Italian front : indecisive results. Italians leave Durazzo. Serbians, Montenegrins and Albanians withdraw from Albania.
27	Battle of Verdun : Germans take Talou Hill, and repulse five attacks on Fort Douaumont. French repulse attack on Eix station.	.. .. ..	Austrians occupy Durazzo.
28	Battle of Verdun : German attacks W. of Douaumont repulsed. Germans carry Navarin Farm (Champ.).	.. .. ..	.. .. ..

Asiatic and Egyptian Theatres.	Naval and Overseas Operations.	Political, &c.	1916. Feb.
.. .. ..	.. .. ..	Vote of Credit ([19]). Germany informs U.S. through a press representative that she regards armed merchantmen as cruisers.	21
Russians approach Trebizond	Japanese warships reported in the Mediterranean. Prize crew from " Moewe " bring a British ship to Santa Cruz and blow her up.	Inter-parliamentary Commission opens at Paris. Blockade policy attacked in the Lords. Duma opens: Tsar well received.	22
Russian capture of Erzerum relieves Egyptian front.	Portuguese seize German steamers in the Tagus. Gen. Smuts arrives at Nairobi.	Lord Robert Cecil appointed Minister of Blockade. Peace debate in Commons.	23
.. .. ..	.. .. ..	German promise of Polish independence announced in Duma.	24
Russians occupy Sakhne and Bideswikh Passes, Kashan and Ispir (Persia).	.. .. ..	President Wilson writes to Senator Stone that he will not abrogate rights of American citizens in the matter of travel by sea.	25
Russians occupy Ashkala (Armen.). Senussi attacked and defeated by B.-Gen. Lukin nr. Agagia (Barani, Egypt). Charge of Dorset Yeomanry; Gaafer Pasha, prisoner.	French transport, " Provence II.", torpedoed in Mediterranean. (930 lost)	Taxation of war profits in Germany ordered.	26
Russians occupy Kermanshah (Persia). Farafra and Dakhla Oases occupied by Arabs.	P. & O. liner, " Maloja," mined off Dover (155 lost).	.. .. ..	27
Barani (W. Egypt) occupied.	.. .. ..	.. .. ..	28

1916. Feb.	WESTERN FRONT.	EASTERN FRONT.	SOUTHERN FRONT.
29	.. .. ..	.. .. ..	.. .. ..
March. 1	Artillery activity round Ypres. Aeroplane raid on Broadstairs and Margate, 1 killed.	.. .. ..	.. .. ..
2	Battle of Verdun: Germans repulsed at Douaumont.	.. .. ..	.. .. ..
3	Battle of Verdun: Germans enter Douaumont village. British regain "International Trench" (Flanders).	.. .. ..	.. .. ..
4	Battle of Verdun: Second phase begins: Germans repulsed at Poivre Hill.	.. .. ..	.. .. ..
5	Battle of Verdun: Germans repulsed E. of Vacherauville. Zeppelin raid on E. and N.E. counties. (18 killed, 52 injured).	.. .. ..	.. .. ..
6	Battle of Verdun: Germans capture Forges Australian siege brigade at Verdun.	.. .. ..	.. .. ..

ASIATIC AND EGYPTIAN THEATRES.	NAVAL AND OVERSEAS OPERATIONS.	POLITICAL, &c.	1916. Feb.
.. .. ..	German raider, " Greif," and British auxiliary cruiser " Alcantara " sink each other in N. Sea. Blockade of Cameroons raised.	Germany formally announces to U.S.A. that she will not postpone her " unlimited " submarine campaign, which is to begin at midnight of Feb. 29. German Note to Portugal. Government recognises National Volunteer Force for Home Defence.	29
Russian advance W. of Kermanshah (Persia).	" **Unlimited** " **submarine campaign begins.** H.M.S. " Primula " torpedoed in Mediterranean.	Order in Council on Government of Ireland Act (1914). Indian budget presented to Supreme Legislature ([20]). Mr. Bonar Law addresses the Associated Chambers of Commerce ([21]).	**March.** 1
Russians capture Bitlis (Armen).	.. .. ..	Death of " Carmen Sylva," Dowager Queen of Rumania,. Lord Derby speaks in the Lords on recruiting ([22]).	2
.. .. ..	.. .. ..	Portugal seizes four German ships at Madeira. U.S. Senate tables resolution warning Americans against sailing in belligerent ships ([23]). Italian Chamber discusses German intrigue in Italy ([24]).	3
Russians land at Atina (E. of Trebizond).	" Moewe " reaches Germany.	Portugal seizes German shipping at Lourenço Marques. Attempted assassination of Enver Pasha.	4
.. .. ..	.. .. ..	Lenten pastoral of Irish R.C. bishops.	5
El Hassana (Sinai) bombed.	German fleet reported to be cruising in North Sea. Chinese rebels defeated in Szechuan.	Women's National Land Service Corps inaugurated. Visit of Russian journalists ([25]).	6

1916. March.	WESTERN FRONT.	EASTERN FRONT.	SOUTHERN FRONT.
7	Battle of Verdun : Germans capture Hills 360 and 265, and Fresnes (S.E. of Verdon).	German artillery active S.W. of Dahlen Island (River Dvina).	.. .. ..
8	Battle of Verdun : French regain ground in Corbeaux wood, N.E. of Mort Homme.	.. .. ..	.. .. ..
9	.. .. ..	German attacks repulsed on Dvina and at Cebrow (Gal.).	.. .. ..
10	Battle of Verdun : Germans reoccupy part of Corbeaux Wood and attack Bois-des-Buttes.	German attacks repulsed E. of Kosloff.	.. .. ..
11	Germans penetrate French positions near Reims. Their first attack on Fort Vaux (Verdun) repulsed.	.. .. ..	.. .. ..
12	.. .. ..	.. .. ..	Italian artillery active on Middle Isonzo.
13	.. .. ..	.. .. ..	.. .. ..
14	Battle of Verdun : Germans penetrate line Béthincourt-Mort Homme.	Great artillery activity on Riga front.	.. .. ..
15	French success S. of Saint-Souplet (Champ.).	.. .. ..	.. .. ..
16	Battle of Verdun : Five successive German attacks on Vaux repulsed.	.. .. ..	.. .. ..

ASIATIC AND EGYPTIAN THEATRES.	NAVAL AND OVERSEAS OPERATIONS.	POLITICAL, &c.	1916. March.
Russians capture Cola (Persia) and Rizeh (E. of Trebizond).	Gen. Smuts advances on Kilimanjaro (Ger. E. Africa).	Mr. Hughes, Prime Minister of Australia, arrives in England. President Wilson secures victory in Congress on submarine question. Mr. Balfour introduces Nav. Estimates ([26]).	7
Failure of attack on Dujailah Redoubt and Es-Sinn. Russians occupy Sennah (Persia).	Second White Paper on the "Baralong" case ([27]).	Special commission on commerce appointed.	8
Turks driven beyond River Kalopotamos (E. of Trebizond). Germans reported to be leaving Ispahan (Persia).	British occupy Taveta (Germ. E. Africa). Russian torpedo boat sunk by submarine in Black Sea.	**Germany declares war on Portugal.** Air debate in Lords ([28]). Mr. Asquith speaks on forthcoming Paris conference.	9
.. .. ..	.. .. ..	Mr. Pemberton Billing (Ind.) elected for E. Herts. F.O. answer to German charges of cruelty published.	10
Russians occupy Kerind (Persia).	H.M.S. "Coquette" destroyer, and T.B. No. 11, mined in North Sea. British success at Kilimanjaro (Reata Nek).	Neutrality of Scandinavian States reaffirmed at Copenhagen ([29]). German memorandum to U.S.A. on submarine warfare ([30])	11
Gen. Gorringe succeeds Gen. Aylmer.	.. .. ..	.. .. ..	12
Turks defeated near River Kalopotamos.	H.M.S. "Fauvette" mined off E. Coast. British occupy Moshi (Germ. E. Africa).	.. .. ..	13
British re-occupy Sollum (Egypt), and scatter Senussi. British air raid on Sinai.	.. ..	Mr. Tennant introduces Army Estimates ([31]).	14
.. .. ..	.. .. ..	**Austria declares war against Portugal.** Lord Derby's pledge to married men with regard to military service.	15
.. .. ..	Dutch liner "Tubantia" torpedoed without warning, off Harwich.	South Wales coal dispute decided ([32]). Von Capelle succeeds von Tirpitz as German Minister of Marine ([33]). Gen. Roques succeeds Gen. Galliéni as French Minister of War. Sofia treason trial begins.	16

c

1916. March.	WESTERN FRONT.	EASTERN FRONT.	SOUTHERN FRONT.
17	.. ..	.. .. ..	.. .. ..
18	Allies bomb Zeebrugge.	First battle of Lake Naroch begins.	.. .. ..
19	Air raid on Kent ([84]). Battle of Verdun : Germans repulsed at Poivre Hill.	Russian success N.W. of Uscieczko (River Dniester).	.. .. ..
20	Allies bomb Zeebrugge. Verdun : Germans attack Avocourt-Malancourt line and enter Avocourt Wood (S.W. of Béthincourt).	.. .. ..	.. .. ..
21	.. .. ..	Russian offensive on the northern front ; Dvina crossed in force near Jacobstadt. Russian success on River Dniester.	.. .. ..
22	Battle of Verdun : Germans gain a footing on Haucourt Knoll, S.W. of Malancourt.	Russian success at Lake Naroch : 1,000 prisoners reported.	.. .. ..
23	British line extended to include Souchez.	German concentration at Dvinsk broken up.	.. .. ..
24	.. .. ..	.. .. ..	... .
25	Battle of Verdun : German artillery active S.W. of Meuse.	.. .. ..	.. .. ..
26	.. .. ..	.. .. ..	.. .. ..

TABLES, 1916.

Asiatic and Egyptian Theatres.	Naval and Overseas Operations.	Political, &c.	1916. March.
Continued Russian advance W. of Erzerum. Duke of Westminster's armoured cars release 91 "Tara" prisoners at Bir-el-Hakim.	Dutch liner "Palembang" torpedoed in North Sea.	Kwangsi province (China) proclaims its independence. Food prices risen 48% in Great Britain.	17
Prince of Wales arrives in Egypt as Staff Capt.	British drive enemy from Ruwu river (E. Africa).	Royal Defence Corps formed.	18
Russians enter Ispahan. Sir A. Murray succeeds Sir J. Maxwell in Egypt.	French t.b. "Renaudin" torpedoed.	.. .. ..	19
.. .. ..	Naval engagement in North Sea between four British and three German torpedo boats.	Recruiting conference at War Office.	20
.. .. ..	British occupy Arusha (Kilimanjaro).	Disturbances at Tullamore, King's County ([35]).	21
Jebel el Hella (Darfur) occupied by Col. Kelly's force.	.. .. ..	Mr. Pemberton Billing attacks the air service in Commons. Central Tribunal for Great Britain set up.	22
.. .. ..	"Minneapolis" sunk in Mediterranean.	Mr. Lloyd George speaks on Paris Economic Conference. Gen. Cadorna received by King George.	23
El Hassana bombed again.	"Sussex" torpedoed in Channel (50 drowned).	Fourth German War Loan stated to have reached £530,000,000. Gaelic Press offices at Dublin raided.	24
.. .. ..	H.M.S. "Cleopatra" sinks a German destroyer. Seaplanes bomb Sylt and coast of Schleswig-Holstein. H.M.S. "Medusa" destroyer, sunk in collision in North Sea.	.. .. ..	25
Turkish base destroyed by air raid on Bir-el-Hassa (N. Africa). Russian progress on upper Chorok (Armen.).	.. .. ..	British delegation arrives in Paris.	26

1916. March.	WESTERN FRONT.	EASTERN FRONT.	SOUTHERN FRONT.
27	Two lines of German trenches captured at St. Eloi (Ypres).	.. .. ..	German air raid on Salonika.
28	Battle of Verdun : German attack on Haucourt-Malancourt front repulsed.	Russian success N. of Bojan (Galicia).	.. .. ..
29	Battle of Verdun : Germans enter Malancourt village ; French recover Avocourt redoubt.	Thaw on the Russian front suspends operations.	Italian success E. of Seltz.
30	Battle of Verdun : Germans repulsed at Fort Douaumont.	Germans driven back over River Oldenevitz.	.. .. ..
31	Battle of Verdun : French evacuate Malancourt and positions between Haucourt and Béthincourt. Zeppelin raid on E. coast : one Zeppelin destroyed ; 48 killed, 64 injured.	.. .. ..	.. .. ..
April. 1	Battle of Verdun: Germans capture part of Vaux village. Zeppelin raid on N.E. Coast, L15 captured ; 22 killed, 130 injured.	.. .. ..	.. .. ..
2	Zeppelin raid on E. Coast and Scotland ; 13 killed, 24 injured.	Germans repulsed in Liakhovichi region.	.. .. ..
3	Verdun : French re-occupy west part of Vaux village. German salient captured, Brit. line advanced on 600 yds. front at St. Eloi. Harmless Zeppelin raid on Norfolk.	Germans repulsed at bridgehead of Üxküll. (Dvina).	Greeks refuse overland route — Corfu - Salonika to Serbian army.
4	Battle of Verdun : French progress N. of Bois de Caillette. Zeppelin raid on E. Coast ; 1 killed, 9 injured.	Gen. Brusilov succeeds Gen. Ivanov in command of southern front.	.. .. ..

Asiatic and Egyptian Theatres.	Naval and Overseas Operations.	Political, &c.	1916. March.
Russians cross River Baltachi Darassi (Armen).	.. .. ..	Paris Conference opens; eight States represented.	27
2nd Anzac Corps formed in Egypt.	Russian torpedo-boats sink ten ships and destroy munition depot on Black Sea.	Paris Conference affirms unity of action ([36]).	28
.. .. ..	.. .. ..	Gen. Polivanov resigns as War Minister; succeeded by Gen. Shuvaiev. Unrest in Holland.	29
.. .. ..	" Portugal," French Hospital ship, torpedoed in Black Sea by German submarine; 115 lost.	Order in Council on Contraband. Reichstag secret debate ends ([37]).	30
Russians defeat Turks at Kara Malachkan (Armen).	Shipping losses in March, 78,769 tons.	Army Council takes over hay and straw. Mr. Asquith in Rome.	31
			April.
.. .. ..	.. .. ..	M. Denys Cochin appointed Minister in charge of blockade in France. Decline of unrest in Holland. King George presents £100,000 for war purposes.	1
Russians cross Upper Chorok, taking fortified mountain positions (Armen).	.. .. ..	Powder explosion in Kent: 172 casualties. Mr. Asquith received by the Pope. Resumption of work advised by Clyde strike committee.	2
British retirement at Alawad (near Aden).	.. ..	Bulgaria informs Greece that Bulgarian troops have been ordered to withdraw across frontier.	3
.. .. ..	British attack Lol Kissale (Germ. E. Africa).	Budget introduced ([38]). Clyde strike ends. Holland reaffirms her neutrality after a secret sitting of the Chamber.	4

1916. April.	WESTERN FRONT.	EASTERN FRONT.	SOUTHERN FRONT.
5	Battle of Verdun: Germans occupy Haucourt; attack on Béthincourt breaks down. Zeppelin raid on N.E. Coast; 1 killed, 9 injured.	..	..
6	Battle of Verdun: German progress between Béthincourt and Hill 265. Germans regain two craters at St. Eloi.	..	..
7	Battle of Verdun: French repulse an attack S. and E. of Haucourt.	Renewed fighting at Lake Naroch (S. of Dvinsk).	Bulgarians and Germans bomb Salonika lines. Italian retirement from trenches on the Rauchkofel (Carnic).
8	Battle of Verdun: French evacuate Béthincourt; German gain at Haucourt reported.	..	..
9	Battle of Verdun: Germans gain footing on Hill 295, but fail in attack on 12-mile front W. of Meuse. Recapture of mine crater at St. Eloi by British reported.	..	..
10	Battle of Verdun: Critical day; general German repulse on Meuse and Mort Homme, but slight German gain at Poivre Hill. Germans gain ground at St. Eloi.	..	Sir C. Monro's Dardanelles despatch published ([41])
11	Battle of Verdun: German attack on Douaumont-Vaux sector fails. German losses since beginning of war 2,730,917.	..	..
12	..	Germans repulsed near Dvinsk.	..

ASIATIC AND EGYPTIAN THEATRES.	NAVAL AND OVERSEAS OPERATIONS.	POLITICAL, &c.	1916. April.
British take Um-el-Hanna and Falahiya position (Mesop.), and positions on right bank of Tigris. Sir J. Nixon's Mesop. desp. of 1.1.16 publ. ([39]).	"Breslau" aids Turks near Trebizond.	List of certified trades under Military Service Act revised. " Military Medal " instituted. Gen. Morone becomes Minister of War in Italy.	5
Russians drive Turks across Kara Dere (Armen.) Failure of preliminary British áttack on Sanna-i-yat.	Lol Kissale (Germ. E. Africa) captured. " Clan Campbell " torpedoed in Mediterranean.	.. .. ..	6
Russians repulse three attacks on Kara Dere. Cars raid Moraisa (18 miles N.W. of Sollum, W. Egypt.)	P. & O. " Simla " torpedoed in Mediterranean	First married groups called up. Dr. Bethmann Hollweg's reply to Mr. Asquith ([40]). Dutch Chamber authorises calling up of 1917 class.	7
.. .. ..	Austrian transport sunk by French submarine in Adriatic.	.. .. ..	8
British attack on main Turkish position at Sanna-i-Yat (Mesop.) fails. Abiad (Darfur) occupied.	.. .. ..	Greco - Bulgarian frontier closed to passenger traffic, mails for Bulgaria and Turkey continue.	9
.. .. ..	Allies decide to form naval bases in Ionian Isles and the Aegean.	Mr. Asquith defines Allied position in a speech to French deputies visiting London. Lords Derby and Montagu resign from Air Committee. Report on Wittenberg prisoners' camp published ([42]).	10
.. .. ..	Kionga (E. Africa) captured by Portuguese troops.	Portuguese Cabinet resigns.	11
Turkish right at Sanna-i-yat forced back 1½ miles ; floods on Tigris increasing.	British occupy Köthersheim (Germ. E. Africa). German note to U.S.A. on the " Sussex " case ([43]).	Clyde strikers tried for sedition. Plot in U.S.A. to blow up ships carrying munitions.	12

1916. April.	WESTERN FRONT.	EASTERN FRONT.	SOUTHERN FRONT.
13	.. .. ..	.. .. ..	.. .. ..
14	.. .. ..	End of first battle of Lake Naroch.	.. .. ..
15	Battle of Verdun : Successful French attack S. of Douaumont.	Russians take two lines of trenches near Lake Naroch.	.. .. ..
16	Battle of Verdun : German bombardment of Avocourt Wood and Hill 304.	.. .. ..	.. .. ..
17	Battle of Verdun : Germans repulsed at Douaumont, but gain footing in Bois de Chaudfour salient.	.. .. ..	Italians blow up Col di Lana and take west part of Monte Ancona (Dol.)
18	Deportation of civilians announced at Lille and elsewhere.	.. .. ..	.. .. ..
19	Battle of Verdun : Germans fail in three attacks at Les Eparges. Germans capture two craters at St. Eloi and positions N. of Langemarck-Ypres.	.. ..	.. .. ..
20	Battle of Verdun : French regain ground near Mort Homme and S. of Douaumont. Russian troops arrive at Marseilles.	.. .. ..	.. ..
21	Battle of Verdun : French make progress near Mort Homme, Vaux fort and Bois de Caillette. British retake ground lost at Langemarck-Ypres.	.. .. ..	Italian progress in the Carso.

Asiatic and Egyptian Theatres.	Naval and Overseas Operations.	Political, &c.	1916. April.
Australian troops break up Turkish camp at Jifjaffa (Sinai P.). Russians repulse Turks after 6 days fighting W. of Erzerum.	.. .. ..	Resignation of Portuguese Cabinet withdrawn.	13
Gen. Gorringe drives back Turks on R. bank Tigris.	British occupy Salanga (Germ. E. Africa), Naval aeroplanes raid Constantinople.	Cabinet Council on the Military Service Act. U.S. cabinet approves President's Note to Germany on submarine campaign ([44]).	14
British advance on Tigris. Russian success near Bitlis. British occupy Kharga Oasis (120 miles S.S.W. of Assiut).	.. .. ..	.. .. ..	15
Russians, after 9 days' fighting take a position on left bank of Kara Dere.	.. .. ..	.. .. ..	16
Russians occupy Surmeneh and reach Assene Kalessi (Armenia). British take Beit Aiessa (Mesop.).	Germans in force at Kondoa Irangi (Germ. E. Africa).	Committee appointed to investigate recruiting ([45]). Italy prohibits trading with Germany.	17
Turkish counter attack forces back British 500 yards at Sanna-i-yat. **Russians take Trebizond.** Russian progress W. of Erzerum.	U.S. Note to Germany on the " Sussex " case, and on submarine policy in general ([44]) despatched.	Lord Milner advocates universal military service in the House of Lords.	18
Field-marshal von der Goltz Pasha assassinated by Albanian officer in Asia Minor.	S. African forces take Kondoa Irangi (Germ. E. Africa).	Cabinet crisis on man-power question reported.	19
Russians take Turkish positions in Bitlis region.	Disguised German warship " Aud " sunk while trying to land arms on Irish coast.	New Volunteer regulations issued. Man-power proposals to be submitted to secret session of both Houses. **Sir Roger Casement lands in Ireland and is arrested.**	20
.. .. ..	.. .. ..	.. .. ..	21

1916. April	WESTERN FRONT.	EASTERN FRONT.	SOUTHERN FRONT.
22	.. .. ..	.. ..	.. .. ..
23	Aerodrome at Mariakerke bombed by naval aeroplanes. British bombard Belgian coast. Battle of Verdun. German attacks at Mort Homme repulsed.	.. ..	.. ..
24	Zeppelin raid on Norfolk and Suffolk coast; 1 killed, 1 injured. Aeroplane raid on Dover, no damage.	.. ..	.. ..
25	Great British aerial activity. Zeppelin raid on Kent and Essex ; 1 injured.	.. ..	.. Fighting in Gevgeli sector (Salonika).
26	Fighting between Ypres and Souchez. Zeppelin raid on Kent ; no damage.	.. ..	.. ..
27	German attack S. of Hulluch repulsed.	.. ..	.. ..
28	.. .. ..	Germans regain all ground lost at Lake Naroch.	.. .. ..
29	German gas attacks at Hulluch and Wulverghem fail.	.. ..	.. Italians take Adamello crest (Trent.).
30	German attack from Messines ridge defeated by artillery.	.. ..	.. ..
May 1	Battle of Verdun : French success at Fort Douaumont. German attacks repulsed E. of Ypres and N. of Albert. Zeppelin raid on E. Coast of England and Scotland.	.. ..	.. .. ..

ASIATIC AND EGYPTIAN THEATRES.	NAVAL AND OVERSEAS OPERATIONS.	POLITICAL, &c.	1916. April.
British repulsed at Sannaiyat.	British progress in Germ. E. Africa.	Easter manœuvres of Sinn Fein volunteers cancelled.	22
s.s. "Julnar" fails to break blockade at Kut. Turks raid Katiya (Sinai) and destroy 2 British posts ; 5th Midland Brig. loses 3½ sq'ns. Yeom'y.	..	..	23
..	..	Rebellion in Ireland ; Sinn Feiners seize Dublin Post Office. Serious fighting in Dublin.	24
..	German battle cruiser squadron raids Lowestoft ; engaged and dispersed by local naval forces. Great Yarmouth bombarded : 4 killed, 19 wounded.	Official report of secret session on Man-power published. Martial law in Dublin.	25
..	..	British reply to U.S. note on blockade.	26
Russian progress in Bitlis district. British occupy Moghara Oasis (90 miles S.W. of Alexandria.).	British submarine sunk in North Sea. H.M.S. "Russell" mined in Mediterranean, 124 lost.	Martial law throughout Ireland. Gen. Sir J. Maxwell takes command in Ireland. New Military Service Bill abandoned. Allied commercial conference at Paris.	27
..	..	..	28
Kut surrenders to Turks : Gen. Townshend, 3,000 British and 6,000 Indian troops taken prisoner ; 143 days' siege.	..	Dublin Post Office, etc., burnt by rebels.	29
..	Belgian column arrives in Victoria Nyanza region.	707 Dublin rebels surrender	30
..	"Aegusa" and "Nasturtium" announced as sunk in Mediterranean.	Herr Liebknecht arrested at Berlin. End of Irish rebellion : leaders surrender (⁴⁶). I. Tribitch Lincoln, M P., extradited.	May 1

1916. May.	Western Front.	Eastern Front.			Southern Front.		
2	Zeppelin raid on E. Coast and Scotland, 9 killed, 30 injured.	..	..	..	French occupy Florina (23 miles S. of Monastir).		
3	Battle of Verdun : French success at Mort Homme ; Germans bombard Hill 304. Aeroplane raid on Deal, 4 injured. L.20 sunk off Norway.	..	..	..	..	..	..
4	Battle of Verdun : Struggle for Hill 304.	..	..	..	..	..	..
5	Battle of Verdun : Germans gain a footing on Hill 304.	..	..	..	..	..	..
6	Battle of Verdun : Continued struggle for Hill 304.	..	..	..	..	..	..
7	Battle of Verdun : Germans make progress on Hill 304 and between Haudromont Wood and Douaumont Fort.	..	..	..	..	..	..
8	Battle of Verdun : Germans repulsed at Hill 304, severe fighting at Thiaumont Farm. Anzacs in line in France.	..	..	..	..	.	..
9	Battle of Verdun : French success N.W. of Thiaumont Farm.	..	..	..	Gen. Milne succeeds Gen. Mahon at Salonika.		
10	Battle of Verdun : French success at Mort Homme and Hill 287.	..	..	..	..	..	..
11	Battle of Verdun : German attack W. of Vaux Pond repulsed. Germans take British trenches N.E. of Vermelles(La Bassée).	..	..	..	..		..
12	Battle of Verdun : French extend position S.E. of Haucourt and repulse attacks on centre.	..	..	..	..	..	..

Asiatic and Egyptian Theatres.	Naval and Overseas Operations.	Political, &c.	1916. May.
King's Message to Mesopotamian Force.	. . .	Germany agrees to British proposal for transfer of prisoners of war to Switzerland.	2
. . .	Belgians occupy Shanzugu on Lake Kivu (Germ. E. Africa).	Three Irish leaders shot ; Mr. Birrell resigns Irish Secretaryship. Military Service Bill, extending compulsion to married men, introduced.	3
. . .	Zeppelin L.7 destroyed by British warships off Schleswig coast.	German reply to U.S.A note on submarine campaign ([47]).	4
Russians defeat Turks at Sermil (Persia).	A Zeppelin destroyed by Allied warships at Salonika.	Four more Irish rebels shot.	5
Russians occupy Serin el Kerind (Persia).	Belgians occupy Kigali (Germ. E. Africa).	. .	6
. . .	. .	. .	7
Turks claim victory over Russians at Pirnakapan (Armenia). Air raid on Port Said.	" Cymric " White Star liner, torpedoed in Atlantic. German attack repulsed at Nhika (Port. E. Africa).	U.S.A. Note to Germany on submarine warfare ([48]). Four more Irish rebels shot.	8
Turks defeat Russians near Bashkeui (Armenia). Gen. Mahon to command W. force, Egypt.	. .	Appeal of Irish Nationalists to Ireland to support the constitutional movement. Duma members received by King George.	9
Russians occupy Kasr-i-Shirin, on road to Baghdad. Sir J. Nixon's despatch of 17.1.16 (Oct., 1915, to 13.1.16), published.	German attack repulsed near Kondoa Irangi (Germ. E. Africa). German note to U.S. on the " Sussex " ([49]).	Commission appointed to enquire into causes of the Irish rebellion ([50]). Lord Wimborne resigns Lord-Lieutenancy. Mr. Hughes speaks in London ([51]).	10
. . .	. .	Debate in Parliament on Irish administration ([52]).	11
. . .	. .	Mr. Asquith visits Dublin.	12

1916. May.	Western Front.	Eastern Front.		Southern Front.
13	Battle of Verdun : German attack N.E. of Mort Homme repulsed. Germans attack on British at Ploegsteert (N. of Armentières) repulsed.	.. ..	.. .. ..	
14	Fighting on Loos salient round Hohenzollern Redoubt and Hulluch.	.. ..	..	**Austrian offensive on Trentino front begins :** " Battle of the Trentino."
15	Fighting on Vimy Ridge.	.. ..	..	Austrians force Italians to retreat S. of Rovereto (Trentino).
16	.. .. ..	.. ..	..	Austrian advance checked at Zugna Torta.
17	Battle of Verdun : German attack in Avocourt Wood. Germans capture British mine crater on Vimy Ridge.	.. ..	..	Austrians claim 6,300 prisoners.
18	Battle of Verdun : German attacks repulsed at Hill 304 and in Avocourt Wood.	.. ..	..	Italians evacuate Zugna Torta and retire from Monte Maggio-Seglio d' Aspio (Trentino).
19	Battle of Verdun : Germans take a work S. of Hill 287. German air raid on coast of Kent; 1 killed, 2 injured ; one German seaplane destoyed off Belgian Coast.	.. ..	..	Italians retreat from Monte Toraro - Monte Campolon - Spitz Tonezza line (Trentino).
20	Battle of Verdun : Great German attack on Mort Homme ; they capture summit of Hill 295. British regain mine crater on Vimy Ridge.	.. ..	.. ..	.. ..

ASIATIC AND EGYPTIAN THEATRES.	NAVAL AND OVERSEAS OPERATIONS.	POLITICAL, &c.	1916. May.
Russians defeated at Ashkale (Armenia).	.. .. ..	.. .. ..	13
. .. ..	" M 30," British monitor, sunk by Turks in Mediterranean.	Speech by M. Poincaré at Nancy. Resignation of Herr Delbrück (Imperial Secretary of State). M. Take Jonescu begins propaganda for Rumanian intervention.	14
Russians take Rowanduz (E. of Mosul). Entente blockade Hejaz coast, and assist Sherif of Mecca.	.. .. ..	Statement on war aims by Sir E. Grey ([53]). Sir R. Casement charged with high treason. Sig. Boselli, Italian Premier; Baron Sonnino, Foreign Minister.	15
Russian advance on Mosul. Anzacs storm Turkish camp at Bayud (Sinai.).	Dutch s.s. " Batavier V." blown up in North Sea. British destroyers and monitors engage German destroyers on Belgian coast. Russian submarine torpedoes 3 German ships off Sweden.	Military Service Bill (extending compulsion to married men) passes the Commons.	16
.. .. ..	.. .. ..	Speech by President Wilson at Washington ([54]). Air Board formed; Lord Curzon president ([55]). Daylight Saving Bill passed.	17
.. .. ..	British advance in Para and Usambara districts. (Germ. E. Africa). British bombard El Arish (N. Sinai).	Royal Commissions on Irish rebellion opens. Mr. Balfour makes a statement on sea power ([56]).	18
Turks evacuate Es Sinn position on R. bank. (Tigris).	.. .. ..	Evidence of Mr. Birrell before Irish Commission ([56]).	19
South bank of Tigris to Shatt-el-Hai cleared of Turks. 3 officers, 110 men, Cossacks from Mahidasht join British on Tigris at Ali Gherbi.	.. .. ..	.. .. ..	20

1916. May.	WESTERN FRONT.	EASTERN FRONT.	SOUTHERN FRONT.
21	Battle of Verdun : French capture quarries of Haudromont and two trenches on Esne Haucourt road ; German attack on Western slopes of Mort Homme succeeds.	..	Austrians capture Armenterra Ridge (S. of the Brenta, Trentino).
22	Battle of Verdun : French gain a footing in Fort Douaumont.	.. .. ..	.. .. ..
23	Battle of Verdun : German assault on Thiaumont-Douaumont front and on Cumières.	..	Italians retreat between Astico and Brenta and in Sugana Valley. (Trenttino).
24	Battle of Verdun : Germans capture Cumières and regain Fort Douaumont.	.. .. ..	.. .. ..
25	Battle of Verdun : German attack between Haudromont Wood and Thiaumont Farm.	.. .. ..	Infantry battle for Buole Pass (Trentino) begins and lasts six days. Austrians take Bettale.
26	Battle of Verdun : French regain part of Cumières trench between Haudromont Wood and Thiaumont Farm : repulse Germans between Avocourt Wood and Mort Homme.	.. .. ..	Austrians capture Monte Civaron (Trentino). Bulgaro - Germans occupy Fort Rupel (Greek Macedonia), Greek Government acquiescing.
27	Battle of Verdun : French take trenches S.W. of Mort Homme.	.. .. ..	Austrians take Monte Moschicce (N. of Asiago) by storm.
28	Germans bombard British line between La Bassée Canal and Arras.	.. .. ..	Austrians close in on Asiago ; are repulsed in Lagarina Valley (Trentino).
29	Battle of Verdun : Germans gain a footing in trench N.W. of Cumières, but are repulsed on Hill 304.	.. .. ..	Italians evacuate Asiago ; Austrians cross Posina, W. of Arsiero.

ASIATIC AND EGYPTIAN THEATRES.	NAVAL AND OVERSEAS OPERATIONS.	POLITICAL, &c.	1916. May.
Russians repulse Turks S of Trebizond. Russians occupy Serdasht (Persia) Port Said bombed.	.. .. ..	German food control board created ; Herr Batocki, president. Daylight Saving Bill comes into operation.	21
British defeat Ali Dinar, Sultan of Darfur, at Beringia.	.. .. ..	M. Briand delivers a speech to the Russian delegates ([58]). Daily cost of war £4,820,000.	22
British occupy El Fasher, capital of Darfur. Ali Dinar flees to Jebel Marra.	.. .. ..	Dr. Bethmann-Hollweg replies to Sir E. Grey ([59]). Vote of credit for £300,000,000.	23
Russians capture Mamakhatun (Armen.)	.. .. ..	Sir E. Grey speaks in Commons on peace terms ([60]).	24
2 Italian battalions land at Moraisa (W. of Sollum).	German retreat in Ger. E. Africa ; British occupy Same, Rufu lager, Lembeni and Ngulu.	Military Service Act becomes law ; Congratulatory message from the King ([61]). Mr. Lloyd George undertakes settlement of the Irish question.	25
.. .. ..	.. .. ..	U.S. note to Great Britain on search of mails ([62]).	26
Russians repulse Turks and Kurds near Serdasht.	.. .. ..	Declaration of M. Sazonov on the alliance and Russian aims ([63]). Speech by President Wilson on the War ([64]). Death of Gen. Galliéni.	27
.. .. ..	.. .. ..	Greek excitement over Fort Rupel incident.	28
White Paper containing Gen. Townshend's views on the advance from Kut published.	W.O. announces new invasion of Germ. E. Africa from Rhodesia and Nyassaland.	British Foreign Office denies German statements as to the Bosnian crisis ([65]). Civilian casualties to date in Great Britain published (v. Index).	29

D

1916. May.	WESTERN FRONT.	EASTERN FRONT.	SOUTHERN FRONT.
30	Battle of Verdun : French retreat from Béthincourt-Cumières road towards Chattancourt; deliver a counter-attack.	.. .. ..	Bulgars occupy Rupel Pass.
31	Battle of Verdun: Fierce fighting between Mort Homme and Cumières; French take a work S.W. of Mort Homme. Much artillery activity on Vimy Ridge.	.. .. ..	Austrians occupy Asiago and Arsiero; Italian prisoners 30,000 since beginning of Austrian offensive. French occupy Poro (Salonika front).
June. 1	Battle of Verdun : Fresh German attack on Fort Vaux: French first line penetrated between Douaumont and Vaux Pond.	Russians repel attack E. of Krevo (Vilna).	Heavy Austrian attack on Italian left centre from Monte Pasubio to S. of Arsiero (Trentino) ; little progress.
2	Battle of Verdun : French recover ground S. of Caurettes Wood ; Germans progress E. of Caillette Wood, on outskirts of Vaux Pond, at Damloup and Vaux Fort. **Third Battle of Ypres ;** two German attacks, second penetrates British trenches to depth of 300 yards on 3,000 yard front towards Zillebeke.	.. .. ..	Austrian attacks from Posina to Astico (Trentino) repulsed. Bulgarians fire on Greeks at Demirhissar.
3	Battle of Verdun : Powerful German attacks on Vaux Fort repulsed. Battle of Ypres : Canadian counter-attack regains much of the lost ground.	Russian bombardment in Riga area, Galicia and Volhynia.	Allies occupy all official buildings in Salonika, and proclaim martial law. Austrians advance on Arsiero-Posina line, but are repulsed on Arsiero-Lagarina line.
4	Battle of Verdun : German attacks on Vaux Fort repulsed. Germans take and lose again three lines of trenches at Casspach (Vosges).	**Great Russian offensive from Pripet (Poland) to Rumanian frontier, under Gen. Brussilov;** 13,000 prisoners reported.	.. .. ..
5	Battle of Verdun : German attacks between Vaux Fort and Damloup repulsed.	Russian offensive continues ; 12,000 prisoners reported. German attacks repulsed near Krevo (Vilna).	Austrians repulsed on Asiago plateau ; Italians gain ground at Monte Cengio (Trentino).

ASIATIC AND EGYPTIAN THEATRES.	NAVAL AND OVERSEAS OPERATIONS.	POLITICAL, &C.	1916. May
Maj.-Gen. Barnardiston's despatch on Tsingtau operations, Sept.-Nov., 1914, published.	British occupy Neu Langenburg (L. Nyassa), and force Germans to retreat from Mikotsheni (Germ. E. Africa).	.. .. ..	30
New Zealand troops raid Bir Salmana (20 miles E. of Katiya), Mamakhatun retaken by Turks.	Battle of Jutland (⁶⁶). Germans retreat from Mombo on Tanga railway towards Hendeni (Germ. E. Africa); British occupy Bwiko and Belgians Usumbara.	Allies protest to Greece against Bulgarian occupation of Fort Rupel. Sir C. Dobell's and Brig-Gen. Cunliffe's despatches of 1.3.16 (27.9.14 to 29.2.16), and 16.3.16 (Aug. 14 to Feb. 16) published.	31
Turkish offensive in Armenia.	Battle of Jutland ends (⁶⁶)	.. .. ..	June 1
Russians repulse Turks between Erzerum and Erzingan Turks retire 25 miles. Turks retire after three days' fighting W. of Rowanduz (E. of Mosul). British drive Turks out of Katiya (N. Sinai).	.. .. ..	Belgians up to the age of 40 called to the colours.	2
Russians defeat Turks at Khanikin (Persia). Turkish attack repulsed by Russians at Diarbekr (Asia Minor).	British occupy Namena (German E. Africa) after 3 days fighting.	.. .. ..	3
Sherif of Mecca starts revolt against Turks.	.. .. ..	.. .. ..	4
Russians evacuate Khanikin.	H. M. S. " Hampshire " mined off Scottish coast : Lord Kitchener and his staff drowned (⁶⁷)	Dr. Bethmann - Hollweg makes a tour of the S. German States to induce acceptance of central control of food supplies.	5

1916. June.	WESTERN FRONT.	EASTERN FRONT.	SOUTHERN FRONT.
6	Battle of Ypres ; Germans again attack, gaining some ground at Hooge.	Russians take Lutsk (Volhynia) ; cross the Ikva and Styr in Lutsk area and make progress S. of Dniester ; 15,000 prisoners reported.	" Pacific blockade " of Greece by Entente Powers begins.
7	Battle of Verdun : Germans take Vaux Fort.	Russian offensive continues ; 11,000 prisoners reported.	Very heavy Austrian attacks S. and S.W. of Asiago repulsed.
8	Battle of Verdun : Violent German attack E. and W. of Thiaumont Farm.	Russian offensive continues ; 13,000 prisoners reported. Austrians reinforced from Italian front. Russians repulse attacks in Vilna district.	Austrians make slight advance near Asiago.
9	Battle of Verdun : German attacks on Hill 304 repulsed.	Russians capture bridgehead at Rojishche (N. of Lutsk) and cross the Strypa ; 500 prisoners reported.	Italian counter - offensive in Trentino begins ; some progress made.
10	German artillery very active near Ypres.	Russians take Dubno (Volhynia) ; enemy retire from Strypa ; heavy fighting on whole front ; 3,500 prisoners reported.	Further Italian progress in Trentino. French occupy Thasos.
11	Battle of Verdun : German attacks W. of Vaux Fort and at Thiaumont repulsed. Germans bombard Ypres heavily.	Russians reach suburbs of Czernowitz ; repel attacks near Dvinsk and Vilna ; are checked at Lutsk and lose ground on Strypa ; 7,000 prisoners reported.	.. .. ..
12	Battle of Verdun : Germans bombard heavily ; German attacks N. of Thiaumont first repulsed and then penetrate French line E. of Hill 321.	Austrians retreat S. of Lutsk. Zaleszczycki (Bukovina) taken by Russians.	Italian advance on Asiago plateau and in Lagarina valley (Trentino).
13	Canadians retake positions lost at Ypres on June 2.	Russians repulsed at Baranovichi (75 miles N. of Pinsk) ; take Torchin and reach the Stokhod (near Lutsk) ; gain ground near Czernowitz ; 6,000 prisoners reported.	.. .. ..

Asiatic and Egyptian Theatres.	Naval and Overseas Operations.	Political, &c.	1916. June.
Russians checked at Diarbekr.	Rhodesian troops drive Germans towards Iringa, N.E. of Lake Nyassa; Belgians advance N.W. of Lake Tanganyika.	Army Order issued *re* Lord Kitchener. Pacific blockade of Greece by the Allies as a result of Greeks allowing Bulgarians to cross frontier. Dr. Taylor's report on Ruhleben Camp published ([68]). Yuan-shi-kai, President of China, dies; succeeded by Li Huan Yung	6
Sherif of Mecca throws off allegiance to Turkey and is supported by the tribes of W. and Central Arabia.	.. .. ..	....	7
.. .. ..	British occupy Bismarckburg and Belgians occupy Usumbara (German E. Africa). British patrols chase Germans into Zeebrugge.	Compulsion replaces voluntary enlistment in Great Britain.	8
.. .. ..	British capture Ukerewe Island (Vict. Nyanza); fighting at Kondoa Irangi (German E. Africa).	Allied War Council meets in London.	9
Turks sink three British munition barges on Tigris.Garrison of Mecca surrenders to Sherif.	British occupy Mkalamo, on Pangani River (German E. Africa).	Compulsory service bill passed in New Zealand. Italian ministry resigns. ([69])	10
Skirmishes at Katiya; Turks bomb El Kántara (Egypt). Russians repulse Turks at Platina (W. of Trebizond).	....	.. .. ..	11
British column (Sir P. Sykes) enters Kerman (S.Persia). Russians take Turkish camp near Diarbekr and repulse attack at Rowanduz	British take Wilhelmstal. Belgians take Kitega (German E. Africa). Italian destroyers raid Parenzo (Istria).	Riots in Greece ([70]). Adm. Jellicoe's message to the Fleet.	12
..	Brit. take Alt Langenburg (Lake Nyassa): Tanga reported to be evacuated by Germans	.. .. ..	13

1916. June.	WESTERN FRONT.	EASTERN FRONT.	SOUTHERN FRONT.
14	Battle of Verdun : Germans take 700 prisoners near Thiaumont Farm.	Fighting at Lokachi and Kolki (Lutsk area); 31,000 prisoners reported.	Italians take trenches at Monfalcone (N. Adriatic).
15	Battle of Verdun : French take a trench on Mort Homme and repulse heavy counter-attacks at Caillette Wood.	Russians advance N.W. of Czernowitz; heavy fighting in the centre.	Artillery activity at Salonika. Austrians repulsed on Asiago plateau; successful Italian counter-attack.
16	.. .. ..	Russians cross Styr and Stokhod N.W. of Lutsk; Austrians retreat across Strypa. German counter offensive in Ukraine.	Austrians repulsed in Lagarina valley on Monte Lemerle ; Italian counter offensive on Asiago plateau.
17	Battle of Verdun : Heavy German attacks repulsed on Mort Homme ; French take some trenches on Hill 321 ; Germans checked at Thiaumont. Capt. Immelmann killed.	Russians occupy Czernowitz ; gain ground W. of Kolki (Lutsk) and repel attacks near Buczacz. Germans retake Svidniki.	Italians repulse counter-attacks at Monfalcone (Isonzo).
18	Battle of Verdun : Germans repulsed N. of Hill 321 ; French repulsed at Fermin Wood. German attack repulsed at Lihons (St. Quentin).	.. .. ..	Italian advance on Asiago plateau and take Monte Isodoro.
19	Battle of Verdun : German night attack repulsed N.W. of Hill 321.	Russians cross Pruth W. of Czernowitz; heavy fighting near Lutsk, Germans reinforcing Austrians.	.. .. ..
20	.. .. ..	Germans penetrate Russian lines at Smorgon (Vilna), but are driven out ; Russians cross Sereth (S. of Czernowitz).	Slight Italian advance on Asiago plateau.
21	Battle of Verdun: Germans repulsed at Mort Homme and W. and S. of Vaux Fort ; German gains in Firmin Wood and Chenois Wood.	Russians occupy Radautz (S. of Czernowitz) ; Germans repulsed in areas of Dvinsk, Vilna and Lutsk ; Russians take trenches on Strypa.	Further Italian advance on Asiago plateau.

ASIATIC AND EGYPTIAN THEATRES.	NAVAL AND OVERSEAS OPERATIONS.	POLITICAL, &c.	1916. June.
Russians regain lost ground near Chorok(S.W. of Trebizond).	Russians attack German convoy in Baltic, sinking an auxiliary cruiser, two torpedo boats and some steamers.	Allied Economic Conference opens at Paris, M. Clémentel presiding ([71]).	14
British cavalry raid an Arab tribe (Mesop.) Heavy fighting at Saripul (Persia).	British secure bridge at Korogwe (W. of Tanga, German E. Africa), and occupy an island in Lake Victoria.	Daylight Saving Act comes into operation.	15
.. .. ..	Germans in force at Hendeni, near Tanga (German E. Africa). " Eden," T.B.D., sunk in collision.	Failure of German intrigues in Afghanistan.	16
British within 200 yards of Sanna-i-yat and 5 miles E. of Kut (Mesop.).	Sir P. Crewe appointed to Lake Command (E.Afr.).	Greek demobilisation begun. Death of Gen. v. Moltke, late Chief of German Gen. Staff.	17
Aerodromes at El Arish (Sinai P.) bombed by British.	.. .. ..	.. .. ..	18
Turks repulsed by Russians at Saripul (Persia).	British occupy Handeni and Germans retreat on central railway (Germ. E. Africa).	New Italian Ministry formed ([72]). 80,000 American Militia called up to police Mexican border.	19
Capture of Mecca, Jeddah and most of Taif, and seige of Medina, by Sherif of Mecca,reported.	Gen. Smuts' despatch on operations in German E. Africa published. ([73]).	.. .. ..	20
Sir J. Maxwell's despatches on operations in Egypt (16.6.15 to 9.4.16) published ([75]).	U.S.A. troops fight Mexicans at Carrizal.	Recommendations of Paris Economic Conference issued ([73]). Allied Note to Greece ([76]). Skouloudhis Greek Cabinet resigns.	21

1916. June.	WESTERN FRONT.	EASTERN FRONT.	SOUTHERN FRONT.
22	Battle of Verdun: Heavy German attacks repulsed on both sides of the Meuse; French regain ground at Firmin Wood. Germans repulsed at Givenchy.	Russians repulse attacks W. of Minsk; Russians advance in Bukovina.	.. .. ..
23	Battle of Verdun; Germans take Hills 321 and 320, and Thiaumont Fort; take, but lose, Fleury; are repulsed at Les Eparges and on left bank of Meuse.	Russians take Kimpolung (Bukovina); heavy fighting near Pinsk (Pripet); total prisoners reported since June 4, 144,000, with 4,031 officers and 219 guns.	.. .. ..
24	Battle of Verdun; French counter-attack regains some ground; Germans occupy part of Fleury, their farthest point of advance.	Russians checked in Lutsk salient; Austrians driven out of Bukovina.	Artillery preparation by Italians from Brenta to Adige (Trentino). Bulgars cross Greek frontier.
25	Battle of Verdun: Heavy fighting at Fleury and W. of Thiaumont. Preliminary British bombardment along Somme front and northwards.	Russian advance from Bukovina; fighting on Dniester.	Great Italian advance from the Brenta to the Adige. Asiago retaken.
26	Battle of Verdun: French gain near Thiaumont work. British patrols active.	.. .. ..	.. .. ..
27	Battle of Verdun: Germans repulsed at Fleury. German attack repulsed at Ypres.	Germans repulsed in Riga and Dvinsk areas. Russian advance from Kolomea (Bukovina).	Italians take Posina and Arsiero; continued advance from the Brenta to the Adige.
28	Battle of Verdun: Heavy fighting at Fleury and Hill 321; Germans repulsed N.W. of Thiaumont.	Heavy fighting on Lutsk salient; Austrians defeated on 25-mile front E. of Kolomea; 10,000 prisoners reported; Germans repulsed in Riga district.	Italians regain half the trenches lost during the Austrian offensive. Italian cavalry reach Pedescala (N.E. of Arsiero).
29	Champagne: German first and second line trenches taken at Tahure; German attack on Hill 304 (Verdun), repulsed	Germans repulsed N.E. of Vilna.	.. .. ..

Asiatic and Egyptian Theatres.	Naval and Overseas Operations.	Political, &c.	1916. June.
.. .. ..	.. .. ..	Demands of Allies accepted. M. Zaimis Premier. Embargo on Greek shipping relaxed.	22
Russians repulse several attacks S. of Trbizond.	" Citta di Messina," Italian auxiliary cruiser, and French torpedo boat " Fourcher " sunk by mines in Strait of Otranto. " Brussels" (G.E.R. steamer) captured by German T.B.D.	.. .. ..	23
.. .. ..	Germans defeated on Lukigura River (German E. Africa). Gen. van Deventer drives them back on to Central Railway.	Embargo on Greek shipping suspended.	24
.. .. ..	.. .. ..	Roger Casement trial begins.	25
Russians advance W. in N. Persia. Turks prepare to leave Mosul. Turks driven from Lake Urmia (Persia).	.. .. ..	General demobilisation ordered in Greece ([76]). Germans threaten to stop Swiss coal supply if their cotton purchases are not delivered.	26
.. .. ..	.. .. ..	Chinese navy threatens to revolt.	27
.. .. ..	.. .. ..	Liebknecht sentenced to 2 years I.H.L. and dismissal from Army. British abandon Declaration of London.	28
.. .. ..	Turkish steamers sunk by Russians in Black Sea.	Roger Casement found guilty of high treason and sentenced to death. U.S. demands apology from Austria for the sinking of the " Petrolite."	29

1916. June.	WESTERN FRONT.	EASTERN FRONT.	SOUTHERN FRONT.
30	Continued Allied bombardment on Western front. French retake Thiaumont.	.. .. ..	.. .. ..
July 1	Great Franco-British offensive begins on 25-mile-front N. & S. of Somme. British capture Montauban and Mametz ; break through towards Bapaume. French attack towards Péronne ; reach outskirts of Hardecourt and Curlu ; take Dompierre, Becquincourt, Bussus, and Fay. 5,000 prisoners taken.	On River Pruth Russians advance N.W. of Kolomea. Austro-Germans progress N.W. of Tarnopol.	Vigorous Italian attacks continued N. of upper Isonzo.
2	British capture Fricourt ; relinquish captured trenches at Gommecourt. French take Curlu, Frise, Bois de Méreaucourt and Herbécourt.	Russians take offensive at Smorgon and Baranovichi, and penetrate German lines. Germans continue advance on Lutsk salient. South of Dniester they regain Tlumacz.	Skirmishes near Salonika ; artillery duels on lower bank of Vardar. Heavy artillery fire and sharp infantry attacks in Trentino and Carso.
3	Fierce fighting continues ; British capture La Boisselle and part of Ovillers. French capture Chapitre Wood, Feuillères, Buscourt, Flaucourt ; also Assevillers to the South. Germans gain and lose Damloup work (Verdun). N. of Ancre actions indecisive. 12,300 prisoners to date.	Battle of Baranovichi continues South of Vilna. Russian sea-attack on German lines near Riga.	French air-raid on Sofia from Salonika.
4	Heavy thunderstorms impede operations. British take Bernafay Wood, E. of Montauban ; make air attacks on Comines, Combles, St. Quentin. French capture Estrées, Belloy-en-Santerre, and Sormont Farm : advance from Curlu towards Hem. Germans regain Thiaumont (Verdun).	Second Great Russian advance in the Ukraine under General Lesch ; they cross Styr at Kolki and Rafalovka and drive the Austrians towards the Stokhod. Further S. they cut Carpathian railway at Mikolichin.	Italians continue to advance in Trentino.

ASIATIC AND EGYPTIAN THEATRES.	NAVAL AND OVERSEAS OPERATIONS.	POLITICAL, &C.	1916. June.
.. .. ..	Baltic : Indecisive small British naval action.	.. .. ..	30
In Persia the Turks defeat Russians ; pursue them to Kermanshah.	.. .. ..	.. ..	July 1
Turks take Kermanshah ; Russians driven E. on road to Hamadan.	.. .. ..	.. .. ..	2
Russians again resume offensive in Armenia, W. of Erzerum.	Belgian advance in E. Africa, in region between Lake Tanganyika and Victoria Nyanza.	Report of Royal Commission on the causes of the Irish Rebellion issued ([77]). Russo-Japanese treaty re the Far East signed.	3
.. .. ..	The " Goeben " and " Breslau " bombard Russian ports in Black Sea.	Ignatius Tribitch Lincoln, ex-M.P., sentenced to 3 years penal servitude for forgery.	4

1916. July.	WESTERN FRONT.	EASTERN FRONT.	SOUTHERN FRONT.
5	English improve their position between Somme and Ancre ; advance slightly in some sectors. French win Hem ; N. of Somme they repel counter attacks at Belloy - en - Santerre. German attacks at Verdun on Avocourt and Hill 304 fail.	On the Riga and Baranovichi fronts, fighting continues. In Galicia, Russians continue their attacks S. of Dniester.	Risings and guerilla warfare in Serbia and Montenegro, owing to weakening of Austrian garrisons
6	British win ground on slopes of Thiépval ; two successful raids on Loos salient. French again repel attacks at Belloy ; lose a small wood N. of Hem. Artillery active at Verdun.	Between the Styr and Stokhod Germans fall back in disorder from Chartorysk salient.	Italian pressure on the Trentino and Isonzo fronts continued.
7	British again advance ; portion of Leipzig Redoubt carried in Thiepval Plateau. Fighting at Ovillers and E. of La Boisselle. Contalmaison won but not held.	Russians reach Manevichi station on Kovel-Sarni railway in N. Lutsk salient.	Italians continue advance between Brenta and Adige ; they carry two enemy positions N. of Asiago.
8	British penetrate S. part of Trônes Wood ; hand to hand fighting in Ovillers. French take Hardecourt. Violent artillery duel at Verdun. Heavy rain hampers operations.	Russians break through N. of Lutsk and cross Upper Stokhod at Ugli and Arsenovich, having advanced 25 miles in 4 days on a 40-mile front. S. of Dniester they capture Delatyn and threaten right flank of Bothmer's army.	.. .. ..
9	Two German aeroplane raids on S.E. coast, no damage. English make slight progress at Ovillers ; fighting continues in Trônes Wood. French advance along Bray-Péronne road ; take Biaches, reach outskirts of Barleux French air sq'drons bomb Ham and Bolancourt.	.. .. ..	.. .. ..
10	Germans regain footing in Trônes Wood. British gain ground E. of Ovillers and in Bois de Mametz. French advance further towards Péronne ; take Hill 97 (S.E. of Biaches) with La Maisonnette Farm.	Germans rally and offer strong resistance on W. Bank of the Stokhod. Austrians concentrate troops for big offensive on S. side of Lutsk salient. Russians claim 300,000 prisoners to date.	.. .. ..

Asiatic and Egyptian Theatres.	Naval and Overseas Operations.	Political, &c.	1916. July.
.. .. ..	.. .. ..	.. .. ..	5
.. .. ..	.. .. ..	Ministerial changes : **Mr. Lloyd George becomes Secretary of State for War.** Lord Derby, Under Secretary for War. Sir Ed. Grey raised to Peerage as Viscount Grey of Fallodon.	6
.. .. ..	In E. Africa **Gen. Smuts occupies Tanga,** the terminus of Usambara railway.	Congratulatory message to troops from King George.	7
.. .. ..	.. .. ..	A Russo-Japanese Agreement in regard to the Far East signed and announced ([78]). **Order in Council rescinds Declaration of London** of Feb. 25, 1909, and all orders arising therefrom.	8
Turks threaten attack on Tigris.	German submarine " Deutschland " arrives at Norfolk (Virg.) from Bremen ; proceeds with mails and cargo to Baltimore. Russian hospital ship " Yperyod " torpedoed in Black Sea.	Mr. E. S. Montagu appointed Minister of Munitions.	9
.. .. ..	Italian destroyer " Impetuoso " torpedoed and sunk by submarine in Lower Adriatic.	.. .. ..	10

1916. July.	WESTERN FRONT.	EASTERN FRONT.	SOUTHERN FRONT.
11	Contalmaison won and held against counter-attacks; British also take parts of Mametz and Trônes Woods. Total prisoners in 10 days fighting 7,500, and 26 field guns. At Verdun Germans gain footing in Damloup battery and E. of Firmin and Chenois Woods.	Germans receive reinforcements and heavy artillery to defend passage of the Stokhod.	.. .. ..
12	British gain Mametz Wood and make progress in Trônes Wood. Successful raids in Loos salient. Germans attack strongly at Verdun; gain some ground at Chapelle St. Fine, at intersection of Fleury—Vaux roads.	Furious fighting continues on the Stokhod, with no decisive results.	An Austrian attack on the Adige driven back.
13	German raids W. of Wytschaete and S. of La Bassée Canal repulsed. On Somme, British capture German howitzers and munitions. French make successful raid in Champagne.	Sharp fighting in Austrian centre, N.W. of Buczacz, on the Strypa. No decisive results on the Stokhod.	.. .. ..
14	British attack German second line; capture Longueval and -Bazentin-le-Petit, and the whole of Trônes Wood. End of first phase of Battle of the Somme.	End of Battle of Baranovichi.	.. .. ..
15	British advance continued; capture of Delville wood, penetrate to Bois des Foureaux and outskirts of Poziéres; 2,000 prisoners taken; second defence line penetrated; British cavalry in action. S. of Somme, Germans re-enter Biaches and La Maisonnette, and are again driven out by French.	On Riga front Russians, supported by sea and land artillery, make slight advance W. of Kemmern. On S. Lutsk salient Russians under Sakharov, anticipating Austrian offensive, attack them on Upper Styr.	.. .. ..
16	British consolidate their positions; withdraw from Bois des Foureaux (High Wood); French make slight advance W. of Fleury (Verdun .	Sakharov drives Austrians back on to the Lipa, captures Mikhailovka, makes 13,000 prisoners.	.. .. ..

ASIATIC AND EGYPTIAN THEATRES.	NAVAL AND OVERSEAS OPERATIONS.	POLITICAL, &c.	1916. July.
Russians begin a fresh offensive in Armenia Gen. Maude succeeds Gen. Gorringe in command of Tigris column.	A German submarine shells Seaham Harbour. One man killed. Three armed trawlers sunk off Scottish coasts, in action with German submarines.	.. ..	11
Russians under General Yudenich advance W. of Erzerum on the Erzingan road and recapture Mamakhatun.	.. .. ..	.. .. ..	12
.. .. ..	German submarine sinks 2 trawlers and 2 fishing boats off Whitby..	Allied Conference on Munition output held in London. Bank Holiday suspended. Bank Rate 6%.	13
.. .. ..	British force under Gen. Sir C. Crewe captures Mwanza, on Lake Victoria Nyanza. Gen. van Deventer takes Mpondi (on Central Railway).	.. .. ..	14
Russian right wing, under Gen. Yudenich, occupies Baiburt ; the left drives back Turks S.W. of Mush.	.. .. ..	.. .. ..	15
.. .. ..	.. .. ..	.. .. ..	16

1916. July.	WESTERN FRONT.	EASTERN FRONT.	SOUTHERN FRONT.
17	**British storm and capture German second line positions** on front of 1,500 yds. Take Waterlot Farm, E. of Longueval; clear Ovillers of the remaining Germans. French repulse attacks at Biaches and La Maisonnette Farm	Russians make progress in the Carpathians.	.. .. ..
18	N. of Ovillers British advance on 1,000 yds. front. Germans make strong counter-attacks at Longueval and Delville Wood; retake part of latter. Germans again repulsed at Biaches (Somme). For third day, close fighting round Fleury (Verdun).	German seaplanes drop bombs on Reval (G. of Bothnia). Sakharov continues pressure against Austrians; drives them S. of the Lipa.	.. .. ..
19	German attacks on Longueval and Delville Wood continued; British regain some lost ground, repulse attack on Waterlot Farm. French take more trenches S. of Estrées. Bombardment of Verdun front.	.. .. ..	.. .. ..
20	Struggle in Longueval and Delville Wood continued. British advance 1,000 yds. between Bazentin and Longueval. N. of Somme French carry enemy trenches from Hardecourt Hill to the river. S. they take enemy first position from Estrées to Vermandovillers, and Barleaux to Soyécourt. French gain a position S. of Fleury (Verdun). French airman drops leaflets over Berlin; is captured in Poland.	Sakharov defeats Austrians on S.W. of Lutsk salient; attacks and carries Berestechko. Heavy fighting on Riga front resumed.	Demobilisation of the Greek army nearly completed.
21	British push their advance to Bois des Foureaux (High Wood). Germans counter-attack and regain some ground. Heavy bombing attacks by enemy S. of Thiepval on Leipzig Redoubt. French repulse counter-attacks on their new front at Soyécourt; also S. of Chaulnes.	Russians drive Austro-Germans over the River Styr, taking 14,000 prisoners.	.. .. ..

ASIATIC AND EGYPTIAN THEATRES.	NAVAL AND OVERSEAS OPERATIONS.	POLITICAL, &c.	1916. July.
In Sinai Peninsula a Turkish and German force under von Kressenstein advances westward on Katiya.	British capture two German steamers on Lake Victoria Nyanza.	Trade Unions recommend postponement of all holidays in connection with munitions production. Daily cost of war, six millions.	17
In Armenia, Russians continue advance ; capture Kighi, an important junction on Erzerum-Baiburt road.	Gen. Smuts reports steady clearance of Usambara district ; enemy forces driven down Pangani river.	Mr. Asquith makes short statement on Mesopotamia in House of Commons and refuses papers.	18
In Persia Russians are defeated and driven back N. of Kermanshah by Turks. 3rd Turkish Division discovered at Bir el Abd (Sinai).	.. .. ..	.. .. ..	19
Russians continue advance in Armenia ; they capture Gumishkhanek, on Trebizond-Erzingan road. Turkish aeroplanes bomb Suez and Port Tewfik.	.. .. ..	Debate on Mesopotamia campaign in both Houses of Parliament. An Anglo-French Loan is made to Greek Government.	20
.. .. ..	.. .. ..	.. .. ..	21

1916. July.	WESTERN FRONT.	EASTERN FRONT.	SOUTHERN FRONT.
22	British attack along whole front from Pozières to Guillemont; violent fighting. French aeroplanes bomb Mülheim (Rhine) and other German towns.	Austrians, retreating before Sakharov, begin to evacuate Brody.	Italian success in the Dolomites; they take and consolidate the Rolle Pass.
23	Second phase of Somme Battle begins. Intense fighting in and round Pozières; British recapture whole of Longueval, but Germans retake N. end of village. Outskirts of G u i l l e m o n t twice change hands.	Kuropatkin's troops drive Germans back S.E. of Riga. Russians advance 12 miles near Kemmern.	.. .. ..
24	Struggle for Pozières continues; British gain some important advantages. Persistent German counter-attacks at High Wood and Guillemont. Near Estrées, French capture enemy battery. They take a redoubt W. of Thiaumont (S.W. of Douaumont, Verdun).	Russians repulse Germans from Üxküll to Riga.	Italian advance on Asiago Plateau and Trentino border continues; after a night attack troops capture Monte Cismone.
25	With fresh reinforcements the Germans counter-attack near Longueval and Bazentin; are repulsed. Pozières almost entirely in British hands. British push along Albert-Bapaume road towards Hill 160. French progress S. of Estrées and N. of Vermandovillers. In Alsace a sharp attack N. of Altkirch is repulsed.	Sakharov again attacks Austrians E. of Styr and advances against Brody. Defeats von Linsingen on River Slonuvka.	The re-constituted Serbian Army comes into action on the Salonika front against the Bulgarians.
26	The whole of Pozières village in British hands. British advance continues northwards towards Hill 160. French capture some fortified houses S. of Estrées.	.. ..	.. ..

Asiatic and Egyptian Theatres.	Naval and Overseas Operations.	Political, &c.	1916. July.
..	..	Gen. Maxwell's despatches on Irish rebellion published in *Times*. Silver badge granted for those disabled.	22
Russians steadily close in on Erzingan (Arm.) ; the Turks retreat.	Running fight in North Sea near mouth of Scheldt between British ships and six enemy destroyers ; no decisive results. Naval force occupies Pangani (E. Afr).	M. Sazonov, Russian Foreign Minister, resigns, and is succeeded by M. Stürmer.	23
..	In E. Africa, Gen. Northey defeats German southern detachment at Malangali; drives enemy towards Iringa.	Vote of Credit for £450,000,000, moved in Commons. British Memorandum in reply to American complaints regarding censorship of neutral mails, published.	24
Capture of Erzingan ; (it formed the advance base for Turkish operations on Caucasus front).	..	The protest of Mr. Gerard (U. S. A. Ambassador) against inhumanity at Ruhleben camp published in *Times*.	25
British-Italian car raid from Sollum.	Adml. Bacon's report on work of Dover Patrol published in *Times*.	Mesopotamia and Dardanelles Commissions (names of members) announced. Lord G. Hamilton and Lord Cromer respective chairmen.	26

1916. July.	WESTERN FRONT.	EASTERN FRONT.	SOUTHERN FRONT.
27	Fresh British gains at Delville Wood and near Pozières; fighting continues at Longueval. French make progress E. of Estrées. Germans make two strong attacks on French centre at Ville-au-Bois, N. of Aisne, and in Champagne, W. of Prosnes.	Sakharov reaches Klekotov position, within 5 m. of Brody.	Hostile aeroplanes drop bombs on Bari and Otranto.
28	British capture whole of Delville Wood and Longueval village; make further progress near Pozières. Enemy raids near Neuve Chapelle repulsed. French gains W. of Thiaumont (Verdun). Zeppelin raid on E. Coast. No damage.	**Sakharov enters Brody,** having captured 40,000 prisoners and 49 guns in 12 days. Further N. Lesch and Kaledin attack on Upper Stokhod, crossing river at many points.	.. .. ..
29	Hand to hand struggle N. and N.E. of Pozières and High Wood. Two German attempts to recapture Delville Wood fail. Activity S. of Ypres and in Loos salient.	.. .. ..	.. .. ..
30	Combined Allied advance N. of Somme, from Delville Wood to the river. British make progress E. of Waterlot Farm and Trônes Wood; French reach outskirts of Maurepas. German attack on L. bank of Meuse repulsed.	In the direction of Kovel and in the region S. of the Dniester towards Stanislau, Russians still pursue Austrians.	Austrian attack in Tofana and in the Adige Valley repulsed. Austrians reinforced, attack three times in Travignolo Valley without success. Russian troops land at Salonika.
31	Zeppelin raid on E. and S.E. Counties; about 60 bombs dropped. No damage.	Russian advance on the Stokhod towards Kovel. Heavy engagements. Russians N. of Dniester have crossed Koropyets River.	In the Astico Valley (Trent.) Austrian attack on positions of Monte Cimone repulsed. S.W. of Castelletto, Austrian attack repulsed by Italians. In the Travignolo valley, Italians occupy Paneveggio.

ASIATIC AND EGYPTIAN THEATRES.	NAVAL AND OVERSEAS OPERATIONS.	POLITICAL, &c.	1916. July.
Russians advance towards Sivas (W. of Erzingan); a Turkish attack near Mosul is repulsed. **Yanbo**, port of Medina, **captured by Grand Sherif** of Mecca. Turks and Germans begin to move from Katiya line.	.. .. ..	**Capt. Chas. Fryatt, of the** G.E. liner "Brussels," is **court-martialled and shot** by German authorities in Belgium for attempt to ram German submarine.	27
Patrol engagements with Turks E. of Suez Canal.	.. .. ..	American Ambassador in London presents formal protest against the policy of the "Black List."	28
.. .. ..	Dodoma (E. Africa) occupied by British.	German Note to U.S.A. Ambassador at Berlin rejects British offer to permit passage of U.S.A. foodstuffs to Poland. Duke of Devonshire appointed Gov.-Gen. of Canada.	29
.. .. ..	British occupy Kikombo (E. Africa).	.. .. ..	30
The pursuit of the Turks from Erzingan (Armen.) continues in the face of a stubborn defence.	British occupy Saranda and Kilimatinde (Central Railway, E. Africa).	Prime Minister in House of Commons denounces murder of Capt. Fryatt; immediate action contemplated by Government. Mr. H. E. Duke becomes Chief Secretary for Ireland.	31

1916. Aug.	WESTERN FRONT.	EASTERN FRONT.	SOUTHERN FRONT.
1	N. of Bazentin-le-Petit, German attack repulsed. High Wood (Somme), German counter attack W. of, failed. French capture strong work between Hem Wood and Monacu Farm. German attacks W. and S. of the Thiaumont work (S.W. of Douaumont, Verdun) repulsed.	.. .. ..	.. .. ..
2	German attack on Delville Wood (Somme) repulsed. German counter - attack on French at Estrées (S. Somme) repulsed. German trenches carried S. of Fleury (Verdun), 800 prisoners taken. British naval air-raid near Ghent.	German gas attack in region of Smorgon (E. Vilna) repulsed.	.. .. ..
3	British gain ground W. of Pozières. French retake Fleury (Verdun) and make progress towards Thiaumont, 1,750 prisoners taken. Zeppelin raid over E. Counties. No damage.	Russians penetrate into Rudka - Mirynska (E. Kovel). Desperate fighting near Lyubashevo and Guledichi (E. Kovel).	.. .. ..
4	British gain German second line system on a front of 2,000 yds. N. of Pozières, several hundred prisoners. Germans retake Fleury (Verdun) but lose it again to French. Furious German counter-attacks at Thiaumont work repulsed.	Fierce fighting in progress on the Graberko and Sereth. Russians take 1,300 prisoners. Germans by an enveloping movement regain Rudka-Mirynska.	.. .. ..
5	.. .. ..	.. .. ..	.. .. ..

ASIATIC AND EGYPTIAN THEATRES.	NAVAL AND OVERSEAS OPERATIONS.	POLITICAL, &c.	1916. Aug.
.. .. ..	.. .. ..	Announcement in House of Commons regarding deaths among troops on trains from Karachi.	1
Turkish counter-attack takes Mush and Bitlis (Armen.).	Loss of Italian Dreadnought "Lionardo da Vinci," at Taranto, by fire and explosion (248 killed.)	Government attitude to Resolutions adopted by Allies at Economic Conference in Paris explained by Mr. Asquith ([71]). Two important State Papers on barbarity of Germans published ([79]).	2
Russians capture Turk trenches at Ognut (Armen.), Turks advance to attack on Maj.-Gen. Hon. H. Lawrence's force at Romani (N. Sinai).	Belgians occupy Ujiji (Lake Tanganyika).	R. Casement hanged. Statement by Mr. Balfour *re* Naval Situation on the 2nd anniversary of war. Prime Minister receives deputation from Miners, Railway Men, and Transport Workers ([80]).	3
Turk attack near Romani (N. Sinai) beaten off ([81]).	.. .. ..	.. .. ..	4
British counter-attack Turks with success near Romani (N. Sinai). British pursuit continues for 18 miles ([81]). Turk attacks held in the region of Mush - Bitlis (Asia Min.). Successful Russian offensive continued 30 miles N. of Erzingan.	British forces in E. Africa begin simultaneous forward movement, through Nguru Mountains, etc., towards Morogoro.	.. .. ..	5

1916. Aug.	Western Front.	Eastern Front.	Southern Front.
6	Slight British progress E. of Pozières towards Martinpuich. German attacks at Thiaumont work and in Vaux-Chapitre Wood repulsed (Verdun).	Russians gain heights and villages on right bank of Sereth and Graberko (S. Brody) and repel German counter-attacks.	**Battle of Gorizia.** Italian attack on Isonzo; several lines of trenches taken in Monfalcone sector, and nearly the whole of Hill 85 ; 3,600 prisoners and many m.g's. taken.
7	British attack outskirts of Guillemont. German attacks N. and N.E. of Pozières, repulsed. French advance N. of Hardecourt (N. Somme). French progress at Fleury and the Thiaumont work(Verdun).	Russian advance in Graberko - Sereth region. Heavy fighting, 2,000 prisoners taken. Russians capture Tlumacz (12 miles from Stanislau) 2,000 prisoners taken.	Italian offensive continues. Monte Sabatino, Monte San Michele and bridgehead of Gorizia captured, 8,000 prisoners, 11 guns and 100 machine guns taken. Austrian attacks beaten off by Italians on Asiago Plateau and in the Upper Cordevole Valley (Dolomites).
8	British move against Guillemont continues, line advanced 400 yds. French progress N. of Hem Wood (S. Somme). Germans, by violent counter-attack, regain trenches. Fierce fighting in Verdun region : Germans gain and lose Thiaumont work. Two German attacks beaten back E. of Monacu Farm (N. Somme).	Russians take Tysmienica (Stanislau, Gal.), 7,400 prisoners.	Italians storm Mount Podgora (covering Gorizia).
9	Germans driven back and French advance N.of Hem Wood. Germans regain Thiaumont work. Zeppelin raid on E. Coast, ten killed. sixteen injured	Russians gain junction of Chryplin (Stanislau).	**Capture of Gorizia** by Italians. Austrians pursued, 10,000 prisoners taken. Italians occupy hills on line Rosenthal-Vertoibica (Isonzo). Heavy Austrian attack beaten back on L. bank Isonzo.
10	British advance N.W. of Pozières.	Russians take Stanislau and 8,500 prisoners. Russians cross the Sereth and repulse repeated enemy counter-attacks. Russians cross the Zlota-Lipa and advance on Halicz.	Allied offensive begins in Macedonia. French bombard Doiran (Serbo-Greek frontier), and occupy Hill 227, S. of Doiran.

Asiatic and Egyptian Theatres.	Naval and Overseas Operations.	Political, &c.	1916. Aug.
Determined Turk attacks repulsed by Russians N. of the Upper Euphrates (Arm.) and in region of Mush-Bitlis. Russians driven back by the Turks E. of Kermanshah (Pers.) British occupy Katiya (N. Sinai).	.. .. ..	.. .. ..	6
Stiff fighting at Romani; British threaten Turkish flanks.	.. ..	..	Admiralty deny allegation in German press that British Hospital Ships are being used as transports.	
Turks occupy Mush and Bitlis (Armenia). Turks abandon Oghratina and fall back to cover Bir el Abd (Sinai).	.. ..	..	Portugal decides to extend her military co-operation to Europe.	8
Turks press back British cavalry E. of Romani (Suez), but are repulsed and lose heavily.	.. .. ..	.. .. ..	9
.. .. ..	.. ..	..	Mr. McKenna, in the House of Commons, spoke on the British financial position (¹²). British protest *re* shooting of Capt. Fryatt published.	10

1916. Aug.	Western Front.	Eastern Front.	Southern Front.
11	French capture German trenches S. of Maurepas. Long distance British air-raids into Belgium.	.. .. ..	Italians land at Salonika. Italians cross the Vallon and make progress on the N. edge of the Carso (Isonzo).
12	British advance on a mile front N.W. of Pozières. French gain the German third line system of trenches from Somme to Hardecourt. Hostile seaplane raid on Dover. Seven injured.	Russians cross the Zlota-Lipa and occupy Mariampol. German retreat from the Strypa (E. Gal.)	Italians capture strong positions on N. edge of the Carso, and take 1,565 prisoners and make progress in Monfalcone sector. End of battle of Gorizia.
13	Grenade attacks in progress-at Fleury (Verdun). French progress S.W. of Estrées.	German attack repulsed in region of the Stokhod (Volhynia).	Italian advance further on N. edge of Carso, and take 800 prisoners.
14	Great artillery activity N. and S. of the Somme.	Russians press retreating Austrians, Halicz (Gal.) threatened, and continue passage of the Zlota-Lipa.	E. of Gorizia, heavy fighting. Italian advance on the N. edge of Carso results in capture of enemy trenches and 1,400 prisoners.
15	The King returns from a visit to the Armies on Western front.	Another Russian force reaches Zlota-Lipa, S. of Brzezany (Gal.), and also Solotwina (W. Stanislau).	Italians take more trenches E. of Gorizia.
16	British advance W. and S.W. of Guillemont. French take trenches on front of 11 miles, Cléry-Maurepas - Guillemont. French take a system of German trenches near Belloy - en - Santerre (S. Somme) on front of 1,300 yds., 1,300 prisoners.	Heavy Russian attacks W. of Sereth (Gal.). Total of Russian captures published (**).	Artillery activity on Isonzo.
17	Violent artillery fighting N. and S. of the Somme. Determined German attack on broad front, N.W. of Pozières, beaten off.	Strong enemy attacks beaten back by Russians on Zlota - Lipa (Gal.) front.	Lively artillery action on upper and middle Isonzo. Considerable activity along whole of Balkan front.

ASIATIC AND EGYPTIAN THEATRES.	NAVAL AND OVERSEAS OPERATIONS.	POLITICAL, &c.	1916. Aug.
Turks attack at Bayud (Sinai), and evacuate it.	German resistance broken at Matamondo (E. of Nguru Mountains, E. Africa) ; they retreat S.	.. .. ..	11
Turks evacuate Bir el Abd (N. Sinai), losing altogether 4,000 prisoners.	British occupy Mpapwa (E. Africa).	.. .. ..	12
.. .. ..	H.M.S. destroyer "Lassoo" torpedoed or mined and sunk off Dutch coast.	.. .. ..	13
Turkish offensive continues W. of Hamadan (Persia).	.. .. ..	Final meeting between Italian and British delegates ; complete understanding on economic questions.	14
.. .. ..	British clear of Nguru Mts., drive enemy force southward and eastward (⁸³). Naval forces take Bagamoyo.	.. .. ..	15
.. . .	Terms of new British War Loan to be raised in U.S.A. announced. Special Register Bill postponed.	16
.. ..	Rumania concludes agreement with Allies for intervention; favourable demonstration at Bucharest.	17

1916. Aug.	WESTERN FRONT.	EASTERN FRONT.	SOUTHERN FRONT.
18	British advance from Pozières to Somme ; ground gained towards Ginchy and Guillemont. French gain part of Maurepas and extend their gains S.E. Violent German counter-attacks N. of Maurepas beaten back by French. French take the whole of Fleury (Verdun) and make progress at Thiaumont.	.. .. ..	Bulgarians having advanced through E. Macedonia, occupy several Greek forts.
19	Heavy fighting on Somme front. British continue to gain ground. German attacks at Fleury (Verdun) repulsed.	.. .. ..	.. .. ..
20	Great artillery activity on the Somme. British and French encounters all along the front.	.. .. ..	Serbs throw back Bulgarians in Moglena sector (Balkans). **General Allied offensive in Macedonia.**
21	Considerable progress made on a front of half mile N.W. of Pozières. British within 1,000 yds. of Thiepval (Somme).	.. .. ..	.. ..
22	Two determined counter-attacks S. of Thiepval beaten off by British. Germans gain a footing in trenches held by French S. of Estrées (S. Somme). Heavy aerial fighting on Somme front.	Russians gain heights S. of Jablonica Pass (Carpath.). Enemy attack with gas S.E. of Vilna, repulsed.	Italian successes in the Dolomites. Allied offensive progresses in the Moglena and Doiran sectors (Maced.).
23	Fighting S. of Thiepval results in a slight British gain. Strong German attacks at Guillemont repulsed. Fierce artillery duel on French section of Somme front. French progress S. of Fleury (Verdun). Zeppelin raid on E. Coast, no casualties.	.. .. ..	Activity on Salonika front, especially on left flank.

Asiatic and Egyptian Theatres.	Naval and Overseas Operations.	Political, &c.	1916. Aug.
.. .. ..	Gen. Northey occupies Lupembe (E. Africa).	.. .. ..	18
.. .. ..	German High Sea Fleet comes out, but retires in face of British forces([88]). H.M.S. " Nottingham " and " Falmouth," light cruisers, torpedoed and sunk; 2 German submarines destroyed. " Westfalen " sunk (?).	Crisis in Greece, owing to Bulgar occupation of Greek territory.	19
.. .. ..	.. .. ..	.. .. ..	20
.. .. ..	.. .. ..	.. .. ..	21
Russian offensive W. of Lake Van (Armenia).	Kilossa, on Central Railway (E. Africa), taken by British. Enemy falls back on Morogoro.	Mr. Lloyd George in the House of Commons gives survey of military situation ; announces 35 Zeppelins destroyed by Allies.	22
Turks defeated at Rayat (Turco-Persian frontier); 2,300 prisoners. Russians retake Bitlis (L. Vau).	Return of submarine " Deutschland " to Germany.	.. .. ..	23

1916. Aug.	WESTERN FRONT.	EASTERN FRONT.	SOUTHERN FRONT.
24	Further British advance towards Thiepval (N. Somme). Hard fighting on E. and N.E. edge of Delville Wood, ground gained and prisoners taken. German attacks W. of Ginchy (Somme) driven off. French capture whole of Maurepas and repulse violent German counter-attacks S. of village. Zeppelin raid on E. and S.E. Coast, nine killed, forty injured.	.. .. ..	Italian progress in Dolomites.
25	Determined German attack S. of Thiepval repulsed. Germans active in Verdun region ; violent German attack repulsed W. of Tahure (Champagne). Zeppelin raid on E. and S.E. Coast and London.	.. .. ..	British warships bombard the forts of Kavalla Seres occupied by Bulgars.
26	British take a short length of German trench N. of Bazentin-le-Petit (Somme).	Russians make slight advance towards Halicz (Gal.).	Activity on left flank of Salonika front. Serbs beat off Bulgar counter-attacks N.W. of Kukuruz and progress in Ostrovo region. Gen. Moschopoulos appointed Chief of Greek General Staff in place of Gen. Dusmanis.
27	German attack in front of Fleury repulsed.	.. .. ..	Ground gained by Serbs near Vetrenik (Salonika) in a general offensive.
28	Artillery activity on Somme front. French gain ground S.E. of Thiaumont work and repulse German attacks against Fleury and against a position near Vaux Fort (Verdun).	Rumanians and Austrians in contact in the passes of the Transylvanian Alps. Austrians withdraw N. of Kronstadt. Austrian monitors bombard Rumanian towns on the Danube.	Serbians progress E. of Cherna River.
29	British capture of German prisoners since the beginning of British offensive July 1st, 266 officers, 15,203 men, 86 guns, 160 machine guns.	Russians capture Mount Pantyr (N.W. of Jablonica Pass, Carpath.). Austrians retreat before Rumanian advance in Trans. Alps. Kronstadt, Petrozseny and Kezdi-Vasarhely occupied by Rumanians.	.. .. ..

Asiatic and Egyptian Theatres.	Naval and Overseas Operations.	Political, &c.	1916. Aug.
Mush (Arm.) recaptured by Russians and 2,300 prisoners taken on way to Mosul.	H.M.S. " Duke of Albany," boarding s.s., torpedoed and sunk.	Conference at Calais on Franco-British war finance ([86]).	24
.. .. ..	.. .. ..	Correspondence between British and Swedish Governments about the detention of mail packets by either Government is published.	25
.. .. ..	British enter Morogoro (E. Africa).	.. .. ..	26
.. .. ..	British capture large artillery dump and occupy Mgeta.	Rumania mobilises and declares War on Austria-Hungary. Greek protest meeting in Athens on King Constantine's policy.	27
Encounters take place S. of Erzerum (Armenia). Gen. Maude succeeds Gen. Lake as C.-i.-C. in Mesopotamia.	.. .. ..	Germany declares War on Rumania. Italy declares War on Germany.	28
.. .. ..	Gen. Northey occupies Iringa.	v. Hindenburg appointed Chief of German General Staff in place of v. Falkenhayn and v. Ludendorff, Chief Quartermaster-General.	29

1916. Aug.	WESTERN FRONT.	EASTERN FRONT.	SOUTHERN FRONT.
30	Somme, Bavarians surrender S. Martinpuich. British list of prisoners ([87])	.. .. ..	Tepeleni (Alb.) occupied by Italians. Venizelis revolution at Salonika.
31	British gas attacks at Arras and Armentières. Heavy German attacks between Ginchy and Bois Foureaux.	Fighting at Halicz and E. of Lemberg; many prisoners taken in Lutsk area by Russians.	Buk (N.E. Drama, Maced air raid on bridges.
Sept. 1	High Wood (Somme front), 4 German attacks failed.	Rumanians capture Hermannstadt. Fresh successful Russian advance in Volhynia.	Bulgars in possession of 1 Greek forts ([88]).
2	Hoboken, near Antwerp, British drop bombs on shipbuilding yards.	Russians cross the Danube into the Dobruja.	.. .. .
3	Somme front, Ginchy and all Guillemont, with many prisoners, captured by British. Le Forest village, E. of Maurepas, Cléry-sur-Somme and German trenches taken by French. 13 airships raided English Eastern counties, one brought down at Cuffley, Essex ([90]). British defeat Prussian Guard attack at Thiepval.	Near Orsova on Danube, Austrians withdraw to W. bank of Cherna. The Dobruja entered by German and Bulgarian troops. Russians close to Zlota Lipa capture position near Brzezany, taking many prisoners. Russian success near Dorna Vatra (Carp.).	Constanza (Rum.) bombed
4	Somme front: French offensive continues, Barleux to S. of Chaulnes, many prisoners taken. French take village of Chilly.	Zlota Lipa front, Gen. Brusilov's troops successful, 19,000 prisoners within 4 days. Unsuccessful German gas attacks near Baronovichi (C.)	.. .. .
5	E. of Guillemont our line is carried forward 1,500 yds.; we hold most of Leuze Wood. Allies occupy whole of enemy's second line on the Somme.	7 miles S.E. of Halicz the Russians claim success; many prisoners taken. Polish autonomy granted by Central Powers.	In the Dolomites operations now developing the whole of Val Cismon free. Bucharest bombed by Bulgars.

Asiatic and Egyptian Theatres.	Naval and Overseas Operations.	Political, &c.	1916. Aug.
.. ..	Germans retire from Morogoro (German East Africa) over Ruwu river.	Turkey declares war on Rumania.	30
British cars raid and capture Senussi convoy 20 miles N.W. of Jaghbub (Tripoli).	.. .. ..	Canadian casualties to date (pub. 22.9.16): 8,644 k. (or d.), 27,212 w., 2,005 missing.	31
Chormuk, N. Euphrates, captured by Russians. 25 bombs dropped on Port Said.	Athens: Naval demonstration of Allied fleet (⁸⁹).	New York, value of German Mark at 30% discount. Bulgaria declares war on Rumania.	**Sept.** 1
.. .. ..	Athens: 3 German vessels seized at Piræus by Allies, Greek arsenal wireless seized.	Greece: Allies demand control of posts and telegraphs.	2
.. .. ..	Ghistelles (5 m. S.E. Ostend) British naval air squadron effectively attacks. **Dar-es-Salaam, capital of German E. Africa, surrenders to British Naval Forces.**	.. .. ..	3
S. of River Elen, W. of Trebizond, Russian offensive continues; over 500 prisoners. S.W. of Lake Nimrud, W. of Lake Van, British armoured cars engage Kurdish forces.	.. .. ..	Athens reports that King Constantine will reconsider the attitude of Greece. The Greek Government accepts the three demands of the Anglo-French note.	4
British bomb Turkish aerodrome at El Arish (90 m. E. of Port Said).	.. .. ..	Mr. Balfour at Glasgow appeals to local trade unions *re* shipyard labour. Trade Union Congress at Birmingham rejects invitation of U.S.A. Federation of Labour, *re* " Terms of Peace " (⁹¹).	5

1916. Sept.	WESTERN FRONT.	EASTERN FRONT.	SOUTHERN FRONT.
6	Somme front : British gain Leuze Wood. S.W. of Barleux and S. of Belloy, Gens. von Stein and Kirchbach make 10 attempts against the French, all hopelessly beaten by " 75's " and " 105 " guns. Capture of Guillemont and advance to Ginchy completed.	.. .. ..	.. ..
7	.. .. ..	Halicz (on the Dniester) on fire, and taken by Russians. Orsova (Austrian bank of Danube) occupied by Rumanians.	Tutrakan (on Danube, S.E. of Bucharest) captured by Bulgars ; the enemy claim 20,000 prisoners and 100 guns.
8	Somme, enemy attack French, Berny to S. of Chaulnes, no success. From Vermandovillers to Chaulnes, Germans make 4 massed attacks ; the French take 200 prisoners. Marschall von Hindenburg reported visiting W. front for first time.	.. .. ..	.. ..
9	N. Somme: British capture Ginchy and make advance of 300 yds. E. of High Wood ; N.E. of Pozières, take 600 yds. of enemy trenches. End of second phase. Before Douaumont, E. of Fleury, French carry whole system of German trenches. French airmen drop bombs on Rottweil (Württemberg).	Fall of Silistria (Danube).	.. ..
10	British line advanced a mile E. of Guillemont, also 1,000 yds. E. of Ginchy. 5 enemy attacks on French line, Berny to region S. of Chaulnes, defeated.	Russian and Rumanian forces in contact. Austrian front withdrawn W. of the Valley of Gyergyo and Czik (Carp.)	British cross the Struma at Neoliori and places above the Tahinos Lake (Maced.). Corfu, Serbian Parliament assembles here, all ministers present.
11	Somme : British heavy artillery caused large fires in enemy ammunition depot, Grandcourt, N. of Pozières.	Bucharest : Gen. Averesco appointed to com. of 3rd Army. Russians capture Mt. Capel Kapul in Carpathians; many prisoners.	.. ..

Asiatic and Egyptian Theatres.	Naval and Overseas Operations.	Political, &c.	1916. Sept.
Mazar (Sinai Pen.), British airmen raid camps, supply depots and camel lines, good results.	British checked N. of Kissaki (Uluguru Mts.)	Birmingham : Trade Union Congress insists on restoration of Trade Union customs and practices after the war. New Zealand : Bill passed for Compulsory military service ; recruiting stimulated. Simla : Viceroy's important speech, re supply of labour to Colonies, and record of India's great services during the War (⁹²).	6
Baghdad railway, over Taurus Mtns. being constructed by Turkish peasants, large bodies of Turkish troops moving to Aleppo, for Mesopotamia.	Kilwa (Kivinje), 135 m. S. of Dar-es-Salaam, and Kilwa Kissiwani, still further S., surrender to British naval forces.	Baron v. Schenck and other Germans and Austrians expelled from Athens.	7
.. .. ..	British naval aeroplanes bomb aerodrome at St. Denis Westrem (5 m. W. of Ghent).	.. .. ..	8
.. .. ..	Naval air raid on Ghistelles, Handzaeme and Lichtervelde (Ostend).	Paris, during last week, French and British Ministers for War and Munitions held conferences. Cardiff : S. Wales railwaymen resolve to strike, demandmanding increase of 10s. weekly on wages.	9
.. ..		Mr. Lloyd George at Verdun, with General Dubois and M. Albert Thomas ; Lloyd George's speech praising Verdun.	10
British defeat Turkish columns at Az Sahilan (Nazariya, Euphrates R.)	.. .. ..	Athens : M. Zaimis tenders resignation.	11

1916. Sept.	WESTERN FRONT.	EASTERN FRONT.	SOUTHERN FRONT.
12	Somme : French take S. of Combles to the river, Hill 145, Marrières Wood, all enemy trench system up to Bapaume-Péronne rd., and many prisoners. Bouchavesnes, and Hill 76, N. of Péronne, taken, and part of German 3rd line.	Dobruja : F.M. von Mackensen in supreme command of German-Bulgarian forces. Rumanians advance on Kronstadt (Brasso), their right flank joining Russians near Dorna Vatra.	4th Greek Corps of 25,000 men at Kavalla deserts (under Col. Hatzopoulos) to the Germans. Sent to Germany as " guests."
13	French carry by assault L'Abbé Wood farm, and trench system S. of Le Priez farm, S.E. of Combles, big success.	.. .. ..	Trieste bombed by 22 Caproni battle-planes. Serbians advance left of Allied line in Macedonia in direction of Florina and Monastir ; Sorovich occupied by Allies. (S.W. end of Lake Ostrovo).
14	Somme · S.E. Thiepval, on a front of 1,000 yds., British storm trenches, including the " Wunderwerk." French carry Le Priez Farm ; fruitless counter-attacks of a German division from Verdun front.	.. .. ..	British gain ground towards Machukova (S. of Gevgeli, Macedonia). W. of Vardar River (Serbia), Serbian troops storm Bulgar entrenchments. Kavalla (Greek Maced.) occupied by Bulgarians.
15	Great British advance (3rd phase) on the Somme, a 6-mile front to depth of 2 or 3,000 yds. Flers, Martinpuich, Courcelette, and whole of High Wood taken. New heavy armoured cars (Tanks) used for first time, N. of Pozières to E. of Guillemont. French capture trenches S. of Rancourt, and system of trenches N. of Le Priez Farm, S. of Somme, E. of Deniécourt, &c.	.. .. ..	Lower Isonzo : Italians take San Grado, strong entrenchments towards Loquizza and E. of Oppacchiasella, and over 1,800 prisoners.
16	Somme, near Courcelette the British front advanced 1,000 yds. ; " Danube " trench taken and Mouquet farm (Thiepval) captured.	Halicz front, Russians capture a position right bank of Zlota Lipa and many prisoners. Along the Narajowka many Germans taken as well as Turks. In the Dobruja, Gen. Averesco (new C.-in-C. Rumanian Army) arrives at front. Rumanians occupy Baraoltu dominating railway from Brasso to Földvar (30 m. from Rumanian frontier).	.. .. ..

Asiatic and Egyptian Theatres.	Naval and Overseas Operations.	Political, &c.	1916. Sept.
.. .. ..	.. .. ..	.. .. ..	12
.. .. ..	British occupy Mikindani (southernmost post in Ger. E. Africa).	Melbourne : Mr. Hughes' bill, referendum for conscription in Australia, read first time. Verdun visited by President Poincaré ; various honours, including M.C., presented to town.	13
.. .. ..	.. .. ..	Popular indignation in Greece at Kavalla news.	14
.. .. ..	Gen. Smuts' columns reach S. of Uluguru Hills, and join near, and occupy, Kissaki ; Van Deventer approaching the Great Ruaha river towards Mahenge (E. Africa). Sudi Bay occupied by British naval forces.	.. .. ..	15
.. .. ..	Lindi (port in S. Ger. E. Africa) occupied by British.	Athens: New Cabinet formed under M. Kalogeropoulos, expected to observe benevolent neutrality towards Entente.	16

1916. Sept.	WESTERN FRONT.	EASTERN FRONT.	SOUTHERN FRONT.
17	S. Somme : French attack, taking Vermandovillers and Berny, Deniécourt surrounded, German reserves much cut up, many prisoners.	Rumanians between Petrozseny and Hatszeg. (W. Transylv.)	Italian success on the Carso.
18	S. of the Ancre, British advance, taking " Quadrilateral " between Bouleaux Wood and Ginchy, on a front of a mile, to a dept of 1,000 yds. French take Deniécourt.	Heavy fighting at Merisor (Transyl.), Rumanians moving towards Hatszeg. In Dobruja, Russo-Rumanians fall back to Rasova-Tuzla line.	Franco - Russian troops enter Florina (Maced.), enemy retreating on Monastir. Serbs occupy parts of Mt. Kaymakchlan.
19	Bad weather hinders both British and French operations.	Desperate fighting on Narajowka river, Halicz region. Germans claim success here and on Stokhod (Pripet); many prisoners. Heavy fighting in defile of Merisor (Transyl.) W. of Petrozseny. Battle lasts two days. Rumanians successful. Rumanians in Dobruja, holding the Rasova-Tuzla position, defending the railway Bucharest-Constanza, heavily engaged. In Galicia, heavy fighting for 3 days past (⁹³).	The Serbo-Russian-French Army advances, making great turning movement in their march on Monastir.
20	Somme : German counteroffensive against French fails. From Combles to the river, an attack with 6 divisions suffered heavy losses. S. of the Ancre, Germans during night attacked New Zealand troops without success.	N. of Vulkan Pass, Transylvania, Rumanians fall back to S. of Petrozseny. Mackensen halts in Dobruja : Germans, Bulgars and Turks in retreat, after severe repulse. On the Stokhod severe fighting, near the Kovel-Rovno railway ; enemy everywhere repulsed.	Italians advance E. of Gorizia, near Santa Caterina, and on the Carso, E. of the Vallone.
21	At Verdun, French take trenches S.E. of Thiaumont Work and over 100 prisoners. S. of the Ancre, during night, British troops advance between Flers and Martinpuich.	In Transylvania, Rumanian left held up near Vulkan Pass (S. of Petrozseny). Fighting in Kealeman and Görgeny mountains (Transyl.), Rumanians taking prisoners.	Allies pressing along the roads N. of Florina. Serbians within sight of Monastir.

Asiatic and Egyptian Theatres.	Naval and Overseas Operations.	Political, &c.	1916. Sept.
British attack and occupy Mazar (N. Sinai). Turks withdraw to El Arish.	.. .. ..	.. .. ..	17
British aeroplanes bomb enemy aerodrome in the Shumran bend (above Kut-el-Amara). British raid Bir el Tawal (30 miles S. of El Kubri, Suez).	.. .. ..	New South Wales : Political Labour League carries resolution expelling Prime Minister, Mr. Hughes, from the Labour movement.	18
.. .. ..	Belgians(under Gen.Tombeur) occupy Tabora. Allied blockade of the GreekMacedonian Coast, from R. Struma to R. Mesto.	M. Briand speaks against the dissident socialist faction of the Chamber.	19
.. .. ..	Portuguese troops cross the Rovuma river, separating German from Portuguese E. Africa ; enemy after feeble resistance abandon their trenches. British occupy Kiswere Port.	Greek Government demands from Germany the return of the 4th Army Corps surrendered at Kavalla and sent to Germany, Albanian Govt. (Essad Pasha) set up in Salonika.	20
.. .. ..	German submarine destroyed at Hagios-Kosmos (E. of Phaleron, Greece).	Paris : Gen. Duport gazetted Chief of the staff, staff attached to Ministry of War.	21

1916. Sept.	WESTERN FRONT.	EASTERN FRONT.	SOUTHERN FRONT.
22	British advance to E. of Courcelette. Strong British aeroplane raid on important railway stations, much damage done. Aeroplane raid on Kent, no damage.	Russians reported about 50 miles from Lemberg.	Left bank of Struma; British troops attacked, on our left Bulgar counter-attacks repulsed.
23	Big raid by German airships on England: 2 airships brought down ([94]).	.. .. ..	.. .. ..
24	Krupp's works at Essen bombed by 2 French airmen; 12 bombs dropped. S. of the Ancre, enemy made 3 attacks on our lines, W. of Lesbœufs, all failed.	A Zeppelin attacks Bucharest, and drops three bombs.	.. .. ..
25	Lesbœufs and Morval captured, Combles hemmed in by Allies. French progress at Rancourt, Le Priez Farm and Frégicourt. Zeppelin raid by 7 airships on England; casualties, 43 killed, 31 injured ([95]).	Bulgarian right wing in Dobruja having retreated, enemy is fortifying new positions.	E. of Florina (N. of Greece) considerable Bulgarian forces attack the French beyond Armenohov. W. of Florina, French and Russian troops engaged, N. of Armensko, taking prisoners and machine guns
26	Capture of Combles and Thiepval. British storm Gueudecourt, and cavalry pursue Germans. Quantity of stores and many prisoners taken. French advance E. of Combles and Rancourt, and enter wood of St. Pierre Vaast.	Vulkan Pass regained by Rumanians.	.. .. ..
27	British storm Stuff Redoubt and advance N. of Flers to the E. of Eaucourt l'Abbaye. At Verdun German strong attack at nightfall against Thiaumont-Fleury front repulsed with great loss.	In the Jiu Valley (Vulkan Pass). Rumanian troops attack and repulse enemy who is retreating towards the N. and N.W. Rumanian Army occupies one-third of Transylvania as the result of one month's War.	.. .. ..

ASIATIC AND EGYPTIAN THEATRES.	NAVAL AND OVERSEAS OPERATIONS.	POLITICAL, &c.	1916. Sept.
.. .. ..	.. .. ..	.. .. ..	22
.. .. ..	.. .. ..	.. .. ..	23
Sherif of Mecca reports he has forced Taif (60 m. S.E. of Mecca) to surrender; garrison Turkish, many prisoners, guns and stores.	.. .. ..	Ottawa: The Canadian War Loan of £20,000,000. Extraordinary success, oversubscribed by sixteen millions.	24
Sir A. J. Murray's despatch of 1.6.16 (10.1 to 31.5.16) published.	.. .. ..	Athens: M. Venizelos with members of his party leaves for Crete, after addressing long message to the *Times*, explaining his position and hopes. Tokyo: Mass meeting of the Doshi-kai (constitutional Unionist party) resolves to amalgamate the three parties supporting the Government.	25
.. .. ..	Athens: Greek ships have joined the Allied fleet under Admiral du Fournet, the French C.-in-C. Gen. Sir C. Crewe occupies Igalulu, E. of Tabora (E. Africa).	.. .. ..	26
.. .. ..	British naval aeroplanes attack sheds near Brussels.	Athens: Greek generals reported in favour of war. Interview with Mr. Lloyd George on the war is published in American papers ([96]).	27

1916. Sept.	WESTERN FRONT.	EASTERN FRONT.	SOUTHERN FRONT.
28	British attack Schwaben Redoubt on crest of Thiepval Plateau ; most of it taken. They advance N. and N.E. of Courcelette, and between Martinpuich and Gueudecourt. French make progress between Frégicourt and Morval.	.. .. ..	.. .. ..
29	S.W. of Le Sars (on road to Bapaume), British take farm.	.. .. ..	.. .. ..
30	Thiepval ridge (except part of Schwaben Redoubt) all occupied. Advance S. of Eaucourt l'Abbaye.	Falkenhayn in Transylvania attacks the Roter Turm pass. Rumanian 1st Army retreats over Fogaras Mts. **Great battle in Galicia** (near Zlota Lipa and Brzezany) **commences.** Russians advance in Brody region.	British cross Struma river at Orliak and capture villages L. bank. Towards Florina, Serbs capture Mt. Kaymakchlan (25 m. E.S.E. of Monastir).
Oct. 1	British attack on line Eaucourt-Le Sars (on Albert-Bapaume road) ; all objectives taken on front of 3,000 yds., Eaucourt occupied. Prisoners, etc., to date (⁹⁷). Zeppelin raid on E. coast, L31 down at Potter's Bar, 1 killed, 1 injured.	In region of Brody, Russians a d v a n c e after severe fighting.	Italians take trenches in Transvenanzis Valley (Trentino). Serbs progress N.E. of Kaymakchlan, and occupy important Bulgar positions. British capture 3 villages on Struma front.
2	Germans regain footing in Eaucourt.	Rumanians rally S. of R o t e r T u r m Pass (S. Transylvania.). On S. front cross Danube at Rjahovo (nr. Ruschuk) threatening Mackensen's rear. In Dobruja they attack and repulse Mackensen. On Zlota Lipa furious fighting continues. Russians take 1,000 prisoners, but front remains unchanged. On Brody - Zloczow road enemy claim recapture all positions lost on 30th.	In Kaymakchlan region Bulgars retire N. in direction Monastir. Bulgars evacuate Mt. Starkov Grob. Bulgar c o u n t e r - attack on Struma front repulsed by British.

ASIATIC AND EGYPTIAN THEATRES.	NAVAL AND OVERSEAS OPERATIONS.	POLITICAL, &c.	1916. Sept.
.. .. ..	.. .. ..	Proclamation by M. Venizelos in Crete.	2S
.. .. ..	Portuguese occupy Bay of Menasi (Germ. E. Africa)	Herr von Kühlmann, GermanMinister at the Hague, appointed Ambassador to Turkey. Greek Provisional Government announced by M. Venizelos and Admiral Condouriotis.	29
.. .. ..	.. .. ..	M. Venizelos, Adm. Condouriotis, and Gen. Danglis form Provisional Government in Crete.	30
			Oct. 1
.. .. ..	.. .. ..	.. ..	
.. .. ..	.. .. ..	Further migration of Greek officers to Venizelos Provisional Government in Crete.	2

1916. Oct.	WESTERN FRONT.	EASTERN FRONT.	SOUTHERN FRONT.
3	.. .. ..	Rumanian 2nd Army takes offensive near Fogaras and in region Roter Turm Pass. Northern Army (4th) L. wing, 12 m. S.E. of Maros Vasarhely, continues to advance. W. of Lutsk (Volhynia), objective Vladimir Volynski, Russians gain some enemy positions.	General Bulgar retreat on whole line Nidje Planina to Krushograd (Florina). After considerable fighting British take Yenikeui on L. bank Struma.
4	Germans driven out of Eaucourt. French carry German line between Morval and St. PierreVaast wood.	Rumanian 2nd Army retreating, Fogaras evacuated. Rumanian progress in Dobruja. Troops who crossed Danube at Rjahovo withdrawn. Battle W. of Lutsk still in progress, enemy obstinately holds positions on Zlota Lipa (Gal.).	Allied forces reach Kenali (10 m. from Monastir). E. of Monastir, Serbs cross Cherna. British make progress (Struma) towards Seres. Italian success in the Travignolo Valley (Avisio region, Trentino).
5	British advance N.E. of Eaucourt. French make progress E. of Morval.	After 3 days' fighting Rumanian Northern Army achieve success in Parajd region. Austrians retire W. In Dobruja, Rumanian offensive continues. Lutsk battle in progress.	Italian success in the San PellegrinoValley (Avisio, Trentino).
6	.. .. ..	Falkenhayn's offensive extending E. against Kronstadt, Rumanian retreat continues. Russian activities removed from Volhynia to N. Gal.; fighting renewed at Brzezany (Zlota Lipa region).	Lively actions within 7 m. of Monastir. Gradual withdrawal Bulgarians from valley of Struma to mountains beyond Demirhissar and Seres. Strong enemy counter-attack on Busa Alta positions repulsed by Italians.
7	British and French advance on Albert-Bapaume road. British advance 1,000 yds. and capture Le Sars. French advance N.E. of Morval to within 200 yds. of Sailly.	Enemy retake Kronstadt and Szekely. Rumanian forces withdrawing to frontier on whole line Predeal to Orsova.	British advance towards Seres continues (Struma front). Italians capture one of the peaks of the Busa Alta (Avisio, Trentino).
8	N. and E. of Courcelette, British line advanced, enemy attack Schwaben Redoubt and regain some trenches.	Germans occupy island in Danube near Ruschuk.	Artillery activity on whole Italian front. Italians inflict heavy losses on Busa Alta. Serbs occupy the Dobropolye summit (E. of Kaymakchlan).

Asiatic and Egyptian Theatres.	Naval and Overseas Operations.	Political, &c.	1916. Oct.
·. ·· ··	·· ·· ··	·· ·· ··	3
·· ·· ··	H.M.S. "Franconia," transport, and French troopship "Gallia" torpedoed in Mediterranean (several hundred lost).	Greek cabinet (M. Kalogeropoulos) resigns.	4
·· ··· ··	·· · ··	Germany and Austria announce an "independent" Kingdom of Poland.	5
·· ·· ··	·· ·· ··	·· ·· ··	6
·· ·· ··	·· ·· ··	·· ·· ··	7
·· ·· ··	Enemy submarine, U.53, outside Newport, Rhode Island, 8 vessels sunk. Atlantic Ports Intern'l. Merc. Marine orders no vessels to sail pending instructions.	·· ·· ··	8

1916. Oct.	WESTERN FRONT.	EASTERN FRONT.	SOUTHERN FRONT.
9	British make progress E. of Le Sars towards Butte de Warlencourt.	Enemy takes Törzburg (S.W. of Kronstadt). E. of Brzezany(Gal.) enemy assumes offensive, fighting on Volhynia front.	Allied forces in Macedonia advance on both wings. Serbs attack enemy's 3rd and last line of defence in Cherna loop, capture positions at Slivitza; Bulgarians retire N. of Brod. British advanced posts within 5,000 yds. of Seres. Italian offensive on the Isonzo front.
10	S. of Somme, French advance on 3 m. front and take all objectives, Bois de Chaulnes and Ablaincourt, and 1,400 prisoners.	Austro-German advance continues in Transyl. Gen. Averescu takes command of 2nd Army. Rumanians make stand in Predeal Pass (S. of Kronstadt).	On Struma front, Seres railway cut by British, enemy falling back to hills. Serbs gain footing in Brod (Cherna front). In Trentino enemy thrust back from N. slopes Mt. Pasubio. Italians clear whole plateau on Mt. Cormagnon. Battle of the Carso commences; whole of enemy's first line, Hill 208 and Nova Villa taken by Italians. 5,034 prisoners.
11	French, after sharp fighting, repulse counter-attacks at Bois de Chaulnes (S. of Somme) and take 1,702 prisoners.	Stubborn fighting in S. Transyl. Passes, 4th Army(Northern) retiring.	French carry enemy's first lines W. of Gevgeli. On Carso front, Austrian second line attacked. Italian front carried forward 2,000 yds. in direction of Mt. Pecenka, attack on Veliki Hriak. Decisive fighting in Mt. Pasubio region. Italian line advanced to foot of Mt. Roite (farther border of Cormagnon).
12	British attack on 4-m. front between Eaucourt and Bapaume - Péronne road, line advanced 500 to 1,000 yds.	Enemy makes progress in Törzburg Pass, 4th Army retreat continues.	Fierce fighting round Brod (Cherna front). On Carso front enemy counter-attacks completely repulsed. Fierce fighting on Hill 208 and in Nova Villa; bag on Isonzo front from Aug. 6 to date, 30,881 prisoners.
13	Big Allied raid (40 aeroplanes) on Mauser factory at Oberndorf. Returns of prisoners (100).	Enemy check in Predeal and Buzeu Passes (S. Trans.).	British forces pushing forward on Struma front. Successful British raids on Doiran front. Fighting in Carso continues.

ASIATIC AND EGYPTIAN THEATRES.	NAVAL AND OVERSEAS OPERATIONS.	POLITICAL, &c.	1916. Oct.
.. .. ..	.. .. ..	New Greek Cabinet formed, Prof. Lambros, Premier ; M. Zalocosta, Foreign Affairs ; Gen. Drako, War. M. Venizelos arriving Salonika receives great ovation. Gradual constitution of Provisional Government. British Royal Commission on Wheat and Flour Control appointed.	9
Sheikh Ahmed es Senussi leaves Baharia Oasis for Siwa.	.. .. ..	Peremptory Allied Note to Greece ; Greek Government complies ([98]).	10
.. ..	.. ..	Mr. Asquith on "No patched-up peace."	11
Publication of Despatch of 12.8.16 from Lt.-Gen. Sir P. Lake relative to operations in Mesopotamia Jan. 19 to April 30, 1916.	.. .. ..	Admiral du Fournet presents a supplementary Note to Greek Government, who comply with all demands ([99]).	12
.. ..	.. ..	Norway prohibits belligerent submarines from using her territorial waters.	13

1916. Oct.	WESTERN FRONT.	EASTERN FRONT.	SOUTHERN FRONT.
14	W. of Belloy-en-Santerre (S. of Somme) brilliant French attack on line of 1½ m., capture German first line, also Génermont, N.E. of Ablaincourt. French bombardment of Sailly-Saillisel (Bapaume - Péronne road) commences.	Enemy advance through Törzburg Pass and reach Rucar (6m. within Rumania). Frontier ridge at Predeal won by enemy and town burnt. Rumanians have now withdrawn from Transylvania, except in N.E. corner.	General indecisive attack by Allies on main Bulgar line (Maced. front). End of offensive in Carso, Italians consolidate all positions, line advanced 2 m.; Italians claim 8,000 prisoners.
15	British make progress in Schwaben Redoubt and Thiepval neighbourhood.	Intense fighting at Rucar. Artillery activity on Danube.	Seres shelled by British. Stubborn fighting on Cherna front. On Mt. Pasubio, Italians continue to advance.
16	French gain footing in Sailly (2 m. E. of Morval).	Fighting continues at Rucar. Rumanians give ground in Buzeu Pass. Enemy's offensive at Dorna Vatra (point of junction Rumanian and Russian armies in Moldavia) and Jablonitsa repulsed.	.. .. ..
17	French gain new group of houses in Sailly-Saillisel.	Rumanians maintain positions at Rucar, but retreat in the Gyimes Pass (Mold.); enemy penetrate 8 m. into Rumania and reach Agas. N. of Korytnitsa (24 m. W.S.W. of Lutsk), obstinate fighting, Germans claim trenches and 1,900 prisoners.	Fighting in Dobropolye region (N. of Kaymakchlan). Italians capture Tooth of Pasubio (Trent).
18	British make progress N. of Gueudecourt. French drive enemy out of Sailly. S. of Somme, French carry whole front between La Maisonnette Chateau and Biaches, facing Péronne.	Rumanians successfully attack enemy in Aluta (S. Trans.) region, Austrians do not take offensive again here until 28th.	Serbs take village of Brod and completely rout enemy. Strong enemy attacks in Doiran region repulsed by British.
19	French returns of prisoners. ([101]).	Enemy check in the Transyl. Passes. Heavy enemy bombardment in Dobruja.	Further Serb successes N. of Brod. Sharp fighting Tooth of Pasubio (Trent.) Austrian counter-attacks repulsed.

Asiatic and Egyptian Theatres.	Naval and Overseas Operations.	Political, &c.	1916. Oct.
.. .. ..	Russian submarine captures " Rodosto," Turk. armed transport in Black Sea.	.. .. ..	14
British raid Magharah (S. Sinai).	.. .. ..	Anti-Entente demonstrations in Athens.	15
.. ..	.. .. ..	In Athens Allies land reinforcements to maintain order, and take possession of 3 Greek warships not previously taken over. Admiral du Fournet hands fresh Note to Greek Government.	16
British raid and take Dakhla oasis (175 miles S.W. of Assiut).	.. .. ..	.. .. ..	17
.. .. ..	" Alaunia," Cunarder, sunk. " München," small German cruiser, torpedoed by British submarine.	.. .. ..	18
British raid and take Baharia Oasis (180 miles S.W. of Cairo).	E. Africa: Last enemy post N. of Central Railway cleared. Gen. van Deventer in touch with Gen. Northey. Enemy begins offensive in Iringa and Ruhuje River districts.	Conference of Allies at Boulogne, whereat Venizelos' Nat. Prov. Government in Crete receives recognition.	19

G

1916. Oct.	WESTERN FRONT.	EASTERN FRONT	SOUTHERN FRONT.
20	Heavy enemy attack on Schwaben and Stuff Redoubts (Thiepval plateau) repulsed.	Mackensen attacks on whole line in Dobruja, gains ground on E. and takes Tuzla.	.. .. ..
21	British advance line on 5,000 yd. front between Schwaben and Le Sars 500 yds., and take 1,018 prisoners.	In Törzburg Pass, enemy drives Rumanians 12 m. across frontier. Austrians 7 m. within Rumanian frontier through Buzeu Pass. In other Passes, Rumanians hold their ground. In Dobruja, Rumanians retiring; enemy take Toprosari and Kobadinu.	Weather breaks and fighting in the Cherna region dies down.
22	French carry ridge W. of Sailly. Aeroplane raid on Sheerness, no damage.	Evacuation of Constanza commences. Stiff fighting N. of Halicz (Gal.) for river heights.	Bulgars reinforced by Germans, counter-attack; everywhere repulsed and lose ground (Cherna front).
23	British advance towards Le Transloy capture 1,000 yards enemy trenches, Weather breaks. Aeroplane raid on Margate; 2 injured.	In Predeal Pass (S. Trans.) Rumanian reverse, lose many prisoners. **Fall of Constanza,** enemy in front of Cerna Voda. Battle in Halicz dies down. Germans claim total repulse of Russians from W. bank of Narajowka.	.. .. ..
24	Verdun front : French attack on line of ½-m.; recapture village and fort of Douaumont and quarries at Haudromont, take 4,500 prisoners (French Army now back to positions held by it in May).	Enemy advances Törzburg region; fighting near Campulung. In Dobruja, Mackensen advancing N. and N.W. of Constanza, reaches Mejidia (on Danube-Black Sea railway); enemy claims 6,700 prisoners.	Serbs take heights on L. bank Cherna. To the W. communications established between Italians (at Koritsa) and the French (S.W. of L. Prespa).

ASIATIC AND EGYPTIAN THEATRES.	NAVAL AND OVERSEAS OPERATIONS.	POLITICAL, &c.	1916. Oct.
.. .. ..	E. Africa : Gen. Smuts reports enemy limited to S.E. portion of Colony of which all ports and main lines of approach held by Allies. Russian battleship " Imperatritsa Maria " sunk by internal explosion.	Greek Government agree to withdraw half Greek troops concentrated at Larissa and practically to place Greek Army on peace footing. German Note to Norway on her submarine policy. Revolution in Abyssinia.	20
.. .. ..	British submarine torpedoes German cruiser, Kolberg class, in North Sea.	Count Stürgkh (Austrian Premier) assassinated by Dr. F. Adler.	21
.. .. ..	Portuguese forces in E. Africa, 8 m. N. of Rovuma River, attack at Nakalala ; enemy retires leaving munitions. Hostile seaplane visits Sheerness, afterwards shot down.	.. .. ..	22
Sir C. Dobell takes over command of Eastern (Sinai) force.	Severe fighting S.W. of Iringa (E. Africa). British mine-sweeper " Genista," sunk, fighting.	.. .. ..	23
.. ..	..	.. .. ..	24

1916. Oct.	WESTERN FRONT.	EASTERN FRONT.	SOUTHERN FRONT.
25	German counter-attacks at Verdun repulsed. Allied (British naval and French) air raid on steel works (Hagendingen) N. of Metz.	Enemy storm Vulkan Pass (W. Transyl.). Rumanians make stand in N. Passes. In Dobruja, Rumanians blow up bridge and abandon Cerna Voda, falling back towards N. Dobruja. Russian victory at Dorna Vatra (Mold.).	.. .. ..
26	.. .. ..	Enemy check in N. Passes (Transyl.). Enemy gain ground in S. Passes,— through Vulkan Pass now 20 m. within Rumania. In Dobruja, Rumanians now 24 m. N. of railway. British and French aircraft reach Bucharest.	.. .. ..
27	.. .. ..	Rumanian 1st Army in Jiu Valley (Wallachia) assume offensive, Rumanians holding positions in Passes. Russian centre (W. bank of Shchara, Minsk) compelled to retire to E. bank of river.	Serbs make progress in Cherna region.
28	.. .. ..	Rumanians successful actions in N. Transyl. Passes. In Jiu Valley, enemy retires leaving 2,000 prisoners.	Bulgar attack in force on Ormali (Struma front), repulsed with heavy loss.
29	Capt. Boelcke. German airman, killed	In Jiu Valley, enemy in retreat. In Dobruja, Rumanians still retiring.	.. .. ..
30	French take trenches N.W. of Sailly-Saillisel. S. of Somme : Germans retake N. part of La Maisonnette.	Enemy retiring in Jiu Valley and in Vulkan Pass. S.E. of Roter Turm Pass, enemy capture heights. Germans and Turks force back Russians near River Narajowka (Gal.). Latter advance towards Lutsk.	Violent fighting along whole line in Cherna region. Bulgar attack on Kalendia (Struma) repulsed.

Asiatic and Egyptian Theatres.	Naval and Overseas Operations.	Political, &c.	1916. Oct.
Sir Reginald Wingate's despatch of 8 Aug. published describing revolt and conquest of Darfur (Jan., 1915 to 22.5.16).	Gen. Gil, with Portuguese, crosses River Rovuma, Germans cut communications between Gen. Northey and Iringa and break through extended British line in following three weeks.	Greek Government issue decree disbanding class 1913 and the men called up on Sept. 10, and agree to transfer of 2 corps to Peloponnesus. Reported at Athens that Protecting Powers had sanctioned loan to Salonika Provisional Government.	25
.. .. ..	.. .. ..	.. .. ..	26
.. .. ..	10 Enemy destroyers raid cross-Channel transport. " Queen Mary " (empty) sunk, torp.-boat destroyer " Flirt " missing, " Nubian " disabled, 2 enemy destroyers sunk.	.. .. ..	27
Fighting near Hamadan (Persia), Russians capture 2 villages.	Donaldson liner " Marina " sunk by submarine.	Venizelos' Provisional Government installed at Salonika.	28
Sherif of Mecca proclaimed King of the Arabs.	German subm. activity in the Ægean. Greek volunteer transport "Angeliki" torpedoed.	Dr. Ernst von Körber appointed Premier in Austria.	29
.. .. ..	British drive enemy over Ruhuje River, and repel them in Iringa district and at Lupembe E. Africa). Main body of enemy S. of Central Railway and about Rufiji river, Tabora force being near Iringa.	Increased wages demanded by Cardiff miners.	30

1916. Oct.	WESTERN FRONT.	EASTERN FRONT.	SOUTHERN FRONT.
31	.. .. ..	Austrians checked at Törzburg, but successful in Predeal Pass. Russians repulse Germans in Narajowka Valley (Gal.), but fall back at Mieczysczow.	On Struma front, British take Barakli Juma (in front of Rupel Pass), also Kumli.
Nov. 1	German attack on Sailly-Saillisel repulsed by French. Allies advance N.E. of Lesbœufs. Germans evacuate Fort Vaux (Verdun). Franco-British captures to date ([102]).	Rumania : Gen. Sakharov takes command of Russians in Dobruja. Advance of Austrians in Törzburg, Predeal, and Roter Turm Passes.	Italians advance on Carso heights S.E. of Gorizia, taking over 8,400 prisoners.
2	British capture trench E. of Gueudecourt.	Austro-Hungarians attack in Predeal Pass ; Rumanians pursue Austrians in Vulkan Pass (N. Wallachia front).	Italians occupy Faiti Hrib (dominating Kostanjevitsa—Isonzo front).
3	French advance to outskirts of Vaux and gain footing on crest.	.. .. ..	Italians storm Mt. Volkovnjak and get within 220yds. of Kostanjevitsa.
4	Verdun : French occupy Damloup.	.. .. ..	.. .. ..
5	French occupy whole of Vaux. Somme front N. : British progress and retreat near Butte de Warlencourt ; attack on Le Transloy. French capture most of Saillisel and attack St. Pierre Vaast Wood.	Enemy success S.W. of Predeal and S.E. of Roter Turm Passes.	.. .. ..
6	Somme front, N. : French progress in N. of St. Pierre Vaast Wood ; In Saillisel Germans regain ground.	Fierce fighting S.E. of Roter Turm Pass.	.. .. ..
7	British progress E. of Butte de Warlencourt and repulse German night attack W. of Beaumont Hamel (N. of the Ancre). French capture Ablaincourt and Pressoir, and advance to outskirts of Gomiécourt.	Russian success S. of Dorna Vatra (S. Bukovina). German attack in Prahova valley (Central sector) ; resume offensive in Vulkan Pass ; repulsed in Tolgyes sector (Mold. front).	.. .. ..

Asiatic and Egyptian Theatres.	Naval and Overseas Operations.	Political, &c.	1916. Oct.
.. .. ..	British reorganised into 2 divisions (Hoskins and van Deventer), former about Kilwa, latter on Ruaha and Central Railway, Northey about Iringa.	.. .. ..	31
			Nov.
.. .. ..	German submarine " " Deutschland " arrives in U.S.A. (New London) for second time. Italian torpedo raid on Pola.	Appointment of Col. L. Stack as acting-Governor-General of Sudan and Sirdar.	1
.. .. ..	Dutch ss.. " Oldambt " rescued from Germans by British scouting craft, 5 German destroyers put to flight. Russian fleet bombards Constanza (Black Sea).	Declaration of Labour Group at Petrograd to working classes ([103]).	2
Major Huddleston occupies Kulme (Darfur).	.. .. ..	.. .. ..	3
.. .. ..	Russian fleet bombards Constanza.	Norwegian Note to Germany ; maintains right to forbid coasts to submarines.	4
.. .. ..	German battleship torpedoed by British submarine in North Sea.	Germany and Austria announce **Poland** to be established **as independent State** (but keep a tight hand on her).	5
Defeat and death of Ali Dinar, ex-Sultan of Darfur at Giuba, near frontier of Wadai.	P. & O. liner " Arabia " sunk in Mediterranean by submarine (2 lost).	Appointment of Gen. Sir F. R. Wingate as High Commissioner of Egypt.	6
.. .. ..	German attack at Kibata repulsed.	**Presidential elections** in U.S.A. result in **return of Pres. Wilson.**	7

1916. Nov.	WESTERN FRONT.	EASTERN FRONT	SOUTHERN FRONT.
8	Repulse of Germans at Saillisel.	Germans advance S. of Roter Turm Pass ; capture Sardoui (16 miles S.)	.. .. ..
9	Aerial battle between 30 British aeroplanes and 36 to 40 Germans near Bapaume. End of 3rd phase of Battle of the Somme	Defeat of Russian centre at Skrobova (C.) 3,400 prisoners taken. Dobruja : Russo-Rumanians occupy Hirshova (right bank Danube) and Dunarea ; fight for Cerna Voda Bridge.	.. .. ..
10	Somme, N. : British capture E. portion of Regina trench (N. of Thiepval). French capture several German trenches N.E. of Lesbœufs.	Serbs advance towards Monastir ; carry Chuke heights, &c.	Review of troops by Greek National Government at Salonika.
11	British bombard Germans on the Ancre ; French recapture most of Saillisel, and repulse German attack near Deniécourt.	Russo-Rumanians occupy Topalu (right bank Danube) and advance S.	Serbs seize Polog village.
12	French conquest of Saillisel completed. German attack near Berny (N.E. of Ablaincourt) repulsed .	Rumanian retreat in valleys of Aluta and Jiu ; severe fighting near Orsova (Danube). Failure of Russo-Rumanians on Cerna Voda and retreat to Dunarea.	French and Serbs capture Iven (15 miles E. of Monastir).
13	**Battle of the Ancre :** British capture St. Pierre Divion (S. of Ancre) and Beaumont Hamel (N. of Ancre) and nearly 4,000 prisoners. 4th phase of Battle of the Somme begins.	German advance S. of Törzburg, Roter Turm and Vulkan Passes continued : capture of Candeshti (S. of Törzburg Pass) and Bumbeshti (Jiu Valley).	Serbs advance on Monastir, masking Bulgar-German positions near Tapavci (15 miles E.S.E. of Monastir).
14	Somme, N. : British capture Beaucourt-sur-Ancre and advance E. of Butte de Warlencourt. Somme, S. : German attack at Ablaincourt and Pressoir largely repulsed.	Rumanians retreat S. of Vulkan Pass ; and below Törzburg Pass ; severe fighting in Prahova Valley (S. of Predeal Pass).	Allies advance on Monastir. Bulgars retreat on River Bistritza.
15	Somme, S. : Germans gain footing W. of St. Pierre Vaast Wood and E. part of Pressoir ; fail to gain Ablaincourt.	Rumanian retreat continued ; Germans bring heavy guns through Törzburg Pass and capture Targu Jiu (Jiu Valley).	Advance on Monastir : French and Serbs capture monastery of Jaratok ; French and Russians at River Viro (4 m. S. of Monastir).

ASIATIC AND EGYPTIAN THEATRES.	NAVAL AND OVERSEAS OPERATIONS.	POLITICAL, &c.	1916. Nov.
.. .. ..	U.S.A. s.s. "Columbian" sunk by German submarine near Cape Finisterre.	Heavy deportations of Belgians by Germans under Decree of 3/10/16.	8
.. .. ..	Malangali post (E. Africa) attacked (8-12.11) and relieved.	Speech of v. Bethmann Hollweg re cause of War and League of Nations([104]) Speech of Mr. Asquith at Guildhall, London ([105]). French War Loan £454,000,000. Portuguese troops ready to leave for European front.	9
.. .. ..	British seaplanes attack Ostend and Zeebrugge. German destroyer attack on Baltic port (W. of Reval), driven off by Russians, 6-9 German destroyers sunk.	German Note to Greek Government re War Material ([106]).	10
British air raid on Beersheba and Maghdaba (100 miles E. of Ismailia).	.. .. ..	.. .. ..	11
.. .. ..	Portuguese occupy Lulindi. British defeat Germans at Malangali (G.E.A.).	.. .. ..	12
Cairo bombed. Little damage done.	.. .. ..	Appeal of Cardinal Mercier to civilised world against Belgian deportations by Germans ([107]).	13
Sir P. Lake's despatch of 27.8.16 (30.4 to 26.8.16) published.	.. .. ..	(British) Publication of White Paper re U.S.A. "Black List" Protest of July 28 ([108]). Pensions Bill introduced. Russian Duma meets.	14
Tunnel through Taurus range on Baghdad railway pierced.	British seaplanes bombard Zeebrugge and Ostend.	Appointment of Food Controller and control of bread foreshadowed. Russian official statement re Poland ([109]). Allied Conference in Paris.	15

1916. Nov.	WESTERN FRONT.	EASTERN FRONT.	SOUTHERN FRONT.
16	Heavy French and German air fights near Amiens. British line extended E. from Beaucourt, retreat from part of ground E. of Butte de Warlencourt. French regain ground E. of Pressoir.	Rumanian retreat continuing; severe fighting S.E. of Tolgyes, near Campulung, and in valleys of Aluta and Jiu.	.. ..
17	French Air raid by Capt. Beauchamp on Munich, crossing Alps, landing near Venice. End of the Battle of the Somme.	Battle of Targu Jiu (in Jiu Valley): Germans break Rumanian front.	Struma front: British capture Kavakli on left bank of Struma.
18	British advance N. and S. of the Ancre, outskirts of Grandcourt reached.	.. .. ..	Germans and Bulgar evacuate Monastir.
19	.. .. ..	Retreat of Rumanians in Jiu Valley where Germans reach Filiasa junction and Aluta Valley.	Capture of Monastir b French and Serbs, an advance E. and N.E. Germans and Bulgar retreat towards Prilep.
20	..	.. .. ..	.. ..
21	.. .. ..	Germans occupy Craiova (cap. of W. Wallachia).	.. .. ..
22	.. .. ..	Fighting near Orsova on the Cherna River.	Fierce fighting N. of Monastir.
23	.. .. ..	German advance on Bucharest. Mackensen crosses Danube at Islatz and Simnitza. On W. Germans take Orsova and Turnu-Severin; repulsed at Slatina (Aluta Valley) but cross Aluta near Caracula.	French and Serbs progress N. of Monastir, taking villages.
24	.. .. ..	Mackensen crosses the Danube at Sistova, Islatz, etc.	.. .. ..

Asiatic and Egyptian Theatres.	Naval and Overseas Operations.	Political, &c.	1916. Nov.
Indian frontier raid: defeat of Pathans near Shabkadar (Peshawar valley) (aeroplanes used).	.. .. ..	German announcement *re* Polish recruiting ([110]). German reorganisation of aircraft forces ([111]).	16
Suez bombed. Waterpipe reaches Romani.	Raid of British naval aeroplanes and seaplanes on Ostend and Zeebrugge,	(British) Food regulations issued ([112]). Note of French Admiral to Greek Government demanding delivery of War material.	17
.. .. ..	Defeat of Germans at Lupembe (G.E.A.) by British. U.S.A. explanation *re* U.53 ([113]).	Protest of Allies *re* Poland.	18
British raid and take Farafra Oasis (180 miles W. of Assiut).	.. .. ..	French Admiral demands dismissal of Ministers of Central Powers and of their Allies from Athens.	19
.. .. ..	.. .. ..	Milk and flour regulations issued by British Board of Trade.	20
.. .. ..	British hospital ship "Britannia" sunk by mine or torpedo in Ægean.	Statement in British press by Venizelos *re* Greek National Defence Movement ([114]). **Death of Emp. Francis Joseph**, aged 86; succeeded by Archduke Charles, b. 17.8.87.	21
.. .. ..	.. .. ..	Protest of Belgium to Neutral Powers *re* deportations and forced labour.	22
.. .. ..	German destroyers raid in Channel, N. end of Downs; little damage.	**Provisional Greek Government** at Salonika **declares war on Bulgaria and Germany.**	23
.. .. ..	British hospital ship "Bræmar Castle" mined or torpedoed in Ægean.	Trepov succeeds Stuermer as Russian Premier. Du Fournet (Fr. Admiral's) ultimatum to Greece ([115]).	24

1916. Nov.	WESTERN FRONT.	EASTERN FRONT.	SOUTHERN FRONT.
25	.. .. ..	German advance on Bucharest; fighting at Curtea de Arges and German occupation of Rymnik; on S., German advance towards Rosiori and Alexandria. Upper Aluta position turned.	.. ..
26	.. .. ..	Mackensen reaches Alexandria and is in touch with Falkenhayn.	French and Serbs captur Hill 1,050 (7 miles N.E of Monastir).
27	Zeppelin raid on N.E. coast and N. Midlands (England), two Zeppelins brought down. 4 killed, 37 injured.	Germans advance on Bucharest, capture Curtea de Arges and Giurgevo and occupy Alexandria. Rumanians abandon Aluta line. Stubborn fighting by Orsova force.	..
28	Mid-day raid on London by 1 aeroplane (subsequently shot down in France). 10 injured.	Russian success in Carpathians, heights E. of Jablonitsa Pass and E. of Kirlibaba captured.	Bulgars occupy Giurgev (on Danube). Successfu British raid near Macu kovo (left bank Varda S.W. of Doiran).
29	.. .. ..	Germans capture Campulung and Piteshti (N.W. of Bucharest). Mackensen at Calugarino (17 miles S. of Bucharest). Russians' Carpathian offensive continues.	Austrians massing troop on Carso front. Fightin E. of Monastir continue in fog.
30	Crown Prince gives up command of German army on Verdun front. French aircraft bomb Thionville.	Germans force passage of River Neajlovu (16 m. S.W. of Bucharest). Russian repulse on Zlota Lipa (Gal.). Fighting in Bukovina.	General artillery actio Italian front. Gree army reported marchin N. Allied troops land a Piraeus.
Dec. 1	.. .. ..	Russians driven off Rukida and Kirlibaba heights (Carpath.). Rumanians retire S.E. from Campulung. Severe fighting S. of Pitesti. Rumanian Government moves to Jassy.	Vicenza bombed. Gree attack on Allied troop at Athens (110)

Asiatic and Egyptian Theatres.	Naval and Overseas Operations.	Political, &c.	1916. Nov.
.. .. ..	.. .. ..	German Patriotic Auxiliary Service Bill presented to Reichstag ([¹¹⁴]).	25
E. Sinai railway reaches Mazar.	German naval raid near L o w e s t o f t; armed trawler " Narval " sunk. Germans surrender at Ilembule (L. Nyassa); French b'ship "Suffren" sunk by submarine	.. .. ..	26
Russians drive back Turks into Persia, taking much war material.	" City of Birmingham " sunk by German submarine (4 lost).	.. .. ..	27
.. .. ..	British seaplanes been bombing Drama and Bulgarian coast for 5 days. Brixham fishing fleet attacked by German submarine. 100 French sailors land at Piræus.	Greek batteries (to be surrendered to Allies) removed to Chalcis, etc. Military Govt. by U.S.A. officers of Dominican Republic proclaimed.	28
.. .. ..	**Adm. Sir J. Jellicoe announced First Sea Lord, and Adm. Sir D. Beatty C.i.C.** of Grand Fleet. British seaplanes bomb Gereviz (Bulgaria).	Board of Trade takes over S. Wales coalfield from Dec. 1, 16. Protest of U.S.A. against deportation of Belgians.	29
Russians 30 m. S. of N. Persian frontier.	.. .. ..	Greek Government refuses Adm. du Fournet's demand for surrender of guns. Greek Reserve officers called up. Lord Derby on New Volunteer Army ([117]).	30
Surrender reported of sons of Ali Dinar (late Sultan of Darfur); organised resistance ended. Publication of despatch of 1/10/16 from Sir A. Murray (operations 1/6–30/9/16).	.. .. ..	Mr. Lloyd George declares his inability to remain in the Government ([119]).	Dec. 1

1916. Dec.	WESTERN FRONT.	EASTERN FRONT.	SOUTHERN FRONT.
2	.. .. ..	Continued Russian offensive in Carpathians. Rumanian front : Heavy fighting at Cerna Voda (Dobruja) ; serious enemy pressure towards Bucharest.	Serbs carry strong Bulgar positions N. of Gum ishta ; Turks assist Bul gars at Seres and Drama Armistice concluded a Athens ; Allied troop withdrawn.
3	.. .. ..	Severe fighting in Carpathian and Moldavian Valleys ; Russians push up the Trotus. Rumanian retreat S.E. ; heavily beaten by Mackensen on Lower Arges. Bulgars repulse Russian assaults in the Dobruja.	Outrages against Venizel ists at Athens ; 1,300 French troops landed a Piraeus, but re-em barked.
4	.. .. ..	Fighting in Stanislau and Tarnopol (Gal.). Russians capture peak commanding Jablonitsa Pass. Struggle continues round Bucharest.	French and Serbs advance eastwards of Monastir Quieter at Athens ; de tachments (Allies) con tinue to re-embark.
5	.. .. ..	Enemy counter-attacks in Carpathians. Mackensen's demand for surrender of Bucharest refused ; enemy advancingon Ploeshti (oilfields); Rumanians abandon Predeal Pass ; their Orsova rearguard gives battle on the Aluta.	Greece : Much unrest a Athens, but comparative order. Reservists con cerned in attacl dismissed.
6	Germans gain footing in salient, Hill 304 (Verdun).	Fighting in Volhynia, W. of Lutsk, round Tarnopol and Stanislau (Gal.) and round Dorna Vatra (Bukovina). **Fall of Bucharest,** Ploeshti and Sinaia. Orsova rearguard on the Aluta capitulates (with 8,000 men).	Enemy activity on the Carso checked. Reci procal air attacks o Trieste and Aquilei (Isonzo mouth). Har fighting round Monastir Royalists at Athens i control. British Legatio prepares to leave.
7	French regain trenches lost on Hill 304.	Russians attack in S.E. Galicia. Fighting in Oitoz and Trotus valleys. Rumanian retreat E. on all fronts ; Wallachia in enemy's hands ; latter checked on Moldavian frontier.	Heavy fighting in Mon astir region. Action S of Seres. Sir G. Milne' despatch of 9.10.1 issued, covering opera tions on Salonika front 9.7.16 to 8.10.16. Troop from the Morea concen trating round Athens Persecution of Veni zelists continues.

ASIATIC AND EGYPTIAN THEATRES.	NAVAL AND OVERSEAS OPERATIONS.	POLITICAL, &C.	1916. Dec.
.. ..	Embargo on all Greek vessels in Allied ports. **Greece declared in state of blockade.**	M. Trepov, new Russian Premier, speaks in Duma. ([120]). Greek Government agrees to surrender 6 (subsequently 8) field batteries.	2
.. ..	German submarines enter Funchal Port, Madeira, sink 3 ships and bombard town.	Mr. Asquith decides on reconstruction of Government. Wage dispute in S. Wales settled in favour of miners. Greek Government gives pledges to Allies.	3
Great aerial activity on Tigris front (Mesop.).	" Caledonia " (Anchor Line) torpedoed in Mediterranean by submarine. Crew saved, Capt. Blaikie prisoner.	The King approves of reconstruction of Government. Lord R. Cecil on situation in Greece ([121]).	4
Reported advance of Turks in Arabia to Yanbu Port.	Portuguese invested by Germans at Newala escape over Rovuma River to Nangadi.	**Resignation of Mr. Asquith,** preceded by that of Mr. Lloyd George. Allies associate themselve with Belgian protest against German slave raids in Belgium.	5
.. .. ..	Further German attacks on Kibata (E. Africa) repelled 7-15.12.	Cabinet Crisis : Mr. Lloyd George asked to form Administration. Greek Provisional Government at Salonika denounces Royalist Government at Athens as unrepresentative. Board of Agriculture given powers to acquire land.	6
E. African situation described ([122]). Sir P. Chetwode assumes command of desert (Sinai) column.	" Suffren," French b.s., reported lost with all hands.	**Mr. Lloyd George becomes Prime Minister.** Germany rejects Belgian protest as unfounded. Official complicity in late outrages at Athens confirmed. Entente Governments announce forthcoming Blockade of Greece.	7

1916. Dec.	WESTERN FRONT.	EASTERN FRONT.	SOUTHERN FRONT.
8	.. .. ..	Heavy fighting in Galicia, in S. of Bukovina, and on Moldavian frontier. Rumanian force retiring on Bucharest from Sinaia captured at Ploeshti. Murman railway opened.	Allied Colonies leaving Athens.
9	.. .. ..	Continuous fighting throughout Russian southern front. Germans claim capture since Dec. 1, of 70,000 Rumanian prisoners and 184 guns.	Bulgarians cross Danube near Silistria and Tutrakan, capturing towns on left bank. Fighting near Monastir. Turk post taken S. of Seres.
10	.. .. ..	Stubborn fighting in Carpathians, S. Bukovina and Trotus Valley. Fighting N. of Ploeshti.	Bulgars capture bridgehead opposite Cerna Voda. Fighting N. of Monastir.
11	Violent artillery action on Somme front. Preparatory French bombardment on Verdun front.	Enemy forces over the Jalomitsa River, N.E. of Bucharest.	.. .. .
12	General Nivelle succeeds Gen. Joffre as C.i.C. N. and N.E. French Armies. Gen. Joffre becomes Technical War adviser to War Cabinet.	Fighting continues round Tarnopol and Stanislau (Gal.) and in S. Bukovina. With help of Russians, Rumanians rally on the Jalomitsa and S.W. of Buzeu.	Fighting near Monastir (Cherna bend). Venizelist troops land at Syra which with other Cyclades comes under National Government.
13	Heavy bombardments on Somme front continue.	Rumanians again forced back from the Jalomitsa and the Ploeshti-Buzeu road. Enemy advances towards Braila and Galatz.	.. .. .
14	Heavy reciprocal raiding near Ypres.	Russians gain in Carpathian struggle, and along Moldavian frontier. Falkenhayn's forces enter Buzeu; Danube army over the Jalomitsa. All Wallachia cleared of Allied troops S. of Bucharest-Cerna Voda line.	Fighting near Monastir; strong artillery action Lake Doiran zone.

Asiatic and Egyptian Theatres.	Naval and Overseas Operations.	Political, &c.	1916. Dec.
.. .. ..	Greek Blockade effective from 8 a.m. Portuguese retire from Nangadi (E. Africa) ; Germans occupy it. Italian B'ship " Regina Margherita " blown up on Italian minefield.	Allies demand explanation of Greek troops concentrated round Athens.	8
.. .. ..	Distress caused in Canary Islands by German blockade.	British and U.S.A. Ministers have audience of King Constantine. Formation of New War Cabinet and 3 new Ministries, and list of New Government. ([123]).	9
.. .. ..	German merchant submarine " Deutschland " returns to mouth of Weser.	Allied Note to Greece demands demobilization.	10
.. .. ..	Allied air-raids on Zeebrugge.	German reply to U.S.A. Note re Belgian deportations. ([124]). Reported Venizelist rising in the Cyclades.	11
British feint on Sanna-i-yat, and move on Shatt-el-Hai.	Vice-Adm. Gauchet succeeds Adm. Dartige du Fournet as C.i.C. Mediterranean Fleet.	Greek Minister in Paris conveys King Constantine's regrets for recent events at Athens. M. Briand completes his War Cabinet .([125]). German " Peace " Note to Allies ([126])	12
British offensive on the Tigris; Sanna-i-Yat bombarded; British cross the Shatt-el-Hai and secure both banks.	Russian ships shell Balchik, to destroy mills supplying Bulgar army	Austrian Premier (Dr. Körber) resigns. Dr. v. Spitzmüller forms new Ministry. M. Briand sums up German " Peace " Note as " Heads 1 win, tails you lose."	13
British advance up the Shatt-el-Hai to within 2½ miles of Kut, and destroy (aeroplanes) Tigris pontoon bridges.	Naval aeroplanes bomb Kuleli-Burgas bridge (20 miles S. of Adrianople). S.S. " Westminster " and empty horse-transport " Russian " torpedoed in Mediterranean.	Allies present 24-hours Ultimatum to Greece ([127]). House of Commons asked for 11th Vote of Credit this financial year. ([128]).	14

H

1916. Dec.	WESTERN FRONT.	EASTERN FRONT.	SOUTHERN FRONT.
15	Gen. Nivelle launches great attack on Verdun front (N. of Douaumont); enemy front pierced to depth of 2 m.; Vacherauville, Poivre Hill (342). Louvemont and Les Chambrettes captured.	Enemy success on Tarnopol Railway, W. of Lutsk. Rumanian and Russians still resisting N. of Buzeu, but retiring from Jalomitsa. Strong Russian defence on Moldavian frontier.	Enemy bombarding Monastir. Fighting on the Struma; repulse of Bulgars.
16	French take Bezonvaux and Hardaumont. 11,000 prisoners and much war material captured.	Russian positions between Kovel and Lutsk captured. Rumanian front enemy continues advance E. and N.E. In the Dobruja, Russians retire northwards.	Greece: Military evacuation of N. Greece begun under supervision of Allies.
17	German counter-attacks near Verdun; they recover Les Chambrettes.	Fighting continues in the Tarnopol region. Rumanians and Russians continue to fall back.	.. .. ..
18	Zouaves recapture Les Chambrettes. End of French offensive at Verdun.	Russian position between Kovel and Lutsk restored. Rumanians and Russians retreat towards Sereth line. Braila and Galatz threatened.	.. .. ..
19	.. .. ..	Enemy's advance from the west checked 30 m. from Braila. Russians in the Dobruja fall back towards Braila.	.. .. ..
20	.. .. ..	Severe fighting W. of Brody (Gal.). German advance on Braila.	Fierce local encounters in Cherna bend (Monastir)

ASIATIC AND EGYPTIAN THEATRES.	NAVAL AND OVERSEAS OPERATIONS.	POLITICAL, &C.	1916. Dec.
.. .. ..	Naval aeroplanes bomb Razlovci, 37 m. E. of Istip (Serbia). British warships shell enemy at head of Gulf of Orfano (S.W. of Kavalla). In E. Africa, fighting still proceeding round Kibata.	Greek Government accepts Allies' Ultimatum. Vigorous speeches in the Duma ([129]). German Minority Socialists' manifesto against "oracular utterances"; demand Government should state peace conditions.	15
Continued bombardment of enemy positions near Kut. Brit. Govmt. recognises "King of the Arabs" as King of the Hejaz.	Gen. Cunliffe's Nigerian brigade reaches Dar-es-Salaam.	Government decides to take over Irish railways, to satisfaction of Irish public. M. Bratianu forms Coalition Gov't. (Rum.),	16
Strong enemy cavalry attacks checked S. of Falahiya (Kut).	Fighting at Kibata continues.	Warrant issued by Greek Govt. for arrest of M. Venizelos. U.S.A. owing to Turkey's conduct to Syrians and Armenians, terminates extra-territoriality agreements.	17
British move round Sanna-i-Yat and reach Tigris above Kut, severing enemy's lateral communications and commanding river upstream of Khadairi Bend.	.. .. ..	German "Peace" Note of 12/12 received at British and French Foreign Offices. Italian Chamber declares solidarity with Allies. Venizelos threatened with arrest for his Press articles.	18
.. .. ..	.. .. ..	Mr. Lloyd George's first speech as Premier ([130]) on Govt. control of Shipping, National Service, &c. German assurance given re Capt. Blaikie ([131]). British Govt. prepared to recognise agents of Venizelist (National) Government. Greek Government protests re Venizelist occupation of islands under Allies' protection. British safe conduct granted to Austr.-Hung. Ambassador (Count Tarnowski) from U.S.A.	19
Turks evacuate El Arish (N. Sinai) and fall back 20 miles S.E. of Magdhaba.	Germans retire from Nangadi (E. Africa).	German War Loan £535,000,000. President Wilson's Peace Conference Note handed to Belligerents ([132]).	20

1916. Dec.	WESTERN FRONT.	EASTERN FRONT.	SOUTHERN FRONT.
21	.. .. ..	N. Russia : Fighting S. of Dvinsk. Also on S. Galician rivers. In Dobruja, Russians drive Bulgars into Lake Ibolota (Babadagh).	.. .. ..
22	.. .. ..	Rumania : Enemy concentrating at Ramnicu, Sarat ; hard fighting ; Russian retreat to Danube completed.	.. .. ..
23	Hostile activity in Champagne.	Fierce struggle for Moldavian frontier positions. Russians from Dobruja retire to Bessarabia, leaving some troops at Macin (Braila).	Bad weather last fortnight on Italian front. Two successful British attacks along Doiran front (Maced.).
24	.. .. ..	Battle continues near Ramnicu Sarat.	Lively British raids on Doiran front.
25	British take over more French line.	Severe fighting W. of Lower Sereth ; Macin bridgehead attacked.	.. .. ..
26	General Joffre created a Marshal of France.	Heavy shelling of Russian positions in Galicia. Severe fighting along whole Rumanian front.	.. .. ..
27	Big French air-raids on German industrial works (Rhineland, etc.).	Falkenhayn takes Ramnicu Sarat. In the Dobruja, the Bulgars seize position E. of Macin.	.. .. ..
28	Heavy enemy attack on Mort Homme front (Verdun).	Enemy pursues northwards from Ramnicu Sarat and advances to S.E. British armoured cars engaged.	.. .. ..

Asiatic and Egyptian Theatres.	Naval and Overseas Operations.	Political, &c.	1916. Dec.
British occupy El Arish. Turkish base removed from Shumran to Baghela (Tigris) ; but shipping at latter bombed by us.	Two British T.B.D.'s sunk by collision in North Sea.	Allies' new Note to Greece ([133]). V. Spitzmüller (Austria) unable to form Cabinet ; duty entrusted to Count Clam Martinic.	21
British positions S. of Kut consolidated ; second air raid on Baghela ; also on Beersheba.	British ships again shell mouth of Struma (Gulf of Orfano).	King's Speech to Parliament ([134]). Swiss Note to Belligerents to support U.S.A. peace efforts.	22
British capture Magdhaba (Sinai), destroying practically whole Turk. force of 3,000. Further success to the S. at Mitla Pass and Abu Aweigila.	Hostile naval night-raid in Straits of Otranto. No material damage.	**Count Czernin** succeeds Baron Burian as **Foreign Minister** (Austria).	23
..	..	..	24
Armenian front : fighting round Van.	Combined offensive (in E. Africa) by Genls. Northey and van Deventer begins, pushing enemy E. and S.	King's Christmas message. Tsar replies to German Peace overtures ([135]). Premiers of self-governing Colonies and Indian representatives invited to War Conference. Coalition Government formed in Rumania, including M. Take Jonescu.	25
Mesopotamia : Weather broken ; operations much hindered.	Naval aeroplanes bomb Turk. camps at Galata (Dardanelles). Naval air-raid on Zeebrugge.	Germany's reply to President Wilson's Note of 20.12 handed to U.S.A. at Berlin ([136]). Austria-Hungary delivers similar reply.	26
..	Naval seaplanes destroy Chikaldir Bridge (Baghdad Railway) Gulf of Alexandretta. French battleship " Gaulois " torpedoed in Mediterranean.	Three Scandinavian Governments agree to present Note to Belligerents in support of peace efforts. Franco-British Agreement re temporary administration of Togoland.	27
Armenia : Turks driven S. of Van.	..	Germany hands appreciative reply to Swiss Note.	28

1916. Dec.	WESTERN FRONT.	EASTERN FRONT.	SOUTHERN FRONT.
29	Issue of Sir D. Haig's despatch dealing with Somme Battle ([137])	Heavy fighting continues on Moldavian frontier; some enemy progress in the Oitoz valley. Enemy advance N. and E. from Ramnicu Sarat continued.	.. .. ..
30	.. .. ..	Very heavy fighting on whole Rumanian front. Enemy progress at various points in mountains and S.E. of Ramnicu Sarat, but checked between here and Focsani. Bulgars and Turks advance slowly towards Macin.	.. .. ..
31	.. .. ..	Further enemy progress in Moldavian mountains and W. and S. of Focsani. Bulgars fail in attack on Braila bridgehead, but carry positions E. of Macin.	.. .. ..

ASIATIC AND EGYPTIAN THEATRES.	NAVAL AND OVERSEAS OPERATIONS.			POLITICAL, &c	1916. Dec.
..	..	..	..	..	French and British ministers, in Conference for last 3 days, arrive at complete agreement. Murder of Russian monk Rasputin ([138]). Sitting of National Socialist Congress in Paris ([139]).	29
..	..	..	..	..	Greek Note to Allies requests raising of the Blockade. Southern Slav Committee issues declaration at Coronation of Austrian Emperor ([140]). **Allies reply to " Peace " Note** of Enemy Powers forwarded to U.S.A. Government ([141]). Spain declines to second President Wilson's proposal.	30
Iagharah Wells, Hassana and Nakhl (Sinai) cleared of enemy.	..	..	..	Entente Note to Greece calling for reparation for events of Dec. 1 and 2, with other demands ([142]).	31

RÉSUMÉ OF MAIN EVENTS IN 1916.

Jan. 10 to Feb. 20	..	Russian offensive in Armenia against Erzerum (captured 16.2).
„ to July ..	..	Baràtov's campaign in Persia.
„ 13 ..	..	Austrians enter Cettinje.
„ 15 ..	..	Russian unsuccessful offensive against Bukovina ends.
„ 20 till April	..	Operations against the Senussi in Western Egypt.
Feb. 18 ..	..	Conclusion of successful Cameroons campaign.
„ 21 to Aug. 3	..	Powerful German attacks on Verdun, eventually unsuccessful
Mar. to May	..	Successful British operations in E. Africa.
„ 9 ..	..	Germany declares war on Portugal.
„ 18 to April 14		Russian offensive about L. Naroch.
Apr. 18 ..	..	Russians capture Trebizond (Black Sea).
„ 20 to May 1	..	Irish Rebellion.
„ 23 to Dec. 23	..	Sinai advance (battle of Romani, 3 to 9.8).
„ 29 ..	..	Fall of Kut-el-Amara.
May 14 to June 27	..	Great Austrian offensive v. the Trentino ; successful at first.
„ 21 ..	..	British lose Vimy ridge.
„ 26 ..	..	Bulgarians occupy Fort Rupel with Greek acquiescence.
„ 31—June 1	..	Battle of Jutland.
„ and June	..	Troubles with Greece.
June 1 to 25 ..	..	Turkish offensive in Armenia.
„ 4 to Aug. 11	..	Brusilov's great Russian offensive in Galicia and the South (capture of Lutsk, 6.6 ; Buczacz, 8.6 ; Dubno, 9.6 ; Czernowitz, 17.6 ; Kolomea, 29.6 ; Brody 28.7 ; Stanislau, 10.8 ; taking 358,602 prisoners).
„ 5 ..	..	Lord Kitchener drowned.
„ 14 ..	..	Allied Economic Conference in Paris.
July 1 to Nov. 19	..	Great Franco-British offensive on the Somme (capture of numbers of villages ; Germans driven back 5 to 7 miles).
„ 25 ..	..	Russians capture Erziŋgan.
„ 28 to Aug. 25	..	Severe Turko-Russian fighting in Armenia.
Aug. 1 to Nov. 3	..	Heavy fighting on Isonzo front (Ital. capture Gorizia, 9.8, and advance their lines).
„ to Dec. ..	..	Renewed troubles with Greece.
„ 10 to Nov. 20	..	Allied offensive in Macedonia (capture of Monastir, 19.11).
„ 15 to Sept. 20	..	Shcherbachev's attack in E. Galicia, checked.
„ 28 ..	..	Rumania declares war on Austria-Hungary.
„ 29 ..	..	Germany declares war on Rumania.
„ 29 to Oct. 6	..	Rumanian offensive in Transylvania, and Bulgar-German attack in South (fall of Turtukai, 6.9 ; Silistria, 9.9).
„ 30 ..	..	Venizelist revolution in Salonika.
Sept. 1 ..	..	Bulgaria declares war on Rumania.
„ 17 ..	..	Greek Corps kidnapped at Kavalla.
Oct. 4 to Dec. 23	..	Austro-German counter-offensive in Rumania (Transylv. cleared of Rumanians by 10.10 ; fall of Constanza, 23.10 ; of Cerna Voda, 25.10 ; of Orsova, 23.11 ; of Bucharest, 5.12 ; and conquest of Wallachia.
Nov. 6 ..	..	Final defeat and death of Sultan Ali Dinar of Darfur.
„ 7 ..	..	President Wilson re-elected.
„ 9 to 18 ..	..	British offensive on the River Ancre.
„ 27 to Dec. 31	..	Russians drive Turks into Persia.
Dec. 1 ..	..	Allied *fiasco* at Athens.
„ 7 ..	..	Mr. Lloyd George succeeds Mr. Asquith as Premier.
„ 11 ..	..	M. Briand French Premier.
„ 20 ..	..	President's Wilson Peace Note to Belligerents.
„ 21 ..	..	British occupy El Arish.
„ 26 ..	..	German reply to Note of 20.12 proposes Peace Conference.

APPENDICES, 1916.

(¹) *Jan.* 1.—Gen. Ivanov began an offensive at the close of December and the beginning of January on a 250-mile front from the Pripet Marshes to the Rumanian frontier. Heavy losses were suffered on both sides and no decisive results obtained, but the offensive gave the Allies time to consolidate their position at Salonika.

(²) *Jan.* 1.—Russian aim in the northern sector was gradually to push the Germans out of their positions before Riga and Dvinsk : by constant local attacks they deprived the Germans of the winter's rest promised to them by Hindenburg.

(³) *Jan.* 4 & 5.—" Baralong " case. German Government in autumn of 1915 accused crew of the British auxiliary cruiser " Baralong " of shooting the crew of a U-boat, sunk on Aug. 19, 1915. Sir. E. Grey offered to submit the case to an impartial tribunal, if the Germans would submit three specific cases of outrages by German sailors to the same tribunal (4.1.16). Germans rejected this offer (14.1.16) on the ground that the cases had already been investigated in Germany.

(⁴) *Jan.* 4.—Lord Derby reported that out of some five million men of military age not already in the forces over one half had offered themselves for enlistment or attestation. The remainder, including 650,000 single men, unattested and unstarred, justified the application of compulsion.

(⁵) *Jan.* 5.—Military Service Bill, introduced by Mr. Asquith to redeem his pledge of Nov. 2, 1915, that married men would not be called up until after single men, provided that unattested single men and childless married men of military age should be regarded as having attested ; that service should be for the duration of the war ; that Ireland should be exempted, etc.

(⁶) *Jan.* 10.—The offensive suddenly launched by the Grand Duke Nicholas culminated in the capture of Erzerum in February. The Turks were forced to withdraw troops from Europe, and pressure on the Salonika front was reduced.

(⁷) *Jan.* 11.—The French took military possession of Corfu to provide a resting-place for the Serbian army, threatened with starvation in Albania. The ministers of the Entente had previously addressed a Note to the Greek Government, which protested but offered no active opposition.

(⁸) *Jan.* 15.—Von Papen, German Naval Attaché at Washington, was expelled from the United States as a *persona non grata*. His papers, seized at Falmouth, contained a cheque-book showing payments to German agents. Photographs of the counterfoils of these cheques were published, with notes on the payees, showing their connection with various outrages in the United States.

(⁹) *Jan.* 27.—The Chief of the Imperial General Staff was made responsible for the issue of orders regarding military operations, which responsibility had previously rested with the Secretary of State.

(¹⁰) *Feb.* 9.—Losses in 18 months were estimated at 2,700,000 : army in the field, 3,600,000 : a total of 6,300,000, to be deducted from a total of 9,000,000 believed to have been available at the outbreak of war. Of these 700,000 would be needed for internal duty, etc.

(¹¹) *Feb.* 9.—M. Skouloudhis, Premier, protested against Allied occupation of Corfu and Kara Buru. M. Gounaris, in reply to the assertion that while Premier he had made proposals to the Entente amounting to departure from neutrality, defended his policy and declared that the interest of the State prevented him from explaining why the Army was not demobilized.

(¹²) *Feb.* 10.—Montenegro had asked for an armistice in order to bring up reinforcements : the request was refused. The Austrian peace terms were then rejected ; the King went to France, one of the Princes and three Ministers being left to continue resistance.

(¹³) *Feb.* 10.—Warns U.S.A. that all armed merchant vessels will be treated as belligerent ships, and warns neutrals that no responsibility is taken for their safety.

(¹⁴) *Feb.* 14.—The Entente Ministers declared that Belgium would be represented at the Peace Conference and that no peace would be made without the restoration and indemnification of Belgium.

(¹⁵) *Feb.* 15.—Mr. Asquith announced further taxation to meet war cost of five millions per diem : British army estimated to be ten times the size of the original Expeditionary Force ; situation in Mesopotamia improved. Lord Kitchener announced that the Mesopotamian campaign would be controlled by War Office henceforth.

(¹⁶) *Feb.* 15.—United States said to be blindly stumbling towards war : " one official declaration of disapproval (of violation of Belgium) would have made the States directors of conscience and morality for all neutrals."

(¹⁷) *Feb.* 19.—Protest against doubts of the good faith of King Constantine. Statement that Greece has never declared that she will not depart from neutrality.

(¹⁸) *Feb.* 21.—King Constantine described the result of the interview as most satisfactory : the Entente need never fear hostile action from Greece.

(¹⁹) *Feb.* 21.—Supplementary vote of £120,000,000, bringing year's war votes up to £1,420,000,000 : vote for next financial year £300,000,000, bringing votes of credit up to £2,032,000,000.

(²⁰) *March* 1.—Import duties increased from 5% *ad valorem* to 7½% ; no change in cotton duties ; export duties on tea and jute ; increase in salt tax ; incomes over 5,000 rupees (£333) to pay 1/3 in £, instead of 9*d*.

(²¹) *March* 1.—Paris Conference to consider trade after the war ; possibility of special *post bellum* trade relations between the Allies ; resources of the British Empire not be to exploited as in the past by Germany ; Empire knit together by war, etc.

(²²) *March* 2.—No fault found with tribunals, but system of exemptions criticised, especially in the case of agriculturists ; stronger measures needed to get men ; women must take the place of men.

(²³) *March* 3.—Senator Gore proposed to warn Americans not to sail in armed merchantmen belonging to belligerents : resolution postponed by 68 votes to 14. A victory for President Wilson's policy.

(²⁴) *March* 3.—Revelation of a German plot to produce sabotage and interfere with output of munitions : said to be organised from Lugano by a German ex-Consul. Enquiries in Switzerland gave no ground for intervention by Swiss authorities.

(²⁵) *March* 6.—Purpose of visit to enlighten Russia as to England's war effort.

(²⁶) *March* 7.—British Navy held command of the sea ; no enemy cruiser at large ; naval air service ten times larger ; programme of late Admiralty Board maintained ; Navy stronger except in armoured cruisers ; personnel doubled since 1914, and tonnage increased over a million.

(²⁷) *March* 8.—Criticism of German answer to charges brought against the German Navy (cf. Appendix 3).

(²⁸) *March* 9.—Lord Montagu urges the setting up of an Air Board, the building of more powerful machines, construction of better anti-aircraft guns, etc.

(²⁹) *March* 11.—Scandinavian Governments will continue to act together and to maintain neutrality ; agreement reached on " some special questions " ; impression that the results of the Conference were small.

(³⁰) *March* 11.—Germany was forced to adopt the submarine by England's refusal to ratify the Declaration of London ; England had rejected United States proposal to allow free passage of food ships for non-combatants and was trying to starve Germany ; English merchantmen armed for offence ; English blockade illegal ; contraband unduly extended, mails interfered with, neutrals oppressed, etc. Therefore, Germany unable to use submarines merely according to provisions of the Declaration of London.

(³¹) *March* 14.—Revision of Exemptions intended ; unmarried men employed on munitions to be reduced to a minimum ; pensions for those discharged owing to illness contracted on service ; four-fifths of full pension for those discharged owing to illness aggravated by service ; measures for providing better defensive weapons for home bases and better anti-aircraft guns ; supply of aeroplanes greater than that of engines and pilots.

(³²) *March* 16.—Sir George Askwith, Chairman of Conference, decided that all miners must become members of recognised unions, to prevent reduction of output ; compulsion to be used if necessary ; difficulties to be reported if necessary to the Chief Industrial Commissioner.

(³³) *March* 16.—Von Tirpitz was appointed Secretary of the Navy in 1897 ; previously in command in Far East ; introduced the first Navy Bill, 1898 ; rather a politician than a sailor ; aim to create a German Navy able to meet the British Navy ; advocate of unrestricted submarine warfare.

([34]) *March* 19.—Four seaplanes over Dover, Ramsgate, Margate and Westgate ; little material damage ; 14 killed, 26 wounded ; one raider brought down at sea by Flight Commander Bone, R.N.A.S.

([35]) *March* 21.—Loyalist crowds demonstrated against Sinn Fein premises ; police stopped disturbance but were fired on from Sinn Fein headquarters ; three police wounded ; four Irish volunteers arrested.

([36]) *March* 27-28.—England represented by Mr. Asquith, Sir E. Grey, Mr. Lloyd George, Lord Kitchener, and Sir W. Robertson. Opening session devoted to military questions ; afternoon session to economic questions. Arranged for an economic conference and a permanent committee in Paris ; measures to be taken to relieve pressure on tonnage.

([37]) *March* 30.—Resolution in favour of free use of submarines adopted by all parties, except the Socialists represented by Herr Ledebour, as being an effective weapon against the British conduct of war.

([38]) *April* 4.—Mr. McKenna stated that expenditure for 1915-6 had been 1,559 millions, 31 millions less than estimate ; revenue 337 millions ; deficit made good by war loans, sale of exchequer bonds, Treasury bills and the Anglo-French American loan. Estimate for 1916-7, 1,825 millions ; revenue 502 millions ; new taxes on amusements, matches and mineral waters ; proposed tax on travel dropped ; owing to rise, income-tax varying up to 5/- in the £ ; 50%-60% increase in taxes on sugar, cocoa, coffee, motor cars and excess profits.

([39]) *April* 5.—Despatch covered period from middle of April to end of September, 1915, and deals with operations on Persian border, the Lower Euphrates and the Tigris, including the first battle of Kut.

([40]) *April* 7.—German food prospects declared to be good ; Allies had refused to consider peace in September, 1915 ; Polish question would be solved by Germany and Austria ; guarantees required that Belgium would not be used as a base against Germany ; nations subject to Russia between Baltic and Volhynian swamps to be freed.

([41]) *April* 10.—Despatch covers period Oct. 28, 1915 to Jan. 9, 1916 ; deals with withdrawal of Allied troops from Gallipoli and the landing at Salonika, to the time of the withdrawal within the Greek frontier.

([42]) *April* 10.—Report is signed by Mr. Justice Younger and covers first six months of 1915 ; deals with the epidemic of typhus, when the German medical staff fled and four English medical officers coped with the disease in a camp of 15,000 prisoners.

([43]) *April* 12.—Note states that the submarine commander believed that the vessel torpedoed on March 24 was a mine-layer ; that the pictures of the " Sussex " do not resemble those of the vessel attacked, and that the " Sussex " must therefore have been sunk in some other way ; Germany is ready to submit the case to a mixed tribunal.

([44]) *April* 14.—Note demanded punishment of submarine commander responsible for the attacks on the " Sussex " and other steamers attacked without warning ; a full indemnity ; guarantees for the future ; delay would mean the breaking off of diplomatic relations.

([45]) *April* 17.—Committee held that there was no case for extension of Military Service Act to all men of military age, but suggested extension of the Act to include those reaching the age of 18 ; the retention of time-expired regulars ; further combing-out of single men ; perseverance with existing methods of recruiting.

([46]) *May* 1.—Casualties : Military and Constabulary, killed, 124 ; wounded and missing, 397 ; civilians, killed, 180 ; wounded, 614.

([47]) *May* 4.—Germany had exercised great restraint in use of submarines and cannot abandon this weapon of self-defence against England ; will not sink vessels without warning and without saving life, unless there is resistance or an attempt to escape ; U.S.A. to insist that Great Britain ceases to interfere with sea-borne trade.

([48]) *May* 8.—U.S.A. unable to discuss suggestion that the safety of American citizens should be made dependent on the conduct of other Governments.

([49]) *May* 10.—Germany admitted torpedoing of " Sussex " by a German submarine ; commander of U-boat punished ; indemnity offered to injured American. Admitted it also to Spain, May 13.

([50]) *May* 10.—Members of Commission : Lord Hardinge, Sir Montagu Shearman, Sir Mackenzie Chalmers.

([51]) *May* 10.—Mr. Hughes argued in favour of industrial re-organisation to win the war and secure fruits of victory ; war was a matter of life and death for labour.

(⁵²) *May* 11.—Mr. Asquith announced the execution of twelve Irish rebels and his own approaching visit to Ireland (73 sentenced to penal servitude, and 6 to imprisonment for life).

(⁵³) *May* 15.—The Allies are fighting for a free Europe ; Prussia for control over Europe ; no coalition against Germany before the war ; no truth in German charges against Great Britain ; war must be avoided for the future if humanity is to be saved.

(⁵⁴) *May* 17.—America anxious to avoid war but may be forced to intervene ; must in any case have a voice in the peace settlement.

(⁵⁵) *May* 17.—Other members, Major Baird, Lord Sydenham.

(⁵⁶) *May* 18.—Freedom of the seas, as interpreted by Germany, meant paralysis of the sea power of other nations ; Great Britain and U.S.A. interested in maintaining unimpaired rights of sea power.

(⁵⁷) *May* 19.—Mr. Birrell stated that Sinn Fein had first been a literary movement but became revolutionary ; strengthened by inclusion of Sir E. Carson in Government ; a serious danger in March, when Mr. Birrell applied for troops to be sent to Ireland.

(⁵⁸) *May* 22.—No peace until Germany has been punished ; durable peace must be based on international right effectively guaranteed.

(⁵⁹) *May* 23.—No distinction between Prussia and Germany ; Great Britain had been militarist at Fashoda, in Algeciras, etc. ; annoyed at Germany preventing war over the Bosnian crisis ; Lord Haldane had been offered a neutrality agreement which would have secured peace ; Germany would make peace on basis of security against attack.

(⁶⁰) *May* 24.—Great Britain could only make peace in concert with her Allies ; no truth in the statement as to British conduct at the time of the Bosnian crisis ; Germany must recognise that the Allies are not defeated ; France has a special right to be heard as to peace negotiations.

(⁶¹) *May* 25.—In the King's message on magnificent response of the people, it is stated that 5,031,000 have voluntarily enrolled since beginning of war.

(⁶²) *May* 26.—No interference with American mails can be tolerated ; stocks, bonds, etc., to be regarded as merchandise ; correspondence to be unmolested.

(⁶³) *May* 27.—Alliance between Great Britain and Russia is eternal and based on community of interest ; Russia has no aggressive aims against Sweden or her other European neighbours ; Poland to be autonomous.

(⁶⁴) *May* 27.—Causes of the war are not the concern of the United States ; America ready to mediate on lines of settlement of immediate interests between belligerents and formation of a universal league to secure freedom of the seas and prevention of war without a first attempt at arbitration.

(⁶⁵) *May* 29.—Extracts from correspondence of British Ambassador at St. Petersburg in 1909 show that Great Britain was opposed to war on behalf of Serbian claims ; war was averted by Russian reluctance to press those claims to the point of war.

(⁶⁶) *May* 31.—Battle of Jutland ; four stages (i.), Admiral Beatty engaged with von Hipper until approach of von Scheer is reported ; (ii.), Beatty steams N. to join Jellicoe, pursued by whole German Fleet, and is joined by advanced guard of Grand Fleet under Admiral Hood ; (iii.), Von Scheer retreats ; (iv.), June 1, Germans escape during night. British loss : " Queen Mary," battleship ; " Indefatigable " and " Invincible," battle-cruisers ; " Defence," " Black Prince " and " Warrior," cruisers ; " Tipperary," " Ardent," " Fortune," " Shark," " Sparrowhawk," " Nestor," " Nomad " and " Turbulent," destroyers. Rear-Admirals Sir R. Arbuthnot and Hon. H. Hood went down with their flagships. German loss at least : two Dreadnoughts, one " Deutschland," " Lützow," battle-cruiser ; five light cruisers ; six destroyers ; one submarine.

(⁶⁷) *June* 5.—H.M.S. " Hampshire " was proceeding to Russia with Lord Kitchener and his staff, Lt.-Col. Fitzgerald, Gen. Ellershaw, Mr. H. O'Beirne, Sir H. F. Donaldson and Mr. Robertson. She struck a mine and sank off the Orkneys ; twelve survivors ; 75 bodies, including that of Col. Fitzgerald, washed ashore.

(⁶⁸) *June* 6.—Rations supplied do not contain enough to support life ; parcels from England sent at random without consideration of the prisoners requirements.

(⁶⁹) *June* 10.—Government said to be out of touch with the country and blamed for reverses in the Trentino.

(⁷⁰) *June* 12.—Riots directed against Venizelos and the Entente ; instigated by secret police and no attempt made to stop them ; belittled by the Greek Government.

(⁷¹) *June* 14 and 21.—Lord Crewe, Mr. Bonar Law, Mr. Hughes (Australia), Sir G. Foster (Canada), British Representatives. Eight Allied States represented. It is recommended that during the war period stringent measures be taken to restrict enemies' supplies and trade ; in period of reconstruction, enemy to be denied most favoured nation treatment for a period to be fixed ; protective measures against enemy trade to be taken by the Allies ; peace period, Allies to be made independent of enemy goods, and new patent laws to be drawn up.

(⁷²) *June* 19.—Nineteen members instead of thirteen ; Signor Boselli, Premier ; Baron Sonnino, Foreign Affairs ; Signor Orlando, Interior ; Signor Bissolati, War, etc. ; a Coalition Ministry pledged to carry on the war.

(⁷³) *June* 20.—Despatch describes attack on Kilimanjaro ; first phase ending with capture of Moschi ; second phase continuing to capture of Usambara ; operations nearing completion.

(⁷⁴) *June* 21.—Great Britain, France and Russia, with Italian approval, demand complete demobilisation of Greek Army ; guarantee of benevolent neutrality ; dissolution and new elections ; dismissal of certain police officials.

(⁷⁵) *June* 22.—Deals with operations against the Senussi who had imprisoned the crews of the " Tara " and " Morina " and attacked Sollum ; they were defeated December, 1915 and January, 1916 ; Said Ahmed, their chief, escaped. Despatch also describes Turkish attack on Suez Canal, February, 1915.

(⁷⁶) *June* 26.—Demobilisation to take effect from July 1 ; half the 1913 class to remain with the colours until August ; other half until the 1915 class is called up.

(⁷⁷) *July* 3.—The Royal Commission appointed to inquire into the causes of the Easter rising in Ireland (April 24, 1916) consisted of Lord Hardinge of Penshurst (Chairman), Mr. Justice Shearman and Sir Mackenzie Chalmers. The terms of reference were to inquire into the causes of the outbreak and into the conduct and degree of responsibility of the civil and military executive in Ireland in connection therewith.

The report deals with :(1) The constitution of the Irish Executive in so far as it is concerned with the maintenance of law and order ; (2) The legal power vested in that Executive ; (3) The history of events leading up to the outbreak of April 24th, with observations thereon.

Discussing the system of Executive Government the report points out that in practice all power and responsibility are taken from the Viceroy and vested in the Chief Secretary who, by the necessity of attending Cabinet meetings and answering questions in the House of Commons, is forced to spend most of his time out of the country.

Reviewing the police organisation, the report shows how there are two separate forces in Ireland, under separate commands ; viz. : the Royal Irish Constabulary and the Dublin Metropolitan Police ; the former armed and quasi-military, the latter unarmed ; consequently when armed rebellion broke out in Dublin the police had to be withdrawn from duty. The Commissioners think that if the Irish system of Government be taken as a whole it is anomalous in quiet times and almost unworkable in times of crisis.

The Commissioners summarise at some length the causes of the outbreak, the Sinn Fein campaign and all the incidents which lead up to the rising of Easter, and they come to the general conclusion, " that the main cause of the rebellion appears to be that lawlessness was allowed to grow up unchecked, and that Ireland for several years past has been administered on the principle that it was safer and more expedient to leave law in abeyance if collision with any faction of the Irish people could thereby be avoided." The Commissioners are of opinion that the general danger of the situation was clearly pointed out to the Irish Government by the military authorities, on their own initiative, but the warning fell on unheeding ears ; and further they are of the opinion " that the Chief Secretary as the administrative head of the Government in Ireland is primarily responsible for the situation that was allowed to arise and the outbreak that occurred."

(⁷⁸) *July* 8.—The object of the Russo-Japanese Agreement of July, 1916, was the maintenance of peace and the safeguarding of special Russian and Japanese rights and interests in the Far East. The text is to the following effect : Article 1. Japan will not be a party to any political arrangement or combination directed against Russia. Russia will not be a party to any political arrangement or combination directed against Japan. Article 2. : Should the territorial rights or the special interests in the Far East of one of the contracting parties recognised by the other contracting party be threatened, Japan and Russia will take counsel of each other as to the measures to be taken in view of the support or the help to be given in order to safeguard and defend those rights and interests. This treaty is a sequel to the Russo-Japanese arrangements concluded in July, 1907, and July, 1910.

(⁷⁹) *Aug.*2.—The French Government issued a Yellow Book, describing the inhumanity of the Germans towards the people of the occupied French territory. The evidence contained therein was summarised in a Note that the French Government despatched to neutral Powers. A British Blue Book contains the evidence of German atrocities perpetrated in the African campaign. The title is " German Atrocities and Breaches of the Rules of Wâr in Africa " (Cd. 8306).

(⁸⁰) *Aug.* 3.—The Deputation (from Miners' Federation, National Union of Railwaymen, and National Transport Workers' Federation) placed before him proposals for dealing with demobilisation problems after the war. The main points of Mr. Asquith's reply were :—(1) War pledges as to the restoration of trade union practices are obligations of honour and indisputably valid. Arbitration provisions for establishments not covered by Munitions Act are being considered. (2) Government to provide special machinery to deal with labour now employed as substitutes. (3) Demobilisation to be gradual and military difficulty to be considered. (4) Local committees to take a large part in the demobilisation.

(⁸¹) *Aug* 4-9.—The attack by a Turkish army about 14,000 strong began early on the morning, August 4. The enemy drove at our front and tried to envelop our southern flank. He failed disastrously. On our flank our cavalry led the enemy into sardhills where they were shattered by our counter-attack. At dawn on August 5th the pursuit began.

Late in the evening our Territorial infantry carried a strong rearguard position. The pursuit was pressed for 18 miles, Katiya-um-Aisha basin cleared of invaders and 45 officers and 3,100 men taken prisoners.

(⁸²) *Aug.* 10.—Mr. McKenna submitted a balance sheet for the end of the financial year on the assumption that the war continued until March 31st, 1917. His estimates worked out at : Total indebtedness, £3,440,000,000 ; Advances to Allies and Dominions, £800,000,000 ; National Indebtedness, £2,640,000,000 ; National Income (about) £2,500,000,000 or perhaps £2,600,000,000 ; Capital wealth, £15,000,000,000.

(⁸³) *Aug.* 15.—Lt.-Gen. Smuts's despatch of August 16 shows that the German force in E. Africa is being driven southward and eastward. From Dar-es-Salaam inland the enemy still holds some 200 miles of the railway, but General Smuts's forces are only 25 miles N. of the line, while from the W. General Van Deventer continues to advance. From the S. General Northey is nearing Iringa.

(⁸⁴) *Aug.* 16.—The Russian official announcement of the total of their captures from the beginning of their offensive in June to August 12th amounts to 7,757 officers, 350,845 men, 405 cannon, 1,326 machine guns, with hundreds of bomb-throwers and ammunition-wagons.

(⁸⁵) *Aug.* 19.—The Secretary of the Admiralty made the following announcement on August 21, 1916 : " Reports from our look-out squadrons and other units showed that on Saturday, 19th inst,the German High Sea Fleet came out,but, learning from their scouts that the British forces were in considerable strength, the enemy avoided engaging and returned to port. In searching for the enemy we lost two light cruisers by submarine attack, H.M.S. " Nottingham " and H.M.S. " Falmouth.". . . . One enemy submarine has been destroyed and another rammed and possibly sunk. There is no truth in the German statement that a British destroyer was sunk and a British battleship damaged."

(⁸⁶) *Aug.* 24.—At the Conference at Calais among the French representatives were the Prime Minister, M. Briand, and the Minister of Finance, M. Ribot. Among the British representatives were the Prime Minister, the Chancellor of the Exchequer, and the Lord Chief Justice. A complete agreement was arrived at on all the subjects with which the Conference dealt. An arrangement was concluded with regard to payments abroad and the maintenance of the exchange between the two countries.

(⁸⁷) *Aug.* 30.—Since July 1st, the British captured on W. front 266 officers, 15,203 men, 86 guns, 160 machine guns, etc. Also 121 German aeroplanes destroyed on Allied front during August.

(⁸⁸) *Sept.* 1.—Bulgarian spoils in Greek Macedonia. The Bulgarians obtained possession of 17 forts without firing a shot. These cost over £4,600,000, whilst they contained large quantities of munitions and provisions and over 100 guns, including several long-range Schneider and Canet cannon.

(⁸⁹) *Sept.* 1.—At Athens a naval demonstration by 23 warships and 7 transports anchored four miles outside the Piræus occurred. French Admiral in command of the squadron which came from Salonika. A semi-military rising at Salonika, organised by Greek patriots, led to the disarming of the local garrison by General Sarrail.

(⁹⁰) *Sept.* 3.—Early on Sunday (the 3rd) 13 airships raided the Eastern Counties of England ; three got near the outskirts of London : at Cuffley, near Enfield, one fell in flames, all the crew being killed. This makes the 7th Zeppelin destroyed during the present year. The experience of all previous raids was surpassed ; measures taken for the protection of outer London came as a great surprise to the people. Four persons killed, and 12 injured, reported ; no military damage. The airship that fell was attacked by Lieut. Wm. Leefe Robinson, R.F.C., given the V.C. He had been in the air for two hours and had previously attacked another airship.

(⁹¹) *Sept.* 5.—The Trade Union Congress at Birmingham decided to reject by a majority of 2 to 1 an invitation from the American Federation of Labour to take part in an International Labour Congress, proposed to be held after the War, and at the same place as the Congress of belligerent nations, to settle the terms of peace. The Delegates refused to parley with the Socialists of Germany and her Allies.

(⁹²) *Sept.* 6.—The Viceroy showed how India in the last two years has supplied and kept up to strength large forces in France, and had also sent troops to E. Africa, Egypt, Mesopotamia, Muscat, and Aden. The Indian Army had proved to be a great Imperial asset. From India 2,600 combatant officers had been withdrawn : to replace them the Indian Army Reserve of officers had been raised from 40 to 2,000. Recruiting had been excellent, more men having joined since the opening of the war than the entire strength of the Indian Army in August, 1914.

(⁹³) *Sept.* 19.—In Galicia for last three days past heavy fighting took place. Gen. Shcherbachev's Army advanced nearly 44 miles since the start of the present operations from the winter line. Since August 31st, 25,000 prisoners taken (8,000 being Germans), and 22 guns, some of them heavy.

(⁹⁴) *Sept.* 23.—German airships, probably 12, made a raid on London and the Eastern, S. Eastern, and E. Midland counties. Two were brought down, one in flames. The crew of one set fire to their craft and then surrendered. The casualties due to the raid were 40 killed, 130 injured. The airships brought down were the new naval Zeppelins, L.32 and L.33.

(⁹⁵) *Sept.* 25.—Another air raid on England occurred on the 25th. Seven airships took part, the South, East, and S. East coasts, and the N. Midlands being visited. The killed numbered 43, and the injured 31.

(⁹⁶) *Sept.* 27.—Interview with Mr. Lloyd George published by Mr. Roy W. Howard, President of the United Press of America. The Secretary of State for War declares Britain has only now begun to fight, " The whole World must know that there can be no outside interference at this stage. There are no quitters among the Allies, and never will be. ' Never again ' has become our battle-cry."

(⁹⁷) *Oct.* 1.—Since July 1, British captures amounted to 588 officers, 26,147 men ; 29 heavy guns, 92 field guns, 103 trench mortars, 397 machine guns. Of 38 German divisions engaged, 29 were withdrawn exhausted or broken.

(⁹⁸) *Oct.* 10.—Admiral du Fournet, in command of Allied Fleets, summoned the Greek Government to surrender to him by mid-day, Oct. 11, the whole of the Greek Fleet. Larger units to be disarmed and crews reduced to one-third ; smaller units to be handed over as they were ; certain coast batteries to be disarmed, mails and Piræus-Larissa Railway to be placed under control of Allies.

(⁹⁹) *Oct.* 12.—Du Fournet presented a Supplementary Note demanding (1) Control by the Allies of the police in Greece, (2) Prohibition of the carrying of arms by citizens, (3) Prohibition of despatch of war material to Thessaly, (4) Lifting of the embargo on the export of wheat from Thessaly.

(¹⁰⁰) *Oct.* 13.—Latest official returns of prisoners :—Germans in British hands, 729 military and 150 naval officers, 36,165 soldiers and 1,976 sailors ; total, 39,020. British in German hands :—Altogether, 30,101.

(¹⁰¹) *Oct.* 19.—German prisoners captured by the French on the Somme, July 1 to Oct. 12, number 40,125.

(¹⁰²) *Nov.* 1.—Franco-British captures, since July 1, amount to 1,449 officers, 71,532 men, 303 guns, 215 trench mortars, and 981 machine guns.

(¹⁰³) *Nov.* 2.—Declaration of Labour Group of Central War Industrial Committee at Petrograd to Working Classes. Warning against listening to alarmist reports *re* riots, accidents in factories, strikes, etc. Danger lest enemy should take advantage of situation ; constructive social work needed.

(¹⁰⁴) *Nov.* 9.—Speech of v. Bethmann-Hollweg in Reichstag in reply to Sir E. Grey. Immediate cause of war, Russian mobilization on July 30.14. Hollweg urged Austria to accept mediation. Vienna consented. Therefore Russia responsible. Deeper cause : British policy of boycott against Germany. Annexation of Belgium not Germany's intention. League of nations to preserve peace after war impossible on Entente terms.

If aggressive coalitions cease, Germany ready to join union of peoples and to be head of such union. Germany fights for safety and development.

(¹⁰⁵) *Nov.* 9.—Speech of Mr. Asquith at Guildhall, London. Assurance given of British sympathy with Armenians and with M. Venizelos. Justification of Allies in Greece. German propaganda aiming at dividing Allies. No separate peace possible.

(¹⁰⁶) *Nov.* 10.—German Note to Greece. Germany would consider Greek giving up of war material to Entente a breach of neutrality.

(¹⁰⁷) *Nov.* 13.—Appeal of Cardinal Mercier to civilized world. Protest *re* deportations made by Cardinals and Bishops, Oct. 19, to Governor-General, who refused to listen. Orders for forced labour, Aug. 15.15, May 2.16 and May 13 (sanction of deportation). Every deported workman equals another soldier for Germany. Liberties of Belgians had been guaranteed by von Hülhe after capitulation of Antwerp, and by von der Goltz as Governor-General at Brussels.

(¹⁰⁸) *Nov.* 14.—British White Paper *re* U.S.A. " Black List " Protest of July 28. Sir E. Grey stated: " Trading with Enemy Act " of 1915 empowers British Government to prohibit British subjects trading with persons in foreign countries who are supporting enemy. This is right of Great Britain as sovereign State. Refusal of bunker coal at British ports to ships of firms on Black List also within British rights. German houses abroad have been used to further German ambitions, *e.g.*, to destroy ships carrying food for Allies. Necessary for British Government to take action against them.

(¹⁰⁹) *Nov.* 15.—Russian official statement *re* Poland. : German-Austrian Proclamation *re* Poland an infringement of International law. Russia at end of war will create autonomous Poland out of all Polish territory to be under Russian Sovereignty.

(¹¹⁰) *Nov.* 16.—Polish recruiting for German Army to begin on 22nd. Hollweg declares German promises to Poland conditional on recruiting results.

(¹¹¹) *Nov.* 16.—German aircraft forces. One board to control aerial and anti-aircraft forces. Von Hoeppner in command.

(¹¹²) *Nov.* 17.—Food regulations. Board of Trade invested with wide powers to prevent waste, regulate manufacture and production, direct sale and distribution, control markets, regulate price, commandeer any article.

(¹¹³) *Nov.* 18.—Letter of Mr. Franklin Roosevelt (Assist.-Sec. U.S.A. Navy) to Mr. Polk (Counsellor of State Dept.) *re* exploits on Oct. 8, for informal use by U.S.A. Ambassador in London. American Navy had not acted in un-neutral manner. Had gone to help of crews forced to abandon ships by U 53 off Nantucket Lightship. U.S.S. " Benham " did not leave Dutch ship " Bloomersdyk " in obedience to signal from U. 53, nor until all on board had left.

(¹¹⁴) *Nov.*21.—Statement by M.Venizelos of aims and policy of Greek National Defence Movement : Greek National Movement fighting to repair wrong done to Serbia by Greek disregard of Treaty obligations, to expel Bulgars from Greek territory, to emphasize conviction that Greek progress and independence can only be maintained in alliance with traditional friends, to ensure right to be masters of own destiny, *e.g.* for triumph over Prussian militarism.

(¹¹⁵) *Nov.* 24.—Ultimatum to Greece. Ten mountain batteries to be handed to Allies by Dec. 1, and remainder of material by Dec. 15, on pain of steps being taken to enforce demand.

(¹¹⁶) *Nov.* 25.—German Patriotic Auxiliary Service Bill presented to Reichstag. Every male between 16 and 60 not serving in army liable to patriotic service (*i.e.*, service in Government offices, war industry, agriculture, nursing). Control of Patriotic Auxiliary Service to be under War Office.

(¹¹⁷) *Nov.* 30.—Conditions of New Volunteer Army : No man to lose civil employment, no compulsion to sign agreement, not to leave home save for defence of country.

(¹¹⁸) *Dec.* 1.—Allied force of 3,000 (British, French and Italian naval troops) landed at the Piræus and marched to Athens. Attacked by King Constantine's troops in the outskirts of the city, scattered fighting continued for 3½ hours, when armistice was concluded, and troops gradually re-embarked. The Zappeion (E. outskirts of Athens) shelled by French ships in afternoon consequent on Greek artillery firing thence at barracks in which were French sailors.

(¹¹⁹) *Dec.* 1.—Mr. Lloyd George, dissatisfied with the leisurely conduct of the war, states that he is unable to remain in the Government ; wrote to Premier proposing reduction of War Committee to four members (including Sir E. Carson). Mr. Bonar Law believed to support scheme.

(¹²⁰) *Dec.* 2.—M. Trepov's speech referred to Agreement with Entente Powers in 1915, whereby Russia's right to the Straits and Constantinople was established. Speaks of effort made to keep Turkey out of the war, guarantees being given by the Entente of her territorial integrity and of certain advantages.

(^{121}) *Dec.* 4.—Lord R. Cecil states that British Government consider King Constantine and his Government deeply involved in recent outrages ; Allies considering measures for radical solution. (In Oct. King Constantine offered artillery, etc., as compensation for that given by Greek officers to enemy, Allies stipulating for Greek neutrality, and offering an indemnity. King and Government failed to keep their word). Greek Minister in London resigns.

(^{122}) *Dec.* 7.—Report of this date states that our northern line—200 miles long— now reaches from Neu Iringa through Kissaki and Kissangire to the coast ; the column advancing S.W. from Kilwa (135 miles S. of Dar-es-Salaam), to join hands with Gen. Northey's force at N. of L. Nyassa, has penetrated 60 miles inland. German main forces between these two lines on the Ruaha River.

(^{123}) *Dec.* 9.—New War Cabinet : Mr. Lloyd George, Lord Curzon, Lord Milner, Mr. Henderson, Mr. Bonar Law. Other Ministers : Mr. Balfour, Foreign Office ; Lord Derby, War Office ; Sir E. Carson, Admiralty ; Lord R. Cecil, Blockade ; Mr. Bonar Law, Chancellor of the Exchequer ; Mr. Austen Chamberlain, India ; Mr. W. Long, Colonies ; Dr. Addison, Munitions. New Ministries : Food, Shipping, and Labour.

(^{124}) *Dec.* 11.—Germany's reply *re* Belgian deputations states : Appalling increase of unemployment in Belgium ; necessary to allot work in Germany ; coercion only used against those who refuse to work ; acting in accordance with humanity and international law ; no protest from neutrals against clandestine removal of Germans to Siberia (!), etc., etc.

(^{125}) *Dec.* 12.—M. Briand, Premier and Foreign Affairs ; Gen. Lyautey, War ; Admiral Lacaze, Marine ; M. Ribot, Finance ; M. Thomas, Munitions War Committee ; M. Malvy, Interior, etc., etc.

(^{126}) *Dec.* 12.—Germany's " Peace " Note (issued through Neutrals) states she was forced to take up arms for justice and liberty ; she has gained gigantic advantages in the war and is anxious to end its horrors and atrocities, and not to shatter her adversaries, hence " the four Allied Powers have proposed to enter forthwith into peace negotiations. The propositions which they bring forward for such negotiations . . . . are an appropriate basis for the establishment of a lasting peace." (But no propositions are brought forward). " If, in spite of this offer of peace and reconciliation, the struggle should go on," the Central Powers " decline every responsibility for this before humanity and history." (The Pope's support for this Note was also invoked). The Note was read in the Reichstag by the Chancellor, who introduced it after a high-sounding preface recapitulating the mighty victories and noble ideals of the great German Empire. An official telegram in the same sense was also issued by Austria at the same time.

(^{127}) *Dec.* 14.—The Allies demand in their Ultimatum the withdrawal of the whole of the Greek force from Thessaly ; that all movement of troops N. ward should be stopped, and a proportion of troops transferred to the Peloponnesus. The blockade will be carried out until reparation for the attack on the Allies has been exacted and guarantee of future security received.

(^{128}) *Dec.* 14.—The House was asked for £400,000,000, bringing total for financial year to £1,950,000,000.

(^{129}) *Dec.* 15.—Russian Foreign Minister on peace negotiations : vigorous speech ; Duma passes resolution for categorical refusal by Allied Powers of any peace negotiations: a lasting peace being possible only after " victory over the military power of Germany."

(^{130}) *Dec.* 19.—Prime Minister states that the Allies arrived at an identical conclusion *re* German " Peace " Note : Conference with Germany without knowledge of proposals would be putting their heads in a noose ; " restitution, reparation, guarantee ; we shall put our trust rather in an unbroken army than in broken faith " ; time come for National Service, and Government control of shipping, mining and food, etc.

(^{131}) *Dec.* 19.—In consequence of our strenuous protests and threats of retaliation, Germany gives assurance that Capt. Blaikie, who had been guilty of the same " crime " as Capt. Fryatt, *i.e.*, defending his ship against an attacking submarine, should not be executed.

(^{132}) *Dec.* 20.—President Wilson's Note *re* a peace conference invites the belligerents to state definite peace terms ; as stated in general terms both sides appear to have similar objects ; counsels interchange of views ; presently too late to accomplish greater things which lie beyond peace conclusions ; these a great concern of his nation, which has been seriously affected by the war.

([133]) *Dec.* 21.—Allies' new Note to Greece demands prohibition of Reservist meetings, control of telegraphs, posts and railways, release of Venizelists, and enquiry by mixed Commission into disturbances of Dec. 1 and 2.

([134]) *Dec.* 22.—King's Speech urges the vigorous prosecution of the war until violated rights vindicated and security of Europe firmly established.

([135]) *Dec.* 25.—Tsar replies to German Peace overtures in an order to his troops : that sense of defeat urged Germany to peace-move ; she must be driven from invaded lands ; Dardanelles and Constantinople regained ; Poland freed ; no thought of peace, etc.

([136]) *Dec.* 26.—Germany's reply to President Wilson's Note proposes immediate meeting of belligerents to discuss peace ; that the great work of preventing future wars can only be begun after present struggle ceases ; reiterates former benevolent statements.

([137]) *Dec.* 29.—Sir D. Haig's despatch of 23rd Dec. covers the operations of our Armies in France from May 19th to date : deals mainly with the operations on the Somme First phase, 1 to 14th July ; second phase, 18th July to 9th Sept ; third phase 15th Sept. to 23rd Oct. Ancre phase, 9th to 18th Nov. During this time were captured : 38,000 prisoners, including over 800 officers ; 125 guns (including 29 heavy) ; 136 trench mortars ; 514 machine guns. Sir Douglas points out that during these operations fully half the German Army was engaged, and defeated, and our own troops, many of whom were only partially trained, surpassed all expectations.

([138]) *Dec.* 29.—Rasputin, a low-class and licentious monk, had obtained great influence at Court, especially over the Tsar and Tsaritsa, by his so-called supernatural powers. The details of his last moments are obscure, but it is believed that the Grand Duke Dmitri, Count Elen, and another lured him to the Yussupov Palace, and there shot him dead, subsequently dropping his body through the ice in the Neva.

([139]) *Dec.* 29.—Resolution at (further) sitting of National Congress of Socialists in Paris states that Germany only offered a trap instead of real peace conditions ; demands more vigorous action from French Government, and that all national forces should be utilized, so as to bring nearer the conclusion of the war.

([140]) *Dec.* 30.—Southern Slav Committee declares that seven millions of Slavs unable to exercise freedom of speech under pressure of war-terror ; in order to fulfil legitimate aspirations all Slav races must sever connection with Habsburgs and unite with Serbia under Karageorgevich Dynasty.

([141]) *Dec.* 30.—Allied Note, handed to U.S.A. in reply to enemy " Peace " Note. The reply is a refusal to enter into negotiations, the proposals of the Central Powers being described as illusory and the peace which they seek as advantageous to those who caused the war. The object of the enemy Note, it is said, was to disturb public opinion in Allied countries and to stiffen it in Germany, to deceive neutrals, and to justify in advance a new series of crimes. The Allies declare that " no peace is possible so long as they have not secured reparation of violated rights and liberties, recognition of the principle of nationalities and of the free existence of small States ; so long as they have not brought about a settlement calculated to end, once and for all, causes which have so long threatened the nations, and to afford the only effective guarantees for the future security of the world." The note concludes with a special reference to the fate and aims of Belgium.

([142]) *Dec.* 31.—The principal Allied demands were : (a) The Greek Army, with all material of war, to be transferred to the Peloponnesus ; (b) Allies' control over Greek public services to be restored ; (c) All political prisoners to be released, with indemnification for those who have suffered unjustly on account of events of Dec. 1 and 2. ; (d) The Greek Government to apologise formally to the Allies, and the Allies' flags to be formally and publicly saluted in Athens. The Allied Powers undertake that Venizelist forces shall not profit by the withdrawal of the Royal troops to make encroachments on Greek territory, but add that the blockade of Greece will be continued until satisfaction is given.

BRITISH MERCHANT VESSELS LOST BY ENEMY ACTION.

	By Cruisers and T.B.D's.		By Submarines.		By Mines.		Total.		
	No.	Lives.	No.	Lives.	No.	Lives.	No.	Lives.	Gross Tonnage.
1914*									
August	8	—	—	—	1	—	9	—	40,254
September ..	19	—	—	—	2	29	21	29	88,219
October	14	—	1	—	4	24	19	24	77,805
November ..	2	—	2	—	1	—	5	—	8,888
December ..	5	—	—	—	5	16	10	16	26,035
Total ..	48	—	3	—	13	69	64	69	241,201
1915*									
January	3	—	7	21	1	—	11	21	32,054
February ..	4	—	8	9	2	21	14	30	36,372
March	2	—	21	161	—	—	23	161	71,479
April	—	—	11	38	—	—	11	38	22,453
May	—	—	19	1,208	—	—	19	1,208	84,025
June	—	—	29	78	2	3	31	81	83,198
July	—	—	19	26	1	2	20	28	52,847
August ..	—	—	42	205	7	43	49	248	148,464
September	—	—	22	44	8	33	30	77	101,690
October ..	—	—	10	35	7	7	17	42	54,156
November ..	—	—	23	25	9	93	32	118	94,493
December ..	—	—	16	416	5	3	21	419	74,490
Total ..	9	—	227	2,246	41	205	278	2,371	855,721
1916.									
January	8	17	5	28	3	19	16	64	62,288
February ..	4	1	7	34	15†	256†	26	291	75,860
March	—	—	19	44	7	29	26	73	99,089
April	—	—	37	119	6	12	43	131	141,193
May	—	—	12	6	8	8	20	14	64,521
June	1	1	11	34	4	29	16	64	36,976
July	2	—	21	58	5	11	28	69	82,432
August ..	—	—	22	4	1	4	23	8	43,354
September ..	1	—	34	16	7	4	42	20	104,572
October ..	1	—	41	182	7	15	49	197	176,248
November ..	—	—	42	55	7	45	49	100	168,809
December ..	10	4	36	91	12	91	58	186	182,292
Total ..	27	23	287	671	82	523	396	1,217	1,237,634

* The corrected returns for 1914 and 1915 were not received in time to be included in Vol. I.

† Includes 1 ship and 13 lives lost by aircraft action

AIR RAIDS ON

(Zeppelin [italic]:

Date.			Locality.		Civilian		
				Killed.			
				Men.	Women.	Children.	Total.
January 19/20 ...	...		*Norfolk*	*2*	*2*	—	*4*
Feb.	21	... ...	Essex	—	—	—	—
April	*14/15*	... ...	*Northumberland*	—	—	—	—
,,	*15/16*	... ...	*Essex and Suffolk*	—	—	—	—
,,	16	... ...	Kent	—	—	—	—
,,	*29/30*	... ...	*Suffolk*	—	—	—	—
May	*9/10*	... ...	*Southend*	—	*1*	—	*1*
,,	*16/17*	... ...	*Ramsgate*	*1*	*1*	—	*2*
,,	*26/27*	... ...	*Southend*	—	*2*	*1*	*3*
,,	*31/June 1*	...	*East London*	*1*	*2*	*4*	*7*
June	*4/5*	... ...	*Kent, Essex and E. Riding* ...	—	—	—	—
,,	*6/7*	... ...	*Hull, Grimsby and E. Riding...* ...	*5*	*13*	*6*	*24*
,,	*15/16*	... ...	*Northumberland and Durham* ...	*18*	—	—	*18*
July	3	... ...	E. Suffolk	—	—	—	—
Aug.	*9/10*	... ...	*Goole, E. Riding, Suffolk and Dover* ...	*1*	*10*	*6*	*17*
,,	*12/13*	... ...	*E. Suffolk and Essex*	*4*	*2*	—	*6*
,,	*17/18*	... ...	*Kent, Essex and London*	*7*	*2*	*1*	*10*
Sept.	*7/8*	... ...	*E. Suffolk and London*	*6*	*6*	*6*	*18*
,,	*8/9*	... ...	*N. Riding, Norfolk and London* ...	*15*	*3*	*6*	*24*
,,	*11/12*	... ...	*Essex*	—	—	—	—
,,	*12/13*	... ...	*Essex and E. Suffolk*	—	—	—	—
,,	13	... ...	Margate	—	*2*	—	*2*
,,	*13/14*	... ...	*E. Suffolk*	—	—	—	—
Oct.	*13/14*	... ...	*Norfolk, Suffolk, Home Counties and London*	*31*	*17*	*6*	*54*
			TOTAL	91	63	36	190

* The corrected returns did not come to

GREAT BRITAIN, 1915.*
Aeroplane.)

Casualties. Injured,				Sailors and Soldiers.		Grand Total.		Remarks.
Men.	Women.	Children.	Total.	Killed.	Injured.	Killed.	Injured.	
9	4	2	15	—	1	4	16	Yarmouth, King's Lynn and neighbourhood.
								Colchester, etc.
—	1	1	2	—	—	—	2	Tyneside.
—	—	—	—	—	—	—	—	Faversham, Sittingbourne, etc.
1	—	—	1	—	1	1	2	
—	1	—	1	—	—	2	1	Zeppelins also raided Dunkirk and Calais.
3	—	—	3	—	—	3	3	
13	13	7	33	—	2	7	35	
3	4	1	8	—	—	—	8	
18	13	7	38	—	2	24	40	Zeppelin destroyed by Lt. R. Warneford, R.N.
72	—	—	72	—	—	18	72	
5	6	7	18	—	3	17	21	One Zeppelin destroyed at Dunkirk
5	10	9	24	—	—	6	24	
16	20	12	48	—	—	10	48	
9	15	13	37	—	1	18	38	
50	32	10	92	2	2	26	94	
—	—	—	—	—	—	—	—	
2	4	—	6	—	—	2	6	
—	—	—	—	—	—	—	—	
71	27	9	107	17	21	71	128	
277	150	73	505	19	33	209	538	

hand in time for inclusion in Vol. I.—Ed.

AIR RAIDS ON

(*Zeppelin* [*italic*]):

				Civilian			
				Killed.			
Date.			Locality.	Men.	Women.	Children.	Total.
Jan.	22/23	...	Dover	1	—	—	1
,,	23	...	Kent	—	—	—	—
,,	31/Feb. 1	...	*West Suffolk and Midland Counties* ...	29	26	15	70
Feb.	9	...	Kent	—	—	—	—
,,	20	...	Kent and E. Suffolk	1	—	—	1
March	1	...	Broadstairs and Margate	—	—	1	1
,,	5/6	...	*Hull, E. Riding, Lincolnshire, Leicestershire, Rutland and Kent* ...	9	4	5	18
,,	19	...	Deal, Dover, Margate and Ramsgate	1	3	6	10
,,	31/April 1	...	*Lincolnshire, Essex and Suffolk* ...	6	7	4	17
April	1/2	...	*Durham County and N. Riding* ...	13	7	2	22
,,	2/3	...	*E. Suffolk, Northumberland, London and Scotland*	10	—	3	13
,,	3/4	...	*Norfolk*	—	—	—	—
,,	5/6	...	*Yorkshire and County Durham* ...	—	—	1	1
,,	24	...	Dover	—	—	—	—
,,	24/25	...	*Norfolk, Lincolnshire, Cambridgeshire, and Suffolk*	—	1	—	1
,,	25/26	...	*E. Suffolk, Essex, Kent and London* ...	—	—	—	—
,,	26/27	...	Kent	—	—	—	—
May	2/3	...	*Yorkshire, Northumberland and Scotland*	4	3	—	7
,,	3	...	Deal	—	—	—	—
,,	19/20	...	Kent and Dover	—	—	—	—
July	9	...	Kent (N. Foreland)	—	—	—	—
,,	9/10	...	Dover	—	—	—	—
,,	28/29	...	*Lincolnshire and Norfolk* ...	—	—	—	—
,,	31/Aug. 1	...	*Norfolk, Suffolk, Cambridgeshire, Lincolnshire, Notts. and Kent* ...	—	—	—	—
Aug.	2/3	...	*Norfolk, E. Suffolk and Kent* ...	—	—	—	—
,,	8/9	...	*Northern Counties and Norfolk* ...	2	4	4	10
,,	12	...	Dover	—	—	—	—
,,	23/24	...	E. Suffolk	—	—	—	—
,,	24/25	...	*E. Suffolk, Essex, Kent and London* ...	3	4	2	9
Sept.	2/3	...	*Midland and N. Home Counties, Kent, and London*	1	2	1	4
,,	22	...	Kent and Dover	—	—	—	—
,,	23/24	...	*Lincolnshire, Notts., Norfolk, Kent and London*	24	12	4	40
,,	25/26	...	*Lancashire, Yorkshire and Lincolnshire*	14	17	12	43
Oct.	1/2	...	*Midland and N. Home Counties, Hertfordshire and London* ...	—	—	—	—
,,	22	...	Sheerness	—	—	—	—
,,	23	...	Margate	—	—	—	—
Nov.	27/28	...	*Durham, Yorkshire, Staffordshire and Cheshire*	1	3	—	4
,,	28	...	London	—	—	—	—
			TOTAL	119	93	60	272

GREAT BRITAIN, 1916.

Aeroplane.)

| Casualties. Injured. | | | | Sailors and Soldiers. | | Grand Total. | | Remarks. |
Men.	Women.	Children.	Total.	Killed.	Injured.	Killed.	Injured.	
2	1	3	6	—	—	1	6	
43	50	19	112	—	1	70	113	*Six Zeppelins seen.*
—	2	1	3	—	—	—	3	Margate and Broadstairs attacked.
1	—	—	1	—	—	1	1	
—	—	—	—	—	—	1	—	
22	22	8	52	—	—	18	52	
4	3	8	15	4	11	14	26	One raider brought down at sea.
2	3	4	9	31	55	48	64	*One Zeppelin brought down.*
67	43	18	128	—	2	22	130	*L15 captured.*
6	13	5	24	—	—	13	24	
3	1	5	9	—	—	1	9	
1	—	—	1	—	—	1	1	
1	—	—	1	—	—	—	1	
—	—	—	—	—	—	—	—	
16	8	1	25	2	5	9	30	*L20 sunk off Norway.*
3	1	—	4	—	—	—	4	
—	1	—	1	1	1	1	2	One raider destroyed off Belgian coast.
—	—	—	—	—	—	—	—	
—	—	—	—	—	—	—	—	*60 bombs estimated dropped.*
5	5	5	15	—	1	10	16	
—	—	—	—	—	7	—	7	Seaplanes.
9	11	5	25	—	15	9	40	*[Cuffley by Lt. W. L. Robinson*
6	5	1	12	—	—	4	12	*13 (?) airships :1 brought down at* No damage.
—	—	—	—	—	—	—	—	*[brought down, one in flames.*
57	44	25	126	—	4	40	130	*L32 and L33, new naval airships,*
7	13	11	31	—	—	43	31	*7 airships seen.*
—	1	—	1	1	—	1	1	*L31 brought down at Potter's Bar.*
1	1	—	2	—	—	—	2	
16	14	7	37	—	—	4	37	*Two Zeppelins brought down.*
4	6	—	10	—	—	—	10	Midday raid by 1 aeroplane, brought down in France.
276	248	126	650	39	102	311	752	

INDEX.

Figures in black type represent the month: *e.g.*, 4.1=4th Jan. ; 23.11 = 23rd Nov. ; etc.

N.B.—In the following index a number of items are included which, by reason of their uncertainty or for some other cause, it has not been found easy or convenient to place in the Chronological Tables. Dates which can at present be only approximately given are indicated thus :—"*c.* 25.8."

ture of Erzerum, 16.2; capture of
Trebizond, 18.4; Sinai advance (Romani
5.8), 23.4 to 23.12; fall of Kut, 29.4;
capture of Erzingan, 25.7; Turkish
offensive and Russian rejoinder, 28.7
to 25.8; defeat and death of Sultan of Darfur, 6.11; occupation of El Arish, 21.12.

ASQUITH, RT. HON. H. H.
Speech on proposed Paris Conference,
9.3; in Rome, 31.3; Dr. Bethmann-
Hollweg's reply to, 7.4; statement to
French deputies, 10.4; introduces Military
Service Bill, 3.5; statement on the Irish
rebellion, 11.5; visit to Ireland, 12.5;
receives Miners' Federation Deputation,
3.8; speech at Guildhall, 9.11; decides to
advise reconstruction of Government, 3.12
King approves reconstruction of Cabinet,
4.12; resigns office, 5.12.

ASSENE KALESSI (Armenia).
Russians occupy Surmeneh and reach,
17.4.

ASSEVILLERS (Somme).
French take, 3.7.

ASTICO (Trentino).
Austrians repulsed near Monte Cimone,
in valley, 31.7.

ASTICO-BRENTA (Trentino).
Italian retreat, 23.5.

ATAB (Mesopotamia).
British infantry cross Shatt el-Hai at,
13-14.12.

ATHENS.
Protest meeting at, against king's
policy, 27.8; reported removal of batteries
from, 28.11; Allied troops attacked at,
1.12; Venizelists ill-treated at, 1.12;
armistice concluded, 2.12; French relin-
quish control of telegraphs at, 4.12;
comparative order restored, 6.12; reported
concentration of Greek troops at, 7.12;
Allied subjects leave, 8.12.

ATINA (Armenia).
Russian troops land at, 4.3.

AUSTRALIA.
Political Labour League carries resolution expelling Mr. Hughes from Labour
movement, 18.9; adoption of "Derby"
scheme reported in, 27.11; Mr. D.
Mackinnon, Director-General of recruiting
in, 29.11.

AUSTRIA-HUNGARY.
Dictates terms to Montenegro, 25.1;
Austro-German note to Rumania, 26.1;
break with Portugal, 15.3; offensive
in Trentino begins, 14.3; checked, 7.6;
Italian counter-offensive begins, 9.6;
Death of Franz Josef and accession of
Karl, Emp., 21.11; new government,
13.12; v. Spitzmüller fails to form ministry,
Count Clam Martinic becomes premier,
21.12; Count Czernin, foreign minister,
replies to Pres. Wilson's note, 26.12.

AVERESCU, GENERAL.
Takes command of Rumanian 2nd
army, 10.10.

AVOCOURT (11 m. W. of Verdun).
Redoubt captured by French : heavy
German losses, 29.3; wood heavily bombarded, 16.4; German attack repulsed,
17-18.5; and 26.5.

AYLMER, MAJ. GEN., F.
In command of force for relief of Kut,
6.1; (see under Kut-el-Amara).

BABADAGH (Dobruja).
Encounter E. of, 21.12.

BADGE, SILVER.
Granted to those disabled in the War,
22.7.

BAGAMOYO (Ger. E. Africa).
Naval forces take, 15.8.

BAGHDAD.
White paper published, containing
General Townshend's views on the ad-
vance from Kut, 29.5; Turks driven back
N.W. of, 26.6.

BAGHDAD RAILWAY.
Reaches Bozanti, at E. foot of Taurus,
7.9.

BAGHELA (Mesopotamia).
British air-raids on new Turkish
base, 21-22.12.

BAHARIA OASIS (200 m. S.W. of Cairo).
Hostile Arab force occupies, 11.2.

BAIBURT (Armenia).
Russians capture, 15.7; advance
beyond, 18.7.

BAKER, MR. NEWTON J.
Becomes U.S. Secretary for War, 6.3.

BALCHIK (S. Dobruja)
Russian ships bombard, 13.12.

BALFOUR, RT. HON. A. J.
Introduces naval estimates, 7.3; answers Mr. Churchill's criticisms, 8.3;
makes a statement on sea-power, 18.5;
becomes Foreign Minister, 10.12.

BALKANS.
Front, considerable activity along
whole of, 17.8.

BALTACHI DARASSI RIVER (Armenia).
Russians cross to left bank, 27.3.

BALTIC.
Encounter between Russian flotilla
and German convoy in, 14.6; indecisive
small British naval action, 30.6.

BANK.
Holiday suspended, 13.7; rate, 6 per
cent.

BAPAUME (N. Somme).
British advance towards, begun, 1.7;
great aerial battle, 9.11.

BILLING, MR. PEMBERTON.
Elected M.P. for E. Herts, 10.**3**;
Attack on the Air Service, 22.**3.**

BIR-EL-ABD (Sinai Pen).
3rd Turkish Division discovered at,
19.**7**; Turks evacuate, 12.**8.**

BIR-EL-HASSANA (Sinai, v. El Hassana).
Successful British air-raid, Turkish
base destroyed, 26.**3.**

BIRRELL, MR. A.
Resigns Irish Secretaryship, 3.**5**; Gives
evidence before the Irish Commission, 19.**5.**

BISMARCKBURG (Ger. E. Africa).
Occupied by British, 8.**6.**

BISTRITSA RIVER (Maced.).
Bulgarian retreat on and from, 14,
15.**11.**

BITLIS (Armenia).
Captured by Russians, 2.**3**; Russian
success in region of, 15.**4**; Russians
dislodge Turks from positions near, 20.**4**;
Russian progress near, 27.**4**; Occupied
by Turks, 8.**8**; Retaken by Russians, 23.**8.**

"BLACK LIST."
Protest against, by U.S.A., 28.**7**;
British White Paper on, in answer to
U.S.A. protest, issued, 14.**11.**

BLACK SEA. (v. also Anatolia).
Russian torpedo boats active in, 17
and 22.**1**; Russian torpedo boat sunk by
submarine in, 9.**3**; Russian torpedo
boat sinks Bulgarian patrol steamer in,
19.**3**; Russian torpedo boats active in,
28.**3**; Turkish sailing ships destroyed in,
29.**6**; Russian ports on, bombarded, 4.**7.**

BLAIKIE, CAPT. (s.s. "Caledonia.").
Taken prisoner, vessel sunk, 4.**12**;
Government enquiries through U.S.A.
Embassy, Berlin, 12.**12**; Government
assurance all necessary steps taken, 13.**12**;
German assurance that fate not same as
Capt. Fryatt, 19.**12.**

BLOCKADE OF GERMANY.
Debate on, in Commons, 26.**1**; in
Lords, 22.**2**; British reply to U.S. Note
of 5.**11**, published, 26.**4.**

BOELCKE, CAPT.
Renowned German airman killed,
29.**10.**

BOESINGHE (Flanders).
British post at, captured, 20.**2**;
Attempted German attack repulsed at,
30.**3.**

BOILER-MAKERS, MERSEY.
Mr. Hodge refuses audience till work
resumed, warning of drastic action,
14.**12**; Strike ends, 18.**12.**

BOIS D'AVOCOURT (Verdun).
See under Avocourt.

BOJAN (Galicia).
Russian success N. of, 28.**3.**

BOLANCOURT (Somme).
French bomb, 9.**7.**

BOLDU (Rum.).
Fine Russian defence, end of December.

BOSELLI, SIGNOR.
Becomes Premier, 15.**5.**

BOSNIAN CRISIS OF 1909.
Statement by Dr. Bethmann Hollweg
on attitude of Great Britain during, 23.**5**;
Answer by Sir E. Grey, 24.**5**; and by
British Foreign Office, 29.**5.**

BOTHMER, GEN. v.
Army of, threatened by Russians, 8.**7.**

BOUCHAVESNES (Somme).
Captured by French, with 1,500
prisoners, 12.**9**; Fighting continues, 14,
20, 25.**9.**

BOULOGNE CONFERENCE.
Recognition of Venizelist National
Provincial Government in Crete, 19.**10.**

BRABANT (Verdun).
Failure of German attack at, 22.**2.**

" BRAEMAR CASTLE " (British Hospital
ship).
Sunk by mine or torpedo in Ægean
Sea, 24.**11.**

BRAILA (Danube).
Enemy advance threatens, 18.**12**;
Enemy checked 30 miles from, 19.**12**;
Russians retiring on, 19.**12.**

BRASSO (v. Kronstadt).

BRENTA, RIVER (Trentino).
Great Italian advance between River
Adige and, 23.**6.**

" BRESLAU " (German cruiser).
Assists Turks near Trebizond, 5.**4**;
Bombards Russian Black Sea ports, 4.**7.**

BRIAND, M. (French statesman).
Visit of, to Italy, 10.**2**; Speech to
Russian delegates at Elysée, 22.**5**; Forms
new war cabinet, 12.**12**; speech on
German peace terms, 13.**12.**

" BRITANNIC " (British Hospital ship).
Sunk by mine or torpedo in Ægean
Sea, 21.**11.**

BRIXHAM FISHING-FLEET.
Attacked by enemy submarine, 18.**11.**

BROD RIVER. (Serbia).
Bulgarian retreat N. of, 9.**10.**

BROD (Serbia).
Serbs gain footing in, 10.**10**; Fierce
fighting round, 12.**10**; Serbs capture, and
progress, 18, 19.**10.**

BRODY (Galicia).
Russians take, 25-28.**7**; Russian pursuit of Austrians near, continues, 30.**7**;
Severe fighting on upper Sereth near,
Russians take 2,000 prisoners, 4, 6, 7.**8**;
Continued Russian advance, after severe
fighting, 30.**9**-1.**10**; Russians lose positions
gained at, 2.**10**; Occasional fighting near,
throughout December.

CARPATHIANS (The).
Severe fighting, Jablonica Pass, Transsylvanian front, December 1916.
CARSO.
Italian progress on N. edge of, 11.8; Strong Austrian positions and 1,565 prisoners taken, 12.8; Nad Logem and 800 prisoners taken, 13.8; Further advance and 1,400 more prisoners, 14.8; Battle on, begins, Italians capturing first line, 10.10; Second line attacked, and front advanced 2,000 yards, 11.10; Counter attacks repulsed, 12.10; Fighting continues, 13.10; Offensive ends, line having been advanced two miles, all gains consolidated and 8,000 prisoners taken, 14.10; Austrians mass troops on W. of Trieste, 29.11; Artillery action, Dec.
CARSON, SIR ED.
Motion for " Equal sacrifice from all men of military age," 12.4; Succeeds Mr. Balfour as First Lord of the Admiralty, 10.12.
CARSPACH (Vosges).
Germans take and lose three lines of trenches at, 4.6.
CASEMENT, SIR ROGER.
Lands in Ireland, and is arrested, 20.4; Charged with high treason, 15.5; Trial begins, 25.6; Found guilty and sentenced to death, 29.6; Hanged, 3.8.
CASTELLETTO (Trentino).
Attack repulsed by Italians, 31.7.
CASUALTIES.
Civilian, in Great Britain, to date, 29.5; Sea attacks: 141 killed, 611 injured; air attacks, 409 killed, 1,005 injured. Canadian (v. Canadian casualties).
CAURES, BOIS DES (Verdun).
Captured by Germans, 24.2.
CEBROW (Galicia).
Night attack repulsed by Russians, 9.3.
CECIL, LORD ROBERT.
Appointed Minister of Blockade, 23.2; Speech on situation in Greece, 4.12.
CENTRAL RAILWAY (German E. Africa).
Enemy retreat towards, 19.6; Gen. van Deventer takes Mpondi, 14.7; British reach and occupy, 14 to 29.7; Saranda and Kilimatinde, 31.7.; Last German posts N. of, cleared, 19.10.
CENTRAL TRIBUNAL (for Gt. Britain).
Appointed, 22.3.
CERNA VODA (Tchernavoda) (Danube).
Mackensen in front of, 23.10; Rumanians blow up bridge and abandon, 25.10; Russians fight for, 9.11; Failure of Russo-Rumanian attempt, 12.11; Fighting at, 2.12; Bulgars capture bridgehead, 10.12.

CETTINJE (Montenegro).
Bombarded by Austrians, 10.1; Taken by Austrians, 13.1.
CHAMBRETTES, LES (Verdun).
Taken by French, 15.12; Enfiladed by enemy guns, 16.12; Germans recover, 17.12; Zouaves recapture, 18.12.
CHAMPAGNE.
German offensive in, 9.1; French success in, 12.2; French lose ground in, 13.2; German liquid fire attack in, between Mont Têtu and Maison de Champagne, 6.3; Three German attacks in, repulsed, 22.6; Fighting at Butte de Mesnil, 9-10.12; Renewed enemy activity, 23.12.
CHAMPNEUVILLE (Verdun).
French organise line Champneuville-Ornes, 25.2; Germans capture, 27.2.
CHAPITRE WOOD (Somme).
French take, 3.7.
CHARTORYSK (Volhynia).
Germans retreat from salient of, 6.7.
CHATTANCOURT (Verdun).
French retreat towards, 30.5.
CHAUDFOUR, BOIS DE (Verdun).
Enemy gain footing in salient at, 17.4.
CHAULNES (Somme).
German attacks near, 21.7; German attacks from Berny to S. of, fail, 8.9.
CHAULNES, BOIS DE (S. of Somme).
Successful French advance, 10.10; Capture of Bois de Chaulnes and 1,400 prisoners, 10.10; French repulse heavy counter attacks, 11.10.
CHELMSFORD, LORD.
Appointed Viceroy of India, 14.1.
CHERNA RIVER (Macedonia).
Serbs cross, E. of Monastir, 4.10; Serbs capture Bulgarian third line, 9.10; Stubborn fighting in bend, 14-30.10; Serbs penetrate N.E. of Monastir, 17.11; Heavy fighting in bend, December.
CHETWODE, Maj.-Gen. SIR P.
Assumes command of Desert Column, (Sinai), 7.12.
CHIKALDIR BRIDGE (Baghdad Rly).
Naval seaplanes destroy (Gulf of Alexandretta), 27.12.
CHIOS.
British land at, 17.2.
CHORMUK (Upper Euphrates).
Capture by Russians, 1.9.
CHOROK, RIVER (Armenia).
Russian advance towards, 1.2; Vigorous Russian advance on upper, 26.3; Russians take fortified position on upper, 2.4.
CHOROK SECTOR (Armenia, S.W. of Trebizond).
Russians regain ground lost at, 1.6.

ture, 24.5; Germans gain footing in trenches N.W. of; 29.5.

CURLU (Somme).
French take, 2.7.

CURTEA DE ARGES (N.W. of Bucharest).
Fighting near, 25.11; Austro-Germans capture, 27.11.

CURZON (EARL).
President of Air Board, 17.5.

CYCLADES, (Is.).
Venizelist rising, reported, 11.12.

" CYMRIC " (White Star Liner).
Torpedoed by German submarine in Atlantic, 8.5.

CZERNOWITZ (Bukovina).
Severe fighting round, 2-9.1; Actions near, 19.1; Russian offensive against resumed, 2.2; Russians gain ground after heavy fighting near, 13.6; Russians reach suburbs of, 11.6; Russians occupy, 17.6; Russians advance N.W. of, 18.6; Russian advance W. of, 19.6.

DAHLEN ISLAND (River Dvina).
German artillery active, 7.3.

DAKHLA OASIS (180 m. S.W. of Assiut).
Occupied by hostile force, 27.2.

DAMLOUP (Verdun).
Fighting for, 3.7; French occupy, 4.11.

DANILOVGRAD (Mont.).
Austrians enter, 23.1.

DANUBE.
Austrian monitors bombard Rumanian towns on, 28.8; Germans occupy island in, near Ruschuk, 8.10; Artillery activity on, 15.10; Bulgarians cross, near Silistria and Turtukai, 9.12; Russians retreating from the Dobruja cross into Bessarabia, 23.12.

DARDANELLES.
Finally evacuated, 9.1; Sir Ch. Monro's despatch on evacuation, dated 6.3, published, 10.4; Commission on the, announced, 26.7.

DAR-ES-SALAAM (Ger. E. Africa).
Capital, surrendered to British naval forces, 3.9; Gen. Cunliffe's Nigerian Brigade reaches, 16.12.

DARFUR.
Gen. Kelly's force occupies Jebel Hella, 22.3; and Abiad, 9.4; El Fasher taken, 23.5; Ali Dinar flees to Jebel Marra, 23.5; Despatch (8.8.16) of Sir F. R. Wingate, describing rising in and conquest of, publ., 25.10; Maj. Huddleston's column occupies Kulme 3.11; Defeat and death of ex-Sultan, 6.11; Surrender of the late Sultan's sons reported, 1.12.

DAULATABAD (Persia).
Occupied by Russians, 13.2.

DAYLIGHT SAVING BILL.
Passed, 17.5; Comes into operation till 1.10, 21.5.

DEAL.
German aeroplane raid, 3.5.

DECLARATION OF LONDON.
Abandoned by British and French, 29.6.

DEDEAGACH (Bulgaria).
Allied ships bombard, 18.1.

DEFENCE REGULATIONS (British).
Forbid entry into enemy's country without special permit, 7.11.

DELATYN (Galicia).
Russians take, 8.7.

DELBRÜCK, HERR.
Resigns German Secretaryship of State for Interior, 14.5.

DEMIRHISSAR (N.E. Greece).
Railway bridge over Struma River, near, blown up by British, 12.1; Bulgarians fire on Greeks near, 2.6; Bulgarians gradually withdraw from, and Seres, into mountains, 6.10.

DENIÉCOURT (Somme).
E. of, French capture ground, 15.9; Successful French offensive, 1,600 prisoners, 17, 18.9; .

DEPORTATIONS.
Of civilians, announced at Lille and elsewhere, 18.4; Further heavy, of Belgians, under German decree of 3.10, 8.11.

DERBY, LORD.
Report on Recruiting, published, 4.1; Speech in Lords, on Recruiting, 2.3; Speeches of, with regard to married groups, 7 and 15.3; Resigns from Air Committee, 10.4; Replies to critics with regard to National Service, 14.4; Under-Secretary for War, 6.7.

" DEUTSCHLAND " (German commercial submarine).
Arrives at Norfolk, Va., 9.7; Returns to Germany, 23.8; Arrives at New London, Conn., 1.11; Returns to the Weser, 10.12.

DEVE BOYUN (Erzerum).
Bombardment of, begun, 29.1.

DEVENTER, MAJ. GEN. VAN.
S. African troops under, occupy Kondoa Irangi (Ger. E. Africa), 19.4;. Further successes, 24.6. (v. East Africa).

DELVILLE WOOD (Somme).
British take, 15.7; Fighting for, 18-28.7; German attack repulsed, 2.8; Heavy fighting, 24.8.

DEVONSHIRE, DUKE OF.
Succeeds Duke of Connaught as Gov.-General of Canada, 29.7.

DIARBEKR (Asia Minor).
Russians repel Turkish attack near, 3.6; Russians checked near, 6.6; Russians take Turkish camp near, 12.6.

K

DURAZZO (Dures) (Albania).
Austrian air-raid on, 25.1; Threatened by Austrians, 16.2; Evacuated by Allies, 24-26.2; Entered by Austrians, 27.2.

DUWEIDAR (N. Sinai).
Unsuccessful Turkish attack on, 23.4.

DVINA, RIVER.
German repulse, 9.3.

DVINSK.
Russian attack S. of repulsed, 11.2; Fighting round continues, 14.2; German concentration near, broken up, 23.3; Germans repulsed near, 12.4; Russians repulse attacks near, 11, 21, 27.6; Fighting in lake district, S. of, 4, 21.12.

EAST AFRICA (German).
Enemy camp captured in, 4.1; Gen. Smuts arrives and takes command, 19.2; Advances on Kilimanjaro, 7.3; British success at Kilimanjaro, 11.3; British occupy Moshi, 13.3; British attack Lol Kissale, 6.4; British occupy Köthersheim, 12.4; And Salanga, 14.4; German concentration, 17.4; Kondoa Irangi taken, 19.4; Further British progress in, 22.4; Belgians occupy Shunzugu, 3.5; and Kigali, 6.5; German attack repulsed at Kondoa Irangi, 10.5; British advance in Para and Usambara districts, 18.5; Further British advance, 25.5; British occupy Neu Langenburg, 30.5; Germans retreat from Mombo, 31.5; British occupy Namena, 3.6; Germans driven N.E. of Lake Nyassa, 6.6; British occupy Bismarckburg and Belgians occupy Usumbara, 8.6; Further British progress, 9-19.6; Gen. Smuts' despatch on operations, 12.2 to 30.4 published, 20.6; Germans defeated on Lukigura River, 24.6; British reach Central Railway, 14.7; Belgian success in (between Lake Tanganyika and V. Nyanza) 3.7; British move S. through Nguru Mts., 5.8, and take Morogoro 26.8; Portuguese occupy Bay of Menasi, 29.8; Dar-es Salaam surrenders, 3.9; Gens. van Deventer and Northey in touch; last enemy post captured N. of Central Railway, 19.10; Gen. Smuts reports enemy limited to S.E. of Colony, 20.10; Nakalala: Successful Portuguese attack, enemy retire N. of Rovuma River, losing guns, ammunition, etc., 22.10; Fighting at Iringa and near Ruhuje River, between 19.10-26.11; British reorganised in two divisions, 27.10; Reported activity of Germans on Portuguese frontier, 2.12; Fighting at British post of Kibata, 5 to 15. 12; Report of action on Portuguese frontier, 5.12; British reported advance island 50 miles from Port Kilwa, 7.12;

Combined offensive by Northey and van Deventer begins, 25.12.

EASTERN FRONT (Main Events).
Russian unsuccessful offensive on Bukovina ends, 15.1; Russian offensive about Lake Naroch, 18.3-14.4; Brusilov's big offensive in the S. begins, 4.6; Brusilov checked, by 20.9.

EAUCOURT L'ABBAYE (Ancre River).
British attack S. of, 30.9, 1.10; Severe fighting, 2-4.10; British advance again, 5, 12.10.

EBOLOWA (Cameroons).
Occupation of, by English and French, 19.1.

ECONOMIC CONFERENCE
Of the Allies, at Paris, opens, 14.6; Recommendations of, issued, 21.6; Mr. Asquith explains in Commons, attitude of Government towards, 2.8; Italian and British delegates reach complete understanding, 14.8.

" EDEN," H.M.S.
T.B.D., sunk in collision, 16.6.

EGYPT (v. also **SINAI**).
Senussi defeated at Agagia, 26.2; Sollum captured, 14.3; " Tara " prisoners released, 17.3; Sir A. J. Murray takes over whole command from Sir J. Maxwell, 19.3; 2nd Anzac Corps formed, 28.3. British occupy Kharga Oasis, 15.4; and Moghara Oasis, 27.4; Despatch on operations in, (16.2.15 to 9.4.16), published, 21.6; Gen. Murray's despatches of 1.6 and 1.10.16 published on 25.9 and 1.12 respectively; British clear Senussi out of Dakhla Oasis, 17.10; Baharia Oasis, 19.10, and Farafra Oasis, 19.11.

EL ARISH (Sinai Peninsula).
Bombardment by British ships, aeroplanes, and seaplanes, 18.5; Aerodrome at, bombed by British, 19.6; Bombed by British, 5.9; Evacuated by Turks, 20.12; Occupied by British, 21.12.

ELBASAN (Albania).
Taken by Bulgarians, 13.2.

ELEN (Black Sea coast).
Russian offensive continues, 500 prisoners taken, 4.9.

EL FASHER (capital of Darfur).
British occupy, 23.5.

EL HASSANA (Sinai).
Bombed by British, 6.2, 20.2. 24.3; Cleared of enemy, 31.12.

EL KANTARA (Egypt).
Bombed by Turks, 11.6.

EL OWASA (Tigris).
Gen. Aylmer at, 25.1.

ENGLISH CHANNEL.
Ten enemy destroyers raid, 27.10.

" FOURCHER " (French T.B.D.).
Sunk by mine in Straits of Otranto, 23.6.

FOUR DE PARIS (Argonne).
Lively encounter in, at, 13.12.

FOUREAUX, BOIS DES (High Wood, Somme).
British at, 15, 16, 21, 24.7; German counter-attack W. of fails, 1.8; Severe fighting at, 1, 9, 10.9.

FOURNET, ADM. DARTIGE DU.
Demands delivery of war material from Greek government, 17.11; Demands dismissal of Ministers of Central Powers at Athens, 19.11; Greeks refuse demand for war uaterial 22.11; Handing over of ten mountain batteries to the Allies by Dec. 1, demanded, 24.11; Interview with the King, 27.11; Replaced in command of French Mediterranean fleet by Vice-Adm. Gauchet, 12.12.

FRANCE.
Government secures a vote of confidence on the question of control in Army zone, 18.2; Minister of Blockade appointed in, 1.4; Allied conferences in, 9.9; Gen. Duport appointed C.G.S. to Ministry of War, and Gen. de Castelnau C.G.S. to French G.H.Q., 21.9; M. Briand forms war cabinet in, 12.12; Disorderly opposition in Chamber to legislation by decree, 15.12.

FRANCIS JOSEPH (Emperor).
Death, aged 86, 21.11.

FREIBURG (Baden).
Bombed, 28.1.

FRESNES (Verdun).
Captured by Germans, 7.3.

FRICOURT (Somme).
British capture, 2.7.

FRISE (Somme).
Captured by Germans, 28.1; Lost trenches regained by British at, 9.2; Germans repulsed at, 10.2; Fighting round, 13.2; French retake, 2.7.

FRYATT, CAPT. CHARLES.
Commander of s.s. " Brussels," judicial murder of, 27.7; Execution denounced by Mr. Asquith, 31.7; British protest sent to Germany through U.S.A., 10.8.

FUNCHAL (Madeira).
German submarine bombards town and sinks French and British vessels, 3.12.

GALATA (Dard.).
Naval aeroplanes bombard, 26.12.

GALATZ (Rumania).
Enemy advance threatens, 18.12.

GALICIA.
Russian offensive in, 3.1; Severe fighting in, 8.1; Russian offensive resumed, 12.1; Austrians claim complete victory in, 18.1; Severe fighting in, 13.2;

Russian success in, 28.3; Gen. Brusilov's offensive begun, 4.6; Continued Russian pressure on retreating Austrians, Halicz threatened, 14.8; Severe fighting in Russian centre and in S.E. during Dec.

" GALLIA " (troopship).
Torpedoed in Mediterranean, 4.10.

GALLIENI, GENERAL.
French War Minister, resigns, succeeded by Gen. Roques, 16.3.; Death of, 27.5.

GALLIPOLI.
Evacuation of, completed, 7-9.1; Gen. Monro's despatch on, 6.3.

GARRAGUA (E. Africa).
Germans attack British and evacuate Garragua, 10.3.

GAUCHET, VICE-ADMIRAL.
Succeeds Admiral Dartige du Fournet in command of French Mediterranean Fleet, 12.12.

" GAULOIS " (French battleship).
Sunk, 27.12.

" GEELONG " s3.
P. & O. boat sunk in Mediterranean, 2.1.

GEORGE V., H.M. KING.
Receives General Cadorna, 23.3; Presents £100,000 for War purposes, 1.4; Receives members of the Duma, 9.5; Returns from visit to armies on Western Front, 15.8.

GEORGE, LLOYD, RT. HON. D.
Receives deputation from temperance council of Christian Churches, 9.3; Speech to Irish deputation, 10.3; Speech on Paris economic conference, 23.3; Secretary for War, 6.7; informs Mr. Asquith that he cannot remain in Government, 1.12; Resigns, 5.12; Invited to form a Government, 6.12; Prime Minister, 7.12; Creates a new War Cabinet, 10.12; Letter of, to Commons, 11.12; First speech as Premier, 19.12.

GERARD, MR.
Protest by (U.S.A. Ambassador at Berlin), re Ruhleben; 25.7.

GERMAN BARBARITY.
State papers on, published, 2.8.

GERMAN FLEET.
Reported to be cruising in North Sea, 6.3; Raid by battle squadron on E. coast, 25.4; Beaten at Battle of Jutland, 31.5-1.6; High Sea Fleet comes out, but retires before British forces, 19.8.

GERMAN PRISONERS.
Total captured on Somme since July 1st (v. Tables), 29.8.

GERMANY.
Herr Liebknecht expelled from Socialist party 12.1; Note on the " Baralong " case, 14.1; Protest with Austria

Ministry (v. App. 123), New War Cabinet sits, 9.12; Lord Devonport Food Controller, 10.12; German "Peace Overtures" announced 13.12; Answered by Prime Minister, 19.12, who desires mobilisation of population 'for labour; Swiss Note to Belligerents, 23.12; Invitation to Dominions for War Conference of Empire, 25.12

GREAT BRITAIN (Naval).

"Unlimited" German submarine campaign begins, 1.3; T.B.D. engagement, 20.3; "Sussex" torpedoed, 24.3; Battle of Jutland, 31.5-1.6; "Hampshire" mined, 5.6; T.B.D. engagement, 23.7; Engagement in North Sea, 2 cruisers sunk, 19.8; Dar es Salaam surrenders to British naval forces, 3.9; Further E. African ports surrender, 7.9; German destroyers raid cross-Channel transport, 27.10; "Oldambt" rescued, 2.11; German raid at Lowestoft, 26.11; Sir J. Jellicoe strikes flag as C-i-C., 27.11; Announced to succeed Sir H. Jackson as First Sea Lord, and Sir D. Beatty to be C-i-C., 29.11; Sir E. Carson First Lord, vice Mr. Balfour, 10.12; Anti-submarine division of War Staff formed at Admiralty, December.

GREECE.

Anti-Ally press campaign in, 3.1; Protest of, against arrest of enemy consuls at Salonika, 3.1; Neutrality of, reaffirmed, 9.2; Protest of, against French action in Corfu, 19.2; Protest of Allies to, on Bulgarian seizure of Fort Rupel, 31.5; Pacific blockade of, by Allies, 6.6; Riots in, 12.6; Demobilisation begun, 17.6; Allied note to, 21.6; Resignation of Cabinet in, 21.6; Embargo on shipping relaxed by Allies, 22.6; and suspended, 24.6; General demobilisation ordered, 26.6; Bulgarians having advanced through E. Macedonia, occupy several Greek ports, 18.8; Crisis in, owing to Bulgarian occupation of Greek territory, 19.8; General Moschopoulos succeeds General Dousmanis as C.G.S., 26.8; Naval demonstration by Allies, 1.9; Three German vessels seized at Piraeus, 2.9; Accepts demands of Anglo-French note, 4.9; Germans and Austrians expelled, 7.9; M. Zaimis resigns, 11.9; M. Kalogeropoulos, Premier, 16.9; Partial blockade of coast declared by Allies from mouth of R. Struma to Bulgarian boundary, 19.9; Demands from Germany the return of the Army Corps surrendered at Kavalla, 20.9; M. Venizelos leaves for Crete, 25.9; Greek ships join Allied fleet, 26.9; King's policy doubtful, 27.9; M. Kalogeropoulos resigns, 4.10; New Cabinet formed, Prof. Lambros, premier, 9.10; Allies' Note to, Government complies, 10.10; Admiral du Fournet

presents supp. Note to Government, compliance with all demands, 12.10; Anti-Entente demonstrations at Athens, 15.10; Allies land reinforcements to maintain order in Athens; Fournet hands fresh Note to Government, 16.10; Govt. agrees to withdraw half Greek troops concentrated at Larissa, 20.10; Decree to disband certain classes, and transfer two corps to Peloponnesus, 25.10; Refusal of war material to Entente, 22.11; Venizelos Government declares war on Germany and Bulgaria, 23.11; Guns to be surrendered to Allies reported removed from Athens, 28.11; Government definitely refuses surrender of guns, 30.11; Attack on Allied troops in Athens, 1.12; Embargo on Greek vessels in Allied ports, 2.12; Royalist Government denounced by Provisional Government at Salonika, 6.12; Official complicity in Athenian outrages confirmed, 7.12; Allied blockade effective, 8 a.m., 8.12; Allies demand explanation of concentration of troops round Athens, 8.12; Hellenic colonies petition Allies for National Government, 12.12; King of Greece sends regrets for recent events through Paris, 12.12; Allies send ultimatum to Greece, 14.12; King accepts ultimatum to Greece, 15.12; Greek military evacuation of N. begun, 16.12; Allies' Note re Venizelist occupation of islands, 19.12; Allies' further Note, 21.12; Greece requests raising of blockade, 30.12; Entente Note to, 31.12.

"GREIF."

German raider, disguised as Norwegian vessel, sunk by Brit. "Alcantara," 29.2.

GREY, SIR EDWARD.

Letter re search of mails, 28.1; Statement of, to *Chicago Daily News* on aims of the Allies and of Germany, 15.5; Speech in Commons on war aims, 24.5; Created Viscount Grey of Fallodon, 6.7.

GUEUDECOURT (E. of Ancre).

British progress N. of, 18.10.

GUILLEMONT (Somme).

British attacks at, 22-24.7; British advance, 7-8.8; Further advance and repulse of German counter attacks, 16, 18, 23.8; British capture with 1,000 prisoners, 5.9.

GUMISHKHANEH (Armenia).

Russians take, 20.7.

GUYNEMER, LIEUT. (French).

Brings down 20th aeroplane, 5.2.

GYIMES PASS (Moldavia, Rum.).

Rumanian retreat; enemy invade Rumania and capture Agas, 17.10.

HABSHEIM (Germany).

Bombed by French, 19.3.

HOHENZOLLERN REDOUBT (Loos).
Germans spring a mine near, 6.3 ;
Fighting at, 14.5.

HOLLAND.
Rationing of by Gt. Britain, 7.1 ; Existence of secret treaty between Germany
and, denied, 29.2 ; Unrest in, 31.3 ;
Excitement abates, 1.4 ; Declaration
strict neutrality, 4.4 ; Dutch mails seized,
4.4 ; Bill in Second Chamber to call up
1917 class if necessary, 7.4 ; Government
report North Sea too dangerous for exchanged prisoners, 7.4.

HOOGE (Ypres.)
British positions at, shelled, 13.2 ;
Germans gain ground at, 6.6.

HOSPITAL SHIPS.
Admiralty deny being used as transports, 7.8.

HUGHES, RT. HON. W. M. (Prime Minister of Australia).
Lands in England, 7.3 ; Series of
speeches by, 9, 15, 17, 20, 24.3 ; Speech
at Queen's Hall, 10.5.

HULLUCH (Loos).
Strong attack accompanied by gas
S. of, repulsed, 27.4 ; German gas attack
at, fails, 29.4 ; Fighting at, 14.5.

HUNGARIAN CHAMBER.
Stormy sitting in, 21.2.

HYMETTUS, MT. (Athens).
Shells dropped on by Allied fleet, 1.12

IGAMBA (18 miles N.E. of Fort Hill,
Nyassaland).
German retreat, 25.5.

ILEMBULE (East Africa).
Germans surrender, 26.11.

IMMELMANN, CAPT.
Renowned German airman killed, 17.6.

" IMPERATRITSA MARIA."
Russian battleship sunk, 20.10.

IMPORTS.
Restriction of, 27.1 ; Returns for
March show highest level during war, 31.3.

INDIA.
Lord Chelmsford appointed Viceroy,
14.1 ; Budget presented, 1.3 ; Mr. A.
Chamberlain speaks on deaths in troop
trains from Karachi, 1.8 ; Viceroy speaks
at Simla on India's services during the
War, 6.9.

INDUSTRIAL UNREST.
Declaration of Russian Labour Group
to working classes, 2.11.

" INTERNATIONAL TRENCH."
Recaptured, 2.3.

INTER-PARLIAMENTARY
Committee in Paris, 22.2.

IONIAN ISLANDS.
Allied Governments to create naval
bases in, 10.4.

IPIANA (21 miles N. of Karonga on Lake
Nyassa).
German retreat, 25.5.

IRELAND (v. also Great Britain).
Order in Council on the Government
of Ireland Act (1914), 1.3 ; Lenten Pastoral of Roman Catholic bishops, 5.3 ;
" Gaelic Press " offices, Dublin, raided,
25.3 ; German attempt to land arms in,
20.4 ; Sir Roger Casement lands in, 20.4 ;
Sinn Fein outbreak in, Dublin Post Office,
etc., seized, 24.4 ; Gen. Sir J. Maxwell
takes command in, 27.4 ; rebels begin to
surrender, 30.4 ; rising ends, 1.5 ; three
rebel leaders shot, 3.5 ; Nationalist party
appeals to people to stand by constitutional movement, 9.5 ; Commission
appointed to enquire into rebellion, 10.5 ;
Debate on, in both Houses, 11.5 ; Commission begins its sittings, 18.5 ; Report
issued, 3.7 ; Casement hanged, 3.7 ; Sir
J. Maxwell's despatches on, issued, 22.7 ;
Mr. H. E. Duke becomes Chief Secretary,
31.7, vice Mr. A. Birrell, resigned.

IRINGA (N.E. of Lake Nyassa).
Rhodesian Col. drive enemy towards,
6.6 ; Germans fall back on, 24.7 ; Gen.
Northey occupies, 29.8 ; Enemy offensive
in, district begins, 19.10 ; Severe fighting
S.W. of, 23.10 ; Germans repulsed in,
district, 30.10.

ISHMI RIVER (Serbia).
Serbians repulse Austrians near, 1.2.

ISLATZ (Danube).
Mackensen's army crosses at, 23.11.

ISONZO RIVER (Italy).
Austrians repulsed, 27.1 ; Italians gain
trenches at Monfalcone, 14.6 ; Austrian
attacks on, repulsed, 17.6 ; Italian offensive on, 1.7 ; Italian success 3,600 prisoners
in Monfalcone sector, 6.8 ; Monte S.
Michele, Gorizia bridgehead and 8,000
prisoners taken by Italians, 7.8 ; Austrians
beaten and pursued, 10,000 prisoners
claimed, 9.8 ; Lively artillery actions on
upper and middle, 16, 17.8 ; Italians
begin offensive, 9.10.

ISPAHAN (Persia).
German colony evacuates, 9.3 ; entered
by Russians, 19.3.

ITALY.
Discussion on German plots in Chamber, 3.3 ; Prohibits trading with Germany,
17.4 ; Ministry resigns, 10.6 ; New Ministry sworn in, 19.6 ; Declares war against
Germany, 27.8 ; Solidarity with the
Allies affirmed by Foreign Minister, 18.12.

JABLONICA PASS (Carpathians).
Russians gain heights S. of, 22.8 ;
success of Russians E. of, 28.11 ; Struggle
for heights during Dec. 1916.

KHADAIRI BEND (Tigris).
British reach Tigris between Kut and, 1S.**12**.
KHANIKIN (100 m. W. of Kermanshah, Persia).
Russians defeat Turks at, 3.**6**.
KHANYS (Armenia).
Turks dislodged from, 13.**2**.
KHARGA OASIS (120 m. S. of Assiut).
British occupy, 15.**4**.
KHRIASK (Galicia).
Russians take, 1.**1**.
KHRYS-KALE (Armenia).
Russians take, 27.**1**.
KIBATA (E. Africa).
Fighting begins at, 5.**12**; Continued reports of fighting at received, 15-17.**12**.
KIGALI (capital of Ruanda in Ger. E. Africa).
Belgians occupy, 6.**5**.
KIGHI (Armen.).
Russians capture, 18.**7**.
KIKOMBO (E. Africa).
British occupy, 30.**7**.
KILIMANJARO (Ger. E. Africa).
British advance towards, 7.**3**; British success near, 11.**3**.
KILINDIR (Maced.).
Allies blow up railway bridge at, 12.**1**.
KILOSSA (E. Africa).
On Central railway, taken by British, 22.**8**.
KILWA KISSIWANI.
Port surrendered to British naval forces, and occupied, 7.**9**.
KILWA (KIVINJE) PORT (Ger. E. Africa).
Occupied by British naval forces, 7.**9**; British 50 miles inland from, 7.**12**.
KIMPOLUNG (Bukovina).
Occupied by Russians, 23.**6**.
"KING EDWARD VII." H.M.S.
Mined and abandoned, 6.**1**.
KIONGA (E. Africa).
Captured by Portuguese troops, 11.**4**.
KIRLIBABA (E. Carpath.).
Russian success E. of, 28 **11**; Fighting near, 30.**11** and part of December.
KISSAKI (Uluguru Mts., E. Africa).
British check at, 6.**9**.
KITCHENER, F.M. EARL.
Drowned in H.M.S. "Hampshire," off the Orkneys, 5.**6**; Army Order issued *re*, 6.**6**.
KITEGA (Ger. E. Africa).
Captured by Belgian River Column E. of Tanganyika, 12.**6**.
KITOVO HILLS (Ger. E. Africa).
Germans defeated at, 7.**3**.
KOLKI (Volhynia).
Fighting at, 14.**6**; Russians cross River Styr at, 4.**7**.
KOLOMEA (S.E. Galicia).
Russian advance E. of, 27.**6**; Aus-

trians defeated on 25-mile front near, 28.**6**; Russians close in on, 28.**6**; Russians take, 29.**6**.
KONDOA IRANGI (Ger. E. Africa).
Enemy encountered in force at, 17.**4**; S. African troops under Gen. van Deventer occupy, 19.**4**; Germans repulsed at, 10.**5**; Fighting at, 9.**6**; British success at, 24.**6**.
KOPRI-KEUI (Armenia).
Russians capture, 17.**1**.
KÖRBER, DR. ERNEST VON.
Appointed Premier of Austria, 29.**10**.
KORITZA (Albania).
French and Italians in touch, 24.**10**.
KORYTNITSA (W. of Lutsk).
Germans claim success, and 1,900 prisoners, 17.**10**.
KOSLOV (Poland).
German counter-attack repulsed E. of, 10.**3**.
KOSTANJEVICA (Carso).
Italians advance close on, 3.**11**.
KÖTHERSHEIM (Ger. E. Africa).
British occupy, 12.**4**.
KOVEL.
Russian advance on the Stokhod towards, continued, 31.**7**; Desperate fighting at Lyubashevo and Guledichi, near, 3.**8**.
KOVEL-ROVNO RAILWAY.
Severe fighting on the River Stokhod (Volhyn.), enemy offensive everywhere repulsed, 20.**9**.
KREVO (Vilna).
Russians repel attack, 1.**6**, 5.**6**.
KROJA (Albania).
Austrians occupy, 5.**2**.
KRONSTADT (=Brasso, Transylv.).
Austrians withdraw from, 28.**8**; Rumanians occupy, 29.**8**; v. Falkenhayn's offensive against and Rumanian retreat, 6.**10**; Austro-Germans reoccupy, 7.**10**.
KUKURUZ (Salonika front).
Serbs beat off repeated Bulgar counter-attacks near, 26.**8**.
KULELI-BURGAS (Turk.).
Naval aeroplanes bomb bridge at, 14.**12**.
KUMLI (Maced.).
British take, 31.**10**.
KURNA (Mesop.).
British repulse near, 18.**1**.
KUROPATKIN, GEN.
Takes command on N. Russian front, 19.**2**; Gains a success near Riga, 23.**7**.
KUT-EL-AMARA (Mesop.).
Shelled by Turks, 2.**1**; Relief expedition sets out for, 4.**1**; Failure of attacks. Um el Hannah, 21.**1**; Es Sinn, 8.**3**; Sanna i-Yat, 9.**4**, 22.**4**. Steamer "Julnar" fails to break blockade of, 24.**4**; Surrenders to Turks, 29.**4**; British positions S. and

LOUVEMONT (Verdun).
French capture, 15.12.
LOVCHEN, MT. (Mont.).
Austrians attack, 9.1; Fall of, 10.1.
LOWESTOFT.
Air-raid on, 20.2; Raid on, by German battle squadron, 25.4; German naval raid near, trawler " Narval " sunk, 26.11.
LUKIGURA RIVER (Ger. E. Africa).
Germans defeated on, 24.6.
LULINDI (Ger. E. Africa).
Portuguese occupation of, 12.11.
LUMI RIVER (Ger. E. Africa).
Germans defeated at, 7.3.
LUPEMBE (E. Africa).
Occupied by Gen. Northey, 18.8; Fighting at, 19.10 and following days; British post attacked 18.11.
" LUSITANIA."
Reported agreement between Germany and U.S. on case of, 9.2; German proposals rejected by U.S., 16.2.
LUTSK (Volhynia).
Russians capture, 6.6; Russians take bridgehead N. of, 9.6; Russians checked at, 11.6; Austrians in retreat S. of, 12.6; Russians reach River Stokhod in region of, 13.6; Russians cross rivers Styr and Stokhod in region of, 16.6; Russian success W. of, 17.6; Heavy fighting round 19.6; Austrian counter attacks N. and N.W. of, 21.6; Russian advance held, 24.6; Heavy fighting in region of, 28.6. 30.6. & German progress, 2.7; Russian success W. of, 3-4.10; Occasional fighting near, from end of November to close of 1916.

MACEDONIA (includes Salonika front).
Gen. Sarrail takes command at Salonika, 16.1; Occupies Kara Burun (15 m. E. of Salonika), 28.1; Serbian troops reach Salonika from Corfu, 27.2; Gen. Milne succeeds Gen. Mahon, 9.5; Bulgars occupy Fort Rupel, 26.5; Gen. Sarrail appointed C.in.C, early August; Allied offensive begins, 10.8; Bulgar offensive begins on both flanks, 17.8; Allied offensive redoubles, 25.8; Teodorov occupies Kavalla, 25.8; Franco-Serb-Russo-Italian offensive on W. flank begins, 7.9; British push forward over Struma River by 10.9; Surrender of Greek 4th Corps at Kavalla, 14.9; Capture of Kaymakchlan (by Serbs), and Florina (by French), 20.9; Hard British fighting nearly to Demir Hissar, 12.9 to 1.11; Heavy fighting for Monastir, 26.9 to 18.11; Capture of Monastir, 19.11.
MACHEMBA (Portug. E. Africa).
Portuguese re-occupation reported, 27.12.

MACIN (Dobruja).
Russian troops concentrated near, 23.12; Enemy attack bridge-head at, 25.12; Severe fighting near, 30, 31.12.
MACKINNON, MR. D.
Director-General of Recruiting, Australia, 29.11.
MAFUB (Ger. E. Africa).
Captured by British, 24.1.
MAGDHABA (N. Sinai).
British air raid, 11.11; Turks retire on, from El Arish, 19.12; British air raid on, 22.12; British capture, 23.12.
MAGHARAH (Wells, E. Sinai).
British raid, 15.10; Cleared of enemy, 31.12.
MAHENGE (E. Africa).
Gen. Wahle's forces make E., 2.12.
MAIL PACKETS.
Correspondence between British and Swedish Governments *re* detention of, published, 25.8.
MAILS (v. also U.S.A.).
U.S. protest against British search of, and British reply, published, 28.1; British Memorandum on, published, 24.7.
MAISONS-DE-CHAMPAGNE.
Germans penetrate French advanced work, 6.3; French recapture trenches, 8.3.
MALANCOURT (Verdun).
French evacuate, 31.3.
MALANGALI (Ger. E. Africa).
British success at, 24.7; Gallant defence of, 8-12.11; Defeat of Germans by British at, 12.11; Relieved 12.11; Brave defence of, by British force, 7.12.
" MALOJA."
P. & O. S.S., mined, 27.2.
MAMAKHATUN (Armenia).
Taken by Russians, 24.6; Retaken by Turks, 31.6; Retaken by Russians, 12.7.
MAMETZ (Somme).
British capture, 1.7.
MAMETZ WOOD (Somme).
British enter, 4.7; Severe fighting for 10 to 12.7; Capture of, 12.7.
MANHEULLES (Woevre).
Captured by Germans in advance, 29.2.
MAN-POWER.
Army Council statement *re* requirements in men, 10.4; Special committee appointed to investigate recruiting facts and figures, 17.4; Cabinet crisis, statement *re* recruiting again postponed, 19.4; Agreement *re* recruiting, proposals to be submitted in each House, 20.4; Official report of secret session, 25.4; Distribution Board appointed, 21.9.
MARGATE.
Air raids on, 1.3, 19.3, 23.10.
MARIAKERKE (Belgium).
Naval aeroplanes bomb aerodrome at, 23.4.

" MARINA " (British ss.).
German assent to indemnify if genuine merchantman, 8.12.

MAROS VASARHELY (Transylvania).
Rumanian Northern (4th) army within 12 miles of, and continues advance, 3.10.

MARRIED MEN.
Groups, first called for service, 7.4.

MARTINPUICH (Somme, N.).
Bavarians surrender at, 30.8 ; Village taken by British, 15.9.

MATAMONDO (E. Africa).
German resistance broken, they retreat south, 11.8.

MAUDE, MAJ.-GEN. F. S.
Succeeds Gen. Gorringe in command of Advanced Force, Mesop., 11.7 ; Succeeds Gen. Lake as C-i-C., 28.8.

MAUREPAS (Somme).
French reach, 30.7 ; French success, 11-16.8 ; French repel counter-attacks, 18-24.8 ; French capture whole of, 24.8.

MAXWELL, GEN. SIR J.
Succeeded in Egypt by Sir A. Murray, 19.3 ; Takes command in Ireland, 27.4 ; Despatches on Egypt issued, 21.6 ; On Irish rebellion, 22.7.

MAZAR (Sinai).
British air raid on, 4.6 ; British attack and occupy, 17.9 ; Railway reaches, 26.11.

McKENNA, RT. HON. R.
Introduces Budget, 4.4.

MECCA, GRAND SHERIF OF.
Proclaims Arabian independence of Turkey, 7.6 ; Occupies Mecca and captures Jeddah, 20.6 ; Captures Yanbo, port of Medina, 27.7 ; Besieges Medina, 30.7 ; Proclaimed King of the Arabs, 29.10 ; Coronation, 4.11 ; Recognised by Brit. Govt. as King of the Hejaz, 16.12.

" MEDUSA " (H.M. T.B.D.).
Sunk in collision, 25.3.

MEJIDIA (Dobruja).
Enemy reach, 7,000 prisoners, 24.10.

MENASI (German E. Africa).
Portuguese occupy Bay of, 29.9.

MÉREAUCOURT, BOIS DE (Somme).
French take, 2.7.

MERISOR (Transylvania).
Rumanians beat Austrians after two days' severe fight in defile of, 19.9.

MERSA MATRUH (Egypt).
Defeat of Senussi at Halazin, 25 miles S.W. of, 23.1.

MESNIL, BUTTE-DE- (Champagne).
Lively encounter near, 9-10.12.

MESNIL (Champagne).
French success near, 11.2.

MESOPOTAMIA.
Gen. Sir P. Lake succeeds Sir J. Nixon, 19.1 ; Imperial Gen. Staff takes charge of operations, 21.1 ; Heavy fighting for relief of Kut, 4.1 to 23.4 ; Gen. Gorringe succeeds Gen. Aylmer in command of relief force, 12.3 ; Fall of Kut, 29.4 ; Sir J. Nixon's despatch of 17.1 on operations Oct.-Dec. 15 publ., 10.5 ; A few Cossacks join British force at Ali Gharbi, 20.5 ; Discussion in Parliament,18, 20.7; Commission on, announced, 26.7 ; Gen. Maude succeeds Sir P. Lake, c. 28.8 ; Publication of Gen. Lake's despatch (Jan. to 30.4), 12.10 ; British feint on Sanna-i-yat, move on Shatt-el-Hai, 12.12 ; British force assumes offensive on Tigris, 13.12 ; Close on Kut, 18.12 ; Move round Sanna-i-Yat and reach Tigris, 18.12.

MESSINES RIDGE.
British repulse German attack from, 30.3.

METZ.
French bomb, 23.1, etc.

METZ SABLONS.
Bombed by French, 8.3, etc., etc.

MEUSE, RIVER.
German attack on 12-mile front fails, 9-10.4 ; German attack on left bank repulsed, 23.6 ; Again, 30.7.

MEXICO.
American militia called out to police frontier of, 19.6 ; Fight between Mexicans and U.S.A.. troops at Carrizal, 21.6.

MIALAMO (Pangani River, German E. Africa).
Occupied by British, 10.6.

MIKINDANI (German E. Africa).
Occupied by British naval forces, 13.9.

MIKOLICHIN (Bukovina).
Russian success at, 4.7.

MIKOTSHENI (on River Pangani, German E. Africa).
Germans stand, but forced to retreat, 30.5.

MILAN.
Bombed, 14.2.

MILITARY MEDAL.
Instituted, 5.4.

MILITARY SERVICE.
Certified trades' list revised, 5.4 ; Cabinet Council on, 14.4 ; Proposed new bill dropped, 27.4.

MILITARY SERVICE ACT (First).
Introduced in Commons, 5.1 ; Opposed by Labour Congress, 6.1 ; Second reading, 12.1 ; Third reading, 24.1 ; Comes into operation, 9.2 ; In operation, 10.2.

MILITARY SERVICE ACT (Second).
Introduced in Commons, 3.5 ; Third reading, 16.5 ; Royal assent, 25.5.

MILITARY SITUATION.
Lloyd George's survey of, in the House of Commons, 22.8.

MILNE, MAJ.-GEN. G.
Succeeds Gen. Mahon on Salonika front, 9.5 ; Despatch covering operations, 9-5 to 8-10 published, 6.12.

MILNER, LORD.
In H. of Lds. moves for universal military service, 18.4.

MINERS' FEDERATION.
Deputation received by Prime Minister, 3.8.

MINE-SWEEPERS.
Attacked off Dogger Bank, 10.2.

" MINNEAPOLIS " s.s.
Sunk in Mediterranean, 23.3.

MITLA PASS (Sinai Peninsula).
British destroy E. defences of, 23.12.

" MOEWE " (German raider).
Reported in Atlantic, 11.1 ; Captures the " Appam," 15.1 ; Sinks five vessels, 9.2 ; Captures ss. " Washburn," 22.2 ; Returns to Germany, 4.3.

MOGHARA OASIS (90 m. S.W. of Alexandria).
British occupy 27.4.

MOGLENA Sector (Balkans).
Serbs throw back Bulgarians in, 20.8 ; Serbians progress, 22. 8 ; Serbians take Moglena ridge, 14.9.

MOLDAVIA (Rumania).
Fierce fighting on frontier throughout December, 1916.

MOLTKE, GEN. v.
Death of, former Chief German General Staff, 17.6.

MOMBO (on Tanga Railway, German E. Africa).
Retreat of Germans, 31.5.

MONACU FARM (Somme).
Repeated German attacks on, beaten back by French, 30.7, 1.2.8.8.

MONASTIR (Serbia).
Bombed by French aeroplanes, 23.1 ; Fortified by Austrians, 9.2 ; Franco-Serbo-Russian offensive on, begins, 7.9 ; Make turning movement to E., 19.9 ; Serbs take Kaymakchlan and French Florina, 20.9 ; Allies within 7 miles of, 6.10 ; Attack Kenali line, 14.10 ; Serbian advance on Monastir, 10.11 ; Serbs outflank Kenali line, 14.11 ; Evacuation by Germans and Bulgarians, 18.11 ; Serbian and French occupation and advance beyond, 19.11 ; Fierce fighting to north, 22.11 ; Continued Franco-Serbian advance north, 23.11 ; Hill, 1,050 (7 miles N.E.) captured by Franco-Serbian troops, 26.11 ; Fighting E. of, in Grunishta region, 29.11 ; Fighting N. and E. of, throughout Dec.

MONFALCONE Sector (Isonzo).
Successful Italian attack, 3,600 prisoners, etc., 6.8 ; Further Italian progress, 12.8.

MONITOR " M. 30."
Sunk by Turkish fire in Mediterranean, 14.5.

MONRO, SIR C.
Despatch on evacuation of Dardanelles dated 6.3, published, 10.4.

MONTAGU OF BEAULIEU, LORD.
Opens air debate in Lords, 9.3 ; Resigns from Air Committee, 10.4.

MONTAUBAN (Somme).
British capture, 1.7.

MONTE ADAMELLO (Trentino).
Italians drive Austrians from main crest of, 29.4.

MONTE ANCONA (Dol.).
Italians blow up Col di Lana and carry W. peak of, 17.4.

MONTE CENGIO (Trentino).
Italians gain ground at, 5.6.

MONTE CIMONE (S.Dol.).
Italians take, 24.7.

MONTE CIVARON (Trentino).
Capture by Austrians, 26.5.

MONTE MAGGIO (Trentino frontier).
Italians retreat from Soglio d'Aspio line, 18.5.

MONTE MOSCHICCE (S. of Asiago).
Austrians storm and occupy, 27.5.

MONTENEGRO.
Austrian attack on, 6.1 ; Fall of Mt. Lovchen, 10.1 ; Armistice with Austria, 12.1 ; Austrians enter Cettinje ; King clears out, 13.1 ; Capitulation of, reported, 17.1 ; Negotiations with Austria broken off, 19.1 ; King Nicholas arrives in Rome ; Austrians occupy Skutari, 23.1 ; Part of army surrenders, 25.1 ; Part of army takes refuge in Corfu, 16.2.

MONTE SABATINO (Isonzo).
Italians take heights of, 7.8.

MONTE SAN MICHELE (Carso).
Italians take heights of, 7.8.

MONT TÊTU (Verdun).
German attack stopped, 6.3.

MONZA (Italy).
Bombed, 14.2.

MORAISA (E. Tripoli).
Raided by British, 7.4 ; Two Italian battalions land at, 25.5.

MOROGORO (German E. Africa).
British enter, 26.8 ; Germans retire S.W. from neighbourhood, 30.8.

MORRONE, GEN.
Becomes Minister of War in Italy, 5.4.

MORT HOMME (Verdun).
French line penetrated near, 14.3 ; French lose ground at, 16.4 ; but recover it, 20.4 ; French progress at, 21.4 ; Germans repulsed, 24.4 ; French carry German positions N.W., 3.5 ; French successful counter-attack, 10.5 ; German attack N.E. repulsed, 13.5 ; Great German

assault, 20.**5** ; French repulse Germans on
W. slopes, 21.**5** ; French take trench S.W.,
27.**5** ; French take work on S.W., 31.**5** ;
French capture trench on, 15.**6** ; German
attacks on, repulsed, 17.**6**-21.**6**.
MORVAL (Somme). ˛
British capture, 25.**9** ; French pro-
gress from, towards Sailly, 4, 5, 7.**10**.
MOSHI (German E. Africa).
Occupied by British, 13.**3**.
MOSUL (Tigris).
Turks driven W. out of their positions
towards, by Russians,26.**6**; Turkish attacks
repulsed by Russians, 27.**7**.
MOUQUET FARM (Somme, N.).
Captured by British, 16.**9**.
MPAPWA (E. Africa).
British occupy, 11.**8**.
MÜLHAUSEN (Alsace).
Bombed by French, 19.**3**.
MÜLHEIM (Baden).
Bombed by French, 22.**7**.
" MÜNCHEN."
Small German cruiser sunk, 18.**10**.
MUNICH.
Air raid by Capitaine de Beauchamp,
18.**11**.
MUNITIONS.
Allied Conference on, 13.**7**.
MURMAN (N. Russia).
Railway declared open, 8.**12**.
MURRAY, LT.-GEN. SIR A.
Succeeds Sir C. Monro as C.-in-C.
Mediterranean Expeditionary Force, 10.**1** ;
His western limit of command in Egypt
defined, 10.**1** ; Succeeds Lt.-Gen. Sir J.
Maxwell in Egypt, 19.**3** ; Despatch of
1.6.16 (10.1 to 31.5.16) published, 25.**9** ;
of 1.10.16 (1.6 to 30.9.16) published, 1.**12**.
MUSEUMS (London). Closing of, 29.**1**.
MUSH (Armenia).
Russians capture, 18.**2** ; Turks de-
feated near, 12.**4** ; Turks recover, 2.**8** .
Russians repulse Turkish attacks E. of,
5, 6.**8** ; Occupied by Turks, 8.**8** ; Recap-
tured by Russians, 24.**8**.
MWANZA (German E. Africa).
British capture, 14.**7**.

NAKHL (Central Sinai).
Raided and cleared of enemy, 31.**12**.
NAMENA (E. Africa).
Occupied by British, 3.**6**.
NANCY (Lorraine).
Shelled by Germans, 24.**1**, etc.
NANGADI (Portug. E. Africa).
Escape of Portuguese garrison from
Newala to, reported, 5.**12** ; German occu-
pation, reported, 8.**12** ; German retreat,
reported, 20.**12** ; Portuguese reoccupation,
reported, 27.**12**.

NARAJOWKA, RIVER (Gali.).
Germans claim total repulse of Rus-
sians, W. bank, 23.**10**.
NAROCH, LAKE (Volhynia).
Russian victory S.W. of, 22.**3** ; Fight-
ing at, renewed, 7.**4** ; Russian success,
15.**4** ; Russians lose all ground gained
near, 28-29.**4**.
" NARVAL " (Brit. armed trawler).
Sunk near Lowestoft by Germans,
26.**11**.
" NASTURTIUM " (Mine-sweeper).
Sunk in Mediterranean by mine, 1.**5**.
NATIONAL DEBT.
Canadian, increased, 16.**2**.
NATIONALIST PARTY (Irish).
Appeal to Ireland to stand by the
Constitutional movement, 9.**5**.
**NATIONAL PROVISIONAL GOVERN-
MENT** (Greece).
M. Venizelos, etc., form, in Crete, 30.**9** ;
Further migration of Greek officers to,
2.**10** ; Allies recognise, 19.**10**.
NATIONAL SAVINGS.
Campaign opened, 9.**2**.
NATIONAL SERVICE.
Lord Derby replies on, issue, 14.**4**.
Memorandum *re* exemptions issued by
Local Government Board, 1.**12**.
NATIONAL UNION
Of Railwaymen and Transport
Workers, Deputation received by Prime
Minister, 3.**8**.
NAVAL AND OVERSEAS OPERATIONS
(Main events).
Cameroons campaign completed, 18.**2** ;
Successful operations in E. Africa, March-
April-May-Sept, Admiral Tirpitz succeeded
by Admiral v. Capelle, 16.**3** ; Battle of
Jutland, 31.**5** ; German submarine
" Deutschland " reaches U.S.A., 9.**7**.
NAVAL SITUATION.
Mr. Balfour's statement surveying,
published, 3.**8**.
NAVARIN (Champ.).
German gas reservoirs at, bombed by
French, 6.**2**.
NEASLOVA, RIVER (Rumania).
Germans force passage S. of Bucharest,
30.**11** ; Rumanians drive enemy back over
river, 1.**12**.
NEU LANGENBURG (German E. Africa).
British occupy, 30.**5**.
NEUVE CHAPELLE.
Heavy German raids near, 28.**7**.
NEUVILLE (St. Vaast) (Arras).
German gains at, 23.**1** ; Heavy fighting
resumed, 24.**1** ; French gains at, 27.**1** ;
Germans hold trenches near, 30.**1**.
NEWALA (E. Africa).
Portuguese garrison invested and then
escaped over Rovuma River, reported. 5.**12**.

NEWPORT (Rhode Is., U.S.).
German submarines sink nine vessels, 8.10.
NEW ZEALAND.
Compulsory Service Bill passed in, 10.6 ; Becomes law, 1.8.
NGOA (Cameroons).
French column reaches, 5.2.
NGULU (E. Africa, Usambara Rly.).
Occupied by British, 25.5.
NGURU MOUNTS. (E. Africa).
British clear, enemy being driven S. and E., 15.8.
NHIKA (on River Rovuma, Portuguese E. Africa).
German attacks repulsed, 8.5 ; and, 12.5.
NICHOLAS II. (Tsar of Russia).
Present at opening of Duma, 22.2 ; Invested with British Field Marshal's bâton, 29.2.
NICHOLAS (King of Montenegro).
Arrival in Rome, 23.1.
NICHOLAS, PRINCE (of Greece).
Letter from, (*Temps*), 9.2.
NIEUPORT (Belgium).
Heavy fighting at, 24.1, etc.
NIKSHICH (Mont.).
Austrians enter, 23.1.
NIMRUD, L. (Armenia).
British armoured cars engage Kurdish forces, 4.9.
NIVELLE, GENERAL.
Succeeds Gen. Joffre as Commander-in-Chief of French armies, 12.12.
NIXON, GEN. SIR JOHN.
Resigns command in Mesopotamia, 10.1 ; Despatches of 1.1.16 (15.4 to 30.9.15) and of 17.1.16 (Oct. 15 to 13.1.16) published, 5.4 and 10.5 resp.
NKAN (German E. Africa).
Germans retire to, 24.1 ; British occupy, 27.1.
NO. 11 (H.M.T.B.).
Mined in North Sea, 11.3.
NON-COMBATANT CORPS.
Army Order authorising, 10.3.
NORTHEY, MAJ.-GEN. E.
Defeats Germans at Malangali (E. Africa), 24.7 ; Occupies Lupembe, 19.8 ; Iringa, 29.8 ; Cut off from Iringa, 25.10 ; Combined offensive with Gen. Van Deventer, 25.12.
NORTH SEA.
Fight between "Alcantara" and "Greif" in, 29.2 ; Naval engagement between British destroyers and German torpedo boats in, 20.3 ; Collision between "Medusa" and "Laverock" in, 26.3 ; Dutch Government report navigation of, to be too dangerous for transport of exchanged prisoners, 7.4 ; British submarine sunk in, 27.4 ; Battle of Jutland, 31.5.

1.6 ; Indecisive naval action near mouth of Scheldt, 23.7 ; British submarine torpedoes German cruiser (Kolberg class), 21.10.
NORWAY.
Prohibits belligerent submarines from using her territorial waters, 13.10 ; German Note to, on her submarine policy, 20.10 ; Note to Germany maintaining her rights in above, 4.11.
"NOTTINGHAM" H.M.S.
Light cruiser, torpedoed and sunk, 19.8.

OBERNDORF (River Neckar).
Big Allied raid on, 13.10.
OBERTYN (Galicia).
Russians capture, 30.7.
OGHNUT (Armenia).
Successful Russian attack, 3.8, 1.9.
OGHRATINA (Sinai).
Turks take British post at, 23.4 ; Turks abandon, 8.8.
OGINSKI CANAL (Pinsk).
Heavy fighting on, 23.6.
OITOZ VALLEY (Moldavia).
Fierce fighting in, throughout December.
"OLDAMBT, " ss. (Dutch).
Captured by Germans, 1.11 ; Rescued by British, 2.11.
OPPACCHIASELLA (Carso).
Italian occupation of Austrian positions to S. of, 1.11.
ORAH (Tigris).
Turks defeated at, 13.1.
ORFANO, GULF OF (Greece).
British warships shell Bulgar entrenchments, 15.12.
ORMALI (Macedonia).
Bulgar attack in force on, repulsed with heavy loss, 28.10.
ORSOVA (Danube).
Austrians withdraw to W. bank of Cherna, 3.9 ; Captured by Rumanians, 7.9 ; Rumanians withdraw from, 7.10 ; Severe fighting near, 12, 22.11 ; Enemy captures, 23.11.
OSTEND.
Bombed by British, 10, 15, 17.11, etc.
OSTROVO (Macedonia).
Serbs progress in the, region, 26.8.
OTRANTO, STRAITS OF.
Italian auxiliary cruiser "Citta di Messina " and French torpedo-boat sunk in, 23.6 ; Town bombed by Austrians, 27.7 ; Enemy naval raid in, 23.12.
OVILLERS (Ancre).
Fight for, 10.7 ; Held by British, 17.7.

" PALEMBANG," ss.
Dutch liner torpedoed North Sea, 18.3.
PANGANI RIVER (Ger. E. Africa).
British report progress towards Tanga

along, 9.**6**; Germans driven down, 18.**7**; Naval force occupies Pangani Port, 23.**7**.

PAPEN, CAPT. von (German military attaché at Washington).
Correspondence published in U.S.A., 15.**1**; in Great Britain, 8.**2**.

PARAJD (Transylv.).
Rumanian N. Army's success in region of, Austrians retire W., 5.**10**.

PARENZO (Istria).
Raided by Italian T.B.D.'s, 12.**6**.

PARIS.
Zeppelin raids on, 29-30.**1**; Magazine explosion at, 4.**3**; Allied Conference at, opens, 27.**3**; Allied Economic Conference at, opens, 27.**4**.

PASUBIO, MT. (Trentino).
Italian success, 10-19.**10**.

"PATCHED UP PEACE."
Mr. Asquith on, 11.**10**.

PEDESCALA (Trentino).
Reached by Italian cavalry, 28.**6**.

PENSION BILL.
Introduced into Commons, 14.**11**; And withdrawn, 27.**11**.

PÉRONNE (Somme).
French advance towards, begins, 1.**7**.

PERSIA.
Barátov takes Hamadan and occupies Kermanshah, January; British Agreement with Bakhtiari, 15.**2**; Sir P. Sykes organises South Persian force, March; Barátov occupies Kerind, 12.**3**; Barátov on frontier, sends patrols to Khanikin, 15.**5**; 3 Officers and 110 Cossacks join British on Tigris, 20.**5**; Sir P. Sykes' column enters Kerman, 12.**6**; Barátov driven back eastwards by strong Turkish forces, summer; Fighting near Hamadan, Russian success, 28.**10**; Russians, advancing from N., drive Turks into, and take much war material, 27.**11**; Russians 30 m. S. of Persian frontier, 30.**11**.

PÉTAIN, GEN.
In command at Verdun, 25.**2**; Appointed to command of N. and N.E. Armies, 15.**5**.

PETER, KING OF SERBIA.
Reaches Salonika, 1.**1**.

"PETROLITE," ss.
U.S.A. demand apology from Austria for sinking, 29.**6**.

PETROZSENY (Transylv.).
Occupied by Rumanians, 29.**8**.

PEYTON, MAJ.-GEN. W. E.
Succeeds General Wallace in command of W. Egypt, 9.**2**.

PILKEM (Ypres).
Germans attack at, 12.**2**.

PINSK.
Russian advance near, 15.**1**.

PIRÆUS, THE (Athens).
Allied squadron at, 1.**9**; French seamen land, 28.**11**; Allied troops land. 30.**11**, 1.**12**; Greeks attack Allied troops, from, 1.**12**; Allied naval and military detachments embark, 4.**12**.

PIRNAKAPAN (Armenia).
Turks claim victory over Russians, 8.**5**.

PITESHTI (Rumania).
Taken by Falkenhayn, 29.**11**; Severe fighting S. of, 1.**12**.

PLOEGSTEERT WOOD (Armentières).
German attack repulsed, 13.**5**.

PLOESHTI (Rumania).
Enemy advancing on, 5.**12**; Enemy captures, 6.**12**; Rumanians check enemy N. of, 10.**12**.

PODGORITZA (Montenegro).
Austrians enter, 23.**1**.

POINCARÉ, PRESIDENT.
Visits Verdun front, 29.**2**; Speech at Nancy, 14.**5**.

POIVRE HILL (Hill 342, Verdun).
German attacks repulsed, 4 and 19.**3**; Germans gain ground at, 10.**4**; French attack and capture, 15.**12**.

POLA.
Italian torpedo boat raid, on, 1.**11**.

POLAND.
German promise of independence to, announced in Duma, 23.**2**; Germany rejects British offer to send U.S. foodstuffs; to, 29.**7**; Autonomy granted by Central Powers, 5.**9**; Establishment as independent State announced by Germany and Austro-Hungary, 5.**11**; Protest of Poles in Duma, 14.**11**; Russia denounces Central Powers' proposals, 15.**11**; Polish recruiting for German Army announced to begin on 22.**11**; German promises dependent on result, 16.**11**; Denunciation of Central Powers' action by Entente, 18.**11**.

POLITICAL, &c. (Main Events).
Germany declares war on Portugal, 9.**3**; Irish rebellion, 24.**4**-1.**5**; Lord Kitchener drowned, 5.**6**; Troubles with Greece, May, June, August to December; Rumania declares War on Austria Hungary, 28.**8**; Germany declares war on Rumania, 29.**8**; Venizelist Revolution in Salonika, 30.**8**; Bulgaria declares war on Rumania, 1.**9**; President Wilson re-elected, 7.**11**; Mr. Lloyd George succeeds Mr. Asquith, 6.**12**; German "Peace" Note, 12.**12**; President Wilson's Peace Note to Belligerents, 20.**12**; German reply proposes Peace Conference, 25.**12**.

PORTO LAGOS (Bulgaria).
Allies bombard, 19.**1**.

PORTO PALERMO (S. Albania).
Italians occupy ground between above and Subasc, 9.**9**.

L

PORT SAID.
Bombed by Turks, 7.5, 21.5, 20.7, 1.9.
PORTUGAL.
Seizes German steamers, 23.2; German Note to, 29.2; More German ships seized, 3.3; Germany declares war against, 9.3; New Ministry formed, 15.3; Austria declares war against, 15.3; War cabinet resigns, 11.4; But withdraws resignation, 13.4; Decides to extend military co-operation to Europe, 8.8; Troops ready to leave for Western front, 9.11.
" PORTUGAL."
French Hospital Ship torpedoed by German submarine in Black Sea, 30.3.
POSINA RIVER (Trentino).
Austrians cross to W. of Arsiero and capture heights on S. bank, 29.5; Italians driven back to Posina village, 3.6; Italians recapture line, 27.6.
POTTERS BAR.
Zeppelin raid on E. Coast, L.31 brought down at, 1.10.
POZIÈRES (Somme).
British approach, 15.7; Fight for, 22-25.7; Capture of, 26.7; Gain ground W. of, 1, 3, 4, 6, 10, 12, 18, 21.8; Heavy counter attacks repulsed, 6, 7, 17.8; British take 600 yards of trench, etc., 9.9; Further advance from 15.9.
PREDEAL PASS (Transylv.).
Rumanians make stand in, 10.10; Enemy checked in Predeal and Buzeu Passes, 13.10; Frontier ridge at, won by enemy and Predeal town burnt, 14.10; Rumanian reverse, heavy losses, 23.10; Austrian pressure, 1,2.11; Germans capture position S.W. of, 5.11; And attack in Prahova valley, 7.11; Rumanians abandon defence, 5.12.
PRESPA LAKE (Macedonia).
French S.W. of, in touch with Italians, 24.10.
PRESSOIR (Chaulnes).
French capture, 7.11; Severe fighting for, 14-16.11.
PRILEP (N.E. of Monastir).
German-Bulgarian troops retreat to, 19.11.
" PRIMULA," H.M.S.
Mine-sweeper torpedoed in Mediterranean, 1.3.
PRISONERS OF WAR.
Germany accepts British proposal for transference of British and German wounded and invalid combatants to Switzerland, 2.5; Russians claim 300,000 prisoners up to 10.7; Return of German prisoners on Somme, 1.10; Returns of British and German prisoners respectively, 13.10; Returns of German, on the Somme, 19.10, 1.11.

PROSNES (Champagne).
German attack at, 27.7.
" PROVENCE II."
French transport, torpedoed in Mediterranean, 26.2.
PRUTH, RIVER (Galicia).
Russian advance near, 1.7.

" QUEEN MARY," H.M.S.
Battleship sunk in Battle of Jutland, 31.5; Transport, sunk in North Sea, by German destroyers, 27.10.

RADAUTZ (S. of Czernovitz).
Occupied by Russians, 21.6.
RADOSLAVOV, M.
Attempted assassination of, Bulgarian Premier, 20.3.
RADZILOV (Brody).
Occupied by Russians, 16.6.
RAFALOVKA (River Styr).
Russian success at, 4.7.
RAILWAYS, IRISH.
Government announces decision to take over, 16.12.
RAMNICU SARAT (Rumania).
Fierce fighting near; Enemy concentrate towards, 22.12; Captured by Falkenhayn, 27.12; Fine Russian defence N. of, 29-30.12.
RANCOURT (Somme).
French progress at, 15, 25, 26.9.
RASPUTIN, GREGORY.
Murder of the monk, by highly-placed personages, 29.12.
RAUCHKOFEL (Carnic).
Italians retire from front trenches on, 7.4.
RAVENNA.
Bombed by Austrians, 12.2.
RAYAT (112 m. E.N.E. of Mosul).
Russians defeat Turks at (2,300 prisoners), 23.8.
RAZLOVCI (Serbia).
British naval aeroplanes bomb, 15.12.
RECRUITING (v. also Man-power).
Lord Derby's report on, 4.1; Conference regarding, at War Office, 20.3; Australia adopts Derby scheme, 29.11.
" RENAUDIN."
French T.B.D. torpedoed in Adriatic, 19.3.
REVAL (Baltic).
Germans bomb, 18.7; German destroyers attack port W. of, and are driven off with loss of six destroyers, 10.11.
RIGA.
Enemy cannonade S.E. of, 1.2; Artillery duel round, 7.2 and 14.3; Russian bombardment in district of, 3.6;

RUPEL, FORT (Macedonia).
Occupation by Bulgaro-German force, 26.5; Greek excitement over, 28.5 Bulgars occupy the Pass, 30.5.

RUSCHUK (Danube).
Germans occupy island near, 8.10.

" RUSSELL," H.M.S.
Sunk by mine in Mediterranean, 27.4.

RUSSIA.
Russian offensive v. Bukovina unsuccessful, but eases Balkan pressure, 1-15.1; Capture of Erzerum, 16.2; Gen. Polivanov succeeded as War Minister by Gen. Shuvaiev, 29.3; Russian offensive about Lake Naroch fairly successful, 18.3 to 14.4; Capture of Trebizond, 18.4; Signs Treaty with Japan, 3.6; Great Russian offensive in S. (Brusilov) begins, 4.6; Capture of Lutsk, 6.6; Buczacz, 8.6; Dubno, 9.6; Leshitski takes Czernowitz, 17.6; and Kolomea, 29.6 Leshitski reaches River Stokhod, 2-8.7; Leshitski takes Delatyn, 8.7; Sazonov succeeded by Stürmer as Foreign Minister, 23.7; Capture of Erzingan, 25.7; Sakharov takes Brody, 28.7; Leshitski takes Stanislau, 10.8; End of Brusilov offensive, 358,602 prisoners taken, 11.8; Leshitski's attack in Carpathians checked, 15.8 to 20.9; Shcherbachev's attack in E. Galicia checked, 29.8 to 20.9; Leshitski joins hands with Rumanians about Dorna Vatra, 11.9; Russian offensive checked, stalemate, 20.9; Political troubles, attacks on reactionary administration, November; M. Trepov, Premier; 23.11; Agrees with Entente of 1915, 2.12; Prince Golitzin, Premier, November; Foreign Minister's and others' vigorous anti-peace-negotiations speeches, 15.12; Tsar's order to troops, reply to German Peace Note, 25.12; Rasputin killed, 29.12.

RUSSIAN CAPTURES.
Total of, to date, published (v. Appendix 84), 16.8.

" RUSSIAN," ss.
British horse transport torpedoed in Mediterranean, 14.12.

RUSSIAN TROOPS.
Arrive in France, 20.4.

RUSSO-JAPANESE AGREEMENT.
Announcement of, 8.7.

RUWU RIVER (E. Africa).
British drive enemy from, 18.3.

SAHILAN, AZ (Euphrates).
British defeat Turkish column at, 11.9.

SAILLY (Somme).
French advance close up to, 7.10; Enemy driven out of, 18.10; French carry ridge W. of, 22.10; French take trenches N.W. of, 30.10.

SAILLY-SAILLISEL (Somme).
French bombard, 14.10; French gain footing in, 16-17.10; French capture larger part, 5.11; After heavy fighting, conquest completed, 12.11.

SALMANA, BIR (N. Sinai).
New Zealand troops raid, 31.5.

SANNA-I-YAT (Mesop.).
Failure of preliminary British attack, 6.4; And of main British attack 9.4; Turkish right driven back, 12.4: Feint on, 12.12; Outflanked, 18.12.

ST. ÉLOI (Ypres.)
British capture first and second lines at, 27.3; Heavy fighting at, 3, 6, 9, 10, 19.4.

STE. MARIE-A-PY (Ypres).
Salient of, carried by British, 25.2; Counter-attack on, repulsed, 26.2.

ST. PIERRE DIVION (Ancre).
British capture, 13.11.

ST. PIERRE VAAST WOOD (Somme).
French attack and progress, 5, 6.11; Germans gain footing in W., 15.11.

ST. QUENTIN.
German attacks repulsed at Lihons near, 18.6; Bombed by British, 4.7.

SAKIZ (S. of Lake Urmia).
Russians occupy, 20.5.

SAKHAROV, GEN.
Begins offensive in E. Galicia, 15.7; Takes Brody and 40,000 prisoners, 28.7; Finishes campaign on River Styr, 10.8; Takes command of Russo-Rumanian army in Dobruja, 1.11.

SALANGA (Ger. E. Africa).
Occupied by S. African troops, 14.4.

SALONIKA.
Gen. Sarrail in command at, 16.1; Zeppelin raid on, 1.2; French troops arrive at, 11.2; Measures taken to protect, 11.2; Serbian troops arrive in March; Air raid on, 27.3; Bulgarians and Germans bomb lines at, 17.4; Hostilities resumed N. of, 30.4; Zeppelin destroyed by Allied fleet at, 5.5; Allied troops occupy Government bureaux in, 3.6; Unusual artillery activity at, 15.6; Russian troops land at, 30.7; Allied offensive begins (v. Macedonia), 10.8; Italian troops land at, 11.8; Venizelist revolution, Committee of National Defence formed, 30.8; M. Venizelos arrives, 9.10; Venizelist Government recognised by Allies, 25.10; Review of troops by Greek National Government, 10.11; National Government declares war on Germany and Bulgaria, 24.11; Denounces Royalist Government, 6.12; Great Britain recognises Diplomatic Agents, 19.12.

SALONIKA FRONT (v. Macedonia).

154 CHRONOLOGY OF THE WAR.

SHIPPING, ITALIAN.
Proposed mobilisation of, 31.1.
SHUMRAN BEND (Tigris).
British aeroplanes destroy pontoon
bridges, 14.12; Turks remove base from,
to Baghela, 21.12.
SILISTRIA (Danube).
German-Bulgar troops occupy, 9.9;
Bulgars cross Danube near, 9.12.
" SIMLA," ss.
P. & O., torpedoed in Mediterranean,
7.4.
SIMNITZA (Zimnicea, Rumania).
Crossing of Danube by Mackensen,
from Sistova to, 19-23.11.
SINAI PENINSULA.
Turkish success at Katiya, 23.4;
Turks advance in force, 19-27.7; Battle
of Romani, British victory, 3-6.8; Turks
fall back, 12.8; British rush Mazar, 17.9;
Railway reaches Mazar (10 m. W. of El
Arish), 26.11; British occupy El Arish,
21.12; British take Magdhaba, 23.12.
SINAIA (Transylv. frontier).
Enemy capture, 6.12; Rumanian
force retires from near, 8.12.
SINN FEIN.
Easter manœuvres of Sinn Fein
volunteers cancelled, 22.4; Outbreak in
Ireland, Dublin Post Office, etc., seized by,
24.4; Sir J. Maxwell takes command,
27.4; Rebellion, and fighting in Dublin,
etc., 24.4 to 1.5; Rebel commanders
surrender, 1.5; Resignation of Mr.
Birrell, 3.5; Commission to enquire
appointed, 10.5; Resignation of Lord
Wimborne announced, 10.5; Report of
Commission issued, 3.7; Mr. Duke
appointed Chief Secretary, 31.7; Lord
Wimborne re-appointed, 11.8.
SISTOVA (v. Simnitza).
SIVAS (Armenia).
Russian advance towards (but do
not reach), 27.7.
" SKODSBORG."
Danish vessel torpedoed by Germans,
19.3.
SKROBOVA (N. of Baranovichi, Polesia).
Defeat of Russian centre, 9.11.
SKUTARI (Albania).
Austrians enter, 23.1.
SLAVS, SOUTHERN.
Declaration against continued slavery
under Habsburg dynasty issued, 30.12.
SMORGON (Vilna).
Germans penetrate Russian lines and
are driven out, 20.6; Russian advance at,
2.7; German gas-attack repulsed, 2.8.
SMUTS, GENERAL J. (v. also E. Africa).
Appointed to command in E. Africa,
25.1; Sails from the Cape, 12.2; Arrives

Mombasa, 19.2; at Nairobi, 23.2; First
despatch published, 20.6.
SOCIALISTS.
Minority Socialists in Germany, mani-
festo against " Oracular utterances,"
15.12; Mr. Henderson's speech at National
Congress of (Paris), 25.12; Further
sitting of, urges more vigorous French
policy, 29.12.
SOFIA.
Treason trial begins, 16.3; French
air raid on, 3.7.
SOISSONS.
Enemy attack near, repulsed, 13.2.
SOLLUM (W. Egypt). (v. Senussi).
Reoccupied by British, 14.3; British-
Italian car raid from, 26.7.
SOMME, RIVER.
Right of British line extended to,
15.4; Big advance begins N. and S. of,
1.7; (For details, v. Tables); Advance
reaches Assevillers, Flaucourt, Hardecourt, Montauban, Mametz Wood, La
Boisselle, Hamel, by 3.7; Advance
reaches Estrées, Biaches, Hem, Hardecourt, Longueval, Bazentin, La Boisselle,
by 14.7 (end of First Phase); Advance
reaches Sormont, Cléry, Maurepas, Guillemont, Bois des Foureaux (High Wood),
Pozières Windmill, by 18.8; Advance
reaches Le Forest, Combles (nearly).
Ginchy, Flers (nearly), by 9.9 (end of
Second Phase); Advance reaches Bouchavesnes, Rancourt, Combles, Lesboeufs,
pt. 2¾ miles S. of Bapaume, Le Sars
(nearly), Thiepval by 1.10; end of Third
Phase, 23.10; Franco-British captures to
date, 1.11; Review of British operations
since second week October, published in
Times of 2.11; Advance reaches Chaulnes
(nearly), Ablaincourt, Belloy-en-Santerre,
Biaches, Sailly, Warlencourt (nearly),
Grandcourt (nearly), Beaumont Hamel,
by 19.11; Ancre Phase, 9-18.11; Ar-
tillery active throughout December; Sir
D. Haig's despatch on Battle of, dated
23.12, published, 29.12.
SONNINO, BARON.
Becomes Italian Foreign Minister, 15.5.
SORMONT FARM (Somme).
French take, 4.7.
SOUCHEZ (Vimy).
Included in extended British line, 23.3.
SOUTH AFRICA.
Political crisis in, averted, 15.2.
SOUTHERN FRONT (Main Events).
Austrians enter Cettinje, 13.1; Big
Austrian offensive v. the Trentino, 14.5-
27.6; Bulgarians occupy Fort Rupel,
26.5; Heavy fighting on Isonzo front,
1.8-3.11; Italians take Gorizia, 9.8; Allied

SWEDEN.
Correspondence between Great Britain and, *re* mail packet detention, published, 25.8; Note to belligerents *re* peace terms, 27.12.

SWITZERLAND.
Threatened with stoppage of coal supply from Germany, 26.6; Note to Belligerent Powers supporting President Wilson, 22.12; Issues Peace Note to Belligerents, 23.12. Receives answer from Germany, 28.12.

SYRA (Cyclades).
Venizelist troops land on, 12.12.

SZEKELY UDVARHELY (S. Transylv.).
Rumanian (4th) Northern Army advances from, 3.10; Enemy retake, 7.10.

TABORA (E. Africa).
Occupied by Belgians, 19.9.

TAHURE (Champagne).
French regain trenches at, 16.2 German first and second lines taken, 29.6; Violent Ger. attacks repulsed, 25.8.

TAIF (S.E. of Mecca).
Turkish garrison of 1,800 surrenders to Sherif of Mecca, 24.9.

TANGA (Ger. E. Africa).
Reported evacuated, 13.6; British secure Korogwe Bridge, 50 miles W. of, 15.6; Occupation by British, 7.7.

TANGANYIKA, LAKE.
Belgian column progresses N.W. of, 6.6.

TANKS.
Employed for first time near Courcelette, 15.9.

TARGU JIU (W. Rumania).
Rumanian evacuation, 16.11; Austro-Germans break Rumanian front, 17.11.

TARNOPOL (E. Galicia).
Russians evacuate trenches S.W. of, 14.2; Shcherbachev attacks W. from, early June; Austrians advance fruitlessly on, 1.7; Fighting near, throughout December.

TAVETA (Ger. E. Africa).
Occupied by British, 9.2.

TEPELENI (Albania).
Italians occupy, 30.8.

TEW (Armenia).
Russians take, 11.1.

THASOS ISLAND (Greece).
Occupied by French troops, 10.6.

THIAUMONT (S.W. of Douaumont, Verdun).
Severe fighting at Farm, 8.5; German attack repulsed, 12.5; German attack between Douaumont and, 29.5; German attacks repulsed N. of, 12.6; Germans penetrate line E. of Hill 321 near, 12.6; Thiaumont Work entered by Germans, 23.6; Heavy fighting W. of, 25.6;

German night attack repulsed, N.W. of, 28.6; French capture, 30.6; Germans recapture, 4.7; Severe fighting near, 24-30.7, 4-6.8; Germans regain, 9.8; French progress, 18, 28.8.

THIEPVAL (River Ancre).
British attacks on, 6, 7.7; British within 1,000 yards of, 21.8; Heavy fighting for, 22-25.8; British repel Prussian Guards, 3.9; British storm "Wunderwerk," etc., 14.9; British capture, 26.9; British take most of Schwaben Redoubt, N.E. of, 28, 30.9; British progress near, 15, 21.10.

THIONVILLE (Lorraine).
French planes bomb, 30.11.

TIGRIS, RIVER (Mesopotamia).
British attempts to relieve Kut, 4.1 to 23.4; Fighting at Sheikh Saad, Turks fall back, 4-9.1; Wadi carried, Turks fall back to Um-el-Hannah, 13.1; Aylmer attacks unsuccessfully, 21.1; Attack on Es Sinn after night march fails, 8.3; Keary takes Um-el-Hannah, 5.4; Gorringe fails in attack on Sanna-i-yat, 9.4; Heavy floods and vile weather, 11.4, etc.; Progress on R. bank, 12-15.4; Beit Aiessia taken and Turks repulsed, 17.4; Attack on N. Sanna-i-yat fails, 22.4; s.s. "Julnar" fails to break blockade and is captured, 23.4; Fall of Kut, 29.4; Turks sink three munition barges, 10.6; British cavalry raid, 15.6; British planes destroy pontoons in Shumran bend, 14.12; British on river between Khadairi bend and Kut, 18.12; British positions consolidated, 26.12.

TIRPITZ, ADMIRAL VON.
Resigns Ministry of Marine, succeeded by Admiral van Capelle, 16.3.

TLUMACH (near Stanislau, Galicia).
Russians capture, 30.6; Germans regain, 2.7; Russians recapture with 2,000 prisoners, 7.8.

TOFANA AREA (Trentino).
Strong attack by Austrians repulsed with heavy loss, 30.7.

TOGOLAND.
Franco-British Agreement, 27.12.

TOLGYES PASS (Carpathians).
Rumanians repulse enemy, 7.11; Rumanians retreat S.E., 16.11.

TORAVO, MONTE.
Italians retreat from, to Monte Campolon-Spitz Tonezza line (Trentino), 19.5.

T.B. DESTROYERS.
Actions in Adriatic, 6.2, 23.6, 1.11; in Baltic, 14.6; in Black Sea, 17, 22.1, 9.3, 28.3; in North Sea 20, 25.3, 31.5, 1.6, 16.6, 23.7, 13.8, 19.8, 27.10, 10, 23.11. Two British, collide and sink, in North Sea, 21.12.

TORTUM, LAKE (Armenia).
Russians surround, 11.1.

TÖRZBURG (Transylvania, Alps).
Enemy capture Törzburg, 9.10;
Enemy progress in Törzburg Pass, 12.10;
Rumanians driven 12 miles back from
frontier, 21.10; Austro-Hungarian pres-
sure, 1.11; Rumanian retreat, 13, 14.11;
Severe fighting near Campu-Lung, S.W. of
16.11.

TRADES UNION.
Congress meets at Birmingham, 4.9;
Refuses to parley with German socialists,
5.9; Insists on restoration of T.U.
practices after war, 6.9.

TRANSYLVANIAN FRONT.
Rumanians cross passes into Transylvania, 28.8; Rumanians occupy Kezdi
Vasarhely, Kronstadt ard Petroszeny,
Austrians retreat, 29.8; Rumanians occupy Hermannstadt and Orsova and near
Hatszeg by 12.9; Rumanians driven
back from near Hatszeg, 15.9; Rumanians take Fogaras, 16.9; Rumanians
evacuate Petroszeny, 20.9; back to
Vulkan, 22.9; Falkenhayn secures Roter
Turm Pass, 26.9; Rumanians driven
back S.E. across mountains from Hermannstadt, 4.10; Remainder of Rumanian armies begin to fall back, 4.10;
Germans in Kronstadt, 7.10; Rumanian
armies back along frontier, except in N.E.
corner, 10.10; Falkenhayn attacks Törzburg Pass and takes Predeal Pass, 14.10;
Rumanians driven from Vulkan Pass,
15.10; Germans take Gyimes Pass, 17.10;
Bavarian attack S.E. of Roter Turm
Pass held up, 18.10; Enemy advance
through Törzburg and Buzeu Passes,
21.10; Rumanians stand in N. Passes,
25, 26, 28.10; Enemy gain groun l in S.
Passes, 26.10; First battle of Târgu Jiu,
Rumanians successful, 27.10 to 9.11;
Rumanians driven back S.E. of Roter
Turm Pass to near Curtea de Arges,
28.10 to 8.11; Strong German offensive
begins, 10.11; Fall of Târgu Jiu, 15.11;
Second battle of Jiu, Rumanian retreat,
17.11; Fall of Craiova, 21.11; Orsova
division cleared out, 25.11; Fall of
Campu-Lung and Piteshti, 29.11; Fall of
Bucharest, Sinaia, and Ploeshti, 5.12;
Orsova force surrenders at Caraculu,
7.12; Fall of Buzeu, 14.12.

TRAVE (German steamer).
Torpedoed by British submarine near
Cape Kullen (Kattegat), 18.5.

TRAVIGNOLO VALLEY (Trentino).
Austrians attack three times without
success, 30.7; Italians occupy Paneveggio,
31.7; Italians beat enemy in, 4.10.

TREBIZOND (Asia Minor).
Threatened by Russian advance, 22.2;
" Breslau " assists Turkish defence of, 5.4;
fall of, 18.4; Russians repulse Turks S. of,
21.5; Turks repulsed at Platina, W. of,
10.6; Several night attacks by Turks
repulsed, 18-23.6.

TRENTINO.
Fierce fighting at Adamello, 11.4;
and Giudicaria, 29.4; Austrian offensive
on large scale begins, 14.5; Italians
fall back S. of Sette Communi, 20-29.5;
Austrian attack on M. Pasubio fails,
25-30.5; Italians repel violent attack on
Buole, but evacuate Arsiero and Asiago,
30.5; Austrian offensive from Monte
Pasubio to Arsiero, 1.6; From Posina to
Astico, 2.6; Austrian attacks repulsed
from Lagarina to Arsiero, and finally
checked, 3.6; Italian progress in, 9.6;
Continued advance, 10.6 - 28.6; Italian
counter-offensive in strength begins, 16.6;
Asiago and Arsiero recovered, 26, 27.6;
Further fighting in Autumn, little definite
result.

TREPOV, M.
Becomes Russian Prime Minister, 24.11.

TRIESTE.
Heavily bombed, 13.9; Further Italian air-raid, 6.12.

TRÔNES WOOD (Somme).
Fighting for, 8-12.7; British take,
14.7.

TSAPUL, MT. (Carpathians).
Russian success, capture 900 prisoners,
12.9.

TSINGTAU.
Publication of Maj.-Ger. Barnardis-
ton's despatches re British at (Sept.-Nov.
1914), 30.5.

" TUBANTIA," ss.
Dutch liner torpedoed by Germans
without warning, 16.3.

TURKEY.
New German loan to, £20,000,000,
16.3; Declares war on Rumania, 30.8;

TURNU-SEVERIN (Danube).
Austro-Germans capture, 23.11.

TURTUKAI (or Tutrakan) (on Danube).
German-Bulgarian troops attack and
take, Germans claim 20,000 prisoners and
100 guns, 6, 7.9; Bulgars cross Danube
near, 9.12.

TYSMIENICA (Stanislau).
Russians take, with 7.400 prisoners, 8.8.

UGANDA RAILWAY.
German bombing parties driven from,
5 and 11.1.

UGLY (Volhynia.).
Russians cross at River Stokhod, 8.7

UJIJI (Lake Tanganyika).
Belgians occupy, 3.8.
UKEREWE ISLAND (Victoria Nyanza).
Occupied by British, 15.6.
ULUGURU MTS. (Ger. E. Africa).
Enemy retreat from, 1.9; British
columns effect junction S. of, 15.9.
UM-EL-HANNAH (Mesopotamia).
Failure of British attack on, 21.1;
Gen. Gorringe carries, 5.4.
UNITED STATES OF AMERICA.
Protest to Great Britain on seizure of
mails, 28.1; War Minister resigns, 10.2;
Refusal to accept German proposals on
"Lusitania" question, 16.2; Senate tables
resolution by Senator Gore, proposing to
warn American citizens not to travel on
armed merchantmen, 3.3: Mr. Newton J.
Baker becomes Secretary for War in, 8.3;
Plot in, to blow up ammunition ships, 12.4;
German Note to, on "Sussex" case, 12.4;
Cabinet approves President's Note to
Germany on "Sussex" case, 14.4; Note
to Germany on "Sussex" case and
submarine campaign published, 18.4;
British Note to, on the blockade, 26.4;
Further Note to Germany on submarine
warfare, 8.5; Further protest to Great
Britain against search of mails, 26.5;
Militia called out to police Mexican
frontier, 19.6; Apology demanded by,
from Austria for sinking of "Petrolite,"
29.6; British memorandum to, re Neutral
Mails published, 24.7; Mr. Gerard's protest
re inhumanity at Ruhleben published,
25.7; Protest against policy of "Black
List," 28.7; German Note to, rejects British offer to pass foodstuffs to Poland,
29.7; Terms of British War Loan in,
published, 16.8; German mark at 30%
discount in, 1.9; Interview with Mr. Ll.
George on War published in, 27.9; British
White Paper re "Black List" published,
14.11; Cables protest to Germany re
Belgian deportations, 29.11; Note to
Great Britain and France re safe conduct
to Austro-Hungarian Ambassador, 30.11;
Germany's reply re Belgian deportations,
11.12; Further message re safe conduct
of Ambassador, 12.12; Denounces Turkey's conduct to Armenians and Syrians,
and terminates extra-territoriality agreements, 18.12; British grant safe conduct
to Austrian Ambassador, American responsibility of request, 19.12; Note to belligerents, re Peace Conference, 20.12;
Note to and from Germany re s.s. "Colum-
bian," 21.12; Peace Note, replies from
Germany and Austro-Hungary, 26.12.;
URMIA (Persia).
Turks driven W. from, 26.6.
USAMBARA (E. Africa).
Germans cleared from, 18.7.

USCIESZKO (Dniester).
Austrian success at, 29.1; Austrian;
repulsed near, 2.2; Russians occupy, 8.2s
Region of, Austrian attacks repulsed,
16.2; Russian success N.W. of, 19.3.
USUMBARA (Lake Tanganyika).
British advance in Para and Usumbara
areas begins, 18.5; Occupied by Belgians,
8.6.
ÜXKÜLL (Dvina).
Germans repulsed at bridgehead of,
3.4.

VACHERAUVILLE (Verdun).
German attack repulsed E. of, 5.3;
French capture, 15.12.
VALLONE (Carso).
Italians cross the, 11.8.
VAN, LAKE (Armenia).
Russian offensive W. of, 22.8; Oc-
casional fighting near, December; Turks
driven back S. of, 28.12.
VARDAR, RIVER (Maced.).
R. Bank of, occupied, by Allies, 11.2;
Artillery duels on, 2.7; Serbs carry Bulgar
trenches on Moglena ridge, W. of, 14.9.
VAUX (Verdun).
Germans deliver five successive assaults
on, 17.3; Germans take village of, 1.4;
French retake village of, 3.4; Failure of
German attack between Douaumont and,
11.4; French progress near fort of, 21.4;
Germans repulsed W. of pond at, 11.5;
Germans gain footing in fort of, 2.6;
German attacks on fort of, 3-5.6; Germans
take fort of, 7.6; Germans repulsed W.
and S. of fort of, 21.6; German attacks
Chapitre Wood to, repulsed, 6, 28.8;
Germans evacuate, 1.11; French advance
and occupy, 3, 5.11.
VENICE.
Austrian seaplanes bomb, 5.9.
VENIZELOS, M.
Message to the *Times* explaining
his position and hopes, 25.9; With Adm.
Condouriotis and Gen. Danglis forms Pro-
visional Government in Crete, 30.9;
Greek officers throng to Venizelos, 2.10;
Arriving Salonika, receives great ovation,
9.10; Allied Boulogne Conference, recog-
nises Venizelos' National Provisional
Government, 19.10; Statement of aims
and policy of Greek National Defence
Movement, 21.11; Petition to protecting
Powers from Congress of Hellenic Colonies
for recognition of National Government,
12.12; Warrant out for arrest of, 18.12.
VERDUN (v. also Vaux, Thiaumont,
etc.).
Battle begins, 21.2; German progress,
French driven back, 21-26.2; Civil
population evacuated, Germans capture

Ridge, 21.5; Allied offensive on the Somme begins, 1.7; British offensive on the Ancre, 9-18.11; End of Somme operations, 19.11.

WESTMINSTER, DUKE OF.
Armoured cars attack and disperse Senussi 20 miles S. of Sollum, 14.3; And release 91 "Tara" prisoners at Bir Hakim, 17.3.

"WESTMINSTER," ss.
Sunk by enemy without warning, 14.12.

WHEAT.
Rumanian crop purchased by Great Britain, 20.1.

WHITBY.
German submarine sinks four boats off, 13.7.

WILHELMSTAL (Ger. E. Africa).
Taken by British, 13.6.

WILSON, DR. WOODROW (President of U.S.A.) (v. also U.S.A.).
Letter from, to Senator Stone, on submarine campaign, 25.2; Letter from, to Rules Committee of Congress, 1.3; Victory of, in Congress on policy towards submarine campaign, 7.3; Speeches on War at Washington, 17, 27.5; Nominated for re-election as President, 7.11.

WIMBORNE, LORD.
Resignation of Lord Lieutenancy, of, Ireland, 10.5; Re-appointed, 11.8.

WINGATE, GEN. SIR F. R.
Despatch from, on conquest of Darfur. 26.10; Appointed High Commissioner of Egypt, 6.11.

WITTENBERG CAMP.
Mr. Justice Younger's report on, 10.4.

WOMEN'S NATIONAL LAND SERVICE CORPS.
Meeting to inaugurate formation of, 6.3.

WULVERGHEM.
German gas attack at, fails, 29.4.

WYTSCHAETE.
German raids near, 13.7.

YANBO.
Port of Medina captured by Grand Sherif of Mecca, 27.7.

YAUNDE (Cameroons).
Occupied by British, 1.1.

YENIKEUI (L. bank Struma River).
Raided by British, 8.9; British take, 3.10.

YOUNGER, MR. JUSTICE.
Report on Wittenberg Camp, published, 10.4.

YPRES.
Germans active round, 13.2; British lose trenches near canal, 14.2; Fighting round, 16, 18, 21.2; Germans capture positions N. of Langemarck, 19.4; British

recapture them, 21.4; Germans repulsed at, 1.5; Germans take 2,000 yards of Canadians' trenches towards Zillebeke, 2.6; But lose much of the ground taken, 3.6; Germans active at, 10.6; Heavy bombardment by Germans, 11.6; Canadians recover lost ground at, 13.6; Germans repulsed at, 27.6; Heavy reciprocal raiding near, 14.12.

YUAN-SHI-KAI (President of China).
Death of, 6.6.

YUDENICH, GEN.
Offensive campaign of, in Armenia, begins, 11.1; Captures Erzerum, 16.2; And Trebizond, 18.4; Further campaign starts, 12.7; Captures Erzingan, 25.7; Beats Turks near Rayat, and captures Mush, 25.8.

YUGO-SLAVS, v. Slavs, Southern.

YUSUFIZZ-ED-DIN, PRINCE.
Turkish Heir-apparent, reported to have committed suicide, 1.2.

"ZEEAREND," ss.
Dutch vessel sunk by submarine, 1.9.

ZEEBRUGGE.
Bombed by Allies, 18.3; Allied naval and air bombardment, of, 20.3; Patrol action off, 8.6; Bombed intermittently, especially on, 10, 15, 17.11, and 11, 26, 27.12.

ZAIMIS, M.
Appointed Greek Prime Minister 21.6.

ZEPPELIN RAIDS ON GREAT BRITAIN.
v Table, p. 122.
Eastern counties, 31.1; N.E. and E. 5.3; E. and N.E., 31.3; N.E., 1.4; Scotland and N.E., 2.4; N.E., 3.4; N.E., 5.4; Norfolk and Suffolk, 24.4; Off Lowestoft, with warships, 25.4; Essex, Kent and E. counties, 25.4; Coast of Kent, 26.4; N.E. coast and S.E., Scotland, 2.5; England, 3.5; Yorkshire, Norfolk and Lincolnshire, 29.7; Kent, Essex, Suffolk, Norfolk, Cambridge and Hunts., 1.8; E. and S.E. counties, 3.8; E. and N.E., 9.8; E. coast, 23.8; E. counties and outskirts of London, 24-25.8; E. counties and Kent, 2-3.9 (13 Zeppelins—one down at Cuffley by Lieut. Robinson, V.C.); E., S.E., Lincoln and London, 23-24.9 (2, brought down); S. and E. coast and N. 25-26.9; E. coast and Lincoln, 1.10 (one L.31 brought down at Potter's Bar); N.E. coast and N. Midlands, 27.11 (2 brought down).

ZEPPELIN RAIDS (elsewhere).
On Paris, 29-30.1, 31.1; On Rouen, 12.2; Other Zeppelins known to have been wrecked, L19, on 3.2; L20, off Norway, 3.5; L7, off Schleswig coast by our ships. Mr. Ll. George announces 35 destroyed by Allies to date, 22.8.

1917

1917. Jan.	WESTERN FRONT.	EASTERN FRONT.	SOUTHERN FRONT.
1	Normal activity proceeding. Sir D. Haig promoted to Field Marshal.	Stubborn fighting in Carpathians on Moldavian frontier; slight enemy p r o g r e s s at various points. Enemy in touch with Sereth lines at Focsani and Fundeni. Further enemy progress at the Macin bridgehead (Dobruja).	.. .. ..
2	.. .. ..	Enemy attack repulsed near Zloczow (N.E. Galicia). Continued heavy fighting in Moldavian mountains. Enemy advance between frontier and Focsani; Russian successful counter-attacks S.E. of that town. Enemy advance near Macin continues.	.. .. ..
3	.. .. ..	Germans take island in Dvina near Glandau, N.W. of Dvinsk. Successful Russian attack near Mt. Botosul (Bukovina). Enemy advance in region of Milcovu, N.W. of Focsani. Germans and Bulgarians take Macin and Jijila (Dobruja).	.. .. ..
4	.. .. ..	Germans fail to cross to right bank of Dvina near Glandau. Enemy advance in Focsani sector, and also take Gurgueti and Romanul, thus piercing the Braila bridgehead; Russians evacuate Braila. Russians defeated at Vacareni (Dobruja).	British airmen bomb Maritza bridge at Kuleli Burgas (S. of Adrianople).
5	British capture two enemy posts near Beaumont Hamel.	Ground gained in Russian offensive between Lake Babit and the Tirul marsh (W. of Riga). Enemy advance at various points on Rumanian front, especially between the rivers Rimnic and Buzeu. **The Dobruja entirely cleared of Russians and Rumanians.**	.. .. ..

ASIATIC AND EGYPTIAN THEATRES.	NAVAL AND OVERSEAS OPERATIONS.	POLITICAL, &c.	1917. Jan.
Gen. Sir R. Wingate becomes High Commissioner of Egypt.	Transport "Ivernia" sunk by submarine in Mediterranean; 153 missing. British carry German lines near Lissaki in the Mgeta valley (Ger. E. Africa), and pursue enemy towards the Rufiji valley at Kibambawe.	Publication of denunciation by Turkey of Treaty of Paris (1856) and Treaty of Berlin (1878).	1
..	..	M. Bratianu, Premier of Rumania, reconstitutes Cabinet.	2
..	..	Admiralty reasserts "immemorial" right of merchant-ships to defend themselves against attack or search by an enemy.	3
..	Russian battleship "Peresvyet" sunk by mine off Port Said.	..	4
Battle of Kut-el-Amara begins.	British occupy Kibambawe in Rufiji valley (Ger. E. Africa).	Conference at Rome between representatives of the British, French, and Italian Governments.	5

1917. Jan.	WESTERN FRONT.	EASTERN FRONT.	SOUTHERN FRONT.		
6	Big daylight raid by British S.E. of Arras	Stubborn fighting between the Carpathians and Focsani ; some enemy progress, especially in the Susitsa valley and near O d o b e s t i. Russian counter - offensive between Focsani and Fundeni ; ground recovered near Obilesti.	..	..	..
7	.. .. ..	R u s s i a n s gain more ground S. of Lake Babit. Russo - Rumanian front broken N.W. of Focsani.	..	..	..
8	.. .. ..	Heavy fighting S. of Lake Babit ; no material change of positions. Russians recover island in Dvina near Glandau. Enemy advance in Casin and Susitsa valleys (Moldavia), capture Focsani, with 5,500 prisoners, and make progress near Fundeni.	..	..	..
9	British take trenches E. of Beaumont Hamel. (Ancre).	Russian advance between Tirul marsh and River Aa. Enemy cross River Putna N. and S.E. of Focsani.	..	..	..
10	.. .. ..	Russian progress S. of Lake Babit. Enemy carry two heights in Oitoz valley (Moldavia), but are thrown back across the Putna N. of Focsani.	..	..	..
11	British carry German trench on front of ¾-mile, N.E. of Beaumont Hamel.	German counter - attack near Kalutsem, S. of Lake Babit, repulsed. Successful Rumanian attack in Casin valley. Enemy p r o g r e s s in Susitsa valley and between Braila and Galatz.	..	..	..

Asiatic and Egyptian Theatres.	Naval and Overseas Operations.	Political, &c.	1917. Jan.
.. .. ..	.. .. ..	.. .. ..	6
.. .. ..	.. .. ..	Close of Rome Conference.	7
.. .. ..	.. .. ..	.. .. ..	8
British carry Turkish positions at Rafa'a (frontier of Egypt and Syria) and defeat relief force ; 1,600 prisoners taken. British take 1,000 yards of trenches on right bank of Tigris N.E. of Kut.	H.M.S. " Cornwallis " sunk by submarine in Mediterranean, 13 lost. " Lesbian " s.s. (Ellerman Liner) sunk.	Resignation of M. Trepov, Russian Prime Minister ; Prince Golitzin succeeds. Allies present ultimatum to Greece demanding immediate acceptance of their demands of Dec. 31.	9
British progress continued N.E. of Kut.	.. .. ..	Allies' reply to President Wilson's " Peace Note," accompanied by special Note from Belgium (¹). Evasive reply by Greek Government to Allies' ultimatum.	10
British occupy Hai (Mesopotamia).	H.M. Seaplane - carrier " Ben-my-Chree " sunk in Kastelorizo harbour (S. Asia Minor).	Terms of new British War Loan announced by Mr. Lloyd George and Mr. Bonar Law at Guildhall(²). Important food orders issued by Lord Devonport (³). Notes from German and Austrian Governments handed to neutral Powers in answer to Entente reply to their " Peace Note " (⁴).	11

1917. Jan.	WESTERN FRONT.	EASTERN FRONT.	SOUTHERN FRONT.
12	.. .. ..	German attack near Kalutsem again repulsed. Enemy capture Mihalea, on Sereth (N.W. of Braila).	.. .. ..
13	.. .. ..	Germans again repulsed near Kalutsem. Enemy repulsed E. of Focsani.	.. .. ..
14	.. .. ..	Enemy thrown back in Casin valley and repulsed N.E. of Focsani, but capture Vadeni (between Braila and Galatz).	.. .. ..
15	.. .. ..	Indecisive fighting in Casin valley sector. Unsuccessful Russian attack in neighbourhood of Fundeni.	.. .. ..
16	Important daylight raid by British W. of Lens.	Rumanians recapture height between Casin and Oitoz valleys. Enemy driven from Vadeni.	.. .. ..
17	Another big British daylight raid W. of Lens. Capture of enemy posts on front of 600 yards N. of Beaucourt-sur-Ancre.	Mackensen's advance in Rumania checked.	.. .. ..
18	.. .. ..	Unsuccessful attacks on enemy positions between Casin and Susitsa valleys.	.. .. ..
19	.. .. ..	Further unsuccessful Rumanian attacks between Casin and Susitsa valleys. Town of Nanesti and bridgehead of Fundeni carried by enemy.	.. .. ..
20	.. .. ..	Germans take Fundeni (on the Sereth).	.. .. ..

ASIATIC AND EGYPTIAN THEATRES.	NAVAL AND OVERSEAS OPERATIONS.	POLITICAL, &c.	1917. Jan.
.. .. ..	.. .. ..	.. .. ..	12
.. .. ..	Italians severely defeat rebels near Zuara (Tripoli).	.. .. ..	13
.. ..	.. .. ..	Provisional Council of State meets at Warsaw.	14
.. .. ..	.. .. ..	.. .. ..	15
.. .. ..	.. .. ..	Despatch from Mr. Balfour in amplification of Allies' Note to U.S.A. communicated to American Government ([5]). Complete acceptance of Allies' ultimatum by Greek Government.	16
.. .. ..	British Admiralty announces that German raider in the Atlantic has sunk 10 British and 2 French ships, and captured 2 British ships.	Gen. Bieliaev appointed Russian Minister of War in place of Gen. Shuvaiev.	17
.. .. ..	.. .. ..	Re-opening of Duma and of Council of the Empire postponed by Russian Government from Jan. 25 to Feb. 27.	18
Right bank of Tigris below Kut cleared of enemy after 10 days' continuous fighting.	.. .. ..	Great explosion at Silvertown, E. London ; 69 killed, 400 injured. Germany initiates negotiations with Mexico, Japan and U.S.A. (v. 1.3.17).	19
.. .. ..	Official despatch from Ger. E. Africa reports progress in Rufiji valley region and W. of Mahenge. Gen. A. R. Hoskins succeeds Gen. Smuts.	The Tsar addresses a rescript to Prince Golitzin laying down the main lines of his policy ([6]).	20

1917. Jan.	WESTERN FRONT.	EASTERN FRONT.	SOUTHERN FRONT.
21	Repulse of German attacks N. of the Bois des Caurières (Verdun).	.. .. ..	.. .. ..
22	.. .. ..	Bulgarians cross southern arm of Danube near Tulcea (Dobruja).	.. .. ..
23	.. .. ..	German counter-offensive between Lake Babit and Tirul Marsh; Russians lose much of recently captured ground. Bulgarians driven back across Danube near Tulcea.	.. .. ..
24	.. .. ..	Further German advance in hard fighting near Lake Babit. Russians fall back.	.. .. ..
25	Suffolk coast (Southwold) shelled at night by enemy vessel; no casualties. Germans attack at four points N.W. of Verdun, and carry mile of French trenches at Hill 304.	Fierce fighting near Lake Babit; Russian counter-attacks fail.	.. .. ..
26	French regain most of ground lost near Verdun.	.. .. ..	.. .. ..
27	British take German position and 350 prisoners near Le Transloy.	Russians carry enemy positions between Kimpolung and Jacobeny (Bukovina), and take 1,218 prisoners.	.. .. ..
28	.. . ..	.. .. ..	.. .. ..
29	.. .. ..	.. .. ..	.. ..

ASIATIC AND EGYPTIAN THEATRES.	NAVAL AND OVERSEAS OPERATIONS.	POLITICAL, &c.	1917. Jan.
.. .. ..	.. .. ..	.. .. ..	21
.. .. ..	Two destroyer actions by night in North Sea. One German destroyer sunk and one (V69) towed damaged into Ymuiden. One British destroyer lost.	President Wilson addresses U.S. Senate on America's attitude towards peace (7).	22
.. .. ..	.. .. ..	Labour Party approves acceptance of office by Labour Members in Ministry.	23
.. .. ..	German force of 289 officers and men surrenders at Likuju (Ger. E. Africa).	Greek Government formally apologises to Allies for events of Dec. 1, 1916.	24
Enemy trenches captured on Hai salient S.W. of Kut ; Turkish counterattacks recover a little ground.	H.M.S. " Laurentic," auxiliary cruiser, sunk by mine off Ireland.	.. .. ..	25
British recapture lost trenches near Kut.	.. .. ..	Compulsory loan or sale to Treasury of certain foreign securities.	26
.. .. ..	S.s. " Artist " torpedoed in a gale by German submarine ; crew left to perish.	.. .. ..	27
Considerable progress by British on right bank of Tigris S.W. of Kut.	.. .. ..	.. .. ..	28
Progress continued near Kut.	Announcement of laying of New British minefield from Yorkshire to Jutland.	Allies' flags formally saluted at Athens.	29

1917. Jan.	WESTERN FRONT.	EASTERN FRONT.	SOUTHERN FRONT.
30	S. of Leintrey (Lorraine) French raiders penetrate to German 2nd line, destroying the garrison and taking prisoners. Further small success S.W. of Leintrey.	Between Tirul swamp and River Aa (Riga) strong German attack succeeds in one sector, 900 Russians taken prisoner. E. of Jakobeny (S. Bukovina) Russians assault and capture important hill fortifications taking over 1,000 prisoners.	.. .. ..
31	On the Ancre near Beaucourt and W. of Serre German attacks fail. Total of German prisoners taken by British in France during January is 1,228, including 27 Officers.	E. of Jakobeny Germans attack three times by night against previous lost positions, but are repulsed with heavy loss.	.. .. ..
Feb. 1	Near Wytschaete Germans in white overalls attack British positions, but are beaten off with heavy casualties. Near Grandcourt (Somme) strong enemy attempt to rush British trenches driven off. N.E. of Gueudecourt (Somme) British raid enemy trenches, taking 56 prisoners.	15 miles S. of Halicz (Gal.) Germans in white overalls break through Russian lines, but are ejected by counter-attack.	.. .. ..
2	.. .. ..	E. of Kalutsem high road, (W. of Riga) Germans launch several attacks, repulsed.	.. .. ..
3	E. of Beaucourt (N. of the Ancre) British line advanced 500 yards on a front of 1,200 yards ; over 100 prisoners taken, and counter-attacks repulsed. First Portuguese contingent arrives in France.	.. .. ..	.. .. ..

ASIATIC AND EGYPTIAN THEATRES.	NAVAL AND OVERSEAS OPERATIONS.	POLITICAL, &C.	1917. Jan.
.. .. ..	.. .. ..	Allied delegates to Russia hold preliminary meetings at Petrograd on military and financial questions. Norway forbids submarines in territorial waters.	30
.. .. ..	Germany declares to all neutrals " Unrestricted naval warfare," i.e., within the war zone. German submarines will sink both combatant and neutral shipping at sight from Feb. 1 (⁸).	Germany announces that the traffic of British hospital ships between Great Britain, France and Belgium will no longer be tolerated. The false reason assigned is misuse of the Red Cross (⁹).	31
Near Kut, E. of the Tigris-Hai junction, British capture all but last line of Turkish trenches, taking 166 prisoners, and repulsing a strong counter-attack.	Dutch s.s. " Gamma " attacked and sunk by German submarine. Dutch Government request an explanation.	Germany's manifesto to sink all ships in the War Zones, taking effect to-day, causes temporary suspension of neutral sailings. The press of U.S.A. takes bellicose view. Norway forbids foreign submarines to use her waters.	**Feb.** 1
.. .. ..	Off Anatolian coast Russian warships sink 18 small Turkish vessels. Bruges harbour bombed by British naval airmen.	Stambul University proposes German Emperor as recipient of Nobel Peace Prize. Appeal to nation for food economy by Lord Devonport.	2
.. .. ..	S.s. " Housatonic ", American grain ship, torpedoed off Scilly Isles. Crew rescued by British ship.	President Wilson severs diplomatic relations between U.S.A. and Germany (¹⁰). Count Bernstorff receives his passports and Mr. Gerard is recalled from Berlin. U.S.A. demands immediate release of over 60 Americans taken prisoner by German Atlantic raider.	3

1917. Feb.	WESTERN FRONT.	EASTERN FRONT.	SOUTHERN FRONT.
4	Near Beaucourt four severe counter-attacks against new British positions defeated. N.E. of Gueudecourt both sides make raids: British take 500 yards of hostile trenches and over 100 prisoners.	Between Tirul Swamp and R. Aa (Riga), Germans make several abortive attacks. E. of Kalutsem road, Germans again attack and take positions, but are ejected.	.. .. ..
5	.. .. ..	10 miles S. of Kieselin (Volhynia) enemy attacks Russian positions, but is repulsed.	Italian line heavily attacked by the Austrians in various sectors. All attacks beaten off.
6	Near Grandcourt (S. of the Ancre) the British advance and occupy 1,000 yards of enemy trench without opposition.	The Sereth river (S.E. of Focsani) being frozen, enemy attacks lightly, but is driven back.	.. .. ..
7	Grandcourt evacuated by the Germans, British occupy the village.	.. ..	.. ..
8	Sailly-Saillisel ridge (Hill 153, Somme) taken by the British with 78 prisoners. From Grandcourt British advance on both banks of the Ancre.	.. ..	.. ..
9	E. of the Meuse an enemy attack fails under the French fire. E. of Sailly-Saillisel Germans counter-attack new British positions, but are repulsed.	.. ..	.. E. of Gorizia, Austrian attack enters certain Italian positions. Austrians claim 1,000 prisoners.

ASIATIC AND EGYPTIAN THEATRES.	NAVAL AND OVERSEAS OPERATIONS.	POLITICAL; &c.	1917. Feb.
At Siwa (Western Egypt) British expedition locates and defeats the forces of the Senussi leader, Said Ahmed.	In Manila Bay German crews wreck the engine-rooms of 9 German steamers.	The U.S.A. demand for release of imprisoned Americans acceded to. Sultan of Turkey accepts resignation of the Grand Vizier, Said Halim ; Talaat Pasha forms new Cabinet ([11]). U.S.A. Note to Neutrals suggesting similar action to its own.	4
Siwa evacuated by the Senussi and entered by British, who capture Munasib Pass, cutting off enemy retreat.	.. .. ..	Referring to the break with U.S.A., Germany says : " The struggle is for our existence. For us there can be no retreat." Switzerland in a message to U.S.A. decides not to break off diplomatic relations with Germany. Russian Conference on future of Poland announced.	5
Near Kut, the Turks evacuate the S. bank of the Tigris E. of the Hai-Tigris junction ; also forward positions W. of the Hai. Second phase of Battle of Kut begins.	S.s. " California," Anchor Line, sunk by submarine without warning, 43 killed and missing.	New Air Board formed with Lord Cowdray as chairman. Mr. N. Chamberlain announces his scheme for National Service.	6
.. .. ..	.. .. ..	Several neutral States refuse Mr. Wilson's invitation to act in conjunction with the U.S. ([12]). Parliament opened by the King.	7
.. .. ..	A British destroyer (old type) sunk by a mine in the Channel ; 5 survivors.	Neutral sources report that Mr. Gerard is being held hostage in Berlin and not allowed to communicate with U.S.A. Spain replies to Germany.	8
Report on Senussi operations issued ([13]).	.. .. ..	German Government admit having prevented Mr. Gerard communicating with U.S.A., stating falsely that Count Bernstorff has not been allowed communication with Germany. Mr. Gerard receives his passports.	9

1917. Feb.	WESTERN FRONT.	EASTERN FRONT.	SOUTHERN FRONT.
10	S. of Serre Hill (N. of Ancre) British capture strong system of hostile trenches on front of 1,250 yards, 215 prisoners taken. Successful Allied raids at Givenchy, Neuville, Grandcourt, La Bassée, Neuve Chapelle, Auberive, (Champ.), and Lunéville. German airmen bomb Dunkirk, Amiens and Nancy.	..	At Valona 2 out of 3 Austrian hydroplanes captured by Italian airmen.
11	N. of the Ancre British take about 600 yards of enemy trenches near the Beaucourt-Puisieux road. S. of Serre Hill enemy attack our new positions, but are decimated.	S. of Halicz small hostile force crosses the Dniester on the ice, but is driven back by a counter-attack.	E. of Gorizia the Italians recover the trenches taken by the Austrians, and make 100 prisoners.
12	S. of Serre several more unsuccessful German attacks. E. of Souchez British raid takes 48 prisoners. Other successful raids at Neuville, Loos and Ypres.	Near Jakobeny (S. Bukovina) the Germans attack and take the new Russian positions and over 1,200 prisoners.	E. of Monastir, Hill 1050 attacked by the Germans, who gain a footing at several points in the Italian front lines.
13	S.E. of Grandcourt British capture a strong point. N.E. of Arras British raid takes 40 prisoners.	Near Jakobeny Russian counter-attacks repulsed.	.. .. ..
14	12 miles N.W. of Compiègne the French carry out successful large-scale raid.	Between Zloczow and Tarnopol (N. Galicia), Germans report successful great raid, taking 6 Russian officers and 275 men prisoners.	E. of Monastir, Italians counter-attack and re-establish their line.

ASIATIC AND EGYPTIAN THEATRES.	NAVAL AND OVERSEAS OPERATIONS.	POLITICAL, &c.	1917. Feb.
Near Kut Turks deliver 4 unsuccessful attacks on British right flank during the night. At Kut British carry the liquorice factory, and establish a new line on a 6,000 yard front, pressing back the Turks from 800-1,200 yards.	.. .. ..	Peru cables protest to Berlin. China sends energetic protest to Germany, and threatens to break off diplomatic relations. Chile sends a reply to Germany refusing to recognise the blockade, and retaining a free hand in case of damage to Chilean ships. Germany declares "period of grace" for neutral shipping expires. Mr. Gerard leaves Berlin.	10
At Kut, British resume attack on R. bank of Tigris, hemming the Turks in on the Dahra bend, taking all but the last line of trenches.	The U.S. s.s. "Lyman M. Law" sunk by a submarine off Sardinia.	German Government state that the restraint placed on Mr. Gerard was an error of minor officials. Swiss Minister sends a message from Germany to U.S.A. suggesting a discussion on ways and means of preventing war.	11
.. .. ..	.. .. ..	Mr. Gerard and staff arrive in Switzerland. The Netherlands Government representative assumes charge of British interests in Germany.	12
.. .. ..	The White Star liner "Afric," of 12,000 tons, reported sunk. Lord Lytton, for the Admiralty, says counter measures against submarine menace have already achieved considerable success.	President Wilson declines to entertain negotiations with Germany unless the Proclamation of ruthless submarine warfare is withdrawn. At Petrograd, Lord Milner, at close of Allied Conference, says much good done in bringing about closer co-operation between Entente countries.	13
.. .. ..	Bruges harbour again bombed by British naval airmen.	The German Ambassador to the U.S.A., with staff, sails from Hoboken in the s.s. "Frederik VIII."	14

1917. Feb.	WESTERN FRONT.	EASTERN FRONT.	SOUTHERN FRONT.
15	Attempted German raids near Loos, W. of Messines, and N.E. of Ypres, break down under our fire. W. of Maisons de Champagne, German attack penetrates French salient, gaining several lines of trenches and taking prisoner 21 officers and 837 men. Interview with Sir D. Haig published.	.. .. ..	.. .. ..
16	At Boulogne German airship drops bombs on town and harbour, doing only slight damage.	.. .. ..	.. .. ..
17	S. of the Ancre British penetrate 1,000 yds. into enemy positions on a front of 1½ miles. N. of the Ancre British take hostile trenches on a 1,000 yd. front. In these two operations 773 prisoners taken. N.W. of Altkirch (Alsace) French raid enemy salient, inflicting heavy loss.	On Lavkassa river (S.W. of Dvinsk) Germans clad in white raid Russian lines, taking about 50 prisoners.	.. .. ..
18	N. of the Ancre strong enemy attack on new British positions above Baillescourt Farm caught by concentrated fire and smashed.	In the Trotus valley (Moldavia), Russian surprise attack captures strong enemy position on high ground.	Junction of French and Italian troops in S. Albania, isolating Greece from Central Powers.
19	S. of Le Transloy (Somme) Germans using *flammenwerfer* capture a British advanced post and 30 prisoners. E. of Ypres British do great damage to enemy positions, and take 114 prisoners in a big raid.	.. .. ..	.. .. ..
20	.. .. ..	.. .. ..	.. .. ..

ASIATIC AND EGYPTIAN THEATRES.	NAVAL AND OVERSEAS OPERATIONS.	POLITICAL, &c.	1917. Feb.
Decisive day of Battle of Kut. Turks driven from R. bank of Tigris.	Italian transport, bound for Salonika, sunk by submarine W. of Matapan.	British Government take over all coal mines in the U.K. for the period of the war. In Brussels, the U.S. Minister is ordered by the Germans to lower the U.S. flag over the Legation. Scandinavian Government's protest v. German submarine warfare.	15
W. of Kut, British capture remaining Turkish positions in the Dahra bend, and take nearly 2,000 prisoners.	Bruges and G h i s t e l l e s bombed by British naval airmen.	Close of War Loan. Opening of S. African Parliament.	16
Near Kut, British progress on S. bank of Tigris. On N. bank an attack on the Sanna - i - Yat positions fails.	.. .. ..	Entente Powers call the Government's attention to hostile attitude of Greek press. Greek Government search private dwellings for hidden arms ([14]). New Australian Government.	17
.. .. ..	.. .. ..	.. .. ..	18
.. .. ..	S.s. " Worcestershire " sunk.	The new British War Loan estimated to be going to reach over £700,000,000 in new money. Government decide to revise exemption certificates for men under 31.	19
At Nakhl and Bir el Hassana (between Suez and Akaba) 2 small Turkish posts surprised and scattered by British.	.. .. ..	President Wilson asks for powers from Congress " to enforce the obligations imposed by the laws of nations and by American statutes." Imperial Preference Report issued.	20

1917. Feb.	WESTERN FRONT.	EASTERN FRONT.	SOUTHERN FRONT.
21	Germans begin to withdraw in front of Serre.	Near Jakobeny the Russians repulse a strong German attack.	At Tarvis (Trentino) Italian artillery destroy Austrian railhead.
22	E. of Vermelles and S. of Neuve Chapelle hostile raids repulsed with heavy loss. N. of Gueudecourt British take enemy trench and 30 prisoners. British push forward cautiously.	.. .. ..	.. .. ..
23	British follow-up retreating Germans.	N.W. of Ocna (Moldavia) the Russians lose the heights of Magyaros, and 1,000 prisoners.	.. .. ..
24	**Great German withdrawal** in full swing. The villages of Serre, Miraumont, Petit Miraumont, Pys and Warlencourt evacuated. (¹⁵).	.. .. ..	.. .. ..
25	German retreat continues on the Ancre. British advance extends over a front of 11 miles from S. of Gommecourt to E. of Gueudecourt, and reaches an extreme depth of 3 miles. Successful raids at Monchy-au-Bois. Lens and in Champagne. Naval air-raid on Brebach (near Metz).	.. .. ..	.. .. ..
26	N. and S. of the Ancre British make further progress, capturing the village of Le Barque (S.W. of Bapaume).	.. .. ..	.. .. ..

Asiatic and Egyptian Theatres.	Naval and Overseas Operations.	Political, &c.	1917. Feb.
.. .. ..	Off Cartagena (S.E. Spain) spare parts for submarines are discovered in a buoy. French transport "Athos" sunk by a submarine in the Mediterranean. Transport "Mendi," S. African labour contingent, sunk in collision.	New British Blockade orders issued. Vessels sailing to and from neutral countries, which have access to the enemy, must put into a British port for examination, or be liable to capture.	21
At Sanna-i-Yat, General Maude launches fresh attack, capturing two lines of enemy trenches.	7 Dutch ships sailing from Falmouth are attacked by submarine U3, in spite of German guarantee of security; four are sunk.	In U.S.A., war tension appears critical. German agents instigating many disturbances. Turkey declares her agreement with Germany on policy of unrestricted submarine warfare. Formation of "Labour Corps."	22
Above Kut British cross the Tigris at the Shumran bend, taking 544 prisoners. Simultaneously at Sanna-i-Yat our troops storm and take the third and fourth line of Turkish trenches.	Submarine sinks 1 Norwegian and 4 British steamers, including the Holt liner "Perseus."	.. .. ..	23
Kut evacuated by the Turks, and whole of enemy positions from Kut to Sanna-i-Yat taken with 1,730 prisoners. Turks retreat toward Baghdad (¹⁶).	.. .. ..	Mr. Gerard is received at Madrid by the King of Spain.	24
Turkish retreat continues, closely pursued by British cavalry. Turks destroy much war material.	Margate and Broadstairs bombarded for 10 minutes by German destroyers. Slight damage. 3 killed, 1 wounded. "Laconia" s.s. (Cunarder) sunk. 4 Americans drowned. The "overt act" for which President Wilson was waiting.	New British War Loan subscriptions amount to (new money) £1,000,312,950.	25
Turkish rearguard covers the retreat 15 miles from Kut. H.M.S. "Firefly" recaptured.	.. .. ..	War Conference at Calais. Wilson asks Congress to establish armed neutrality and arm merchant vessels. British Govt. requisitions Dutch ships in British ports	26

1917. Feb.	WESTERN FRONT.	EASTERN FRONT.	SOUTHERN FRONT.
27	Ligny (E. of Le Barque) and Gommecourt occupied by the British. Also the Western and southern defences of Puisieux. E. of Armentières British raiders seriously damage 3 lines of enemy trenches and take 17 prisoners.	Near Jakobeny the Germans take several Russian positions on high ground and 1,300 prisoners.	At Salonika German airmen bombard Allied camps. One enemy machine shot down.
28	Thilloy, Gommecourt, Puisieux and Sailly-Saillisel taken by British.	Rumanian counter-attacks in Bukovina partially successful.	Austrian attacks on Asiago Plateau and N. of Gorizia repulsed.
March 1	G.H.Q. reports capture of 2,133 German prisoners and 11 villages during past month. German air losses during February twice those of Allies. Aeroplane raid on Broadstairs : 6 injured.	..	..	..	..	..	..
2	British line advanced N.W. of Puisieux and N. of Warlencourt (Ancre). Unsuccessful enemy counter-attacks from near Bapaume.	Fighting continues in S. Bukovina. Activity round Riga and on Narajowka river (Gal.), where Germans claim success.	..	..	..
3	British progress N. of Puisieux and E. of Gommecourt. German War Minister's announcement re prisoners under fire ([21]).	Russian gas attack N. of Lake Naroch. German attack S.W. of Brzezany (Gal.) and near Voruchin (W. of Lutsk).	Fierce fighting near Monastir ; Italian troops in action.

ASIATIC AND EGYPTIAN THEATRES.	NAVAL AND OVERSEAS OPERATIONS.	POLITICAL, &c.	1917. Feb.
Pursuit of Turks continued, 7,000 prisoners taken.	.. .. ..	The German Chancellor proclaims great success of submarine campaign, and justifies breaking of Germany's agreement with U.S.A., saying it was conditional on America insisting on Great Britain respecting international law concerning " Freedom of the Seas." Reopening of Duma.	27
Turkish losses in Mesopotamia in last 3 months estimated at over 20,000.	French destroyer " Cassini " torpedoed in Mediterranean.	Allied Ministers present Memo. to Chinese Govt. ([17]). Particulars of German plot re Mexico and Japan pub. in U.S.A. (v.19.1) ([19]).	28
			March.
.. .. ..	First weekly statement of shipping, sailings, arrivals and losses issued ([18]). Germany announces end of safe period for sailing vessels in Atlantic.	Speech by Herr Zimmermann on torpedoing of neutrals ([20]). Government of India's offer of £100,000,000 towards cost of war accepted.	1
Turks fall back towards Baghdad, one column from Hamadan and one to Dauletabad. Russians occupy Hamadan.	.. .. ..	U.S. Congress passes resolution for arming merchant-ships. State Council, Warsaw, reported organising national army against Russia, using Polish legions as cadres. French recruits of 1918 called up.	2
.. ..		Governments of Japan and Mexico deny having received proposals from Germany ([22]). In U.S. Senate obstructionist minority prevents Vote on President's armed neutrality policy. 15,000 British women volunteer for National Service in three days. Mr. Wilson takes the oath as President of the United States.	3

N

1917. March.	WESTERN FRONT.	EASTERN FRONT.	SOUTHERN FRONT.
4	French *coup-de-main* between Oise and Aisne, S. of Mouvron. Germans gain footing in Caurières Wood (Verdun). Enemy front and support lines captured E. of Bouchavesnes (N. of Somme). E. of Gommecourt British continue advance.	Russian gas attack near Krevo (S.E. of Vilna). On the Sereth Rumanians bombard region of Calieni.	Enemy attack in force E. of Gorizia driven back with heavy loss. Austrians massing in Trentino. Italians occupy heights in Costabella group (Avisio).
5	German attack W. of Pont-à-Mousson fails; attempts to recapture Bouchavesnes repulsed. British progress on Ancre front towards Bapaume Ridge.	.. .. ..	Sharp fighting in the Dolomites.
6	British line extends S. of Somme to neighbourhood of Reims, twice the length of a year before.	Night attack on German positions S. of Brzezany fails.	.. .. ..
7	.. .. ..	.. .. ..	.. .. ..
8	In Champagne, French regain most of salient lost on Feb. 15 between Butte de Mesnil and Maisons de Champagne. Slight British advance in Ancre valley. Great air activity. Five enemy raids against British positions N. of Wulverghem (Messines).	Rumanians lose three heights (late Russian positions) N.W. of Ocna (Moldavia). Enemy repulsed near Mitau (Riga).	Several days' shelling of Monastir reported.

Asiatic and Egyptian Theatres.	Naval and Overseas Operations.	Political, &c.	1917. March.
.. .. ..	Naval aeroplanes bomb Brebach (Saarbrücken).	Chinese cabinet crisis due to disagreement as to policy with regard to Germany. " Flemish " deputation received by German Chancellor.	4
Engagement with Turkish rearguard at Laj (9 miles S.E. of Ctesiphon). Russians occupy Kangavar, S. of Hamadan. Turks abandon strong position W. of Shalal (Sinai Peninsula).	.. .. ..	Austrian reply to U.S. memorandum re new submarine warfare ([23]). Pres. Wilson's inaugural address at opening of his second term ([24]). Lord Milner returns from Allied Conference at Petrograd ([25]). British food items ([26]).	5
British cavalry 14 miles from Baghdad.	.. .. ..	U.S. Supreme Court decides " Appam " case in favour of British owners.	6
Three Turkish columns in W. Persia continue retreat, converging on Baghdad road at Kangavar ; main column thrown from Assadabad Pass by pursuing Russians. Proclamation by Ulema of Mecca to the Faithful published ([27]).	.. .. ..	Recruiting for W.A.A.C. temporarily completed. 114,803 enrolled for National Service to date. National manifestation at Sorbonne, Paris, for triumph of right. 1920 class called up in Austria.	7
Tigris bridged and Turks driven from position 6 miles from Baghdad. British effect surprise crossing of Diala river (Mesop.). Russians on road from Hamadan rout Turks, who withdraw to Hajiabad.	Norwegian relief ship " Storstad " torpedoed.	Civil mobilisation report tabled in French Senate : civilians of both sexes, 17 to 60, included. Speech by Sir E. Carson ([28]). Interim report of Dardanelles Commission issued ([29]). British Government accepts Nizam of Hyderabad's offer of £100,000 towards anti - submarine campaign. Wireless communication between U.S.A. and Germany suspended. Pres. Wilson decides to arm American ships against submarines. Death of Count Zeppelin.	8

1917. March.	WESTERN FRONT.	EASTERN FRONT.	SOUTHERN FRONT.
9	French repulse attacks in Champagne and N. of Bois des Caurières.	.. .. ..	.. .. ..
10	British capture Irles (Ancre) : 292 prisoners.	Rumanians and Russians counter-attack to regain Magyaros Ridge (Moldavia) lost on March 8.	.. .. ..
11	Continuous air fighting ; loss of 26 Allied and enemy machines reported.	Russian gas attack E. of Mitau.	**Spring campaign in Macedonia begins :** Allies attack N. and N.W. of Monastir.
12	French gain ground in E. Champagne. British raid near Arras. Soissons bombarded with incendiary shells.	Successful German raids near Zloczow-Tarnopol railway, near Brzezany and on Narajowka (Gal.).	British advance on Doiran front.
13	British occupy Loupart Wood and Grévillers, 1½ miles from Bapaume. Enemy abandons ground E. and N.E. of Gommecourt. Lively fighting N.E. of Soissons. Germans fail to retake Hill 185. Fighting in St. Mihiel region (S.E. of Verdun).	Bulgarians bombard Galatz from the Danube.	Field hospitals at Vertekop (Serbia) bombed: two British nurses and others killed. British line S.W. of Doiran advanced 1,000 yards.

Asiatic and Egyptian Theatres.	Naval and Overseas Operations.	Political, &c.	1917. March.
Passage of Diala forced: British advance on Baghdad. Russians attack retreating Turks near Sivas (Asia Minor). Russian scouts advance S.W. from Sakis; Sinnah (Persian Kurdistan) captured. General retreat of Turks in Persia. Russian troops invite Persian Govt. to resume possession of towns occupied by Russians in Persia.	.. .. ..	British loan of £40,000,000 to Rumania. World shortage of wheat foreshadowed in French Chamber. Lord Devonport sanctions maximum food prices. Food prolem at Petrograd becomes urgent. Dutch authorities officially notified by Germany that safety is guaranteed for shipping along a strip of North Sea from Holland to Norway.	9
Turks forced back to within three miles of Baghdad.	.. .. ..	.. .. ..	10
British enter Baghdad after three days' fighting. Cavalry occupy Kazimain, 4 miles N.	.. .. ..	Strikers' food demonstrations and rioting increase in Petrograd; Govt. agrees to hand over food question to local bodies. Chinese Parliament votes for breach with Germany. Sugar-cards in Paris.	11
Italians occupy Bukamez (W. of Tripoli).	American steamer " Algonquin " torpedoed without warning.	Tsar orders suspension of Duma and Council of the Empire. Three Guard and several line regiments join Parliamentary party. **Russian Revolution begins: Provisional Government formed** ([30]). Canada's 3rd War Loan launched. U.S. State Dept. rules that merchant-vessels armed fore and aft may clear from U.S. ports. Speech by Gen. Smuts on landing in England ([31]).	12
Russians take Kermanshah (Persia) after two days' fighting. Another column approaches Bana (140 miles N.W. of Kermanshah). British 30 miles N. of Baghdad.	Norwegian relief ship " Lars Fostencs," carrying grain, torpedoed outside blockade zone.	Gen. Smuts sworn of the Privy Council. Statement on mastery of air in Commons ([32]). Government intends to stand by new Indian cotton duties. Impending cabinet crisis in Austria. Revolutionary movement at Petrograd continues ([33]). China **breaks off relations** with Germany.	13

1917. March.	WESTERN FRONT.	EASTERN FRONT.			SOUTHERN FRONT.		
14	British advance W. and S.W. of Bapaume and S. of Achiet-le-Petit (Ancre). Progress towards Les Essarts on extreme left.	..	..	..	Monastir front lively: Austrians attack W. and Italians advance E. of town.		
15	British progress on 2½ mile front between St. Pierre Vaast Wood and Saillisel (N. of Somme). German attack E. of Achiet-le-Petit. French progress between Avre and Oise.	..	..	..	..	..	..
16	Big advance on Somme: British occupy St. Pierre Vaast Wood, dominating Péronne. Zeppelin raid on Kent and Sussex : no casualties. Aeroplanes over Westgate.	..	..	..	Austrians destroy Italian defences in San Pellegrino valley (Dolomites) and occupy positions there.		
17	British take Bapaume and 7 other villages after hard fighting ; advance S. of Somme and occupy Fresnes and 6 other villages. Germans abandon line between Andechy and Oise held by them for two years. French enter Roye and Lassigny. Frankfurt bombed in reprisal for destruction of Bapaume. Aeroplane raid on Kent : no casualties.	..	..	..	..	.	..

Asiatic and Egyptian Theatres.	Naval and Overseas Operations.	Political, &c.	1917. March.
British 35 miles N.E. of Baghdad. Fighting on W. bank of Tigris. Turks hurrying N. to position at Mushaidiya (20 miles N. of Baghdad).	.. .. ..	Moscow, Kharkov and Odessa declare for Provisional Government; Grand Duke Cyril with his sailors place themselves under M. Rodzianko's orders. German minister at Pekin handed his passports. Gen. Lyautey, French Minister of War, resigns. Both Houses accept India's war contribution of £100,000,000 and authorise increase in cotton duties.	14
Turkish concentration in Asia Minor contemplated. British take Mushaidiya ; Turks in full flight towards Samarra (Tigris).	British T.B. mined in Channel.	Tsar Nicholas abdicates and resigns rights of his son (³⁴); preparations for calling a Constituent Assembly based on universal suffrage (³⁵). Sixth German War Loan floated. U.S. railwaymen threaten strike. Vote of Credit in Commons. French Chamber pass summer-time bill.	15
Russians dislodge Turks from summit of Naleshkian (Persia) and occupy Alliabad, engaging enemy near Kerind.	.. .. ..	British labour leaders send telegram of sympathy to Russian labour party. Winter Palace declared State property. Speech by M. Kerenski in Duma (³⁶). Turkish Senate approves agreement with Baghdad Railway Co. Acute potato famine in England. Sheikh - ul - Islam again proclaims Holy War ; general mobilisation of Turks ordered.	16
British stated to be 35 miles N. of Baghdad. Russians occupy Kerind on |Tehran road after heavy fighting and continue to pursue Turks.	Enemy destroyers shell Ramsgate and sink a destroyer.	Germans send many prisoners into war zone as " reprisal." M. Briand and cabinet resign owing to Lyautey crisis. Albert Hall meeting in favour of national service for women.	17

1917. March.	WESTERN FRONT.	EASTERN FRONT.	SOUTHERN FRONT.
18	British occupy Chaulnes and Péronne and advance on 45-mile front from Chaulnes to Arras. Great air activity. French occupy Noyon, Nesle, Guiscard, etc., and advance on 40-mile front. Zeppelin brought down at Compiègne. Germans launch heavy attack against Avocourt-Mort Homme sector (Verdun). Ramsgate etc., shelled : no casualties.	.. .. ..	After 5 days' fighting French capture 1,200 Bulgarians, a mile of trenches N.E., and village of Svegovo, N., of Monastir.
19	40 more villages in British hands; over 170 taken by Allies in 3 days. French advance beyond Ham (Somme) and take Chauny (Oise). Heavy German attacks between Avocourt Wood and Hill 304 (Verdun) repulsed.	.. .. ..	Continued fighting near Monastir. Germans reoccupy railway station at Poroj, previously entered by British. Renewed activity in Pass of Tonale, in areas of Pasubio, Asiago, Tolmino, E. of Gorizia and on Carso.
20	Despite bad weather, British advance towards Cambrai and St. Quentin; 14 villages occupied. Department of Oise entirely liberated. French take Tergnier and cross St. Quentin Canal. Historic ruins of Château de Coucy blown up by Germans. French carry railway junction of Jussy (E. of Ham). German casualties reported at 4,148,163 (to end of February).	.. ..	.. ..

Asiatic and Egyptian Theatres.	Naval and Overseas Operations.	Political, &c.	1917. March.
Russians enter Van (Armenia).	German destroyers fire on Kent coast towns (Ramsgate, etc.) : no casualties. Sinking of three U.S. steamers, 14,600 tons gross shipping, reported.	Russian Press urges loyalty to Allied cause ; commission inquires into delinquencies of former ministers ; food question, in hands of Zemstva, etc., becomes less acute.	18
Proclamation by Sir Stanley Maude to people of Baghdad, promising freedom for Arabs. Capture of Feluja (Euphr.), Deltawa and Sindia.	French battleship " Danton " torpedoed in Mediterranean : 296 lost.	British Government opens relations with M. Miliukov, but Government not officially recognised. Committee of Workmen's and Soldiers' Delegates orders resumption of work in Petrograd. Attempted murder of M. Kerenski. Pres. Wilson settles U.S. railway strike ; 8-hours day legalised. Financial statement by Mr. Bonar Law in Commons ([37]).	19
.. .. ..	British hospital ship " Asturias " torpedoed without warning during night of 20-21 : 41 lost.	Ex-Tsar reviews troops, urging loyalty to Government and prosecution of war. Appointment of Grand Duke Nicholas to supreme command of army annulled. Casualties at Petrograd 2,500. Proclamation by Provisional Government ([34]). American note to General Carranza (Mexico) pubd. ([39]). New French Ministry under M. Ribot ([40]). First meeting of Imperial War Cabinet ; Ministry of National Service formed. Important developments in Board of Trade ([11]) Dardanelles debate in Commons ; Mr. Asquith defends Lord Kitchener.	20

1917. March·	WESTERN FRONT.	EASTERN FRONT.	SOUTHERN FRONT.
21	British advance S.E. and E. of Péronne; occupy 40 more villages, approaching St. Quentin. Progress towards Cambrai continues. French force passage of Somme Canal and progress N. of Soissons.	Germans active near Lida (Beresina), in Galicia and on Rumanian front.	Fighting by French, lasting for over a week, frees Monastir from daily bombardment. Enemy makes serious counter-attack but is repulsed.
22	Increased enemy resistance on British front from W. of St. Quentin to S. of Arras. Heavy snowstorms. French progress gress N. of Tergnier (Oise) and N. of Soissons, despite stiffening defence.	Russians retake lost trenches near Lida (Vilna).	.. .. ..
23	French success at Artemps (S. of St. Quentin). Oise valley and La Fère flooded by enemy. New detachments cross Ailette; progress N. of Soissons. Enemy thrown back to Grand Seraucourt. Some fighting on British front between Arras and Bapaume-Cambrai road.	Russians lose trenches W. of Moinesci, near River Trotus (Rumanian front). Germans massing troops on Riga-Dvinsk front seriously menacing Petrograd.	Bombs on Mudros from German airship.
24	British take Roisel E. of Péronne. French occupy right bank of Oise from N. of Vaudreuil to suburbs of La Fère and progress on E. bank of Ailette Canal.	Russian armies declare their loyalty to the Provisional Government.	.. .. ..
25	Hard fighting S. of St. Quentin. French reach neighbourhood of Coucy-le-Château. 395 shells on Reims.	Gen. Alexeiev, C.-i.C. of Russian army. German attack with gas in Dvinsk region repulsed.	.. .. ..

ASIATIC AND EGYPTIAN THEATRES.	NAVAL AND OVERSEAS OPERATIONS.	POLITICAL, &c.	1917. March.
Russians continue to pursue Turks from Sakiz (Persia) towards Kermanshah.	.. .. ..	Imperial War Conference inaugurated by Premier. Ex-Tsar and Tsaritsa deprived of liberty ; general political amnesty. Munitions and food problem in Petrograd being satisfactorily dealtwith. Proposed 8-hours day. Vote of confidence in French Chamber. French Military Mission leaves for New York.	21
.. .. ..	" Moewe," German raider, reported returned to a home port after second cruise in Atlantic, having sunk 111,000 tons of British shipping. American steamer " Healdton " sunk.	Ex-Tsar reaches Tsarskoye-Selo. Great Britain, France and Italy recognise Provisional Govt. in Russia. Death penalty in latter abolished. Speech in Reichstag by Dr. Helfferich (Interior) ([12]). Archangel route in danger zone. British danger zone in North Sea extended towards Holland and Jutland from April 2.	22
.. .. ..	.. .. ..	Telegram from Mr. Lloyd George to Russian Prime Minister ([13]). Lord Devonport on food consumption.	23
.. .. ..	.. .. ..	France protests to neutrals against barbarity and devastation by Germans in evacuated French territory. Allied ministers return to Athens. Greek Govt. demands withdrawal of Italian troops from Epirus.	24
.. . ..	French take Oujjan (Marocco). Dunkirk bombarded from sea.	Russian Provisional Govt. accepts responsibilities of former régime ; all decorations (except St. George) abolished. U.S. Legation at Brussels removed to Havre : Belgian relief-work to be undertaken by other neutrals.	25

1917. March.	WESTERN FRONT.	EASTERN FRONT.	SOUTHERN FRONT.
26	British take Lagnicourt (6 miles N.E. of Bapaume); French repulse several attacks S. of St. Quentin, throw back enemy beyond Barisis-Servais line, and take village of Coucy-le-Château.	Russians attacked S.W. of Baranovichi (centre), retire on E. bank of Shchara, losing 300 prisoners.	French take trenches W. of Monastir and 2,000 prisoners. Austrians occupy Italian advanced trenches S. of the Vipacco (Carso).
27	British attack N.E. of Bapaume and occupy villages N.E. of Péronne. French reach Forest of St. Gobain and, N. of Soissons, the Aisne-Oise Canal.	.. ..	.. .. ..
28	French repulse enemy in Maisons de Champagne, but lose a few trenches. They recapture Hill 304 (Verdun). British established along Bapaume-Cambrai road beyond Beaumetz. Ground gained round Croisilles - Arras. German long-range gun shells Soissons.	Germans report that spring thaw prevents fighting on large scale. Russian attacks on Magyaros Ridge (Moldavia) fail.	Unsuccessful Austrian attacks in the Carso.
29	British take Neuville-Bourjonval (7 miles E. of Bapaume) after sharp fighting. German retreat slackens.	.. ..	.. Heavy Austrian attacks in the Carso repulsed.
30	British progressing towards Cambrai, take 8 villages. Infantry in touch with whole German front from Arras to 6 miles S.W. of St. Quentin. French recapture lost trenches in E. Champagne.	.. ..	.. .. ..
31	British advance N.E. of St. Quentin. Four villages taken.	.. ..	.. .. ..

ASIATIC AND EGYPTIAN THEATRES.	NAVAL AND OVERSEAS OPERATIONS.	POLITICAL, &C.	1917. March.
First battle of Gaza. Gen. Murray attacks; thick fog; Gaza surrounded, but not penetrated.	.. .. ..	Enlistment for U.S. Navy to be increased to maximum of 87,000. Statement *re* prisoners of war in Commons ([44]). Mr. Bonar Law appeals to engineers on strike at Barrow to resume work. Bread rises to 1s. per 4-lb. loaf, and new standard of flour applied to bakers.	26
After two days' fighting, British take 950 Turkish prisoners near Gaza, including several generals and whole 53rd Divisional Staff. Obliged to fall back, mainly through water difficulties.	.. .. ..	French Chamber votes for calling up of 1918 class in April. Blockade debate in Commons. Russian proclamation in favour of self-determination and peace.	27
Turks claim battle at Gaza as a victory.	Two British destroyers reported to have been sunk recently.	All members of Romanov family have taken oath of fidelity to Provisional Govt. Export of wheat from Argentina prohibited. Electoral reform debate in Commons; Mr. Asquith announces his conversion to woman suffrage.	28
.. .. ..	.. .. ..	Speech by German Chancellor ([45]). Speech by Mr. Bonar Law; 100,000 men needed. Military service (Review of Exemptions) Bill passed. Hamarskjöld (Conservative) Ministry in Sweden resigns.	29
.. .. ..	Hospital ship "Gloucester" torpedoed in Channel; no lives lost.	Russian Provisional Govt. acknowledges independence of Poland. Electoral Reform debate in Prussian Parliament.	30
British occupy Deli Abbas (River Diala).	.. .. ..	Order limiting output of beer in United Kingdom issued.	31

1917. April.	WESTERN FRONT.	EASTERN FRONT.	SOUTHERN FRONT.
1	British capture Savy (4 miles W. of St. Quentin) and Savy Wood. French drive back Germans to Vauxaillon (N.E. of Soissons). A German bombardment of Reims begins.	.. .. ..	Bulgar-Germans bombard Monastir (asphyxiating shells).
2	British advance W. and N. of St. Quentin ; to W., capturing 3 villages ; to N. between Arras and Bapaume-Cambrai road, taking Croisselles and 5 other villages ; and to N.W., at Templeux.	.. ..	
3	British capture Hénin-sur-Cojeul (S.E. of Arras), and Maissemy (St. Quentin), and occupy Ronssoy Wood (N. of Templeux). German night attack W. of St. Quentin fails. S.W. and S. of St. Quentin French take 4 villages.	German success on the Stokhod (Volhynia).	.. .. ..
4	British capture Metz-en-Couture (towards Cambrai). French (S. of St. Quentin) capture 3 villages and advance to S.W. suburb of St. Quentin.	.. ..	
5	British capture 3 villages between Cambrai and St. Quentin. Germans bombard French N. of Urvillers. Great air battle begins, lasting two days. Aeroplane raid on Kent and Ramsgate, no casualties.	Manifesto of M. Guchkov (Russian War Minister) to soldiers to do their duty.	.. .. ..
6	Beginning of French bombardment of German positions E. of Vauxaillon (N.E. of Soissons) to N. of Reims.	.. ..	
7	British advance N.W. of St. Quentin to Fresny-le-Petit. Severe fighting round Berry - au - Bac (N.W. of Reims.)	.. ..	

ASIATIC AND EGYPTIAN THEATRES.	NAVAL AND OVERSEAS OPERATIONS.	POLITICAL, &c.	1917. April.
Russian progress towards Khanikin (85 miles N.E. of Baghdad). Turks retreat towards Kasr-i-Shirin (Persia). British occupy Kizil-Robat (26 miles S.W. of Khanikin) on Diala river.	.. .. ..	British Government decide to interfere in Barrow strike. They adhere to principle of an independent Poland.	1
British and Russians in touch at Kizil-Robat.	"Aztec," armed liner (U.S.A.) sunk by German submarine off France.	President Wilson asks Congress to declare " a state of war " with Germany ([46]) Speeches of Sir R. Borden and Lt.-Gen. Smuts re Empire and War ([47]). British Government give Barrow strikers 24 hours to resume work.	2
Russian cavalry occupy Kasr-i-Shirin and Khanikin.	Brazilian steamer, "Paranà," torpedoed by German submarine in Channel.	Barrow strike over. Russian Provisional Government forms War Committee, and repeals anti-Jewish legislation. Kaiser and Emperor Charles meet at Homburg.	3
.. .. ..	Belgian relief ship, "Trévier," torpedoed off Scheveningen.	Speeches of Gen. Robertson and Adm. Jellicoe to Trade Unions re sacrifice required from nation ([48]). British Food Order for hotels, etc. ([49]). British Flour Order ([50]).	4
.. .. ..	.. .. ..	British Food Hoarding Order ([51]). Dutch Note to British Government re armed merchantmen ([52]). Gen. Lyautey appointed to Marocco.	5
.. .. ..	U.S.A. seize German ships in U.S.A. ports.	U.S.A. declare war on Germany. Decree of Russian Provisional Government abolishing legal, religious, etc., restrictions.	6
.. .. ..	British night raid (7-8) on Zeebrugge	Cuba declares war on Germany.	7

1917. April	WESTERN FRONT.	EASTERN FRONT.	SOUTHERN FRONT.			
8	British progress N. of Louveral (half-way between Bapaume and Cambrai). Evacuation of Reims by civil population.	..	..	.. ..	..	..
9	**Battle of Arras** (on 12-mile front from Hénin-sur-Cojeul, S.E. of Arras, to Givenchy-en-Gohelle, N. of Arras). **British (Canadians) take Vimy Ridge**(N. end excepted), 5 villages and 6,000 prisoners. N. of St. Quentin and towards Cambrai British take 6 villages and enter Havrincourt Wood.	..	..	.. ..	..	..
10	British complete capture of Vimy Ridge, occupy Farbus (N.E. of Arras) and Fampaux (4 miles E. of Arras). Great French bombardment of Moronvillers *massif* (group of hills E. of Reims) begins.	..	..	.. ..	..	..
11	Repulse of British E. of Bellicourt (St. Quentin). British capture village of Monchy - le - Preux (5½ miles E.S.E. of Arras).	..	..	.. ..	..	..
12	British advance N. of Vimy Ridge, taking the " Pimple " and Bois en Hache, and S. of Arras-Cambrai road take Héninel and Wancourt.	..	..	.. ..	..	..
13	S. of Bapaume-Cambrai road, British capture village and wood of Gouzeaucourt. N. of Scarpe, British capture Vimy, Givenchy-en-Gohelle, Angres, and 2 other villages.	..	..	.. ..	..	..

Asiatic and Egyptian Theatres.	Naval and Overseas Operations.	Political, &c.	1917. April.
British capture Belad station on Baghdad-Samarra railway.	.. .. ..	Kaiser promises Prussia electoral reform ([53]). Austria-Hungary severs diplomatic relations with U.S.A. Panama joins U.S.A. to defend Panama Canal.	8
Russians occupy Kizil Robat. British occupy Harbe (4 miles N. of Belad.)	Spanish steamer, " San Fulgencio," carrying British coal for Barcelona, torpedoed.	Total Canadian oversea enlistments to date :— 407,302, of which Ontario 170,205, Montreal 36,282, Quebec 8,145. Brazil severs diplomatic relations with Germany.	9
.. .. ..	British hospital ship " Salta " sunk by mine in Channel (52 drowned). Severe explosion of ammunition factory at Eddystone, near Philadelphia.	Proclamation, dated 9.4, of Russian Provisional Government re Russia and war aims. ([54]). Note of Argentina to U.S.A. approving of U.S.A. action re war.	10
British defeat Turks near Ghaliya (N.E. of Deltawa, N. of Baghdad).	.. .. ..	Note of Argentina to U.S.A. deciding on benevolent neutrality to U.S.A. in war.	11
Turks retreat towards Deli Abbas (between Tigris and Diala).	.. .. ..	London meetings celebrating entry of U.S.A. into war ([55]). Spanish protest to Germany re " San Fulgencio." Costa Rica places territorial waters and ports at disposal of U.S.A.	12
British drive Turks from Seraijik (on Deli-Abbas-Mosul road).	.. .. ..	Russian Provisional Government receives representatives of British Labour and French Socialists ([56]). All-Russian Conference of workmen and soldiers' delegates at Petrograd. Bolivia severs diplomatic relations with Germany.	13

1917. April.	WESTERN FRONT.	EASTERN FRONT.	SOUTHERN FRONT.
14	British capture Vimy Station, Liévin, and Cité St. Pierre (Lens). German attack on British at Monchy-le-Preux repulsed British and French air raid on Freiburg. End of first phase of Battle of Arras.	.. .. ..	.. .. ..
15	British repulse German attack on Bapaume-Cambrai road; severe fighting at Lagnicourt. British capture Villeret (N.W. of St. Quentin).	.. .. ..	.. .. ..
16	**Second battle of the Aisne** (between Soissons and Reims). French take first German positions between Soissons and Craonne, and second positions to S. of Juvincourt, and advance line to Aisne Canal between Loivre and Courcy.	.. .. ..	.. .. ..
17	German attacks near Hurtebise Farm (between Troyon and Craonne) and at Courcy (N. of Reims) repulsed. Battle of Moronvillers (E. of Reims) begins. French capture heights of the *massif* and 3,500 prisoners.	.. .. ..	.. .. ..
18	French advance continued. E. and N.E. of Soissons. French capture 5 villages; on Aisne capture Condé bridgehead and Vailly, repulse enemy near Juvincourt, and consolidate positions in Moronvillers *massif*. British capture Villers-Guislain (12 miles S. of Cambrai).	.. .. ..	.. .. ..

ASIATIC AND EGYPTIAN THEATRES.	NAVAL AND OVERSEAS OPERATIONS.	POLITICAL, &c.	1917. April.
.. .. ..	.. .. ..	Appeals to farmers by Mr. Lloyd George and Board of Trade ([57]). Note of Allies (France, England, Italy) to Russia re Poland ([58]). U.S.A. War Bill (loan of £1,400,000,000) passes House of Representatives.	14
Turks driven back to Jebel Hamrin (tableland from Tigris to Persian hills).	.. .. ..	Appeal of President Wilson to American citizens re war ([59]). Austrian feelers for separate peace with Russia apparent. Venizelist régime in Greek islands in force.	15
British advance towards Istabulat (12 miles S.E. of Samarra).	.. .. ..	Strike in Berlin and Leipzig due to defective food distribution. British food orders re wheat, barley, and oats ([60]).	16
British on night 17-18 force passage of Shatt-el-Adhaim (left trib. of Tigris below Samarra). Second advance against Gaza begins.	British hospital ships "Donegal" and "Lanfranc" torpedoed in Channel.	Measures of Senate (U.S.A.) to suppress export of foodstuffs, etc., to Germany ([61]). Sixth German War Loan closed:£656,100,000.	17
British defeat Turks on right bank of Tigris, taking 1,200 prisoners.	.. .. ..	U.S.A.War Bill("OldGlory" loan of £1,400,000,000) passes Senate. British Food Order restricting pastry and cake making. German Government grants concessions to strikers ([62]). Death of Gen. v. Bissing, Gov.-General of Belgium.	18

1917. April.	WESTERN FRONT.	EASTERN FRONT.	SOUTHERN FRONT.
19	French capture Fort of Condé (E. of Soissons, on Aisne) and 3 villages, and capture Le Teton (in Moronvilliers *massif*) and village of Auberive.	.. .. ..	.. .. ..
20	French occupy Sancy (N.E. of Soissons). British capture Gonnelieu (8 miles S.W. of Cambrai).	.. .. ..	.. .. ..
21	British gain ground E. of Fampoux (E. of Arras).	Decree of Russian War Minister *re* Army([64]).	.. .. ..
22	British capture S. part of Trescault (E. of Havrincourt Wood, below Bapaume - Cambrai road). Germans bombard Reims; French repulse German attack on Moronvilliers *massif*.	.. .. ..	.. .. ..
23	British capture rest of Trescault and greater part of Havrincourt Wood —Second phase of **Battle of Arras** begins. **British attack N. and S. of the Scarpe** (Arras), capturing 2 villages.	.. .. ..	.. .. ..
24	Severe fighting from Croisilles to N. of Gavrelle (Arras). S. of Bapaume-Cambrai road British advance to St. Quentin Canal near Vendhuil and capture Bithem.	.. .. ..	British night attack on W. side of Lake Doiran (N.W. of Salonika).

ASIATIC AND EGYPTIAN THEATRES.	NAVAL AND OVERSEAS OPERATIONS.	POLITICAL, &C.	1917. April.
Second Battle of Gaza. Heavy fighting and much ground gained, but, owing to severe looses, attack not pushed through.	Adm. K o l c h a k (Commander of Black Sea fleet) appointed C.i.C. of Baltic Fleet.	Speech of Mr. Fisher (Minister of Education), *re* educational reform (⁶³). Señor G. Prieto (Marquis of Alhucemas) succeeds Count Romanones as Spanish Premier. U.S.A. announces food policy : provision for Allies before neutrals ; and seizes German liner docks in New York. Pastry restrictions in France. " Kadaver-Verwertungs - Anstalt " question.	19
.. .. ..	Germans shell Calais and Dover, no casualties ; B r i t i s h destroyers " Swift " and " Broke " successfully engage 6 German destroyers.	Senhor D'Almeida resigns Premiership in Portugal. Flour Mills' Order (British) extending powers of Food Controller.	20
British capture Turkish front line at Istabulat (evacuated by Turks during night). Cossacks repulse Kurds on Diala (N.W. of Kasr-i-Shirin).	.. .. ..	Premier returns from Savoy Conference.	21
British attack Turks in retreat from Istabulat on W. bank of Tigris and on W. bank of Shatt-el-Adhaim.	.. .. ..	Arrival of British Mission, headed by Mr. Balfour, at Washington.	22
British occupy Samarra (60 miles N. of Baghdad), 937 prisoners.	Between Blankenberghe a n d Z e e b r u g g e 3 British seaplanes attack 5 German destroyers and sink 1.	**Diplomatic relations broken off between U.S.A. and Turkey** (no state of war followed).	23
Retreat of Turks up Shatt-el-Adhaim towards Jebel Hamrin.	... .	Arrival of French Mission (Marshal Joffre and M. Viviani) in New York. Ukraine demands autonomy. Sen. Costa (Democrat) becomes Premier in Portugal.	24

1917. April.	WESTERN FRONT.	EASTERN FRONT.	SOUTHERN FRONT.
25	German attack on Hurtebise Farm (Vauclère Plateau, Chemin des Dames) repulsed.	.. .. ..	British success at Lake Doiran.
26	German attacks on Gavrelle (Arras) and Chemin des Dames (Aisne) repulsed.	.. ..	British repulse Bulgar night attack (26-27) on Hill 380 (Doiran-Vardar front).
27	French offensive on the Aisne checked.	.. .. ..	.. .. ..
28	British thrust E. of Vimy and capture Arleux ; progress N.E. of Gavrelle. French advance towards Suippe valley (Champ.).	.. .. ..	.. .. ..
29	British capture German trenches S. of Oppy (E. of Vimy Ridge). Gen. Pétain appointed Chief of French General Staff.	.. .. ..	.. .. ..
30	Damage at Zierikzee (Holland) by unknown aeroplane.	.. .. ..	.. .. ..
May. 1	Successful air-day. S. of Moronvilliers two heavy enemy counter - attacks fail. Number of prisoners published (⁶⁸).	.. .. ..	.. .. ..
2	In Champagne and Moronvillers region enemy raids beaten back.	.. .. ..	.. .. ..

Asiatic and Egyptian Theatres.	Naval and Overseas Operations.	Political, &c.	1917. April.
.. .. ..	German destroyer flotilla bombards Dunkirk: repulsed by French and British patrols.	Second reading of Corn Production Bill carried in Commons ([65]). Court intrigues in Athens cause dissatisfaction.	25
.. .. ..	German Naval raid on Ramsgate, night 26-27; 2 killed, 3 wounded.	French Socialists refuse to send representatives to Stockholm Conference on May 15.	26
.. .. ..	Australian transport " Ballarat " torpedoed and sunk; no casualties.	Speech of Mr. Lloyd George re present position and future policy ([66]). Spanish Note to Germany re " San Fulgencio " published. **Guatemala breaks diplomatic relations with Germany.**	27
.. ..	U.S. s.s. " Vacuum " torpedoed ; 1 officer and 9 men of U.S. Navy lost.	**U.S.A.** Congress passes Army Bill and **decides for Conscription** ([67]).	28
.. ..	.. ..	British and French Missions visit Washington's tomb.	29
Gen. Maude defeats 13th Turkish Corps at Gorge of Shatt-el-Adhaim and Kifri.	.. .. ..	Jockey Club stops racing after May 4. Polish scheme for Galicia published.	30
			May.
Mush (Lake Van) occupied by the Turks. N.W. frontier (India) : Mahsud tribesmen attack British convoy ; beaten off, our losses 60 killed, 55 wounded.	British s.s. " Gena " sunk off Suffolk by German seaplane.	New schedule of Protected Occupations published ([69]). Marshal Joffre and M. Viviani enthusiastically received by U.S. Senate. M. Miliukov's Note on Russian foreign policy. Polish Council of State presents demands to Central Powers.	1
.. .. ..	British destroyer sunk by mine in Channel ; one officer, 261 men lost.	Argentina receives reparation from Germany for sinking of " Monteprotegido " ([70]). Fresh Food Order extending powers of Controller. M. Zaimis again becomes Premier. Talaat Pasha visits Kaiser. Mr. Bonar Law introduces Budget ([71]).	2

1917. May.	WESTERN FRONT.	EASTERN FRONT.	SOUTHERN FRONT.
3	British attack E. of Arras on 12 mile front, take Fresnoy and break through "Hindenburg" switch at Quéant; progress also at Chérisy and Fontaine Wood.	.. ..	.. ..
4	French take Craonne, and trenches on 3-mile front, 17 miles N.W. of Reims. They bomb factories near Metz. 19,343 prisoners secured by British during April.	.. ..	.. ..
5	French, co-operating with British, on front of 20 miles N. of the Aisne, take crest of Craonne ridge, including Chemin des Dames with 6,000 prisoners.	.. ..	.. French and Greek troops take Bulgar trenches on the Lyumnitsa River (Gevgeli). Gorizia bombed. Italians repulse enemy on Carso.
6	French successfully resist all German counter-attacks on the Aisne : 29,000 prisoners taken by French since 10.4. Third big German counter-attack near Souchez River (Lens) unsuccessful.	.. ..	.. Violent artillery actions on Trentino and Julian front.
7	British position between Bullecourt and Quéant improved by Australians. Daylight aeroplane raid on N.E. London, 1 killed, 2 wounded.	.. ..	.. Bulgar counter-attack on Franco-Venizelist forces near Gevgeli repulsed.
8	Fresnoy attacked in great strength by Germans and recaptured. French attack and capture German trenches beyond Chevreux (Craonne) ; German counter-attacks repelled.	.. ..	.. British capture Bulgar position S.W. of Lake Doiran. Serbs seize useful points in Moglenitsa Valley.

ASIATIC AND EGYPTIAN THEATRES.	NAVAL AND OVERSEAS OPERATIONS.	POLITICAL, &c.	1917. May.
.. .. ..	.. .. ..	Members of Imperial War Conference received by King at Windsor. British Trade Corporation founded with capital of 10 millions. Gen. Alexeiev protests v. " no annexation, etc. " propaganda.	3
.. .. ..	British transports "Arcadian " and " Transylvania " torpedoed in Mediterranean. 19 officers and 258 men, and 31 officers and 382 men respectively, lost. British Admiralty reform announced ([72]).	Russian Provisional Government secures narrow vote of confidence.	4
Russian detachments withdraw about Oghnut and Mush.	.. .. ..	War Conference in Paris ([73]). Gen. Kornilov reorganises reserves. Mr. Balfour addresses Congress ([74]). Flat racing discontinued ([75]).	5
.. .. ..	.. .. ..	Mass Meeting at Salonika demands deposition of King Constantine.	6
.. .. ..	.. .. ..	German Chancellor uses Social Democrats to influence Soviet delegates towards German terms of peace.	7
.. .. ..	.. .. ..	Australian elections result in Nationalist majority in both Houses. " Combing out " of munition workers begins. Liberia breaks off relations with Germany.	8

1917. May.	WESTERN FRONT.	EASTERN FRONT.	SOUTHERN FRONT.
9	German attack on the Chemin des Dames, as well as Craonne and Corbény, fail.	.. .. ..	.. .. ..
10	Small British gains S.W. of Lens and on S. bank of River Scarpe. French success near Chevreux (Craonne).	Gen. Russki relieved of command on N. front by Provisional Government.	French and Venizelists take enemy position near the Lyumnitsa. Two attacks on Krastali driven off by British.
11	Repulse of various German attacks on ground gained by Allies (Arleux, Souchez river, Cerny, Craonne, etc.).	.. ..	French carry Srka di Legen (W. of Lyumnitsa). Serb raids on Moglena hills (Dobropolye), and N. of Pozar.
12	British storm most of Bullecourt, and Roeux trenches. Enemy's counter-attack fails.	.. .. ..	Artillery activity on Julian front from Tolmino to the sea. Italians bomb Prosecco (N. of Trieste).
13	British establish themselves in Roeux, and progress on "Greenland Hill." French repulse heavy German attacks N. of Reims and in Maisons de Champagne.	Gen. Kornilov, Commandant of Petrograd, and M. Guchkov, Minister of Marine and War, resign.	.. .. ..
14	British line advanced N. of Gavrelle. Strong hostile reconnaissances N.E. of Vauxaillon (Soissons), W. of Craonne, Berry au Bac and in Champagne fail.	.. .. ..	Strong Italian attack N. and S. of Gorizia and in N. sector of Carso, E. of Faiti Hrib ([n]).

Asiatic and Egyptian Theatres.	Naval and Overseas Operations.	Political, &c.	1917. May.
.. .. ..	.. .. ..	British Labour Party decides not to attend Stockholm Conference. Mr. Henderson and deputation appointed to visit Russia. Vote of Credit demanded for £500 millions ; daily expenditure £5,600,000.	9
.. .. ..	British scouting force from Harwich chases 11 German destroyers into Zeebrugge.	British Ministerial Conference with Engineer, etc. representatives. Secret Session of House of Commons on submarine warfare. Plot to assassinate M. Venizelos discovered at Salonika. President of Duma (M. Rodzianko) affirms Russian loyalty to Allies.	10
.. .. ..	.. .. ..	House of Commons Secret Session continues. Sir E. Carson refuses to alter form of weekly shipping losses.	11
.. .. ..	Heavy naval bombardment of Zeebrugge by Dover Division, etc.	Two new groups for attestation announced : 41 to 45, and 45 to 50. Bombs and seditious leaflets seized in Calcutta. Both Houses, Canadian Parliament, addressed by M. Viviani.	12
Mesopotamia : Russian detachments compelled to retire across Diala river towards Kifri (⁷⁶).	Spanish s.s. "Carmen" sunk in protected zone by German submarine.	Socialist Conference opens at Stockholm. Marshal Joffre reviews garrison troops at Montreal; much enthusiasm.	13
.. .. ..	British Naval forces destroy Zeppelin L.22 in the North Sea. Sir J. Jellicoe to be Chief of Naval Staff, Sir E. Geddes Controller.	King George tours industrial centres in the North. British labour unrest ; engineers on strike, ditto omnibuses in London, weavers in N. threaten strike	14

1917. May.	WESTERN FRONT.	EASTERN FRONT.	SOUTHERN FRONT.
15	Heavy fighting round Bullecourt. Severe fighting also on Chemin des Dames. French raids in the Woevre and Lorraine. **Gen. Pétain appointed to command N. and N.E. French Armies, Gen. Foch succeeding him as C.G.S., with wide powers.**	.. .. ..	Italians hold M. Kuk and Vodice, and reach slopes of M. Santo (Gorizia). On Doiran front, British advance S.W. of Krastali ; French, Serbs and Greeks also successful.
16	Enemy attacks on Gavrelle, N. of River Scarpe, fail with heavy losses. British hold on " Siegfried " line, N.E. of Bullecourt, extended. French make appreciable advance E. of Craonne. End of Battle of Arras.	.. .. ..	Italians take 4,021 prisoners in last two days' advance in Carso and on Vodice. Austrians claim 2,000 prisoners in the Carso.
17	British complete capture of Bullecourt. King of Belgians visits the Somme, Ancre and Arras battlefields.	Intense enemy fire on Russian trenches near Kukhary (Kovel).	Italians, supported by British heavy artillery, stick to M. Kuk, Vodice, and M. Santo.
18	Artillery activity near Fresnoy. Germans concentrate on California Plateau, Chemin des Dames ; slight attacks repulsed.	.. .. ..	Italians extend their hold on Vodice and Hill 652.
19	British push forward beyond Bullecourt. Fighting about Chemin des Dames, hostile attack on La Bovelle repulsed.	Russian Army at the front remains passive.	Austrians fail to recover heights N. of Gorizia ; their surprise attack at night on Vodice collapses.

ASIATIC AND EGYPTIAN THEATRES.	NAVAL AND OVERSEAS OPERATIONS.	POLITICAL, &c.	1917. May
.. .. ..	U.S.A. destroyer - flotilla arrives in British waters. Austrian light cruiser sinks 14 British drifters in Adriatic. Is hunted back to Cattaro by Allied vessels, but H.M.S. "Dartmouth" torpedoed, not sunk. British transport "Cameronia" torpedoed in Mediterranean, 140 men lost.	German Socialists are refused passports for Stockholm.	15
.. .. ..	French s.s. "Sontay" torpedoed in Mediterranean, 45 lost. Gen. Van Deventer succeeds Gen. Hoskins in E. Africa.	Russian Coalition Cabinet, M. Kerenski, War and Marine ; M. Tereshchenko Foreign Minister vice M. Miliukov. Mr. Lloyd George proposes Home Rule at once and suggests Convention (⁷⁸). German Chancellor indicates lines of peace with Russia.	16
Kurds attack Russian rear near Khanikin. Mesopotamian Commission's report presented.	.. .. ..	Annual meetings of Imperial Cabinet announced. Herr Zimmermann on "Kadaververwaltungsanstalten." Honduras severs diplomatic relations with Germany. U.S.A. Minister in Belgium issues damning report on German deportations.	17
.. ..	.. .. ..	The Duma urges loyalty to Allies on Provisional Government. U.S.A. Congress passes Army Bill : 500,000 to be mustered in September. Unit of U.S.A. Medical Corps reaches England.	18
.. .. ·. ..	.. .. ..	Settlement with Amalgamated Society of Engineers agreed on. Nicaragua severs diplomatic relations with Germany.	19

1917. May.	WESTERN FRONT.	EASTERN FRONT.	SOUTHERN FRONT.
20	British force line near Fontaine-lez-Croisilles. Germans gain 200 yards N.E. of Cerny. They lose 500 prisoners on Moronvilliers sector. End of 2nd battle of the Aisne.	..	Austrian attacks on the Carso beaten off.
21	British capture " Siegfried " line from Bullecourt to 1 mile E. of Arras (bar 2,000 yards). French claim great success on Moronvilliers ridge and ground held. Activity on California Plateau and near Craonne.	..	Severe fighting in the Travignolo Valley (Trent.) ; enemy penetrate and are later ejected.
22	Confused fighting on Arras front ; successful French actions on the River Aisne front.	..	Italians frustrate hostile attacks in Travignolo valley.
23	Zeppelin raid E. Counties, 1 killed. Germans make early attack on Vauclère Plateau (Craonne), heavily repulsed.	..	S. Carso : Great Italian advance from Kostanjevica to the sea, capturing several important positions. Ten British batteries and British monitors engaged. 9,000 prisoners taken.
24	French line round Craonne improved.	..	Further Italian gains in S. Carso. Austrian counterattacks fail.
25	British advance towards Fontaine - lez - Croisilles. Aeroplane raid on S.E. Coast, 95 killed, 192 injured ; 3 raiders brought down. German success near Braye (Chemin des Dames) ; French success round Mt. Cornillet (Moronvilliers).	..	Italian progress on the Isonzo (Plava to M. Kuk), and on S. Carso.

Asiatic and Egyptian Theatres.	Naval and Overseas Operations.	Political, &c.	1917. May.
.. .. ..	.. .. ..	U.S.A. Division to start at once for France under Gen. Pershing ([79]). Mr. Roosevelt's offer declined. Conscription bill in Canada announced and well received. Russian Provisional Government recognises debt of honour to Allies and repudiates peace talk.	20
.. .. ..	.. .. ..	M. Albert Thomas, French Minister of Munitions, speaks with effect in Moscow. Debate in House of Commons on proposed Irish Convention.	21
Demolition of 13 miles of Hejaz Railway by Anzac Mounted Brigade and Camel Corps.	.. .. ..	Brig.-Gen. Nash succeeds Sir E. Geddes as I.-G. Transportation. Crisis in China ; President replaces Tuan-chi-jui by Wu Ting Fang, as Prime Minister. Count Tisza, Hungarian Prime Minister, resigns.	22
Demonstration and raid by mounted troops on Bir-es-Saba (Palestine).	.. .. ..	M. Isvolski appointed Ambassador in London (subquently cancelled). Return to France of Marshal Joffre and M. Viviani from U.S.A.	23
.. .. ..	Japanese flotilla announced in Mediterranean ([80]).	Mr. Bonar Law on German finance ([81]).	24
.. .. ..	.. .. ..	Mr. Lloyd George issues statement *re* submarine menace and food supplies.	25

1917. May.	WESTERN FRONT.	EASTERN FRONT.	SOUTHERN FRONT.
26	Three German attacks in Champagne, all successful.	.. ..	..	Italians take and lose Kostanjevica, but capture 10 guns.
27	Small actions along Moronvilliers, Verdun and Alsace fronts.	.. ..	..	Italians take S. Giovanni (Carso, third Austrian line), and cross River Timavo; lose and regain Hill 126, E. of Gorizia. Austrians claim 13,000 prisoners.
28	German attacks near Hurtebise repulsed.	.. ..	..	Italian guns within 10 miles of Trieste. In Plava sector Italians drive enemy to end of Globna valley. Claim nearly 24,000 prisoners in last fortnight.
29	Near St. Quentin and in Champagne heavy artillery and small patrol actions.	.. ..	..	Italians win trenches near Medeazza (S. Carso). Austrian attacks on Vodice fail.
30	Stubborn fighting on Moronvilliers *massif*.	.. ..	..	Austria reported asking for German aid for Trieste.
31	Artillery action in Ypres and Wytschaete salients. Violent German attacks on Moronvilliers *massif* fail. 442 German to 271 Allied aeroplanes brought down in May.	.. ..	..	Austrian counter-attack in Vodice sector repulsed. Venizelist forces in Macedonia now amount to nearly 2,000 officers and 60,000 men.

Asiatic and Egyptian Theatres.	Naval and Overseas Operations.	Political, &c.	1917. May.
.. .. ..	Hospital ship " Dover Castle " torpedoed twice in Mediterranean, and sunk, 6 lost.	Mr. Balfour arrives in Canada. French Minister of Marine states Germans have sunk 2,400,000 tons in first four months. Brazil annuls its neutrality decree.	26
.. ..		Germans threaten to sink at sight all hospital ships in Mediterranean. Announced that 600 German daily papers ceased publication since beginning of war.	27
.. ..		Mr. Balfour's remarkable reception at Toronto University. French Socialists decide to attend Stockholm Conference. MM. Ribot, Cambon, Painlevé and Gen. Foch's agreement with War Cabinet in London.	28
.. .. ..	French liner " Yarra " torpedoed in Mediterranean : 56 lost. H.M.S. " Hilary " sunk, 4 lost. Russian naval raid on Anatolian Coast.	Mr. A. Henderson goes to Russia on special Mission. Mr. Balfour addresses Canadian Parliament in French and English.	29
.. .. ..	E. Africa : German forces break S. from Rufiji towards Portuguese territory.	Soviet announces International Conference at Stockholm. Austrian Reichsrat meets for first time since war broke out.	30
.. ..		Emperor Charles promises a more liberal Constitution after the war. Meat Sale Order in Great Britain published.	31

1917. June.	WESTERN FRONT.	EASTERN FRONT.	SOUTHERN FRONT.
1	Continued artillery duel in Wytschaete salient. German attack near Laffaux Hill (Chemin des Dames) gains some ground. During " Spring offensive," Allies have captured 52,000 Germans (including 1,000 officers), 446 guns, and 1,000 m.g.'s. Since beginning of war, British have taken 76,067 prisoners on the Western front.	.. .. ..	Successful Italian attack S. of Kostanjevica (Carso).
2	Artillery activity near Wytschaete. British advance S. of Souchez river.	.. .. ..	.. ..
3	Intense artillery duel in Wytschaete salient. Germans recover ground S. of Souchez river. Five heavy German attacks repulsed on Chemin des Dames front.	.. .. ..	Austrians repulsed on San Marco (E. of Gorizia). They open a great counter-offensive on the Carso.
4	Continued artillery activity in Wytschaete salient. French air-raid by night on Treves.	Gen. Brusilov appointed commander-in-Chief of Russian armies in succession to Gen. Alexeiev.	Very heavy fighting on the Carso ; Italians forced back S. of Jamiano, but hold line elsewhere.
5	Daylight aeroplane raid on Thames estuary and Medway, 13 killed, 34 injured ; at least six enemy machines destroyed while returning. Artillery still active near Wytschaete. British make small advance S. of Souchez river, and begin an attack N. of river Scarpe. German attack near Hurtebise (Chemin des Dames) fails.	.. .. ..	Italians withdraw further S. of Jamiano.
6	In attack N. of Scarpe river British carry positions on Greenland Hill. Unsuccessful German attacks on Chemin des Dames front.	.. .. ..	Further heavy fighting on Carso ; no material change of front. Austrians claim 10,000 prisoners in last 3 days.

ASIATIC AND EGYPTIAN THEATRES.			NAVAL AND OVERSEAS OPERATIONS.	POLITICAL, &c.	1917. June.
..	..	..	Zeebrugge, Ostend and Bruges heavily bombed by R.N.A.S.	Lord Devonport resigns office of Food Controller. French Government announces no passports to French delegates to Stockholm Conference. British Labour Party appoints deputation to Stockholm and Petrograd. Socialist revolt at Kronstadt against Russian Provisional Government.	1
..	..	..	British transport "Cameronian" sunk in Mediterranean, 63 lives lost.	**Brazil revokes her neutrality** as between U.S.A. and Germany, and seizes German ships in Brazilian waters.	2
..	..	..	Aerodromes at Zeebrugge, Bruges, etc., again heavily bombed. Austrian torpedo-boat sunk by submarine.	**Proclamation of Albanian independence** under Italian protection. Socialist Conference at Leeds. Provisional Government formed in China.	3
..	..	..	.. .. ..	.. .. ..	4
..	..	..	Naval action between light craft in N. Sea ; German destroyer sunk. Ostend bombarded from the sea.	.. .. ..	5
..	..	..	.. .. ..	Arrival in Greece of M. Jonnart, High Commissioner of the Protecting Powers . Collapse of Kronstadt revolt after negotiations with Provisional Government. Lord Northcliffe to go to U.S.A.	6

1917. June.	WESTERN FRONT.	EASTERN FRONT.	SOUTHERN FRONT.
7	Battle of Messines begins. **British capture Messines-Wytschaete ridge,** after explosion of 19 mines; front of 9 miles stormed; 6,400 prisoners taken.	.. ..	.. Austrian attack on Vodice ridge repulsed.
8	Gen. Pershing and staff arrive in England. Repulse of German counter-attacks E. of Messines ridge. Big British raids near Lens.	.. ..	.. Italians occupy Jannina (Greek Epirus).
9	.. .. ..	.. ..	.. ..
10	British gain ground in Messines region.	.. ..	.. Italians carry pass of Agnello and advance on Mt. Ortigara (Trentino).
11	British progress on mile front S.E. of Messines; La Potterie system captured.	.. ..	.. French troops land at Corinth, and Franco-British force enters Thessaly.
12	British advance on 2-mile front E. and N.E. of Messines.	.. ..	.. Allied forces occupy Larissa (Thessaly) and Corinth.
13	Daylight aeroplane raid on London : 162 killed, 432 injured.	.. ..	.. Austrian attack on Mt. Ortigara repulsed. Trikala and Volo (Thessaly) occupied by Allies.
14	German withdrawal between St. Yves and the Lys. Successful British attacks near Messines, and on Infantry Hill (E. of Monchy-le-Preux). End of Battle of Messines.	.. ..	.. ..

ASIATIC AND EGYPTIAN THEATRES.	NAVAL AND OVERSEAS OPERATIONS.	POLITICAL, &c.	1917. June.
.. .. ..	.. .. ..	.. .. ..	7
.. .. ..	.. .. ..	.. .. ..	8
.. .. ..	.. .. ..	Spanish Cabinet resigns. Russian Soviet rejects German wireless proposal for unlimited armistice.	9
.. .. ..	Opening of operations which drive Germans from estuary of Lukuledi river (Ger. E. Africa).	.. .. ..	10
.. .. ..	.. .. ..	Señor Dato forms Cabinet. Publication of message from President Wilson to Russian Government ([82]). Sailors and Firemen's Union refuse to let Mr. R. Macdonald, etc., sail for Russia. **Abdication of King Constantine** of Greece in favour of his second son, Alexander.	11
Fort of Salif (Red Sea) destroyed by British naval forces.	.. .. ..	Publication of British reply to Russian Note on war aims, and of French message regarding Russian proclamation of 9.4.17 ([88]).	12
.. .. ..	H.M.S. " Avenger," merchant cruiser, sunk by submarine.	Serious explosion in munitions factory at Ashton-under-Lyne.	13
.. .. ..	Zeppelin L43 destroyed by naval forces in North Sea.	Arrival in Petrograd of Senator Root and U.S. Mission. Count M. Esterhazy becomes Hungarian Prime Minister.	14

1917. June.	WESTERN FRONT.	EASTERN FRONT.			SOUTHERN FRONT.
15	German counter - attack S.E. of Ypres repulsed. Small British advance near Bullecourt.	..	..	..	Italians carry position on Corno Cavento (W. Trentino) and repulse attack on Mt. Ortigara. British withdraw on wide front from advanced positions in Struma Valley.
16	.. .. ..	..	..	..	.. .. ..
17	Two Zeppelins raid Kent and the Eastern Counties; one destroyed, 3 killed, 16 injured. Germans capture French trenches near Hurtebise. Portuguese in action for first time.	..	..	..	Austrian attacks on Asiago Plateau (Trent.) and Vodice repulsed. Italian advance near Jamiano (Carso).
18	British lose ground on Infantry Hill. French advance between Mont Cornillet and Mont Blond (Champagne).	..	..	..	.. .. ..
19	Small British advances on Arras front.	..	..	..	Italian offensive on Asiago plateau; ground gained on Mt. Ortigara.
20	German attacks on Souchez river repulsed. British recover ground on Infantry Hill. Violent German attack near Vauxaillon (Chemin des Dames) gains ground.	..	..	..	Italians carry height on Piccolo Lagaznoi (Carnia front).
21	French recover nearly all ground lost near Vauxaillon and make small advance near Mont Cornillet. German attack on the Teton (Champagne) repulsed.	..	..	..	.. .. ..
22	Heavy German attack on Chemin des Dames front; French lose ground S.E. of Filain.	..	..	..	.. .. ..

ASIATIC AND EGYPTIAN THEATRES.	NAVAL AND OVERSEAS OPERATIONS.	POLITICAL, &c.	1917. June.
.. ..	..	Lord Rhondda's appointment as Food Controller announced. Release of Irish rebels announced. Haiti breaks off relations with Germany.	15
.. ..	..	Peace terms of German Socialist delegates to Stockholm published (⁸⁴). Opening in Petrograd of All-Russian Congress of Workmen's and Soldiers' Delegates.	16
.. ..	..	Paris Economic Conference concludes agreements as to future economic policy.	17
.. ..	..	Gen. Smuts to attend War Cabinet meetings. Herr Hoffmann, Swiss Foreign Minister, resigns over German peace-terms incident (⁸⁴ᵃ).	18
.. ..	..	British peerages conferred by the King on Teck and Battenberg families.	19
.. ..	..	Baron Sonnino on Italian aims.	20
.. ..	..	Warrant instituting "Order of the British Empire" published. Brit. Govt. place embargo on disposal of U.K. securities in neutral countries by residents in enemy countries.	21
.. ..	.. Unsuccessful attack on U.S.A. transports by German submarines.	.. .. ..	22

1917. June.	WESTERN FRONT	EASTERN FRONT.	SOUTHERN FRONT.
23	Further German attacks near Vauxaillon and Filain repulsed.	..	..
24	French r e c o v e r more ground near Vauxaillon. British advance on 1½ mile front near Lens.	..	..
25	British advance on Souchez river continues. French carry crest near Hurtebise (" Dragon's Cave "). **First fighting contingent of American troops lands in France.**	..	Austrian counter-attacks on Mt. Ortigara.
26	British advance astride Souchez river; La Coulotte occupied.	..	Small Italian withdrawal on Mt. Ortigara.
27	..	..	Austrian attack on Agnello pass repulsed.
28	British advance on 2-mile front S. of Souchez river. German positions near Oppy carried. German attack N.W. of Verdun; French trenches on Hill 304 captured.	..	..
29	Continued British advance S. of Souchez river; Avion entered. German attacks on Chemin des Dames front; French lose ground N.E. of Cerny. German attack near Reims repulsed.	..	Austrian attack in Dolomites repulsed. Italians evacuate advanced position on Asiago Plateau (Trent.).
30	British capture further enemy defences S.W. and W. of Lens. German attack on Chemin des Dames. Violent infantry a c t i o n W. of M o r t Homme (Verdun).	Heavy artillery action in Galicia.	..

ASIATIC AND EGYPTIAN THEATRES.	NAVAL AND OVERSEAS OPERATIONS.	POLITICAL, &C.	1917. June.
.. .. ..	P. & O. liner " Mongolia " sunk off Bombay by mine.	Return of M. Thomas to Paris from Russia. Resignation of M. Zaimis, Greek Premier.	23
.. .. ..	Mutiny of Russian Black Sea Fleet at Sevastopol	New Austrian Ministry, Dr. v. Seidler Premier. British and German delegates on Prisoners of War question meet at The Hague. The £400,000,000 U.S.A. Liberty Loan largely over-subscribed. M. Pashich forms new Serbian Government.	24
.. .. ..	Raid in Black Sea by " Breslau " ; Russian wireless station and lighthouse on island of Fidonisi destroyed.	M. Venizelos returns to Athens and succeeds M. Zaimis as Premier. Recall of German Minister to Norway, consequent on bomb-plot.	25
Russians take Serdesht (Persia).	.. .. ..	Report of Mesopotamia Commission published ([85]).	26
.. .. ..	French cruiser " Kléber " sunk by mine. British transport " Armadale " sunk in Atlantic.	Greek declar'n of 23.11.16 becomes effective ; state of war v. Austria-Hungary and Turkey declared.	27
.. .. ..	.. .. ..	In recognition of New Zealand's services, " Governor " changed to " Governor-General." Czech Socialist memo. published.	28
Announcement that Gen. Allenby has arrived in Egypt and assumed command of Allied forces, in succession to Gen. Murray.	.. .. ..	Speech by Mr. Lloyd George at Glasgow ([36]).	29
.. .. ..	German forces driven from Nyassaland to the Rovuma border by British and Portuguese.	Greece breaks off relations with Germany and Austria-Hungary. Soviet delegates leave Russia for Socialist conferences in Stockholm, England, France and Italy.	30

1917. July.	WESTERN FRONT.	EASTERN FRONT.	SOUTHERN FRONT.		
1	Violent bombardment, followed by German attacks in Cerny-Ailles sector (N. Aisne); enemy losses heavy. Successful French counter-attack N.W. of Verdun.	**Russian offensive, under Gen. Brusilov, opens** on 50-mile front, on either side of Brzezany (Gal.); 3 lines of trenches and 12,000 prisoners taken. To the S. stubborn fighting, heavy Russian losses.	Austrians very active in the Trentino. Attacks repulsed by Italians.		
2	British aeroplanes bomb Bruges. British advanced posts driven back short distance from Lens. German attacks repulsed N. of the Aisne.	Russian offensive progresses in the region of Zborow (E. of Lemberg); 6,300 prisoners taken.	..	..	..
3	German offensive on a front of 11 miles N. of the Aisne repulsed with heavy loss. German attacks towards Verdun repulsed. British air raid on Belgian towns.	Russian attack on Brzezany (Gal.) fails. Artillery activity growing in the Stokhod area (Volhynia).	..	..	..
4	Aeroplane raid on Harwich (17 killed, 30 injured).	..	..	..	..	..
5	British line slightly advanced S. of Ypres. Artillery engagements in the Aisne and Champagne sectors.	Artillery and infantry action in the Brzezany region.	..	..	..
6	Aerial activity S. of Ypres. German towns bombed by French aeroplanes.	Russian attack in Galicia spreading in region of Stanislau. Heavy fighting near Brzezany.	..	..	..

ASIATIC AND EGYPTIAN THEATRES.	NAVAL AND OVERSEAS OPERATIONS.	POLITICAL, &c.	1917. July.
.. .. ..	.. .. ..	Announcement in Holland of assurance by Lord Derby that Britain will not strike at Germany through Holland if she remains neutral. Young Chinese Emperor, Hsuan Tung, restored.	1
.. .. ..	.. .. ..	King and Queen attend service at Westminster Abbey for jubilee of Canadian Federation.	2
.. .. ..	.. .. ..	Riots in Amsterdam. Statement in House of Lords by Lord Hardinge (Ex-Viceroy of India) on report of Mesopotamia Commission.	3
Turkish cavalry reconnaissance from Beersheba (Palestine); shelled and forced to retreat.	German submarine attack in force on U.S. transports defeated. Issue of report on operations in E. Africa ([87]). British mine-sweeper sunk in Mediterranean. Ponta Delgada (Azores) shelled by enemy submarine.	.. .. ..	4
Improvement in comfort and health of troops in Mesopotamia announced.	British destroyer mined in North Sea (announced), 18 survivors.	Belgian Socialists announce at Stockholm their determination to make no peace with German Imperialism. Reichstag opens..	5
.. .. ..	British destroyer torpedoed in North Sea, 8 lost.	Crisis in Germany owing to the demand in the Reichstag for reforms in domestic and foreign policy and a peace without annexations or indemnities. Second reading of Conscription Bill in Canada carried.	6

1917. July.	WESTERN FRONT.	EASTERN FRONT.	SOUTHERN FRONT.
7	French gain ground at Cerny (N. Aisne) and at Verdun. Big German aeroplane raid on London, 57 killed, 193 injured; 11 enemy aeroplanes accounted for. British aeroplanes bomb Ghistelles (Belgium).	.. .. ..	.. .. ..
8	Heavy fighting on the Aisne; German attacks repulsed.	Austrian front broken W. of Stanislau by Gen. Kornilov; 7,000 prisoners taken, cavalry pursue enemy, rout stemmed by German reserves.	.. ..
9	British line advanced slightly on Messines front. German counter - attack on Aisne front repulsed. French counter - attacks successful at Braye - en - Laonnois (Aisne).	Russian offensive progresses S.W. of Halicz, enemy driven back behind River Lomnica; 1,000 prisoners.	Austrian attacks on Italian positions W. of Tolmino (Up. Isonzo) repulsed.
10	After intense bombardment Germans gain ground to the E. of the mouth of the Yser (Nieuport) and cut off and destroy parts of 2 British battalions, taking over 1,000 prisoners. British counter - attack drives Germans from advanced positions gained near Lombaertzyde.	Capture of Halicz (Gal.) by Russians; enemy pursued across River Lomnica, 2,000 prisoners taken.	.. .. ..
11	Great aerial activity on British front.	Capture of Kalusz (W. Stanislau, Gal.) by Russians.	Statistics of health of British army at Salonika published.
12	British air raid into Belgium.	Russian progress towards Dolina (Gal.). Gen. Kornilov crosses the Lomnica river.	.. ..

ASIATIC AND EGYPTIAN THEATRES.	NAVAL AND OVERSEAS OPERATIONS.	POLITICAL, &c.	1917. July.
Despatches on winter operations in Egypt published ([86]).	.. .. ..	French Government affirm their right of control in respect of army services. Chinese Emperor abdicates.	7
.. .. ..	.. .. ..	America declares an embargo on exportation of foods, metal and coal.	8
British aeroplanes bomb Constantinople and the Turkish-German fleet. Russians report evacuation of towns on Mesopotamian front owing to Turkish pressure.	H.M.S. "Vanguard" blown up as a result of internal explosion; 3 survivors of those on board at the time.	Secret Session of House of Commons on London air raids.	9
.. .. ..	.. .. ..	Official statement gives British captures on all fronts since beginning of war as 117,772 prisoners and 759 guns.	10
British column from Feluja (Euphrates) engages Turkish force up the river and inflicts considerable loss. Despatch on operations in Mesopotamia published ([89]).	Report of British operations in E. Africa published ([90]).	Announcement of judicial enquiry into the conduct of all persons affected by Mesopotamia Report. Prussian Reform : Kaiser promises an equal franchise in the next elections to the Prussian Diet. Sinn Fein candidate defeats Nationalist in East Clare election.	11
Announced that Turks have been routed by King of Hejaz in N. Arabia, 700 killed, 600 prisoners.	.. .. ..	Mesopotamia Debate : Mr. A. Chamberlain, Secretary of State for India, resigns. Chinese Republicans enter Pekin ; Tuan Chi Jui, P.M. ; Fen Kwo Chang, President.	12

1917. July.	WESTERN FRONT.	EASTERN FRONT.	SOUTHERN FRONT.
13	.. .. ..	Further Russian progress around Kalusz (Gal.); 1,600 prisoners ([91]).	.. .. ..
14	German attacks repulsed in region of Lombaertzyde (Nieuport). French gain and hold against counter-attacks German trench system on Moronvillers, E. of Reims. German thrust on Chemin des Dames and Cerny partially resisted N. of the Aisne.	.. .. ..	.. .. ..
15	German assault on captured positions on Mont Haut (Moronvillers) defeated. British air raid on Belgium.	Enemy opposition stiffening in Galicia; slight enemy success S. of Kalusz.	Italian raid in the Carso, 275 prisoners.
16	German counter-attacks repulsed at Moronvillers (Champagne).	Russian withdrawal in Galicia; Kalusz evacuated.	.. .. ..
17	Successful British raids in the Ypres sector. French regain positions N.W. of Verdun lost during last 18 days.	Russians hold their positions in Galicia against German counter-thrust.	.. .. ..
18	German attacks held S. of St. Quentin and N.W. of Verdun.	Russians gain and lose Nowica (Gal.); heavy fighting.	.. .. ..

ASIATIC AND EGYPTIAN THEATRES.	NAVAL AND OVERSEAS OPERATIONS.	POLITICAL, &c.	1917. July.
.. ..	.. .. ..	Deputation on London Air Defences received by Prime Minister.	13
Successful British raid on Turks near Gaza.	.. .. ..	Herr von Bethmann Hollweg resigns ; succeeded as German Imperial Chancellor by Dr. Michaelis. U.S. House of Representatives votes *nem. con.* £128,000,000 to send 22,000 aeroplanes and 100,000 airmen to Western Front. The King and Queen return from visit to Western Front. Sir D. Haig made K.T.	14
.. ..	.. .. ..	Crisis in Russia : resignation of 4 Ministers of Cadet Party, as protest against recognition of the Ukraine.	15
.. ..	6 German steamers intercepted off Dutch coast, 2 driven ashore, damaged by gunfire, 4 captured.	Disorders in Petrograd engineered by Maximalists commence.	16
.. ..	.. .. ..	Continued disorder in Petrograd ([92]). Royal Proclamation changing name of Royal House and family to W i n d s o r. Changes in the Government announced ([93]). Resolution in favour of extension of Canadian Parliament passed.	17
.. ..	Sir E. Geddes succeeds Sir E. Carson as First Lord of the Admiralty.	Revolt in Petrograd crushed ; order being restored. Mesopotamia R e p o r t : Government announce further decision ([94]). Petition to extend the Canadian Parliament will not be put forward. Australian repatriation scheme introduced.	18

1917. July.	WESTERN FRONT.	EASTERN FRONT.	SOUTHERN FRONT.
19	Heavy German attacks S. of Lombaertzyde (Nieuport sector), S. of St. Quentin, and N. of the Aisne repulsed.	German counter-offensive opens; Russian positions E. of Zloczow (E. Lemberg) pierced as a result of troops insubordination.	.. .. ..
20	.. .. ..	German breach of Russian front in Galicia growing; retreat stayed in Brzezany and Halicz regions.	.. .. ..
21	Heavy artillery battle in Flanders.	Germans progress S. of the Dniester, reach suburbs of Tarnopol. Russians retreating on the Sereth.	.. .. ..
22	Intense artillery activity in Flanders. Heavy enemy attacks launched on French on the Aisne front. Stubborn resistance. Germans active on Verdun front. German aeroplane raid on E. Coast (13 killed, 26 injured).	Russian retreat in Galicia extending. Russians penetrate German defences E. of Vilna to a depth of 2 miles, taking 1,000 prisoners; further success jeopardised by indiscipline.	British raid Bulgar trenches on Struma front.
23	Numerous raids by British and Canadians.	Russian undisciplined retreat in Galicia continues on a front of 150 miles; fall of Halicz, Stanislau evacuated. Russian diversion at Dvinsk and Smorgon followed by voluntary withdrawal of troops. Rumanian front: Russo-Rumanian success, 2,000 prisoners, 57 guns taken.	.. .. ..
24	French counter-attack and regain ground lost N. of the Aisne.	Fall of Stanislau and Tarnopol. Russian Government restore death penalty at front.	.. .. ..

ASIATIC AND EGYPTIAN THEATRES.	NAVAL AND OVERSEAS OPERATIONS.	POLITICAL, &c.	1917. July.
Turkish cavalry force encountered W. of Beersheba (Palestine) and driven back.	Report on operations in E. Africa ([95]) published. Main German positions in the region of Narongombe (E. Africa) attacked; heavy casualties on both sides.	German Imperial Chancellor speaks in the **Reichstag** on the " **Majority Resolution** " ([96]). Statement issued on Russian and German Socialists meeting at Stockholm. Attempted assassination of M. Kerenski.	19
Record heat at Baghdad 123 deg.	.. .. ..	.. .. ..	20
.. .. ..	H.M.S. " Otway " torpedoed, 10 lost.	Mr. Lloyd George replies to Herr Michaelis ([97]). Arrest and deportation to Germany of Gen. Pilsudski (Polish patriot).	21
Successful British raid at Gaza.	.. .. ..	M. Kerenski succeeds Prince Lvov as Prime Minister, retaining offices of War and Marine. **Siam declares state of war** with Germany and Austria-Hungary.	22
.. .. ..	.. .. ..	Amendment to Corn Production Bill defeated ([98]).	23
.. .. ..	.. .. ..	Vote of Credit for £650,000,000 moved. Announcement of transfer of Recruiting system from the control of the War Office to the Local Government Board. Canadian Military Service Bill passed.	24

1917. July.	WESTERN FRONT.	EASTERN FRONT.	SOUTHERN FRONT.
25	Intense artillery battle in progress in Flanders. French repel German counter attack N. of the Aisne front.	Russian retreat in E. Galicia continues; towns evacuated, positions in Carpathians abandoned. Russo - Rumanian advance in S. Moldavia.	.. .. ..
26	Repeated German attacks N. of the Aisne and at Mont Haut (Champagne) repulsed.	Austro-Germans cross the Sereth and take Kolomea (Gal.).	.. .. ..
27	Further fighting N. of the Aisne. German attacks on Champagne front repulsed.	.. .. ..	.. .. ..
2S	Successful British raids. British air raid into Belgium.	Further Russian retreat in Galicia; enemy reach Russian frontier. Rumanian advance in Moldavia continues.	.. .. ..
29	Furious artillery battle in progress in Flanders and in region of Lens.	Russians offer resistance in the region S. of the Dniester, but retirement in Bukovina continues. Rumanian advance continues in Moldavia; all objectives and many prisoners taken.	.. .. ..
30	Heavy artillery fire on the Aisne front.	Fall of Zaleszczycki and Sniatyn.	.. .. ..
31	**Third Battle of Ypres begins.** British and French attack on 15-mile front in Flanders; take 12 villages and claim 5,000 prisoners ([102]). French make successful attack S. of La Royère, W. of the Chevregny Ridge (Aisne).	Enemy extends his hold on Galician front and stands on W. bank of Zbrucz on front of over 30 miles. Russians retiring in Czernovitz region.	.. .. ..

Asiatic and Egyptian Theatres.	Naval and Overseas Operations.	Political, &c.	1917. July.
.. .. ..	.. .. ..	Allied Balkan Conference in Paris opens. Irish Convention, opening meeting, Sir H. Plunket in the Chair.	25
.. .. ..	.. .. ..	Food policy outlined by Lord Rhondda. Announcement by French and German Governments of agreement as to treatment of prisoners. Balkan Conference in Paris closes ([99]).	26
.. .. ..	Over 3,000 merchant ships armed (official statement).	Mr. R. Macdonald's motion to approve Reichstag " Peace Resolution " of 19.7 defeated by 148 to 19. Serbian Government's Yugo-Slav manifesto.	27
.. .. ..	.. .. ..	Royal Warrant authorising formation of " Tank Corps." Imperial and Prussian Cabinets reconstructed ([100]).	28
.. .. ..	.. .. ..	.. .. ..	29
.. .. ..	Sharp fighting reported in E. Africa ; enemy driven from River Lugungu (half-way between Lake Nyassa and sea). Announcement of H.M.S. " Ariadne " torpedoed and sunk, 38 lost.	Speech to the Press by Mr. Lloyd George ([101])	30
.. .. ..	.. .. ..	.. .. ..	31

1917. Aug.	WESTERN FRONT.	EASTERN FRONT.	SOUTHERN FRONT.		
1	Germans counter-attack, retake St. Julien and regain some positions in Ypres-Roulers railway district. French gains on W. bank of Yser Canal.	Enemy advance on Czernowitz; occupy positions near Bessarabian frontier. Russians retiring E.; S. of Dniester to Rumanian frontier, Russians retiring rapidly. Enemy now holds 50 m. on W. bank Zbrucz.	..	..	..
2	Positions Ypres-Roulers retaken by British. Germans attack Infantry Hill (E. of Monchy-Arras) and carry some trenches.	Generals Brusilov and Dmitriev resign. Gen. Kornilov appointed C.-in-C.	..	..	..
3	British retake St. Julien and positions on Infantry Hill.	Fall of Czernowitz. Kimpolung (Rumanian front) evacuated.	..	..	..
4	.. .. ..	Russians rally and attack enemy on Zbrucz River; elsewhere Russian retreat continues.	..	..	..
5	Germans regain footing in Hollebeke, but are driven out in course of day.	Enemy now 10 miles E. of Czernowitz. Vama (Bukovina front) occupied by enemy.	..	..	..
6	.. .. ..	Slight Russian rally in Czernowitz region. On Rumanian front v. Mackensen storms positions N. of Focsani.	..	..	.
7	.. .. ..	v. Mackensen crosses the Susitza river, and takes 3,000 prisoners.	..	..	..
8	Wet weather continues in Flanders. French make progress N.W. of Bixschoote.	Retirement of Russo-Rumanians in Trotus valley S.W. of Ocna.	..	..	..

Asiatic and Egyptian Theatres.	Naval and Overseas Operations.	Political, &c.	1917. Aug.
.. .. ..	.. .. ..	The Pope sends out Peace Note (v. 14.8.17).	1
.. .. ..	German raider " Seeadler " wrecked on Lord Howe Island, Pacific.	M. Kerenski resigns. Adm. Lacaze (Minister of Marine) and M. Denys Cochin (Under Secty. Foreign Affairs) resign from French Cabinet.	2
.. .. ..	Heavy fighting German E. Africa ; enemy compelled to withdraw along Lindi-Masasi road (80 miles S.W. of Port Lindi).	.. .. ..	3
.. .. ..	.. .. ..	King and Queen attend special service at Westminster Abbey for third anniversary of war. M. Kerenski withdraws resignation at request of All Parties Conference ; new Cabinet constituted.	4
.. .. ..	.. .. ..	New German Ministry announced ([100]) (v. Kühlmann Foreign Minister).	5
.. .. ..	.. .. ..	M. Kerenski (Prime Minister, War and Marine) forms National Ministry. M. Tereshchenko, Foreign Minister.	6
.. .. ..	Vice - Admiral Sir R. Wemyss succeeds Adm. Sir C. Burney as 2nd Sea Lord ; Mr. A. G. Anderson, Controller.	Liberian declaration of war on Germany, dated 4.8, published.	7
.. .. ..	.. .. ..	Mr. Ll. George and Lord R. Cecil on Serbia.	8

1917. Aug.	WESTERN FRONT.	EASTERN FRONT.	SOUTHERN FRONT.
9	Successful British raids in Lens district.	Mackensen presses his offensive, threatening communications of Russo-Rumanian armies; after 3 days fighting Russo-Rumanians repulsed.	.. .. ..
10	British advance on 2-mile front E. of Ypres, capture remainder of Westhoek, and occupy Glencorse Wood. French make progress E. and N. of Bixschoote. Nancy bombed; French bomb Frankfurt.	Mackensen beyond Susitsa river, strikes N. at Rumanians, always threatening rear of Russo-Rumanian armies; enemy also advancing in N. Moldavia.	.. .. ..
11	Heavy German counter-attack E. of Ypres repulsed. British line pressed back in Glencorse Wood.	Mackensen crosses River Sereth at one point; claims 7,000 prisoners, Rumanians stubbornly resisting, retire at Ocna.	.. .. ..
12	Aeroplane raid on Southend and Margate; 32 killed, 46 injured: one raider destroyed.	On mountain front of Moldavia, Russo-Rumanians take offensive.	.. .. ..
13	.. .. ..	Russo-Rumanian offensive continues favourable to Allies (Ocna region).	.. .. ..
14	.. .. ..	.. .. ..	.. .. ..
15	British attack on wide front N.W. of Lens to Bois Hugo, N.E. of Loos, carry German first lines and penetrate enemy positions to depth of 1 mile. Hill 70 taken by assault, also villages of Cité Ste. Elizabeth, Ste. Emile and St. Laurent, Bois Rasé and Bois Hugo. Five German counter-attacks repulsed.	Rumanian thrust in Ocna region carried no further. Rumanian 2nd Army and Russian 4th army retreating S. toward the Sereth; enemy take Soveia, renew offensive in Focsani region.	.. .. ..

Asiatic and Egyptian Theatres.	Naval and Overseas Operations.	Political, &c.	1917. Aug.
.. .. ..	.. .. ..	Third reading of Compulsory Military Service Bill for Canada passed. Count Esterhazy, Hungarian Prime Minister, resigns.	9
.. .. ..	.. .. ..	Labour Party Conference decides, by large majority, to send delegates to Stockholm Conference.	10
.. ..	Liner " City of Athens " mined off Cape Town, 21 lost.	U.S. Government refuses to issue passports for Stockholm Conference. Mr. Henderson resigns position as member of War Cabinet.	11
.. .. ..	.. ..	Ex-Tsar removed to Tobolsk.	12
.. .. ..	.. ..	Martial law in Spain. Mr. Barnes appointed to War Cabinet. Mr. Bonar Law announces that no passports for Stockholm Conference will be issued.	13
.. .. ..	.. ..	China declares War on Austria and Germany. Papal Note with proposals for peace sent to belligerent Governments published ([103]).	14
.. .. ..	.. ..	Text of Papal Note published. American troops pass through London on their way to the front; Stars and Stripes and Union Jack flown side by side from House of Lords.	15

1917. Aug.	WESTERN FRONT.	EASTERN FRONT.	SOUTHERN FRONT.
16	**Allies attack on 9-mile front N. of Ypres-Menin road, crossing Steenbeek River,** and capturing all objectives. British carry Langemarck, and establish positions ½-mile beyond; on high ground N. of Menin Road Germans press back British from ground won earlier in the day. French advance on Craonne ridge.	Russo - Rumanian army still retreating before Mackensen's offensive up Sereth valley. Baltareta bridgehead lost. In Ocna region enemy take offensive, also in Susitsa valley. Rumanians hold their ground.	.. .. ..
17	Germans counter - attack near Lens repulsed. French hold all gains and secure possession of ground E. of Bixschoote. Big French air operations on the Meuse.	.. .. ..	.. .. ..
18	French counter-attack on R. bank of Meuse and recapture trenches lost on Aug. 16.	Rumanian front fighting less intense, situation unchanged. Rumanians retire towards Marasesti (20 m. N. of Focsani).	Great fire at Salonika.
19	British line slightly advanced on a front of one mile in neighbourhood of Ypres-Poelcapelle road.	Rumanian front fighting in Slanie region S. of Ocna; enemy gain trenches in Focsani region. Germans claim 22,000 Russian prisoners in recent fighting in Galicia and Bukovina.	**Italian attack on 30-mile front in Carso** (between Mrzli Vrh and sea). Carry Austrian first line E. of Isonzo from Plava to sea (25 m.); 7,500 prisoners. Italians take Austrian bridgehead near Anhovo on R. bank Isonzo and attack Bainsizza plateau.
20	N. of Ypres slight British advance. **French carry enemy defences N. of Verdun** (third offensive) on 11-mile front to a depth of 1¼ miles, and hold Avocourt Wood, Mort Homme and Hill 240; 5,000 prisoners.	Rumanians gain ground N. of Focsani on 19th. In Ocna region enemy gain ground. Indisciplined Russians forced to retire on Riga front.	Battle continues in favour of Italians; enemy defences between Korite and Sella (right wing) carried.
21	British capture enemy positions W. and N.W. of Lens on front of 200 yards. On Verdun front, French take Cote de l'Oie, Regnéville (on L bank), Samogneux and fortified trenches connecting village with Hill 344. Zeppelin raid on Yorkshire; 1 injured.	Enemy attack on Riga front commences, Russians evacuate positions between Tirul Marsh and River Aa. Enemy attack town of Sereth (Bukovina) and take one of fortified heights.	Battle in Carso region continues.

Asiatic and Egyptian Theatres.	Naval and Overseas Operations.	Political, &c.	1917. Aug.
.. .. ..	British and German destroyers in action in Bight of Heligoland.	Mr. Ll. George on shipping losses.	16
.. ..		Mr. Balfour on the Balkans. Brig.-Gen. A. Geddes succeeds Mr. N. Chamberlain as D.-G. National Service.	17
.. ..		Government proclamation forbids threatened strike of Associated Society of Engineers and Firemen.	18
.. ..	.. ..	19
.. ..		Dr. Wekerle appointed Hungarian Prime Minister.	20
.. ..		Labour Party reaffirm their decision to send delegates to Stockholm. Parliament adjourns.	21

1917. Aug.	WESTERN FRONT.	EASTERN FRONT.	SOUTHERN FRONT.
22	Heavy fighting on Ypres front; British line advanced 500 yds. on 1-mile front. Also advance ½-mile on 2½ mile front (objective Lens). Aeroplane raid on Dover, Ramsgate and Margate; 12 killed, 25 injured. Zeppelin destroyed by naval forces off Jutland.	At Raggazen (Gulf of Riga) Russians retire from 3 to 8 miles, to shorten line. Situation unchanged on Rumanian front, where fighting continues.	Fierce fighting in Carso region, Italian progress on both R. and L. wings.
23	S.W. of Lens and N.E. of Langemarck British line slightly advanced.	.. .. ..	Battle continues. Italians carry new positions.
24	British advanced line forced back from positions gained on 22nd. Enemy post captured near Lombaertzyde (coast section). French advance 1½ miles on 2,000-yards front at Verdun, carrying Hill 304 and Bois Camard, reach S. bank of Forges Brook, between Haucourt and Béthincourt, make progress N. of Mort Homme. Official figures of enemy prisoners taken ([104]).	.. .. ..	Italians occupy summit of Monte Santo and continue their advance towards E. border of Bainsizza Plateau. Italian advance in this region 4 miles on 12½ mile front. Battle further S. dies down. Italians consolidating positions.
25	Enemy recapture some of positions lost on 19th, but are driven out later in the day. French progress N. of Hill 304.	Lull on Riga and Rumanian fronts, some activity on Volhynia front.	Intense fighting Bainsizza Plateau.
26	British capture enemy positions E. of Hargicourt (N.W. of St. Quentin) on front of over 1 mile to depth of ½ mile. Enemy recapture post lost on 24th. French make progress on R. bank of Meuse, reaching outskirts of Beaumont.	Renewed enemy attacks E. of Czernowitz; Germans claim 1,000 prisoners.	**Practically whole of Bainsizza Plateau in Italian hands;** 23,000 prisoners to date; Italians fail at Jenelik.

Asiatic and Egyptian Theatres.	Naval and Overseas Operations.	Political, &c.	1917. Aug.
War Office reports Turkish defeat in Hejaz.	.. .. ..	Earl Granville appointed Minister at Athens.	22
. .. ..	.. ..	.. .. ..	23
. .. ..	.. ..	.. .. ..	24
. .. ..	.. ..	Russian National Conference opened at Moscow by M. Kerenski, who warns extremists of the danger of their methods.	25
. .. ..	.. ..	.. .. ..	26

1917. Aug.	WESTERN FRONT.	EASTERN FRONT.	SOUTHERN FRONT.
27	Ypres region : British line advanced 2,000 yards astride St. Julien-Poelcapelle road. Renewed activity on the Aisne. On R. bank of Meuse heavy enemy counter-attack repulsed.	.. .. ..	.. .. ..
28	**Verdun : French positions** on this front almost completely **restored to those** before the great attack of **February, 1916.**	Enemy attack Focsani region (Rumanian front) ; Russian defection (of a division) in face of enemy, who advance throughout day and penetrate positions in region of Vainitza. Heavy fighting in Ocna valley, Rumanians stubbornly resisting.	Austrian counter-attacks on Bainsizza Plateau broken down. Italians claim 1,000 prisoners.
29	.. .. ..	Fighting continues in Focsani region.	.. .. .
30	Attempted German night raid on British lines S.E. of Lens repulsed.	.. .. ..	.. .. .
31	Germans force British to evacuate advanced posts N. of St. Julien-Poelcapelle road. British air raid on aerodromes on Belgian coast. French success near Hurtebise (Aisne).	.. .. ..	Heavy fighting at Mont San Gabriele (N.E. of Gorizia) ; Austrian counter - attacks repulsed. Italians claim 27,000 prisoners since Aug. 19.
Sept. 1	Enemy attack on Havrincourt (S.W. of Cambrai), at first successful, beaten back later. N.E. of Craonne, German counter-attack broken up.	German attack on E. of Riga ; their troops enter the city. Dvina river evacuated by Russians, and crossed by Germans at Üxküll.	Julian front : Slight Italian advance, taking 34 prisoners.
2	Enemy attack unsuccessfully British advance posts near Havrincourt. At Hurtebise (Aisne), 4 German attempts to recover lost positions crushed. Aeroplane raid on Dover, 1 killed, 6 injured.	Some Russian troops fall back to W. of Riga ; fighting on Mitau road. Germans cross Dvina river 18 m. above town.	.. .. .

Asiatic and Egyptian Theatres.	Naval and Overseas Operations.	Political, &c.	1917. Aug.
.. .. ..	Publication of official communication regarding operations in E. Africa; enemy slowly being pressed back, 8 miles in Masasi district. Belgian columns from Kilossa drive enemy to S. bank Ruaha river. Midway between Lake Nyassa and sea, considerable German force closely invested.	At Russian National Conference, Gen. Kornilov appeals for measures to restore discipline in the army.	27
British aeroplanes successful about Maan (Hejaz railway).	German aeroplanes drop 90 bombs on Russian shipping in Gulfs of Riga and Finland.	Moscow National Conference closed.	28
.. .. ..	.. .. ..	Polish State Council resigns. U.S. reply to the Papal Peace Note ([105]).	29
British advance on front of 600 yards S.W. of Gaza.	.. .. ..	.. .. ..	30
.. .. ..	British seaplanes drop many bombs on aerodromes near Belgian coast.	M. Malvy, French Minister of the Interior, resigns.	31
.. .. ..	Jutland coast: British destroyers drive four German mine-sweepers ashore, two on fire.	.. .. ..	Sept. 1
.. .. ..	Naval airmen bomb Bruges Docks. E. Africa: British and Belgian operations drive German detachments from River Ruaha to Mahenge.	At Trades Union Congress at Blackpool, Stockholm programme partly settled, but strongly opposed.	2

1917. Sept.	WESTERN FRONT.	EASTERN FRONT.	SOUTHERN FRONT.
3	Six German aeroplanes bomb Sheerness, etc. ; 132 killed, 96 injured, mostly naval ratings. British front slightly advanced near St. Julien (Ypres). Champagne : French raid gas tanks on Souain-Somme Py road.	**Riga finally evacuated by Russians,** forts and bridges blown up, etc. Germans claim many thousands of prisoners and 150 guns.	Pola bombed.
4	Verdun : Red Cross stations in rear of, bombed during night. Aeroplane raid on London and S.E. Counties, 19 killed, 71 injured.	Russians fall back 30 miles along Riga-Petrograd-road.	Heavy fighting N.E. of Gorizia and on S. Carso ; Italians take positions round Monte S. Gabriele and 1,600 prisoners. Italians fall back from, but recover, positions between Brestovica valley and sea.
5	Air raids over British lines kill 37 and wound 43 German prisoners. They bomb 3 British hospitals and kill 19 and wound 26 patients in French hospital at Vadelaincourt, Meuse.	Germans capture line of River Dvina to Friedrichstadt.	Struggle continues N.E. of Gorizia.
6	British detachments pressed back near Frezenberg (Ypres).	12th Russian Army falls back clear of enemy. Kaiser reviews troops in Riga.	Stubborn fighting N.E. of Gorizia.
7	American hospitals near coast bombed, 3 killed, 10 wounded.	.. .. ..	British activity on Struma front (E. Maced.). Italians attack Monte S. Gabriele. Austrians bomb Venice.
8	Verdun : French attack on Meuse front and seize Fosses, Caurières and Chaume Woods and 800 prisoners.	Gen. Kornilov dismissed ; Gen. Kemborski appointed C-i-C. Owing to misunderstanding with M. Kerenski, Gen. Kornilov marches on Petrograd.	.. .. ..
9	British take 600 yards of German trenches at Villeret (N.N.W. of St. Quentin). Meuse, R. bank : heavy fighting, Germans repulsed. End of Third Fr. offensive at Verdun.	.. .. ..	Austrians claim 6,000 prisoners near Hermada (Carso). French advance near Lake Ochrida (S.W. Macedonia).

Asiatic and Egyptian Theatres.	Naval and Overseas Operations.	Political, &c.	1917. Sept.
.. .. ..	Bruges again bombed. German warships break into Gulf of Riga and shell Livonian villages.	.. .. ..	3
.. .. ..	Scarborough shelled by submarine ; 30 rounds, 3 killed, 6 injured.	Trades Union Congress declares against Stockholm Conference by overwhelming majority. Mr. Morel sent to prison. Corresponsspondence between Kaiser and Tsar (anti-British proposals) published ([106]).	4
.. .. ..	E. Africa : Germans lose 500 men altogether from 30.8 to 2.9, and particularly severely in retreat to Mahenge.	" Bonnet Rouge " newspaper case being investigated : treasonable intrigue ; French Government accused of weakness in connection.	5
.. .. ..	German force surrenders to British c o l o u r e d troops at Kakera (N.N.E. of Kilossa).	Petrograd and Moscow closed to strangers. Mr. Henderson on Stockholm. Australian £80,000,000 War Loan Bill.	6
Health of troops in Mesopotamia reported greatly improved.	.. .. ..	U.S.A. contemplate seizing 400,000 tons of neutral shipping in American ports. M. Ribot's ministry resigns. M. Pashich in Rome.	7
.. .. ..	Enemy H.Q. at Mahenge threatened by Belgian troops from N. Enemy retreats towards Liwale, 120 m. S.W. of Kilwa. German positions occupied by British at Mponda's, S. of Mahenge.	Russian Government re-imposes death penalty everywhere for treason, desertion and cowardice. British Food Controller fixes price of milk for 3 months after October at 8d. per quart.	8
.. .. ..	Cadiz : German submarine, U 293, short of oil, enters, and is interned.	U.S.A. publishes disclosures re Swedish Legation at Buenos Aires ([107]). King's special decoration for 1914 campaign announced.	9

1917. Sept.	WESTERN FRONT.	EASTERN FRONT.	SOUTHERN FRONT.
10	British take 400 yards more trench at Villeret.	Russian 12th Army takes up position 30 m. N.E. of Riga; German pursuit.	French and Russian troops extend their occupation near Lake Ochrida.
11	British bomb S. of Lille and Roulers region heavily.	.. .. ..	Austrian counter-attacks on Bainsizza Plateau and N.E. of Gorizia heavily repulsed.
12	French headquarters estimate German losses to end of July at 4 millions.	.. .. ..	Italians hold on stubbornly N.E. of G o r i z i a. French and Russian troops cross River Devoli (Albanian frontier), driving back enemy 20 miles.
13	German attack near Langemarck repulsed. German raids W. of Craonne. Germans penetrate French advanced line N. of Caurières Wood (Meuse).	Odessa and Black Sea t r a n q u i l; population sympathise with Provisional Government.	.. .. ..
14	French drive enemy out of Caurières Wood (Verdun).	Enemy approach trenches near Focsani; repulsed everywhere by Rumanians.	.. .. ..
15	2nd Phase of 3rd Battle of Ypres: London troops capture strong point N. of Inverness Copse (Ypres). Enemy repulsed by Portuguese at Neuve Chapelle.	.. .. ..	Four successive Austrian counter-attacks on Bainsizza Plateau fail; Italians gain ground to S.E.
16	German attack on Apremont Forest (St. Mihiel) fails. Stuttgart, Colmar, Thionville and Saarburg bombed by French.	.. .. ..	.. .. ..
17	.. .. ..	Riga front: fighting between advanced posts continues.	.. .. ..

ASIATIC AND EGYPTIAN THEATRES.	NAVAL AND OVERSEAS OPERATIONS.	POLITICAL, &c.	1917. Sept.
.. .. ..	.. .. ..	Gen. Kornilov approaches Petrograd. M. Kerenski assumes dictatorship. Provisional Government resigns.	10
.. .. ..	British seaplanes bomb Zeebrugge mole and air sheds.	First party of British prisoners from Switzerland arrives. Russian crisis : M. Kerenski declares Gen. Kornilov a traitor.	11
.. .. ..	Gulf of Riga still controlled by Russian warships ; bombard German batteries on Courland shores.	M. Painlevé forms Ministry. Russia on point of civil war. Argentina hands passports to Count Luxburg. Polish Regency Council created.	12
.. .. ..	.. .. ..	Gen. Alexeiev treats with Gen. Kornilov. Latter's revolt fails ; his commander, Gen. Krimov, kills himself. Gen. Kalédin and Cossacks revolt. Soviet bans Cadets. New French Cabinet announced ([108]).	13
.. .. ..	.. .. ..	U. S. A. have spent £400,000,000 for naval construction in little over a year. Lord Reading arrives on financial mission. Sir J. Allen on New Zealand spirit ([109]). Gen. Kornilov submits.	14
Hottest season on record at Baghdad. Troops' health and spirits excellent.	Seaplanes successfully attack shipping between Blankenberghe and Ostend.	Provisional Council of 5 declares Russia a Republic under M. Kerenski ; new War Cabinet formed.	15
.. .. ..	German position at Kalimoto (N. of Mahenge) captured. Belgian troops (Col. Huyghe) pursue.	Gen. Kalédin, Hetman of Don Cossacks, declares loyalty to Government.	16
.. .. ..	.. .. ..	Central Powers issue decree appointing Polish Regency Council. Germany apologises to Argentina over Count Luxburg affair. 9d. loaf order in operation. " Summer Time " ends 2 a.m.	17

R

1917. Sept.	WESTERN FRONT.	EASTERN FRONT.	SOUTHERN FRONT.
18	.. .. ..	.. .. ..	Italians capture 200 prisoners, etc., in Carzano (Val Sugana, Trentino).
19	.. .. ..	German infantry attack Lemburg (E. of Riga) repulsed with loss by Letts.	Fighting dying down on Italian front.
20	British advance E. of Ypres and take Inverness Copse, Glencorse Wood, Veldhoek and part of Polygon Wood and 2,000 prisoners.	Enemy attack thrice in Susitza valley (Moldavia), repulsed by Rumanians.	French and Albanian troops raid Austrians in Skumbi valley (Alb.); 400 prisoners.
21	Enemy's attacks on Tower Hamlets' ridge (Ypres) repulsed. Prisoners now exceed 3,000.	After holding enemy here for 18 months, Russians retire N. from Jakobstadt (River Dvina).	Second phase of Isonzo battle closed; neither side can hold Mte. S. Gabriele.
22	Stuttgart, Trèves, Coblenz, and Frankfurt bombed.	.. .. ..	Slight Italian push in Marmolada region (Carnic).
23	.. .. ..	.. .. ..	.. .. ..
24	Aeroplane raid on London and S.E. Coast, 21 killed, 70 injured. German attack N. of Bezonvaux, Fosses and Chaume Woods, Verdun (N.E.), repulsed.	.. .. ..	Capt. Marchese di Laureati flies from Turin to London, non-stop, 650 miles, 7 hours 22 minutes.
25	Germans penetrate between Tower Hamlets ridge and Polygon Wood; repulsed later. S.E. London raided by German aeroplanes; 9 killed, 23 injured. Zepps. attack Yorkshire and Lincolnshire coasts, 3 injured.	.. .. ..	.. .. ..

Asiatic and Egyptian Theatres.	Naval and Overseas Operations.	Political, &c.	1917. Sept.
.. .. ..	.. .. ..	M. Painlevé re - defines French War Aims : Alsace-Lorraine and reparation.	18
.. .. ..	.. .. ..	M. Kerenski tries to limit powers of Extremists. Vote of confidence in French Government. 343,500 U.S.A. conscripts joined to date.	19
Gen. Cassini's column defeats Nuri Pasha at Zanzur (W. of Tripoli City) ; enemy losses 1,600 etc. Trans-Caucasia declares itself a Republic.	.. .. ..	Sir A. Yapp, Food Controller. National War Convention of U.S.A. Chambers of Commerce meets for better understanding of British war aims ; addressed by Lord Northcliffe.	20
British bomb and cause surrender of Diwaniya (Euphrates).	German groups broken up W. of Kilwa and Lindi ; flee S. to River Mbemkuru.	Central Powers' reply to Papal Note ([110]). Gen. Alexeiev resigns. Publication of Count Bernstorff's correspondence with Berlin *re* bribing Congress.	21
.. .. ..	Ostend attacked by British coast patrol.	Relations much strained between Germany and Argentina.	22
.. .. ..	British destroyer sunk in Channel, 50 survivors.	Costa Rica breaks off relations with Germany.	23
.. .. ..	British destroy German food depôts W. of Kilwa ; Belgian column within 10 miles of Mahenge.	Satisfactory Japanese Mission (Viscount Ishii) to U.S.A. Great Britain apologises to Denmark for Jutland violation on 1.9.17, and offers indemnity.	24
Russian detachments attack Turks successfully near Ortobo (Bitlis).	Ostend bombarded again. Brig. - Gen. Northey's summary of his operations in E. Africa published ([111]).	New Fatherland's Party meeting and declaration of v. Tirpitz's policy ([112]). U.S.A. not one of the " Allies "([113]).	25

1917. Sept.	WESTERN FRONT.	EASTERN FRONT.	SOUTHERN FRONT.
26	British advance on 6-mile front E. of Ypres ; Polygon Wood cleared, Zonnebeke stormed ; advance towards Passchendaele. Four hostile counter-attacks fail after fierce fighting.	.. .. ..	Fighting in Marmolada region.
27	Seven enemy counter-attacks E. of Ypres repulsed	.. .. ..	Pola and Olivi Rock (Austrian submarine base) heavily bombed.
28	Aeroplane raid on S.E. Coast ; raiders headed off from London ; no damage.	.. .. ..	Italians gain ground on Monte S. Gabriele.
29	Aeroplane raid on London ; 3 machines penetrate defences, 14 killed, 87 injured.	.. .. ..	Italians improve position on Bainsizza Plateau, taking 1,400 prisoners.
30	Aeroplane raid on London : 4 machines penetrate defences ; 14 killed, 38 injured. Three German flame attacks between Tower Hamlets and Polygon Wood repulsed. Germans gain temporary footing at Berry-au-Bac (Aisne river). 5,296 prisoners and 11 guns, etc., taken by British during September.	.. .. ..	Successful Italian attack on Bainsizza Plateau ; 600 prisoners taken.
Oct. 1	Five powerful German attacks repulsed between Ypres-Menin road and Polygon Wood and at Zonnebeke. Between Chaume Wood and Bezonvaux (Verdun) temporary German success. French and British airmen bomb Rhine towns and Roulers ; Dunkirk bombed by Germans, serious material damage. Aeroplane raid on London : 11 killed, 41 injured.	German airmen bomb Oesel Island (Riga).	Austrian attack on Bainsizza Plateau repulsed.

Asiatic and Egyptian Theatres.	Naval and Overseas Operations.	Political, &c.	1917. Sept.
Hejaz railway bridge destroyed near Maan; train derailed, 80 prisoners.	E. Africa : enemy retire from strong post in Lukuledi valley (22 m. S.E. of Lindi).	Australian strike: 50,000 unemployed in Sydney, etc. etc. M. Venizelos resigns War portfolio. Reichstag President denounces Mr. Wilson. Central Georgian Council formed. M. Kerenski resigns from Soviet.	26
Russians fight Kurds near Oromaru (Van).	Seaplanes raid St. Denis Westrem aerodrome : 15 Gothas hit.	Russian Democratic Congress at Moscow opens. National War Bonds (5% and 4%, latter free of Income Tax) started. Arrest of Lenin ordered.	27
British defeat Turks near Ramadiya (Euphrates), and take Turkish commander, 3,455 prisoners, and 13 guns. Red Cross river work ([115]).	Zeebrugge and aerodromes bombed. Big German supply centre 82 m. S.W. of Kilwa captured. Rhodesian column arrives 66 miles S.W. of Liwale.	Bolo Pasha arrested ([116]). v. Kühlmann on Papal Note in Reichstag ([117]). Dr. Michaelis refuses to state German war aims.	28
.. .. ..	.. .. ..	King of Italy returns after visiting French and Belgian fronts.	29
.. .. ..	St. Denis Westrem again bombed.	Sun-yat-Sen arrested for organising revolution at Canton. Non-Slav Congress at Kiev demands autonomy for all Russian nationalities.	30
			Oct. 1
.. .. ..	E. Africa : Fighting proceeding in Mbemkuru Valley ; 75 miles S. of Kondoa Irangi (N. of Cent. Rly.) a German guerrilla detachment surrenders. Our troops meet strong resistance 30 m. S.W. of Lindi.	Great typhoon in Japan does vast damage.	

1917. Oct.	WESTERN FRONT.	EASTERN FRONT.	SOUTHERN FRONT.
2	Germans attack in Beaumont (Reims), and between Samogneux and Hill 344 (Verdun) gain footing. French counterattacks all day fail to drive out Germans. French and British airmen bomb towns in Metz region, Cambrai and Courtrai and St. Denis Westrem aerodrome.	.. .. ..	Austrian attack on slopes of San Gabriele (Isonzo) fail. Italians gain ground in counter-attack.
3	German attack repulsed N. of Menin road between Tower Hamlets and Polygon Wood (Ypres). Preparations for German attack E. of Reims broken up. Violent artillery duel on Verdun front.	Intense artillery duel in Jakobstadt region (Dvinsk). Artillery stop fierce enemy attack 7 m. N. of Rumanian frontier (Bukovina). Bulgars attack Rumanians N. of mouth of Buzeu river.	Italians repel continued Austrian attacks on San Gabriele.
4	British advance on 8-mile front, anticipating by a few minutes a German attack E. of Ypres; 3,000 prisoners. In counter-attack Germans regain some ground S.E. of Polygon Wood. Small German attack repulsed on Hill 344 (Verdun).	.. .. ..	.. .. ..
5	Number of German prisoners taken last 5 days on Ypres front totals 4,446. Congratulations from the King.	.. .. ..	.. .. ..
6	German attack penetrates trenches at Hill 344 (Verdun), but French drive them out again. Enemy attack at dusk on Polygon Wood (Ypres) repulsed; British take 380 prisoners.	Heavy fighting 25 m. S. of Czernovitz; no change, Russians take 750 prisoners.	.. .. ..
7	German attacks near Reutel (Ypres) repulsed. Powerful German raid in Champagne repulsed by French.	German attack 28 m. E.N.E. of Riga repulsed.	Artillery active on Bainsizza Plateau (Isonzo), and on Carso. Austrian attack on Massif of Costabella repulsed.

Asiatic and Egyptian Theatres.	Naval and Overseas Operations.	Political, &c.	1917. Oct.
.. .. ..	H.M.S. "Drake" torpedoed off the Irish Coast: 19 killed. Reichstag informed of mutiny at Wilhelmshaven.	British War Loan issued. Russian Democratic Conference decides against Coalition Government. Swedish Government resigns. 2nd Papal Note to Allies announced in Italy.	2
Russians take Nereman village, 50 m. N. of Mosul.	Italian airmen bomb vessels in harbour of Cattaro.	Meeting of Democratic Conference in Russia ([118]). Count Czernin issues Peace programme. Sir W. Laurier (Canada) resigns.	3
.. .. ..	.. ..	Figures re losses of British Overseas troops are published ([119]). Peruvian Government issues ultimatum to Germany re sinking ships. M. Radoslavov (Bulg.) on peace.	4
.. .. ..	In Mbemkuru Valley (S.W. Kilwa), enemy retiring before British, reach Nangano (35 m. S.E. Liwali). Column from Ruhuji river advance W.	Serious position in Argentina ([120]). Swedish Government protest against seizure of their ships lying in British ports.	5
.. ..	Mbemkuru column (E. Africa) reaches point 30 m. from Nangano; Belgian troops engaged N. and N.E. of Mahenge; British troops in close touch with enemy 50 and 25 m. further South.	**Peru breaks off diplomatic relations** with Germany. Socialist Conference at Bordeaux. Georgia starts a separate Army.	6
Great artillery activity on Gaza front (Palestine).	German U.293, interned at Cadiz, escapes from Spain. Enquiry ordered by Spanish Prime Minister.	M. Kerenski forms Coalition Government. **Uruguay breaks off diplomatic relations** with Germany. Paris Chamber announces scantiest harvest for 50 years in France. Luxuries cut down to make tonnage for import of grain.	7

1917. Oct.	WESTERN FRONT.	EASTERN FRONT.	SOUTHERN FRONT.
8	Aisne front : both German and French attacks round Craonne fail. Germans claim to have broken up French attack S.W. of Beaumont (Reims).	..	..
9	3rd Phase of 3rd battle of Ypres : Franco - British attack E. and N.E. Outskirts of Houthulst Forest taken. 1 m. advance on Passchendaele Ridge, 2,000 prisoners. Enemy counter-attack drives in advance troops S. of Ypres-Staden railway on 2,000 yards front. Keen artillery struggle, N. of Chaume Wood (Verdun).	Enemy air activity very marked round Oesel Island (Riga).	..
10	French extend their hold up valley of Corverbeck (Ypres). Germans gain footing in first line trenches N. of Chaume Wood (Verdun).	..	..
11	French stop a German counter-attack E. of Dreibank, Ypres. Germans gain temporary footing in advanced trenches N. of Hill 344 (Verdun), but driven out by French.	Germans gain some ground S.E. of Segewold (Riga). Germans attempt to fraternize in Riga sector.	..
12	British attack N.E. of Ypres on 6 m. front from French right to Ypres-Roulers railway. Some progress all along line, but rain stops big advance. German attacks repulsed all along French front, notably in Champagne.	Germans land at Tagga Bay N. of Oesel Island (Riga) and on Dago Island Part of Oesel Island occupied and traversed to E. end ; attempt to capture pier on Moon Island repulsed.	Austrian attack repulsed in region of Mnt. Costabella.
13	Control of British Air Service reorganised ; Maj.-Gen. Salmond succeeds Lt.-Gen. Sir D. Henderson as Director-General.	Germans continue landing on Oesel Island. Detachments landed on Dagö Is. promptly ejected, Arensburg occupied.	Considerable artillery activity on Upper Isonzo.

ASIATIC AND EGYPTIAN THEATRES.	NAVAL AND OVERSEAS OPERATIONS.	POLITICAL, &c.	1917. Oct.
.. .. ..	Russian encounter with enemy scouting-vessels between Oesel Island and N.W. Courland.	Railway strike begins in Russia. Ukraine inaugurates autonomous Government. Inter-ally Parliamentary Committee commences 3 days'conference. M. Kerenski forms new Russian Cabinet.	8
Death of Hussein Kamel, Sultan of Egypt ; succeeded by Ahmed Fuad, his youngest brother, b. 1868.	German Naval mutiny announced to-day. Independent Socialist Party involved ([121]). 11 enemy motor boats reconnoitring near Riga. N. of Lake Eyassi (S.E. Victoria Nyanza) last enemy guerrilla detachment captured. Belgians occupy Mahenge, old German H.Q. in Highlands; 260 prisoners.	German intrigue in Spanish Marocco ([122]).	9
.. .. ..	Portuguese capture German post at Mauta, 26 m. N. of Rovuma river (E. Africa). Germans bomb Russian transports at S. end of Oesel Island (Riga).	v. Kühlmann discussing Peace proposals says Germany will never give back Alsace-Lorraine ; French press virulent on the subject.	10
Turkish attack in Armenia, 16 m. S.W. of Erzingan, repulsed.	E. Africa : Column in Mbemkuru valley occupies Ruponda on flank of enemy retreating before Nahango column. Large quantities corn and ammunition captured.	4 ships flying Swedish flag and lying in British ports taken over by British, being mainly British owned and liable to be treated as such by Germans. British Government stops commercial cable communication with Holland ([123]). Kaiser visits Sofia.	11
.. .. ..	Combined German naval and military landing at Oesel Island (Riga). Russian coast batteries destroyed (German 8 Dreadnoughts, 12 light cr., 40 t.b.d.,etc.).Russian ships hinder German fleet entering between Dagö and Oesel Islands.	Count Luxburg is interned in Argentina. Sir Robert Borden forms Coalition Government in Canada.	12
.. .. ..	Belgians repel German attack S.E. of Mahenge. German mine-sweepers between Courland and Oesel Island.	.. .. ..	13

1917. Oct.	WESTERN FRONT.	EASTERN FRONT.	SOUTHERN FRONT.
14	.. .. ..	Tserel and Arensburg in flames. Russians guarding Irbek Strait cut off on Sworbe Peninsula.	.. .. ..
15	Bruges dock raided by British airmen.	Germans cut off retreat of Russians from Oesel Island to Moon Island *via* Mole and capture 3,500 prisoners. Germans advance along Sworbe Peninsula.	.. .. ..
16	Enemy air raid on Nancy. French attack W. of Craonne is repulsed by Germans.	Oesel Island fully in German possession. Germans claim 10,000 prisoners and 50 guns. German attempt to throw bridge across Dvina frustrated.	.. .. ..
17	Great artillery activity N.E. of Soissons. Germans enter French trenches at Hill 344 (Verdun).	German attempt to land on Dagö Island (Riga) supported by naval guns is repulsed. Government prepares to move to Moscow from Petrograd.	.. .. ..
18	.. .. ..	Moon Island (Riga) evacuated by Russians.	Renewed local fighting on Trentino and Carnia fronts.
19	13 Zeppelins raid E. and N.E. England and London; 5 brought down. Larger type of Zeppelin used; 36 killed, 55 injured.	Germans land on Dagö Is. Germans fail in effort to fraternize on Rumanian front.	.. .. ..
20	Violent artillery action on Aisne front.	Islands of Dagö and Schilden captured by Germans. Germans retire to Skuli - Lemburg line 30 m. E. of Riga to prepared positions.	Germans report French attack repulsed between Skumbi valley and L Ochrida (Maced.).

Asiatic and Egyptian Theatres.	Naval and Overseas Operations.	Political, &c.	1917. Oct.
.. .. ..	German warships land detachments on Islands of Runo and Abro (Riga). British mine-sweeper "Begonia"and merchant cruiser "Champagne" sunk, 56 lost. Russian t.b.d's repel German effort to force passage of Moon Sound (Oesel Is'd.)	More drastic measures taken in Great Britain to compete with growing shortage of foodstuffs, petrol, and coal. Ukraine declares itself an autonomous nation and claims participation in future Peace Conference.	14
.. .. ..	E. Africa : Lindi column drives enemy on Nyangoa by enveloping movement from N.	.. .. ..	15
.. .. ..	Belgians rescue convoy of prisoners S.E. of Mahenge (E. Africa). Russian fleet assists defence in Moon Sound. "Slava" battleship sunk.	Pan-German propaganda ([124]). Mr. Bonar Law announces future Air Ministry Bill.	16
.. .. ..	U.S. transport "Antilles" torpedoed : 67 lost. E. Africa : Column from Lukuledi Mission drives enemy eastward ; 2 columns occupy Nyangoa. Naval engagement Gulf of Riga ([125]). German raiders sink 9 merchantmen and 2 destroyers out of convoy off Bergen ; 135 lost.	Australian trans-continental railway joined up. Holland replies to British note re transport of gravel and sand ([126]).	17
Report re German activity near Jibuti (Fr. Somaliland) ([126]).	Fighting continues round Nyangoa (E. Africa) ; considerable casualties on both sides.	Dutch shipping in American ports to be utilised ([127]).	18
.. .. ..	British armed mercantile cruiser "Orama" torpedoed and sunk ; no lives lost.	Liberal Swedish Cabinet formed by Prof. Eden. U.S.A. embargo on trade with Northern Neutrals ([128]). Munition works removed from Petrograd.	19
Turkish troops driven across Diala river (Mesopotamia).	British submarine sinks German Dreadnought and transport in Gulf of Riga.	Archbishop of Athens degraded for "Anathema" ceremony of 25.12.16. Allies recognise Polish National Committee.	20

1917. Oct.	Western Front.	Eastern Front.	Southern Front.
21	Germans make strong attack at Bezonvaux (Verdun) ; Saarbrücken bombed by British ; Dunkirk bombed by Germans.	Russians repel German attempt to land 8 m. N. of Verder Peninsula (Riga). Germans land on Russian mainland at Verder. Germans claim 20,000 prisoners and 100 guns in last nine days' fighting.	Considerable artillery activity on Italian front. Monastir shelled again.
22	Franco-British advance on 2½ m. front between Poelcapelle (Ypres) and Houthulst Forest, S. end of Forest captured, 200 prisoners.	On night 21-22 Germans retire on wide front between Riga Bay and River Dvina.	Italians repulse strong Austro-German attack on Cadore front (Dolom).
23	**Great French Victory on the Aisne**, N.E. Soissons ; French advance up to 2 m. on 6 m. front, capture 8,000 prisoners, 70 guns. Germans gain footing N.E. Hill 344 (Verdun) but driven out. Germans regain a little ground S. end Houthulst Forest (Ypres). German attack near Poelcapelle repulsed. In evening Germans seventh counter-attack on Ypres front since 22nd repulsed.	Attempted German landing 8 m. S. of Verder repulsed. N.E. of Riga, Germans retire 20 m. in 2 days, destroying bridges.	Strong hostile concentration towards Upper Isonzo and Bainsizza Plateau ; Mt. Rombon to Bainsizza heavily shelled.
24	French reach banks of Oise-Aisne Canal ; 11,000 prisoners to date. German attack Chaume Wood (Verdun) repulsed. German attack repulsed Houthulst Forest (Ypres.)	Russians begin to evacuate Kronstadt. Russian advance to Dvina 30 m. S.E. Riga.	**Austro-Germans attack in** thick fog on 20-mile front **breaking through 2nd Italian Army** at Tolmino, Caporetto and Plezzo ; 10,000 prisoners.
25	Germans gain footing N. of Chaume Wood (Verdun). Further French advance on Aisne front ; Filain captured ; 160 guns taken since 23rd.	German attempt to consolidate on Verder Peninsula frustrated.	Italians retreat from Plezzo to S.W. of Tolmino and prepare to evacuate Bainsizza Plateau. Germans claim 30,000 prisoners and 300 guns.

ASIATIC AND EGYPTIAN THEATRES.	NAVAL AND OVERSEAS OPERATIONS.	POLITICAL, &c.	1917. Oct.
· · · · · ·	Russian fleets escapes N. out of Moon Sound. Ostend bombarded by British ships.	Russian Soviet's Peace Terms issued.	21
· · · · · · · ·		Petrograd Soviet hold stormy meeting; Trotski demands peace; accuses Kerenski of treason; defence of Petrograd arranged. U.S.A. begin appropriation of raw material for war purchased and stored by Germans in U.S.A. during first two years of war.	22
Turkish troops approaching Samarra (N.W.Baghdad) repulsed by British.	· · · · · ·	M. Ribot resigns, succeeded as Foreign Minister by M. Barthou. Mr. Redmond's motion on Irish Government.	23
· · · · · · · · · ·	· · · ·	· · · · · ·	24
· · · · · ·	German ships from Moon Sound bombard Kuno Island near Pernau (Riga).	Fall of Boselli Cabinet in Italy. Franco-British convention for Military Service ([136]). Sinn Fein convention in Dublin.	25

1917. Oct.	WESTERN FRONT.	EASTERN FRONT	SOUTHERN FRONT.
26	Franco-British attack E., N.E. and N. of Ypres. British positions improved from Passchendaele to Poelcapelle. French capture Draibank; bad weather.	.. .. ..	Bainsizza Plateau evacuated. Germans claim 60,000 prisoners and 500 guns.
27	French progress on Aisne front, occupy Froidmont Farm, fail to cross Canal. French and Belgians advance astride Ypres-Dixmude road. U.S.A. troops in action.	Germans retire from Verder Peninsula (Riga). Germans again attempt to fraternize with Russians North and Centre.	Cividale (W. of Isonzo) in flames and occupied by Germans, who claim 80,000 prisoners.
28	French attack on Oise-Aisne Canal and German counter-attack both fail. German attack in Champagne repulsed. French continue progress in Belgium. Germans gain footing from Chaume Wood to Bezonvaux (Verdun).	.. .. ..	Italian 2nd and 3rd armies retreat. Italians retreat from Carnia front. Austrians occupy Gorizia and 8 m. further W. Germans claim 100,000 prisoners.
29	Attempted air - raid on Essex driven off. Dunkirk, Calais, Belfort bombed.	Enemy attack repulsed in Riga area, Janinzen to Skuli.	Germans capture Udine, former Italian G.H.Q. Austrians drive Italians back along Carnia front.
30	British attack in bad weather at Ypres from Poelcapelle to Passchendaele ; enter latter but are driven back to outskirts. Five German counter-attacks repulsed. Saarbrücken and Pirmasens bombed by British.	.. .. ..	Italians fall back towards the River Tagliamento.
31	Aeroplane raid on Kent and Dover : no damage. Another raid at night on Kent, Essex and London ; 10 killed, 22 injured.	German attempts at fraternization met with artillery fire.	2nd and 3rd Italian armies withdrawn behind River Tagliamento. Germans claim over 180,000 prisoners and 1,500 guns.
Nov. 1	British airmen bomb Kaiserslautern.	.. ..	.. ..

ASIATIC AND EGYPTIAN THEATRES.	NAVAL AND OVERSEAS OPERATIONS.	POLITICAL, &c.	1917. Oct.
.. .. ..	German squadron bombards Khainash, 40 m. S. of Pernau (Riga). Transports appear 12 m. further S.	**Brazil declared in a state of War** with Germany.	26
British cavalry in action in centre of Gaza front (Palestine).	.. .. ..	**U.S.A. infantry and artillery in action in France for first time.** Army brings about fall of Cabinet in Spain. Polish Regency Council takes office.	27
.. .. ..	.. .. ..	U.S.A. second Liberty Loan: £1,000,000,000 has been subscribed. Count Luxburg's plot to invade S. Brazil ([131]). Sig. Orlando Italian Prime Minister.	28
.. .. ..	General Northey captures Liwale ; Germans driven S.E.	Parliament's thanks voted to Navy and Army.	29
Maj.-Gen. L. J. Bols succeeds Maj.-Gen. Sir A. Lynden Bell as C.G.S. in Palestine.	.. .. ..	Signor Orlando forms new Italian Cabinet ([132]). Mr. Balfour on the Balkans.	30
British capture Beersheba, with 1,800 Turks and 9 guns.	.. .. ..	Dr. Michaelis resigns German Chancellorship ; latter offered to Count Hertling.	31
Turkish defeat near Gaza ; British capture outer defences on a front of 5,000 yards.	.. .. ..	Recruiting taken over by Ministry of National Service.. Unrest in Petrograd ; Maximalists threaten armed action. **Count Hertling becomes Imperial Chancellor.**	Nov.

1917. Nov.	WESTERN FRONT.	EASTERN FRONT.	SOUTHERN FRONT.
2	Hostile artillery active E. of Ypres. Big French success on Aisne; Germans retreat from Chemin des Dames on 12½ mile front.	.. .. ..	Italy reorganises her forces behind the Tagliamento; Germans reach E. bank of river.
3	Skirmishing activity round Ypres. French push forward in region of Corbeny and reach S. bank of Ailette river.	German and Russian soldiers fraternise on northern front.	German pressure on Tagliamento increases. French troops arrive. W. of L. Garda Germans make strong attacks on Italian advanced posts.
4	Raiding on Ypres and Arras fronts. Artillery active N. of Chaume Wood (Verdun). French consolidate new positions along Chemin des Dames.	.. .. ..	British Troops arrive in Italy.
5	.. .. ..	.. .. ..	Enemy cross Tagliamento N. of Pinzano, capture many prisoners. Pressure on Italian left wing intensified. British and French troops arrive in Italy.
6	British attack launched at dawn on Ypres ridge. Canadians capture Passchendaele. End of Third Battle of Ypres.	Limited fighting on Russian fronts.	Italians again in retreat; they abandon the Tagliamento; enemy troops reach Maniago. Renewed German attacks in Trentino.
7	British consolidate new positions at Passchendaele; no German counter-attacks. Germans attack French defences at Chaume Wood (Verdun).	.. .. ..	Italians in retreat W. from Tagliamento reach River Livenza. Germans claim many thousand prisoners.
8	Two successful British raids near Fresnoy and Armentières. Lively artillery actions along whole front.	.. .. ..	Germans force crossing of Livenza river and pursue Italians towards Piave river. Between Tolmezzo and Gemona, 17,000 Italians are outflanked and surrender.

ASIATIC AND EGYPTIAN THEATRES.	NAVAL AND OVERSEAS OPERATIONS.	POLITICAL, &c.	1917. Nov.
British capture positions N. of Beersheba. On Tigris, British rout Turks near Dur, 85 m. above Baghdad.	In Kattegat, British destroyers sink a German auxiliary cruiser and 10 armed patrol craft.	Mr. Balfour's letter to Lord Rothschild, giving Government approval to Zionism, published.	2
Operations against Gaza continued.	In E. Africa British and Belgian forces make good progress; drive German detachments eastward.	.. .. ..	3
.. .. ..	.. .. ..	Mr. Ll. George and M. Painlevé leave for Italy. Gen. Tumanov succeeds M. Verkhovski as Russian Minister of war.	4
British carry Turkish line of defences between Gaza and Beersheba. Sir S. Maude routs Turks at Tekrit (Tigris).	.. .. ..	Correspondence of British and German Governments re alleged misuse of British hospital ships issued as White Paper (Cd.8692).	5
Gen. Allenby captures Khuweilfeh, 11 m. N. of Beersheba. Gen. Maude occupies Tekrit.	.. .. ..	Conference at Rapallo (near Genoa) between Allied statesmen and generals on critical situation in Italy. War aims debate in House of Commons. Maximalists gain increased power.	6
Capture of Gaza by Gen. Allenby; the troops push on and reach the Wadi Hesi, 8 m. N. of Gaza. British and French warships co-operate off coast.	.. .. ..	Notes of agreement between U.S.A. and Japan, concerning their interests in China, published ([133]). Maximalist ("Bolshevik") revolution spreading in Petrograd.	7
Gen. Allenby follows up his victory in Palestine. Turks in retreat N. on Hebron and Jerusalem.	.. ..	Arrival in London of U.S.A. Mission under Col. House. Coup d'Etat and fighting in Petrograd ; Bolsheviks under Lenin depose Kerenski, who takes to flight. Revolutionaries announce " an immediate democratic peace " their first object ([134]).	8

S

1917. Nov.	WESTERN FRONT.	EASTERN FRONT.			SOUTHERN FRONT.
9	Heavy air fighting	..	..	..	Italians establish themselves behind the Lower Piave. Germans continue advance ; in Trentino they recapture Asiago. Gen. Fayolle C.-in-C.of Franco-British forces in Venetia. Allied Ministers visit King of Italy on front. Gen. Diaz succeeds Gen. Cadorna.
10	English and Canadian troops make successful attacks along ridge N. and N.W. of Passchendaele. Germans repulsed at Chaume Wood by French.	..	..	..	Austrian advance checked on Asiago front ; on Upper Piave enemy capture Belluno.
11	Heavy rain ; enemy artillery active against new positions on Passchendaele ridge. Germans repulsed at Hartmannsweilerkopf.	..	..	..	From Belluno Austrians advance down the Piave towards Feltre. They renew attacks on Asiago Plateau without success.
12	Heavy shelling on Ypres front.	..	..	..	On Lower Piave Austrians establish bridgehead at Zenson, 20 m. N.E. of Venice. Italians evacuate Fonzaso and mountain positions overlooking the Brenta.
13	Concentrated shelling of Ypres and Passchendaele salient by Germans, followed by infantry attack ; repulsed by British. Successful Belgian raid S.E. of Nieuport. German raids near Reims repulsed ; they bomb Calais.	..	..	..	Great efforts by Austrians to force the Piave lines guarding Venice ; they cross main stream at Zenson and Grisolera ; further N. they occupy islands in the river.
14	British improve their line N.W. of Passchendaele. Artillery active in French sector.	..	..	..	Italians make firm stand on whole length of Piave, enemy held everywhere.

ASIATIC AND EGYPTIAN THEATRES.	NAVAL AND OVERSEAS OPERATIONS.	POLITICAL, &c.	1917. Nov.
Much war material collected at Tekrit.	.. .. ..	Lord Mayor's Banquet: important speeches. Conference at Rapallo decides on creation of a **Supreme Allied War Council** for Western front ([¹³⁵]). Lenin and the Revolutionary Military Committee remain in command of Petrograd ; Soviets issue appeals for support of army. Cossack Confederation forming.	9
Further advance of Gen. Allenby's forces ; Ascalon occupied ; fighting near Esdud.	Good progress in E. Africa; British troops occupy Ndonda, in Lukuledi valley. Enemy's N. force in retreat from Mahenge.	Text of Air Force Bill published in " Times " ([¹³⁶]). Anti-Bolshevik reaction, troops loyal to Kerenski and Provisional Government march on Petrograd.	10
Turks organise new line of defence covering Jerusalem and Hebron.	In E. Africa two British columns meet at Ndonda, Germans flee to hills near Portuguese border.	Reports from Petrograd of disorder spreading ; Kerenski's forces reach Tsarskoe Selo.	11
Gen. Allenby attacks new Turkish position on the Wadi Sugheir, 12 m. N. of Ascalon.	.. .. ..	Mr. Lloyd George in Paris on urgent necessity of new Allied War Council. New scale of voluntary rations ([¹³⁷]). Russians in London repudiate Leninists. Fighting at Tsarskoe Selo: Trotski and Lenin claim victory over Kerenski's forces.	12
British troops drive Turks from Wadi Sugheir ; take many prisoners and guns. Turks seek refuge behind Wadi Surar, 8 m. S. of Jaffa.	.. .. ..	M. Venizelos arrives in London. Painlevé Ministry resigns after defeat on vote of confidence in Chamber. Fighting in Moscow and Petrograd between Bolsheviks and followers of Kerenski.	13
Gen. Allenby continues advance in Palestine ; Jerusalem railway reached.	Loss announced of one of H.M. destroyers and a small monitor by submarine, while co-operating with Army in Palestine.	In House of Commons, Mr. Ll. George explains Allied War Council. " Reprisal " Bill against Germans adopted in Brazilian Chamber ([¹³⁸]). Defeat of Kerenski ; civil strife and much confusion in Petrograd.	14

1916. Nov.	WESTERN FRONT.	EASTERN FRONT.	SOUTHERN FRONT.
15	Enemy attacks N. of Menin road and N.E. of Passchendaele repulsed.	.. .. ..	Italians give ground both sides of the Brenta; enemy capture Cismon. On Lower Piave resistance maintained. Allied reinforcements arrive daily.
16	Intense firing round Passchendaele. Good air work by Allies behind battle front.	.. .. ..	Strong enemy onslaughts on whole Italian front. Italians give ground between Brenta and Piave, are driven from Mt. Prassolan, and retreat to Mt. Grappa. They hold enemy on Lower Piave.
17	British salient widened on Passchendaele ridge. Successful raid S. of River Scarpe. Surprise attacks by French S.E. of St. Quentin and in Champagne.	.. .. ..	Fierce mountain fighting: Germans take Quero and Monte Cornella.
18	Artillery very active on both sides; German raids N.W. of St. Quentin.	.. .. ..	Italians driven from fortified positions on Mt. Tomba, but offer strong resistance. Austrians attack in S. Albania and attempt to cross River Voyusa, 12 m. N. of Valona.
19	Hostile raids repulsed by British. French success at Chaume Wood.	.. .. ..	Italians make determined stand in the mountains and defeat Austrians' attacks. On Lower Piave enemy make no progress.
20	Surprise **British Advance at Cambrai**. 3rd Army under Lt.-Gen. Byng attacks on 10 m. front, between St. Quentin and River Scarpe. "Hindenburg Line" broken, numerous villages captured, over 8,000 prisoners taken ([110]).	.. .. ..	Failure of enemy attacks along whole front. On the coast the Italian navy and British monitors co-operate with land forces.

Asiatic and Egyptian Theatres.	Naval and Overseas Operations.	Political, &c.	1916. Nov.
Gen. Allenby advances to within 3 m. of Jaffa. Since Oct. 31 over 9,000 prisoners taken.	Further actions on Makonde Plateau (E. Africa). Enemy driven from Chivata ; make for Portuguese territory.	M. Clémenceau accepts office and forms a new Ministry. Himself P.M. and Minister of War, M. Pichon Foreign Minister. Georgian Nobility declares its property national. Flight of Kerenski. Bolsheviks in power in Petrograd. Bitter fighting in Moscow, over 4,000 killed.	15
.. .. ..	.. .. ..	Lord Cowdray resigns Chairmanship of Air Board. M. Venizelos welcomed at Mansion House.	16
British troops capture Jaffa ; Turks again retire N.	Naval engagement between light cruisers in Heligoland Bight ; one German mine - sweeper sunk. In E. Africa British troops pursue enemy and occupy Lutshemi.	.. .. ..	17
Death from cholera of Sir Stanley Maude in Mesopotamia ([139]).	In E. Africa force of 262 Germans and 700 Askaris surrenders to British, 18 m. S.E. of Chivata. British patrol boat sunk in Mediterranean by enemy submarine, 9 killed.	Petrograd completely held by Bolsheviks. Rumours current that Russia will shortly withdraw from war.	18
British advance further in the hills of Judea ; arrive within 6 m. of Jerusalem.	.. .. ..	Mr. Ll. George on Allied War Council in House of Commons. Georgian National Council meets. Bolsheviks issue offer to the nations for immediate armistice on all fronts for the purpose of discussing a democratic peace.	19
Turks stubbornly defend road to Jerusalem.	.. .. ..	Conference between U.S. Mission, War Cabinet and Heads of Departments re America's co-operation in War. M. Clémenceau makes statement of policy.	20

1917. Nov.	WESTERN FRONT.	EASTERN FRONT.	SOUTHERN FRONT.
21	British success continued; villages taken; our troops at Fontaine Notre Dame within 2½ m. of Cambrai; more guns and prisoners captured. French carry a salient on Craonne Plateau, S. of Juvincourt.	Bolsheviks dismiss Gen. Dukhonin (C.-in-C.) for refusing to negotiate an armistice with enemy; Ensign Krilenko C.-in-C.	Strong enemy attacks in mountains between the Brenta and Piave are everywhere repulsed by Italians, except at Mt. Fontana Secca.
22	All gains on British front consolidated, except at Fontaine Notre Dame, which Germans retake. Unsuccessful German counter-attack S. of Juvincourt.	Lenin authorises troops the at front to negotiate peace with the enemy.	Fighting in mountains continues. On Lower Piave enemy make no progress. Austrian attacks in Albania on Italian line between rivers Osum and Voyusa
23	British attack in the night and advance on line S.E. of Ypres. Further advance on enemy positions W. of Cambrai; British attack Bourlon Wood. Byng promoted to General.	Lenin Government issues decree for further disbandment of Russian army.	.. .. ..
24	Fierce fighting at Bourlon Wood and village; both change hands frequently. British gains near Mœuvres, Quéant, Bullecourt, and Banteux. Successful French attack on Verdun front.	.. .. ..	Austrian assaults fail on Asiago Plateau; also attempts to cross Lower Piave. Gen. Sir H Plumer appointed to command British forces in Italy.
25	Strong German counter-attacks at Bourlon; enemy regain parts of the village. French attack in Samogneux district, N. of Verdun; they take 800 prisoners.	In Russian centre (near Baranovichi) the troops continue to fraternize with the enemy.	Heavy mountain fighting between the Brenta and Piave; enemy attacks repulsed. Fresh Austrian attacks in Albania; on night of 25th-26th enemy force passage of River Osum.
26	Heavy shelling about Ypres.	.. .. ..	Sharp enemy attack repulsed in Brenta valley 2 m. E. of San Marino.
27	Severe village fighting at Fontaine Notre Dame and Bourlon; British line advanced and 500 prisoners taken; enemy attack W. of Mœuvres repulsed. French success near Hill 344 (Verdun).	.. .. ..	.. ..

Asiatic and Egyptian Theatres.	Naval and Overseas Operations.	Political, &c.	1917. Nov.
Gen. Allenby's troops storm the Nebi Samwil ridge, 5 m. N. of Jerusalem; fruitless counterattacks by Turks.	Considerable captures of Germans in E. Africa by British columns, at Simba and Nevala.	Disfranchisement of Conscientious Objectors passed in Commons. Ukranian Republic proclaimed and declared member of Russian Federal Republic.	21
British troops capture Turkish post of Jabir, 15 m. from Aden.	.. .. ..	U.S.A. Mission under Col. House leaves London for Paris. Germany announces extension of the " barred zone " for shipping ; Dutch indignation (¹⁴¹).	22
. .. ..	.. .. ..	Lord R. Cecil on Bolsheviks.	23
Lt.-Gen. Sir W. R. Marshall succeeds Sir S. Maude in Mesopotamia.	.. .. ..	Trotski begins publication of Russian secret treaties with other Powers.	24
Mounted troops capture Ain Karim, 4 m. W. of Jerusalem. British patrols, after crossing Auja river forced back by hostile infantry.	.. ..		25
. . .. ..	.. .. ..	Lord Rothermere appointed President of the Air Council. Increase of pay to both Navy and Army announced.	26
. . .. ..	Unconditional **surrender** near Nevala (E. Africa) **of Mahenge force,** under Col. Tafel, consisting of over 3,500 German and native troops.	Brazil concludes agreement with France for the use of 30 interned German ships, to carry food for the Allies.	27

1917. Nov.	WESTERN FRONT.	EASTERN FRONT	SOUTHERN FRONT.
28	Enemy shell Bourlon Wood and Ypres front.	.. .. ..	Italian batteries shel enemy boats on Lower Piave. In Albania Aus trians assault Italian positions 9 m. N.E. from Avlona.
29	Slight British gain W. of Bourlon Wood. Enemy attack Belgian positions near Aschhoop. Artillery activity in Ypres sector.	Cessation of hostilities on Russian front. Russian artillery in Trotus (Mold.) valley breaks up enemy operations.	Enemy efforts on the River Piave fail.
30	Cambrai front : enemy attacks salient at Vendhuille, Bourlon Wood and Mœuvres ; penetrating British position as far as La Vacquerie and Gouzeaucourt. British counter-attack regains La Vacquerie.	.. .. ..	In Doiran region and N of Monastir, French and British batteries destro enemy dumps and brea up positions. Frenc bomb valley of the Var dar and N. of Monasti
Dec. 1	S.W. Cambrai : Gonnelieu recovered, but British withdraw from Masnières salient. Enemy attacks heavily at Bourlon Wood and claims 4,000 prisoners and 60 guns. Verdun : Violent German attack N. of Fosses Wood.	M. Lenin demands surrender of Gen. Dukhonin, C.-in-C. Russian General Staff surrenders at Mohilev. Partial cessation of hostilities.	.. ..
2	Cambrai : Enemy in vain try to recover high ground about La Vacquerie. Further fighting N. of Passchendaele.	Brest-Litovsk : Russian and German Peace Delegations welcomed by Prince Leopold of Bavaria (C.-in-C.).	Intense artillery action o Asiago Plateau (Trent.
3	British withdraw at La Vacquerie and E. of Marcoing. British gain ground S.W. of Polygon Wood (Ypres).	Gen. Dukhonin murdered by mob of soldiers and sailors at Mohilev station. Gen. Kornilov escapes.	.. ..
4	Bourlon Wood evacuated by British ([111]). W. Verdun : enemy efforts to reach Avocourt and Forges sectors fail.	.. .. ..	Austrian artillery ver active towards Bren river.

ASIATIC AND EGYPTIAN THEATRES.	NAVAL AND OVERSEAS OPERATIONS.	POLITICAL, &c.	1917. Nov.
.. .. ..	Russian t.b.d. mined in the Baltic.	Esthonia declares itself independent.	28
.. .. ..	British monitor destroys bridge of boats at Passarella, 5 m. up the Piave.	Inter - Allied Conference opens in Paris. Letter in " Daily Telegraph " from Lord Lansdowne calling for a re-statement of Allies' War Aims. Germany accepts Lenin's offer of an armistice. Russian delegates cross German lines. Count Hertling willing to treat with Bolsheviks.	29
At Auja, Palestine, Australian Light Horse surround Turks, taking 148 prisoners. British raid Turks at Beth Horun Upper (10 m. W. of Jerusalem), taking 300 prisoners.	.. .. ..	Prisoners in all theatres taken by British during November, 26,869 and 221 guns. Coventry aircraft works on strike, 50,000 men and women idle. German press approves Lord Lansdowne's letter.	30
			Dec.
.. .. ..	German E. Africa clear of enemy ([142]) ; v. Lettow-Vorbeck retires across Rovuma river (Portuguese boundary).	Inter-Allied Council at Versailles inaugurated ([143]). Canadian Victory Loan ; over 70 million £ subscribed.	1
.. ..	.. .. ..	.. .. ..	2
British drive Turks out of Kara Tepe ; Turks flood country between Nahrin and Diala rivers. Russians co-operate from Persia.	.. .. ..	First day of compulsory food rationing in Rome. Bulgaria declares readiness to negotiate war settlement.	3
Minor actions N. of Jaffa and on Jerusalem road. British seaplanes active.	Operations at Aden described in House of Lords ([145]).	Pres. Wilson's message to Congress ([146]).	4

1917. Dec	WESTERN FRONT.	EASTERN FRONT.	SOUTHERN FRONT.
5	British airmen raid Zweibrücken and Saarbrücken.	Negotiations at Brest Litovsk *re* Russian Armistice ; **preliminary suspension of hostilities signed** ([147]).	Enemy progress at Asiago, storm M. Zomo and Castelgomberto and attack Melette, claiming 11,000 prisoners.
6	London and S.E. counties raided by 25 aeroplanes, 2 brought down ; 8 killed, 28 injured.	Rumania obliged to suspend hostilities in consequence of Russian action.	Austrians capture Mount Sisemol ; attacks in Val Frenzela frustrated.
7	British line improved N. of La Vacquerie. End of Battle of Cambrai.	.. .. ..	Asiago : Italians continue withdrawal to Melette lines. Austrians claim 15,000 prisoners since 4.12.
8	Small actions W. of Graincourt (S.W. Cambrai). Great artillery activity N.E. of Verdun.	.. .. ..	French and British join Italian line, latter in Montello district (Piave). Combined airwork (150 planes) in Frenzela valley.
9	.. .. ..	Definite truce on Rumanian front begins.	Stiff fighting for bridgehead on Lower Piave (15 m. from Venice) ; Italians hold on.
10	Enemy post carried E. of Boursies (Cambrai). Verdun : German attacks on Chaume Wood, etc., checked.	Bolsheviks defeat Gen. Kornilov at Tamarovka (N. of Kharkov).	.. .. ..
11	.. .. ..	Forces from Russian front sent against Don Cossacks.	.. .. ..
12	Enemy capture small salient between Bullecourt and Quéant (W. of Cambrai).	Fighting between Cossacks and Bolsheviks at Rostov (River Don). **Rumanians sign armistice.**	Battle begins on Monte Grappa front between Brenta and Piave heavy Austrian attacks
13	Moderate fighting on Ypres, Cambrai and Verdun fronts.	Gen. Kornilov's troops worsted by Bolsheviks near Bielgorod (S. Russia).	.. .. ..

Asiatic and Egyptian Theatres.	Naval and Overseas Operations.	Political, &c.	1917. Dec.
British take Sakaltutan Pass (on Deli Abbas-Kifri road) and 230 prisoners.	Successful British air-raids on Belgian coast. S.S. "Apapa" (Elder-Dempster) torpedoed; 79 lost.	.. .. ..	5
.. .. ..	U.S. destroyer "Jacob Jones" torpedoed; 37 survivors.	Nationalisation of railways in U.S.A. announced. Rising in Lisbon ([148]). Halifax (N.S.) wrecked ([149]).	6
Hebron (17 m. S. of Jerusalem) captured.	.. .. ..	**Pres. Wilson signs declaration of war v. Austro-Hungary.** Ecuador breaks off relations with Germany.	7
British, by cutting Jerusalem-Jericho and Shechem roads, isolate city. Local authorities arrange to surrender.	Germans capture Portuguese force at Ngoma (River Rovuma).	.. .. ..	8
Surrender of Jerusalem. Holy City surrounded by our troops.	Italian light boats enter Trieste Harbour and sink the "Wien" (old).	.. .. ..	9
.. .. ..	British seaplanes bomb aerodromes near Ghent, and Bruges Docks.	Panama declares war against Austro-Hungary.	10
Gen. Allenby enters Jerusalem and reads proclamation.	British airship lost (with crew of 5) over the North Sea.	Mr. Balfour announces receipt in September of German peace proposals ([151]). Non-Ferrous Metals Bill passed. Constituent Assembly meets at Petrograd.	11
British have taken 562 officers and 11,474 men prisoners in Palestine to date.	Convoy to Norway sunk ([152]); 3 vessels also sunk off the Tyne. Funchal (Madeira) shelled by submarine; much damage.	Enquiry into the reverse at Cambrai ordered by Government. French Government decides to bring M. Caillaux before Court Martial. Cuba declares war on Austro-Hungary.	12
British line extended N.E. of Jerusalem and advanced between latter and Jaffa.	.. .. ..	Constituent Assembly at Taurida Palace dispersed by Bolshevist troops.	13

1917 Dec.	WESTERN FRONT.	EASTERN FRONT.	SOUTHERN FRONT.
14	.. .. ..	Rostov occupied by Bolshevist troops.	Italians surrender Col Caprile (Valstagna, Brenta river); otherwise enemy repulsed.
15	Snow interferes with operations. Germans repulsed at Chaume Wood (Verdun).	**Russian Armistice** (28 days) agreement **signed** ([153]). After 6 days' fighting, Gen. Kalédin (Cossacks) enters Rostov; local Bolshevist chiefs flee to Black Sea fleet.	Gen. Guillaumet succeeds Gen. Sarrail at Salonika as C.-in-C.
16	E. of Avion (S. of Lens) British position improved.	.. .. ..	Italians regain some positions in Brenta valley. Allied aeroplanes bomb depots at Cestovo (Macedonia).
17	Fighting near the Ypres-Comines Canal.	.. .. ..	Austrians repulsed on Upper Brenta.
18	Aeroplane raid on London, Essex and Kent; 14 killed, 85 injured. Heavy air fighting in Allies' favour on N. front.	Area of civil war extends to the Ukraine. Rada rejects Bolshevist demands for passage.	Italian 4th Army heavily attacked near Mt. Asolone (Mt. Grappa), Austrians claim 2,000 prisoners.
19	.. .. ..	The Ukraine defies the Bolsheviks; Odessa supports it.	Brisk fighting in Piave delta; enemy stopped. British guns heavily engaged at Montello.
20	W. of Messines, Germans capture British advanced post in fog.	.. .. ..	Italians recapture part of M. Asolone.
21	Stiff fighting at Hartmannsweilerkopf (Als.).	.. .. ..	Italians recapture whole of M. Asolone.
22	Germans drive in British advanced posts on Ypres-Staden railway.	Peace negotiations proceeding at Brest-Litovsk ([156]).	Austrian massed attack carries hills near Valstagna.
23	Fighting at Poelcapelle, near Epéhy (S.W. Cambrai) and Caurières Wood (Verdun).	.. .. ..	.. ..

Asiatic and Egyptian Theatres.	Naval and Overseas Operations.	Political, &c.	1917. Dec.
.. .. ..	Naval Allied Council to be created (Ministers of Marine and Chiefs of Staffs).	Mr. Ll. George at Gray's Inn on " No halfway house between victory and defeat."	14
British left centre in Palestine advanced 1½ m. on 5 m. front.	.. .. ..	Bolshevist ultimatum to the Ukraine demands free passage for troops.	15
Gen. Allenby made G.C.M.G.	Ionian Sea: French destroyer sinks 2 submarines.	New Portuguese Government declare they will honour all Portuguese engagements.	16
.. .. ..	.. .. ..	Count Hertling replies to Mr. Ll. George's speech of 14.12 ([154]).	17
British clear ground S.E. of Jerusalem, beyond Abu Dir.	.. .. ..	.. .. ..	18
.. .. ..	Two U.S.A. submarines collide in fog; F.1 sunk, 19 lost.	Unionist success in Canadian elections. Conscription Law becomes effective.	19
.. .. ..	.. .. ..	Tentative German peace terms in Washington ([155]). M. J. Cambon, adviser for U.S.A. affairs in Paris.	20
.. .. ..	.. .. ..	Italian war industry establishments number 3,500 as against 125 in 1915. Mr. Ll. George appeals for increase of agricultural cultivation.	21
Arabs under Sheikh Feisul capture Turkish troop train on Hejaz railway. British advance N. and E. of Jaffa.	Three British destroyers sunk off Dutch coast; 13 officers, 180 men lost.	Lord Rhondda's scheme for rationing by localities comes into force; main cause of queues removed.	22
.. .. ..	H.M.S. " Stephen Furness " sunk by submarine in Irish Channel; 6 officers and 95 men lost.	The Kaiser on the Almighty as a German ally ([157]). Moldavian Republic, including Bessarabia, proclaimed at Kishinev.	23

1917. Dec.	WESTERN FRONT.	EASTERN FRONT.	SOUTHERN FRONT.
24	Mannheim (Rhine) heavily bombed by British airmen.	German forces not sent W. or to Italy being massed on S. and Rumanian fronts. Telegraph between Petrograd and S.W. interrupted by Ukraine authorities.	Italians regain much of lost ground near the Brenta. Enemy claims 9,000 prisoners in last 2 days. Snow severe on Italian front. French raids in Albania.
25	.. .. ..	.. .. ..	Heavy fighting continues on Asiago plateau for passage of Brenta river.
26	Hostile artillery activity near Vimy and E. of Ypres. Germans repulsed in Caurières Wood (Verdun).	.. .. ..	Big aerial fight 18 m. N. of Venice.
27	.. .. ..	Bolsheviks try to get Ukraine to fight Cossacks.	.. .. ..
28	Much activity on both sides N. of St. Quentin.	.. .. ..	Enemy bridges at Zenson bend (L. Piave) destroyed. Padua bombed, 13 killed, 60 injured.
29	Local German attacks S. of St. Quentin and near Ypres-Staden railway.	.. .. ..	Padua again bombed, 3 killed, 3 injured.
30	S. of Marcoing (Cambrai) British regain portions of Welsh Ridge.	.. .. ..	French storm Austrian trenches E. of M. Grappa. Padua again bombed.
31	Renewed German attacks on Welsh Ridge repulsed.	Civil war raging in Russia; large numbers of officers have joined Gen. Kaldin.	Austrians forced to abandon bridgehead in Zenson bend. Austrians bomb Treviso, Vicenza, Castelfranco and Bassano.

ASIATIC AND EGYPTIAN THEATRES.	NAVAL AND OVERSEAS OPERATIONS.	POLITICAL, &c.	1917. Dec.
.. .. ..	British seaplanes bomb Bruges Docks and other aerodromes.	.. .. ..	24
.. .. ..	E. Africa : British pursue Germans 40 m. S. of River Rovuma ; latter broken up.	Count Czernin replies to Russian peace proposals of 22.12 ([158]).	25
Palestine : Sharp fighting during night ; British picquets attacked.	Adm. **Sir R. Wemyss** appointed **First Sea Lord** *vice* Sir J. Jellicoe (peerage conferred on latter).	U.S.A. Shipping Board promises five million tons in 1918. Mr. McAdoo appointed Director of Railways.	26
Turko-Germans attempt to recapture Jerusalem ([159]).	.. .. ..	Sir F. E. Smith emphasises British solidarity in New York.	27
Enemy driven back N. of Jerusalem ; Ramah and Bertunia captured.	.. .. ..	Labour memo. on War Aims accepted in special Conference. French war aims outlined by Foreign Minister.	28
Further British advance N. of Jerusalem.	German Naval Mission under Adm. Kaiserling arrives at Petrograd.	First batch of British prisoners arrives in Holland for internment. Efforts of U.S.A. Shipping Board bent on steel ships ([160]). Finnish Republic asks for recognition ([161]). Bolsheviks seize all banks.	29
British continue advance N. ; take Bethel, etc.	H.M.S. " Aragon " torpedoed in Mediterranean.	.. .. ..	**30**
.. .. ..	Progress reported in E. Africa ([162]). H.M.S. " Osmanieh " sunk by mine in Mediterranean.	Anglo-Turkish agreement for exchange of prisoners signed at Berne. Lord Rhondda issues model rationing scheme.	31

RÉSUMÉ OF MAIN EVENTS IN 1917.

Jan. 1 to Feb. 20 ..	Fighting on the Ancre.
„ 1 to Mar. 31 ..	Scattered fighting on Eastern front (Russians and Rumanians cleared out of Dobruja, 5.1 ; Focsani lost, 8.1), in Riga, N. Galicia, Bukovina and Moldavia theatres.
„ 31 *et sqq.* ..	" Unrestricted submarine warfare " announced for following day by Germany ; and carried out.
Feb. 3	U.S.A. sever diplomatic relations with Germany ; tension through February and March.
„ 21 to Mar. 31 ..	Great German withdrawal (extending from Soissons to Arras), to Siegfried line, followed up, fighting, by French and British.
„ 24	British capture Kut el Amara.
„ 26	British War Loan reaches £1,000,312,950.
Mar. 9	Food riots in Petrograd develop into Revolution ; Provisional Government formed 12.3 ; Tsar abdicates, 15.3 ; and is interned, 21.3.
„ 11 *et sqq.* ..	Capture of Baghdad ; British push on.
„ 11 to May 11 ..	Spring campaign in Macedonia ; fighting round Monastir, etc.
„ 18 *et sqq.* ..	British occupy Péronne and French Noyon ; both close on St. Quentin, 23.3 ; heavy fighting continues.
April 6	U.S.A. declares War on Germany, and Austro-Hungary on U.S.A., 8.4 ; French and British (Mr. Balfour, 22.4) Missions in U.S.A.
„ 9 *et sqq.* ..	Battle of Arras ; Canadians capture Vimy Ridge, etc.
„ 16 *et sqq.* ..	Second Battle of the Aisne.
„ 23	U.S.A. severs relations with Turkey.
„ 28	U.S.A. introduces Conscription.
May 3 *et sqq.* ..	British break Quéant switch and progress E. of Arras and towards Cambrai.
„ 4 „	French take Craonne and Chemin des Dames ; fighting on Moronvillers *massif*, 21 to 31.5.
„	Russians fall back in Mesopotamia, Persia and Armenia.
„ 12 „	Italians attack on Isonzo front, and on Carso, 23.5, etc.
„ 13	Socialist Conference in Stockholm opens.
June 7 *et sqq.* ..	British capture Messines-Wytschaete ridge and progress.
„ 11	Abdication of King Constantine in favour of his son Alexander.
„ 14 to July 27 ..	Heavy fighting on Aisne, in Champagne, on Arras-Cambrai front, and in Trentino, etc.
„ 25	First U.S.A. fighting contingent arrives in France.
„ 30	Greece breaks off relations with Germany and Austro-Hungary.
July 1	Russian offensive under Brusilov in Galicia (German counter-offensive, 19.7 ; Russian retreat, 20-22.7 ; rout, 23.7, etc.).
„ 14	Herr v. Bethmann-Hollweg succeeded as German Chancellor by Dr. Michaelis.
„ 31 to end of year	British and French attack in Flanders—largely spoilt by foul weather.

Aug.	3 *et sqq.*	.. Allied push in German E. Africa, eventually driving Germans over Portuguese border by 1.12.
,,	5 to 29	.. Enemy offensive v. Russo-Rumanian junction in Moldavia, etc. ; stubborn resistance.
,,	10 to Sept. 30	.. Stockholm Conference causes awkward situations in Great Britain, France and U.S.A.
,,	14	.. .. China declares war on Germany and Austro-Hungary ; Papal Peace Note issued.
,,	19 to Sept. 20	.. Great Italian attack on Isonzo-Carso front ; heavy fighting ; Italian successes on Bainsizza Plateau and Carso.
,,	21 to Sept. 21	.. Germans attack Riga front (Riga evacuated, 2.9 ; Russians fall back 30 miles).
Sept.	1 to 28	.. French Government takes action against treasonable intrigues.
,,	2 to 30	.. Numerous air-raids on London, S.E. counties, etc.
,,	8 to 13	.. Kornilov " revolt."
,,	9 to 17	.. Luxburg disclosures in Argentina.
,,	15	.. .. Russian Republic under M. Kerenski declared.
Oct.	12 to 21	.. Naval fighting in Gulf of Riga.
,,	24 *et sqq.*	.. Austro-German attack breaks through Second Italian Army (Boselli Ministry falls, 25.10 ; Italian retreat to River Tagliamento, 30.10 ; Italians fall back to River Piave and hold it, 9.11 ; heavy fighting on Asiago Plateau and between the Upper Brenta and Piave Rivers, 15.11–25.12).
,,	31 to Nov. 1	.. Dr. Michaelis succeeded as German Chancellor by Count Hertling.
Nov.	1 *et sqq.*	.. Bolsheviks cause trouble (*coup d'état* and flight of M. Kerenski, 8.11 ; latter defeated at Tsarskoe Selo, 14.11 ; Bolshevist Government formed, 16.11 ; Ukraine defies Bolsheviks, 18.12).
,,	6	.. .. Capture of Passchendaele and ridge.
,,	7	.. .. Capture of Gaza.
,,	9	.. .. Supreme Allied War Council decided on at Rapallo ; Inaugurated, 1.12.
,,	15	.. .. M. Clémenceau forms Ministry.
,,	20	.. .. Surprise British advance at Cambrai ; driven back, 25.11 to 4.12.
Dec.	2 *et sqq.*	.. Brest Litovsk meeting (preliminary suspension—seven days— of hostilities, 5.12 ; armistice for 28 days, 15.12 ; peace negotiations entered on).
,,	6	.. .. Rumanians obliged to suspend hostilities.
,,	7	.. .. U.S.A. declares war on Austria Hungary.
,,	9	.. .. Capture of Jerusalem ; entry of Gen. Allenby, 11.12.
,,	26	.. .. Sir J. Jellicoe succeeded as First Sea Lord by Sir R. Wemyss.

T

APPENDICES, 1917.

(¹) *Jan.* 10.—The Allies "associate themselves whole-heartedly with the plan of creating a League of the Nations," but judge it impossible at the moment to conclude a peace that will assure to them "the reparation, the restitution, and the guarantees to which they are entitled." While deploring the sufferings of neutrals, they disclaim responsibility for them, as they did not desire or provoke the war; and they "hold themselves bound to make a stand . . . against the establishment in the American Note of a likeness between the two belligerent groups," this protest being enforced by a recital of some of Germany's crimes and atrocities. The Allies consider that their reply to the German Peace Note sufficiently indicates their views as to the terms of peace; their war-aims "are well-known" and "will only be set forth in detail . . . at the moment of negotiation." These aims are then stated to imply "necessarily and first of all, the restoration of Belgium, Serbia, and Montenegro, with the compensations due to them; the evacuation of the invaded territories in France, in Russia, in Rumania, with just reparation; the reorganisation of Europe, guaranteed by a stable régime and based at once on respect for nationalities and on the right to full security and liberty of economic development possessed by all peoples, small and great, and at the same time on territorial conventions and international settlements such as to guarantee land and sea frontiers against unjustified attack; the restitution of provinces formerly torn from the Allies by force or against the wishes of their inhabitants; the liberation of the Italians, as also of the Slavs, Rumanes, and Czecho-Slovaks from foreign domination; the setting free of the populations subject to the bloody tyranny of the Turk; and the turning-out of Europe of the Ottoman Empire as decidedly foreign to Western civilisation." The intentions of the Tsar regarding Poland are said to have been "clearly indicated by the manifesto he has just addressed to his armies." Lastly, it is declared that "the extermination and political disappearance of the German peoples" have never formed part of the Allies' designs.

(²) *Jan.* 11.—Interest 5 per cent.; issue price 95; principal repayable in 1947; or, as an alternative, interest 4 per cent., free of income-tax; issue price 100; principal repayable in 1942.

(³) *Jan.* 11.—The most important of these orders, which were to come into force on various dates, required millers to add to the percentage of flour hitherto extracted from wheat a further 5 per cent., either by additional milling, or by means of flour from certain other cereals. This other flour, if the miller chose, might amount to as much as 10 per cent. The use of wheat, except as seed or for making flour, was forbidden. Among the other orders was one fixing a maximum price for chocolates and other sweet-meats.

(⁴) *Jan.* 11.—The German Note states that Germany and her allies were compelled to take up arms "to defend their freedom and their existence, mentioning among the causes of the war "provocation by Serbia" and the "complete Russian mobilisation." A protest is raised against the Allies' description of the Central Powers' "Peace Note" as a war manœuvre. The sincerity of the Allies' concern for the rights of small States is impugned on the ground of "the fate of the Irish people, the destruction of the freedom and independence of the Boer Republics, the subjection of North Africa by England, France, and Italy, the suppression of foreign nationalities in Russia, and finally the oppression of Greece, which is unexampled in history." As to the violation of international rights, the Note adduces as instances the renunciation by the United Kingdom of the Declaration of London, her violation of the Declaration of Paris, her "starvation campaign" against Germany, her pressure on neutrals, the use of coloured troops in Europe, the extension of the war to Africa, and the deportation of the civil population from East Prussia, Alsace-Lorraine, Galicia, and the Bukovina. In regard to Belgium, Germany cannot admit "that the Belgian Government has always observed its obligations." Before the war Belgium was "under the influence of England, and leaned towards England and France, thereby herself violating the spirit of the treaties which guaranteed her independence and neutrality." The Note recalls Germany's offers to the Belgian Government at the outbreak of war, and states that in 1887 the British Government were known to be determined not to oppose the right of way through Belgium on these conditions. The "calumnies" about German methods and measures in Belgium are then denied. The Austrian Note is of the same general tenor, but has a special reference to the ultimatum to Serbia, asserting that Austria had for years shown the greatest forbearance towards Serbia, till the Serajevo murder made this impossible.

(⁵) *Jan.* 16.—Mr. Balfour's despatch is a vindication, in general terms, of the Allies' aims as stated in their Note to President Wilson and of their refusal to enter into negotiations. The following passage summarises his main argument : " The people of this country . . . do not believe that peace can be durable if it be not based on the success of the Allied cause. For a durable peace can hardly be expected unless three conditions are fulfilled. The first is that the existing causes of international unrest should be, as far as possible, removed or weakened. The second is that the aggressive aims and the unscrupulous methods of the Central Powers should fall into disrepute among their own peoples. The third is that behind international law and behind all treaty arrangements for preventing or limiting hostilities some form of international sanction should be devised which would give pause to the hardiest aggressor."

(⁶) *Jan.* 20.—The Tsar states that the first objects of the Government's attention should be (a) the strenuous and unremitting prosecution of the war ; (b) the provisioning of the armies and the civil population ; (c) the improvement of transport. The hope is expressed that the Duma and the Council of the Empire will support the efforts of the Ministry. " It is furthermore the duty of all persons called upon to serve the State to act with goodwill, uprightness, and dignity towards the Legislative Institutions." It is added that in organising the economic life of the country the Government will find " invaluable support in the Zemstva."

(⁷) *Jan.* 22.—President Wilson said that while the United States would not have a voice in determining what the terms of peace should be, they would have a voice in determining whether they should be made lasting or not by the guarantees of a universal covenant. He laid down certain essential elements of any peace that the peoples of America would join in guaranteeing : (a) It must be a peace without victory, *i.e.,* a peace based on negotiations conducted as between equals. (b) There must be equality of rights of nations whether small or great. (c) Government must be based on the consent of the governed—e.g., there must be a united, independent, and autonomous Poland. (d) The paths of the sea must be free, a question closely connected with that of the limitation of military and naval armaments, which will also have to be faced, and which is " the most immediately and intensely practical question connected with the future fortunes of nations and of mankind."

(⁸) *Jan.* 31.—*German Submarine Campaign.*—On this date the German Manifesto to all Neutrals was published, declaring " that she must now abandon the limitations hitherto self-imposed in the employment of her fighting weapons at sea, by imposing ' unrestricted Naval Warfare ' on all ships entering the War zones—whether Neutral or Belligerent—on and from February 1." These " War Zones " as mapped by Germany to consist of wide areas round Great Britain, France and Italy, and in the Eastern Mediterranean. The United States of America to be allowed access to Falmouth with one vessel per week, and one Dutch paddle-steamer to be allowed to sail weekly between Flushing and Southwold, both of these exceptions to be subject to certain stringent conditions. This German declaration, which constituted the greatest crime against International Law ever committed, was immediately put into practice with resultant heavy loss to both Belligerent and Neutral shipping, and numerous instances of cold-blooded murder on the high seas. As a consequence, Neutral shipping was temporarily confined to its own harbours, and the direct affront to Neutrals, and especially to the United States of America, was at once challenged by the latter. Counter-measures were at once put in practice by the British Admiralty, and after the Nation had been warned of the seriousness of the menace by Mr. Lloyd George ; Lord Lytton, speaking for the Admiralty on February 13, said that the British counter-measures had already met with considerable success.

(⁹) *Jan.* 31.—*War on Hospital Ships.*—On this date the British Foreign Office published a further announcement by Germany to the effect that "the passage of Hospital Ships would no longer be tolerated between Great Britain, France, and Belgium. The threat implied that in future all Hospital Ships would be sunk at sight, and that no difference would be made between them and merchant shipping. The excuse given for this additional crime was that Hospital Ships had often been misused for the transport of troops and munitions. The falsity of this excuse is apparent from the fact that although the enemy have the right to search hospital ships, they have never once availed themselves of this privilege.

(¹⁰) *Feb.* 3.—As a result of the German declaration against neutral shipping, and their refusal to modify the terms of same, President Wilson on this date broke off diplomatic relations between the U.S.A. and Germany. In his speech to Congress the President recalled the solemn undertaking by Germany on the occasion of the sinking of the " Sussex " when American lives were lost, and stated that the German Note of January 31 was a clear breach of their undertaking, to which Americans could not with honour submit. In spite of the rupture the President still hoped that Germany would not persevere in her policy of unrestricted Naval Warfare, but if she did, and American ships and lives were sacrificed, he would summon Congress to demand the means to protect them. He considered that all neutrals would take the same view, and invited them to follow the example of the U.S.A by breaking off diplomatic relations. On the conclusion of his speech to Congress the President was accorded a great and enthusiastic ovation. On February 4 Count Bernstorff, the German Ambassador to the U.S.A., was handed his passports, and Mr. Gerard, the U.S.A. Ambassador to Germany, was instructed to leave Berlin.

(¹¹) *Feb.* 4.—On February 4 the Sultan accepted the resignation of the Grand Vizier, Said Halim, for health reasons. Talaat Bey formed a New Ministry, becoming Pasha and Grand Vizier, and having as his chief associates Mussa Effendi, Messimi Bey, Halil Bey, and Jemal Pasha, with Enver Pasha as Minister of War.

(¹²) *Feb.* 7.—During the week following the rupture of diplomatic relations between the U.S.A. and Germany, replies were received from other Neutrals to the American invitation to sever diplomatic relations. Switzerland, Holland, Denmark, Norway, and Sweden all declined the suggestion, chiefly on the score of geographical situation. Spain and other countries decided to maintain neutrality, and satisfied their national honour by sending Notes of Protest to Germany. On the other hand, Brazil, China, Chile, and the Argentine sent spirited protests to Germany threatening rupture if the threats to their shipping were carried out.

(¹³) *Feb.* 9.—On February 4 a British Expedition, which had set out from Egypt for the purpose of breaking the power of Said Ahmed, the Senussi leader and his followers, located the enemy at the Oasis of Siwa and other neighbouring camps in the Western desert. An all-day engagement ensued, and towards evening the Senussi were defeated and retired on to their camps. They evacuated these camps during the night, and by morning were in full flight towards Shiyata. The pursuing cavalry cut off the enemy retreat by gaining possession of the Munasib Pass, where they captured a convoy, and forced the tribesmen to disperse southwards into the waterless desert. The enemy losses were estimated at 200 killed, and the Senussi power in the Western Desert was utterly broken.

(¹⁴) *Feb.* 17.—On February 17 the Entente Powers in a joint Note called the attention of the Greek Government to the continued hostile attitude of a certain section of the Greek Press, which was causing much dissatisfaction and unrest. As a result strict action was taken against all such pro-German activities, and many suspected buildings and private houses were searched for hidden arms and ammunition, of which a considerable store was found and confiscated.

(¹⁵) *Feb.* 24.—*German Retreat on the Ancre.*—Great British activity on both banks of the River Ancre was the chief feature on the Western Front during this month. On February 3 our lines were successfully advanced on a 1,200 yard front East of Beaucourt, while on the 5th and 6th strong German positions were carried near Gueudecourt and Grandcourt. On the 7th, owing to the continued pressure the enemy evacuated Grandcourt, and on the 8th the Sailly-Saillisel ridge was stormed and taken. The enemy made strong efforts to recapture the latter position, but totally failed, and South of Serre Hill our gains were extended on February 10 on a front of 1,250 yards. German counter-attacks were again cut to pieces, and British troops continued to make ground in various sectors until February 24, when the enemy found he could no longer hold the salient and retreated, leaving in our hands the villages of Serre, Miraumont, Petit Miraumont, Pys, and Warlencourt. On the 26th and 27th the villages of Le Barque and Ligny were also captured; the ground gained extended over a front of 11 miles from South of Gommecourt to East of Gueudecourt, and to an extreme depth of 3 miles.

(¹⁶) *Feb. 24.—Résumé of Operations in Mesopotamia by Anglo-Indian Troops under General Maude.*—On January 31 and February 1 the British offensive against the Turkish forces in and around Kut-el-Amara was continued, and practically the whole of the enemy positions were captured East of the Tigris-Hai junction. Continued pressure compelled the Turks to evacuate their forward positions on the South bank of the Tigris, and also to the West of the Hai on February 6. Fighting in the immediate vicinity of Kut then became desperate, particularly round the Liquorice Factory and in the Dahra bend of the Tigris. On February 16 General Maude's troops finally cleared the Dahra bend, taking about 2,000 prisoners. The strong Turkish lines at Sanna-i-Yat were then attacked, at first unsuccessfully, but after continuous fighting from the 17th to 23rd February the greater part of the defences were in British hands. On February 23 General Maude executed a clever turning movement by successfully crossing the Tigris at the Shumran bend, thus compelling the Turks to evacuate Kut, and at the same time forcing the Sanna-i-Yat positions. Nearly 2,000 prisoners were again taken and the enemy beat a hasty retreat towards Baghdad, with Indian Mounted troops and other columns in close pursuit.

(¹⁷) *Feb.* 28.—The Memorandum expressed sympathy with the attitude taken up by China towards Germany, and promised favourable consideration of suspension during the war of the Boxer indemnity payment and revision of the tariff in the event of China severing relations with Germany and Austria.

(¹⁸) *March* 1.—Week ending February 25, 1917, arrivals and sailings of merchant vessels of all nationalities (over 100 tons net) at and from United Kingdom ports (exclusive of fishing and local craft) : arrivals, 2,280 ; sailings, 2,261. British merchant vessels sunk by mine and submarine : 1,600 tons (gross) or over, 15 ; under 600 tons (gross), 6. British merchant vessels unsuccessfully attacked by submarine, 12 ; British fishing vessels sunk, 4. (Complete list for the year given at the end of Appendices.)

(¹⁹) *March* 1.—This contains instructions to negotiate an offensive alliance with Gen. Carranza, and the suggestion is made that Gen. Carranza should approach Japan, apparently with the object of getting her to join in an attack on the United States.

(²⁰) *March* 1.—German Foreign Secretary expressed regret of his Government at torpedoing of Dutch ships. The Government, he explained, was only able to give relative security to Dutch ships because orders to let them pass might not reach all submarines. He expressed his desire that neutral vessels should remain in port, so that the freedom of the seas might be quickly attained.

(²¹) *March* 3.—German War Minister announces that until German prisoners are removed at least 50 kilometres from firing line, British and French prisoners will be employed within range of our own guns.

(²²) *March* 3.—Germany admits having intended to negotiate alliance with Mexico in event of United States declaring war, but does not mention Japan.

(²³) *March* 5.—Austria declares herself at one with Germany and places responsibility of submarine warfare on Great Britain. She argues that violation of right of freedom of the seas by Allies for two years has forced her to return " like for like " in order to obtain restoration of the right.

(²⁴) *March* 5.—Speaking of the war he said : " We stand fast on an armed neutrality, since it seems that in no other way can we demonstrate what it is that we insist upon and cannot forego. We may even be drawn on by circumstances . . . to an active assertion of our rights as we see them."

(²⁵) *March* 5.—Speaking to a representative of the Press Lord Milner said result had exceeded his expectations. " About the continuance of the war and the part Russia was playing, I could find no difference of opinion. On all hands there is only one aim—to bring it to a rapid and successful conclusion. . . . It is quite wrong to suppose that in Russia there is any controversy about the waging of the war ; it is as I say, merely a question of administration ; in fact, much the same kind of controversy as we have in England."

(²⁶) *March* 5.—Scarcity of potatoes foreshadowed. London consumption of meat falls from 31,600 tons in January to 23,450 tons in February.

(²⁷) *March* 7.—The Proclamation sets forth the grounds of the rebellion of the Holy Places of Islam against the Young Turks and of the assumption of the title of King of the Hejaz by the Grand Sherif of Mecca. It condemns the fact that Moslem women are employed by Government unveiled, under the new régime, and deplores the usurpation of Osman's Empire by puppets in the hands of the Janissaries.

(²⁸) *March* 8.—The First Lord of the Admiralty warned the Nation of the danger ahead. The situation threatened the food of the people to an extent that no one could have thought possible, and he hinted at further drastic restrictions. Great Britain has 3,000 patrol boats, in spite of which German mines have been sown as far as the Cape of Good Hope, Aden, and Colombo. In February 500,000 tons of food had been sunk.

([29]) *March* 8.—The Commission is of opinion that a combined Naval and Military attack on the Peninsula would have been possible had it not been for unnecessary delay in despatching troops : the combination being the only way of achieving success. They consider that the decision to abandon the Naval attack after the bombardment of March 18 was inevitable. Lord Kitchener is blamed for not sufficiently availing himself of the services of the General Staff, and Lord Fisher's policy of concurrence or resignation is condemned. Certain political advantages were gained by the Expedition.

([30]) *March* 12.—The Executive Committee includes M. Rodzianko, M. Kerenski, M. Miliukov, M. Vladimir Lvov, M. Karajulov, Col. Engelhart. First Proclamation as follows : " The Provisional Committee of Members of the Imperial Duma finds itself compelled, by the onerous circumstances of internal chaos resulting from the measures taken by the old Government, to take in hand the re-establishment of State and public order. Fully appreciating the responsibility it has assumed, the Committee feels confident that the people and Army will help it in the difficult task of creating a new Government capable of meeting the wishes of the Nation and deserving its confidence." M. Rodzianko informed Tsar of unanimous demand for a new Government. Insurgents take possession of Law Courts and sack Ministry of Interior. Fortress of Peter and Paul Headquarters of revolutionary armies.

([31]) *March* 12.—He said East African campaign was practically over, but heavy rains had caused delay, and he emphasised the fact that no German colony could possibly be returned to Germany.

([32]) *March* 13.—Mr. Macpherson said mastery on British front was undecided; the best type of machine was being used. With the advent of fine weather severe contests were to be expected before achieving definite superiority.

([33]) *March* 13.—Russian Admiralty surrenders. Prefect prisoner in Duma with M. Shcheglovitov, M. Stürmer, Archbishop Pitirin, etc. M. Protopopov gives himself up. Petrograd garrison goes over to Provisional Government. British and French ambassadors cheered by crowd. Second proclamation of Duma appealed to people of Petrograd to spare all public institutions and services, also not to endanger lives and property of private people. The shedding of blood and plundering of property might cause privations to the inhabitants besides being a blur on the conscience.

([34]) *March* 15.—The Tsar gives as his reasons for decision the need for close union and organisation of all forces for rapid victory. He names his brother, the Grand Duke Michael, Regent, and relies on him to rule in conjunction with the National Government.

([35]) *March* 15.—The Grand Duke Nicholas and Gen. Alexeiev adhere to new cause. The Ministry includes :—

Prince George Lvov	Prime Minister and Interior.
M. Miliukov	Foreign Affairs.
M. Guchkov	War and Marine.
M. Kerenski	Justice.
M. Vladimir Lvov	Holy Synod.

Proclamation by Provisional Government, following principles adopted : Political and religious amnesty, freedom of Press, association, speech and labour organisation, and freedom to strike, with extension of these liberties to officials and troops so far as conditions permit. Abolition of all social, religious, and national restrictions. Immediate preparations for a Constituent Assembly. Substitution for police of a National Militia, etc., etc.

([36]) *March* 16.—The Minister announced that the Provisional Government had taken office in virtue of an agreement with the workmen and soldiers' delegates. He proceeded to proclaim the freedom of Russia and asked for co-operation of the soldiers.

([37]) *March* 19.—Total financial expenditure for financial year, April 1, 1916 to March 31, 1917, would average £6,000,000 a day, with an additional million per day during last six weeks. Nominal total of National Debt, £3,900,000,000. Total due from Allies and Dominions to this country in respect of advances made during war, £964,000,000.

([38]) *March* 20.—The Proclamation appeals for support from citizens and soldiers, discipline, and unity. The Provisional Government will be supreme pending election of a Constituent Assembly.

(³⁹) *March* 20.—It declines his proposal for neutral action with a view to forcing peace on Europe by cutting off supplies. The refusal is based on the hopelessness of peace at the present time, on Germany's attempt to embroil Mexico and Japan in war with the United States and the belief that any restrictions of commerce with belligerents would be un-neutral discrimination.

(⁴⁰) *March* 20.—

M. Ribot ..	..	..	..	Prime Minister.
M. Painlevé	..	..	..	War.
M. J. Thierry	..	..	..	Finance.
M. Viviani	..	..	..	Justice.
M. Malvy..	..	..	..	Interior.

(⁴¹) *March* 20.—Chief points : Government intends to establish a British Trade Corporation, whose principal object would be to form a Trade Credit Bank for developing British trade abroad. Shortage of petrol and coal. Steps for dealing with evasion by foreigners of Business Names Act.

(⁴²) *March* 22.—After recording the usefulness of the Auxiliary Service Law and the measures for reconstructing a number of minor industries after the war, he announces that the effects of the restrictions in food have not been injurious, the general state of health being surprisingly good and the infant mortality lower than in peace time. In spite of the Paris Conference Germany would renew her economic relations with foreign countries after the war.

(⁴³) *March* 23.—He congratulates Russia on her freedom and says he believes that the revolution is the greatest service which has yet been made to the cause for which Allies are fighting, and is a sure promise that Prussian military autocracy, which is still the only barrier to peace, will before long be overthrown.

(⁴⁴) *March* 26.—Throughout the Empire there were on that date : 55,397 German prisoners, 16 Austrians, 763 Bulgarians, 15,512 Turks. Germans held about 32,500 British prisoners.

(⁴⁵) *March* 29.—Herr von Bethmann-Hollweg declared that Germany had no intention of taking any part in Russian internal problems, and that the Russian aristocracy was mainly responsible for the war. He also disclaimed for Germany any responsibility with regard to the hostile attitude of America or the rupture of relations with China, which were entirely due to pressure from the Entente.

(⁴⁶) *April* 2.—Speech of President Wilson to Congress asking for War on Germany. Warfare against commerce is warfare against mankind. Object of U.S.A. in declaring war is vindication of principles of peace and justice against selfish autocratic power. No quarrel between U.S.A. and German people, but with German Government autocracy as a foe to peace. Fall of Russian autocracy heartening for future peace of the world. " World must be made safe for democracy." U.S.A. desire no conquest, no dominion, no indemnities, no material compensation, will fight for democracy, rights of small nations, universal domination of right by consent of free peoples.

(⁴⁷) *April* 2.—Speeches to Empire Parliamentary Association *re* Empire and War. Sir R. Borden described war work of Dominions, difference between German and British ideals, dawn of new era marked by rise of Imperial War Cabinet. Gen. Smuts stated Co-operation of South Africa due to " one of wisest political settlements ever made." Empire not founded on force, but on freedom, equality, and equity. In future constitution-making of British Empire precedents not to be followed but to be made. No final solution to be reached. " We are built on freedom."

(⁴⁸) *April* 4.—*Trade Union Conference.*—Sir Wm. Robertson : We cannot win war unless and until every man and woman does full day's work of essential nature. Germans not beaten ; her man-power increased. Army requires half-million men between now and July; self-denial and self-sacrifice needed. Sir J. Jellicoe : Serious time before country, need of economy in food consumption.

(⁴⁹) *April* 4.—British food order *re* hotels, boarding-houses, clubs, restaurants. A weekly meatless day ; 5 potato-less days ; 5½ lbs. of meat, 3½ lbs. of bread, 14 oz. flour, ¼ lb. sugar for each person.

(⁵⁰) *April* 4.—Flour Order directs an increasing percentage of non-wheaten flour to be mixed with wheaten flour.

(⁵¹) *April* 5.—Food Hoarding Order forbidding (1) anyone to acquire food in excess of household needs for use ; (2) dealers to sell food where reason to suppose amount of food allowed will be exceeded ; and authorising entry of premises for examination.

([52]) *April* 5.—Holland refused to admit armed merchantmen in her ports, referred to insistence by British representatives at Hague Conference that Neutrals were not to alter neutral regulations in course of war except to make them stricter.

([53]) *April* 8.—Electoral reform promised Prussia by Kaiser. The promises were those of abolition of class franchise, direct and secret election of deputies ; proposals of reform ordered to be made by Ministry to Kaiser.

([54]) *April* 10.—Proclamation of Russian Provisional Government states that Defence of Country is seriously disorganized ; Germany threatening Russian liberty ; deliverance from invader is vital problem ; Russia not aiming at domination nor annexations, but at durable peace on basis of rights of nations to decide own destinies. Every effort must be made to save the State.

([55]) *April* 12.—Mr. Page (U. S. Ambassador) on aim of war : " To save the earth as a place worth living in." Mr. Lloyd George : " Entrance of U.S.A. and Russian revolution prove war to be one for freedom. For fifty years Europe under menace of Prussia. Germany relying on submarine war and unreadiness of U.S.A. Ships needed for victory. We are marching with the dawn."

([56]) *April* 13.—British representatives : Messrs. Will Thorne,. J. O'Grady, C. W. Bowerman, S. W. Sanders. Speech of M. Kerenski—Dream of brotherhood of nations approaching realization. Russian democracy opposed to Imperialism. Speech of M. Miliukov—Russia fighting for annihilation of German Militarism and to prevent future wars.

([57]) *April* 14.—Appeals of Mr. Lloyd George and of Board of Trade *re* food production to farmers. Mr. Lloyd George : " We may have to depend on home-grown food ; the line which British Empire holds against the Germans is held at home as well as abroad." Board of Trade : " Farmers asked to limit use of human food-stuffs in fattening cattle and feeding horses not doing productive work.

([58]) *April* 14.—Allies are in accord with Russia in her desire to restore Poland to integrity and independence.

([59]) *April* 15.—Aid is needed from America by Allies in food, clothing, ships, steel, coal, etc. Appeal to various classes to do utmost. " The supreme test of the Nation has come, and we must all speak and act together."

([60]) *April* 16.—British Food Orders : Prices of wheat, barley, and oats fixed. Wheat, 78s. per quarter of 480 lbs. ; Barley, 65s. per quarter of 400 lbs. ; Oats, 55s. per quarter of 312 lb. Requisition of barley (other than home-grown not kiln-dried) by Food Controller.

([61]) *April* 17.—President to be empowered to restrict or prohibit export ; imprisonment for five years for any naturalized or non-naturalized resident attempting to violate order ; imprisonment for three years and confiscation of cargo and ship for any in command of vessels seeking to export prohibited articles.

([62]) *April* 18.—German concessions to strikers. Permission granted to form Committee of Workers to watch over interests *re* food.

([63]) *April* 19.—Speech of Mr. Herbert Fisher (Minister of Education) *re* educational reform. Estimated expenditure, £40,000,000 (almost quarter expenditure on alcohol). Experience of war proves good value given for educational expenditure. Average pay of teachers too low. Additional grants to be given to elementary and secondary education. Social fusion needed in schools. Desire of Government—people to be good citizens, reverent, dutiful, sound in mind and body, skilled in avocations, capable of using leisure rationally.

([64]) *April* 21.—Decree of Russian War Minister *re* Army. Election of Officers by soldiers forbidden. Russian deserters to present themselves to military authorities by May 14.

([65]) *April* 25.—Corn Production Bill. Object : To increase arable land and guarantee minimum prices to farmer and minimum wages to labourer.

([66]) *April* 27.—Submarine peril to be met by increased land cultivation, lessened imports, ship-building, self-rationing. Ideas of Empire to be revised. Dominions and India must have partnership in Imperial Government ; system of Imperial preference to be introduced ; settlement of Ireland essential.

([67]) *April* 28.—U.S.A. Army Bill. President empowered to raise Regular Army to 287,000 men and National guard to 625,000 men, and to obtain additional drafts.

([68]) *May* 1.—Since April 9 British have captured 19,736 prisoners (including 393 officers), 227 guns (including 98 heavy), 227 trench mortars and 470 machine guns. French have taken, since April 18, 20,780 prisoners and 157 guns; 717 aeroplanes altogether brought down during April.

(⁶⁹) *May* 1.—A new list of scheduled occupations to which protection is afforded by the War Office, Admiralty, and Ministry of Munitions was issued to-day. Agriculture occupies a special position. Under the new scheme very few men—and those only in very special circumstances—who are classified A and B1 escape Military Service.

(⁷⁰) *May* 2.—Germany agreed to pay an indemnity for the sinking of the Argentine ship "Monte Protegido." The German Minister at Buenos Aires sent a note to the Argentine Minister for Foreign Affairs, stating that at the first opportunity an Imperial Squadron would salute the Argentine flag ; and meanwhile, in Berlin, that flag would be saluted with 101 guns.

(⁷¹) *May* 2.—No new taxes. Total estimated expenditure, £2,290,000,000 ; revenue, £639,000,000.

(⁷²) *May* 4.—Admiralty Staff reform on considerable scale determined on ; the formation of a War Staff, each of whose members will be free from Departmental duties of any kind, to be the main principle of the change. The Inventions Board to be reorganized. Hoped that these changes will lead to greater success in dealing with the submarine menace. Admiral Jellicoe to be Chief of the enlarged Staff, his position to correspond with that of C. I. G. S. at the War Office.

(⁷³) *May* 5.—Mr. Lloyd George, Lord Robert Cecil, Gen. Sir W. Robertson, and Sir John Jellicoe have been three days attending meetings in Paris with the French Government : M. Ribot, Gen. Nivelle, Gen. Pétain, and Vice-Adm. Le Bon, to discuss and determine operations in France and the East ; complete agreement was reached.

(⁷⁴) *May* 5.—At Washington, U.S.A., Mr. Balfour addressed Congress in connection with the French and British Mission ; he was splendidly received by the House and made a characteristic speech felicitously expressed. This is the first time that anyone not American has addressed the House.

(⁷⁵) *May* 5.—The Racing Calendar published full report of the Jockey Club Meeting of April 30, at which it was decided to discontinue racing and cancel fixtures after May 4. It was agreed that public opinion was strongly opposed to racing, and that severe restrictions on the provision of oats made further sport impossible. The War Cabinet had agreed to the suggestions made by the Club concerning thoroughbred horses.

(⁷⁶) *May* 13.—*Mesopotamia*.—The retirement of the Russians to the left bank of the Diala was of consequence ; had they maintained their position the Turkish line of retreat was threatened, the troops of General Maude facing them from the South.

(⁷⁷) *May* 14.—*Isonzo Offensive*.—A big bombardment for fifty-six hours opened the offensive on a front of twenty-five miles. The chief Italian attack was on the Plava sector. The Isonzo was bridged below Plava, and the infantry crossed on the 14th : the enemy shelled the river ; Italian trench mortars supporting, the attack was successfully launched.

(⁷⁸) *May* 16.—The replies to Mr. Lloyd George's Home Rule proposals favoured a convention—the Ulster members alone being willing to agree to the Prime Minister's offer, subject to reconsideration at the end of five years. The financial proposals of the Home Rule Act to be reconsidered. A conference to meet on the lines of the Speaker's Conference on Electoral Reform. Nationalist Ireland considered the "clean cut" impossible ; no partition could be endured.

(⁷⁹) *May* 20.—General John J. Pershing, who took command of the 1st U.S.A. Division of regular troops sent to France, is a West Point cavalryman. He fought with distinction in Cuba and in the Philippines, and gained the reputation of a hard fighter and good administrator. In 1906 Mr. Roosevelt promoted him Brigadier. He was born in 1861. A total of from 35,000 to 40,000 men might be sent as the first instalment of an army for which it was estimated ten million would be available between the ages of 21 and 30 years.

(⁸⁰) *May* 24.—Lord Robert Cecil announced that the Japanese Navy had sent considerable forces to the Mediterranean, including several light cruisers, to assist and co-operate with the Allies. In the Indian and Pacific Oceans fast and powerful Japanese cruisers were assisting us.

(⁸¹) *May* 24.—Mr. Bonar Law stated in the House of Commons that the German National Debt equalled our own, but that whilst the Germans had only raised by taxes 85 millions above pre-war taxes, we had been able to raise 400 millions by additional taxation.

(⁸²) *June* 11.—President Wilson, after declaring that the United States seek no material profit or aggrandisement in the war, urges that the *status quo ante* must be altered with a view to preventing the recurrence of such a calamity. No people, consequently, must be "forced under a sovereignty under which it does not wish to live.

No territory must change hands except for the purpose of securing to its inhabitants a fair chance of life and liberty." There must be no indemnities apart from compensation for " manifest wrongs." Finally, " the free peoples of the world must draw together in a common covenant, some genuine and practical co-operation that will combine their force to secure peace and justice in the dealings of nations with one another." The message concludes with an appeal for the unity of the forces of liberty.

(⁸³) *June* 12.—The British Note quotes the Russian declaration that " free Russia does not propose to dominate other peoples or to take from them their national patrimony or forcibly to occupy foreign territory," and states that the British Government agrees with the principles here implied. The purpose of the United Kingdom " at the outset " was to defend its existence " and to enforce respect for international arrangements. To these objects has now been added that of liberating populations oppressed by alien tyranny." The British Government, it is asserted, heartily accept and approve the "principles laid down by President Wilson in his message to Congress. They " believe that, broadly speaking, the agreements which they have from time to time made with their allies are conformable to these standards. But if the Russian Government so desire, they are quite ready with their allies to examine, and, if need be, to revise, these agreements." The French Note is couched in general terms, but becomes more specific regarding Alsace and Lorraine, the restoration of which is declared to be essential.

(⁸⁴) *June* 16.—The principal points were : (*a*) no annexations " detrimental to the cause of nationality," (*b*) no indemnities, (*c*) Belgium to be restored to independence, (*d*) the Balkans to be dealt with as proposed by the Austrian Socialists, (*e*) Russian-Poland to be independent, (*f*) cultural autonomy should be granted to portions of States with a different language from the rest—*e.g.*, Schleswig, Posen, Alsace-Lorraine, (*g*) an international tribunal to be set up, (*h*) armaments to be limited, (*i*) new rules for blockade in war to be framed, (*j*) no commercial war after the war ; free trade to be everywhere adopted, (*k*) no secret diplomacy ; all diplomatic agreements to be submitted to representatives of the people.

(⁸⁴*a*) *June* 18.—Herr Hoffmann, Swiss Foreign Minister, sent a message in cypher, containing an outline of conciliatory German peace-terms to be conveyed to the Russian Government, to Herr Odier, Swiss Minister in Petrograd, instructing him to inform Herr Grimm, a Swiss Socialist Member of Parliament then in Petrograd. It was expected that Herr Grimm would bring these terms to the knowledge of the Russian Government. Herr Grimm did so, and was promptly expelled ; and Herr Hoffmann, after publishing (16.6) an explanatory apology, resigned, 18.6. He was succeeded by Herr G. Ador, of anti-German tendencies.

(⁸⁵) *June* 26.—The Mesopotamia Commission Report, after full investigation, finds that though the Expedition was a justifiable military enterprise, it was entered into too light-heartedly and without sufficient care and preparation. The division of responsibility between the India Office (policy) and the Indian Government (management) was unworkable ; whilst the scope of the objective was not sufficiently thought out. The Report goes deeply into the manner in which affairs were conducted in higher quarters, and makes pointed recommendations. As to the advance on Baghdad, it was " under the conditions existing in October, 1915, an offensive movement based upon political and military miscalculations and attempted with tired and insufficient forces and inadequate preparation." The chief responsibility, in sequence, lay respectively on Gen. Sir J. Nixon, Lord Hardinge, Gen. Sir B. Duff (C.-i.-C.), Gen. Sir E. Barrow (Mil. Sec., India Office), Mr. Austen Chamberlain (S.S.I.), and the War Committee of the Cabinet ; and blame is apportioned in detail, more especially in the matter of River Transport, Supplies and Medical Provision, in which the Expedition had broken down badly. For the latter the responsibilities of the C.-i.-C., the D.M.S. in India (Surgeons-General Sir W. Babtie and J. G. MacNeece) and the S.M.O. of the Force (Surgeon-General G.H. Hathaway) are seriously dealt with, and the general inefficiency of the Medical Service in India (largely owing to financial cheeseparing) is exposed. At the same time full credit is given to the " magnificent courage and pertinacity " of the fighting ranks, and it is pointed out that " with the exception of a few months during which there was a serious setback, the war has been an unbroken success." Allowance is also made for the fact that the internal situation in India was giving considerable cause for anxiety at the time. A Minority Report, by Commander J. Wedgwood, D.S.O., M.P., emphasised considerably the actions of certain high authorities who were in his opinion most severely to blame.

(⁸⁶) *June* 29.—Mr. Lloyd George reviewed the Military and Naval situation, speaking optimistically regarding the ultimate effect of the Russian Revolution and regarding the submarine menace. He said that the Government had come to the conclusion that the submarines could neither starve us out nor cripple our Military effort, and added " we are beginning to get them." He afterwards discussed the prospects and terms of peace, arguing that no honourable peace was at the moment attainable. No detailed exposition of war aims was given, but he declared that Mesopotamia would never be restored to Turkey and that the question of the German Colonies must be settled by the Peace Conference. The conditions of peace, he stated, must be " guaranteed by the destruction of the Prussian Military Power," or, better, by the " democratisation of the German Government." While disclaiming any desire to dictate to the Germans their form of Government, he said that the Allies would enter into negotiations with a free Government in Germany with a different temper and with more confidence than they could with a Government dominated by the spirit of Prussian Militarism.

(⁸⁷) *July* 4.—The chief fighting is reported from the Coast district South of Kilwa and in the region between Lake Nyassa and the Central Railway. The main German force is retreating South. In the South German forces marching across Portuguese territory reached the British border east of Lake Nyassa, but were driven back by British and Portuguese columns from the south.

(⁸⁸) *July* 7.—The despatches cover the operations in Egypt from October 1, 1916, to February 28, 1917, during which period Sinai was cleared of the Turks and the Egyptian force won the victories of Maghdaba and Rafa'a, and on the western front the Senussi were defeated near Siwa.

(⁸⁹) *July* 11.—The operations leading up to the capture of Baghdad are described by Lt.-General Sir Stanley Maude. The record begins on August 28, 1916, and closes on March 31, 1917. The first half of the period was occupied in preparation, the second in heavy fighting round Kut and Sanna-i-Yat, the passage of the Tigris and the advance on Baghdad.

(⁹⁰) *July* 11.—A converging movement of British columns compelled the German forces on the coast hills S. and W. of Kilwa to fall back. German detachments further inland between Lake Nyassa and the sea were being pressed from the N.W. and south to Mahenge.

(⁹¹) *July* 13.—Since July 1, 834 officers and 35,809 men have surrendered to the Russians.

(⁹²) *July* 17.—Due to the disbandment of recalcitrant regiments on July 16, the Maximalists under M. Lenin organised a mutiny of the garrison ; the following day mutineers and workmen from Kronstadt arrived in the capital. There was random machine-gun and rifle fire in the streets. The outbreak was denounced by the Council of Workmen's and Soldiers' Delegates.

(⁹³) *July* 17.—Sir Edward Carson joins the War Cabinet and is succeeded as First Lord of the Admiralty by Sir Eric Geddes ; Dr. Addison becomes Minister in charge of Reconstruction and is succeeded as Minister of Munitions by Mr .Churchill ; Mr. Montagu becomes Secretary of State for India in succession to Mr. Chamberlain.

(⁹⁴) *July* 18.—No enquiry to be set up as a preliminary to further action against persons impugned. As regards the soldiers, they will be dealt with by the Army Council in the ordinary way.

(⁹⁵) *July* 19.—Near the Coast at Kilwa, British columns are closing in on one of the larger bodies of enemy troops. In the South, the enemy are being driven towards Mahenge.

(⁹⁶) *July* 19.—The Centre, Radicals, and Majority Socialists passed a so-called " Majority Resolution," declaring that no desire for conquest actuated Germany ; that " declining all thoughts of the forcible acquisition of territory, the Reichstag strives for a peace by agreement and a permanent reconciliation of the nations " ; it also " rejects all plans which aim at economic exclusion and enmity between peoples after the war "— and aims only at an economic peace and freedom of the seas as preparatory for permanent friendly relations and the strengthening of international law. " So long as hostile Governments reject such a peace and threaten Germany and her Allies with schemes of conquest and oppression, the German people are determined unshakably to stand together," etc. Passed by 212 to 126. On this resolution Dr. Michaelis made a long speech, which appears to have pleased nobody—especially as, whilst nominally accepting the Resolution, he qualified his acceptance by talking of " your resolution. as I interpret it." He declared , in fact, for a victor's peace and the inviolability of German territory, and stated that Germany would not again offer peace.

(⁹⁷) *July* 21.—The new Chancellor's speech, he said, meant that the military party had won. As for the U-boat menace, our losses were decreasing and our shipbuilding increasing. Our food supply for 1917-18 was secured.

(⁹⁸) *July* 23.—It proposed to raise the minimum wage to agricultural workmen from the 25s. per week proposed by the Bill to 30s. per week.

(⁹⁹) *July* 26.—A resolution was passed that the Allies are determined only to lay down arms when they have rendered impossible any return in the future of acts of criminal aggression, such as those for which the autocracy of the Central Empires has been responsible.

(¹⁰⁰) *July* 28.—

Imperial:		
Dr. G. Michaelis	..	Chancellor.
Herr Helfferich ..	..	Interior and Vice-Chancellor.
Baron v. Kühlmann	..	Foreign Affairs.
Count Rödern ..	..	Finance.
Adm. v. Capelle	..	Marine.
Herr Solf	..	Colonies.
Herr v. Waldow	..	Food Controller.
Etc.		Etc.
Prussian:		
Dr. G. Michaelis	..	Prime Minister.
Herr Helfferich ..	..	Vice-Chairman of Cabinet.
General v. Stein	..	War.
Herr Drews ..	..	Interior.
Etc.		Etc.

(¹⁰¹) *July* 30.—He said that the French spirit was better than he had almost ever known it. If France and Britain held together they would be able to get through their Russian troubles. It was his conviction, based on information, that the Russians would recover and become as formidable as ever.

(¹⁰²) *July* 31.—The Allies attacked from La Basse Ville (River Lys) to Steenstraate (River Yser), taking both those villages and, besides, Hollebeke, Sanctuary Wood, Hooge, Westhoek, Verlorenhoek, Frezenberg, St. Julien, Pilkem, Bixschoote, and Kortekeer Cabaret. The object of this attack was eventually to drive the enemy off the high ground, or, rather, low ridge, commanding Ypres from the South to the North-east.

(¹⁰³) *August* 14.—The Papal Note invited heads of belligerent States to consider the following proposals: Diminution of Armaments, Institution of Arbitration, " Freedom of the Seas," general condonation as to damage with certain exceptions, reciprocal restitution of occupied territory and an examination in a conciliatory spirit of other territorial questions.

(¹⁰⁴) *August* 24.—Prisoners taken by Allies between April 9 and August 22 :—

British ..	..	..	46,155
French ..	..	..	43,723
Italians ..	..	..	40,681
Russians ..	..	..	37,221

Total German prisoners in British hands to date,102,218. Total British and Indian prisoners in German hands, about 43,000.

(¹⁰⁵) *August* 29.—The American Note, in answer to the Papal Note, stated that the mere cessation of hostilities ought not to be sought unless such cessation could be obtained on conditions which would ensure a stable and enduring peace. The object of this war is to deliver the free peoples of this world from the evil power of a vast military establishment controlled by an irresponsible Government which, regardless of Treaty obligations or humanity, aimed at the domination of the world and " now stands baulked, but not defeated, the enemy of four-fifths of the world." " We cannot take the word of the present rulers of Germany as a guarantee of anything that is to endure, unless explicitly supported by such conclusive evidence of the will and purpose of the German peoples themselves as the other peoples of the world would be justified in accepting." The remaining Allied Powers concurred in this Note and did not issue separate replies to the Pope.

(¹⁰⁶) *Sept.* 4.—In the autumn of 1904 and summer of 1905, after the Dogger Bank incident, the Kaiser sought to exploit the Tsar's resentment of the British attitude. The *New York Herald* reports a series of telegrams exchanged between the Kaiser and Tsar Nicholas, the intention being the formation of a Triple Alliance between Germany,

France and Russia against Great Britain. The Tsar at one moment seemed disposed to agree.

([107]) *Sept.* 9.—The United States publish disclosures of German official cypher messages passing between Count Luxburg (German Chargé d'Affaires at Buenos Aires) and Berlin, transmitted through the Swedish Legation at Buenos Aires and the Swedish Foreign Office. Luxburg recommends that neutral ships should either be spared altogether or sunk without leaving a trace (" spurlos versenkt "). Diplomatic relations between Argentina and Germany severely strained in consequence.

([108]) *Sept.* 13.—

Prime Minister and War	..	M. Painlevé.
Foreign Affairs	.. ..	M. Ribot.
Marine	.. .. ..	M. Chaumet.
Munitions	.. .. ..	M. Loncheur.
Interior	.. .. ..	M. Steeg.
Etc.		Etc.

War Committee formed of the four first-mentioned Ministers and four " Secretaries of State." (MM. Barthou, L. Bourgeois, Doumer and Dupuy.)

([109]) *Sept.* 14.—Col. Sir J. Allen, Minister of Defence, states that New Zealand has sent 86,000 men oversea, and that of the men returned over 1,200 had gone out to fight again. 61 per cent. of the wounded had recovered and rejoined the ranks.

([110]) *Sept.* 21.—The German reply repeats the Kaiser's assertion that he had tried to maintain peace. No reference is made to Belgian or any other territorial questions.

([111]) *Sept.* 25.—Brig.-General E. Northey, C.B., reporting on his operations on March 10 last, states that the New Langenburg and Bismarckburg districts (between Lakes Nyassa and Tanganyika), covering an area of 20,000 square miles, have been cleared of the enemy.

([112]) *Sept.* 25.—Gross Admiral v. Tirpitz, at the first propaganda meeting of the " Vaterlandspartei " in Berlin, declares that Great Britain is the enemy that counts ; that not wrong but right had been done to Belgium, and that peace without indemnification of a tangible kind signified Germany's defeat and the triumph of Anglo-American capitalism. He saw no difficulties in the East ; the enemy that mattered was England.

([113]) *Sept.* 25.—President Wilson states that it is not the desire of the United States Government to give the impression to the world that it is allied with the other Governments at war with Germany, other than that the U.S.A. and the Entente Allies have a common object in defeating any world-conquering aspirations of Prussian Militarism and in " making the world safe for Democracy."

([114]) *Sept.* 26.—Herr Kaempf in the Reichstag denounced Mr. Wilson for attempting to sow distrust between the Kaiser and his people—" doing so is like biting on granite, on account of the common sense of the German people." " In the air the Germans have gained supremacy ; and the U-boat crews have done more than they promised."

([115]) *Sept.* 28.—The Red Cross motor-launches, employed on the Tigris in February and March last, followed the Army close in its advances, acting as feeders to river-going and ocean-going Hospital Ships, and dealing promptly with sick or wounded. Thirty-five launches were sent out from home and twenty-one from Bombay. The motor-driven hospital ship, " Nabha," also working on the Tigris as far as Baghdad, did wonderfully good work.

([116]) *Sept.* 28.—Bolo Pasha, a Marseilles adventurer who had been in close touch with ex-Khedive Abbas, was arrested in France on suspicion of being an enemy agent— trying to purchase control of the " Journal " in order to influence public opinion, acting in various treasonable financial intrigues, and having received £320,000 from the Deutsche Bank in 1916.

([117]) *Sept.* 28.—In the Reichstag v. Kühlmann delivered himself, on the subject of the Papal Note, of a cloud of generalities concerning the general state of Europe. He did not descend to discussion of facts nor to answers to definite questions.

([118]) *Oct.* 3.—Democratic Conference meets. M. Kerenski objects to an entirely Socialist Ministry and threatens to resign if a Coalition Government is not approved. Meeting declares for active policy towards general peace. Bolsheviks leave assembly in a body.

([119]) *Oct.* 4.—Owing to an agitation *re* the over-employment of overseas troops in the fighting line, official figures are published showing overseas forces engaged and casualties to the same. The total shows overseas forces engaged : Casualties thereto represent .08 of whole force. In the fighting since July 31, the proportions engaged were :   84 per cent. Home Troops, 16 per cent. Overseas ; in casualties 92 per cent. Home Troops, 8 per cent. Overseas.

([120]) *Oct.* 5.—Count Luxburg was reported as having sailed for Spain, but he had not done so ; Argentina was suffering from shortage of flour and worried by strikes ; the country wanted war—the President opposed it.   Cabinet crisis imminent.

([121]) *Oct.* 9.—Four Battleships, 1 cruiser involved.   Mutineers wanted to paralyse Fleet and force peace on country.   Cause imputed to bad food and absorption of Russian Revolutionary ideas.   Independent Socialist Party involved.

([122]) *Oct.* 9.—Attention is drawn to German intrigue in Spanish Marocco ; working up disaffection among Moslems against British and French ; rebel detachments attacking French and withdrawing into Spanish territory ; continual assistance given to German submarines from Moorish Coast.

([123]) *Oct.* 11.—Commercial cable communication with Holland was interrupted by British Government until Holland consented to stop transit of sand and gravel and scrap metals through their country from Germany to Belgium ; supplies so transmitted being out of all proportion to Belgium's civil needs.

([124]) *Oct.* 16.—The Germans maintain that the " Wilhelmshaven Mutiny " was exploited deliberately by the Government to meet unanswerable exposures concerning Pan-German propaganda in the Army, about which there is considerable disaffection. Dr. Michaelis held responsible.   Independent Socialist Party say they are given no chance, Pan-Germanism being officially encouraged.

([125]) *Oct.* 17.—The Germans held Irbe Strait, preventing the Russian exit, and drove the Russian Fleet into Moon Sound.   Russians fought at the entrance, but had to retire into Moon Sound, where an enemy torpedo boat destroyer in rear from the North was repulsed.   The Russians lost a battleship—" Slava ", and had some coast batteries knocked out.   The Germans had several Dreadnoughts and many destroyers engaged.

([125]a) *Oct.* 17.—Holland maintains the legality of transport of material required for upkeep of roads and maintenance of State on peace conditions ; says Germany wanted supplies ahead of her needs, as transit by canal in the winter months is impossible ; requests Great Britain to prove that the material transported is for war works.

([126]) *Oct.* 18.—A report was received of the capture of a German and an Austrian with Arab and Somali followers, who tried to capture a small fort near Jibuti and destroy the railway and create trouble and disorder.

([127]) *Oct.* 18.—Dutch shipping in American ports to be used by America outside war zone in exchange for food and raw material, which Holland guarantees not to re-export to Germany.   Neutral stocks of raw material for war-stores may be seized by America.

([128]) *Oct.* 19.—The U.S.A. refuse to send further supplies to Holland and Scandinavian countries until the latter prove that supplies are not demanded in excess of normal requirements and are not being re-exported to Germany.

([129]) *Oct.* 21.—Fifteen clauses.   General principles are :   No annexations and no indemnities ;   Nationality of disputed territories to be settled by a plebiscite after all troops removed :   Neutrality of Suez and Panama Canals and all straits leading to inland seas ;   no economic blockades ;   general disarmament and creation of militia system.

([130]) *Oct.* 25.—French in England and British in France not serving are now liable to be conscripted under the convention just signed.

([131]) *Oct.* 28.—The Brazilian Foreign Minister has discovered a plot to send a squadron of submarines to Buenos-Aires to assist the German invasion of S. Brazil.

([132]) *Oct.* 30.—Signor Orlando, Prime Minister ;   Baron Sonnino, Foreign Affairs ;   Gen. Alfieri, War ;   Admiral del Buono, Marine ;   etc.

([133]) *Nov.* 7.—In the Notes exchanged between Mr. Lansing and Viscount Ishii, dated November 2, 1917, the U. S. Government recognises that Japan has special interests in China, and both Governments declare their adhesion to the principle of " the open door " in that country.

([134]) *Nov.* 8.—The social and political unrest which had been stirring in Russia all through the summer of 1917 came to an head when the Bolsheviks under Lenin, assisted by German intrigue, overthrew the Provisional Government.   Already in July the Bolsheviks had organised an armed rising in Petrograd, and though at that time they did not wield a majority in the Soviet, false reports telegraphed by their agents to the front made the troops believe that they had obtained control and that the war was practically over.   Some divisions opened the front to the enemy and the rest would have followed but for the strong intervention of General Kornilov, who assumed the

High Command and took stern measures to re-introduce discipline in the Army. Meanwhile the Bolsheviks fast increased their hold upon the Soviet, and were insistent with their cry for an immediate " democratic peace " with no annexation and no indemnity. Kerenski temporised with these opposing elements and lost the confidence of all. Kornilov having already been overthrown, the Extremists in the Soviet seized the supreme power, and ordered the arrest of Kerenski, who, after a brief struggle, only saved himself by flight.

([135]) *Nov.* 9.—The object of the Allied War Council was to set up a central body charged with the duty of continuously surveying the field of operations as a whole and, from the information derived from all fronts, co-ordinating the plans prepared by the different General Staffs. The War Council was to have no executive power, and the final distribution and movements of the various armies in the field were to rest with the several Allied Governments.

([136]) *Nov.* 10.—The " Air Force Act " established an Air Council as a first-class Government Department, with a Secretary of State at its head ; this Air Council to have a status similar to the Admiralty and Army Council.

([137]) *Nov.* 12.—Sir A. Yapp announced a new scale of voluntary rations, in which meat was limited to 2lb., butter and fats to 10oz., sugar to 8oz., and bread 3½lb. to 8lb. per head per week, according to sex and occupation.

([138]) *Nov.* 14.—The " Reprisal " Bill passed by the Brazilian Parliament authorised the Government to proclaim a state of siege in such parts of the country as was necessary ; to cancel contracts for public works with enemy subjects or other contracts prejudicial to the national defence ; to prohibit trade with Germans abroad ; to intern enemy suspects, and to revise eventually the concession of land to colonists.

([139]) *Nov.* 18.—*General Sir Stanley Maude.*—Born in 1864 ; joined the Coldstream Guards in 1884 ; served in the Sudan in 1885. In the South African War he took part in the advance on Kimberley and the actions at Poplar Grove, Driefontein, Diamond Hill and Belfast. From 1901 to 1904 he served as Military Secretary to the Governor-General of Canada, and on returning home did valuable work in connection with the Territorial Force. At the outbreak of war in 1914, Sir S. Maude was on the Staff and rejoined the 5th Division in November in Flanders. He was given command of the 14th Infantry Brigade and was severely wounded. On his recovery he received command of the 13th Infantry Division, which was transferred from France to the Dardanelles, thence to Egypt, and subsequently to Mesopotamia. In August 1916 he succeeded Sir Percy Lake in the Mesopotamian Command and made it his first duty to reorganise his Army and improve his lines of communication. This difficult task accomplished, he marched with all his forces against the Turks in the middle of December, 1916, and carried through a brilliant winter campaign culminating in the fall of Baghdad in March, 1917. There followed another long period of preparation, devoted to improving the means of communication by river and rail, and developing local resources to supply the requirements of the Army. In September, 1917, by a succession of swift blows he again routed the Turks and was preparing to meet an enemy force concentrated at Mosul, when he died of cholera, from drinking coffee and milk at a native reception, on Sunday evening, November 18, 1917.

([140]) *Nov.* 20.—The outstanding feature of Gen. Byng's advance on Cambrai in the third week of November, 1917, was that it was not preceded by any preliminary bombardment, the British command relying entirely on the use of tanks to break down the dense masses of the enemy's wire. Though the extreme limits of the attack were Epehy and Fontaine, places some thirty miles apart, the main assault was concentrated on the front between the Bapaume-Cambrai and Péronne-Cambrai roads. Having quietly accumulated a large number of tanks in this section, at the pre-arranged moment early in the morning these moved forward, the infantry following in their wake. The novelty and daring of this manœuvre took the Germans by surprise, and the " Hindenburg line," considered by them impregnable, was swiftly penetrated to a depth of several miles by the British.

([141]) *Nov.* 22.—In November the German Government, through its wireless stations, announced that on and from November 22, 1917, there would be an extension of the field of operations of its submarines :—(1) The " barred zone " round England and France was extended. (2) A new " zone " round the Azores defined. (3) The channel to Greece in the Mediterranean was closed. This fresh restriction of the safe zone along the Dutch Coast was much resented in Holland.

([142]) *Dec.* 1—General Van Deventer, commanding British Forces in East Africa, reported that since the 1st of August his troops have captured 1,400 German and 4,149 native prisoners and 11 field guns. The War Cabinet sent him a message of thanks, describing the behaviour of his troops as beyond all praise.

(143) *Dec.* 1.—At the first meeting of the Versailles Allied Council were present M. Clémenceau, Mr. Lloyd George, Col. House (U.S.A.), Signor Orlando, and Generals Foch, Robertson, Wilson, Cadorna and Bliss.

(144) *Dec.* 4.—The withdrawal of British Troops from Bourlon Wood was rendered necessary on account of the poisonous gas, pools of stagnant water and numbers of dead bodies. Our men had almost to live in their gas-masks, and the wood was a loathsome place. It did not command our positions, though when in our possession it was inconvenient to the enemy, and he therefore made every effort to gain it.

(145) *Dec.* 4.—Lord Curzon stated that our line at Aden was the same as in July, 1915, and described an arc at about 11 miles outside Aden. In the interval there had been constant patrol skirmishes and small actions. Our most important success had been the capture of Jabir on November 22. A modified transfer to the War Office had been carried out, and political charge handed to Sir F. R. Wingate (Egypt). It would doubtless tend to strengthen our position if we could drive out the enemy altogether, but at present troops could not be spared for the process.

(146) *Dec.* 4.—President Wilson stated that when the German people say that they are ready to agree to a settlement based on justice and reparation for the wrongs their rulers have done, peace will come.

(147) *Dec.* 5.—M. Trotski at Petrograd maintained that the Russian Government sought a general peace negotiated in concert with the Allies ; they were against Imperialism in all countries, Great Britain included, and against all secret diplomacy.

(148) *Dec.* 6.—Senhor d'Almeida's Government resigned, and after three days street fighting Major Sidonio Paes formed a Provisional Government. President Machado was driven from Office, Major Paes subsequently becoming Provisional President, and taking over the Ministries of War and Foreign Affairs. Solidarity with the Allies was reaffirmed.

(149) *Dec.* 7.—Halifax (Nova Scotia) was wrecked by the explosion of a munition-ship coming into collision with another vessel. The damage to property was reckoned at four millions sterling ; 25,000 people were rendered homeless, and the loss of life was subsequently estimated at over 10,000. Five British steamers were damaged, two-thirds of their crews being lost. The British Government subscribed a million pounds.

(150) *Dec.* 11.—The Commander-in-Chief and a small staff, with a guard of less than 150 all told of Allied troops, passed through the Mount Zion part of the city some 200 yards from the walls and out again, on foot. Outside the Jaffa Gate, Sir Edmund Allenby was received by the Military Governor and a guard of honour composed of men who had done their full share in the campaign. At the base of the Tower of David the Proclamation was read to the people assuring them of good treatment and of the sanctity of all Holy Places being respected. Dr. Hertz, Chief Rabbi in London, also addressed a letter of thanks on behalf of all Jews to the King on the British victories in the Holy Land, and British Jewry congratulated General Allenby on the entry into Jerusalem of the British forces.

(151) *Dec.* 11.—The British Government replied, concerning German peace proposals in September last, that they would be prepared to receive the communications suggested and to discuss them with their Allies. The Allies had been informed. No answer had been returned by the German Government.

(152) *Dec.* 12.—A convoy from Scotland to Norway of five neutral and one British vessels was sunk in the North Sea by four German destroyers. One British destroyer (H.M.S. " Partridge ") and four armed trawlers forming part of the escort were also lost. The covering force did not arrive on the scene of action in time to prevent the disaster.

(153) *Dec.* 15.—The main provisions of the ten articles of the "definite" armistice-treaty were :—Armistice from December 12, 1917, to January 14, 1918—seven days' notice of termination. (This article was broken by the Germans, who resumed operations at only two days' notice). No German troops during the armistice to reinforce on the Russian front, nor to reinforce the Western from the Russian front. (This article was also broken by the Germans, at least seven divisions being so transferred during the Armistice). Centres of fraternization fixed. Turkish and Russian troops to withdraw from Persia. Peace negotiations to begin at once. The Powers then at once entered into peace negotiations, Count Hertling, Herr v. Kühlmann, Count Czernin (Austrian Foreign Minister), MM. Joffe, Kamenev, etc., coming to Brest Litovsk ; but up to the end of the year the negotiations had not got much forwarder (v. App. 156-158).

(154) *Dec.* 17.—Count Hertling said : " It is not Mr. Lloyd George who is the world judge, but history ; as on August 2, 1914, so also to-day, we can look forward to its verdict with equanimity. It was not we who brought about the murders at Serajevo ; The Sukhomlinov trial in Petrograd made absolutely clear what we knew from the end of July, 1914, that the Order of Nicholas II. for a general mobilisation forced on us a war on two fronts."

(155) *Dec.* 20.—Washington : The latest proposals included various feelers circulated among the Diplomatic Corps here. A plebiscite for Alsace-Lorraine ; England to pay for German African Colonies, the proceeds to restore Belgium, Northern France, Serbia and Rumania. Russian territory under German protectorate ; Turkey to remain intact, and some few other impossible propositions purporting to be the Kaiser's Christmas Peace Terms. This represented Germany's expected peace " drive " in the U.S.A., through a neutral Legation.

(156) *Dec.* 22.—The Russian suggestions for peace terms were : (1) No forcible annexations of territory taken during the war. (2) Complete restoration of independence to the nationalities who had lost it during the war. (3) Nationalities not hitherto enjoying independence to have the right to decide by plebiscite whether they would be united to other States or acquire independence. (4) Safeguarding of the rights of minorities in territories inhabited by several nationalities. (5) No war indemnities, but war requisitions to be returned. (6) Colonial acquisitions to be decided on the same principles. Economic war was condemned by the Russians.

(157) *Dec.* 23.—The Kaiser, visiting the Second Army (West Front) addressed the troops and announced : "The year 1917 has proved that the German people has in the Lord of Creation above an unconditional and avowed Ally on whom it can absolutely rely."

(158) *Dec.* 25.—Count Czernin dealt with Russian terms (see App. 156) as follows : He accepted 1,2, and 4, and refused 3. *Re* 5, he suggested a modification, and *re* 6, he said that Germany demanded the return of her Colonies, plebiscites there being impracticable.

(159) *Dec.* 27-28.—The Turks with German assistance made a determined attempt to retake Jerusalem. The attack began on the 27th and lasted for 26 hours. Gen. Allenby counter-attacked the Turkish right flank and made a general advance on the 28th. By the morning of the 29th, the British had reached the line Burkah-Ram Allah-Wadi el Kelb and inflicted heavy losses.

(160) *Dec.* 29.—Admiral Dowles at the Senate Investigation of Shipping Board Construction stated that it was considered possible to produce fabricated steel ships in much less time than wooden ships, and that enough lumber to build the number of ships required by Mr. Denman's plan was not available—hence the unsatisfactory tonnage situation.

(161) *Dec.* 29.—A deputation from Finland, received by the King of Sweden, was assured of that country's sympathy. A second Finnish delegation went to Berlin and a third to London, Havre and Paris. The Republic was recognised in Paris, but not in London.

(162) *Dec.* 31.—East Africa : Progress during the month. German forces escaped over Portuguese border closely pursued by British. The Germans have since spread over the country between coast and Lake Nyassa and captured Portuguese posts. Three columns of British troops are working inwards from N., W. and E., and have obtained contact with enemy E. of Nyassa.

BRITISH CAPTURES AND LOSSES IN PRISONERS IN 1917.

	Captures.		Losses.	
	Men.	Guns.	Men.	Guns.
Western Theatre	73,131	531	27,200	166
Salonica	1,095	—	202	—
Palestine	17,646	108	610	—
Mesopotamia	15,944	124	267	—
East Africa	6,728	18	100	—
Total	114,544	817	28,379	166

BRITISH MERCHANT VESSELS LOST BY ENEMY ACTION.

	By Cruisers. T.B.D's, etc.		By Submarines.		By Mines.		Total.		
	No.	Lives.	No.	Lives.	No.	Lives.	No.	Lives.	Gross Tonnage.
1917.									
January	6	—	35	245	8	31	49	276	153,666
February	7	—	86	355	12	47	105	402	313,486
March	11	18	103	630	13	51	127	699	353,478
April	—	—	155	997	14	128	169	1,125	545,282
May	1	11	106	507	15*	73	122	591	352,289
June	1	—	116	384	5*	32*	122	416	417,925
July	—	—	88	401	11	67	99	468	364,858
August	1	—	84	415	6	47	91	462	329,810
September ..	—	—	68	293	10*	63*	78	356	196,212
October	1	—	79	578	6	30	86	608	276,132
November ..	—	—	56	376	8	44	64	420	173,560
December ..	1	—	76	520	8	65	85	585	253,087
Total ..	29	29	1,052	5,701	116	678	1,197	6,408	3,729,785

* Including 3 ships and 6 lives altogether lost by aircraft action.

AIR RAIDS ON GREAT BRITAIN, 1917.

AIR RAIDS ON

(Zeppelin [italic].

Date.		Locality.	Civilian Killed.			
			Men.	Women.	Children.	Total.
March	1	Kent	—	—	—	—
March	16	Kent and Margate	—	—	—	—
March	*16/17*	*Kent and Sussex*	—	—	—	—
,,	17	Kent	—	—	—	—
April	5	Kent and Ramsgate	—	—	—	—
May	6/7	London	1	—	—	1
,,	23/24	*Essex, Norfolk and Suffolk*	2	1	—	3
,,	25	Kent and Folkestone	17	34	26	77
June	5	Essex and Kent	3	—	—	3
,,	13	Margate, Essex and London	90	25	43	158
,,	*16/17*	*Kent and Suffolk*	2	1	—	3
July	4	Essex and Suffolk	3	—	—	3
,,	7	Margate and London	38	9	8	55
,,	22	Essex and Suffolk	1	—	—	1
Aug.	12	Essex and Margate	10	13	9	32
,,	*21/22*	*East Riding*	—	—	—	—
,,	22	Kent	6	1	1	8
Sept.	2/3	Dover	—	—	—	—
,,	3/4	Kent (Sheerness)	—	1	—	1
,,	4/5	Home Counties and London	7	8	1	16
,,	24/25	Kent, Essex and London	5	4	2	11
,,	*24/25*	*Lincolnshire and Yorkshire*	—	—	—	—
,,	25/26	Kent and London	6	2	—	8
,,	28/29	Home Counties	—	—	—	—
,,	29/30	Kent and London	4	5	4	13
,,	30/Oct. 1	Kent, Essex and London	5	4	—	9
Oct.	1/2	Kent, Essex and London	7	4	—	11
,,	*19/20*	*Midlands, Eastern Counties and London*	3	12	16	31
,,	29/30	Essex	—	—	—	—
,,	31	Kent and Dover	—	—	—	—
,,	31/Nov. 1	Kent, Essex and London	4	3	1	8
Dec.	6	Kent, Essex and London	1	5	1	7
,,	18	Kent, Essex and London	5	5	4	14
		TOTALS	220	137	116	473

GREAT BRITAIN, 1917.

Aeroplane.)

| Casualties. | | | | Sailors and Soldiers. | | Grand Total. | | Remarks. |
| Injured. | | | | | | | | |
Men.	Women.	Children.	Total.	Killed.	Injured.	Killed.	Injured.	
—	1	5	6	—	—	—	6	
—	—	—	—	—	—	—	—	
—	—	—	—	—	—	—	—	
1	1	—	2	—	—	1	2	
5	7	2	14	—	2	3	16	*Four Zeppelins came over.*
28	51	15	94	18	98	95	192	Three aeroplanes downed.
3	4	1	8	10	26	13	34	Four aeroplanes downed.
213	110	102	425	4	7	162	432	
5	7	2	14	—	2	3	16	*One Zeppelin downed out of two.*
1	—	—	1	14	29	17	30	
95	45	50	190	2	3	57	193	
1	2	—	3	12	23	13	26	
13	19	12	44	—	2	32	46	Two aeroplanes downed.
1	—	—	1	—	—	—	1	*One Zeppelin downed off Jutland.*
4	2	7	13	4	12	12	25	Three aeroplanes downed.
—	4	2	6	1	—	1	6	
1	3	2	6	131	90	132	96	Casualties mostly Naval.
20	29	10	59	3	12	19	71	
24	24	2	50	10	20	21	70	Only two out of twenty-four penetrated London defences.
—	3	—	3	—	—	—	3	S.E. outskirts of London.
9	9	3	21	1	2	9	23	Headed off from London.
—	—	—	—	—	—	—	—	
41	34	7	82	1	5	14	87	Only three penetrated defences.
17	13	3	33	5	5	14	38	Four aeroplanes reach London.
18	19	4	41	—	—	11	41	
24	17	11	52	5	3	36	55	*Thirteen Zeppelins reported (?)*
—	—	—	—	—	—	—	—	
8	9	4	21	2	1	10	22	
13	8	6	27	1	1	8	28	
42	23	14	79	—	6	14	85	
587	444	264	1,295	224	349	697	1,644	

INDEX.

Figures in black type represent the month : *e.g.*, 4.1=4th Jan. ; 23.11 = 23rd Nov. ; etc.

N.B.—In the following index a number of items are included which, by reason of their uncertainty or for some other cause, it has not been found easy or convenient to place in the Chronological Tables. Dates which can at present be only approximately given are indicated thus :—" *c.* 25.8."

BOIS HUGO (Loos).
British capture, 15.8.
BOLIVIA.
Severs diplomatic relations with Germany, 13.4.
BOLO PASHA.
Arrested, 28.9.
BOLS, MAJ.-GEN. L. J.
Succeeds Sir A. Lynden Bell as C.-of-S. in Palestine, 30.10.
BOLSHEVIKS (Maximalists), see also Russia.
Rise to power of, Nov., 1917; Demonstrations, 1.6; Lord R. Cecil on, 26.11; Obtain surrender of Russian General Staff, 1.12; After fight with Cossacks, occupy Rostov (Don), 14.12; Ultimatum to the Ukraine, 15.12; Try to make terms with Ukraine, 27.12.
BOMBARDMENTS OF ENGLISH PORTS.
Southwold (no cas.), 25.1; Margate and Broadstairs (3 k. 1 in.), 25.2; Ramsgate and Broadstairs (no cas.), 17.3; Dover and neighbourhood (no cas.), 20.4; Ramsgate, Broadstairs, etc. (2 k. 3 in.), 26.4; Scarborough (3 k. 6 in.), 4.9.
BONAR LAW, Mr.
Makes financial statement, 19.3; Appeals to strikers, 26.3; Introduces Budget for £2,290,000,000, 2.5; Asks for Vote of Credit, 500 millions, 9.5; Announces no issue of passports for Stockholm Conference, 13.8.
" BONNET ROUGE."
French Government action *re*, 5.9.
BORDEN (SIR ROBERT).
Speech to Empire Parliamentary Association (war work of Dominions, etc.), 2.4; Speech at Edinburgh, 11.4.
BOUCHAVESNES (Péronne).
Lines captured at, 4.3.
BOULOGNE.
Bombed by German airship, 16.2.
BOURLON (Cambrai).
Fighting at, 23-29.11; Enemy attacks in strength, 30.11, 1.12; British evacuate, 4.12.
BOURSIES (W.S.W. of Cambrai).
British capture, 9.4.
BRAILA (Rum.)
Captured by enemy, 4.1.
BRATIANU, M.
(Premier of Rumania) reconstructs Cabinet, 2.1.
BRAYE-EN-LAONNAIS (N.E. of Soissons)
French capture, 18.4; Heavy German attacks repulsed, 15-24.5; French regain ground, 9.7.
BRAZIL.
Severs diplomatic relations with Germany, 9.4; Neutrality Decree issued, 28.4; Neutrality decree annulled, 29.5; Seizure

of 240,000 tons of German shipping, *c.* 4.6; State of war with Germany, 26.10; Count Luxburg's plot to invade, revealed,, 28.10; Legislation v. Germans in, 14.11; Cedes ships to France, 27.11; French Government to use 30 German vessels, 5.12.
BREAD.
1s. per 4-lb. loaf, 26.3.
BREBACH (Saarbrücken).
Air raids on, 25.2; 4.3.
BRENTA RIVER (Trent.).
Italian retreat on, 15.11; Italians recover positions, 16, 24.12; Fail to hold heights above, 25.12.
" BRESLAU."
Makes raid in Black Sea, 25.6.
BREST-LITOVSK.
German and Russian delegations meet at, 2.12; Preliminary suspension of hostilities signed, 5.12; Russian armistice signed, 15.12; Peace negotiations entered on, 17.12; Peace negotiations proceeding (v. App. 156), 22.12.
BRESTOVICA VALLEY (Carso).
To the sea, fighting with varying fortune, 4.9.
BRIAND, M. (French Premier).
Resigns, 17.3.
BRITISH LINE.
Extension of, on French front, 6.3.
BRITISH LOSSES AT SEA.
Some Naval; Destroyers, 8.2, 28.3, 2.5, 6.7, 23.9, 23.12; Transports, 8.2.3, 2.5, 4.5; "Transylvania," 15.5, "Cameronia," 15.5; Mine-sweepers, 4.7; Convoys, 9 ships and 2 destroyers, 12.12. (For merchant vessels v. p. 294).
BRITISH TRADE CORPORATION.
Founded, with capital of 10 millions, 3.5.
BROADSTAIRS.
Air raid on, 1.3.
" BROKE," H.M.S. (Destroyer).
And " Swift " engage 6 German destroyers off Dover, 20, 21.4.
BRUGES.
Attacked by British naval airmen, 2, 14, 16.2; 2.7, 2, 3, 4.9, 15.10, 10, 24.12.
BRUSILOV, GENERAL.
Commander-in-Chief of Russian army, 4.6; Great offensive under, 1-19.7; Resigns, succeeded by Gen. Korniloff, 2.8.
BRUSSELS.
Mr., Whitlock, U.S. Minister, ordered by Germans to lower Legation flag, 15.2; He reports on German deportations as one of the foulest deeds in history, 17.5.
BRZEZANY (E. Gal.).
Night attack near, 6.3; Further German attacks, 8, 12.3; Russian offensive opens either side of, 1.7; Successful to

" CASSINI."
French destroyer, torpedoed, 28.2.

CASTAGNEVIZZA, v. Kostanjevica.

CASUALTIES, GERMAN.
To end of February, 1917, pub. 20.3.

CATTARO.
Italian airmen bomb, 3.10, etc.

CAURIÈRES, BOIS DES (Verdun).
Repulse of German attacks near, 21.1 ;
German attacks, slight gains, 4.3, 13.9.

CERIZY (St. Quentin).
French capture, 3.4.

CERNY (Aisne River).
Violent German attacks repulsed, 11.5.;
German attacks gain ground, 20.5, 1.7.;
French gain ground, 7.7.

CHAMBERLAIN, Mr. N.
Succeeded by Brig. Gen. E. Geddes as
D. G. National Service, 17.8.

CHAMPAGNE FRONT.
Fighting with varying results, mostly
German attacks and repulses, 12,28, 30,3 ;
5, 27.7 ; 7, 12, 28.10 ; 22.12.

CHARLES, EMPEROR.
Meets the Kaiser at Homburg, 3.4.

CHAULNES (S. of Péronne).
British occupy, 18.3.

CHAUME WOOD (Meuse, Fr.).
Germans attack, 4-7.11.

CHAUNY (E. of Noyon).
French capture, and move on, 19 to
24.3.

CHAVONNE (E. of Soissons).
French capture, 18.4.

CHEMIN DES DAMES (N. of R. Aisne).
French advance on, 16.4, et seqq ;
French take Craonne, 4.5 ; German
attacks on this front, 15, 18, 19, 25.5 ; 1, 3,
5-6, 17, 20-24, 29-30.6 ; French attack,
26.6 ; Germans retreat from, 2.11.

CHERISY (Arras-Cambrai Rd.).
British progress, later retire, 3.5.

CHEVREUX (N.E. of Craonne).
Successful French attacks, 8, 10, 22.5 ;
French lose position, 24.5.

CHILE.
Refuses to recognise German blockade,
10.2 ; New Cabinet, c. 6.7.

CHINA.
Threatens rupture with Germany on
Submarine question, 10.2 ; Allies memo-
randum to, 28.2 ; Cabinet crisis, 4.3 ;
Breaks off relations with Germany, 13.3 ;
Tuan Chi Jui, Prime Minister, dismissed,
22.5 ; Provisional Government formed,
dangerous situation, 3.6 ; Parliament
dissolved by President Li Yuan Hung,
12.6 ; Gen. Chang Hsun restores the
Empire, Hsuan Tung young Emperor, 1.7 ;
Pekin threatened, fighting, Emperor abdi-
cates, 7.7 ; Republicans enter Pekin, 12.7 ;
Tuan Chi Jui Premier again ; Fen Kwo

Chang President ; Declares war on
Austro-Hungary and Germany, 14.8 ;
Americo-Japanese agreement re, 7.11.

CHIVATA (E. Africa).
German defeat at, 15, 18.11.

CHIVRES (E. of Soissons).
French capture, 18.4.

CISMON (Italy).
Germans capture, 15.11.

CITÉ STE ÉLIZABETH (Lens).
Taken by British, 15.8.

CITÉ STE ÉMILE (Lens).
British take, 15.8.

CITÉ ST. LAURENT (Lens).
British take, 15.8.

CITÉ ST. PIERRE (N.W. of Lens).
British capture, 14.4.

CIVIDALE (Friuli).
In flames and captured by Germans
under von Below, 7.10.

CIVIL MOBILISATION REPORT.
Tabled, 8.3.

CLÉMENCEAU, M.
Accepts Premiership, 15.11 ; Statement of policy, 20.11.

COAL MINES.
British Government assumes control
of, 15.2.

COCHIN, M. DENYS
(Under Sec, Foreign Affairs) and Adm.
Lacaze resign from French Cabinet, 2.8.

COMMITTEE. (Inter-Ally Parliamentary).
Meets, 8.10.

COMPIÈGNE.
Successful large-scale French raid,
12 miles N. of, 14.2.

COMPULSORY MIL. SERV. BILL.
For Canada, third reading passed, 9.8.

CONDÉ (River Aisne).
French capture bridgehead, 18.4 ; and
fort, 19.4.

CONFERENCE, ALLIED BALKAN.
In Paris, 25. 26,7.

CONFERENCE, ALLIED WAR.
Meets in Rome, 5 to 7.1 ; at Calais,
26.2 ; In Petrograd, 5.3 ; InSavoy (French
and Italian), 19-20.4 ; In Paris, 5.5 ; In
London, 28.5 ; At Rapallo, 6 to 9.11 ; In
Paris, 29.11 ; At Versailles, 1.12 ; and on
other occasions, in varying proportions,
personalities and places, chiefly in Paris
and London.

CONFERENCE, ECONOMIC.
Concludes agreements in Paris, 17.6.

CONFERENCE, IMPERIAL (British)
WAR.
Inaugurated by Premier, 21.3.

CONFERENCE, SOCIALIST.
Opens at Stockholm, 13.5 ; German
Socialists refused passports for, 13.5 ;

French Socialists decide to attend, 28.5;
Soviet announces an International, at
Stockholm, 30.5; French Socialists refused passports for Stockholm, 1.6; Socialist,
at Leeds, 3.6; U.S. Govt. refuses passports for Stockholm, 11.8, Gt. Britain
ditto, 13.8; Labour decides to send delegates, 21.8; Trades Union declares against,
4.9; Mr. Henderson, 6.9.

CONSCIENTIOUS OBJECTORS.
Disfranchisement of, 21.11.

CONSCRIPTION.
U.S.A. decides for, 29.4; In Canada—
v. Canada.

CONSTANTINE, KING OF GREECE.
Abdicates in favour of second son,
Alexander, 11.6.

CONSTANTINOPLE.
British aeroplanes bomb town and
Turkish-German Fleet, 9.7.

CONSTITUENT ASSEMBLY (Russia).
Preparations for, 15.3.

CONVOY.
Nine merchantmen and two destroyers
sunk off Bergen, 17.10; Five merchantmen, etc., sunk in North Sea, 12.12.

CORINTH.
French troops land, 11.6.

CORMONS. (8 miles W. of Gorizia).
Captured by Germans, 28.10.

CORNELLA, MONTE.
Italians lose, 17.11.

CORN PRODUCTION BILL.
To increase arable land, second reading,
25.4; Amendment to defeated, 23.7.

" CORNWALLIS," H.M.S.
Sunk by torpedo in Mediterranean, 9.1.

COSSACKS (Russia).
Revolt against Government, 13.9;
Gen. Kalédin declares loyalty to Government, 16.9; Bolshevist forces fight Don,
11-12.12.

COSTA (Dr. Affonso).
Becomes Portuguese Premier (Demo-
crat), 24.4.

COSTABELLA, MT. (Trent.).
Italian success, 4.3; Austrian attack
repulsed, 12.10.

COSTA RICA.
Places territorial waters and ports at
disposal of U.S.A., 12.4; breaks off relations with Germany, 23.9.

CÔTE' DE L'OIE (Verdun).
French take, 21.8.

COTTON DUTIES.
New Indian, 13.3; Increase In, 15.3.

COUCY-LE-CHÂTEAU (10 miles N. of
Soissons).
Historical old castle blown up by
Germans, 20.3; French reach and take
town, 25-26.3.

COUNCIL OF EMPIRE.
Suspended, 12.3.

COURCY (N. of Reims).
Russians repulse Germans, 17.4.

COVENTRY.
Aircraft works strike, 30.11.

COWDRAY, LORD.
Resigns Presidency of Air Board, 16.11.

CRAONNE (N. of River Aisne).
Taken by French; also, in co-operation
with British, crest of ridge, 26,000 prisoners, 4.5; Violent fighting in neighbourhood and along Chemin des Dames, 9, 13,
16, 24.5.; French attack repulsed, 16.10;
French success near, 21.11.

CROISILLES (S.E. of Arras).
British gain ground near, 28.3; British
capture, 2.4; Severe fighting from Croisilles to N. of Gavrelle, 24.4.

CUBA.
Declares War on Germany, 7.4; and
on Austria-Hungary, 12.12.

CZERNIN, COUNT O. (Austro-Hung. For.
Minister).
Peace programme issued, 3.10; At
Brest Litovsk, and dealing with Russian
Peace proposals, December.

CZERNOWITZ (Bukovina).
Enemy approach and Russians retire,
29.7 to 1.8; Fall of, 3.8; Russians rally
E. of, 6.8; Renewed German attacks,
taking 1,000 prisoners, 26.8; Heavy
fighting indecisive, 25 m. S. of, 6.10.

DAGÖ ISLAND (Riga).
Germans land on, 12.10; German
landing parties ejected, 13.10; Germans
land again, 17, 19.10; Islands captured,
20.10.

DALLON (S.W. of St. Quentin).
French capture, 3.4.

" DANTON."
French battleship torpedoed in Mediterranean, 19.3.

DANUBE, RIVER (Rumania).
Fighting on, 1-4.1; crossed by retreating Russians, 5.1; enemy advance on left
bank, 11, 14.1; enemy checked on left
bank, 16.1; Southern arm crossed by
Bulgars, 22.1; Bulgars driven back, 23.1.

DARDANELLES COMMISSION.
Interim report of, issued, 8.3; debate,
20.3.

" DARTMOUTH," H.M.S.
Chases Austrian light cruisers to
Cattaro, etc., 15.5.

DAULETABAD (Persia).
Turks fall back on, 2.3; Offered to
Persian Government, 9.3.

DEATH PENALTY.
Abolished in Russia, 22.3.

DECORATIONS.
Russian, abolished, 25.3; "1914 Star" announced, 9.9.

DELI ABBAS (between Tigris and Dialah rivers).
Turks retreat towards, 12.4.

DEMICOURT (S. of Bapaume-Cambrai Road).
British capture, 9.4.

DENMARK.
Declines invitation of President Wilson to break with Germany, 7.2; Danish West Indies transferred to U.S.A. for £5,000,000, latter recognise Danish sovreignty over Greenland, 1.4; British Government express regret for violation off Jutland on 1.9, 24.9; Iceland demands autonomous powers, at intervals.

DESTROYERS, BRITISH.
Following sunk during year: 1 in action, 23.1; by mine action, torpedoed, etc., 1 on 8.2; 1.3; 15.3; 2 on 27.3; 1 on 10.4, 2.5, ? 5, ?.7, 6.7, ?.8, 23.9, ?.10, 2 on 17.10; 1 on 12.12; 3 off Dutch Coast, 23.12; Destroyer action Schouwen Bank, 23.1; Destroyer action ("Broke" and "Swift") off Dover, 20-21.4.

DESTROYERS (German).
Fire on Kent coast towns, 18.3.

DEVENTER, GENERAL T. L. van.
Succeeds Gen. Hoskins in E. Africa, 16.5.

DEVONPORT, LORD.
Issues Food Orders, 11.1; Appeals for economy, 2.2; Warning by, 22.3; On food consumption, 23.3; Fixes meat prices, 31.5; Resigns, 1.6.

DIALA, RIVER (trib. of Tigris).
British force passage of, 8-9.3; British and Russian forces in touch on left bank, 2.4; Turks driven across the, 20.10.

DNIESTER, RIVER.
Germans progress south of, 21.7; Russians evacuate Zalesczycki bridgehead, 29.7; Russians retire rapidly to Rumanian frontier, 1.8.

DOBRUJA (Roumania).
Enemy advance in, 1-4.1; evacuated by Allies, 5.1.

DOIRAN (Maced.).
British line at, advanced, 13.3; British night attack, 24.4; British success 25.4; Enemy's attack in force fails, 28.4; British attack and advance on 2-mile front, 9.5; French and British artillery destroy dumps, etc., 30.11.

DOLINA (Gal.).
Russian progress towards, 12.7.

DOLOMITES.
Severe fighting in, 5.3; Austrian attack repulsed, 29.6.

DOMINICAN REPUBLIC.
Declares War on Germany, 7.4.

"DONEGAL" (British hospital ship).
Torpedoed in Channel, 17.4.

DOVER.
German raid in night, 20-21.4.

DOVER CASTLE (hospital ship).
Torpedoed and sunk in Mediterranean, 26.5.

"DRAKE," H.M.S.
Torpedoed off Irish Coast, 2.10.

DUKHONIN, GENERAL (Russian C.-in-C.)
Dismissed by Bolsheviks, 21.11; Lenin demands surrender of, 1.12; Murdered by mob of soldiers and sailors, 3.12.

DUMA, THE.
Re-opening postponed, 18.1; Tsar signs Ukase suspending, 12.3; Elects Committee of twelve, 12.3.

DUNKIRK.
Bombed by German airmen, 10.2; Bombarded, 25.3; German destroyers bombard, driven off by Allied patrols, 25.4: Bombed, 1, 21, 24.10.

DUR (Tigris).
Turkish defeat near, 2.11.

DUTCH NOTE.
Reply to British Note re Armed Merchantmen, 5.4.

DUTCH SHIPPING.
In American Ports to be utilised, 18.10.

DVINA, RIVER.
Fighting on, 3-4, 8.1; Country west of, evacuated by Russians, 1.9; Russians retire to Bilderlingshof (Gulf), 2.9; Germans cross the, 18 miles above Riga, 2.9; Germans claim 1,000 prisoners near Jakobstadt, 21.9; Intense artillery action near Jakobstadt, 3.10.

DVINSK.
German attack near, 25.3; Russian diversion near, followed by withdrawal, 23.7; Russian peace delegates assemble at, 2.12.

EAST AFRICA. (British).
Raid in N. Turkana country driven off, May; Compulsory Service Act of 1916 put in force, June-July.

EAST AFRICA (German).
General Smuts succeeded by Gen. van Deventer, 20.1; Base formed at Lindi, British move S. to Rufiji, trying to combine with Gen. Hoskins from Kilwa to cut off enemy, 1, 5, 20, 24.1; Enemy slips through, rainy season till June; Van Deventer resumes operations, 10.6; drives Germans to Rovuma border, 30.6; Issue of Reports on Operations, 4, 11, 19.7; Enemy driven from R. Lugungu, 30.7; Heavy fighting in Masasi District, 3-20.8; (reported, 27.8); Belgians from Kilossa

British troops gain ground near, 25-26.5,
Hostile raiders repulsed in night near;
30.5.
FONTAINE-NOTRE-DAME. (Cambrai).
Heavy fighting for, 21, 22, 27.11.
FONTANA SECCA, MT. (Friuli).
Germans reach, 21.11.
FONZASO (Trent.).
Italians evacuate, 12.11.
FOOD HOARDING.
Made criminal offence, 22.3.
FOOD ORDERS.
Re hotels, restaurants, etc., 4.4; For-
bidding hoarding, etc., 5.4; Appeal by
Government to agriculturists, 14.4; Price
of cereals fixed, 16.4; Pastry forbidden,
18.4; Food Controller's powers extended,
20.4.
FOOD POLICY.
Outlined by Lord Rhondda, 26.7.
FOOD PRICES.
Fixed, 9.3; 16.4.
FOREIGN SECURITIES.
Compulsory loan or sale to Treasury
of, 26.1.
FRANCE (Political).
General Lyautey crisis in Chamber,
14.3; M. Briand resigns Premiership
(held since October, 1915), 17.3; M. Ribot
Prime Minister, 19.3; Military Mission to
U.S.A., 21.3; 1918 Class called up, 2, 27.3;
Protest by French Government against
German acts of barbarity, 24.3; Socialists
and Stockholm Conference, May and June;
Renaudel's proposal to accept invitation
passed, 29.5; Passports to Stockholm
refused, 1.6; Government affirms right
of control over Army Services, 7.7;
Admiral de Lacaze and M. D. Cochin resign, 2.8; Almereyda dies in prison, early
August; M. Malvy (Interior) resigns, 31.8;
M. Ribot resigns Premiership, 7.9; be-
comes Foreign Minister, 13.9; M. Pain-
levé becomes P.M. and War Minister, 8.9.
War Committee of 8 formed, 13.9;
M. Ribot resigns Foreign Secretaryship,
14.10; M. Barthou succeeds him, 17.10;
M. Painlevé resigns, 13.11; M. Clémen-
ceau Prime Minister, 14.11; M. Caillaux
arrested, November; Vote of confidence
in Government, 20.11; War credits voted
during year, £1,660,000,000; no real
War Loans.
FRANCILLY-SÉLENCY (W. of St. Quen-
tin).
British capture, 2.4.
FRANCO-AMERICAN RELATIONS.
Clearing-office established, 20.12.
FRANCO-BRITISH CONVENTION.
For Military Service, 25.10.
FRANKFORT.
Bombed by Allies, 17.3. &c.

FREIBURG (Baden).
British and French air-raid on, 14.4.
FRENCH HARVEST.
Chamber announces scantiest harvest
for 50 years, 7.10.
FRENZELA RAVINE (Trent.)
Enemy attempts to break through,
stopped; terrain N. of, in enemy's hands,
6.12; 150 aeroplanes operate, 7.12; Enemy
gain ground, pushing eastwards, 25.12.
FRESNES (Arras).
Occupied by British, 17.3.
FRESNOY (E. of Vimy).
British attack on 12-mile front and
take, 3.5; Enemy attack on, our troops
withdraw, 8.5.
FRESNOY-LE-PETIT (N.W. of St. Quen-
tin).
British advance to outskirts, 7.4; and
capture, 9.4.
FREZENBERG (Ypres).
British take, 31.7; British detach-
ments withdraw from N. of, 6.9.
FUNCHAL (Madeira).
Shelled by German submarine, 12.12.
FUNDENI (Rumania).
Fighting near, 1, 6, 15.1; bridgehead
carried by enemy, 19.1.
GALATZ (Rumania).
Threatened by enemy, 11 to 16.1;
bombarded, 13.3.
GALICIA, EAST.
German activity in, 21.3; Enemy
opposition stiffens, success S. of Kalusz,
15.7; Russians begin to withdraw, evacuate Kalusz, 16.7; Russians withstand
counter-thrust, 17.7; Russian troops
insubordinate, Zloczow positions pierced,
19.7; Russians begin to retreat, except
at Brzezany and Halicz, 20.7; German
breach of Russian line extends, Russian
retreat degenerates into rout, 22 to 28.7;
Enemy over Russian frontier, 30.7.
GAVRELLE (on Arras-Douai Road).
British capture, 23.4; British progress N. E., 28.4; Strong German attack
repulsed,16.5.
GAZA (Palestine).
Indecisive action at, Turks claim
victory, 27-28.3; Successful British raids,
14, 22.7; British advance towards, 30.8;
Artillery activity near, 7.10; Cavalry, etc
engagements near, 27.10; 5.11; British
capture the town, 7.11.
GEDDES, BRIG. GEN. AUCKLAND.
Director of Recruiting, succeeds Mr.
N. Chamberlain as Director of National
Service, 10.8.
GEDDES, SIR ERIC.
To be Controller, Admiralty, 14.5;
Succeeded, as I. G. Transportation, by

GIVENCHY-EN-GOHELLE (N. of R. Scarpe).
British capture, 13.4.

GLENCORSE WOOD (Ypres).
British occupy, 10.8; British line pressed back in, 11.8.

GOLITZIN, PRINCE.
Becomes Russian Prime Minister, 9.1; receives instructions from Tsar, 20.1.

GOMMECOURT (S. of Arras).
Occupied 27.2; British progress E. of, 3, 4, 13.3.

GONNELIEU (S.W. of Cambrai).
British capture, 20.4; Withdraw from 30.11; Recover from enemy, 1.12.

GORIZIA.
Austrians take some Italian trenches, 10.2; And are expelled, 11.2; Austrians attack E. of, 4.3; Hard fighting N. of, and on M. Vodice, M. Kuk and M. Santo, Italian success, 18, 20.5; Renewed fighting, Italians repulse attacks E. of, 5 to 12.9; Captured by Germans, 28.10.

GOUZEAUCOURT (S. of Bapaume-Cambrai Road).
British capture village and wood, 12-13.4; Enemy attacks in strength and carries, 30.11.

GRANDCOURT (River Ancre).
Futile German attempt near, 1.2; British occupy, 7.2; Successful British actions, 10, 13.2.

GRAND SERAUCOURT (St. Quentin).
Enemy thrown back to, 24.3.

GRANVILLE, EARL.
Appointed Minister at Athens, 22.8.

GRAPPA, MONTE (Trent).
Italians fall back on, 16.11; Austrians attack heavily between Rivers Brenta and Piave, 12.12; Italian artillery smashes enemy efforts, 17.12.

GREAT BRITAIN (Naval).
" Cornwallis " sunk in Mediterranean, 9.1; Destroyer action Schouwen Bank, 23.1; New Minefield Proclamation, 31.1; Government denies German accusation of mis-using Hospital Ships, etc., 10.2; German flotilla chased back to Zeebrugge; " Swift " and " Broke " action off Dover, 20-21.4; Ramsgate bombarded, 26-27.4; Belgian coast often bombarded by heavies during year; Sir E. Geddes Controller of Admiralty, 14.5; " Vanguard " blown up, 9.7; Four German merchantmen captured off Dutch coast, 16.7; Sir E. Geddes succeeds Sir E. Carson as First Lord, 18.7; Scarborough bombarded, 4.9; " Drake " torpedoed, 2.10; Norway-Shetlands convoy attacked by German raiders, 17.10; Losses 1.11.16 to 31.10.17: 2 battleships, 2 cruisers, 1 auxiliary, 5 armed liners, 19 destroyers; Re-organisation of Higher

administration in Admiralty, 1.11; German raider sunk in Kattegat, 2.11; convoy and torpedo boat destroyer sunk in North Sea, 12.12; Sir J. Jellicoe relieved by Sir R. Wemyss. 26.12.

GREAT BRITAIN (Political).
War Loan announced, 5 per Cent. at 95, 4 per Cent. at par, 11.1; India and U.S.A. War Loans announced, 18.1; Food Control Orders issued in January, February, April, June, September, October, November; Labour Party Conference resolutions, 25.1; Speaker's Electoral Reform Conference Report issued, 29.1; United Kingdom Food Supply Report issued, 2.2; National Service Scheme launched, 6.2, etc.; King opens Parliament, 7.2; Vote of Credit for £550,000,000, 12.2; Submarine Debates, 13.2, 21.2, 3.5; Scheme of State Food assistance, 23.2; War Loan yields over £1,000,000,000, 25.2; Dutch ships requisitioned, 26.2; Government on Home Rule, 7.3, 16.5, etc.; Dardanelles Commission Report issued, 8.3; Imperial War Cabinet meets, March; Vote of Credit for £60,000,000, March; Strike at Barrow, 21.3; Official welcome to Russian Revolution, 23.3; Entry of U.S.A. into War celebrated, 12.4; Education Estimates (Mr. H. Fisher), April; Statement of Economic Policy, 27.4; Budget, estimated expenditure, £2,290 millions, no new taxation, 3.5; Engineers' Strike, 4 to 23.5; Vote of Credit £500 millions, 9.5; Franchise Bill introduced, 15.5; Irish Convention announced, 21.5; Racing restrictions, 24.5; Embargo on disposal of Securities, 21.6; Air-raids, June and July; Mesopotamia Commission Report issued, 26.6 (Mr. A. Chamberlain resigns, 11.7); Anglo-German Prisoners of War Conference, 25.6, etc. (agreement signed, 2.7); Stockholm Conference proposals, June, July, August; Secret Session, 10, 11.7; Reconstruction of Cabinet (Sir E. Geddes to Admiralty, Mr. Churchill to Munitions, etc.), 17.7; Vote of Credit £650 millions, 24.7; Stockholm Conference Labour meetings, 14 to 21.8, etc.; Railway Strike forbidden, 18.8; Air-raids numerous, September; National War Bonds 5 per Cent. and 4 per Cent. issued, 2.10; Voluntary Rations Scale, 12.11; Allied War Council at Versailles announced, November; Lord Lansdowne's first letter appears, 29.11; Vote of Credit £550 millions, 12.12; Speeches on War Aims, c. 20.12; Sir R. Wemyss First Lord vice Sir J. Jellicoe, 26.12.

GREECE.
Presented with Ultimatum by Allies

of 4 out of 7 Dutch ships sailing under German safe conduct, 22.**2**: Ships requisitioned by Gt. Britain, 26.**2**; German notification to Dutch shipping, 9.**3**; Lord Derby's assurance that Great Britain will not strike at Germany through, published, 1.**7**; Food riots in Amsterdam, July; British protests *re* armed merchantmen forbidden in Dutch ports, August; British Government stops cables to Dutch East Indies, 11.**10**; Replies to British Note *re* gravel transit, 17.**10**; First train of British prisoners from Germany, 29.**12**.

HOLLEBEKE (Ypres).
British take, 31.**7**; German regain footing in, but are driven out later in day, 5.**8**.

HOLNON (W. of St. Quentin).
British capture, 2.**4**.

HOLY WAR.
Again proclaimed by Sheikh-ul-Islam, 16.**3**.

HONDURAS.
Severs relations with Germany, 17.**5**.

HOOGE.
British take, 31.**7**.

HOSKINS, MAJ.-GEN. A. R.
Succeeds to command in E. Africa, 20.**1**

HOSPITAL SHIPS.
German Government announces intention of sinking between Great Britain, France and Belgium, 31.**1**; "Donegal" torpedoed in Channel, 17.**4**; "Dover Castle" torpedoed in Mediterranean, six lives lost, 26.**5**; King of Spain's measures *re* safeguarding of, summer; Alleged misuse of, 5.**11**.

HOUSE, COLONEL (of U.S.A).
In London, 8-22.**11**.

HOUSE OF COMMONS.
Secret Session, 11.**5**.

HUNGARY.
Count Tisza resigns Premiership, 22.**5**; Count Esterhazy becomes Premier, 14.**6**; Resigns, 9.8; Dr. Wekerle appointed Premier, 20.**8**.

HURTEBISE FARM (between Troyon and Craonne).
French repulse two German attacks, 17.**4**; German attack repulsed, 25.**4**; More German attacks repulsed, 20, 28.**5**; Further fighting near, 5, 17, 25.**6**.

HYDERABAD, NIZAM OF.
Generous offer by, 8.**3**.

IMPERIAL PREFERENCE.
Report issued, 20.**2**.

IMPERIAL WAR CABINET.
First meeting of, 20.**3**.

INDIA.
War Loan issued, 18.**1** (v. War Loans); Compulsory Military Service for white men Ordinance, Indian Defence Bill, 21.**2** Offers £100,000,000 towards cost of war, 1.**3**; Mahsudi's attack British convoy, heavy British losses, 1.**5**; Mahsudis sue for peace, *c.* 5.**7**; Joint meeting of Committee of Indian National Congress and Moslem League demands India as self-governing unit in Empire, July; late Mr. Gokhale's memo published, 14.**8**; Enlistment statement (276,000 Indians enlisted, of whom 155,000 Punjabis), 13.**9**; Secretary of State for India (Mr. Montagu) arrives, 9.**11**.

INFANTRY HILL (Monchy-le-Preux).
Fighting on, 14, 18, 20.**6**.

INVERNESS COPSE (E. of Ypres).
Taken by British, many prisoners, 20.**9**.

IRELAND.
House of Commons Debate on proposed Convention, 21.**5**; Release of rebels announced, 15.**6**.

IRISH CHANNEL.
"Stephen Furness" torpedoed, 23.**12**.

IRISH CONVENTION.
Debate on proposed, 21.**5**; Opening meeting, 25.**7**.

IRLES (River Ancre).
Captured by British, 10.**3**.

ISONZO, R. (v. also Julian Front).
Great artillery activity from Tolmino to the sea, 12 to 14.**5**; Severe fighting. Italians reach slopes of M. Santo, 14 to 17.**5**; Enemy attacks on M. Vodice repulsed, 19.**5**; After heavy fighting with varying fortunes, Italians make progress, taking heights E. of Plava (Italians claim 23,000, Austrians 13,000, prisoners, in two weeks), 20 to 30.**5**; Attacking on 30-mile front, Italians carry most of Austrian first line from Plava to the sea, 19.**8**; Enemy lines broken on wide front, 26.**8**; Italians gain ground and take 2,000 prisoners, 1 to 4.**9**; Austrians fail to drive Italians from M. Gabriele, second phase closed, 21.**9**; Great artillery activity on Upper, 7 to 13.**10**; Strong hostile concentration on Bainsizza Plateau, Austro-German offensive and defeat of Second Italian Army (Caporetto), 23 to 25.**10**.

ISTABULAT (on Baghdad-Samarra Railway).
British advance towards, 16.**4**; British capture front line of Turkish positions, 21.**4**; Turks evacuate, 21-22.**4**.

ITALY (Military).
Austrian attacks on various sectors repulsed, 5.**2**; Italian thrust on Carso-Julian front, 19 to 25.**8**; Overwhelming hostile attack on N.E. front (Caporetto); Enemy overruns Friuli Plain, 23 to 30.**10**; Italians fall back and occupy the Tagliamento line, 29.**10** to 3.**11**; Withdrawal to

KALIMOTO (E. Africa).
German positions at, captured, Belgian troops pursue, 16.9.

KALUSZ (Galicia).
Russians capture, 11.7; Russians take 1,600 prisoners, 13.7; Russians evacuate, 16.7.

KALUTSEM (Riga).
Germans repulsed, 11 to 13.1; 2, 4.2.

KANGAVER (Persia).
Occupied by Russians, 5.3; Offered to Persian Government, 9.3.

KARA TEPE (Mesopotamia).
Turks driven out of, 3.12.

KASR-I-SHIRIN (Persia).
Turks retreat towards, 1.4; Occupation by Russian cavalry, 3.4; Cossacks repulse attack of Kurds to N.W., 21.4.

KATTEGAT.
Naval action in, 2.11.

KAZIMAIN (Baghdad).
British cavalry at, 11.3.

KENTISH COAST TOWNS.
German aeroplane raid on, 5.4.

KERENSKI, M.
Russian Minister of Justice, strong speech by, 16.3; Orders abandonment of Rasputin enquiry, 18.3; Minister of War, attempted assassination of, 19.7; Succeeds Prince Lvov as Prime Minister, 22.7; Resigns, 2.8; Withdraws resignation, 4.8; Opens National Conference at Moscow, 25.8; Dismisses Kornilov, 11.9; Prime Minister and Commander-in-Chief, 12.9; Action to limit powers of extremists, 18.9; Resigns from Soviet, 26.9; Flight of, 8.11; Marches on Petrograd, 10-12.11; Defeat and flight of, 14,15.11.

KERIND (Persia).
Russians occupy, 17.3.

KERMANSHAH (Persia).
Taken by Russians, 13.3; Turks scattered near, 21.3.

KHANIKIN (near Persian border).
Russian progress towards, 1.4; Occupation by Russian cavalry, 3.4.

KIEV.
Non-Slav Congress meets at, 30.9.

KHUNEILFEH (Palestine).
Capture of, 6.11.

KIESELIN (Volhynia).
Ten miles S. of, enemy attack on Russian line fails, 5.2.

KILOSSA (E. Africa).
Belgian columns from, drive enemy to S. bank of Ruaha River, published 27.8.

KIMPOLUNG (S. Bukovina).
Enemy makes progress, 29.7; Russians evacuate, 3.8.

KITCHENER, LORD.
Defended in House of Commons, 20.3.

KIZIL ROBAT (R. Diala).
British and Russians in touch at, 2.4; Russian occupation, 9.4.

" KLÉBER " (French Cruiser).
Sunk, 27.6.

KOLCHAK (Admiral).
Appointed Commander-in-Chief Baltic Fleet, 19.4.

KOLOMEA (Galicia).
Taken by Germans, 26.7.

KONDOA IRANGI (E. Africa).
German detachment surrenders 75 miles S. of, 1.10.

KORITE (Carso Front).
Italians carry enemy defences between, and Sella, 20.8.

KORNILOV, GEN.
Proclamation to soldiers by, 20.3; appointed Commander-in-Chief, 2.8; Dismissed, 8.8; Approaching Petrograd with Army, 10.9; Arrested by Kerenski, movement fails, 11 to 13.9; Escapes Bolsheviks at Mohilev and Byelgorod, 3 to 13.12.

KOSTANJEVICA (Carso Front = Castagnevizza).
Italians take and lose, 26.5.

KRASTALI (Doiran, Macedonia).
British drive enemy from Goldie's Hill, 9, 10.5; Italians advance successfully, 15.5.

KREVO (Vilna).
Russian attack near, 4.3.

KRILENKO, ENSIGN.
Appointed Commander-in-Chief Russian Army, 21.11; Captures Russian Headquarters Staff, 3.12.

KRONSTADT.
Socialist revolt at, 1 to 6.6; Russians begin to evacuate, 24.10.

KUCHARZEWSKI, M. (Poland).
Forms Cabinet, c. 14.11.

KÜHLMANN, BARON, v.
Becomes Foreign Secretary, c. 20.7. vice Herr Zimmermann; Speeches to Main Committee, 28.9; and Reichstag, 9.10.

KULELI BURGAS (Turkey).
Bridge bombed by British, 4.1.

KUT-EL-AMARA.
British progress towards, 9, 10, 19. 25 to 28.1; British advance at Tigris-Hai junction and repel counter-attacks, 29.1, 1.2; British make further advance at junction, 6.2; British capture Liquorice Factory and repulse counter-attack, 10.2; British surround Turks in Dahra Bend, 11.2; British capture all positions in Dahra Bend, 16.2; But fail in attack on Sanna-i-Yat, 17.2; Further attacks on Sanna-i-Yat are successful, 22, 23.2; Turks evacuate, and retreat towards Baghdad.

British occupy, 24.2; British continue pursuit and attack Turkish rearguard 15 to 30 miles N. of, 25, 26.2.

LABOUR, BRITISH.
Leaders congratulate Russian do.,16.3; Unrest—Engineers, Omnibus, Weavers— May ; Party decide not to attend Stockholm, but to send deputation to Russia, 9.5 ; Settlement with A.S.E., 19.5 ; Party decides to send delegates to Stockholm, 11.8 ; Passports refused, 13.8 ; Conference accepts memo. on War Aims, 28.12.

LABOUR CORPS.
Formation of Military, 22.2.

" LACONIA, " s.s.
Cunarder, sunk, 25.2.

LA COULOTTE (Lens).
Occupied by British, 26.6.

LADJ (Ctesiphon).
Engagement at, 5.3.

LAFFAUX (Soissons).
French capture, 19.4.

LA FOLIE FARM (Vimy Ridge).
British capture, 9.4.

LAGNICOURT (N.E. of Bapaume).
British take, 26.3; Severe fighting, Germans capture and are expelled, 15.4.

" LANFRANC " (British Hospital Ship).
Torpedoed in Channel, 17.4.

LANGEMARCK (Ypres).
British carry, 16.8 ; N.E. of British line advanced, 23.8 ; Further British progress,27.8; German attacks repulsed, 13.9.

LANSDOWNE, LORD.
First letter of, to " Daily Telegraph," 29.11 ; German Press approves, 30.11 ; Allies and U.S.A. object to, 1.12.

LARISSA (Thessaly).
Occupied by Allies, 12.6.

" LARS FOSTENES," s.s.
Norwegian relief ship, sunk, 13.3.

LAUREATI, CAPT. MARCHESE DI.
Flies from Turin to London, 24.9.

" LAURENTIC," H.M.S.
Sunk, 25.1.

LA VACQUERIE (Cambrai).
Enemy attacks in strength, British counter-attack regains, 30.11 ; Enemy in vain try to recover, 2.12 ; British withdraw, 3.12 ; Ulster troops capture German trenches, 7.12.

LAVKASSA R. (S.W. of Drinsk).
Successful German raid, 17.2.

LE BARQUE (R. Ancre).
British capture, 26.2.

LEINTREY (Lorraine).
Very successful French raid, 30.1.

LEMBURG (E. of Riga).
Letts drive back Germans with loss, 19.9.

LEMPIRE (St. Quentin).
British capture, 5.4.

LENIN, M. (Serge Uliakov).
Rise of to power, early in November ; Orders troops to negotiate with enemy, 22.11.

LENS.
British raids near, 16, 17.1, 22.7. 9.8, etc. ; Fighting S. of, 8.6 ; British gain German trenches S.W. of, 30.6 ; British advanced posts driven back, 2.7 ; Heavy artillery battle, 29.7 ; British attack N.W. of, successful, 15 to 23.8.,

LE TÉTON (Moronvilliers massif, Reims).
French capture, 19.4.

LE TRANSLOY (Bapaume).
British take position near, 27.1 ; Germans take British post, 19.2.

LE VERGUIER (St. Quentin).
British capture, 9.4.

LIBERIA (West Africa).
Severs relations with Germany, 8.5 ; Sympathetic proclamation issued, 1.6 ; State of War with Germany declared, 4.8.

LIDA (Vilna).
German activity near, 21.3 ; Russians re-take trenches near, 22.3.

LIÉVIN (S.W. of Lens).
British capture, 14.4.

LIGNY (River Ancre).
British capture, 27.2.

LIKUJU (E. Africa).
Germans surrender at, 24.1.

LINDI (E. Africa).
Heavy fighting, enemy compelled to withdraw, 3.8 ; Strong German resistance 30 miles S.W. of, 1.10 ; Column from, envelops and drives enemy on Nyangoa, 15.10.

LIVENZA, RIVER (between Rs. Tagliamento and Piave).
Italians reach, 7.11 ; Germans cross, 8.11.

LIWALE (E. Africa).
British capture, 29.10.

LOANS. —v. War Loans.

LOMBAERTZYDE (Nieuport).
British counter-attack drives Germans from advanced positions gained, 10.7 ; German attacks repulsed, 19.7 ; British capture, 24.8 ; Enemy retake, 26.8.

LONDON, AIR-RAIDS ON—v. Table (pp. 295, 296) for details.

LOOS.
Successful British raid, 12.2 ; German raid fails, 15.2.

LORRAINE.
Successful French raids in, 15-18.5 ; German surprise attack at Veho broken up, 28.12.

LOUPART WOOD (Bapaume).
British occupy, 13.3.

LOUVEMONT (Verdun).
East of, French repel German attacks, 6.2.

LOUVERVAL (Bapaume).
British progress to N. of, 8.4.

LUDD (12 miles S.E. of Jaffa).
British advance N.E. of, 15.12.

LUKULEDI RIVER (E. Africa).
Operations on, 10.6 ; Right column established at Mission, 17.10 ; Further operations on, 10.11.

LUNGUNGU RIVER (E. Africa).
Enemy driven from positions on, 30.7.

LUTSHEMI (E. Africa).
British occupy, 17.11.

LUXBURG, COUNT (German Chargé d'Affairs in Argentina).
Offensive cipher messages through Swedish Legation published in U.S.A., 9.9 ; Receives passports, 12.9 ; Germany says she disapproves his telegrams, 17.9 ; Interned on Island of Martin Garcia, 12.10.

LYAUTEY, GEN.
Resignation of, 14.3 ; Appointed Governor-General of Marocco, 5.4.

LYS, RIVER.
German withdrawal on, 14.6.

LYUMNITSA (Maced.).
French and Venizelists take Bulgarian trenches, 5.5 ; Bulgarian counter-attacks repulsed, 6.5 ; French and Venizelists take enemy position near, 10.5.

MAAN (60 miles S.S.E. of Dead Sea).
British aeroplane raid on, 20.8 ; successful attack on railway, 26.9.

" MACAO," ss. (Brazilian).
Sunk by German submarine, c. 15.10.

MACDONALD, MR. RAMSAY.
Sailors' and Firemen's Union refuse to let sail for Russia, 11.6 ; Motion re " Peace Resolution " defeated, 27.7.

MACEDONIA.
Spring campaign commences, 11.3 ; Italian front advanced 500 yds. S.W. of Krastali, 15.5 ; British raid at L. Bulkova (Doiran), 21.12.

MACIN (Galatz).
Captured by enemy, 1-3.1.

MAGYAROS RIDGE (Moldavia).
Struggle for, 10.3 ; Russian attacks on fail, 28.3.

MAHENGE (East Africa).
Occupied by Belgian troops, 9.10 ; Prisoners' convoy rescued S.E. of, 10.10 ; Belgians repel German attack, 13.10 ; German retreat from district, 10, 27,.11.

MAISONS DE CHAMPAGNE.
French success near, 8.3 ; Germans seize French salient, 15.2.

MAISSEMY (St. Quentin).
British capture, 2.4.

" MAJORITY RESOLUTION."
In the Reichstag, 19.7, and v. App. 96.

MAKONDE PLATEAU (E. Africa).
Actions on, 15.11.

MALANCOURT WOOD (Verdun).
French raid, 21.2.

MALVY, M. (French Government).
Minister of the Interior, resigns, 31.8.

MANIAGO (Italy).
Germans reach, 6.11.

MANILA BAY.
Crews wreck engines of 9 German steamers in ; these with 8 other vessels seized by U.S.A., 4.2.

MANNHEIM.
Often raided by Allied airmen, especially 24.12.

MARASESHTI (Moldavia, 20 miles N. of Focsani).
Rumanians retire towards, 18.8 ; Rumanians make successful attack at, 21.8.

MARGATE and BROADSTAIRS.
Bombarded by German Destroyers, 25.2.

MARMOLADA (Carnic).
Fighting in region, 24, 26.9.

MAROCCO.
German intrigues in Spanish, 9.10. (v. App. 4).

MARSHALL, LT.-GEN. W.
Commands in Mesopotamia, 24.11.

MASASI (E. Africa).
Heavy fighting, enemy compelled to withdraw, 3 to 20.8 ; Official report on fighting, 27.8.

MASNIERES (S. of Cambrai).
British withdraw from salient, 1.12.

MAUDE, GEN. SIR STANLEY.
Captures Baghdad, 11.3 ; Death of, from cholera, 18.11.

MAXIMALISTS (v. Bolsheviks, Russia).

MBEMKURU VALLEY (E. Africa).
Fighting proceeding in, 1.10.

McADOO, MR.
Appointed Director-General of U.S. Railways, 26.12.

MEAT.
Consumption falls, 5.3.

MECCA.
Ulema of, Proclamation by, 7.3.

MEDALS.
" 1914 Star " announced, 9.9.

MEDEAZZA (Carso).
Italians approach and gain trenches near, 26 to 29.5.

MEDWAY, RIVER.
Valley raided by aircraft, 5.6.

" MENDI " s.s.
Transport, sunk, 21.2.

MENIN.
Allies' successful attack N. of Ypres

MONTE SAN MARCO (Gorizia).
Fighting on, 3.**6**.
MONTE SANTO (Carso).
Italians occupy summit of, and continue advance, 24.**8**.
MONTE TOMBA.
Italians driven from, 18.**11**.
MONT HAUT (Reims).
German assault defeated, 15, 26.**7**.
MOON SOUND (Riga).
Russian Fleet assists defence in, 16.**10**; Russians evacuate Island, 18.**10**.
MOREL, Mr. E. D.
Sent to prison, 4.**9**.
MORONVILLIERS MASSIF (group of hills E. of Reims).
French bombard, 10.**4**; French capture Mounts Cornillet, Blond, Sans Nom, Haut and Le Téton, 17 to 19.**4**; Heavy fighting, Germans repulsed, 22.**4**, 1, 4, 20 to 22.**5**; Germans attack again with some success, 27, 31.**5**; German counter-attacks repulsed, 16.**7**.
MORT HOMME (Verdun).
Violent infantry action W. of, 30.**6**; French take, 20.**8**; And progress N. of, 24.**8**.
MOSCOW.
Declares for new Russian Government, 14.**3**; Workmen resume work, 20.**3**; National Conference opened by Kerenski, 25.**8**; Closed, 28.**8**; Moscow closed to strangers, 6.**9**.
MOSUL (Tigris).
Russians take Neleman Village 50 miles N. of, 3.**10**.
"MÖWE."
Atlantic raider returns to home port, 22.**3**.
MUDROS.
German airship bombs island, 23.**3**.
MUNITION WORKERS.
Combing-out begins, 8.**5**.
MUSH (Mesopotamia).
W. of Lake Van, occupied by the Turks, 1.**5**.
MUSHAIDIA (Baghdad).
Turks hurry towards, 14.**3**; Position at captured by British, 15.**3**.

NAHRIN RIVER (Mesopotamia).
Turks flood the country between Diala River and, 3.**12**.
NAKHL (Sinai Pen).
At, and at Bir-el-Hassana British surprise small Turkish posts, 20.**2**.
NALESHKIAN (Armenia).
Turks dislodged from, by Russians, 16.**3**
NANCY.
Bombed by German airmen, 10.**2**; Air-raid on, 16.**10**.

NANESHTI (Rumania).
Captured by enemy, 19.**1**.
NANTEUIL-LA-FOSSE (N.E. of Soissons).
French capture, 18.**4**.
NARAJOWKA RIVER (Galicia).
German success on bank of, 2.**3**; Further raids on, 12.**3**.
NAROCH, LAKE.
Russian gas-attack N. of, 3.**3**.
NARONGOMBE (E. Africa).
Main German positions attacked, heavy casualties both sides, 19.**7**.
NATIONAL SERVICE.
Mr. N. Chamberlain announces his scheme for, 6.**2**; Ministry formed, 20.**3**; Brigadier-General A. Geddes succeeds him as Director-General, 10.**8**; and takes over Recruiting, 1.**11**.
NATIONAL SERVICE FOR WOMEN.
15,000 women ready, 3.**3**; Meeting in favour of, 17.**3**.
NAVAL WARFARE (v. also Great Britain (Naval), Submarine Warfare, etc.).
New British Minefield declarations 31.**1**; Germany declares commencement of unrestricted, from 1.**2**, and announce, intention of sinking hospital ships, 31.**1**; This causes temporary suspension of neutral sailings, 1.**2**; Turkey declares agreement with German policy, 22.**2**; Ditto Austro-Hungary, 5.**3**; German Chancellor attempts to justify, 27.**2**; Atlantic raider "Möwe," after destroying 23 ships (19 British), returns to Germany, 23.**3**; U.S.A. t.b.d. flotilla arrives in British waters, 4.**5**; Admiral Lacaze's statement *re* tonnage sunk, 25.**5**; Energetic U.S.A. preparations during year. Indian Ocean raider "Wolf" at work, February to June; Austrians sink 14 British drifters in Adriatic, 15.**5**; German submarine attack on U.S.A. transports, driven off, 22.**6**; King of Spain and Hospital Ships, summer; "Seeadler," German Pacific raider, after sinking 11 vessels, wrecked, 2.**8**; Germany extends Barred zone, 15.**11**; Allied Council on, 14.**12**.
NDONDA (E. Africa).
British occupy, 10.**11**.
NEBI SAMWIL (Palestine).
British capture, 21.**11**.
NESLE (S. Somme).
British and French occupy, 18.**3**.
NEUVE-CHAPELLE.
Successful British raids, 10, 17.**2**; German raid fails, 22.**2**.
NEUVILLE VITASSE (S.E. of Arras).
British capture, 9.**4**.
NEWALA (E. Africa).
Germans captured at, 21, 27.**11**.
NEW ZEALAND.
"Governor" changed to "Governor-

General," recognition of status as "Dominion," 28.6 ; £12,000,000 War Loan 4½ per Cent. issued, August ; 74,000 men sent to the fronts by August.

NICARAGUA.
Severs relations with Germany, 19.5.

NICHOLAS II., TSAR.
Abdicates, and issues decree at Pskov, 15.3 ; Counsels loyalty to Provisional Government, 20.3 ; Interned at Tsarskoe Selo, 21.3 ; Transferred to Abalak Monastery, and disfranchised, 12.8.

NICHOLAS MIKHAILOVICH, GD. DUKE.
Letter to Tsar published, 22.3.

NICHOLAS NICHOLAIEVICH, GRAND DUKE.
Appointment to Command of Army annulled, 20.3.

NIEUPORT (Belgian Coast).
Germans bombard British seaward positions, 9.7 ; Isolate British contingent on R. bank of Yser and destroy it, 10.7.

NOBEL (Peace) **PRIZE.**
Stambul University proposes the German Emperor as recipient of the, 2.2.

NON-FERROUS METALS.
Bill passed, 11.12.

NORTHEY, MAJ. GEN.
Success in E. Africa, 29.10.

NORTH SEA.
British scouts drive 11 German destroyers to Zeebrugge, 10.5 ; British Naval force destroys Zeppelin L22, 14.5. Heavy Naval patrol duties throughout year.

NORWAY.
Forbids submarines in territorial water, 30.1 ; Declines President Wilson's invitation to break with Germany, 7.2 ; Rautenfels bomb-outrage, recall of German Minister to, 25.6 ; Great fire at Trondjem, 15.7 ; Conference of three Scandinavian Kings at Christiania, 28.11.

NOWICA (Galicia).
Russians gain and lose, 18.7.

NOYON.
French occupy, 18.3.

NYANGAO (E. Africa, S.E. Coast).
Occupied by British, 17.10 ; Heavy fighting continues round, 18.10.

OCHRIDA, LAKE (S.W. of Monastir).
French and Russians make progress near, 9, 10.9.

OCNA (River Trotus, Moldavia).
Russians lose the heights of Magyaros, 23.2 ; Rumanians lose further heights, 8.3 ; Russo-Rumanian thrust, 13 to 15.8 ; Enemy take offensive and gains ground, 16 to 20.8 ; Heavy fighting, stubborn Rumanian resistance, 27, 28.7.

ODESSA.
Declares for new Russian Government,

14.3 ; Tranquil under Russian reverses, 13.9.

OESEL ISLANDS (Gulf of Riga).
Bombed by German airmen, 1.10 ; German troops land and occupy most of, 12.10 ; Russians cut off on Sworbe Peninsula (S.W.), 14.10 ; Russo-German Naval action in Dagö-Oesel Sound, 14.10 ; Germans capture 3,500 prisoners, part of garrison escapes, 15.10 ; Entirely in German hands, 16.10.

OISE, RIVER.
French progress between R. Avre and, occupy part of R. bank, 24.3 ; Advance between R. Aisne and, 27.3.

OITOZ, RIVER (Rumania).
Fighting on, 10.1.

OLIVI ROCK (Adriatic).
Austrian submarine base attacked by Italian airmen, 27.9.

OPPY (E. of Vimy Ridge).
British capture trenches S. of, 28, 29.4 ; Fighting near, 28.6.

" ORAMA," H.M.S.
British armed mercantile cruiser, torpedoed and sunk, 19.10.

" ORDER OF THE BRITISH EMPIRE."
Warrant instituting, 21.6 ; First appointments published, 25.8.

" ORDER OF THE COMPANIONS OF HONOUR."
Warrant instituting, 21.6 ; First appointments published, 25.8.

ORLANDO, SIGNOR.
Italian Premier, 28.10.

ORTIGARA, MT. (Trentino).
Fighting on, 10, 15, 19, 25, 26.6.

OSTEND.
Bombarded, 5, 6, 23.9, 21.10, etc., and frequently bombed ; Enemy shipping damaged by British aircraft, 15, 22.9.

OSUM, RIVER (Albania).
Austrians at, 22, 25.11.

OTTOMAN EMPIRE (v. Turkey).

" OTWAY," H.M.S.
Torpedoed, 21.7.

OUJJAN (Marocco).
French take, 25.3.

OVERSEAS TROOPS (British).
Statement re numbers engaged and losses to, 4.10.

PADUA.
Bombed by the enemy, 28, 29.12.

PAES, MAJOR SIDONIO.
Becomes Prime Minister of Portugal, and subsequently President, 6.12.

PAINLEVÉ, M.
Becomes Premier and War Minister, 8.9 ; Forms Ministry, 12.9 ; Defines War Aims, 18.9 ; In Italy, 4.11 ; Resigns on Supreme Army Command and Propaganda

Questions, 13.11; Succeeded by M. Clémenceau.

PALESTINE.

British reverse at Gaza, 26.3; General Allenby succeeds General Murray, 29.6; Capture of Beersheba, 31.10; Capture of Gaza, 7.11; Surrender of Jerusalem, 9.12.

PANAMA.

Joins U.S.A. in defence of Canal, 8.4; Declares war on Germany, 10.4; Declares War on Austro-Hungary, 11.12.

PAPAL NOTE.

With proposals for peace sent to belligerent Governments (App. 103), 14.8; U.S. reply to, 30.8; Germany and Austria-Hungary reply to, 21.9; Second Note to Allies announced in Italy, 2.10.

" PARANA " (Brazilian s.s.).

Torpedoed by German submarine in Channel, 3.4.

PARROY (Nancy).

French repel German attacks, 6.2.

PASHICH, M.

Serbian Premier, in Rome, 7.9.

PASSCHENDAELE (Ypres).

Canadians capture, 6.11; Fighting near, 10 to 17.11, 2.12.

PASUBIO (Trentino).

Renewed activity in area of, 19.3.

PAY, OF ARMY AND NAVY.

Increase of, 26.11.

PEACE TENTATIVES.

Austrian feelers for Peace with Russia apparent, 15.4. Put forward by Central Powers throughout year.

PEKIN.

German Minister at, leaves, 14.3.

PÉRONNE.

British occupy, 18.3.

PERSHING, GENERAL.

Infantry Division to be sent to France at once under, 20.5; Arrives in England, 8.6.

PERSIA.

5,000 recruits for Sir P. Syke's force, February; Russians enter Hamadan, 2.3; Kermanshah, c. 15.3, Piatak Pass, 30.3; General Turkish retreat, c. 9.3; Persians rejoice at Russian Revolution, March; Baratov's force withdrawn, July.

PERU.

Cables protest to Berlin re sinking ships, 10.2; Issues Ultimatum to Germany, 4.10; Breaks off relations with Germany, 6.10.

PÉTAIN, GENERAL.

Appointed Chief-of-Staff, French Army, 30.4; Appointed to Command N. and N.E. Armies, 15.5.

PETROGRAD.

Allied Delegates visit, 30.1 to 13.2; Food troubles and demonstrations, 9, 11.3;

Revolution breaks out, 13 to 15.3; Resumption of work ordered, 19.3; Serious casualties (2,500) announced, 20.3; Disorders, revolt crushed, 16, 17, 18.7; Closed to strangers, 6.9; General Kornilov approaches, in force, 10.9; Government prepares to move to Moscow, 17.10; Munition works removed from, 19.10; Stormy Soviet meeting, 22.10; Constituent Assembly meets at, 11.12; Dispersed by Bolsheviks, 13.12; Martial Law proclaimed, 19.12; German Naval Delegates arrive, seizure of private banks, 29.12.

PHILADELPHIA (U.S.A.).

Explosion of ammunition factory at Eddystone, near, 10.4.

PIAVE, RIVER.

Fighting on, 8 to 28.11; British monitor destroys enemy bridge, 29.11; Italians destroy bridges at Zenson, 5.12, 28.12; Stiff fighting in the Delta, 9 to 19.12.

PICCOLO LAGAZNOI, MOUNT (Carnic).

Fighting on, 20.6.

PICHON, M.

Becomes Foreign Minister under M. Clémenceau, 15.11.

PILKEM (Ypres).

British take, 31.7.

PINZANO (Italy).

Austrians reach, 5.11.

PLAVA (Julian).

Italian attacks from, to sea, carry Austrian first line E. of Isonzo, 19.8.

PLUMER, GEN. SIR H.

Commands British force in Italy, 24.11.

POELCAPELLE.

British line slightly advanced astride of Ypres Road, 19.8.

POGRADEC (Macedonia).

French consolidating positions won, 13.9.

POLA (Istria).

Italian airmen bomb, 3, 27.9.

POLAND.

Provisional Council of State meets at Warsaw, 14.1; Russian Conference on future of, announced, 5.2; National Army to be formed, 2.3; Russian Provisional Government acknowledges correspondence of, 30.3; Allies' sympathetic Note to Russian Government re ,14.4; Council of State presents demands, 1.5; Galician Poles vote for independent Poland, 28.5; Crisis in Polish Legions, July; Arrest of Gen. Pilsudski, 21.7; Central Powers create Polish Regency Council and Cabinet, 12.9; Council takes office, 27.10; M. Kucharzewski forms his first Cabinet, c. 11.11.

POLYGON WOOD (Ypres front).

British troops advance, 26-27.9; British gain ground S.W. of, 2, 3.12.

6.9; 12th Russian Army takes up defensive position 30 miles E. of town, 2 to 18.**9**; Russian advance S. of Riga-Pskov Railway, 30.**9**; German attacks repulsed, 7.**10**; Hostile Naval activity round Oesel Islands, 9 to 12.**10**; German attempts to fraternize, 11.**10**; Naval engagement at entrance to Gulf, 17.**10**; British submarine sinks German transport and torpedoes battleship, 20.**10**; Germans retire 20 miles, 20 to 23.**10**; Russians advance to Dvina River, 30 miles S.E. of, 24.**10**; German ships bombard coast near Pernau, 25,26.**10**; German attacks repulsed on Dvina, 29.**10**.

RODZIANKO, M.
Intimation to Tsar by President of Duma, 12.**3**; Affirms Russia's loyalty to Allies, 10.**5**.

ROEUX (Arras).
Heavy fighting in and round, 13, 14 to 29.**5**.

ROISEL (E. of Péronne).
British take, 24.**3**.

ROMANONES, COUNT.
Resignation of Spanish Cabinet, 19.**4**.

ROME.
Conference of Allies in, 5-7.**1**; First day of compulsory food rations, 3.**12**.

RONSSOY WOOD (N.W. of St. Quentin).
Occupied by British 3.**4**; Village occupied, 5.**4**.

ROOSEVELT, MR.
To work in advisory capacity *re* U.S.A. War preparations, 29.**12**.

ROOT, SENATOR E.
With U.S.A. Mission arrives in Russia, 14.**6**.

ROSTOV (River Don).
Cossacks fight the Bolsheviks at, 12.**12**; Bolsheviks occupy, 14.**12**; General Kaledin enters, 15.**12**.

ROTHERMERE, LORD.
Becomes President of Air Council, 26.**11**.

ROULERS.
Germans regain some positions near, 1.**8**; Retaken by British, 2.**8**.

ROYE (River Aisne).
French enter, 17.**3**.

RUA, (Region, Armenia).
Russian detachments drive back Kurds in, 29.**9**.

RUAHA RIVER (E. Africa). .
Belgian columns from Kilossa drive enemy to S. Bank of, reported, 27.**8**.

RUFIJI RIVER (E. Africa).
Operations near, 1, 5, 20.**1**.

RUMANIA.
British loan to, 9.**3**; German attacks in Susitsa Valley, etc., repulsed, 11 to 16.**1**; Indecisive Rumanian attacks, 18 to 23.**1**; General Iliescu blames Russia

for disasters of previous autumn, *c.* 20.**3** ; Electoral and Agrarian Reform Bills passed, 4.**7**; Russo-Rumanian success, 2,000 prisoners taken, 23.**7**; Von Mackensen storms positions N. of Focsani, 7.**8**; Enemy strikes severe blow on Suzitsa and Sereth Rivers, 9 to 11.**8**; Russo-Rumanian Armies retreat up Sereth Valley, 16.**8**; Germans fail to fraternize, 19.**10**; Agree to armistice with Central Powers, 6.**12**; Truce begins, 9.**12**; Headquarters report no other course possible, 11.**12**; and sign Armistice, 12.**12**.

RUSSIA.
Prince N. Golitzin Premier *vice* M. Trepov, 9.**1**; Allied Delegates in Petrograd, 30.**1** to 13.**2**; Conference on future of Poland announced, 5.**2**; Re-opening of Duma, 27.**2**; Bread riots in Petrograd, 8.**3**; Order forbidding street assemblies disregarded, 11.**3**; Mutiny among troops, street fighting, Tsar suspends Duma, Lower House disregards order and forms Executive Committee, 12.**3**; M. Rodzianko and Committee take over Government, 14.**3**; and appoint Provisional Government under Prince Lvov, 15.**3**; " Soviet " formed, 14.**3**; Tsar abdicates by decree, 15.**3**; Provisionaal Government recognised by Allies representatives, 15.**3**; and Governments, 22.**3**; Grand Duke Michael Alexandrovich refuses Crown except by will of people, 16.**3**; Provisional Government issues Manifesto, 16.**3**; M., Miliukov issues foreign policy statement 17.**3**; Press urges people to loyalty to Allied cause, 18.**3**; Death penalty abolished, 22.**3**; Ditto Decorations 25.**3**; General Alexeiev, Commander - in - Chief, Army votes for defence of country, 24.**3**; Provisional Government accepts financial responsibilities, 25.**3**; Imperial Family take oath of fidelity to Provisional Government, 28.**3**; Provisional Government proclaims independence of Poland, 30.**3**; Committee of War formed, Repeal of anti-Jewish legislation, 3.**4**; All-Russia Conference of Soviets, 13.**4**; Proclamation of War aims, 10.**4**; Reception of British Labour and French Socialists, 13.**4**; Disciplinary decrees of War Minister Guchkov, 21.**4**; Miliukov's Note to Allies *re* Foreign policy, 1.**5**; Kornilov orders re-organisation of Reserve, 5.**5**; Collapse of Army discipline, desertions and murders of officers, April to June ; Soviets' resolution for International Socialist Peace Conference, 9.**5**; General Russki relieved of command on N. Front, 10.**5**; Rodzianko and Duma affirm loyalty to Allies, 10 and 18.**5**; General Kornilov resigns Commandantship of Petrograd, 13.**5**;

SAN MARINO (River Brenta).
Austrian attack at, 26.**11.**
SANNA-I-YAT.
(v. Kut-el-Amara).
SAN PELLEGRINO VALLEY (Dolomite).
Defences destroyed by enemy, 16.**3.**
SARY (St. Quentin).
Village and wood captured by British,
1.**4.**
SCARBOROUGH.
Hostile submarine fires 30 rounds at
the town, 4.**9.**
SCARPE, RIVER (Arras).
Operations in valley, ,, 10.**5**, 5.**6** ; etc.
SCHILDEN ISLANDS (Riga).
Captured by Germans, 20.**10.**
" SEE-ADLER."
German raider wrecked off Lord Howe
Island in Pacific, 2.**8.**
SELENCY (St. Quentin).
British capture, 2.**4.**
SELLA (Carso).
Italians carry enemy defences between
Korite and South, 20.**8.**
SENUSSI.
Report on operations against the,
issued, 9.**2.**
SERAIJIK (on Deli Abbas-Mosul Road).
British drive out Turks, 13.**4.**
SERBIA.
M. Pashich forms new Government,
24.**6** ; Yugo-Slav Conferences, June and
July ; " Corfu Pact " (Union of Serbia,
Yugo-Slavs and Montenegro) signed, 20.**7.**
SERDESHT (Persia).
Taken by Russians, 26.**6.**
SERETH RIVER (Galicia).
Russians retreating on the, 21.**7** ;
Germans cross the, 26.**7.**
SERETH (Rumania).
Enemy attack on Rumanian lines,
1, 2, 4, 16, 19.**1** ; German attack on Rus-
sian position near Focsani fails, 6.**2** ;
Von Mackensen crosses, Rumanians resist,
11.**8**, Rumanian 2nd and Russian 4th
Armies retreat up valley, 15, 16.**8.**
SERETH, RIVER (town, Bukovina).
Successful enemy attack S.W. of town,
21.**8.**
SERRE HILL (River Ancre).
British line advanced, 10.**2** ; German
counter-attacks fail, 11, 12.**2.**
SHALAL (Sinai Peninsula).
Turks abandon, 5 **3.**
SHATT-EL-ADHAIM, RIVER (left trib.
of Tigris).
British force passage in night of
17-18.**4** ; British defeat Turks on river
bank, 18.**4** ; British attack Turks on river
bank above junction, 22.**4.**
SHEERNESS.
Chatham district bombed, 107 naval
ratings killed and 86 wounded, 3.**9.**

SHIPPING LOSSES.
French Minister of Marine's statement,
26.**5** ; For general table, v. p. 294.
SHUVAIEV, GEN.
Resigns position of Russian Minister
of War, 17.**1.**
SIAM.
Declares war on Germany and Austro-
Hungary and seizes 9 German vessels, 22.**7.**
SIMBA (E. Africa).
Germans captured at, 21.**11.**
SINNA (Persia).
Captured by Russians from Turks and
offered to Persian Government, 9.**3.**
SINN FEIN.
Candidate defeats Nationalist in East
Clare Election, 11.**7** ; Recrudescence of
movement, autumn ; Convention in Dub-
lin, 25.**10.**
SIVAS (Asia Minor).
Turks attacked by Russians near, 9.**3.**
SIWA (W. Egyptian Desert).
Senussi Arabs defeated and dispersed
by British, latter enter town, 4, 5.**2.**
SKUMBI VALLEY (Albania).
French and Albanian troops success-
fully raid Austrian positions, 20.**9.**
SMUTS, GEN.
Relinquishes command in E. Africa,
20.**1** ; Made Member of Privy Council,
13.**3** ; Speeches in London, 12.**3**, 2.**4** ; at
Edinburgh, 11.**4** ; To attend War Cabinet
meetings, 18.**6.**
SMORGON (Vilna).
Russian diversion at, 23.**7.**
SNEGOVO (Monastir).
Captured by French, 18.**3.**
SOCIALIST ACTIVITY (v. also Stock-
holm Labour Party, Conference, etc.).
Conference at Stockholm proposed,
April, begins to sit, June ; French Govern-
ment refuses passports to, 1.**6** ; Confer-
ence at Leeds, 3.**5** ; Great Britain grants
passports to Russian Conference, 8.**6** ;
Seamen and Firemen's Union prevents
delegates leaving, 11.**6** ; Peace terms of
German delegates published, 16.**6** ; Czech
memo. published, 28.**6** ; British Labour
Party accepts invitation to Stockholm,
10.**8** ; Mr. Henderson resigns from War
Cabinet, 11.**8** ; Government refuses pass-
ports to Stockholm, 13.**8** ; Majority of
Labour Party for Stockholm much reduced
20.**8** ; Trades Union Congress against
International Conference, 4.**9** ; Conference
at Bordeaux, 6.**10.**
SOFIA.
Kaiser visits, 11.**10.**
SOISSONS.
Bombarded, 12, 28.**3** ; Fighting N.E.
of, 13.**3** ; French progress N. of, 22, 24.**3** ;
SOMME CANAL.
Passage forced by French, 21.**3.**

SWISS MINISTER (Berlin).
Forwards to U.S.A. a Berlin suggestion for discussion on means of preventing war, 11.2.

SWITZERLAND.
Declines President Wilson's invitation to break with Germany, 5.2 ; Herr Grimm expelled from Russia, for communicating German Peace proposals, 16.6 ; Herr Hoffmann (Foreign Minister) resigns, 18.6 ; Herr Ador appointed Foreign Minister, 20.6 ; General Election, Radical majority, 28.10 ; Dr. F. Calonder elected President, 13.12.

SYDNEY (Australia).
Australian election results in majority for Nationalist Party, 8.5 ; Serious strike, 50,000 unemployed, 26.9.

TAFEL, COL. (E. Africa).
Surrender of, 27.11.

TAGLIAMENTO RIVER.
Italian retreat on, 29.10 to 3.11 ; Austrians cross, 5.11.

" TANK CORPS."
Royal Warrant forming, 28.7.

TARNOPOL (Galicia).
Germans in the suburbs of, 21.7 ; Fall of, 24.7.

TARVIS (Trentino).
Austrian railhead at destroyed by Italian artillery, 21.2.

TECK.
British Peerage (Cambridge, M.) conferred on family, 19.6.

TEKRIT (Tigris).
British beat Turks at, 5.11 ; British occupy, 6 and 9.11.

TERGUIER (La Fère).
Taken by French, 20.3 ; French progress N. of, 22.3.

TÉTON HEIGHT (Champagne).
Moronvilliers, enemy gain some ground later retaken by French, 26.5 ; Germans attack, 21.6.

THAMES, RIVER.
Estuary raided by aircraft, 5.6.

THÉLUS (N.E. of Arras).
British capture, 9.4.

THESSALY.
Entente troops in, 11-13.6.

THILLOY (Bapaume).
Occupied by British, 28.2.

THOMAS, M. ALBERT (French Minister Munitions). In Moscow, 21.5.

TIGRIS, RIVER.
British cross, 23.2 ; Bridged below Baghdad, 8.3 ; Fighting on, 15.3 ; British attack on W. bank, S. of Samarra, 22.4.

TILLOY-LEZ-MOFFLAINES (E. of Arras).
British capture, 9.4.

TIRUL MARSH (Gulf of Riga).
Russian offensive near, 5 to 13.1 ; German counter-offensive, 23 to 25.1 ; German attack partially successful, 30.1 ; Further German attacks fail, 4.2 ; Russians evacuate positions between, and Aa River, 21.8.

TISZA, COUNT (Hungarian).
Prime Minister retires, 22.5.

TOLMEZZO (Venetia).
Italian defeat near, 8.11.

TOLMINO (Upper Isonzo).
Activity in area of, 19.3 ; Austrian attacks repulsed, 9.7 ; Italian line ruptured by Austro-Hungarians about, 24.10.

TONALE (Trentino).
Renewed activity on, 19.3.

TORPEDO-BOAT DESTROYERS.
v. Destroyers.

TOWER HAMLETS RIDGE (Ypres sector).
Fighting, 21 to 25.9.

TRADE UNION CONFERENCE.
Addressed by Sir Wm. Robertson and Sir John Jellicoe, 4.4.

TRANSCAUCASIA.
Declares itself a Republic, 20.9.

" TRANSYLVANIA," H.M.S.
Transport torpedoed in Mediterranean, 4.5.

TREATIES, RUSSIAN.
Publication by Trotski of Secret, 24.11.

TRENTINO.
Austrians massing in, 4.3 ; Austrians very active in, attacks repulsed, 31.5-17.6 ; 1.7 ; Renewed local fighting in, 18.10.

TREPOV, M.
Resigns position of Russian Prime Minister, 9.1.

TRESCAULT (S.W. of Cambrai).
British capture, 22, 23.4.

TREVES (=Trier, Moselle).
Air-raid on, 4.6, etc.

" TREVIER " (Belgian relief ship).
Torpedoed off Scheveningen, 4.4.

TRIESTE.
General Cadorna's progress towards, continues, 4,021 prisoners, 14-16.5 ; Italian guns within 10 miles of, 27.5 ; Italian boats sink Austrian battleship, 9.12.

TRIKALA (Thessaly).
Occupied by Allies, 13.6.

TRIPOLI.
Revolting natives defeated by General Latini at Zuara, 13.1, 16.1 ; Nuri Pasha defeated by General Cassini, 20.9.

TROTSKI, M.
Comes to the front politically, 12.11.

TROTUS VALLEY (Moldavia).
Russians capture strong position and beat off counter-attacks, 18.2 ; Russian guns stop enemy operations, 29.11.

TSAR (v. Nicholas II.)

"VACUUM," U.S.S.
Torpedoed and sunk, 28.4.

VADELAINCOURT (Meuse).
Germans bomb French Military Hospital, 19 patients killed, 26 wounded, 5.9.

VADENI (Rumania).
Captured by enemy, 14.1; Retaken, 16.1.

VAILLY (River Aisne).
French raids, 26.2; French capture, 18.4.

VALEPUTNA (Rumania).
Austro-German success near, 27.2.

VALLERET (Bapaume).
British take 400 yards of enemy trenches, 10.9.

VALONA (=Avlona, Albania).
Austrian advance on, 18.11; Continued, 28.11.

VALSTAGNA (Asiago, River Brenta).
Italians surrender Col Caprile, 14.12; Austrians advancing on held by concentrated fire, and withdraw, 16.12.

VAN (Armenia).
Russians enter, 18.3.

"VANGUARD," H.M.S.
Blown up as result of internal explosion (3 survivors), 9.7.

VARDAR RIVER (Macedonia).
Heavy fighting between the Cherna and, 11.5; French airmen bomb valley of, 30.11.

VARNITZA (Rumania).
Enemy attack Focsani region; Russian defection in face of enemy, 28.8.

VAUCLÉRE PLATEAU (W. of Craonne).
Great activity on California Plateau and E. of Chevreux, 25.4, 21.5; French attack at three points with success, taking 400 prisoners, 22.5; Unsuccessful German counter-attack, 23.5.

VAUXAILLON (N.E. of Soissons).
French drive German to, 1.4; French bombardment E. of, 6.4; Fighting near, 20, 21, 23, 24.6.

VENDHUILLE (St. Quentin Canal).
British advance to, 24.4.

VENICE.
Austrians bomb, as reprisals for attack on Trieste, 7.9; Austrians approach, 12.11.

VENIZELOS, M.
Becomes Premier of Greece, 25.6; In London, 13 to 19.11.

VERDER (Riga).
Russians repel German attempt to land 8 miles N. of, but Germans land at town. 21.10; Germans attempted landing S. of repulsed, 23.10; Peninsula evacuated by Germans, 27.10.

VERDUN.
Germans capture trenches, French counter-attacks, 21 to 26.1; French repulse attacks N. of Bois des Caurières, 9.3; Germans attack N.W. of, 28.6; French counter-attacks successful, 1.3, 7. 17.7; Germans again busy, 22.7; French push to the N., 20, 24.8; German attacks on Fosses Wood—Caurières Wood line repulsed, 9, 14.9; French attack on R. bank of Meuse, 8, 14.9; Germans repulsed in heavy fighting on the N., 1 to 11.10, and 24 to 27.10; Further German efforts on the N. fail, 4, 10, 13, 26.12.

VERLORENHOEK (Ypres).
British take, 31.7.

VERMELLES (Hulluch).
German raid fails, 22.2.

VERSAILLES.
Inter-Allied Supreme War Council inaugurated at, 1.12.

VERTEKOP (Macedonia).
British hospitals at bombed, by enemy, 13.3.

VESSELS, ARMED.
U.S.A. ruling concerning armed merchant vessels, 12.3.

VICTOR EMMANUEL, KING.
Receives Allied Ministers at front, 9.11.

VILLE-AUX-BOIS (Craonne).
Capture by French, 18.4.

VILLERET (Le Catelet).
British troops take trenches on 600 yards front, and prisoners, 9.9.

VILLERS-GUISLAIN (12 miles S. of Cambrai).
British capture, 18.4.

VILNA.
E. of, Russians penetrate German defences 2 miles (1,000 prisoners), further success jeopardised by indiscipline, 22.7.

VIMY (Village N. of River Scarpe).
British capture, 13.4; And Station, 14.4.

VIMY RIDGE (N. of Arras).
British (Canadians) capture, 9, 10.4; Two German positions captured N. of, 12.4.

VODICE (Sector, Trent).
Fighting on, 31.5, 7.6, 17.6.

VOJUSA RIVER (Albania).
Austrians at, 18, 22.11.

VOLHYNIA FRONT.
Some activity on, 25.8.

VOLO (Thessaly).
Occupied by Allies, 13.6.

VOLUNTARY ENLISTMENT (British).
S.S.W. announces two new groups for men under 45, and 45 to 50, 12.5.

VORONCHIN (Lutsk).
German attack near, 3.3.

VOTES OF CREDIT.
v. Great Britain (Political).

WADI HESI (Palestine).
British reach, 7.11.

YPRES.

German raid fails, 5.2; British raids near, 12, 13, 19.2, 17.7; Fighting near, 31.5, 14, 15.6; Slight British advance S. on, 5.7; Fighting in,—Roulers railway region, 1, 2.8; British advance on 2 miles front, 10.8; And repel German counter-attacks, 11.8; Allies attack on 9 miles front across Ypres-Menin Road and capture all objectives, 16.8; British line advances with heavy fighting to N.E., 19 to 27.8; Further advance E. of, 20, 26.9; German attacks repulsed along Menin Road and towards Polygon Wood, 1 to 7.10; Franco-British advance E. and N.E. of, 9, 10.10; French stop German counter-attack N. of, 11.10; British attack on 6 mile front from Passchendaele northwards, 12.10; Desperate fighting between Poelcapelle and Houthulst ends slightly in our favour, 22 to 24.10; French-Belgian advance across Dixmude Road, 27.10; British advance between Poelcapelle and Passchendaele, 30.10; Canadians capture Passchendaele, 6.11; Further fighting near Polderhoek, 13 to 17.12; Enemy attack near,—Staden Railway, repulsed, 29.12.

YSER (Nieuport Front).

Germans gain ground E. of the mouth of the, 10.7.

YUSSUPOV, PRINCE (Rasputin murder).

Returns to Petrograd, 18.3.

ZAIMIS, M. (Greek Premier).

Resigns, 23.6; Succeeded by M. Venizelos, 25.6.

ZALESZCZYCKI (Bridgehead on Dniester).

Russians evacuate, 29.7.

ZÁNZUR (W. of Tripoli City).

General Cassini's column defeats Nuri Pasha, enemy loss 600 killed, 1,000 wounded, 20.9.

ZBOROW (E. of Lemberg).

Russian offensive progresses, 6,500 prisoners, 2.7.

ZBRUCZ RIVER (Russian-Galicia Frontier).

Enemy cross at many points, 29.7; Enemy stands on broad front on W. bank, 31.7, 1.8; Russians rally and attack enemy on, 4.8.

ZEEBRUGGE.

British raid, 7-8.4; Sea and air fight between Blankenberg and Zeebrugge, 23.4; Heavy Naval bombardment of, by Dover Division and R.N.A. Service, 12.5; Bombed by Naval Air Force, and on other occasions, 1.6, 3.6, 11.9, 28.9, etc.

ZENSON (Lower River Piave).

Austrians at, 12.11.

ZEPPELIN, COUNT.

Death of, 8.3.

ZEPPELIN RAIDS.

On Kent, 16.3; One brought down at Compiègne, 18.3; 4 over E. counties, little damage, 1 killed, 23.5; One downed in North Sea, 14.5; L43 downed in North Sea, 14.6; On E. counties, 3 killed, 16 wounded, 17.6; On Yorkshire coast, one destroyed by Naval forces off Jutland, 21.8; On York and Lincoln coasts, 3 casualties, 25.9; On London, 36 killed, 55 wounded, 19.10 (see pp. 295, 296).

ZIMMERMANN, HERR (German Foreign Secretary).

Speech on torpedoing of Neutrals, 1.3; succeeded by Herr von Kühlmann, 20.7.

ZIONISM.

Letter from Mr. Balfour acknowledging, principles, 2.11.

ZLOCZOW (N. Galicia).

Enemy attack repulsed, 2.1; Successful big German raid between and Tarnopol, 14.2; Further German raid, 12.3.

ZUARA (Tripoli).

Italian victory at, 13.1.

PART III
1918–1919

TABLE OF CONTENTS

1918. Jan.	WESTERN FRONT.	EASTERN THEATRE.	SOUTHERN FRONT.
1	German raids near Loos, Méricourt, and on other portions of front fail. French repulse raid at Beaumont (Verdun).	Reported German peace term cause consternation in Russia and denounced as annexationist([1]). M. Litvinov appointed Bolshevik Plenipotentiary in London.	Austrians bomb Bassano Treviso and Mestre (Venice). Successful Britisl raid across Piave river Austrians driven fron Zenson.
2	British repulse raid near La Bassée.	Central Committee of Soviets meets to receive reports of Peace pourparlers. German conditions denounced.	Austrians bomb Caste franco, Veneto (W. c Treviso) and hit hosp tals.
3	Allied air raids on Metz district. S. of Lens British line is advanced slightly. French repulse attack near Anspach (Alsace) with heavy loss.	Sir J. Buchanan, British Ambassador in Petrograd, granted leave of absence.	Austrians bomb Trevis and Padua.
4	Further British air raid on Metz district.	Bolshevik Government recognises independence of Finland.	Austrians bomb Mestr Bassano and Caste franco.
5	Strong German attacks on British positions E. of Bullecourt (Cambrai) repulsed ; also two raids near Hollebeke. British bomb Conflans station.	Turkey communicates peace terms to Russia([6]).	Artillery activity fro Asiago to Adriatic a aerial activity on whe front.
6	... ...	... ...	Patrol actions betwe Brenta and Piave rive Austrian patrols act N. of Costalunga. bania : Italians repu large enemy deta ments on Osum river
7	Germans raid British post near Flesquières (Cambrai). Another raid near Ypres repulsed. French repulse enemy attempts at Béthincourt (Meuse).	Trotsky and Russian peace delegates return to Brest-Litovsk and negotiations continue([8]).	... ...

Asiatic and Egyptian Theatres.	Naval and Overseas Operations.	Political, &c.	1918. Jan.
British advance continues N. of Jerusalem.	H.M.S.S. " Arbutus " and " Grive " (small vessels) reported torpedoed.	Inter-allied War Purchases Committee meets in Paris. Calcutta : All-India Moslem Association formed (²)	1
... ...	... ...	Air Council established by Order in Council (³). U.S.A. : Statement showing result of American War Mission in Europe issued (⁴). Newfoundland : Sir E. Morris, Prime Minister resigns.	2
... ...	... ...	Man-power Conference between Government and Trades Unions addressed by Sir A. Geddes (⁵).	3
British again advance for a mile N. of Jerusalem.	British naval aircraft bomb Ghistelles aerodrome. Hospital ship " Rewa " torpedoed in Bristol Channel ; all wounded saved.	... ...	4
Aden : British make strong reconnaissance towards Hatum and Jabir and destroy the former. Lt.-Col. R. Storrs made Governor of Jerusalem.	... ...	Mr. Lloyd George addresses Man-power Conference on War Aims (⁷). Independence of Finland recognised by Sweden. Newfoundland : Mr. Lloyd forms new Cabinet.	5
Arabia : Arabs raid Hejaz railway S. of Maan.	... ...	Independence of Finland recognised by France and Germany.	6
... ...	East Africa : British column from Fort Johnston engages enemy force and drives it northwards (¹⁰).	Lord Reading appointed High Commissioner to U.S.A. (⁹) Naval mutiny in Lisbon arrested.	7

1918. Jan.	WESTERN FRONT.	EASTERN THEATRE.	SOUTHERN FRONT.
8	Strong enemy local attack near Bullecourt repulsed. French make successful raid on large scale near Seicheprey (Woëvre). Sir D. Haig's 4th Despatch published([10]).	... ...	... ...
9	Successful raid by Canadians S. of Lens.	Russo - German negotiations at Brest-Litovsk ([12]). Bolsheviks issue appeal for volunteers to march against "Bourgeoisie of the world."	... ...
10	British raids near Ypres. Ammunition depot near Courtrai bombed.	Central Powers and Bolsheviks recognise the Ukraine as separate state; latter to be represented at negotiations. British Government assure ·Russian Government of their support in creation of an independent Poland.	... ...
11	Unsuccessful German raid S. of Armentières. French raids in Argonne, Vosges and Champagne.	Bolshevik excesses in Sevastopol and Kilia.	... ...
12	British make successful raid at Loos and disperse four German raids S. of Lens and E. of Monchy. French repel "flame" attack on Chaume Wood (Meuse).	Russo-German Peace Conference adjourns. Rumanian Minister in Petrograd arrested by Bolsheviks.	... ...
13	Raid by Canadians N. of Lens.	Esthonian Government issue declaration of independence.	... ...
14	British bomb successfully, by day, Karlsruhe, Thionville and Metz area. French repulse attacks on Chaume Wood and make successful raid in Lorraine. British raid N. of Lens.	Von Kühlmann warns Russians that German terms have now reached extreme limit. Attempted assassination of Lenin at Petrograd.	Italians advance E. of Brenta Valley in Asolone District and to lesser extent in Piave Delta.

ASIATIC AND EGYPTIAN THEATRES.	NAVAL AND OVERSEAS OPERATIONS.	POLITICAL, &c.	1918. Jan.
... ...	... ...	U.S.A. : Pres. Wilson addresses Congress—" 14 Points " speech — on peace programme ([11]). Australia : Mr. Hughes and Nationalist Cabinet resign.	8
War Office announces further Arab activity on Hejaz railway.	H. M. S. " R a c o o n " founders in snowstorm off coast of Scotland : all hands lost.	Mr. Hughes forms new Ministry.	9
Gen. Maude's despatch of 15.10.17 issued ([12]).	Board of Admiralty reconstituted, with Sir E. Geddes as First Lord and Sir R. Wemyss as First Sea Lord.	House of Lords adopts Women's Suffrage clause. Australia : Conscription Referendum : majority against — 165,000. Mr. Balfour in Edinburgh ([11]).	10
... ...	Three columns of British troops pursuing Germans in Mozambique.	U.S. Labour supports War Aims declarations. Denmark recognises independence of Finland.	11
... ...	Two British destroyers lost in gale off Scottish coast. British column disembarks at Port Amelia, Portug. E. Afr.	... ...	12
... ...	Japan despatches warships to Vladivostok.	... ...	13
Rafile, S.E. of Dead Sea, captured by Hejaz troops.	Yarmouth bombarded by enemy destroyers ; 6 killed, 6 injured.	House of Commons reassembles. Sir A. Geddes introduces Man-power Bill ([13]). Allies sign wheat convention with Argentine. M. Caillaux arrested.	14

1918. Jan.	Western Front.	Eastern Theatre.	Southern Front.
15	Results of Cambrai enquiry published ([16]).	Bolsheviks issue 24 hours' ultimatum to Rumania ([17]). Corps Diplomatique secure release of Ambassador. Arrest of King of Rumania ordered by Bolsheviks.	Austrian counter-attacks on new Italian positions are repulsed.
16	Successful French raid S.E. Verdun. British again bomb Metz area.	Settlement in principle arrived at between Central Powers and Ukraine.	Austrian attack on Italian positions at Capo Sile (lower Piave) repulsed with heavy loss.
17	... ...	... ...	... ...
18	German raids near Neuve Chapelle and Lens repulsed.	Bolsheviks send further two hours' ultimatum to Rumania demanding passage of troops. Germany refuses undertaking to withdraw troops from Russia. Constituent Assembly meets in Petrograd and denounces Bolsheviks.	Italian patrols active on Asiago plateau.
19	Raids and counter raids in Cambrai sector.	Constituent Assembly forcibly dissolved by Bolsheviks.	... ...
20	... ...	... ...	... ...
21	French raid in Argonne. British bomb Thionville and Metz district and aerodromes in Belgium.	Germany announces agreement with Ukraine ([21])	... ...

ASIATIC AND EGYPTIAN THEATRES.	NAVAL AND OVERSEAS OPERATIONS.	POLITICAL, &c.	1918. Jan.
Considerable air and patrol activity in Palestine. Amman (Hejaz railway) bombed.	... ...	Draft of compulsory rationing scheme issued to Control Committees. U.S.A. : War labour administrator appointed. Strikes in Austria.	15
... ...	Hospital ship "Rewa" : Spanish Commissioner guarantees all conditions were observed.	U.S.A. publishes documents referring to Caillaux case. Prussian Finance Minister Hergt declares sufficient American troops cannot reach Europe. Committee of Enquiry into expenditure of Government Departments announced.	16
... ...	W.O. announces progress in East Africa ([18]).	... ...	17
British advance at Dura, 12 miles N. of Jerusalem. Arabs capture important Turkish convoy E. of Medina. British bomb Samaria.	... ...	Mr. Lloyd George again addresses Man - power Conference ([19]). Australia : Mr. Hughes' Government defeats "No confidence" vote. Hungary : Serious strikes in Buda Pest	18
... ...	... .	... .	19
Samaria again bombed. Troops of King of Hejaz active.	Naval action at entrance to Dardanelles : German cruiser "Breslau" and British monitor "Raglan" sunk and "Goeben" damaged ([20]). H.M.S. "Mechanician" torpedoed in English Channel. Two German destroyers mined in North Sea.	... .	20
Mesopotamia : British bomb Turkish aerodrome at Kifri, N. of Baghdad.	War Office reports further progress in East Africa ([22]). British occupy Mwembe. H.M.S. "Louvain" torpedoed and sunk in Mediterranean.	Sir E. Carson resigns ([21]). Man-power Bill passes Committee stage. Austria : Strikes reported at an end.	21

1918. Jan.	WESTERN FRONT.	EASTERN THEATRE.	SOUTHERN FRONT.
22	German raids near St. Quentin and La Bassée. Much British bombing at Roulers, Menin and Courtrai.	Russians protest against omissions in German report of peace proceedings.	... ...
23	Germans occupy trenches E. of Nieuport (Belgian Coast) after heavy bombardment. French restore position later. British bomb aerodromes at Courtrai and Ghent. French raid E. of Auberive (Champagne).	M. Trotski declares policy of Central Powers to be "a monstrous annexation." Rioting with much bloodshed in Moscow. Congress of Soviets meets in Petrograd.	... ...
24	Great aerial activity in Flanders. Courtrai, Ledeghem and Douai bombed. Air raids into Germany on Mannheim, Trèves and Thionville. French repulse raids N. of Aisne river and at Caurières Wood.	... ...	Italians occupy Austrian advanced post at Capo Sile.
25	E. of Loos, Germans make raid after heavy bombardment. Great Allied air activity: Courtrai, Tournai, Ghent and Douai districts heavily bombed by British and Thionville, Freiburg and Ludwigshafen by French.	Fight between Rumanians and Bolsheviks at Galatz.	... ...
26	Germans report air attack on Dunkirk, Calais and Boulogne. Extension of British line to S. of St. Quentin reported.	Ukraine declares its complete independence. Provisional Siberian Government elected by Regional Government at Tomsk.	Austrian attempt at Capo Sile repulsed. Austrians bomb Mestre and Treviso and damage hospitals.

Asiatic and Egyptian Theatres.	Naval and Overseas Operations.	Political, &c.	1918. Jan.
Samaria again bombed.	... ...	First meeting of Allied Naval Council in London ([24]). Japan: Prime Minister warns Russia that Japan will intervene in Eastern Asia if necessary. Resignation of v. Seidler (Austrian P.M.).	22
... ...	Action between a British submarine and three German submarines reported from Canary I'ds.	Great Britain: Public Meals Order issued. Average daily expenditure $7\frac{1}{2}$ millions. Appointment of Sir H. Lawrence to be C.G.S., France, vice Sir L. Kiggell; other H.Q. appointments announced ([25]). New Army officers to be employed more in staff and higher ranks. Labour Party Conference meets in Nottingham ([26]). Signor Orlando, Italian Prime Minister, arrives in London.	23
... ...	Naval aircraft continue to bomb "Goeben." Enemy post at Pamuni Hill (E. Africa) taken.	Mr. Lloyd George and Signor Orlando confer. Lord Rhondda outlines comprehensive scheme of national food distribution. Germany: Counts Hertling and Czernin reply to war aims speeches for Germany and Austria ([27]).	24
Palestine: British bomb troops S. of Shechem. General Allenby's despatch issued ([30]).	Unsuccessful bombing of "Goeben" continues. War Office report progress in East Africa ([28]).	Great Britain: 36th Meeting of Irish Convention considers letter from Prime Minister ([29]).	25
Turkish attacks near Tafile and Maan repulsed by Hejaz troops.	Submarines sink Dublin steam packet s.s. "Cork" and (50th) Spanish steamer "Giralda."	... ...	26

1918. Jan.	WESTERN FRONT.	EASTERN THEATRE.	SOUTHERN FRONT.
27	Trèves bombed by British, Conflans and Metz district by French.	Bolshevik Government breaks off diplomatic negotiations with Rumania.	... ...
28	Aeroplane raid on London : 67 killed, 166 injured; one enemy machine down. French make two small attacks in Champagne and one in Upper Alsace. Air attacks by British on Roulers and other aerodromes. German raid repulsed between Lens and Arras.	Heavy fighting between Bolsheviks and Ukrainians at Lutsk. Rumanian Legation ordered to leave Petrograd. **Civil War in Finland :** Helsingfors captured by Socialists and Russian troops.	Italians attack between Asiago and Brenta Valley and capture Col del Rosso and 1,500 prisoners.
29	Aeroplane raid on London: bombs dropped in outskirts, 10 killed, 10 wounded. Successful British raids and patrol encounters near Havrincourt and Bullecourt (Cambrai).	... ...	Italian attack continues. Monte di Val Bella captured ([33]).
30	14 tons of bombs dropped on Paris, 1 raider brought down; 49 killed, 206 injured.	... ...	Battle dies down on Asiago plateau; Italians gain ground along Frenzela Gorge and at Val Bella and Rosso.
31	... ...	... ...	Strong Austrian counter-attack on Monte di Val Bella defeated.
Feb. 1	... ...	Central Powers recognise Ukraine Republic as independent state.	Mutiny of Greek troops at Lamia suppressed ; MM. Skouloudhis and Lambros arrested.
2	U.S. troops reported in front line.	... ...	... ...
3	About 185 German divisions on W. Front.	... ...	Austrians bomb Venice, Padua, and other towns in Venetian plain.

ASIATIC AND EGYPTIAN THEATRES.	NAVAL AND OVERSEAS OPERATIONS.	POLITICAL, &c.	1918. Jan.
... ...	Cunard liner s.s. "Andania" torpedoed off Ulster coast. Naval aircraft bomb Aertrycke and Engel. Argentine s.s. "Ministro Iriondo" torpedoed by Germans. "Goeben" refloated.	... ...	27
War Office reports further operations near Hejaz railway (³¹).	Further naval air attacks on Aertrycke and Engel. H.M.S. "Hazard" sunk in collision in Channel. Ankwalu (E. Afr.) occupied by British.	U.S.A. : Mr. Baker makes statement on strength of Army (³²). Germany : Great strikes in Berlin,&c.	28
... ...	Naval aircraft bomb Coolkerke aerodrome (Bruges). Allied air raid on Zeebrugge. Enemy driven down Lujenda Valley towards Mtarika (E. Africa).	Signor Orlando's visit to London ; official communiqué records complete understanding.	29
British line advanced near Arnutiya, 12 m. N. of Jerusalem.	Brazil to send naval squadron to Europe. British submarine E.14 sunk off Kum Kale in endeavour to sink "Goeben."	Allied War Council meets at Versailles. German strikes spread to Kiel, Munich, and Hamburg (³⁴).	30
... ...	... ...	Martial Law in Berlin, Hamburg, etc. ; Trade Unions refuse strike pay.	31
			Feb.
... ...	Austrian Naval mutiny at Cattaro.	German strikes die down. Sir E. Geddes states submarines being sunk as fast as Germany can build them.	1
... ...	... ...	End of Supreme War Council meeting ; vigorous combined prosecution of war.	2
... ...	Mtarika (E. Africa) occupied by British troops.	Enlargement of powers of Supreme War Council at Versailles announced.	3

1918. Feb.	WESTERN FRONT.	EASTERN THEATRE.	SOUTHERN FRONT.
4	Considerable aerial activity; more American troops occupy portion of W. battle front.	Gen. Kaledin reported to have relinquished leadership of Cossacks to Gen. Alexeiev, who with 30,000 men advances towards Moscow against Bolsheviks.	... ...
5	French airmen bomb Saarbrücken junction.	First Duma of Independent Siberian Republic opened.	Venice again bombed.
6	... ...	German ultimatum to Rumanian Government, giving 4 days in which to enter into peace negotiations (afterwards denied) ; Bratianu Cabinet resigns. Bolshevist campaign against Orthodox Church rousing opposition.	... ...
7	... ...	Civil war in Finland still raging.	... ...
8	Gen. Cadorna succeeded by Gen. Giardino on Versailles Committee. Repulse of Germans on Chemin des Dames.	Lenin and Trotski alleged by Paris press to be receiving pay from German agents.	... ...
9	... ...	**Peace signed between Central Powers and Ukraine Rada :** boundary defined. Gen. Averescu forms new Rumanian Cabinet.	... ...
10	... ...	Trotski states that Russia, while desisting from signing formal peace, is no longer at war with Quadruple Alliance. Order given for demobilisation of Russian forces. **Russia out of the War.** Publication of peace treaty between Central Powers and Ukraine ([35]).	Renewed Austrian activity on Asiago front.

Asiatic and Egyptian Theatres.	Naval and Overseas Operations.	Political, &c.	1918. Feb.
... ...	... ...	Bolo Pasha trial commences. British Government renew to King of Hejaz pledges for freeing Arab peoples.	4
... ...	U.S. trooper " Tuscania " torpedoed off Irish coast, 166 lives lost.	... ...	5
... ...	... ...	President Wilson asks for new powers to reorganise the Government and war machine. Reprisals threatened if British leaflet-scattering airmen improperly treated.	6
... ...	... ...	... ...	7
... ...	British destroyer " Boxer " sunk by collision in English Channel.	... ...	8
... ...	... ...	Embargo on Dutch commercial cables provisionally raised. Economic Allied Council sits in London.	9
... ...	... ...	Lord Beaverbrook appointed Minister in charge of Propaganda. Death of Abdul Hamid, ex-Sultan of Turkey.	10

1918. Feb.	WESTERN FRONT.	EASTERN THEATRE.	SOUTHERN FRONT.
11	Metz raided by French airmen.	Polish Cabinet resigns as protest against Ukraine treaty.	Fighting in Asiago region to advantage of Italians.
12	Allied planes bomb Offenburg, Metz, etc. Fighting in Passchendaele region.	... ...	... ...
13	French win salient between Tahure and Butte de Mesnil (Champ.).	Bolsheviks defeat Gen. Alexeiev; suicide of Gen. Kaledin reported.	British line in Italy extended.
14	... ...	Resignation of M. Kucharzewski, P.M., and Cabinet, Warsaw.	... ...
15	... ...	... ...	... ...
16	Fighting in Cambrai section. Air raid on London and Dover: 1 enemy machine down, 12 killed, 6 injured.	... ...	... ...
17	Air raid on London: 21 killed, 32 injured. 1 ton of bombs dropped in and near Metz.	... ...	... ...

Asiatic and Egyptian Theatres.	Naval and Overseas Operations.	Political, &c.	1918. Feb.
... ...	(Feb. 11 to . 18) : Main German force dislodged from Lujenda Valley, moves southwards from Mtarika area towards Upper Rio (frontier of Mozambique).	President Wilson restates War Aims. Lord Reading arrives in U.S.A. as Ambassador, etc.	11
... ...	... ...	Parliament meets. Mr. Asquith asks for explanation of extension of powers of Versailles Council ; answer refused.	12
... ...	... ...	Pacifist group in House of Commons defeated.	13
British troops advance at Mukhmas, N.E. of Jerusalem ; line advanced 2 m. on 6 m. front.	... ...	Bolo Pasha and Cavallini condemned to death. Death of Sir Cecil Spring Rice, British Ambassador, U.S., at Ottawa.	14
... ...	Submarine shells Dover, 1 killed, 7 injured. British trawler and 7 drifters sunk in Straits of Dover. Maloktera (on Upper Lurio) reoccupied by Portuguese troops. In Coastal area British column from Port Amelia approaching Meza.	U.S. Government takes over complete control of foreign trade.	15
... ...	... ...	Sir Henry Wilson succeeds Sir Wm. Robertson as Chief of Imperial Staff([2e]).	16
... ...	... ...	... ...	17

1918. Feb.	WESTERN FRONT.	EASTERN THEATRE.	SOUTHERN FRONT.
18	German raiders fail to get through defences in attempted air raid on London.	End of Russian armistice. German army crosses Dvina and marches on Dvinsk and Lutsk. A second army advances into Ukraine against Bolsheviks. Russians evacuate Armenia. Turks within 8 m. of Trebizond. S. Finland now in hands of Bolsheviks. Gen. Mannesheim (commanding Constitutional forces, "White Guards") gathers an army together in the North.	... ...
19	... ...	Germans occupy Dvinsk and Lutsk, and advancing on whole line from Riga to Volhynia, enter Esthonia and press towards Reval and Petrograd. Bolshevik Government formally declare willingness to sign peace upon conditions dictated at Brest-Litovsk by Quadruple Alliance([37]). Austria-Hungary and Ukraine sign agreement by which Kholm district of Poland will not necessarily be included in Ukraine Republic.	... ...
20	Successful extensive French raid N. of Bures (Lorraine): 500 prisoners.	German armies still advancing towards Reval, Petrograd, Moscow and Kiev, meeting with little resistance, and occupy Hapsal and Minsk. German troops reach Finland to reinforce White Guard.	Great bombing raids from both sides; Venice, Padua, etc., again bombed.
21	... ...	Main Committee of German Reichstag adopts peace treaty with the Ukraine. New peace terms for Russia formulated by Germany. Germans within 60 m. of Reval.	... ...

ASIATIC AND EGYPTIAN THEATRES.	NAVAL AND OVERSEAS OPERATIONS.	POLITICAL, &c.	1918. Feb.
.. ..	... ...	... ...	18
British troops attack on 15-mile front E. of Jerusalem ; all objectives secured. British now within 8 miles of Jericho.	... ...	Gen. Sir H. Rawlinson appointed British Army representative at Versailles. Premier defends arrangements *re* latter.	19
British troops N. of Jerusalem advance on 4-mile front on Shechem road ; within 4 miles of Jericho. Khan Abu Rayan occupied by British patrols within 10 miles of Hit (Mesop.).	... ...	Inter-Allied Labour and Socialist Conference meets at Westminster.	20
Jericho taken. British established on line of the Jordan to E. and Auja to N., threatening Hejaz railway.	... .	.. ..	21

1918. Feb.	WESTERN FRONT	EASTERN THEATRE.	SOUTHERN FRONT.
22	... ...	... ...	... .
23	... ...	... ...	... .
24	... ...	Russia accepts German terms of peace ([37]). Novocherkask, capital of Don Cossack territory, in Bolshevik hands.	... .
25	... ...	Reval and Pskov occupied by Germans. In Ukraine Germans reach Zhitómir, temporary capital of Ukraine Republic. Fresh meeting of German-Austrian and Rumanian peace delegates at Bukarest.	Venice, Castelfranco and Mestre damaged by Austrian airmen.
26	... ...	... ...	... .
27	Big British raid in Houthulst Forest (Flanders).	Ukraine Central Soviet accepts treaty concluded with Germany by the Rada. Japan proposes military action in Siberia.	... .
28	Repulse of German attack near Chavigeron (N.E. of Soissons).	Russian delegates return to Brest-Litovsk. Continued German advance in the Ukraine: armed Pripet flotilla captured. Austrians invade the Ukraine N. of the Pruth River.	... ...
Mar. 1	Germans recapture trenches S.W. of Butte de Mesnil, but fail in local attacks elsewhere in Champagne and near Reims. Big German raids at Haucourt (N.W. of Verdun) and Seicheprey (Lorraine), the latter against Americans.	... ...	... ...

ASIATIC AND EGYPTIAN THEATRES.	NAVAL AND OVERSEAS OPERATIONS.	POLITICAL, &c.	1918. Feb.
Retreat of Turks beyond River Jordan.	German rearguard dispersed between Mtende and Msalu (Portug. E. Africa) ; v. 21.3.18.	... ...	22
Patrol activity on wide front N. of Jerusalem, E. of Jericho.	... ...	End of Inter-Allied Labour Conference ; statement of War Aims ([38]).	23
Turks re-occupy Trebizond.	German auxiliary cruiser " Wolf " returns to Pola after 15 months' absence, having sunk 11 vessels, 33,000 tonnage.	Count Motono states if Russia concludes separate peace Japan will take decided and adequate steps to meet occasion.	24
... ...	... ...	Meat, butter and margarine rationing comes into force in London and Home counties.	25
Patrols reach Rujm el Bahr (at N. end of Dead Sea, 2 miles E. of mouth of Jordan).	Hospital ship " Glenart Castle," outward bound, torpedoed in Bristol Channel. 162 lost.	Lawlessness in Ireland ; additional troops sent to aid police.	26
... ...	... ...	... ...	27
... ...	... ...	Grant of £25,000 to Lady Maude. Resignation of M. Pashich and Serbian Cabinet.	28
			Mar.
... ...	H.M.S. "Calgarian," armed merchant cruiser, torpedoed and sunk off Irish coast ; 21 officers, 46 men lost.	... ...	1

1918. Mar.	WESTERN FRONT.	EASTERN THEATRE.	SOUTHERN FRONT.		
2	Many German raids on British lines.	Capture of Kiev by Germans and continued advance of Austrians in the Ukraine. Rumania agrees to negotiate for peace on basis of enemy demands.	...	...	...
3	Great raiding activity by British.	Peace between Russia and enemy Powers signed at Brest-Litovsk ([39]).	...	...	...
4	Continued raiding by both sides, including an important enterprise by the French at Les Éparges.	Germans claim capture of 6,000 officers, 57,000 men, 2,600 guns, and 5,000 m.-guns in recent invasion.	...	...	...
5	... ...	Rumania accepts enemy terms and signs at Buftea preliminary treaty of peace ([40]). Germans land on Aaland Islands at request of Finnish Government.	...	...	...
6	Failure of German night attack on Belgians near Ramscapelle and Stuyvenskerke. Unusual aerial activity on British front.	... ...	...	...	...
7	Aeroplane raid on Kent, Essex, Herts, Bedfordshire and London; 23 killed, 39 injured; one Gotha downed.	Peace signed between Germany and Finland ([42]).	...	...	...
8	Failure of heavy local attacks on British near Ypres. Big aeroplane raid by night on Paris; 13 killed, 50 injured; one Gotha downed.	... ...	...	...	...
9	Daylight air-raid by British on Mainz.	... ...	...	...	...

Asiatic and Egyptian Theatres.	Naval and Overseas Operations.	Political, &c.	1918. Mar.
British advance on 12-mile front astride Jerusalem-Nablus road.	... ...	... ...	2
British advance in Palestine continued, reaching maximum of 3,000 yds.	... ...	Germany notifies Sweden of forthcoming occupation of Aland Islands.	3
... ...	... ...	... ...	4
... ...	... ...	Sir E. Geddes reviews shipping situation in House of Commons ([41]).	5
... ...	Further shipping-loss figures issued ([42]).	Death of Mr. J. Redmond.	6
British advance in Palestine, pressed continuously for some days, reaches maximum of 3 miles on front of 18.	... ...	Entente note to Holland demanding unconditional use of Dutch shipping in ports of Allies ([44]). Vote of credit for £600,000,000.	7
... ...	... ...	Patriotic speech by M. Clémenceau : Vote of confidence in Government.	8
British cross Wadi Auja (Jordan valley) and advance 2-3 miles on front of 13, astride Jerusalem-Nablus road, taking height of Tel Asur. British occupy Hit (on Euphrates).	... ...	War Bonds Week produces £138,870,240.	9

1918. Mar.	WESTERN FRONT.	EASTERN THEATRE.	SOUTHERN FRONT.
10	Many German raids on French. Daylight air-raid by British on Stuttgart.	Enemy advance on Odessa continues.	... ...
11	Big German raids near Ypres and Armentières repulsed. Big aeroplane raid by night on Paris ; 4 Gothas downed.	... ...	Seaplane raid by night on Naples.
12	Repulse of big German raid on Portuguese near Laventie. Daylight air-raid by British on Coblenz. Zeppelin raid on Yorkshire ; Hull bombed, one woman killed.	German troops land at Aabo (Finland), and advance inland.	... ...
13	Daylight air-raid by British on Freiburg. Zeppelin raid on Co. Durham, Hartlepool bombed ; 8 killed, 39 injured.	Germans and Austrians occupy Odessa.	... ...
14	French recover trenches near Butte de Mesnil lost on March 1. Severe aerial fighting ; 223 enemy machines disabled since March 1.	Congress of Soviets at Moscow ratifies Brest-Litovsk treaty by 704 votes to 261.	... ...
15	... ...	Germans occupy Nicolaiev (Odessa). German Protectorate over independent Courland announced.	... ...
16	Big French raids near Cheppy and Malancourt (W. of Verdun). Daylight air-raid by British on Zweibrücken (Pfalz).	... ...	... ...
17	Big German raid N.E. of Verdun. Daylight air-raid by British on Kaiserslautern (Pfalz).	—	... ...

ASIATIC AND EGYPTIAN THEATRES.	NAVAL AND OVERSEAS OPERATIONS.	POLITICAL, &c.	1918. Mar.
British advance 3,000 yds. on front of 12 miles astride Jerusalem-Nablus road.	Hospital ship "Guildford Castle" torpedoed in Bristol Channel, but not sunk.	... ...	10
Further British progress astride Nablus road.	... ...	Mr. Lloyd George on connection between Government and Press. National Expenditure Committee report on extravagance in munitions, etc.	11
British advance 3 miles on 11-mile front in coastal sector of Palestine. Turks report recapture and burning of Erzerum.	Enemy driven from Poluvu (Portuguese East Africa).	... ...	12
. ...	... ...	Lts. Sholtz and Woolley released by Germans (v. 6.2.18).	13
British make small advance in Jordan valley.	... ...	Mr. Balfour, speaking in House of Commons, defends proposed Japanese intervention in Asiatic Russia. Meeting of Supreme War Council in London, attended by Entente Premiers and Foreign Ministers.	14
. ...	... ...	Publication by "Politiken" of Prince Lichnowsky's memorandum([227]) Strikes in Austro-Hungary.	15
... ...	... ...	... ...	16
... ...	... ...	... ...	17

1918. Mar.	WESTERN FRONT.	EASTERN THEATRE.	SOUTHERN FRONT.
18	Belgians repulse heavy local attacks in Flanders. Daylight air-raid by British on Mannheim.	... ...	... ...
19	... ...	Germans still advancing in Ukraine.	... ...
20	Repulse of strong German local attacks in Champagne, near Verdun, in the Woëvre, and in Lorraine.	... ...	... ...
21	Second Battle of the Somme. Great German offensive on 50-mile front between Sensée and Oise rivers. British battle positions penetrated at various points, especially near St. Quentin.	... ...	... ...

ASIATIC AND EGYPTIAN THEATRES.	NAVAL AND OVERSEAS OPERATIONS.	POLITICAL, &c.	1918. Mar.
. ...	... ...	Publication of manifesto by Premiers and Foreign Ministers of Entente regarding Germany's policy towards Russia and Rumania ; they refuse to recognise the peace treaties. Holland accepts Entente demands in regard to Dutch shipping, with reservations (⁴⁴).	18
nall British advance in coastal sector of Palestine.	... ...	Allies demand unconditional acceptance of their demands by Dutch (⁴⁴). Debate in House of Lords on resolution approving principle of League of Nations : debate adjourned.	19
.. ..	... ...	Dutch ships in ports of U.S.A. seized by Government (⁴⁴). Sir E. Geddes, speaking in House of Commons, gives figures relating to submarine warfare and shipbuilding, and announces that Lord Pirrie is to be Controller-General of Merchant Shipbuilding(⁴²). M. Marghiloman, Rumanian P.M. Mr. A. Henderson declares that Labour cannot accept peace of Brest-Litovsk.	20
.. ..	Great activity off Flanders coast : Dunkirk bombarded by German destroyers, Ostend by British monitors ; two destroyer actions, 3 enemy vessels sunk. Official report of fighting 22.2.18 at Msalu (Port. E.Africa) and of occupation of Nampula by column from Mozambique.	Dutch shipping question to the fore (⁴⁴).	21

1918. Mar.	WESTERN FRONT.	EASTERN THEATRE.	SOUTHERN FRONT.
22	Germans generally held on northern part of battle-front, but **British defences broken through W. of St. Quentin,** and troops here and in adjoining sectors retreat hastily. Germans claim 16,000 prisoners and 200 guns.	... ...	... ...
23	**Germans** take Monchy-le-Preux, cross Tortille river (between Bapaume and Péronne), capture **Péronne and Ham, and reach line of Somme.** French troops enter battle on British southern wing. Bombardment of Paris by long-range gun (74 miles) begins. British air-raid on Konz (near Trèves) by night.	... ...	... ...
24	Germans held in desperate fighting round Bapaume, cross Somme between Péronne and Ham, and take Nesle and Péronne, and further south capture Guiscard and Chauny. They now claim 30,000 prisoners and 600 guns. British aeroplanes raid Mannheim by day and Cologne by night.	... ...	...
25	**Germans carry Bapaume** in night attack; subsequently their advance, though less rapid than on previous two days, continues on whole front from Ervillers (N. of Bapaume) to the Oise. Germans claim 45.000 prisoners since beginning of attack.	... ...	...

Asiatic and Egyptian Theatres.	Naval and Overseas Operations.	Political, &c.	1918. Mar.
British cross Jordan and advance eastward.	... ...	Dutch Government informed that **Allies have decided to seize Dutch ships** in their ports ([44]). New Spanish Cabinet under Señores Maura and Dato.	22
.. ..	British destroyer sunk in collision.	Russian and Rumanian treaties adopted by Reichstag.	23
British advance 9 miles towards Es Salt (Jordan).	... ...	... ...	24
British take Es Salt ...	... ...	... ...	25

1918. Mar.	WESTERN FRONT.	EASTERN THEATRE.	SOUTHERN FRONT.
26	British make stand N. of Somme on line Rœux-Ayette - Beaumont Hamel - Albert - Bray, but lose Albert and Bray. Very heavy fighting S. of Somme ; Germans capture Lihons, Chaulnes, Roye and Noyon. Momentous Franco-British Conference at Doullens on unity of command (⁴⁵).	... ...	... ...
27	Germans advance on both sides of Somme in night attack, reaching Sailly le Sec (12 m. from Amiens), but lose ground in British counter-attacks. Germans afterwards fail in attacks from Bucquoy to Rosières and are checked near Lassigny and Noyon, but take Montdidier after rapid advance.	... ...	... ...
28	Great German attack on wide front N. and S. of Scarpe river defeated with very heavy loss. Between Somme and Avre rivers Germans advance, reaching Hamel. Strong French counter - attacks gain ground near Montdidier and between Hainvillers and Pont l'Évêque (Oise).	... ...	... ...
29	No serious fighting N. of Somme. Between Somme and Avre Germans continue to advance, taking Hamel, Mézières and Demuin. French hold line W. of Mézières-La Neuville - Sire Bernard - outskirts of Montdidier. Continued French counter-attacks on southern flank. Germans claim 70,000 prisoners and 1,100 guns since opening of offensive. General Foch appointed to co-ordinate action of Allied Armies. Long-range gun causes 160 casualties in Paris church.	Germans ratify Brest-Litovsk treaty of 3.3. Turks ratify peace with Russia and Ukraine.	... ...

Asiatic and Egyptian Theatres.	Naval and Overseas Operations.	Political, &c.	1918. Mar.
British cavalry advancing towards Amman (E. of Jordan). British carry Turkish positions at Khan Baghdadiya (on Euphrates) and take 3,000 prisoners.	... ...	Prime Minister of Japan says gravity of situation in Siberia may shortly compel action.	26
... ...	British destroyer sunk by mine.	... ...	27
.. ..	H.M. boarding - steamer "Tithonus" torpedoed. British destroyers sink 3 German armed trawlers and capture crews.	Gen. Pershing asks for employment of U.S.A. troops ([46]). Australian Cabinet reconstituted.	28
.. ..	... ...	... ...	29

1918. Mar.	WESTERN FRONT.	EASTERN THEATRE.	SOUTHERN FRONT.
30	On a 37½-mile front, between Moreuil and Lassigny, French offensive continued ; desperate resistance to enemy attacks. N. of Somme in Boivy and Boyelles region (Cojeul river) heavy German attacks break down. S. of Somme in Luce valley, Demuin is lost and retaken by British. Attack on Belgian trenches E. of Nieuport repulsed.	... ...	Albania : Enemy attempt against bridgehead in Avlona sector fails.
31	Indecisive fighting in Luce and Avre valleys. Hangard taken and retaken. French make some progress between Montdidier and Lassigny. W. of Albert German attack is stopped. 1,059 aeroplanes reported brought down on all fronts in March, of which Allies claim 838, and Germans 221. Comparative statement of bombing activity by British and German aircraft issued (⁴⁷).	Russo - Rumanian agreement on subject of Bessarabia completed.	Announced that British troops in Italy are now holding sector on Asiago Plateau instead of Montello.
April 1	Local attacks near Albert repulsed. Grivesnes (S. Moreuil) heavily attacked but remains in French hands. At Hébuterne (Bucquoy) local fighting in favour of British.	Berlin reports the despatch of ultimatum to Russia on subject of Finland.	... ...
2	On Scarpe river British repulse attack near Fampoux and further south capture Ayette. Local fighting between Moreuil and Lassigny. Generally fighting has died down. U.S.A. agrees to brigade troops with British and French.	New Polish Cabinet formed by M. Steczkowski. Siberia reported dominated by Bolsheviks, German and Austrian prisoners being armed.	... ...

ASIATIC AND EGYPTIAN THEATRES.	NAVAL AND OVERSEAS OPERATIONS.	POLITICAL, &c.	1918. Mar.
British raid Hejaz railway near Amman (E. of Jordan).	... ...	H.M. the King returns from a visit to the front. Mr. Lloyd George issues statement on course of present battle and announces appointment of General Foch ([45]).	30
War Office reports progress in Mesopotamia ([48]), Palestine ([49]), and the Hejaz ([50]).	... ...	Mr. Lloyd George in message to Dominions says "the last man may count." U.S.A.: Agreement between Capital and Labour to refer all questions to arbitration announced. Austria: "Arbeiter-Zeitung" on Sea-power ([51]).	31
Mesopotamia: British troops 73 miles beyond Ana (Middle Euphrates). Palestine: Strong Turkish resistance near Amman; British retire to Es Salt.	British destroyer sunk in collision.	Royal Air Force (under Air Ministry) formed from R.N.A.S. and R.F.C. Canada: Anti-conscription riots in Quebec. Troops fire on rioters.	April 1
... ...	... ...	"Curfew" order comes into force. Canada: Prime Minister intends to enforce Military Act on Quebec rioters.	2

1918. Apr.	WESTERN FRONT.	EASTERN THEATRE.	SOUTHERN FRONT.
3	Local fighting in Scarpe river region and at Hébuterne. Heavy air fighting and bombing. One long-range gun reported blown up.	Indications of coalition between local authorities and Entente to safeguard Murman railway. German troops (30,000 ?) land at Hangö in Finland; White Guards capture Tammerfors with 1,000 prisoners.	... ...
4	Germans again attack in force between Somme and Avre rivers. British pressed back near Hamel and Villers-Bretonneux, and French between Avre and Luce rivers. N. of Somme, attack near Albert is repulsed. French counter - attack between Grivesnes and Noyon ([54]). Germans claim 90,000 prisoners since 21.3.	... ...	... ...
5	Germans again attack from Somme to beyond Bucquoy. British take 200 prisoners in counter-attack near Hébuterne. French attack N. of Montdidier and near Noyon. End of Second Battle of the Somme.	German landing in Finland confirmed ([56]). Siberia: Japanese marines land at Vladivostok, followed by a British detachment.	60 Austrian sailors captured on land by Italians near Ancona.
6	Severe fighting in Aveluy Wood (Albert), near Hébuterne, in Luce Valley, N. and S. of Montdidier, and in Oise region. Strong German attacks near Beaumont (Meuse). Reims heavily bombarded.	Ukraine: Ekaterinoslav (N.E. of Odessa) occupied by Germans. Siberia: Disorders in Vladivostok are confirmed.	... ...
7	Heavy artillery work on the Oise and between the Somme and Armentières; two attacks on Bucquoy repulsed.	Russian protests to Germany about landing in Finland and to foreign Consuls in Moscow about Vladivostok. Bolsheviks evacuating Helsingfors.	... ...

Asiatic and Egyptian Theatres.	Naval and Overseas Operations.	Political, &c.	1918. Apr.
Baluchistan: Successful progress of operations against the Marris.	Seven British Submarines blown up in Baltic (between 3rd and 8th April) to save them from German hands ([52]).	British Shipping output for first quarter 320,280 tons. Austria: Count Czernin speaks([53]) on international situation and declares he has received peace offer from France (M. Clémenceau denies this). Cape Town: Gen. Botha appeals to "Fellow South Africans" for recruits. Allied Blockade Committee meets.	3
Sarikamish (Transcauc.) occupied by Turks.	Marocco: Reported German intrigues in ([55]). British destroyer sunk in collision. Petrograd reports sinking of 3 Russian warships in Finnish waters and destruction of others to avoid capture.	Mr. Ll. George returns from visit to the front.	4
Van (Armenia) retaken by the Turks.	Sir J. Van Deventer's despatch on East Africa published ([57]).	51st Meeting of Irish Convention adopts draft report. Convention adjourns sine die.	5
Turks occupy Ardahan (Transcauc.).	... ...	The King sends greetings to U.S.A. on anniversary of entrance into the war. President Wilson speaks at Baltimore on war aims and resolves ([58]).	6
Kerak (S. of Dead Sea) occupied by Hejaz troops. Transcaucasia: Turkish Troops reported to be marching on Batum.	... ...	Paris: M. Clémenceau receives Mr. Baker, U.S. Secretary of War.	7

D

1918. Apr.	WESTERN FRONT.	EASTERN THEATRE.	SOUTHERN FRONT.		
8	On Oise river French are forced back in Forest of Coucy, and Coucy le Château and Landricourt are lost. German attempts in districts of Reims, Verdun and Vosges. Heavy German bombardment on whole British front, up to Armentières.	Germany answering Russian protests demands disarmament of Russian Fleet. Bessarabian Council of Land vote for autonomous union with Rumania.	...	...	...
9	**Battle of the Lys begins.** Heavy bombardment from La Bassée Canal to Armentières, followed by strong attacks, force British and Portuguese back to Lys river at Estaires. Neuve Chapelle lost. Fine stand by Guards Division. Hangard lost and retaken by French ; between it and Noyon all enemy attempts repulsed.	... ...	... ...	..
10	Battle extends northwards. Germans reach left bank of Lys river. From Estaires S. to Givenchy position is maintained. N. of Armentières, line forced back to Wytschaete, Messines Ridge and Ploegsteert ; Armentières evacuated with practically no loss.	Siberia : Bolsheviks at Vladivostok reported to have fired on Japanese troops.	...	...	..
11	Fighting general on whole battle-front. British forced back beyond Ploegsteert and Steenwercke to S. of Neuve Église and Bailleul. At Hollebeke and Messines attacks repulsed. Enemy captures Merville. Strong local attacks repulsed S. of Arras. Germans claim 20,000 prisoners in Northern fighting.	... ...	... ...	.

ASIATIC AND EGYPTIAN THEATRES.	NAVAL AND OVERSEAS OPERATIONS.	POLITICAL, &c.	1918. Apr.
... ...	... ...	Rome : **Conference of Nationalities oppressed by Austria** opens. Paris : M. Clémenceau discloses contents of Emperor of Austria's letter ([59]). Canada : Sir Sam Hughes speaks on conditions in Quebec ([60]).	8
Transcaucasia : Turks reported before Batum and marching on Kars. Palestine : British advance 1½ miles on 5-mile front E. of Tul-Keram-Ramleh railway. Arabs claim 800 miles of Red Sea coast, and to have put 40,000 Turks out of action since declaration of independence.	German torpedo-boats bombard Belgian coast.	Mr. Lloyd George introduces Man-Power Bill ([61]), reviews battle situation ([62]), and refers to Irish affairs ([63]).	9
Palestine : Turco - German troops attack British position in coastal sector and after preliminary success are driven back, and British line is slightly advanced.	Monrovia (Liberia) bombarded by German submarine and wireless destroyed.	Man-Power Bill read second time (majority 223); order for thinning - out issued by Sir A. Geddes— to have effect on April 24. Rome : Conference of Oppressed Nationalities ends. Canada : Bill appropriating £100,000,000 for war expenditure introduced.	10
Palestine : Turks attack near El Ghoraniya (E. Jordan) ; defeated and pursued by cavalry 6 m. towards Es Salt. Further attack astride Jericho-Shechem road repulsed.	E. Africa : British columns from coast and Lake Nyassa in touch with enemy forces at Medu and Msalu river. British naval forces bombard Ostend and aircraft bomb Zeebrugge. American s.s. "Lakemoor" sunk by submarine.	Maj.-Gen. Hon. C. Sackville-West succeeds Sir H. Rawlinson (to the front) at Versailles. Report issued of Government Committee on treatment of prisoners of war behind lines ([64]j. Food riots in Holland.	11

1918. Apr.	WESTERN FRONT.	EASTERN THEATRE.	SOUTHERN FRONT.
12	Strong enemy pressure, especially at Bailleul and Wulverghem ; Neuve Église and Messines penetrated. In Apremont Forest Franco-Americans repulse continued attacks. 110 German Divisions engaged till now. Zeppelins raid Eastern and Midland Counties (7 killed, 20 injured). Air raid on Paris, one raider shot down at Compiègne.	... ...	Sir H. Plumer's despatch from Italy published (**).
13	British reoccupy Neuve Église and repel further attack. Continuous fighting round Wulverghem, Bailleul and Meteren, and at Festubert. On Lys river front remains firm. Sir Douglas Haig issues special Order of the Day (**). On Meuse river, Americans N.W. of Toul are twice attacked. Long-range gun shells Paris by night. Zeppelin Works near Friederichshafen burnt out.	... ...	... ...
14	Neuve Église taken by Germans. Seven attacks in Merville sector repulsed. Near Bailleul, British line penetrated, but position restored. E. of Robecq, British take prisoners and machine guns. **General Foch appointed Commander-in-Chief** of Allied Armies in France.	... ...	... ...
15	Fighting continues on Bailleul - Wulverghem line, and Germans capture both places. Very violent artillery action in Luce Valley (Somme).	Finland : Germans report occupation of Helsingfors.	Macedonia : Greek troops cross Struma river and occupy villages in Seres district. British troops take two villages S.W of Demirhissar.

ASIATIC AND EGYPTIAN THEATRES.	NAVAL AND OVERSEAS OPERATIONS.		POLITICAL, &c.	1918. Apr.
... ...	... ...	...	Man-Power Bill : Military service for Ireland agreed to by majority of 165. Holland : Food riots quelled by troops. Germany : Food Dictator says that no satisfactory solution of economic situation can be expected.	12
Turks occupy Batum. Sir A. A. Barrett's Gazette on Mahsud operations of 1917 published. Trans-caucasian Council break off peace negotiations with Turks.	... ...	...	Irish Convention Report published (**). South Africa : Mr. Hertzog's seditious speech, demanding separation. National Assembly of Yugo-Slavs, Croats and Slovenes at Agram take oath of solidarity.	13
... ...	... ...	...	M. Clémenceau issues statement that France does not recognise present Russian Government nor its acts. Maj. - Gen. Sykes appointed Chief of Air Staff.	14
... .	British Naval forces sink 10 German armed trawlers in Kattegat.		Austria : Count Czernin's resignation announced.	15

1918. Apr.	WESTERN FRONT.	EASTERN THEATRE.	SOUTHERN FRONT.
16	Heavy attacks develop at Wytschaete and S.W. of Vieux Berquin. Wytschaete and Meteren lost and retaken. Attacks near Bailleul repulsed. German progress on Lys river forces British withdrawal from Passchendaele. Sir Douglas Haig issues special despatch "The 55th Division at Givenchy." Heavy fighting in Boyelles district, S. of Arras.	Ukraine : Renewed fighting between Soviet troops and those of Gen. Kornilov. Ukraine Government protests against union of Bessarabia and Rumania.	... ...
17	Intense bombardment, followed by infantry attack, on whole line from Nieppe Forest to Wytschaete. Wytschaete and Meteren again lost. N.W. of Dixmude, Belgians take 700 prisoners and 42 machine guns. French repulse attacks on Meuse and in Champagne.	... ...	... ...
18	Heavy attacks from Givenchy to Lys river. Fighting particularly severe at Givenchy, where enemy make slight advance. In the N., attacks S. of Kemmel repulsed. French progress on Avre river and take 650 prisoners at Castel. Belgians repulse attack N.W. of Passchendaele.	... ...	Macedonia : Enemy detachments attack Italians in Cherna Bend and are repulsed.
19	On Scarpe river British capture prisoners and machineguns. Position restored at Givenchy. Sharp fighting at Robecq. N. of Merville heavy shelling, but no infantry attacks.	Ukraine : Germans report occupation of two stations on main Sevastopol line.	Asiago Plateau : Successful minor action. British announce Macedonia: British withdraw from positions in Struma valley occupied on 15th.

ASIATIC AND EGYPTIAN THEATRES.	NAVAL AND OVERSEAS OPERATIONS.	POLITICAL, &c.	1918. Apr.
.. ..	... ...	Military Service Bill passes House of Commons; majority 198. U.S.A.: Mr. Schwab appointed Director-General of U.S. Shipbuilding. Hungary: Dr. Wekerle (Premier) resigns. Dutch Government decides to send convoy to East Indies.	16
Transcaucasia: Turks approach Kars, and claim 250 guns at Batum.	E. Africa: War Office reports progress ([68]). British monitors bombard Ostend.	Canada: Government makes proposals for increase of man-power. ([69]). France: Gen. Belin succeeds Gen. Weygand on Supreme War Council. Bolo is executed. Austria: Baron Burian succeeds Count Czernin as Minister for Foreign Affairs. Hungarian Cabinet (Wekerle) resigns.	17
... ...	Enemy destroyers bombard Adinkerke (Belgian coast).	Military Service Bill (Man-Power) receives Royal Assent ([70]). Lt.-Gen. Sir D. Henderson resigns from Air Board. Dublin Mansion House Conference, after consultation with Bishops, denies right of Government to enforce conscription. Cape Town: In House of Assembly, Sir P. FitzPatrick denounces Mr. Hertzog for sedition. Earl of Derby appointed Ambassador to France, vice Lord Bertie. Mr. A. Chamberlain joins War Cabinet. Viscount Milner to be Secretary of State for War.	18
... ...	... ...	British Government announces right of search re Dutch Convoy of 16.4. U.S.A. State Department says American landing in Vladivostok is merely police precaution.	19

1918. Apr.	WESTERN FRONT.	EASTERN THEATRE.	SOUTHERN FRONT.		
20	Minor operations near Hébuterne, Robecq and S. of Scarpe go in favour of British. N.E. of Ypres German attempt fails. At Seicheprey (Woëvre) Germans gain partial success against French and Americans.	Finland : Details of intentions of Finnish "White Party" are published ([71]) in Stockholm.	...	...	...
21	Position at Seicheprey restored. Local fighting round Albert, Villers Bretonneux and Robecq. Great aerial activity and much bombing on whole front. German airman, Capt. von Richthofen, killed. Result of 29 days' bombardment of Paris : 118 killed, 236 injured.	... ...	...	...	...
22	Local fighting to British advantage in Albert, Robecq and Wytschaete sectors. Near Villers Bretonneux and on Ancre river, enemy concentrations are dispersed. Austrian troops reported to be arriving in Belgium.	United Diets of Baltic Provinces request German Government to form them into a monarchy under King of Prussia.	...	...	...
23	Violent artillery fire from Avre river to Albert, followed by heavy infantry attacks at Albert and in region between Somme and Avre. Paris raided by one aeroplane, which is brought down. Special despatch from Sir Douglas Haig mentions 14 divisions ([76]) ; 102 German divisions employed against British alone during great offensive.	Finland : Finnish Western White Army reported to have reached Russian frontier. Bolshevik Government again protests against union of Bessarabia and Rumania.	...	...	...

ASIATIC AND EGYPTIAN THEATRES.	NAVAL AND OVERSEAS OPERATIONS.	POLITICAL, &c.	1918. Apr.
. ...	British and German destroyers in contact in Heligoland Bight. One German destroyer damaged.	Gt. Britain : First National Emergency Proclamation, withdrawing exemptions up to 23½ years, issued. Nationalist M.P.s unanimously decide to oppose conscription; Irish Bishops support them. South Africa : Governor-General (Lord Buxton) issues warning to Nationalists.	20
... ...	... ...	Australian Roman Catholic Bishops protest against Government action in Ireland. New constitution of Versailles Council announced (⁷²). The King sends message to munition workers. Sir M. de Bunsen sent on Mission to S. America.	21
Baluchistan : India Office announces unconditional surrender of Khotran Tribe. Transcaucasian Council decides to declare independence and reopens negotiations with the Turks.	Brilliant Naval Raid on Zeebrugge and Ostend, night of 22-23 ; Zeebrugge entrance blocked by sinking ships. Blockships also sunk in Ostend Harbour (⁷³). Destroyer action in Adriatic.	Severe tension reported between Holland and Germany (⁷⁴). Germany : "Das neue Europa" publishes estimate of German losses up to 31.7.17 as exceeding 5,000,000. Mr. Bonar Law introduces the Budget (⁷⁵).	22
Palestine : War Office reports progress in Hejaz (⁷⁷). Bayazid (Armenia) occupied by Turks.	Naval aircraft bomb docks at Zeebrugge and Ostend Durazzo (Albania) bombed by Naval aircraft:—only one warship seen in harbour.	Newfoundland : Conscription Bill introduced. Japan : Viscount Motono succeeded by Baron Goto as Foreign Minister. Hungarian Premier on Emperor's letter (⁷⁶). Maj.-Gen. Bridges, Military Adviser to Lord Reading in U.S.A. Guatemala declares war on Germany.	23

1918. Apr.	WESTERN FRONT.	EASTERN THEATRE.	SOUTHERN FRONT.
24	Violent attacks on junction of British and French in Amiens sector S. of Somme; Villers—Bretonneux lost. Battle very severe at Hangard; Germans finally capture village. Attacks beaten off E. of Robecq and N.E. of Bailleul. Heavy artillery fire in Woëvre.	Manchuria: Cossacks under Col. Semenov defeat 500 armed Hungarian prisoners of war and drive them back towards Chita.	Macedonia: Lively fighting W. of Doiran and in Cherna Bend.
25	Very strong attack on British and French from Bailleul to Hollebeke. Germans reach Mt. Kemmel; Allied line forced back. S. of Somme Allies recapture Villers-Bretonneux with 600 prisoners. German tanks in action for first time. In the Woëvre, after heavy bombardment, German attack is stopped.	Finland: Germans report junction with Finnish army 30 m. N. of Helsingfors. Ukraine: Germans announced to be near Sevastopol.	In Asiago basin British patrols force enemy detachments to retire.
26	In Kemmel region, Germans occupy Kemmel Hill and village and Dranoutre after very severe fighting. Locre is lost and retaken by French. On Ypres-Comines Canal, Allied line falls back; at Voormezeele (Ypres) heavy fighting results in repulse of Germans. In Luce Valley and at Givenchy, fighting is to the advantage of the Allies. Hangard Wood recaptured.	... ...	... ...
27	In Ypres sector Voormezeele is twice attacked by Germans without success. Local fighting astride Ypres-Comines Canal.	... ...	... ...

Asiatic and Egyptian Theatres.	Naval and Overseas Operations.	Political, &c.	1918. Apr.
During past week, a 53-mile section of Hejaz railway S. of Maan effectively occupied by Arab troops.	Naval aircraft over Zeebrugge and Ostend ([79]).	Rectification of Anglo-Turkish agreement for exchange of prisoners announced. French papers publish Lichnowsky memorandum in full. Hungary: Count Serenyi tries to form Ministry; and fails next day.	24
... ...	... ...	Mr. Churchill reviews work of Ministry of Munitions. ([80]). Lord Rothermere (Air Ministry) resigns. Australia: Mr. Hughes and Mr. Cook appointed to represent Australia at War Conference. Mr. Loudon, Dutch Foreign Minister, says relations with Germany difficult. German demands for use of Limburg railway agreed to. Red Cross sale £151,000.	25
... ...	... ...	Ministry of Reconstruction issues report of Balfour Committee on commercial and industrial policy after the war.	26
Armenia: Turks report capture of Kars with 860 guns. Rapid British advance N. of Baghdad; Kifri captured.	... ...	Announcement of Sir W. Weir's appointment as Secretary of State for Royal Air Force. Independence of Georgia (Trans-Caucasia) declared by its Diet. Important War Conference at Delhi.	27

1918. Apr.	WESTERN FRONT.	EASTERN THEATRE.	SOUTHERN FRONT.
28	Germans again attack at Locre and are repulsed. Great artillery activity in Luce Valley and S. of Lassigny. Further attacks on Hangard Wood are repulsed. At Langemarck, Belgians repulse a big enemy raid. Announced that an American force has entered the line under French command on Northern battle front.	Polish Government addresses Note to Central Powers ([81]).	... ...
29	Heavy bombardment between Meteren and Voormezeele followed by violent infantry attacks by 13 Divisions; 3 British divisions repulse every attack; latter continuous; enemy losses very heavy. French at Scherpenberg (N.W. of Kemmel) and Belgians N. of Ypres are unsuccessfully attacked. French regain Locre. **End of the Battle of the Lys.**	Viborg taken by White Guards.	... ...
30	Fierce fighting in Noyon sector.	Russia: Rumoured that a counter-revolution is about to take place.	Operations during the month confined to artillery, air and patrol actions.
ay. 1	Comparative quiet on W. front. French improve their positions before Locre. U.S. troops join Amiens front.	Germans occupy Sevastopol, establish military dictatorship in Ukraine under F.M. von Eichhorn. Gen. Skoropadski proclaimed Hetman. Germans occupy Odessa.	British airmen in Balkans bomb Bulgarian aerodromes n Vardar valley.
2	Minor infantry actions. Enemy guns active on Villers-Bretonneux sector. French gains in Avre valley, seize Hill 82, between Hailles and Castel. British airmen bomb Thionville. Zeebrugge again bombed.	Ex-Tsar is removed to the Urals. Germans occupy Taganrog in Donetz region.	... ...

ASIATIC AND EGYPTIAN THEATRES.	NAVAL AND OVERSEAS OPERATIONS.	POLITICAL, &C.	1918. Apr.
British forces reach the Ak Su river (Tigris).	... ...	Senhor Sidonio Paes, Provisional President, is elected President of the Portuguese Republic.	28
British capture Tuz Khurmati (Tigris).	East Africa : British columns from coast and Lake Nyassa have forced Germans to River Lurio; other British and Portuguese columns approaching this river from the South.	France : Bonnet Rouge treason trial opens. Germany : Formation of State Grain Bureau in Ukraine announced.	29
British reach Tank river on Mosul road and capture 12 guns and 1,800 prisoners. British advance E. of Jordan to attack S. of Es Salt. Line advanced at Mezra. (Jerusalem).	Canadian Pacific liner, s.s. " Oronsa," sunk by submarine. Further prohibited area in North Sea announced for May 15th.	Mr. Ian Macpherson, Under-Secretary of State for War, appointed Vice-President of Army Council. Maj.-Gen. Harrington to be Deputy C.I.G.S.	30
British advance E. of Jordan, capture Es Salt. British mounted brigade, guarding ford at Jisr ed Damiya, attacked and compelled to fall back, leaving 9 guns.	British in E. Africa capture important convoy from Germans retreating towards Nanungu. Zeebrugge lock gates heavily bombed.	Mr. Ll. George, M. Clémenceau and Signor Orlando attend Fifth War Council in France. Further increase of U.S. Army sanctioned. France and Germany arrange for exchange of prisoners of war.	May. 1
Heavy fighting in Palestine; Turks cross Jordan at Jisr ed Damiya; attack troops holding Es Salt.	... ...	... ...	... ...	2

1918. May.	WESTERN FRONT.	EASTERN THEATRE.	SOUTHERN FRONT.
3	Quiet on front, artillery active locally. British bring down 36 enemy planes.	Germans and Finns surround and defeat Red Guard forces in S.W. Finland.	... ...
4	Germans open intense bombardment of French and British positions, from Locre and S. of Ypres; no attack develops. French make progress in Locre sector.	Germans take Sevastopol.	Activity increased on Italian front. Serbians capture and hold Bulgarian advanced positions on Dobropolye sector.
5	Artillery fire on both sides and local encounters on whole front. Our line advanced at Morlancourt between Ancre and Somme. A German long-range gun put out of action by French guns.	... ...	... ...
6	French repulse raids S. of Locre.	Russian ships bombard Germans in Mariupol Harbour (Azov). Russian Black Sea Fleet arrives at Odessa, surrenders to local authorities.	... ...
7	Rain prevents all but artillery fighting at front.	**Peace of Bukarest** signed by Rumania and Central Powers ([82]).	British successfully raid enemy trenches near Lake Doiran, on Balkan front.
8	Strong local attack by enemy between La Clytte and Voormezeele; they enter front line at certain points S. of Morlancourt. Australians push forward. Activity in Avre valley.	German forces occupy Rostov, on the Don.	In Balkans Allied airmen bomb aerodrome at Drama and cantonments at Beranci.
9	Enemy attacks in La Clytte-Voormezeele sector repulsed; French and British positions re-established. Germans gain small success at Albert. French success at Grivesnes, N.W. of Montdidier.	M. Ustemovich proclaimed President of the Ukraine.	Italians storm Monte Corno, in the Vallarsa (Upper Piave) during night; take 100 prisoners.

ASIATIC AND EGYPTIAN THEATRES.	NAVAL AND OVERSEAS OPERATIONS.	POLITICAL, &c.	1918. May.
attacked by superior forces, British withdraw from Es Salt and retire to W. of Jordan.	... ...	Mr. Ll. George returns with cheering message from Paris.	3
...	... ...	... ...	4
... ...	v. Lettow-Vorbeck defeated at Nanungu (E. Africa) by Gen. Northey's forces; enemy driven to N.E. with much loss.	Lord French appointed Lord-Lieutenant of Ireland; Mr. Ed. Shortt, Chief Secretary.	5
Turko-German delegates arrive at Batum to negotiate peace with Georgia.	... ...	... ...	6
British troops enter Kirkuk, on Baghdad-Mosul road. Turks retire towards Lesser Zab river.	... ...	**Nicaragua declares war on Germany.** Letter of Maj.-Gen. Sir F. Maurice in "Times" charging Ministers with mis-statements on the military position ([228]).	7
Operations continued on Baghdad - Mosul road. Enemy troops attacked by British airmen on Tigris, N. of Tekrit.	... ...	... ...	8
... ...	... ...	Debate in House of Commons on Gen. Maurice's letter; motion by Mr. Asquith defeated by large Government majority. Entente Trade Committee formed in Holland.	9

1918. May.	WESTERN FRONT.	EASTERN THEATRE.	SOUTHERN FRONT.
10	British eject Germans from front trench N.W. of Albert. Great activity of British bombing-machines on whole front. French improve positions N. of Kemmel village.	... ...	... ...
11	Minor local actions on front; hostile artillery active in Ancre sector.	Fighting between Bolsheviks and Anarchists in Moscow. Conflicts at Kiev between German troops and supporters of Rada. Congress of Ukraine peasants demand land, etc.	Italians retain Monte Corno against Austrian counter-attacks.
12	Quiet on all sectors; artillery duel on right bank of Meuse. Between May 6th-12th B.A.F. contingents from Dunkirk attack Zeebrugge and Ostend continuously.	In E. Siberia, Col. Semenov's forces, acting against Bolsheviks, move W. from Manchurian border towards Lake Baikal ([55]).	British airmen make raids in Balkans and bomb aerodrome at Drama. Naval base of Cattaro successfully bombed by Italians.
13	German artillery active on Lys and Somme battlefields; heavy rain throughout day. Local fighting N. of Kemmel.	... ...	Increased raids and bombing activity on Balkan front. 11 enemy planes destroyed on Italian front.
14	Germans attack on a mile front S.W. of Morlancourt; fine counter-attacks by Australians.	... ...	Great massing of enemy troops and artillery along Alpine lines and Friuli Plains for new offensive.
15	Heavy artillery fire on whole front; infantry actions locally. N. of Kemmel, French advance their line; capture a wood S. of Hailles in Avre Valley.	... ...	Reconnoitring raids on both sides along Italian front. In Balkans lively artillery actions near Lake Doiran; British airmen bomb depôts near Seres.
16	Big-gun duel still in progress; few infantry actions; successful British raid near Beaumont Hamel (Ancre river). Sharp air fights, Saarbrücken raided. Germans bomb hospitals at Hoogsbade and Calais.	... ...	... ...

Asiatic and Egyptian Theatres.	Naval and Overseas Operations.	Political, &c.	1918. May.
... ...	**Attack on Ostend ;** H.M.S. " Vindictive " filled with concrete and sunk inside harbour mouth in early hours of morning ([53]).	... ...	10
a Mesopotamia, Gen. Marshall drives Turks over Lesser Zab river at Alton Keupri, 70 miles from Mosul. Turks advance in W. Persia, occupy Uskner and Suj Bulak :—Enzeli on Caspian Sea being their objective.	British submarine sinks large cruiser U-boat in Atlantic in lat. of C. St. Vincent ; the first submarine of this type to be destroyed ([84]). Sir R. Keyes thanked by War Cabinet.	The King reviews American troops in London. Peace signed in Berlin between Finland and Turkey.	11
uccessful Arab raids on Hejaz railway line and the Turkish defences round Maan.	Italian destroyers attack enemy convoy off Durazzo ; sink a transport.	The Kaiser and Emperor Charles confer at German headquarters. Return of Mr. Montagu from India.	12
... ...	... ...	Government announce policy denouncing all commercial treaties which contain " most favoured nation " clauses ([86]).	13
... ...	Daring Italian sea-raid into military post of Pola ; enemy warship torpedoed.	First million tons of ships ordered by U.S.A. on the seas.	14
... ...	Official account of Ostend raid issued.	" Bonnet Rouge " trial ends in Paris ; Duval sentenced to death, other accused men imprisoned. Chino - Japanese Agreement signed at Pekin to ensure co-operation in Far East against German menace ([87]).	15
... ...	... ...	U.S.A. delegates received by King and Queen.	16

E

1918. May.	WESTERN FRONT.	EASTERN THEATRE.	SOUTHERN FRONT.
17	Much artillery and aerial activity along front. Metz station bombed by British airmen.	... ...	In S. Albania, Franco-Italian troops drive back Austrians W. of Koritsa and advance 12 m.
18	Successful raid by Australians W. of Morlancourt; in the night they capture Ville-sur-Ancre, take 360 prisoners, 20 machine guns. Daylight raid by B.A.F. on Cologne; 33 bombs dropped, all machines return safely.	... ...	Air fights in Upper Adriatic, W. of Pola, between Italian and Austrian seaplanes.
19	British raid S.W. of Meteren. Heavy air fighting and many bombing raids behind enemy front. Shameful bombing of British hospitals at Étaples, etc., outside war zone, by German airmen; 300 casualties. Air raid on London by over 20 Gothas; considerable damage, 49 killed, 177 injured; 5 raiders destroyed.	... ...	At Capo Sile (N.E. corner of Venetian Lagoons) Italian storming party captures and holds Austrian advanced positions.
20	French carry out successful operation E. and N.E. of Locre, 400 prisoners; also big raid near Berméricourt, penetrating enemy's third line. Local fighting N. of Albert; successful operation N.W. of Merville by a Surrey battalion. Coblenz bombed.	... ...	British airmen bomb Cattaro, return undamaged. Italian seaplanes bomb Durazzo and Lagosta (off Dalmatia).
21	Hostile counter-attack N.W. of Merville fails. Successful British raids on Lys front and Arras district. Mannheim, etc., heavily bombed by British airmen. Raid on Paris by 2 Gothas, one downed.	Increasing unrest at Kiev; acts of terrorism ineffectually repressed by Germans.	... ...

Asiatic and Egyptian Theatres.	Naval and Overseas Operations.	Political, &c.	1918. May.
ritish mounted troops occupy Fatha on Tigris, 45 miles N. of Tekrit; Turks retire N. Arab troops raid Turkish post at Wadi Jerdun (Palestine) on Hejaz railway.	... ...	Sudden arrest of about 150 Sinn Fein leaders in Ireland for plotting with Germany. "Denaturalization of Dangerous Aliens " Bill issued.	17
lexandropol (Georgia) occupied by the Turks.	... ...	Proclamation by Lord French (Ld. Lt. of Ireland) re pro-German conspiracy.	18
. ...	In East Africa Gen. Edwards occupies Nanungu without opposition; Germans retire S.W. towards Mahua.	... ...	19
.. ..	... ...	... ...	20
.. . .	General Edwards' troops come up with enemy's rearguard 9 miles S.W. of Nanungu.	... .	21

1918. May.	WESTERN FRONT.	EASTERN THEATRE.	SOUTHERN FRONT.
22	Liége and Metz railways bombed by British airmen; Mannheim again attacked. Raid attempted on Paris by about 30 German machines, but only one reaches capital.	... ...	Increased artillery fighting along Piave; an attack at Capo Sile bridgehead repulsed. Allied airmen active.
23	Infantry fighting unimportant. Successful local raids round Arras. Artillery active S. of the Avre. French raids on Kemmel front.	... ...	Infantry fighting on Italian mountain front increases; much aerial activity.
24	Many raids by both sides. British at Nieppe Forest bombed by gas shells.	Gen. Semenov makes steady progress, organising anti-Bolshevist forces in Siberia. Gen. Poole lands at Murmansk to organise N. Russia Expeditionary Force.	... ...
25	Day and night raids by British. Heavy shelling by enemy of Villers-Bretonneux area. British raid on Bruges docks.	... ...	... ...
26	No infantry actions of importance; increased artillery activity at certain points N. and S. of the Avre.	... ...	Good progress made by Italian troops in mountain passes between Lake Garda and Swiss frontier (Monticello and Adamello region).
27	Third Battle of the Aisne begins; New German thrust for Paris. After heavy bombardment enemy deliver great attack on Aisne between Soissons and Reims; Allies' line pressed back; Germans carry Chemin des Dames Ridge; smaller attack between Locre and Voormezeele. Long-range guns bombard Paris.	... ...	Italians storm Austrian positions at Capo Sile, N.E. of Venice. British air raid on Durazzo (Albania); Austrian torpedo-boat sunk.

Asiatic and Egyptian Theatres.	Naval and Overseas Operations.	Political, &c.	1918. May.
.. ..	Air-raids on Zeebrugge; a German destroyer sunk in harbour. In E. Africa British engage enemy between Nanungu and Mahua; capture guns and ammunition, drive Germans westward.	U.S.A. Sedition Bill passed, and £300,000,000 voted for ordnance.	22
ʌrabs successfully attack Turks near Abu Naam (80 miles N. of Medina).	British armed mercantile cruiser "Moldavia," carrying American troops, torpedoed and sunk in Channel; 56 lost.	Georgia (Caucasus) proclaims its independence. U. S. A. National Conscription (fight or work) after 1 July decided on.	23
.. ..	... ...	Government issues statement exposing Sinn Fein intrigues with Germany and the revolutionary movement in Ireland ([88]).	24
ʌrabs raid El Hasa and Ferafrai stations (Hejaz railway, N. of Maan).	... ...	King Albert thanks U.S.A. **Costa Rica declares war** on Germany.	25
ʌranscaucasian Federal Government dissolved. Georgia forms National Government. Armenian National Council takes charge of Armenian affairs.	H.M. Transport "Leasowe Castle" sunk in Mediterranean by enemy submarine, 101 lost. In Portuguese E. Africa Germans driven S. towards Upper Lurio river.	... ...	26
ʌatar National Council proclaims establishment of " Republic of Azerbaijan " (N. Persia).	... ...	Interesting Parliamentary Paper (Cd. 9059) published on methods used by Germany in the past to influence British trade.	27

1918. May.	WESTERN FRONT.	EASTERN THEATRE.	SOUTHERN FRONT.
28	Enemy across the Aisne on 18-m. front; battle on plateau between Aisne and Vesle, Allies fall back, Germans force passage of Vesle. Allies left and right wings make stand at Vregny plateau and heights of St. Thierry. Line restored S. of Ypres. Big British R.A.F. raids into Germany.	The Cossacks of the Don notify Ukraine Government of their opposition to the Soviets and of independence of the rest of Russia. Col. Semenov forced by Bolsheviks to retire to right bank of Onon (Mong.).	Two Austrian counter-attacks repulsed at Capo Sile. British aeroplanes bomb Cattaro.
29	Further Allied retreat. On left enemy sweep over Vregny Plateau, take Soissons; in centre gain heights S. of the Vesle, make progress towards the Marne. On right, Allied troops covering Reims fall back behind Aisne Canal. Enemy repulsed near Kemmel. Bombs on Metz and Thionville.	... ...	Artillery actions on the Doiran-Vardar front and in Serbian sector. Bad weather hampers activity.
30	French hold enemy up S. of Soissons, preventing further advance. In centre Germans capture Fère-en-Tardenois and Vezilly, increase their pressure towards Ville-en-Tardenois, reach the Marne near Jaulgonne, and gain some forts N.W. of Reims. Enemy claim capture of 35,000 prisoners and much war material. British bomb various towns on German front.	... ...	Franco-Greek success at Srka di Legen, 1,500 prisoners taken (11 miles W. of River Vardar).
31	Germans reach Marne river from Château Thierry to Dormans and advance on Compiègne. French retire from River Ailette, drive Germans E. of Sempigny, and recover Thillois (W. of Reims). British bomb Karlsruhe.	... ...	... ...

ASIATIC AND EGYPTIAN THEATRES.	NAVAL AND OVERSEAS OPERATIONS.			POLITICAL, &c.	1918. May.
vere fighting near Alexandropol (90 miles S. of Tiflis). British advance 2 miles N. from Jaffa.	...	...	...	British Government opens negotiations with Germany for direct exchange of prisoners on lines of Franco-German Convention. Further revelations of brutal treatment of our prisoners.	28
...	...	...	...	...	Report of Food Production Department issued, showing that four million acres have been added for tillage ; and that four-fifths of country's food for the year will be home-grown. U.S.A. communiqué sympathising with Czecho - Slovaks and Yugo-Slavs.	29
ritish bomb Turks at Fatha (Tigris, above Tekrit) and at junction of Lesser Zab river.	...	...	...	Publication of Chino-Japanese Note *re* military agreements ([89]).	30.
ritish bomb Turkish camps near Amman (Hejaz railway).	British destroyer sunk in collision. " Pres. Lincoln," U.S.A. transport, torpedoed. Fighting near Imagu Hills (160 miles N.E. of Blantyre).			Great fire at Constantinople for 27 hours. Dutch Government refuses to tolerate British examination of convoyed ships.	31

1918. June.	WESTERN FRONT.	EASTERN THEATRE.	SOUTHERN FRONT.
1	Germans advance down River Ourcq, taking Chouy and Neuilly St. Front. French lose and retake Fort de la Pompelle (dominating Reims-Châlons Railway, S.E. of Reims) ; French retreat between Oise and Aisne to line Carlepont Wood (S. of Noyon)—Fontenoy (N. of Soissons). German bombardment of, and raid on, Paris.	... ...	... ...
2	Violent battle on Ourcq ; Germans take and lose Longpont, Corcy, Faverolles (again retaken) and Troesnes. German attack on Château-Thierry road, S.E. of Bouresches (N.W. of Château-Thierry), repulsed. French capture Champlat (12 miles S.W. of Reims). Fierce fight at Choisy Hill, S. of Noyon. **End of Third Battle of the Aisne.**	Defeat of Bolsheviks by Semenov in E. Siberia.	... ...
3	Choisy Hill retaken by French. Germans capture Pernant (W. of Soissons). French check German attempts to enter Forest of Villers-Cotterets, re-capture Faverolles. French and Americans force Germans back over Marne at Jaulgonne (N. E. of Château-Thierry).	Retreat of Semenov on Borsia (120 miles from Karimskaya on Siberian Railway).	... ...
4	Germans capture Veuilly-la-Poterie (half-way between Ourcq and Château-Thierry). Americans check Germans at Veuilly Wood.	Ukraine Government recognised by Central Powers.	... ...

Asiatic and Egyptian Theatres.	Naval and Overseas Operations.	Political, &c.	1918. June.
Withdrawal of British in Kirkuk area (E. of Tigris, between Mosul and Baghdad).	Germans retreat in E. Africa, crossing River Lurio (to E. of S. end of Lake Nyassa). Fighting near Imagu Hills (160 miles N.E. of Blantyre, Nyassaland).	... ...	1
. ...	U.S.A. have 150 vessels in European waters.	Publication in *Politiken* (Swedish Socialist paper) of Secret Convention between Germany and Finland ([90]).	2
British air raid on Amman (on Hejaz railway, 25 miles N.E. of Jericho).	German retreat in E. Africa ; Germans dislodged from crossings of Upper Lurio. German submarines off New Jersey (U.S.A.) sink vessels.	British Government admits recognition of Czecho-Slovak aims ([91]). Declaration of Premiers of Great Britain, France and Italy at Versailles *re* Poles, Czecho-Slovaks and Yugo-Slavs ([92]). Proclamation of Lord French *re* Irish recruiting ([93]).	3
British air raid on Amman.	... ...	M. Cooreman succeeds Baron de Brogneville as Belgian P.M. M. Clémenceau praises armies of French and Allies. German article on main Continental idea ([94]). Renewal of Anglo-American Arbitration Treaty.	4

1918. June.	WESTERN FRONT.	EASTERN THEATRE.	SOUTHERN FRONT.
5	Near Vingre (N.W. of Soissons) German attempt to cross Aisne checked. German attacks at Longpont (N. of Forest of Retz) and at Chezy (S. of Ourcq) defeated by French. Sir W.R. Robertson appointed to command of British home forces.	... ...	... ...
6	Germans capture village and height of Bligny (S.W. of Reims) ; height re-taken by British ; Counter-attacks by Allies, especially in region nearest to Paris. Gotha raid on Paris ; Third British air-raid on Coblenz.	Capture of Gurks (93 miles N.E. of Borsia on Kharbin - Karimskaya Railway) by Semenov.	... ...
7	French and Americans capture Veuilly-la-Poterie and Vinly (W. of Château Thierry), Bouresches and Hill 204 (W. of Château-Thierry). British regain Bligny.	Kern (N. Russia) occupied by Entente forces. Omsk (Siberia) taken by Czecho-Slovaks.	... ...
8	... ...	Bolshevik Government orders Entente forces in the N. to leave the country.	... ...
9	First Battle of Lassigny begins. New German offensive from between Montdidier and Noyon towards Compiègne. Germans enter Thiescourt Wood (S.W. of Noyon) and Ressons-sur-Matz ; are checked on line Mortemer-Cuvilly.	... ...	... ...

ASIATIC AND EGYPTIAN THEATRES.	NAVAL AND OVERSEAS OPERATIONS.	POLITICAL, &c.	1918. June.
... ...	British armed boarding-steamer torpedoed and sunk by German submarine.	Speech of Count Tisza in Hungarian Diet *re* Dual Alliance extension ([95]). Madsen machine-gun debate in House of Commons. General Robertson C.i.C. Home Defences.	5
... ...	" Koningen Regentes," Hospital Ship accompanying British delegates to Hague, torpedoed—4 lost.	... ...	6
... ...	... ...	Installation of Signor Avezzano as Italian Minister at Athens : friendly speech.	7
Arab raid on Hejaz railway near Toweira (105 miles N.W. of Medina) ; British advance N. of Jaffa. Germans land at Poti (N. of Batum.)	" Pinar del Rio " (American steamer) sunk by U-boat off Maryland.	Prisoners of War Conference at the Hague opens ([96]). Arrival in London of Sir R. Borden and Mr. W. Massey (Canadian and New Zealand Premiers). Georgians and Armenians sign peace treaties with Turkey.	8
... ...	Commander Rizzo torpedoes and sinks Austrian Dreadnought " Szent Istvan " off Premuda Island, Dalmatia.	Speech of President Wilson to Mexican Mission ([97]).	9

1918. June.	WESTERN FRONT.	EASTERN THEATRE.	SOUTHERN FRONT.
10	German advance on Compiègne. On E. French withdraw from Carlepont Wood on Ribécourt. In centre Germans take heights of Marquéglise and reach Antheuil. French retreat on River Aronde, re-capture Méry. Courcelles (S.E. of Montdidier) taken by Germans, retaken by French. Bombardment of Paris by long-range gun continues. Australians advance S. of Morlancourt (between Ancre and Somme).	Retreat of Col. Semenov in Siberia.	French carry Mt. Kami (S.W. of Lake Ochrida and villages of Streks and Proptisti.
11	Check to German advance. Successful French counter-attack from Rubescourt to St. Maur; re-capture of Belloy. Germans driven out of Antheuil. Americans capture Belleau Wood (W. of Château-Thierry).	Soviet delegates arrive in Berlin. Czecho-Slovaks in control of Siberian Railway between Cheliabinsk and Nizhni-Udinsk (W. of Irkutsk); Bolsheviks retreat to Slatust. Czechs threaten Samara (on Volga).	... ...
12	French advance near Belloy and St. Maur; Germans cross Matz, enter Mélicocq (S. of Lassigny). Americans capture Belleau Wood (Nancy). German advance on Cutry plateau (Villers-Cotterets). 700,000 U.S. soldiers reported in France.	... ...	... ...
13	Germans gain footing on edge of Forest of Villers-Cotterets; otherwise held up. **End of First Battle of Lassigny.**	Fighting at Irkutsk (Siberia) between Red and White Guards.	Austrian attack again Cady summit and Mon cello ridge (N. and S. Tonale Pass, W. Tren defeated by Italians.
14	British successful midnight attack N. of Béthune along La Bassée Canal. General Guillaumont appointed Military Governor of Paris.	... ...	... ...

Asiatic and Egyptian Theatres.	Naval and Overseas Operations.	Political, &c.	1918. June.
ccessful British raid on Turks N. of Kefr Malik (between Shechem Road and Jordan Valley).	... ...	International Seamen's Congress at Copenhagen forms International Federation; Mr. Havelock Wilson, President, Mr. Damm (Dane), Secretary. Officially stated that between May 15th and June 1st Germans had bombed hospitals on seven occasions, with resulting loss of 248 killed and 693 wounded.	10
itish air raid on Amman.	... ...	Bill for new Constitution of Finland presented to Finland Diet ([98]). Speech of von Stein *re* military position ([99]).	11
flis, capital of Georgia, occupied by Germans; Kurdamir (Transcauc.) and Ujari (N. Persia) occupied by Turks.	Allies enter Malema (Portuguese E. Africa). Germans retreat to River Ligonya.	1st Meeting of Imperial War Conference ([100]). Warm speech of Mr. Balfour *re* Japan. Czecho-Slovak movement recognised also by France and Italy.	12
... ...	British armed cruiser "Patia" torpedoed and sunk by German submarine.	... ...	13
rkish capture of Tabriz (N.W. Persia) reported; they repulse British on Hejaz line (Maan region, S. of Dead Sea).	... ...	Inadequate majority in Finnish Diet for bill to establish monarchy. Protocol of agreement between Don and Kuban Cossack Governments. Provisional Treaty between Russia and Ukraine ([101]).	14

1918. June.	WESTERN FRONT.	EASTERN THEATRE.	SOUTHERN FRONT.
15	German air-raid on Paris. French regain Cœuvres (Villers-Cotterets).	... ...	**Second battle of the Pia** begins. **Great Austri** offensive from **Lagari** Valley to sea; British li in Asiago section pe trated and restored. Grappa front Austria gain footing in Mts. Val Bella, Asolone a Solarolo, and are eject Austrians cross the m dle Piave in Nervesa a Fagare-Musile regions
16	... ...	... ...	Violent fighting on Pia Austrians capture grou S.E. of Montello a Capo Sile (N.E. Venice). British che Austrian advance the hills.
17	Aeroplane raid on Kent; no damage.	... ...	Italians and French ca ture Razea Pizzo a heights S.E. of Sas (Asiago). In Grap region Allies gain grou On Lower Piave (b tween S. Andrea a Fossalto) Italians pulse Austrian attemp to cross.
18	French repulse German at- tack on Reims front from Sillery (S. of La Pompelle Fort) to Trigny (7 miles W. of Reims).	... ...	Piave in flood. Austri attempts to cro between S. Andr and Candelu repulse Italians recapture Ca Sile.
19	... ...	Reported overthrow of Bolshevist Government in W. Siberia. Anti- Bolshevist Government set up at Nizhni-Udinsk (330 miles N.W. Lake Baikal). Tomsk taken by Anti-Bolsheviks.	Allies regain initiativ furious fighting fr Montello to sea; A trian lines on Monte thrown back; On Asia Plateau French captu Mts. Bertigo and Pe nar; Italians captu Mt. Costalunga.

Asiatic and Egyptian Theatres.	Naval and Overseas Operations.	Political, &c.	1918. June.
... ...	Germans retreat in E. Africa at Alto Mulocue (225 miles W. of Port of Mozambique).	Formation of Committee of Ministers for Home Affairs under Chairmanship of Sir G. Cave.	15
British air raid on El Kutrani on Hejaz railway (30 miles E. of S. end of Dead Sea). Yekaterinenfeld (Tiflis) occupied by Germans.	... ...	Bulgarian Cabinet (M. Radoslavov) resigns ; M. Malinov becomes Premier: **beginning of the end foreshadowed.**	16
.. ..	... ...	Disturbances and partial strike in Vienna, etc., *re* reduced bread ration.	17
British air raid on Amman. German troops land at Poti (Black Sea, 35 miles N. of Batum).	Dutch Government sends to investigate cause of loss of " Koningen Regentes." Germans in retreat reach Mujebu (80 miles N. of Quilimane, Portuguese E. Africa). Russian battleship " Svobodnaya Rossiya " destroyed in Black Sea to avoid surrender to Germans.	Arrival of Prince Arthur of Connaught in Japan. Vote of credit for £500 million. Publication of Secret Treaty between Bolsheviks and Germans *re* Poland ([102]). Publication of Agreement between Entente and Sweden ([103]).	18
.. ..	British squadron in N. of Heligoland Bight attacked by German seaplanes. 1 German seaplane destroyed.	M. Malinov becomes Foreign Minister. Decision *re* Finnish Monarchy postponed till 1920. Report of British Sub-Committee of Re-construction Committee *re* increase of home-grown food ([104]). Swiss Government adopts project of subvention of port at Basle.	19

1918. June.	WESTERN FRONT.	EASTERN THEATRE.	SOUTHERN FRONT.
20	... ...	... ...	Italian advance continue in Montello, Fagare an Zenson (Lower Piave sectors. Austrian line a Cortelazzo (mouth o Piave) broken. Nerves re-captured.
21	... ...	... ...	Italians enlarge bridge head at Cavazuccherin (near mouth of Piave) Austrian attempts t regain initiative i Montello and Grapp regions checked ; 12,00 prisoners to date.
22	Enemy attack on Bligny (Reims) repulsed.	Appeal of General Horvath to Allies for help against German invasion.	Piave in flood ; Austria retreat across Piav begins.
23	British line on Lys front advanced S.W. of Meteren.	... ...	Austrians in disordere retreat from Montello t the sea ; heavy losses **End of Second Battle o the Piave.**
24	... ...	... ...	Right bank of Piav cleared of Austrians Italians attack Austrian N.W. of M. Grapp without much success Further 8,000 prisoners

Asiatic and Egyptian Theatres.	Naval and Overseas Operations.	Political, &c.	1918. June.
... ...	Appointment of General Northey as Governor and Commander-in-Chief of E. African Protectorate and High Commissioner for Zanzibar Protectorate.	Re-establishment of Civil Law Courts in occupied territory of Palestine. Publication of Lord Grey's "League of Nations" [105]; Report of Shipping Committee [106]; Speech of Lord Curzon re Ireland [107]; Speech of Mr. Balfour re peace [108]; Reception of Sir M. De Bunsen's Mission by President of Chile. Food riots in Vienna. Refusal of passport to M. Troelstra (Dutch Socialist leader) to visit England.	20
.. ..	... ...	Food crisis in Vienna eased; Empire gathering in London. Von Kühlmann on the Balkans [109]. Mr. Balfour censures Pacifists. Labour Ministers' Manifesto [110]. Lord Curzon announces abandonment of Home Rule and conscription in Ireland for the present.	21
Turkish attack at El Haza (N. Hejaz) repulsed.	... ...	Turkish war aims published [111].	22
.. ..	... ...	Resignation of von Seidler (Austrian Premier); Anglo-American Union proposed by Lord Reading.	23
.. ..	... ...	Speeches of Mr. Lloyd George in House of Commons [112] and of von Kühlmann, on the situation [113]. Emperor Charles refuses resignation of von Seidler. Appeal of Irish Recruiting Council: Irish overseas aghast at inaction in Ireland.	24

F

1918. June.	WESTERN FRONT.	EASTERN THEATRE.	SOUTHERN FRONT.
25	American success near Belleau Wood. British air attacks on Saarbrücken, Offenburg (13 miles S.E. of Strassburg) and Karlsruhe.	M. Markiewicz (Socialist) forms cabinet in Ukraine, vice M. Lyshub resigned.	Italians take bridge-head of Capo Sile.
26	British take point W. of Vieux Berquin (10½ miles W. of Armentières). German air-raid on Paris.	Peace Treaty between Germany and Finland ratified.	... ...
27	Air-raid on Paris, 11 killed, 14 injured.	650 newly-elected members of Soviet enrolled. ([116]).	... ...
28	French capture Cutry Plateau. British success E. of Forest of Nieppe (N.W. of Béthune). Another air-raid on Paris.	... ...	... ...
29	French, S. of River Ourcq, carry hill between Mosloy and Passy-en-Valois.	Provisional Government proclaimed at Vladivostok (some members remaining at Tomsk).	... ...
30	Two air-raids on Paris. French success between Marne and Ourcq. German attack on British near Merris (River Lys) repulsed; British success N.W. of Albert.	Murman Council decides to support Entente against Bolsheviks.	Italians capture Monte d Val Bello and Col del Rosso (Asiago). 2,000 prisoners.
July. 1	French capture St. Pierre Aigle (village N.W. of Forest of Villers-Cotterets). Americans capture Vaux (W. of Château-Thierry). British air raids on Mannheim, Coblenz, Thionville and Trèves.	... ...	Italians gain positions in N.W. of Monte Grappa

Asiatic and Egyptian Theatres.	Naval and Overseas Operations.	Political, &c.	1918. June.
...	...	Speech of Chief Secretary for Ireland in House of Commons ([114]).	25
...	...	Labour Conference in London ([115]). House of Lords approves principle of League of Nations. Strike of aircraft workers.	26
...	Hospital ship "Llandovery Castle" torpedoed S.W. of Fastnet—all boats (except one) rammed and sunk: 244 lost. Four British destroyers fight eight German ones: no damage received.	Agreement between Sweden, Finland and Germany for abolition of forts on Aaland Islands. Yugo-Slav deputation at Rome ([117]). Mr. Hughes in London. Chamber of Commerce declares for abandonment of policy of open door. Speech of M. Kerenski at Labour Conference, London.	27
Arabs capture Kalaat el Almar (200 miles N. of Medina) from Turks.	...	2nd U.S.A. communiqué in favour of deliverance of all Slavs from German or Austro-Hungarian rule.	28
...	...	...	29
...	...	...	30
			July.
...	U.S. transport "Corrington" torpedoed and sunk, 6 lost. Five British aeroplanes bomb Austrian base at Cattaro. (Portuguese E. Africa): Germans under Lettow-Vorbeck fight British and Portuguese at Nhamacurra (26 miles N. of Quilimane).	Appointment of five M.P.'s to investigate Alien question and to advise action to be taken. Publication of Mr. Lloyd George's reply to deputation of Federalists ([119]). Serious explosion at shell factory in Midlands, 100 killed, 150 injured.	1

1918. July.	WESTERN FRONT.	EASTERN THEATRE.	SOUTHERN FRONT.
2	Germans re-capture ground N.W. of Albert. French advance N. of River Aisne near Moulin sous Touvent (N.W. of Soissons). 1,019,115 U.S. troops embarked for France up-to-date : 291 lost at sea.	... ...	Successful Italian attack on Austrians in Piave delta begins—1,900 prisoners.
3	French advance N. of Aisne between Autrèches on E. and Moulin sous Touvent on W.; 1,000 prisoners.	Germans prepare to advance on Murman railway. New Provisional Government established at Vladivostok ([121]).	... ...
4	Australians and Americans re-capture village of Hamel and Vaire Wood (E. of Amiens).	Czecho - Slovaks defeat Bolsheviks near Nikolaievsk (50 miles N. of Vladivostok) and occupy the town.	Continued Italian advance in Piave delta and on Grappa front.
5	Australians advance line N.E. of Villers-Bretonneux (S.E. of Amiens).	... ...	French and Italian offensive in S. Albania begins.
6	... ...	Cossacks fight Bolsheviks N.W. of Nikolsk (between Vladivostok and Khabarovsk) and Czecho - Slovaks take Nikolsk. Assassination of Count Mirbach (German Ambassador at Moscow).	Piave delta cleared of Austrians by 23rd Italian Corps; 21,000 men and 63 guns, etc., taken by Italians since 15.6.
7	Australian advance continued on each side of River Somme. German air-raid on ambulance park at La Panne (village behind Yser); 43 girls killed.	Czecho-Slovaks defeat Bolsheviks near Chita (E. of Irkutsk).	Italians attack on Middle and Lower Vojusa (S. Albania).

ASIATIC AND EGYPTIAN THEATRES.		NAVAL AND OVERSEAS OPERATIONS.			POLITICAL, &c.	1918. July.
.	...	...	...	...	Opening of International Commercial Conference at Westminster. Establishment of (British) Central Council of Agriculture. Statement of General Botha *re* military and police measures ([119]). Publication of Austrian Socialists' Declaration *re* Peace ([120]).	2
••	...	...	Retreat of Germans at Nhamacurra.		Proclamation of Sinn Fein as dangerous organisation. Death of Lord Rhondda (British Food Controller). Death of Mohammed V., Sultan of Turkey; succeeded by Mohammed VI. (Vahided-Din).	3
.	...	...	...	...	British Government reiterates British right of search, but waives it *re* Dutch Convoy to E. Indies ([122]). American Independence Day Celebrations ([123]). Proclamation at Constantinople of Vahid-ed-Din as Sultan.	4
••	...	...	Dutch Government accepts conditions *re* convoy; Convoy sails.		Treaty of Bukarest passes Reichstag.	5
••	...	...	...	...	Publication of Montagu–Chelmsford Report *re* Indian Constitutional Reforms ([124]). U.S. first large aeroplane launched near New York. Silver Wedding of Their Majesties.	6
••	...	...	...	...	Agreement between Great Britain, U.S., France and Murman Council *re* Allied help.	7

1918. July.	WESTERN FRONT.	EASTERN THEATRE.	SOUTHERN FRONT.
8	Successful French attack N.W. of Longpont (W. of Villers - Cotterets); 346 prisoners.	Czecho - Slovaks occupy Irkutsk. Declaration of aims to Allies by Siberian Government.	Italians win passage of Vojusa and occupy Fieri (20 miles N. E. of Valona); French and Italians threaten Berat (N.E. of Valona).
9	... ...	Bolsheviks take Sizran and Bulgulma, and reach Stavropol (N.W. of Sa-mara). Martial law at Moscow.	Successful Italian progress in Albania.
10	French capture whole of Courcy (village E. of Villers-Cotterets).	General Horvath (Czecho-Slovak Commander) establishes new Siberian Government at Grode-kovo (N.W. of Vladi-vostok) ([125]).	Italians occupy Berat (Albania).
11	Successful Australian raid near Merris (N. of River Lys). 74 British air-raids in Germany during June announced.	... ...	... ...
12	... ...	Announcement of Allied force on Murman coast. Czecho-Slovaks capture Kazan (on River Volga); Czecho-Slovaks control Siberian Railway E. of Penza.	French advance on both sides of River Devoli (S. Albania); Austrians retreat.
13	... ...	... ...	French General Gramat appointed C. of S. to Greek Army.
14	... ...	... ...	French capture Austrian positions on River De-voli (Albania).

Asiatic and Egyptian Theatres.	Naval and Overseas Operations.	Political, &c.	1918. July.
... ...	British monitors aid Italian advance on Lower Vojusa.	Report of five M.P.'s *re* enemy aliens, recommending stricter treatment. H. of C. prolongs life of Parliament to 30.1.19.	8
... ...	Announced that ships lost ·homeward bound to U.K. since 1.1.18 rather more than 1 per cent.	Salzburg Conference opens *re* economic relations of Central Powers. Resignation of von Kühlmann (German Foreign Secretary); succeeded by Admiral von Hintze. Appointment of Mr. J. R. Clynes, M.P., as (British) Food Controller.	9
... ...	"Carpathia" s.s. (Cunard Liner) torpedoed and sunk in Atlantic, W. of Ireland, 5 lost.	Mr. Asquith on President Wilson and League of Nations.	10
... ...	U.S. supply ship "Westover" torpedoed and sunk in European waters, 10 lost.	Count Hertling in Committee of Reichstag on foreign policy; to be unchanged ([126]). British Government announces stricter treatment of enemy aliens to be adopted.	11
... ...	Japanese battleship "Kawachi" blown up and sunk in Tokuyama Bay, 500 casualties.	Count Hertling in Reichstag on Belgium as a pawn. Prussian Upper House expels Prince Lichnowsky. Mr. Hughes (Australian Premier) *re* Pacific islands ([127]). Denaturalisation Bill passes first and second reading in Commons.	12
Turks attack British positions on Jordan and on Abu Tellul ridges (7 miles N. of Jericho).	... ...	Haiti declares war on Germany.	13
Defeat of Turks at passages of Jordan and on Abu Tellul ridges, 510 prisoners.	... ...	Provisional agreement between British and German delegates to Hague *re* Prisoners of War ([128]).	14

1918. July.	Western Front.	Eastern Theatre.	Southern Front.		
15	**Second Battle of the Marne** begins. Great German offensive on front of 50 miles E. and W. of Reims, from Château-Thierry on W. to Main de Massiges on E. On E. Germans held in check. On W. Germans penetrate 2 or 3 miles on 20-mile front; cross Marne between Dormans and Fossoy (W. of Château-Thierry). Americans repulse Germans at Vaux.	...	...	...	...
16	S. of Dormans French and Americans counter-attack and take villages of St. Agneau and La Chapelle. Germans advance up Marne to Montvoison (7 miles from Épernay).	**Ex - Tsar Nicholas and family shot** at Ekaterinburg, capital of Red Ural, by order of Ural Regional Council ([129]).	...	...	...
17	E. of Reims French defeat Germans S. of Prunay. S.W. of Reims French retake and lose Montvoisin. S.E. of Villers-Bretonneux. Australians advance line. 30 German divisions engaged.	...	...	...	...
18	**High-water mark of the War.** Great Allied counter attack on 27-mile front between Fontenoy (6½ miles N.W. of Soissons) and Belleau (6 miles N.W. of Château - Thierry). French reach Mont de Paris (1 mile from Soissons) and 5 miles of Crise Valley, E. of Buzancy. S. of Ourcq, French and Americans secure line Marizy – Hautvesnes – Belleau. S. of Marne Germans reach St. Agneau. E. of Reims French retake Prunay and defeat Prussian Guard E. of Prosnes. Aeroplane raid on Kent; no casualties.	...	...	...	...

ASIATIC AND EGYPTIAN THEATRES.	NAVAL AND OVERSEAS OPERATIONS.	POLITICAL, &c.	1918. July.
... ...	British transport " Barunga " sunk by German submarine. French transport " Djemnah " torpedoed and sunk in Mediterranean, 442 lost.	Field-Marshal Conrad von Hötzendorf (Austria) placed on retired list.	15
... ...	... ...	Trial of M. Malvy, former French Minister of Interior, on charge of treason.	16
... ...	... ...	General Pershing, commanding U.S. Army, made G.C.B., and Generals Bliss and March G.C.M.G.	17
... ...	... ...	Debate in Reichsrat re " German Course " of Austrian policy ([130]). Japanese Diplomatic Council approves U.S.'s proposal for intervention in Siberia.	18

1918. July.	WESTERN FRONT.	EASTERN THEATRE.	SOUTHERN FRONT.		
19	French and Americans advance on Soissons-Thierry line, taking Vierzy (N. of Ourcq) and Neuilly St. Front (S. of Ourcq). S. of Marne, French re-take Montvoison. British capture Meteren (W. of Bailleul), taking 300 prisoners.	...	...	... ...	... ...
20	Germans re-cross Marne. 20,000 prisoners and 400 guns since 18th. British French and Italians advance in Ardre valley. in Bois de Courton, and towards St. Euphraise. Aeroplane raid on Kent; no damage.	...	...	... ...	... ...
21	French recapture Château-Thierry. Allied progress in Ardre valley continued; Bois de Courton captured.	...	...	... ...	... ...
22	Allies hold German counter-attacks between Ourcq and Marne, and cross Marne near Dormans at Chassons and Passy. Germans in retreat. General Gouraud reoccupies former positions between the Suippe river and Massiges.	...	...	Allied offensive in Albania checked.	
23	British take Marfaux (S.W. of Reims). French and Americans continue advance N. and S. of Ourcq, reaching Oulchy la Ville and occupying Bois du Châtelet. N. of Montdidier French occupy Mailly - Raineval, Sauvillers and Aubervillers.	Appointment of Herr Helfferich (German ex-Minister of Interior) as Ambassador at Moscow. Siberian Government at Vladivostok resigns; Proclamation of Siberian Government Council ([133]).	...	...	...

ASIATIC AND EGYPTIAN THEATRES.	NAVAL AND OVERSEAS OPERATIONS.	POLITICAL, &c.	1918. July.
.. ..	British airmen, supported by detachment of Grand Fleet, bomb Zeppelin base near Tondern (Schleswig - Holstein). French liner "Australien" (Messageries Maritimes) torpedoed in Mediterranean, 20 lost. U.S. armoured cruiser "San Diego" sunk off Fire Island, off New York, 6 lost. "Justicia" (White Star Liner) torpedoed off N. coast of Ireland, 10 lost.	**Honduras declares War on Germany.** British Ministerial changes ([131]). Admiral Sims made G.C.M.G. Statement of Lord R. Cecil *re* Allies Trade Policy ([132]). Denaturalisation Bill read third time in Commons. Sedition Committee Report (Rowlatt) published in India.	19
.. ..	British destroyer "Marne" sinks German submarine attacking "Justicia"; "Justicia" sinks after long fight.	Mr. Balfour replies to Hertling's "pawn" speech. Threatening meeting of munitionworkers at Birmingham.	20
.. ..	Portuguese E. Africa: battle between British and Germans at Namirrue (near confluence of Rivers Namirrue and Ligonya).	Appeal of Ministry of Munitions to workers not to strike during critical battle.	21
.. ..		Dr. von Seidler resigns Austrian Premiership. Resignation of Lord Lee as Director - General of Food Production.	22
.. ..	Retreat of Germans at Namirrue. British armed mercantile cruiser "Marmora" torpedoed and sunk by German submarine, 100 lost.	Munition-workers' strike at Coventry. Mr. Herbert Hoover (U.S. Food Controller) at Mansion House, London. King visits Grand Fleet.	23

1918. July.	WESTERN FRONT.	EASTERN THEATRE.	SOUTHERN FRONT.
24	French and Americans advance S. of Ourcq towards Fère-en-Tardenois and along Marne in Forest of Fère (between Chartèves and Jaulgonne).	... ...	Successful French and Italian fighting in Albania.
25	Allies advance continued. French re-take Main de Messiges (E. of Reims). Allies take Villemontoire (6 miles S. of Soissons), Oulchy-le-Château (N. of River Ourcq) and S. half of Forest of Fère.	Czecho-Slovaks capture Simbirsk (corn granary on W. bank of Volga, 130 miles from Samara).	... ...
26	General retreat of Germans on Marne towards Épernay. Partial capture of Buzancy by Scottish Division.	French troops join the N. Russian Expeditionary Force at Murmansk.	... ...
27	General German retreat N. of Marne; Cavalry pursue. Allied troops reach line Bruyères-Chaumuzy. (Bruyères 3 miles W. of Fère-en-Tardenois. Chaumuzy on River Ardre, S.W. of Reims).	... ...	... ...
28	French advance, occupying Fère-en-Tardenois; British re-take Montagne de Bligny (Ardre valley).	... ...	... ...
29	German positions N. of Oulchy-le-Château stormed. French capture Grand Rozoy. French and British capture Buzancy. Australians capture Merris and advance in Morlancourt sector, S. of Albert.	... ...	... ...

Asiatic and Egyptian Theatres.	Naval and Overseas Operations.	Political, &c.	1918. July.
... ...	... ...	Dr. von Hussarek, Austrian Premier. General Smuts in London *re* future of S. Africa. Birmingham munition-workers' strike. Scheme of Imperial Preference adopted.	24
... ...	... ...	Speech of Mr. Lloyd George at dinner to Food Controllers of France, Italy and U.S.A. Mr. Balfour at inauguration of Yugo-Slav National War Aims Committee. Conference of National Engineering and Allied Trades' Council decides for strike if no settlement before July 30.	25
... ...	... ...	Japan accepts U.S.'s proposals for joint action in Siberia on behalf of Czecho-Slovaks. Government warning to munition-workers : After 29th, alternative is return to work or military service.	26
... ...	... ...	Mr. Montagu, Secretary of State for India, on Indian Constitutional Reform ([134]).	27
... ...	... ...	... ...	28
... ...	... ...	Munition-workers' strike at end.	29

1918. July.	Western Front.	Eastern Theatre.	Southern Front.
30	Strong German resistance all along line. At St. Euphraise (S. W. of Reims) German counter-attack fails. Remigny captured.	Murder of F.M. von Eichhorn (German Military dictator in Ukraine) at Kiev.	... ...
31	Severe fighting round Seringes (N. E. of Fère-en-Tardenois) ; finally left to Americans.	... ...	... ...
Aug. 1	Allies advance on Ourcq, on N. reaching line Cramoiselle-Cramaille (N.W. of Fère-en-Tardenois), on S. taking Cierges (S.E. of Fère-en-Tardenois). French capture Romigny (S.W. of Reims).	**Allied forces land at Archangel** and capture defences.	... ...
2	French re-take Soissons. Germans retreating to River Vesle.	Pro-Entente revolution in Archangel.	... ...
3	Allies reach Fismes (on River Vesle), and re-take 50 villages. Germans retreat behind River Ancre from Hamel (N. of Albert) to Dernancourt (S. of Albert).	**British force lands at Vladivostok.**	... ...
4	Americans take Fismes ; Allies on right bank of Vesle. **End of second battle of the Marne.**	General Kirchbach takes command at Kiev.	... ...
5	Five German airships attack E. Anglia : no casualties. One brought down in flames 40 miles from land.	... ...	... ...

ASIATIC AND EGYPTIAN THEATRES.	NAVAL AND OVERSEAS OPERATIONS.	POLITICAL, &c.	1918. July.
... ...	... ...	Onondaga Indians declare war on Germany.	30
... ...	... ...	Lord R. Cecil accepts recommendations of Royal Commission on F. O. Reforms ([135]). Lord Lansdowne's letter *re* conditions of Peace discussions. Speech of Mr. Lloyd George to Manufacturers ([136]). Sir Charles W. Fielding appointed D.G. of Food Production.	31
... ...	... ...	Speech of Mr. Balfour on League of Nations.	Aug. 1
Turks occupy Urmia, N.W. Persia.	... ...	Japanese Government decides to act with U.S.A. in sending troops to Vladivostok.	2
... ...	British Ambulance transport "Warilda," homeward bound, torpedoed and sunk, 123 lost.	... ...	3
... ...	... ...	... ...	4
... ...	... ...	Message of Mr. Lloyd George to British Empire to "Hold Fast." U.S.A. Man-Power Bill introduced into Congress; military age from 18 to 45.	5

1918. Aug.	WESTERN FRONT.	EASTERN THEATRE.	SOUTHERN FRONT.
6	Germans attack S. of Morlancourt (S. of Albert), re-taking part of Australian gains. General Foch promoted Marshal of France.	... ...	... ...
7	... ...	... ...	... ...
8	**Second and decisive Battle of Amiens begins.** Great Franco-British advance (British 4th and French 1st Armies) on Amiens front from Morlancourt to Montdidier. General line advanced to Plessier-Rozainvillers, Beaucourt, Caix, Framerville, Chipilly, and W. of Morlancourt.	... ...	... ...
9	**Second battle of Lassigny begins.** British occupy Morlancourt and reach Lihons (2 miles from Chaulnes). French 3rd Army advances on Montdidier from N. and S., capturing Assainvillers (on S.) and Pierrepont (on N.).	News of arrest of Messrs. Lockhart (British Consul-General at Moscow) and Wardrop (British Consul) by Bolsheviks.	Italian air raid on Vienna dropping leaflets, not bombs.
10	French retake Montdidier.	... ...	... ...
11	Allied advance between River Avre and River Oise reaches line Armancourt (S.W. of Roye), Tilloy, Cambronne (between Matz and Oise); British air raid on Karlsruhe.	1st Japanese contingents arrive at Vladivostok. Semenov defeats Bolsheviks N. of Manchuria Station. Arrival of German Embassy (Helfferich) from Moscow at Pskov.	... ...
12	**Close of battle of Amiens. German General Staff loses heart**	... ...	... ...

ASIATIC AND EGYPTIAN THEATRES.	NAVAL AND OVERSEAS OPERATIONS.	POLITICAL, &c.	1918. Aug.
.. ..	... ...	Speech of Mr. Montagu on Indian Constitutional Reform ([131]). M. Malvy sentenced to five years' banishment. Czechs, Yugo-Slavs, some Poles vote against Austrian Budget. Retirement of Herren Ballin and Holtzendorff from Council of Central Europe.	6
.. ..	French cruiser " Dupetit Thouars " torpedoed in Atlantic, 13 lost.	Mr. Lloyd George on War position([138]).	7
.. ..	... ...	(British) Education Act receives Royal Assent. Reply of Mr. Balfour in Commons to Pacifists ([139]).	8
... ...	... ...	Declaration (dated 6.8) of British Government to Peoples of Russia published ([140]). Appeal of Executive of Miners' Federation of Great Britain to miners to increase output of coal by avoiding unnecessary absenteeism.	9
... ...	... ...	... ...	10
... ...	Off W. Frisian coast fight between British naval light forces and aircraft and German aircraft; German airship burnt N. of Island of Ameland; 6 British motor-boats lost.	... ...	11
... ...	... ...	Speech of Sr. Giolitti on reconstruction after War.	12

G

1918. Aug.	Western Front.	Eastern Theatre.	Southern Front.		
13	French capture Belval (1½ miles S. from Lassigny).	Appeal of General Dieterichs to Allied Naval and Military Commanders at Vladivostok for help. Release of Messrs. Lockhart and Wardrop.	...	...	...
14	**German retreat from River Ancre begins:** evacuation of Beaumont-Hamel, Serre, Puisieux, Bucquoy. N. of Oise French capture Ribécourt. On Lys salient British establish posts S. and E. of Vieux Berquin (6 miles E.S.E. of Hazelbrouck).	...	...	...	...
15	French complete capture of Lassigny Massif by capture of Alliche farm. **End of second battle of Lassigny.** Last German air raid on Paris. British cross Ancre to Thiepval Wood and make progress between Beaucourt (N. of Albert) and Puisieux (N.E. of Beaucourt).	Announcement of British troops at Baku (on W. of Caspian Sea) and at Krasnovodsk (on E. of Caspian, terminus of Central Asiatic Railway).	...	...	...
16	Anglo-French advance on Roye progresses. German counter attack at Damery (N.W. of Roye) repulsed.	General Otani (Japanese) commanding Allied expedition, arrives at Vladivostok. Sir Charles Eliot appointed British High Commissioner in Siberia.	...	...	...
17	French capture Cæsar's Camp trenches (W. of Roye) and Canny-sur-Matz (N.W. of Lassigny). New advance of French in angle between Oise and Lower Aisne. French advance 1 mile N. of Autrêches.	Arrival of U.S.A. troops at Vladivostok. Announcement of re-capture of Irkutsk by Czecho-Slovaks and Siberian troops. Reported defeat of Bolsheviks on Ussuri front by Czecho-Slovaks.	...	...	...
18	French advance between Oise and Lower Aisne, capturing plateau about Nampeel and village of Nouvron-Vingre. British advance between Vieux Berquin and Bailleul, capturing Oultersteene.	...	...	...	...

ASIATIC AND EGYPTIAN THEATRES.	NAVAL AND OVERSEAS OPERATIONS.	POLITICAL, &c.	1918. Aug.
... ...	... ...	British declaration recognising Czecho-Slovaks as Allied nation ; latter declare war on Germany.	13
... ...	Portuguese E. Africa : Germans 60 miles inland from coast at Angoche (seaport 100 miles S.W. of Mozambique).	... ...	14
... ...	... ...	Relations between U.S.A. and Bolshevist Government in Russia severed. Spanish Note to Germany *re* Shipping losses ([141]). Meeting of Kaiser Wilhelm and EmperorCharles at Main Head Quarters.	15
... ...	... ...	National Yugo-Slav Council Meeting at Laibach.	16
... ...	... ...	... ...	17
... ...	... ...	British Government announcement *re* representation of Dominions in Imperial War Cabinet ([142]).	18

1918. Aug.	WESTERN FRONT.	EASTERN THEATRE.	SOUTHERN FRONT.
19	N. of Oise French capture Le Hamel; between Oise and Aisne French capture Morsain; British retake Merville (Lys front).	Successful Bolshevist attack on Ussuri front. Allied line withdrawn 6 miles.	... ...
20	French between Oise and Aisne reach Lombray.	British War Office announces Japanese to be advancing beyond Nikolaievsk (at mouth of Amur).	
21	French capture Lassigny. **Battle of Bapaume begins.** British 3rd and 4th Armies attack N. of River Ancre on 10-mile front between Beaucourt-sur-Ancre and Moyenneville. British line reaches Albert-Arras Railway.	Reported Bolshevist advance towards Grodekoro (on Kharbin-Vladivostok Railway). Announcement of appointment of M. Regnault(ex-French Ambassador at Tokyo) to be French representative at Vladivostok.	... ...
22	**British** attack between Ancre and Somme, **recapture Albert** and Bray-Albert road. French advance on Noyon, to Quierzy (S. of Oise) and to River Divette from Evricourt to mouth (N. of Oise).	Statement of Allies at Archangel of aims ([146]).	Austrians begin counteroffensive in Albania.
23	British attack on front of 33 miles from Mercatel (5 miles S. of Arras) to Lihons (N.W. of Chaulnes). British cross Arras-Bapaume road, advancing on Bapaume from N. and N.W. About Albert British capture high ground to E. S. of Somme British capture Chuignolles (on Péronne road).	Semenov advances from Manchuria Station and defeats Bolsheviks.	Austrians renew attacks on Italian positions (S. Albania).

Asiatic and Egyptian Theatres.	Naval and Overseas Operations.			Political, &c.	1918. Aug.
... ...	...	...	...	Italian newspapers begin discussion *re* difference in Foreign policy between S'ri. Orlando (Premier) and Sonnino (Foreign Secretary).	19
British and Arab attacks continued against Hejaz Railway.	...	...	...	Speech of Dr. Solf (German Colonial Secretary) in reply to Mr. Balfour's speech of 8.8.18 [143]. Committee of Representatives established by Inter-Allied Food Council [144].	20
... ...	...	...	...	Speech of Lord Reading *re* U.S.A. and War [145].	21
Japanese detachment joins Semenov at Manchuria Station.	...	...	...	... ...	22
... ...	...	...	...	Lord Robert Cecil (Assistant Foreign Secretary) on Dr. Solf's speech of 20.8.18 [147].	23

1918. Aug.	WESTERN FRONT.	EASTERN THEATRE.	SOUTHERN FRONT.
24	British advance on Bapaume, capture Bray (S. of Albert), Thiepval Ridge (N.E. of Albert), Miraumont (W. of Bapaume), Biefvillers (N. of Albert) and reach Avesnes les Bapaume (W. outskirt of Bapaume).	Successful attack of Allies on Bolsheviks, who retreat to Kraevsk, (Ussuri front). Announcement of tunnel, 39 miles E. of Lake Baikal, blown up by Bolsheviks.	... ...
25	British advance on Bapaume ; on N. capture Behagnies, Sapignies and Favreuil ; on S. hold Albert–Bapaume road.	Czecho - Slovaks occupy Kazan (on River Volga). Coup d'état of General Horvath ([148]).	Austrians recapture Fier and Berat (S. Albania)
26	**Battle of the Scarpe** (E. of Arras) **begins.** British 1st Army attack Germans on River Scarpe, capture Monchy-le-Preux (S. of Scarpe) and reach outskirts of Roeux (N. of Scarpe).	Allied and Czech patrols disarm 400 Russian volunteers supporting Horvath.	... ...
27	British capture Chérisy, Bois du Sart (S. of Scarpe), Roeux, etc. (N. of Scarpe). Severe fighting N. and S. of Bapaume. British take Trônes Wood (E. of Albert). S. of Somme, British advance towards Péronne, reaching line Fontaine - les - Coppy— Vermandovillers. French occupy Roye.	German and Russian Governments conclude Supplementary Treaty of Peace. ([150])	... ...
28	British advance N. and S. of Somme towards Péronne, reaching line Fresnes – Herbécourt – Curlu ; British capture Hardecourt (E. of Albert). French advance on Noyon, occupying Chaulnes, Nesle, Vauchelles (2 miles from Noyon).	Japanese report retreat of Bolsheviks to Ussuri. Mr. Miliukov leaves Cadets and forms Constitutional Monarchist Party. General Semenov captures Borzia Station (Siberia) ; Bolsheviks retreat towards Onon River.	... ...

Asiatic and Egyptian Theatres.	Naval and Overseas Operations.	Political, &c.	1918. Aug.
... ...	... ...	U.S.A. House of Representatives pass Man-Power Bill (336 votes to 2).	24
... ...	... ...	Germany accepts Spanish terms *re* Spanish losses caused by submarines.	25
... ...	... ...	Letter of Lord Hugh Cecil on Lord Lansdowne's policy ([149]). Finnish Government repudiates alleged intention of supporting German Murman expedition. Manifesto of Ukrainian National Council in Paris appealing for moral support against Germany. Announcement that Duke Adolf-Friedrich of Mecklenburg-Schwerin no longer candidate for Finnish throne.	26
onstantinople bombed by British airmen.	... ...	... ...	27
... ...	... ...	Announcement of retirement of Mr. Page, U.S.A. Ambassador in London.	28

1918. Aug.	WESTERN FRONT.	EASTERN THEATRE.	SOUTHERN FRONT.
29	British re-capture Bapaume. French re-capture Noyon and cross River Ailette.	British Embassy at Petrograd attacked by Bolshevist troops; Capt. Cromie, Naval Attaché, killed.	Austrian offensive in Albania checked.
30	British advance on Péronne, crossing Somme at Feuillères (W. of Péronne) and taking Cléry (N.W. of Péronne). British advance towards Cambrai, attacking between Haucourt and Hendecourt (N. and S. of Arras–Cambrai road) ; Violent fighting at Bullecourt (S. of Hendecourt). Germans retreat on Lys front ; British re-occupy Bailleul.	Attempt on Lenin's life in Moscow.	... ...
31	British capture Mont St. Quentin (overlooking Péronne). **End of Battle of Bapaume.** Germans evacuate Mt. Kemmel.	Supplementary Peace Treaties signed at Berlin. Bolshevik position 75 miles S. of Archangel on Vologda Railway carried by Allies.	... ...
Sept. 1	Capture of Péronne; British take Bouchavesnes and Rancourt and make general progress S. of Scarpe ; On Lys front they advance and capture Neuve Eglise. Over 57,000 prisoners and 650 guns re-taken by British during August. French advance continues N. of Noyon; Above Soissons they capture Leury, Juvigny, Coucy and other places.	Terrorism in Moscow ; 5,000 social-revolutionaries sentenced to death by Bolsheviks.	... ...

ASIATIC AND EGYPTIAN THEATRES.	NAVAL AND OVERSEAS OPERATIONS.	POLITICAL, &c.	1918. Aug.
... ...	"Casara," Spanish s.s. torpedoed and sunk by German submarine.	Mr. Ryan (U.S.A.) to be A.S. of War, with title and functions of Director of Air Service. Visit of Kaiser Wilhelm to Tsar Ferdinand ot Bulgaria at Nauheim.	29
ublication of General Marshall's 1st Despatch re Mesopotamia.	... ...	(British) Government welcome to Mr. Gompers (President of American Federation of Labour). London Police strike.([151])	30
... ...	British attack Germans successfully near Lioma, in Lurio valley (Portuguese E. Africa), and drive them S.	London Police strike settled ; men return to work.	31
urks begin attack on Baku.	... ...	... ...	Sept. 1

1918. Sept.	WESTERN FRONT.	EASTERN THEATRE.	SOUTHERN FRONT.
2	Battle on 23-mile front; **Troops** of First Army, supported by tanks, **break through Drocourt-Quéant "Switch" line,** S. of Scarpe, capture Cagnicourt and Villers, encircle and take Quéant by nightfall; 10,000 prisoners. On Lys front British also gain ground, and N. of Péronne, where Sailly - Saillisel and whole of St. Pierre-Vaast Wood re-taken. General Mangin continues advance N. of Soissons, captures Neuilly and Terny Sorny.	In Siberia Czech forces advancing E. from Lake Baikal effect junction with Cossacks from Manchurian border under General Semenov. On Vladivostok front Japanese continue to drive back enemy.	... ...
3	**End of battle of the Scarpe.** British advance rapidly beyond Drocourt-Quéant line towards Canal du Nord, capture Lécluse, Rumancourt and Baralle. Germans evacuate Lens, retreat rapidly between Quéant and Péronne. On Lys front we capture Richebourg - St. Vaast. S. of Péronne French cross Somme at Épenancourt. E. of Noyon they reach outskirts of Salency.	... ...	Austrians re - take tw observation posts fro Italians between M Mantello and S. Matte
4	Germans retreat on wider front; Canal du Nord forced by British and villages of Manancourt and Étricourt carried. Ruyaulcourt also taken and outskirts of Havrincourt Wood reached. British reach Moeuvres. On Lys front Ploegsteert and Hill 63 carried. Prisoners since 2nd number 15,000. Germans retreat before French in Noyon pocket, between Canal du Nord and Oise. French line now passes through Guiscard and Apilly.	Oboserskaia (73 miles S. of Archangel) occupied by Allied forces, after severe fighting with forces led by Germans. Execution at Moscow of Dora Kaplan, the assailant of Lenin.	... ...

ASIATIC AND EGYPTIAN THEATRES.		NAVAL AND OVERSEAS OPERATIONS.			POLITICAL, &c.		1918. Sept.
...	...	...	...	...	...	...	2
...	...	...	...	...	The United States recognise the Czecho-Slovaks as a co-belligerent nation.		3
...	...	...	...	...	...	...	4

1918. Sept.	WESTERN FRONT.	EASTERN THEATRE.	SOUTHERN FRONT.
5	British still advance N. and S. of Péronne ; approach high ground on Athies–Nurlu front ; local fighting about Moeuvres and Neuville-Bourjonval. Steady advance of General Humbert's Army from Noyon towards St. Quentin ; crosses Somme canal and approaches within 3 miles of Ham. On Vesle front (E. of Soissons) Franco-American troops drive Germans N. towards the Aisne.	North of Vladivostok Japanese capture Khabarovsk, an important enemy base, with much booty and 120 enemy guns.	...
6	On Amiens–St. Quentin road British press forward. Germans in full retreat from the Somme. Ham and Chauny retaken by French. In N. English troops advance N.W. of Armentières and re-take Bailleul. Americans reach S. bank of Aisne river.	... ...	... ...
7	Rapid British and French pursuit of Germans, who retreat towards " Hindenburg " Line. British take Roisel (railway junction for St. Quentin and Cambrai) and greater part of Havrincourt Wood. On Somme French capture Pithon, Dury and Ollezy, E. of Ham, cross Crozat canal at Pont de Tugny and St. Simon after heavy fighting. On Lys front enemy display strong resistance.	First instalment of Russian War Indemnity to Germany, consisting of £12,500,000 in gold and bank notes is sent from Moscow to the frontier.	... ...
8	Enemy show increased resistance. Violent fighting N. and E. of St. Simon. Avesnes lost and re-taken by French, who also take Artemps, Happencourt, Fluquières, Vaux and gain ground both sides of Oise river. Over 19,000 prisoners taken by British in past week. Over 150,000 taken by Allies since 18.7.	Representatives of neutral countries make strong protest against the wholesale arrests and executions carried out in Russia. Junction of the Czecho - Slovaks at Olovyanna in Siberia with other Czech forces from the E.	... ...

ASIATIC AND EGYPTIAN THEATRES.	NAVAL AND OVERSEAS OPERATIONS.	POLITICAL, &c.	1918. Sept.
The Hejaz Arabs continue to harry the Turks in frequent raids round Medina.	... ...	Arrest in London of M. Litvinov and other Bolsheviks, as guarantees for the safety of British subjects in Russia.	5
.. ..	In E. Africa von Lettow's forces are overtaken on Upper Lurio river near Anguros and attacked by two British columns from S. and S.E. Enemy retreat W. after severe losses in killed and captured.	... ...	6
.. ..	Publication by Admiralty of names of commanders of 151 " U " boats disposed of by Navy.	... ...	7
.. ..	... ...	... ...	8

1918. Sept.	WESTERN FRONT.	EASTERN THEATRE.	SOUTHERN FRONT.
9	After sharp fighting British gain high ground between Havrincourt and Gouzeaucourt, overlook-Hindenburg Line. French push well across Crozat Canal towards St. Quentin and La Fère ; main progress made E. of St. Simon ; they capture Grand Seraucourt, Montescourt, Remigny and Liez Fort. Two strong counter-attacks at Laffaux (between Soissons and Laon) repulsed.	Complete anarchy reported in Petrograd ; Bolsheviks massacre the " bourgeoisie." Threat to execute British officials.	Greek new advanced line heavily bombed in Struma Valley.
10	Local fighting in Epéhy and Gouzeaucourt sectors. British patrols make progress N.E. of Neuve Chapelle. E. of Crozat Canal between St. Quentin and La Fère, French make further progress ; they occupy Hinancourt and Travecy. Special Order of the Day issued : 75,000 prisoners and 750 guns taken by British in four weeks.	Fight for Kazan (Volga) and reported Soviet success.	... ...
11	Sharp fighting on Cambrai front, where enemy make counter-attacks at Gouzeaucourt and Mœuvres. British line advanced further S. : Vermand, Attilly and Vendelles are taken. British rush and hold the "Railway Triangle" position, S.W. of La Bassée. Counter-attacks round Laffaux repulsed by French. Belgians gain ground N. of Ypres.	Arrival of American troops at Archangel announced.	... ...

ASIATIC AND EGYPTIAN THEATRES.	NAVAL AND OVERSEAS OPERATIONS.	POLITICAL, &c.	1918. Sept.
... ...	... ...	... ...	9
... ...	... ...	... ...	10
... ...	... ...	Prince Frederick Charles of Hesse (brother-in-law of the Kaiser), candidate for Kingdom of Finland.	11

1918. Sept.	WESTERN FRONT.	EASTERN THEATRE.	SOUTHERN FRONT.
12	**Battle of Epéhy begins :** British .success on Cambrai front, Mœuvres, Havrincourt and Trescault taken ; over 1,000 prisoners. **Battle of St. Mihiel begins :** Americans supported by French, begin attack on St. Mihiel salient, S. of Verdun ; they advance 5 miles on a 12-mile front ; about 8,000 prisoners. Heavy rain and high wind impedes air work.	... ...	Artillery activity on whole Struma front.
13	British and French nearing St. Quentin : they take Holnon Wood and Savy respectively. Complete success of Americans in St. Mihiel salient, they make over 13,000 prisoners. **End of battle of St. Mihiel.**	... .	
14	Continued German retreat between the Meuse and Moselle, closely followed by French and Americans. Between the Oise and Aisne the French capture Allemant village and Laffaux Mill in local attacks. German counter-attacks at Havrincourt fail.	... .	
15	British capture Maissemy, 5 miles N.W. of St. Quentin. Germans make ineffective counter-attacks S. of the Oise. Americans continue advance on 33-mile front ; they come within reach of fortress guns of Metz. Karlsruhe and Mainz heavily bombed by R.A.F.	... ...	**Battle of the Vardar begins.** French and Serbian offensive in the Balkans ; Bulgarian position carried on front of 7 miles, and 800 prisoners taken.

ASIATIC AND EGYPTIAN THEATRES.	NAVAL AND OVERSEAS OPERATIONS.	POLITICAL, &C.	1918. Sept.
.. ..	The Union-Castle liner "Galway Castle" torpedoed without warning in Channel; 154 lives lost.	Blue Book (Cd. 9146) and (Cd. 8371) issued, describing German rule in S.W. Africa and ill-treatment of the natives.	12
.. ..	... ...	Registration in U.S.A. of 13 million citizens between 18 and 21, and 32 and 35 for military service. British Railway strike begins in S. Wales.	13
British force withdrawn from Baku (Caspian Sea) owing to failure of Armenians to support them (¹⁵²).	... ...	Germany makes peace offer to Belgium on the basis of no indemnity or reparation, etc.	14
. ...	... ...	Austria-Hungary sends a Note to U.S.A. and all belligerent and neutral powers suggesting a " confidential and non-binding " discussion on peace terms.	15

1918. Sept.	WESTERN FRONT.	EASTERN THEATRE.	SOUTHERN FRONT.
16	Slight advance by British in neighbourhood of Ploegsteert and E. of Ypres. French capture Vailly (N.E. of Soissons) and Mt. des Singes. Americans advance along W. bank of Moselle. Air Raid on Paris by Gothas during the night: 6 killed, 15 injured, 2 raiders brought down.	Archangel front; successful operation by naval units and Allied troops on the River Dvina; two enemy ships sunk, three guns captured.	Franco-Serbian advance continues; the troops advance to a depth of 5 miles on 16-mile front in region of Dobropolje. Italians make successful raid N. and N.W. of Mt. Grappa; capture over 300 prisoners and some machine guns.
17	British make local progress N. W. of St. Quentin and in the north near Ploegsteert. Germans counterattack at Mœuvres. French gain ground N.E. of Soissons, capture several strong points. Americans consolidate their line between the Meuse heights and the Moselle. Good bombing attacks by R.A.F. on German objectives.	... ...	Italians repulse strong counter-attacks N. of Mt. Grappa. In Macedonia the Franco-Serbian advance continues; Allied troops reach the Cherna river.
18	Great British advance on 16-mile front N.W. of St. Quentin, extending from Holnon Wood to Gouzeaucourt; over 6,000 prisoners and a number of guns captured; outer defences of Hindenburg Line stormed in many places. French, in liaison with British, capture Savy Wood and Fontaineles-Clères. End of battle of Epéhy. Germans continue strong counterattacks N. and S. of Mœuvres.	Murmansk front: Karelians defeat German-led forces from Finland at Ukhtinskaya and drive them back over the border. Japanese converging from E. and S. take Blagoveshchensk (on the Amur) and Alexeievsk. 2,000 Germans and Austrians lay down their arms.	Bulgarians in full retreat before French, Serbians and Yugo-Slavs; Serbian cavalry reaches Polosko; communication with Prilep (Bulgarian advanced base) cut Anglo - Greeks attack in neighbourhood of Lake Doiran and take the town.

ASIATIC AND EGYPTIAN THEATRES.	NAVAL AND OVERSEAS OPERATIONS.	POLITICAL, &c.	1918. Sept.
... ...	... ...	President Wilson refuses suggestion of peace conference put forward by Austria-Hungary. Recognition by Japan of Czecho-Slovaks as belligerent Allies.	16
... ...	... ...	... ...	17
Arab force surrounds Dera'a and blows up railway junction.	... ...	Complete failure of the Austro-Hungarian peace offer, which is rejected by Great Britain, France, U.S.A. and Belgium in turn.	18

1918. Sept.	WESTERN FRONT.	EASTERN THEATRE.	SOUTHERN FRONT.
19	Further British and French gains in direction of St. Quentin; heavy fighting round Gouzeaucourt and Mœuvres, all German attacks finally repulsed. British capture Lempire and the French advance beyond Contescourt; they capture Essigny le Grand at end of the day.	... ...	Bulgarian rout continues; Serbians cross the Cherna and march on Prilep; over 5,000 prisoners taken.
20	British line pushed forward in the Lempire-Epéhy sector; recapture of Mœuvres completed. N. W. of La Bassée British front advanced. French repulse 5 attacks against their new positions near Allemant (N. of the Aisne). They advance E. of Essigny le Grand.	Reported set-back of Czecho-Slovaks on the Volga; they are driven from Volsk, Simbirsk and Kazan by Bolshevist and German forces.	Bombs and leaflets dropped on Constantinople by R.A.F. in co-operation with Greek Navy
21	British encounter stubborn resistance but gain ground E. of Epéhy, capturing Le Petit Priel farm and other strong positions. British line improved at Mœuvres. Further French gains S. of St. Quentin, they take Benay.	... ...	Franco - Serbian troops pursue Bulgarians past Kavadar and threaten Babuna pass. They reach the Vardar near Demirkapu and Negotin Bulgarians begin destroying their stores and war material preparatory to a retreat.
22	Hostile attacks N.W. of La Bassée fail. S. of St. Quentin French reach outskirts of Vendeul and gain ground E. of Sancy.	... ...	**Great Allied victory in** Balkans; Brilliant Serbian attack; Bulgarian retreat on 100-mile front, from Monastir to Lake Doiran. Allies cut Vardar railway and line from Prilep to Gradsko They advance on Babuna Pass.

ASIATIC AND EGYPTIAN THEATRES.	NAVAL AND OVERSEAS OPERATIONS.	POLITICAL, &c.	1918. Sept.
Great Offensive (Battle of Samaria) in Palestine. General Allenby advances on 16-mile front between Rafat and the sea ; pierces Turkish lines. Infantry reach railway junction of Tull Keram, cavalry push forward E. & N.E. to cut off enemy retreat. 3,000 prisoners taken by British.	... ...	Mr. J. Davis appointed U.S.A. ambassador to Great Britain.	19
Further brilliant progress in Palestine. The cavalry continue wide outflanking movement to the north. They cross the Field of Armageddon and reach Beisan, Afulah, and Nazareth.	... ...	... ...	20
Advance of British Infantry in Palestine ; they reach Shechem and Samaria, and drive Turks into arms of cavalry operating southward from Jenin and Beisan. E. of Jordan the Hejaz Arabs cut the Damascus railway in numerous places. 18,000 prisoners taken.	... ...	Sir M. de Bunsen returns from successful mission to S. America.	21
British seize passages of Jordan N. of Dead Sea and close enemy's last means of escape. 25,000 prisoners and 260 guns taken. The 7th and 8th Turkish armies are virtually wiped out.	... ...	... ...	22

1918. Sept.	WESTERN FRONT.	EASTERN THEATRE.	SOUTHERN FRONT.
23	Series of local battles along front; Germans make stubborn resistance round Epéhy. French advance their line E. of St. Quentin Canal; they reach the Oise, three miles N. of La Fère. Actions round Haumont on American front.	... ...	Bulgarian rout; French cavalry enter Prilep, enemy stream northward toward Veles pursued by Allied troops. Serbians in neighbourhood of Demir Kapu are well N. of the Vardar. British advance N. of Lake Doiran and their cavalry pursue Bulgarians along road to Strumitsa.
24	French and British co-operate in attack in St. Quentin sector, good progress made, in spite of strong resistance, around hamlets of Salency (Noyon) and Gricourt. Allies within two miles of St. Quentin. French capture Francilly-Selency and Dallon; approach Giffecourt.	... ...	Allies continue to advance on both sides of Vardar river. Bulgarians offer strong rearguard resistance. French advance beyond Prilep and Serbians approach Babuna Pass.
25	Sharp local fighting renewed in neighbourhood of Selency (2 miles W. of St. Quentin). Surprise attacks by enemy near Mœuvres and Epéhy are repulsed. Artillery actions on French front.	... ...	**Bulgaria proposes an Armistice,** but General Franchet d'Esperey, (C.-i-C. of Allied forces) declines any suspension of hostilities. Serbians in possession of Babuna Pass, they capture Veles and Ishtip, press on to Usküb. British cross Bulgarian frontier at Kosturino. Over 10,000 prisoners and 200 guns. **End of battle of the Vardar.**
26	**Great Franco - American attack** on 40-mile front, from middle of **Champagne to the Meuse.** French under General Gouraud, Americans under General Pershing. Both armies advance several miles, capture Montfaucon, Varennes and many villages.	... ...	**British enter Strumitsa** (Bulgaria). Serbian cavalry, striking E. from Ishtip, capture Kochana. Bulgarians make hard fight to retain Usküb.

ASIATIC AND EGYPTIAN THEATRES.	NAVAL AND OVERSEAS OPERATIONS.	POLITICAL, &c.	1918. Sept.
East of Jordan, Colonial and Jewish troops pursue Turkish 4th Army in retreat towards Amman on Hejaz railway ; British reach Es Salt. Arab forces occupy Maan (S. of Dead Sea) ; harass enemy retreating north. Increasing number of prisoners. On coast, British capture Acre and Haifa.	... ...	... ...	23
General Allenby's troops in pursuit of Turkish 4th Army approach Amman on Hejaz railway. Arab forces cut the line farther N. and press enemy in retreat from Maan. 40,000 prisoners and 265 guns taken.	... ...	Railway strike, which began in South Wales, spreads to other lines ; Great Western, Midland and London and South Western affected. Yugo-Slav charter signed at Agram. Resignation of Japanese Cabinet announced.	24
In Palestine British cavalry reach Sea of Galilee in pursuit of Turks, who are fleeing towards Damascus. E. of Jordan British cavalry occupy Amman on Hejaz railway. Total of prisoners 45,000 and 265 guns.	... ...	Yugo-Slav State recognised by Italy as independent.	25
U.S. s.s. "Tampa" sunk on convoy duty (117 lost).	... ...	Railway strike in England ended. Count Tisza's Mission to Bosnia a complete failure.	26

1918. Sept.	WESTERN FRONT.	EASTERN THEATRE.	SOUTHERN FRONT.
27	**Great British attack on Cambrai front,** extending from Sauchy l'Estrées to Gouzeaucourt. **Second battle of Cambrai and battle of St. Quentin begin.** Hindenburg Line pierced. Beaucamp, Graincourt, etc., taken; Canadians capture Bourlon Wood. Further Franco-American advance between Reims and Verdun, converging move on the Argonne. 23,000 prisoners taken.	... ...	
28	**Battle of Flanders begins.** Successful **Anglo-Belgian attack** on a 23-mile front from Dixmude to Ploegsteert under King Albert; Houthulst Forest captured and over 4,000 prisoners. Further Franco-American progress; General Mangin advances in Champagne and on the Aisne. Germans retire to the Ailette. Italians force crossing of the Aisne E. of Condé. American line advanced to Exermont and Brieulles, many villages taken. Long-range bombardment of Dunkirk.	... ...	Bulgaria makes request for an Armistice with a view to peace negotiations. Austrian attack in Val Giudicaria (Dol.) repulsed.
29	Good progress of Anglo-Belgian attack; Dixmude, Passchendaele, Messines, Gheluvelt and other places occupied; Allies reach Roulers-Menin road. British reach outskirts of Cambrai and break Hindenburg Line on a 6-mile front. 22,000 prisoners taken in three days. Stiff fighting by Australian and American troops about St. Quentin tunnel. General Mangin reaches the Ailette.	... ...	**Armistice between Bulgaria and Entente signed** [153]. Serbs close to Bulgarian frontier S. of Küstendil and storm Bulgarian position, 11 miles N.E. of Veles. French cavalry enter Üsküb. Severe fighting with Austrian rearguards in Albania.

ASIATIC AND EGYPTIAN THEATRES.	NAVAL AND OVERSEAS OPERATIONS.	POLITICAL, &c.	1918. Sept.
.. ..	... ...	Reported from Christiania that British flag hoisted over (destroyed) German property at Spitsbergen.	27
British troops under General Allenby cross the Upper Jordan at Jisr Benat Yakub and effect a junction with Arab forces near Deraa. British cavalry at El Kuneitra, 40 miles from Damascus.	British ships and aeroplanes co-operate in attack on Zeebrugge.	Germany refuses British proposal *re* Prisoners agreement.	28
Cavalry and car movement towards Damascus continues. 10,000 Turks, part of 2nd corps, 4th army, between Maan and Amman, surrender at Ziza (17 miles S. of Amman).	... ...	Japanese Cabinet formed under Mr. Kei Hara. Czecho-Slovak resolution for liberty proclaimed at Prague (text in Tables of 18.10).	29

1918. Sept.	WESTERN FRONT.	EASTERN THEATRE.	SOUTHERN FRONT.
30	Important progress on St. Quentin-Cambrai front, Thorigny-Guistain-Rumilly taken. Cambrai fired by enemy. General Gouraud, on 20-mile front in Champagne takes Ste. Marie-à-Py, etc. General Mangin progresses on Aisne and Vesle. Belgians take Dixmude and threaten Roulers. Stiff American fighting in Argonne Forest. British progress N. of Neuve Chapelle.	... ...	**Bulgaria surrenders a** noon and accepts th Allied terms. Openin of Sobranje and King Speech.
Oct. 1	British progress and take ground S. of Le Catelet; stiff fighting near Bony and S. of Cambrai. French take part of St. Quentin. Germans fall back from Reims-Aisne plateaux; steady French advance in Champagne; Flanders ridge occupied and Ledeghem seized by British.	... ...	Austrians take defensiv measures on their S frontier in consequence of Bulgarian Armistice Italians occupy Bera and push rapidly for ward in Albania.
2	Germans withdraw on wide front N. and S. of La Bassée Canal; British recapture Armentières. **French eject enemy from St. Quentin.** Advance N. of the Vesle to near Cormicy. Lille being evacuated. French capture Challerange (Argonne).	M. Litvinov arrives at Bergen (Norway). M. Kucharzewski appointed Polish P.M.	... ...
3	Germans withdraw from Lens – Armentières line and past La Bassée. British successfully attack on 8-mile front and take Le Catelet, etc. Stiff fighting by French N. of St. Quentin, N.W. of Reims and in Champagne. British capture Gheluwe; French and Belgians reach Hooglede. Brutal order by Ludendorff re prisoners ([157]). Successful Allied air fighting, 55 German planes down.	The Ufa (S. Urals) loyal Government declare all Soviet treaties void and propose All - Russian Constituent Assembly. Fighting in the Urals. Japanese reported to have joined Semenov at Ruchlevo (Siberia); 1,500 Magyar prisoners.	Allied forces in touch with Austro-Germans in S. Serbia; Serbs capture 7,000 Bulgars. Big British raid on Asiago front.

ASIATIC AND EGYPTIAN THEATRES.	NAVAL AND OVERSEAS OPERATIONS.	POLITICAL, &c.	1918. Sept.
Damascus taken by British and Arabs. 7000 prisoners. **End of Battle of Samaria.**	British seaplane squadron over Heligoland Bight. U.S. ss. " Ticonderoga " torpedoed (121 soldiers lost).	The Chancellor of the Exchequer opens a " Feed-the-Guns " campaign to raise a second War Loan of £1,000,000,000 (154). Mr. Balfour . on the League of Nations. Count Hertling and all German Secretaries of State resign (155).	30
			Oct.
Damascus occupied by British and Arab forces ; 7,000 prisoners taken. (*v.* T. 3.10.18.)	British Flag hoisted at Ebeltoft Harbour, Spitsbergen.	Wages (men and women) Committee begins. German majority programme issued(156). Baron Hussarek (Austrian Prime Minister) on situation : open to Peace offers ; great row in Reichsrath. Milk to be controlled in Great Britain.	1
... ...	British and Italian warships bombard Durazzo, destroy Austrian base and ships and 2 submarines. German submarine shells and sinks Spanish s.s. " Francoli " off Cartagena.	Allies recognise belligerent status of Arab Allies in Palestine and Syria. Grand conference in Berlin under Kaiser's presidency.	2
... ...	... ...	Germans witholding ratification of Prisoners of War Agreement because of Germans interned in China. Sir G. Cave Chairman of Inter-departmental P. of W. Committee. General Moiner appointed Governor of Paris.	3

1918. Oct.	WESTERN FRONT.	EASTERN THEATRE.	SOUTHERN FRONT.
4	British and French heavy fighting St. Quentin to Cambrai. French and Americans increase gains in Champagne as far as the River Arnes. Announcement *re* prisoners, etc.([158]). American attack W. of the Meuse gains ground N.E. of Argonne Forest. German guns being removed from Flanders coast.	... ...	Greek troops occupy Seres and Demir Hissar. French and Serbs drive back Austrians in Vranya region, and French and Italians drive back Austrians in Albania. Sharp fighting in Monte Grappa (Upper Brenta) region.
5	Enemy falls back between Le Catelet and Crève-coeur and burns Douai. British carry Beaurevoir, etc. (E. of Le Catelet). **End of Second Battle of Cambrai, and of Battle of St. Quentin.** Germans fall back towards the Suippe river ; fighting on the Arnes (Champagne). French occupy Moron-villiers Massif (E. of Reims). Stiff American fighting W. of Meuse. Much successful bombing by Allies.	... ...	German troops reported withdrawn from Bulgar front. Franco - Serbs take Vranya (50 miles S. of Nish). Dibra (Albania) occupied. Italians active on their own mountain fronts.
6	British take Fresnoy (N. of Arras). **Second Battle of Le Cateau begins.** French press enemy back along Suippe front. Italian advance N. of Ostel (9 miles S. of Laon) ; Laon on fire. Stiff American fighting on Meuse – Argonne front continues.	British officials from Petrograd reach Swedish frontier. Bolsheviks repulsed by Allied troops at Seletskaya (170 miles S. of Archangel).	65,000 Bulgars have surrendered altogether. Prince Regent of Serbia accepts promotion to General. Italians pushing on in Albania, N. of Berat, towards Elbasan.
7	British advance N. of Scarpe river. Heavy French fighting all along their line ; they take Berry - au - Bac (Aisne river). Americans drive enemy back S.E. of Grand Pré.	M. Guchkov (late Minister of War) executed by Bolsheviks.	Italians occupy Elbasan (Albania).

ASIATIC AND EGYPTIAN THEATRES.	NAVAL AND OVERSEAS OPERATIONS.	POLITICAL, &c.	1918. Oct.
.. ..	Japanese steamer "Hirano Maru" torpedoed off Ireland, 292 lost.	Prince Max of Baden appointed Chancellor. Germany ([159]) and Austria ([160]) address pleas for Armistice to President Wilson. Ferdinand of Bulgaria abdicates ; succeeded by his son Boris, who signs decree for demobilisation of Bulgar Army.	4
... ...		Prince Max speaks in the Reichstag ([161]). Messrs. Gröber, Erzberger and Scheidemann Secretaries of State, and Dr. Solf Foreign Minister. Figures *re* U.S.A. forces in Europe published ([162]). Formation of Yugo – Slav National Council at Laibach.	5
Reported 79,000 prisoners taken since 18.9.18. Zahleh and Rayak (N.W. of Damascus) occupied by our cavalry. French and British warships find Beirût evacuated.	H.M.S. " Otranto," carrying U.S.A. troops, collides and sinks, 431 lost ; T.B.D. " Mounsey " rescues 596.	Peaceful Manifesto by King Boris. Prince Max's letter of 12.1.18 revealed ([163]). France warns Germany *re* crimes on French territory. Canton Government declares war on President Hsuh Shih Chang.	6
British occupy Sidon (Saida). British and French occupy Beirût.	... ...	U.S.A. solid views on answer to be given to Central Powers. Sir E. Geddes and Naval Mission arrive New York. Vice-Admiral Ritter von Mann German Naval Secretary.	7

1918. Oct.	Western Front.	Eastern Theatre.	Southern Front.
8	**Great Allied (3rd and 4th British Armies, 30th U.S.A. Division and French)** 3-mile advance on St. Quentin–Cambrai 20 m. front ; over 10,000 prisoners and 150 guns. N. of Scarpe British take Fresnes – Rouvroy line. French drive Germans back on the Arnes, Aisne and Suippe. Americans and French take Cornay and Consenvoye, and drive enemy back N. of Verdun.	M. Trepov (ex-Premier) reported shot.	Greeks occupy Drama.
9	**British take Cambrai.** Advance continued. Since 21.8, entire Hindenburg system broken through, 110,000 prisoners and 1,200 guns. British arrive within 2 miles of Le Cateau. N. of Verdun French and Americans push beyond 1915 line. Hostile counter - attacks on River Arnes repulsed.	Finnish Lantdag elects Prince Friedrich Karl of Hesse King of Finland. Proclamation of Regency Council in favour of an independent and re-united Poland.	Serbs enter Leskovats ; fighting on River Toplitsa. Greek troops enter Kavalla.
10	**British take Le Cateau** and Rouvroy (S.E. of Lens) and Sallaumines. King's congratulations. Germans forced back by French beyond Oise Canal and in Champagne (losing Grand Pré) and from part of the Chemin des Dames. Argonne Forest cleared.	Death of General Alexeiev. ſ	Allies approach Nish, held by Mackensen. French occupy Prishtina.
11	Strong German resistance N. of River Selle (Le Cateau) ; Germans retreat from strong positions N. of River Sensée ; British close to Douai. Enemy retreats on 38-mile front N. of Rivers Arnes and Suippe. Big French advance. Germans strip Flanders coasts of ships and aeroplanes.	... ...	Heavy fighting on Asiago plateau ; 500 prisoners. General Jekor, Bulgarian C.-i.-C., dismissed. Allied raid N. of Monte Grappa.

Asiatic and Egyptian Theatres.	Naval and Overseas Operations.	Political, &c.	1918. Oct.
Turkish Divisions reported wiped out in Syrian and Mesopotamian campaigns.	... ...	President Wilson's temporizing answer to German Peace Note ([164]). Polish manifesto summoning popular Government. Spanish Cabinet (Sr. Maura) resigns.	8
British armoured cars enter Baalbek and take 500 prisoners.	... ...	Talaat and Enver Pashas reported resigned, and replaced by Ahmed Tewfik and Izzet Pashas. Milk controlled; jam to be rationed. Spanish Premier remains; crisis over.	9
. ...	The Irish mail-boat "Leinster" torpedoed in Irish Channel; 527 lost. v. Lettow-Vorbeck reported moving to N. end of Lake Nyassa.	Lord Grey on the League of Nations ([165]). Gen. v. Scheuch succeeds v. Stein as German War Minister. Cuban troops offered to U.S.A. French Socialist Congress passes a "Bolshevist" resolution. Severe "flu" epidemic in S. Africa. Tuan Chi Jui, Chinese P.M., retired.	10
.. ..	... ...	Herr Erzberger announces German militarism is dead. Huge military appropriations demanded in U.S.A. Emperor Karl receives nationality deputations of Reichsrat. Dr. Wekerle, Hungarian P.M., resigns. Martial law in parts of Portugal.	11

1918. Oct.	WESTERN FRONT.	EASTERN THEATRE.	SOUTHERN FRONT.
12	Fighting on River Selle. **End of Second Battle of Le Cateau.** French take Vouziers. **End of Champagne Battle** (since 26.9) ; 21,500 prisoners and 600 guns taken. French N. of Craonne and within 3 miles of Laon.	... ...	Serbs capture Nish after stiff fight. French occupy Mitrovitsa and Prisrend 90,000 Bulgars and 2,000 guns captured in 27 days. Italians take Kavaya (Albania).
13	More fighting on River Selle line ; progress N.W. of Douai. French capture La Fère and Laon and push well on. Stiff fighting on Meuse, N. of Verdun.	French, British and Japanese troops enter Siberia.	French cavalry enter Pirot. Serbs storm enemy positions N. of Nish.
14	**Great Allied attack in Flanders** under King of Belgians ; advance of 5 miles. French storm Roulers and Sissonne. German attacks on Selle river repulsed. French advance on River Aisne W. of Rethel.	British, Indian and Turkoman troops attack Bolsheviks, and after severe Indian losses drive enemy from Dushak (90 miles W. of Merv). British troops from Vladivostok reach Irkutsk.	Italians take Durazzo from land side ; enemy evacuate Jakova and retire on Ipek (Montenegro).
15	Further advance in Flanders ; British take Menin and close on Courtrai ; Belgians close to Thourout. British advance N.E. of Lens. French advance along River Serre and in the Argonne.	... ...	... ...
16	Enemy retreats from Douai–Lille front, pursued by British. Flanders army advances, taking part of Courtrai, etc. Americans enter Grand Pré after hard fight. Strong German counter-attack on River Selle. Dunkirk finally shelled by long-range gun.	M. Lenin again wounded. Bolsheviks try to stop Middlesex battalion at Zema (Siberia).	Greece cleared of Bulgarians ; Proclamation issued.

Asiatic and Egyptian Theatres.	Naval and Overseas Operations.	Political, &c.	1918. Oct.
... ...	... ...	German reply to President Wilson despatched ([166]). Luxemburg begs President Wilson to protect her rights. Polish National Army recognised by Allied Powers. U.S. troops overseas number over 1,900,000.	12
British advanced forces enter Tripolis (Syria).	... ...	M. Venizelos arrives in London.	13
... ...	S.S. " Brussels " at Zeebrugge torpedoed by British destroyers.	Announced that Germany refuses to ratify Prisoners of War Agreement. British reply ([167]). President Wilson answers German Note of 12.10 ([168]). Turkey's Peace Note received in U.S.A. The King presents £10,000 to Red Cross. Mr. Justice Younger's report on Prisoners of War in 1918 issued ([169]). Spaniards take over seven German ships as compensation ([170]). Izzet Pasha Grand Vizier and Minister of War.	14
British enter Homs (Syria)	... ...	Yugo-Slav demand for peace based on popular rights issued. Two Committees on Indian reform announced.	15
Armenian General Andranik harassing Turkish communications about Erivan (Russian Armenia).	... ...	Peace demonstrations in Berlin ; public opinion much disturbed. Manifesto by Emperor Karl granting autonomy to Yugo-Slavs ([171]). Row in Hungarian Parliament.	16

1918. Oct.	WESTERN FRONT.	EASTERN THEATRE.	SOUTHERN FRONT.
17	**Battle of the Selle begins.** British-American attack on 9-mile front carries line of Selle S. of Le Cateau. **British enter Douai and capture Lille** (stripped). **Belgians enter Ostend** by land, their King and Queen and Sir R. Keyes by sea ; Cavalry at gates of Bruges. British reach outskirts of Tourcoing. Americans fight W. of Grand Pré.	British troops in Transcaspia capture Dushak, driving back Bolsheviks (announced).	Franco - Serbs occupy Knyazhevats and Kr shevats. Montenegrin rise against Austrian French capture Ipe Over half of Serb cleared of enemy.
18	British advance 6 miles E. of Douai-Lille, and 3 miles E. of Le Cateau. Belgians approach Bruges after strong resistance. Stiff fighting on Grand Pré - Vouziers line. Germans pushed back.	British troops repel far superior number of Bolsheviks at Seletsko (160 miles up Dvina river from Archangel). Allies push on to Soroka (S.W. White Sea) from Murmansk. Czecho-Slovaks pressed back by Bolsheviks in E. Russia.	Bulgaria cleared of Ge mans who pillaged t the last. Italians acti on their mountain front
19	British-American advance continued between the Oise and Le Cateau. British advance E. of Douai and Lille and take Marchienne. **Belgians occupy Zeebrugge and storm Bruges,** their left on Dutch frontier ; whole coast and W. Flanders liberated. French break Hunding Line between Sissonne and River Serre.	Allied troops from Murmansk have cleared Karelia of enemy, and from Archangel have occupied Kadish (100 miles S. of Archangel) (announced).	Serbs occupy Zayecha (Austrian - Bulgaria Serb frontier). Frenc reach Danube at Vidi (Bulgaria).
20	British cross the Selle river in face of heavy resistance. British 2 miles from Tournai. Flanders armies continue advance; British across whole of Lys river on their front. Entire Belgian coast in hands of Allies.	... ...	... ...

ASIATIC AND EGYPTIAN THEATRES.	NAVAL AND OVERSEAS OPERATIONS.	POLITICAL, &c.	1918. Oct.
igris railway extended by British beyond Tekrit.	... ...	British Government recognises Polish Army as autonomous. **Proclamation in Prague of Czech Republic, and at Agram of Yugo-Slav independence.** Bolshevik-German correspondence published in Washington. London subscribes 31 million pounds National War Bonds in nine days.	17
ritish hold Turks at Fatha (30 miles N. of Tekrit, Tigris).	Spanish zone in Marocco in complete anarchy : Raisuli and Abdul Malek and German influence supreme.	President Wilson declines suggestions in Austro-Hungarian Note of 4.10. Higher allowances to dependents of fighters granted. Count Tisza admits defeat. Count Burian resigns. Czecho-Slovak Council in Paris declares independence. Prince of Wales gives £3,000 to Red Cross.	18
... ...	German submarines ordered to return to their bases (announced from Madrid).	... '... ...	19
... ...	S.S. " Dundalk " torpedoed in Irish Channel.	Denmark proposes to Germany a plebiscite (as to nationality) for Schleswig Holstein. 4th Liberty Loan in U.S.A. exceeds 1,200 million pounds.	20

1918. Oct.	WESTERN FRONT.	EASTERN THEATRE.	SOUTHERN FRONT.
21	British push on ; stubborn resistance. Belgians 3 miles from Ghent, across Derivation Canal to Eede (Dutch frontier). French advance between Rivers Serre and Oise ; stubborn fighting N. of Verdun. Sir D. Haig's despatch of 20.7, on March and April withdrawal([172]), publ'd.	... ...	Italians fighting on Asia and Grappa front French capture conv of lighters at Lo Palanka (Danube).
22	**British enter Valenciennes.** French and Czecho - Slovaks push enemy back on the Serre river. Fierce fighting by Americans on both banks of Meuse, N. of Verdun and in the Woëvre.	New Polish Cabinet formed under M. Swiezynski.	Lord Cavan's despatc dated 14.9 (10.3 to 13.9 issued ([174]).
23	**Big British attack between Le Cateau and Valenciennes** carries line forward 1 to 3 miles after stiff resistance ; Bruay taken and Scheldt reached. Heavy fighting by French on Serre and Vouziers fronts. King and Queen of Belgians fly to Bruges.	Bolsheviks attack Allied position of River Dvina (S. of Archangel) and are repulsed.	Croat troops seize Fium but are suppressed.
24	British attack resumed ; advance of 3 miles after heavy fighting. 9,000 prisoners and 150 guns taken in last two days. German counter - attack on Derivation Canal repulsed by Belgians. Slight French advance on S. fronts.	... ...	Serbs force enemy back disorder along Morav **Third Battle of th Piave begins.** 7th Briti Division seizes part Grave di Papadop Island (River Piav (night of 23-24). St successful fighting Monte Grappa regio 2,800 prisoners.
25	Further British advance between Le Quesnoy and Maing. **End of Battle of the Selle.** Successful French attacks between Rivers Serre and Oise, and between Rethel and Sissonne. Stiff American fighting N. of Verdun. French and British advance to 10 miles E. of Courtrai.	... ...	Serbs reach Kraguyeva and Chrupriya (60 mil S. of Danube).

Asiatic and Egyptian Theatres.	Naval and Overseas Operations.	Political, &c.	1918. Oct.
... ...	... ...	German reply to U.S.A. Note of 14.10 issued ([173]). King George receives Inter-Parliamentary delegates. German Governor-General of Belgium " pardons " Belgians and neutrals convicted by Court Martial. Belgian Bill for German damage already nearly 400 million pounds.	21
... ...	Italian ships shell S. Giovanni di Medua (Albania).	Hindenburg's order " approving peace-steps " captured. Prince Max announces programme of some reforms ([175]). Karl Liebknecht released.	22
urks retire, pursued, 20 miles from Fatha (Tigris).	239,000 tons Allied shipping (including 151,000 British) lost in September (announced).	Mr. Balfour on the Empire ([176]). U.S.A. Note in reply to German one of 20.10 ([177]). Impudent German reply *re* prisoners ([178]). House of Commons approves of female M.P.s. Karl Liebknecht amnestied. Dr. Solf and German War Minister on the situation. Baron Hussarek still Austrian Premier.	23
ritish cavalry within 4 miles of Kirkuk (100 miles S.E. of Mosul, Tigris river). British successfully attack Turks at Fatha.	... ...	Growing desire in Germany for Kaiser to abdicate. National Council in Croatia meets. German mark drops to 33 to the £.	24
Iritish columns turn Turkish position at mouth of Lower Zab river (Tigris). Cavalry occupy Kirkuk.	... ...	... ...	25

1918. Oct.	WESTERN FRONT.	EASTERN THEATRE.	SOUTHERN FRONT.
26	British progress S. of Valenciennes and repulse German attack on Maing. Heavy French fighting on Rethel-Oise front. Slight advance E. of Courtrai. **General von Ludendorff resigns.**	... ...	Remainder of Grave di Papadopoli Island seized by British and Italians.
27	German attack N.W. of Le Quesnoy repulsed. Enemy gives way on Serre-Oise salient; French pursue. Americans take Bois Belleu (E. bank of Meuse). General von Ludendorff succeeded by von Lossberg.	... ...	British–Italian advance continued across the Piave; 9,000 prisoners. Lord Cavan commands 10th Italian Army. Serbs drive enemy back N. of Kraguyevats.
28	Slight British advance S. of Valenciennes. Heavy French fighting at Verly (Oise) and (American) about Grand Pré. Great French bombing raid on Seraincourt (N.W. of Rethel).	Siberian Coalition Ministry formed under Admiral Kolchak (War and Marine); MM. Shekin (Foreign Affairs), Orlov (Commerce) and Ostrugov (Communications).	**General advance by 10th and 12th Italian (including British) Armies.** Stiff fighting, Austrians driven back. Severe fighting in Grappa region. Italians enter Allessio (Albania).
29	Successful French attack on 7½-mile front N.W. of Château . Porcien (W. of Rethel).	... ...	Main Italian (and British) forces advance 5 miles on 30-mile front. Enemy are weakening.

Asiatic and Egyptian Theatres.	Naval and Overseas Operations.			Political, &c.	1918. Oct.
tish advanced troops ccupy Aleppo. Turks n Tigris retreat during ight 26/27 to Kalaat hergat.	...	...	...	Count J. Andrassy succeeds Count Burian as Foreign Mimister. King of Montenegro suggests a Confederated Yugo-Slavia with autonomons States.	26
tish cavalry seize Musmie junction (N. of leppo, on Baghdad railay). British main body n touch with Turks on ower Zab. Turks fall ack to hills covering hergat.	...	...	...	Colonel House arrives in Paris as U.S.A. special representative. German reply to President Wilson's Note published [179]. **Austro-Hungarian Note asks for Armistice** [180]. (published 29.10).	27
rks attack British on E. ank of Tigris, but are eavily beaten on W. ank, and retreat. Brith beat Turks at Sherat.	...	...	...	Allied Conference in Paris. Professor Lammasch succeeds Baron Hussarek as Austrian P.M. Fresh Austrian Note to President Wilson urging immediate Armistice. Czech National Council takes over administration in Prague. Admiral Prince Yorihito arrives in London. Kaiser's decree to Chancellor states " Kaiser's office is one of service to German people."	28
rsuit of Turks contines : position cut off and aptured.	...	...	...	Archduke Joseph charged by Emperor Karl with scheme for independence of Hungary. Indictment of Caillaux in French Senate. Independence of Croatia and Yugo-Slav lands agreed to by Croat Congress at Agram.	29

1918. Oct.	WESTERN FRONT.	EASTERN THEATRE.	SOUTHERN FRONT.
30	Over 30,000 prisoners taken in Flanders during past month. Region above Valenciennes flooded by Germans. Mannheim bombed by British.	... ...	Serbs reach Danube E. Semendria and occu Pozharevats. Itali advance continues tween Upper Brenta a sea ; 33,000 prisone Severe fighting at Gr pa. Fiume surrende to the Croats by Hungarians.
31	British captures in last 3 months : 172,659 prisoners, 2,378 guns, 17,000 machine guns, 2,750 trench mortars, etc. British successful attack S.W. of A u d e n a r d e (Courtrai), carrying all objectives ; 1,000 prisoners.	... ...	Scutari (Albania) c tured by Italia Austrians in Trent and Venetian A separated and cha back, losing all positi between the Brenta a Piave. **Austrian C.** **applies to General D** **for an Armistice.**
Nov. 1	Americans and French advance between Aisne and Meuse in Argonne Forest. **Battle of the Sambre begins.** British reach outskirts of Valenciennes. British, French and Americans reach Gavere, on Scheldt (10 miles S. of Ghent).	Ukraine National Council assumes administration of E. Galicia. Collisions between Polish and Ukrainian troops. Lemberg proclaimed to be in state of seige.	Serbs re-enter Belgra Austrians retreat fr Venetian Alps and pl towards River Tag mento.
2	Allied advance continued. Germans retreat in Argonne Forest. Americans capture Buzancy. French capture S. bank of Canal des Ardennes between Semuy and Neuville.	Polish Regency Council orders formation of regular Standing Army.	Austrian retreat in Ve tian Alps and pl continued. Allies e Belluno.

ASIATIC AND EGYPTIAN THEATRES.	NAVAL AND OVERSEAS OPERATIONS.	POLITICAL, &c.	1918. Oct.
rkish Army on Tigris urrenders to British.	... ...	Serious influenza epidemic in London : 2,200 deaths last week. Hungarian Republic proclaimed : Count Hadik P.M. German Note to U.S.A. received saying armistice terms are being awaited. National Council of Fiume proclaims independence of city and desires union with Italy. **Armistice between Turkey and Entente Powers signed at Mudros.**	30
... ...	Austrian Fleet handed to Yugo-Slav Council and Danube flotilla to Hungarians.	Revolution in Vienna. Count Tisza assassinated in Vienna. **Hostilities between Turkey and Entente cease at noon.** End of the Dual Monarchy. Italians and Slovenes take over Trieste.	31
... ...	Austrian Dreadnought "Viribus Unitis" sunk at Pola by two Italians.	Versailles Conference opens. Abdication of King Boris of Bulgaria announced ; peasant Government established at Tirnova under leadership of Mr. Stambuliski. Revolution in Vienna. Hungarian National Council assumes power. Count Michael Karolyi becomes Premier. Great Serbian National Council proclaimed at Serajevo (Bosnia).	**Nov.** 1
... ...	von Lettow attacks Fife (frontier post of Rhodesia) and is repulsed.	Publication of armistice terms with Turkey ([181]). Mass-Meeting of Trade Unionists in London to consider Labour's part in the Peace. Baron Flotow succeeds Count Andrassy as Minister for Austria - Hung. Foreign Affairs. Slovenes take over administration of Carniola.	2

1918. Nov.	WESTERN FRONT.	EASTERN THEATRE	SOUTHERN FRONT.
3	Argonne Forest cleared of Germans. Advance of French and Americans. Allied forces reach approaches to Ghent.	Fighting in Lemberg; Poles victorious.	Italians advance on who Italian front; occu? Trent and Udine.
4	**Great British (1st, 3rd and 4th Armies) and French offensive on 30-mile front** from E. of Scheldt at Valenciennes to Guise on Oise, reaching to E. of Le Quesnoy, half way through Mormal Forest, past Landrecies on Sambre and across Sambre – Oise Canal. 10,000 prisoners and 200 guns captured. Belgians advance to N.W. and S. suburbs of Ghent. French reach Le Chesne on Ardennes Canal. Americans advance to Stenay on Meuse.	... ...	**Hostilities between Aust? Hungary and Ente? cease at noon.**
5	Allied advance from Scheldt to Meuse continued. Between Scheldt and Sambre British capture Le Quesnoy and Mormal Forest. Between Oise and Aisne French capture Château-Porcien (on Aisne) and Guise (on Oise). Between Aisne and Meuse French cross Ardennes Canal; Americans cross Meuse at Brieulles and Cléry-le-Petit and take Beaumont. Marshal Foch in supreme strategical direction.	Resignation of Siberian Government in favour of " All-Russian Government."	... ...

ASIATIC AND EGYPTIAN THEATRES.	NAVAL AND OVERSEAS OPERATIONS.	POLITICAL, &c.	1918. Nov.
Mosul occupied by British.	Italians land at Trieste and occupy Lissa (isle in Adriatic). **German sailors mutiny at Kiel.**	**Armistice with Austria-Hungary** signed (v. 6 Nov.). Count Karolyi resigns Presidency of National Council of Hungary, and is succeeded by M. Johann Hock. Yugo Slav National Council announces intention of forming a common State with Serbia and Montenegro.	3
... ...	German battleship mutiny at Kiel ([182]). Italian occupation of Adriatic. Italian ships enter Fiume and Zara, occupy Rovigno, isles of Lagosta, Meleda and Curzola, and ports of Dulcigno and Antivari (Montenegro).	U.S.A. recognise Polish army as autonomous and co-belligerent. Spread of revolution to Hamburg, etc.	4
... ...	Italians enter Pola.	U.S.A. elections for Congress ; Republican majority returned. British Ministerial changes : Sir A. Geddes becomes President of Local Government Board in place of Mr. W. Hayes-Fisher, resigned. Announcement of Mr. Lloyd George in Commons *re* Armistice ([183]). President Wilson replies to Germany *re* Armistice ([184]).	5

1918. Nov.	WESTERN FRONT.	EASTERN THEATRE.	SOUTHERN FRONT.
6	German armistice delegates leave Berlin for Western Front ([184]). German retreat from Scheldt to Meuse becomes general. British advance towards Mons, Maubeuge and Avesnes. French between Oise and Aisne capture Vervins and Rethel on Aisne. Americans enter Sedan. Main German lateral line of communications cut.	Directorate of Polish Republic formed with seat at Cracow.	... .
7	Marshal Foch informs German armistice delegates they may advance to French outposts by Chimay – Fourmies – La Capelle–Guise road. Allies' advance continues. British make formal entry into Valenciennes, gain W. outskirts of Avesnes, reach Haumont (3 miles from Maubeuge) and Élouges (9½ miles S.W. of Mons). French and Americans threaten Charleville–Mézières.	... ...	... ..
8	Marshal Foch receives German armistice delegates at Réthondes (4 miles from Compiègne), refuses request for provisional armistice, terms of armistice to be accepted or refused by 11 a.m. on November 11. Allies continue advance : French reach outskirts of Hirson and Mézières ; French and Americans clear heights E. of Meuse; **British capture** Avesnes and **Maubeuge**, advance towards Mons capturing Condé, cross Scheldt Canal and occupy W. part of Tournai. Over 18,000 prisoners taken by British since November 1. German prisoners since January 1 ([185]).	Polish Government informs Austrian Premier that Polish sovereignty has been assumed over Galicia.	... .

ASIATIC AND EGYPTIAN THEATRES.	NAVAL AND OVERSEAS OPERATIONS.	POLITICAL, &c.	1918. Nov.
... ...	... ...	Publication of terms of Austrian Armistice ([186]). U.S.A. promises to exercise influence to secure for Rumania political and territorial rights.	6
... ...	German naval revolt spreading. Admiral Sir R. Wemyss appointed British Naval representative with Marshal Foch to receive German Delegates.	(British) Appointment of Civil Department of Demobilisation and Resettlement. Health Ministry Bill introduced into Commons([187]). Yugo-Slav-Serbian Government to be formed. Kiel and Hamburg in hands of " Soviets." Flight of King of Bavaria from Munich. British and French Governments proclaim deliverance of Eastern peoples from Turkish oppression.	7
... ...	... ...	Prince Max of Baden issues proclamation to Germans abroad declaring Germany beaten, and resigns Chancellorship ([189]). Abdication of King of Württemberg and Duke Ernest of Brunswick. Bavarian Republic declared at Munich. (British) Minister of Blockade informs neutral countries that transfer of enemy ships to neutrals will not be recognised.	8

1918. Nov.	WESTERN FRONT.	EASTERN THEATRE.	SOUTHERN FRONT.
9	British enter Maubeuge, approach Mons, capture Tournai. French surround Mézières and occupy Hirson.	Polish Goverment formed at Lyublin.	Rumanian ultimatum Marshal von Mackense German troops to lea Rumania within 24 hour
10	French and Americans cross Meuse, capture Hirson, and advance towards Montmédy; surround Mézières.	... ...	Rumania takes up arm again. Allied force cross Danube and joi hands with Rumania.
11	British capture Mons before dawn. **Armistice signed at 5 a.m. Hostilities on all fronts cease at 11 a.m.** End of the Battle of the Sambre. British front extends about 60 miles from near Montbliart (E. of Avesnes) to just N. of Grammont; held from S. to N. by 4th 3rd, 1st, 5th and 2nd Armies. Positions unchanged until 17 November.	British recognise Lettish Government as independent. New National Government in Esthonia orders general mobilisation. Polish Directorate established at Warsaw; Regency Council deposed.	... .

Asiatic and Egyptian Theatres.	Naval and Overseas Operations.	Political, &c.	1918. Nov.
French occupy Alexandretta (N. Syria).	H. M. S. " Britannia" (battleship), torpedoed and sunk off Gibralter. (40 drowned).	Nominal Abdication of Kaiser. Flight of Kaiser and Crown Prince to Holland. Revolution in Berlin. Prince Max becomes Regent; Herr Ebert becomes Chancellor. Herr Kurt Eisner assumes Premiership and Ministry of Foreign Affairs of Bavarian Republic. Reported resignation of Marghiloman Cabinet at Jassy; General Coanda to form New Cabinet. Swiss Federation of Workmen's Unions orders general strike. Speech of Mr. Lloyd George at Mansion House ([190]).	9
British join French at Alexandretta.	British mine - sweeper " Ascot" torpedoed and sunk by German submarine off N.E. coast of England (53 lives lost).	Tewfik Pasha (ex-ambassador to London) is appointed by Sultan Grand Vizier and forms pro-Entente Government at Constantinople. Kaiser crosses into Holland. Death of Herr Ballin.	10
... ...	... ...	Appeal of Dr. Solf, German Foreign Minister, to President Wilson for mitigation of armistice terms. Abdication of Grand Dukes of Hesse, Mecklenburg and Saxe-Weimar. King of Saxony and Grand Duke of Oldenburg dethroned. German Socialist Coalition Ministry formed. Message of King George to British Empire ([191]). Great rejoicings in England. Speech of President Wilson at Washington ([192]). Expulsion of Bolshevist Mission from Switzerland.	11

1918. Nov.	WESTERN FRONT.	EASTERN THEATRE.	SOUTHERN FRONT.
12	... ...	Anti-Semitic pogroms in Poland reported.	... .
13	... ...	... ...	... .
14	Marshal Foch warns German High Command that acts of violence still being committed in occupied regions by German troops must cease.	... ...	... .

ASIATIC AND EGYPTIAN THEATRES.	NAVAL AND OVERSEAS OPERATIONS.	POLITICAL, &c.	1918. Nov.
.. ..	Allied Fleet passes through the Dardanelles.	**Publication of Armistice terms** ([193]). Dr. Solf appeals to President Wilson for immediate peace negotiations. Speech of Mr. Lloyd George at Meeting of Liberals on National policy ([194]). Letter of Mr. Lloyd George to Unionist Meeting expounding domestic policy ([195]). Statement of Dr. Addison, Minister of Reconstruction *re* Government plans for demobilisation, in Commons ([196]).	12
.. ..	**Allied Fleet at Constantinople.** German cruiser " Königsberg " sails with plenipotentiaries of Workmen's and Soldiers' Council of German Fleet to meet representatives of British Admiralty ([197]).	Abdication of Emperor Karl officially announced in Vienna, and resignation of Lammasch cabinet. Abdication of Prince Leopold of Lippe. Publication of assignment of officers in new German Government ([197a]). Appeal to Germany of 302 Danish Associations of N. Schleswig for right of self-determination. Message of President Wilson to Germany *re* food ([198]). Speech of Mr. Lloyd George in London at Meeting of Employers and Trade Unions ([199]).	13
.. ..	**General von Lettow-Vorbeck surrenders** on Chambezi river, south of Kasama (N. Rhodesia).	**Republic of German-Austria proclaimed in Vienna.** Swiss strike ended. (British) Labour Conference decides to leave Coalition Government ; Mr. Barnes, Labour M.P. of War Cabinet, leaves Labour Party. Issue of Labour Programme ([200]).	14

K

1918. Nov.	WESTERN FRONT.	EASTERN THEATRE.	SOUTHERN FRONT.
15	... ...	... ...	Fiume occupied by Italian naval forces and Serbian troops. Hungarian Government concludes separate armistice with Allies at Belgrade.
16	Allied troops begin to move towards Germany.	German troops leave Finland. Polish officers demand surrender of Posen. Polish President (M. Pilsudski) proclaims Poland an Independent and Sovereign State. Baku re-occupied by British and Russian troops.	... ...
17	Allied armies begin march to the Rhine. In British sector 4th (Rawlinson) and 2nd (Plumer) Armies, preceded by 2nd, and 1st and 3rd, Cavalry Divisions respectively, advance. Each Army consists of 4 Corps, each of 4 Divisions. Tribute of Marshal Foch to British armies as " decisive factors in final German defeat."	... ...	Fiume occupied by Italian troops.
18	American troops enter Longwy and Briey (Lorraine) Belgian troops re-enter Antwerp and Brussels.	Siberian coup d'état. Directorate abolished, Admiral Kolchak made Dictator.	... ...

ASIATIC AND EGYPTIAN THEATRES.	NAVAL AND OVERSEAS OPERATIONS.	POLITICAL, &c.	1918. Nov.
... ...	Sir David Beatty receives Rear-Admiral von Meurer on board H.M.S. " Queen Elizabeth " in Firth of Forth.	German-Austria requests of German Government complete union with German Republic. Appeal of Dr. Solf to President Wilson *re* a Hague Conference ([201]). New German Ministry ([202]). **National Assembly of Czecho-Slovak State** holds 1st sitting at Prague: Professor Masaryk elected 1st President of Republic; M. Franz Tomasek, President of National Assembly; Dr. Kramarzh, Premier.	15
... ...		Appeal of Dr. Solf to President Wilson to allow German Commissioners to leave for U.S.A. ([203]). Reply of U.S.A. Government to Germany: all communications *re* armistice to be sent to all Allied Governments. Announcement at Budapest of **Emperor Karl's abdication of throne of Hungary.** (British) Government election campaign opens with meeting in London ([204]).	16
... ...		Hungarian Republic proclaimed at Budapest. Formation of Serb-Coalition Ministry at Paris, M. Pashich Premier ([205]). **Abdication of Duke of Saxe - Coburg Gotha.** Yugo-Slav National Council protests against Italian occupation of Fiume.	17
... ...		Appeal of Dr. Solf to Allied Governments to mitigate armistice conditions. Mr. Asquith's election address to London Liberals ([206]).	18

1918. Nov.	WESTERN FRONT.	EASTERN THEATRE.	SOUTHERN FRONT.
19	**King and Queen of Belgians re-enter Antwerp. French troops enter Metz.** Luxemburg entered by American troops. General Pétain promoted Marshal.	... ...	Serbian troops withdraw from Fiume.
20	Great difficulties of supply and transport in ruined area surmounted by British Transport Services during this week.	General Manishevski C.i.C. of Russian forces in Archangel, etc.	... ...
21	British enter Namur.	... ...	French troops land in Constantinople.
22	**King Albert re-enters Brussels.**	... ...	... ...
23	... ...	... ...	... ...
24	**British and American troops reach German frontier.**	... ...	... ...

ASIATIC AND EGYPTIAN THEATRES.	NAVAL AND OVERSEAS OPERATIONS.	POLITICAL, &c.	1918. Nov.
... ...	Surrender of 20 German submarines to Rear-Admiral Sir Reginald Tyrwhitt at Harwich.	... ...	19
... ...	... ...	Italian Parliament opens. Speech by Signor Orlando. Mr. Bonar Law states re-victualling of Germany to be dependent on proper arrangements for returning prisoners.	20
... ...	"Capitulation of Rosyth." Surrender of German Navy off Firth of Forth. Surrender of 39 German submarines off Harwich.	Resignation of Lord Robert Cecil (Assistant Foreign Secretary) and of Mr. Clynes (Food Controller) ([207]). Greece, Serbia and Rumania announce decision to strengthen union.	21
... ...	... ...	Issue of Mr. Lloyd George's and Mr. Bonar Law's Election Manifesto ([208]).	22
... ...	... ...	Assembly of S. Slavs at Agram proclaim union of all S. Slav districts of Austria-Hungary with Serbia and Montenegro and of all Yugo-Slav military forces with the Serbian Army.	23
... ...	28 German submarines surrender at Harwich.	Publication of despatches of Count Lerchenfeld (Bavarian Minister in Berlin, 1914) ([209]). Soldiers' and Workers' Council in Oldenburg, E. Friesland, Bremen, Harburg-on-Elbe, Hamburg and Schleswig - Holstein decide to form Republic with Hamburg as capital. Grand Duke of Baden abdicates. Bukovina desires union with Rumania.	24

1918. Nov.	WESTERN FRONT.	EASTERN THEATRE.	SOUTHERN FRONT.
25	Marshal Foch enters Strasburg.	... ...	... ...
26	Last German troops withdraw from Belgium. French troops cross German frontier.	Bolshevik troops take Pskov and Dvinsk and bombard Narva (Gulf of Finland).	American troops enter Fiume.
27	—	... ...	... ...
28	Patrols of 2nd Cavalry Division reach German frontier near Beho (just N. of N. point of Luxemburg).	Narva captured by Bolsheviks.	... ...
29	... ...	... ...	... ...
30	Belgians occupy Aix-la-Chapelle.	... ...	... ...
Dec. 1	British 2nd Army enters Germany ([212]) between Oudler and Eupen. American forces enter Germany and occupy Trier (Treves).	... ...	Bukarest re-occupied by Rumanian and Allied troops.
2	Belgians occupy Jülich.	... ...	... ...
3	... ...	... ...	Last Bulgarian troops evacuate the Dobruja.

Asiatic and Egyptian Theatres.	Naval and Overseas Operations.	Political, &c.	1918. Nov.
... ...	5 German battleships leave Firth of Forth for internment at Scapa Flow (Orkney Isles).	British Parliament dissolves. Conference of German States at Berlin to consider future Government of Germany; opened by Herr Ebert. Montenegrin Skupshtina votes for union with Serbia.	25
... ...	**Entente Squadrons arrive at Odessa and Sevastopol;** surrender of German submarines and Russian ships in German hands.	Bavaria threatens to break off relations with Berlin.	26
... ...	27 German submarines surrender at Harwich.	Visit of King George to Paris. Labour Election Manifesto ([210]). Mr. Asquith's address to East Fife electors ([211]).	27
... ...	British squadron anchors off Copenhagen.	**Bavaria breaks off relations with Berlin.** Speech of Mr Asquith at Huddersfield attacking Coalition. **Kaiser signs formal deed of abdication** ([212]).	28
... ...	... ...	Speeches of Mr. Lloyd George at Newcastle.	29
... ...	... ...	King of Württemberg formally abdicates.	30
			Dec.
... ...	Eight German submarines surrender at Harwich: total surrendered now 122.	M. Clémenceau, Marshal Foch, Signor Orlando, and Baron Sonnino arrive in London. Prince Regent of Serbia approves Yugo-Slav constitution.	1
... ...	British destroyers arrive at Libau.	Conference in London between British ministers and French and Italian visitors.	2
... ...	... ...	Inter - Allied Conference continued and concluded.	3

1918. Dec.	WESTERN FRONT.	EASTERN THEATRE.	SOUTHERN FRONT.
4	Owing to supply difficulties, British 2nd Army resumes march only to-day. Belgian cavalry enters Neuss; British occupy Düren.	... ...	... ...
5	Belgians occupy München-Gladbach.	... ...	... ...
6	Belgians occupy Crefeld. 2nd British Cavalry Brigade and armoured cars enter Cologne.	... ...	... ...
7	28th Infantry Brigade reaches Cologne.	... ...	... ...
8	Belgians occupy Urdingen (left bank of Rhine, N.E. of Crefeld). Americans enter Coblenz. British 1st Cavalry Division reaches Rhine and secures crossings.	Bolshevik forces advancing in Esthonia; reach point 40 miles from frontier.	... ...
9	After advancing for several days, **Americans reach Rhine** from Brohl to Rolandseck (between Coblenz and Bonn). **French enter Mainz.**	... ...	... ...
10	Americans occupy strips of left bank of Rhine (either side of Coblenz): from Andernach to Rolandseck and from Trechtingshausen (N. of Bingen) to Boppard.	... ...	... ...
11	Sir C. Fergusson, Military Governor, reaches Cologne and hoists Union Jack. **Americans occupy Coblenz,** and hold Rhine bank from Trechtingshausen to Rolandseck.	Odessa occupied by Ukrainian revolutionary forces.	... ...

ASIATIC AND EGYPTIAN THEATRES.	NAVAL AND OVERSEAS OPERATIONS.	POLITICAL, &c.	1918. Dec.
... ...	Publication of official estimate of world's shipping losses during war ([216]).	Nomination of candidates for General Election in United Kingdom. President Wilson sails from France. Yugo-Slav Union proclaimed. Rumanians of Transylvania and Banat vote union with Rumania.	4
... ...	H. M. light cruiser "Cassandra" sunk by mine in Baltic. Announced that all Turkish warships and all Russian warships in Black Sea have been surrendered.	Mr. Lloyd George publishes statement of aims and policy of British Government ([215]).	5
... ...	... ...	British railway dispute settled ([216]). Fighting in Berlin between Government troops and "Spartacus" party.	6
... ...	... ...	... ...	7
... ...	Naval action in Caspian between British and Bolshevik vessels.	... ...	8
Lahej (S. Arabia) re-occupied by British. Turkish garrison surrenders.	... ...	... ...	9
... ...	... ...	Mr. Lloyd George announces 6 "points" of his election programme ([217]).	10
... ...	... ...	Speech by Mr. Lloyd George at Bristol, principally on conscription, indemnities, and punishment of Kaiser ([218]).	11

1918. Dec.	WESTERN FRONT.	EASTERN THEATRE.	SOUTHERN FRONT.
12	**British Cavalry cross Rhine and begin occupation of Cologne bridgehead.** American sector contracted, extending now from Brey to Rolandseck.	... ...	... .
13	British Infantry (29th, 9th and 2nd Canadian Divisions) complete occupation of Cologne bridgehead. **Americans cross Rhine and occupy Coblenz bridgehead.** Armistice prolonged to 17.1.19.	... ...	... .
14	... ...	... ...	... .
15	... ...	... ...	... .
16	... ...	Announced that British squadron in Gulf of Finland has bombarded Bolshevik position at Wesenberg (Esthonia), but that the Bolsheviks continue to advance near Pskov. Bolshevik reverse N. of Ekaterinburg (Urals).	Marshal Mackensen and his force surrender to the Hungarians near Buda-Pest.
17	... ...	Complete evacuation of Finland by German troops announced. Kiev occupied by Ukrainian revolutionary forces.	... ...
18	... ...	Announced that Bolsheviks have entered Walk (Livonia) after its evacuation by Germans. Dorpat (Esthonia) evacuated by Germans.	... ...

Asiatic and Egyptian Theatres.	Naval and Overseas Operations.	Political, &c.	1918. Dec.
... ...	British naval squadron arrives at Reval.	Publication of order for demobilisation of men over 41 called up under British Military Service Act of 1918.	12
... ...	... ...	**Prolongation of armistice** with Germany for one month (to Jan. 17) agreed upon ([219]). Further announcement regarding conscription by Mr. Lloyd George ([220]). President Wilson lands at Brest.	13
Hodeida (S. Arabia) occupied by British.	... ...	**General election in United Kingdom.** President Wilson arrives in Paris. Assassination of Senhor Paes, President of Portuguese republic.	14
... ...	... ...	Bessarabia votes for union with Rumania.	**15**
... ...	... ...	Imperial Conference of Workers' and Soldiers' Councils opens at Berlin.	16
... ...	... ...	... ...	17
... ...	... ...	Conference at Berlin decides on form of provisional government of Germany, pending meeting of National Assembly ([221]).	18

1918. Dec.	Western Front.	Eastern Theatre.	Southern Front.		
19	Sir D. Haig and 5 generals commanding British armies on western front visit London and are entertained by the King.	... ...	...	...	...
20	... ...	French troops land at Odessa.	...	...	...
21	... ...	... ...	...	...	...
22	... ...	... ...	...	...	...
23	... ...	... ...	...	...	...
24	... ...	Perm taken by the Russo-Czechs, with many prisoners and guns.	...	...	...
25	... ...	... ...	...	...	...
26	... ...	Continued advance of Bolsheviks in Esthonia reported.	...	...	...
27	... ...	Batum occupied by British.	...	...	...
28	... ...	Fighting between Germans and Poles at Posen, following arrival of M. Paderewski. Reported that British squadron has landed Esthonian troops in rear of invading Bolsheviks.	...	...	...

Asiatic and Egyptian Theatres.	Naval and Overseas Operations.	Political, &c.	1918. Dec.
.. ..	... ...	Sir E. Geddes appointed co-ordinator of demobilisation of British army. Publication of statement of Lord Milner regarding British policy in Russia ([222]).	19
... ...	... ...	Conference at Berlin passes resolution in favour of socialisation of industry, and fixes 19 Jan. as date of elections for National Assembly. Independent Socialists refuse to co-operate in Provisional Government.	20
... ...	... ...	... ...	21
... ...	... ...	... ...	22
... ...	... ...	... ...	23
... ...	... ...	Fighting in Berlin between discontented sailors and Government troops ends in success of latter.	24
... ...	... ...	... ...	25
... ...	... ...	Arrival of President Wilson in London.	26
... ...	Announced that H.M.S. "Calypso" has captured two Bolshevist destroyers near Reval.	President Wilson in conference with Mr. Lloyd George and Mr Balfour, and entertained by King at State banquet.	27
... ...	... ...	**Results of British General Election announced** ([223]). President Wilson receives address of welcome from City of London at Guildhall ([224]). Resignation of Signor Bissolati, Italian socialist minister, owing to disagreement with Government's peace policy.	28

1918. Dec.	WESTERN FRONT.	EASTERN THEATRE.	SOUTHERN FRONT.
29	... ...	British troops landed at Riga.	... ...
30	... ...	Kadish (N. Russia) taken by Entente forces. Birsk (E. Russia) taken by Russo-Czechs.	... ...
31	... ...	Ufa and Sterlitamak (E. Russia) taken by Bolsheviks. Two French (African) battalions landed at Odessa.	... ...

ASIATIC AND EGYPTIAN THEATRES.		NAVAL AND OVERSEAS OPERATIONS.			POLITICAL, &c.	1918. Dec.
..	... ...	...	...	...	Important speeches by MM. Clémenceau and Pichon in French Chamber of Deputies regarding peace terms and international relations after war ([225]).	29
...	... ...	...	...	...	President Wilson receives freedom of Manchester, and makes important speeches ([226]).	30
...	... ...	...	...	...	Draft of German Constitution published by the *Vorwärts*.	31

RÉSUMÉ OF MAIN EVENTS IN 1918.

Jan. 8	... ...	President Wilson's "Fourteen Points" speech.
,, 19	... ...	Bolsheviks forcibly dissolve Constituent Assembly.
,, 20	... ...	"Breslau" sunk and "Goeben" damaged near Dardanelles.
,, 28	... ...	Civil war in Finland begins.

Feb. 4	... ...	Alexeiev advances v. Moscow; defeated by Bolsheviks, 13.2.
,, 6	... ...	German ultimatum to Rumania.
,, 9	... ...	Peace signed between Central Powers and the Ukraine.
,, 18	... ...	German advance in Russia begins; Russians begin to evacuate Armenia.
,, 19 to May 4	...	Allenby secures his right flank in Palestine by minor operations: Jericho, 21.2, Es Salt, 4.5.

Mar. 3	... ...	Treaty of Brest-Litovsk signed between Russia and Central Powers.
,, 5	... ...	Preliminary Peace Treaty (Rumania and Central Powers) signed at Bukarest.
,, 6	... ...	Germans land on Aaland Islands. Death of Mr. J. Redmond.
,, 7	... ...	Peace between Germany and Finland.
,, 9 to May 10	...	British take Hit and progress along Tigris; take Kirkuk, 7.5.
,, 15	... ...	Prince Lichnowsky's revelations published.
,, 19	... ...	Allies demand unconditional acceptance of their conditions by Dutch; and seize ships, 22.3.
,, 21 to April 29	...	Great German offensive of Western Front: British lines penetrated, 21.3; long-range gun bombardment of Paris begins, 22.3; Germans reach Somme, Péronne lost, 23.3; desperate fighting round Bapaume, 24, 25.3, etc.; Albert and Noyon lost, 26.3; very heavy fighting both sides of Somme, 27.3, etc.; Great German attack on both sides of River Scarpe defeated with very heavy losses, 28.3; strong French counter-attacks check Germans in Somme region, 28, 29.3; Gen. Foch appointed to co-ordinate action of Allies, 29.3; Germans held, 31.3; Germans attack again between Somme and Avre, 4.4; severe fighting North and South of Albert and North of Verdun, Reims heavily shelled, 6.4; heavy local fighting again Avre to Albert, 22, 23.4; severe German attacks gain Villers-Bretonneux, 24.4.
,, 26	... ...	Conference at Doullens on unity of command.

April 1	... ...	Royal Air Force formed.
,, 3	... ...	Germans land in Finland; confused situation.
,, 8 to 10 ...	...	Conference of oppressed Yugo-Slav nationalities in Rome.
,, 9 to 29 ...	...	Battle of the Lys: Heavy German attacks drive British and Portuguese towards Estaires, 9.4; Heavy fighting from here to South of Ypres and strong enemy pressure about Bailleul, latter lost, 15.4, and more ground, Wytschaete and Meteren, 16, 17.4; Germans take Kemmel and Dranoutre in very heavy fighting, 25.4.
,, 9	... ...	Man-Power Bill introduced; passed, 16.4.
,, 13	... ...	Turks occupy Batum; Hertzog seditions in South Africa.
,, 14	... ...	Gen. Foch appointed C.i.C. Allied Armies in France.
,, 20	... ...	Irish Nationalists and Priesthood oppose conscription.
,, 22	... ...	Trans-Caucasia declares independence.
,, 22, 23	... ...	Brilliant naval raid on Zeebrugge.

April 25, et seq.	...	Penetration of South Russia by Germans; latter near Sevastopol; in Tiflis, 16.6.
„ 29 to May 15	...	" Bonnet Rouge " trial in Paris.
May 1	... ...	U.S. troops join Amiens front.
„ 7	... ...	Peace of Bukarest signed by Rumania and Central Powers.
„ 10	... ...	H.M.S. " Vindictive " sunk at Ostend.
„ 14	... ...	Fighting in Italy; first million U.S. tons of shipping on seas.
„ 15 to June 1	...	Germans bombard hospitals, killing 248 and wounding 693.
„ 23	... ...	Georgia declares her independence.
„ 24	... ...	British land at Murmansk; Sinn Fein intrigues with / Germany exposed.
„ 27 to June 2	...	Third Battle of the Aisne : Germans drive French back across Aisne, and take Soissons, 29.5; Germans press forward between Reims and Soissons and reach the Marne, 30.5.
„ 27	... ...	British detachments sent to Persia and the Caspian.
June 3	... ...	Germans checked in the Marne " pocket " and on the Ourcq.
„ 8	... ...	Prisoners of War Conference at the Hague.
„ 9 to 13	...	New German offensive towards Compiègne, the 1st Battle of Lassigny; Germans checked, 11.6.
„ 15 to 23 ...	...	Second Battle of the Piave : Great Austrian offensive, successful at first, eventually repulsed with heavy slaughter.
„ 16	... ...	Beginning of the end foreshadowed by change of Bulgarian Premiers (Malinov for Radoslavov).
„ 18, 22 ...	...	French repulse German attack at Reims.
July 6	... ...	Publication of Montagu-Chelmsford Report on India; Assassination of German Ambassador Count Mirbach at Moscow; Franco-Italian attack begins in South Albania.
„ 15 to Aug. 4	...	Second Battle of the Marne : Great German offensive on 50-mile front East and West of Reims ; held on the East they cross the Marne on the West, 16.7; high-water mark of German offensive and great Allied counter-attack on south-west of Marne " pocket," 18.7; Germans recross Marne, 20.7; in retreat, 22.7; Allied progress in Marne " pocket " and on flanks, 22 to 26.7; strong German resistance, 30.7; French retake Soissons, 2.8.
„ 16	... ...	Ex-Tsar and family shot at Ekaterinenburg.
„ 30	... ...	Assassination of F.M. von Eichhorn at Kiev.
Aug. 1	... ...	Allies land at Archangel.
„ 3	... ...	British land at Vladivostok; Japanese, 16.8; U.S. troops, 17.8.
„ 6	... ...	Gen. Foch created Marshal.
„ 8 to 12 ...	...	Second Battle of Amiens. British on 11-mile and French on 4-mile front, 2,000 guns and 200 tanks, drive in German line, " black day " for Germany, 8.8; German retreat from Ancre begins, 14.8.
„ 9 to 16 ...	...	Second Battle of Lassigny. French advance and capture it, 15.8.
„ 17 to 20 ...	...	Gen. Mangin drives Germans from the Aisne heights.
„ 21 to 31 ...	...	Battle of Bapaume. Heavy fighting; British take Albert 22.8, Bapaume 29.8, Péronne 31.8.
„ 24	... ...	U.S.A. pass Man-Power Bill.
„ 26 to Sept. 3	...	Battle of the Scarpe. British take Monchy-le-Preux, 26.8; break through Drocourt–Quéant switch, 2.9.
„ 30, 31 ...	...	London Police Strike.

L

Sept. 3 to 9 ...	...	Germans fall back on Hindenburg Line, evacuating Lens, etc.; British force Canal du Nord, 4.9; take Ploegsteert, 4.9, Bailleul, Kemmel, Merville and Neuve Chapelle, 6.9; French take Ham, 6.9; Americans reach the Aisne, 6.9.
„ 7 ...	...	List of 151 German submarines destroyed published.
„ 12, 13 ...	...	Americans attack and take St. Mihiel salient. Allied Front now clear for final drive.
„ 13 ...	...	Registration of 13 million American citizens for military service.
„ 14 ...	...	Germans retreat between Meuse and Moselle; Austria-Hungary proposes informal Peace Conference; rejected.
„ 15 to 25 ...	...	Battle of the Vardar (Macedonia): Franco-Serb offensive 15.9; Anglo-Greek offensive, 18.9; Bulgarians in full retreat; British enter Bulgaria, Ishtip taken by Serbs 25.9.
„ 19 to 30 ...	...	Great British offensive in Palestine: Brilliant progress and cavalry dash; British seize Jordan crossings and wipe out 7th and 8th Turkish Armies by 22.9; capture Acre and Haifa, 23.9; pursue and destroy 4th Turkish Army, 24.9, etc.; enter Damascus, 30.9.
„ 24 to 26 ...	...	Railway strike in England.
„ 26 to 29 ...	...	Great American attack between the Meuse and Argonne; storm Montfaucon, 28.9; seize first and second German lines by 29.9, and threaten German lateral communications.
„ 26 to 30 ...	...	Simultaneous successful attack by Gen. Gouraud in Champagne: German line penetrated 6 miles by 29.9.
„ 26 to Oct. 5 ...	...	Great British bombardment by 1st and 3rd Armies, 26.9; and attack (second Battle of Cambrai) on 30-mile front between St. Quentin and the Sensée; storm Canal du Nord and threaten Cambrai from North, taking 10,000 prisoners, 27.9; Cambrai enveloped, 30.9.
„ 28 to Oct. 22 ...	...	Battle of Flanders under King of Belgians: Belgians, two French divisions and 2nd British Army seize ridges by 30.9, and reach Menin outskirts by 1.10; transport and supply difficulties; fresh attack, Roulers captured, 14.10; Menin, 15.10; Courtrai, 16.10; Belgians enter Ostend, 17.10, and Zeebrugge and Bruges, 19.10; British enter Douai, 17.10, and Lille, 18.10; whole Belgian coast in our hands by 20.10.
„ 28 to Oct. 5 ...	...	Battle of St. Quentin: Fourth British Army, with Americans and French, attacks on 12-mile front, crosses St. Quentin Canal and takes Bellecourt, etc., 29 and 30.9; French take St. Quentin 1.10; Hindenburg Line stormed in strongest place and 36,500 prisoners, etc., taken by 3.10.
„ 28 to 30 ...	...	Bulgaria asks for Armistice; signed, 29.9; Bulgaria surrenders, 30.9.
„ 28 to Oct. 18 ...	...	Fierce American fighting through Argonne Forest, 28.9 to 10.10; transport and supply difficulties; 630,000 Americans engaged; Germans evacuate Argonne, 9.10; driven on to Kriemhilde system by 14.10; Americans take Grandpré, 16.10; Kriemhilde system pierced on 16, 17 and 18.10.
Oct. 4 ...	...	Prince Max of Baden, Chancellor, addresses plea for Armistice to U.S.A. King Ferdinand of Bulgaria abdicates.
„ 5 to 16 ...	...	French occupy Moronvilliers Massif, 5.10; Gen. Gouraud attacks towards Aisne and drives Germans to Rethel–Vouziers line, 8.10; French enter Laon, 13.10, and cross Aisne at Vouziers, 16.10.

Oct. 6 to 12	...	Second Battle of Le Cateau : Allied attack on 20-mile front, 8.10 ; British capture Cambrai, 9.10 ; entire Hindenburg system broken through by 10.10 ; British take Le Cateau, 10.10.
,, 8 to Nov. 16	...	Correspondence of President Wilson with German and Austro-Hungarian Governments.
,, 9	...	Talaat and Enver Pashas resign.
,, 10	...	R.M.S. " Leinster " torpedoed and sunk.
,, 12	...	Serbs capture Nish from Germans and Austrians.
,, 14	...	Turkish Peace Note received by U.S.A.
,, 17	...	Proclamation in Prague of Czecho-Slovak Republic, and in Agram of Yugo-Slav independence.
,, 17 to 25	...	Battle of the Selle : Stiff fighting by Allies ; Germans forced behind Sambre–Oise Canal by 19.10 ; Allies cross the Selle, 20.10 ; 4th, 3rd and 1st British Armies advance 15 miles on 23.10.
,, 18 to 25	...	British advance on Tigris and take Kirkuk, 25.10.
,, 21 to 31	...	Stubborn fighting North of Verdun and on Meuse by Americans and French.
,, 24 to 30	...	Third Battle of the Piave begins : British cross river ; general Italian–British advance, 28.10 ; Austrians routed.
,, 25 to 30	...	British advance in Mesopotamia ; Turkish Army surrenders, 30.10.
,, 26	...	Ludendorff resigns. British occupy Aleppo.
,, 27	...	Austro-Hungary applies to U.S.A. for Armistice.
,, 29	...	Successful French attack West of Rethel.
,, 30	...	Armistice signed with Turkey.
,, 31	...	Austrian troops apply for Armistice ; revolution in Vienna ; Fleet handed to Yugo-Slavs ; Scutari (Albania) captured by Italians. Hostilities between Turkey and Entente cease.
Nov. 1 to 11	...	Franco-American attack on Forêt de Bourgogne, 1.11 ; Buzancy captured, forest cleared, 2.11 ; rapid American advance, 4, 5.11 ; French enter Rethel and Americans Sedan, 6.11 ; Allies drive enemy back to Montmédy by 11.11.
,, 1	...	Serbs re-enter Belgrade.
,, 1 to 11	...	British advance between Sambre and Scheldt (Battle of the Sambre) : Enter Valenciennes, 2.11 ; great attack by 4th, 3rd and 1st Armies on 30-mile front, 4.11 ; clear Forêt de Mormal, 4.11 ; with French 1st Army drive enemy back in confusion ; enter Bavai, 7.11 ; Avesnes, 8.11 ; Maubeuge, 9.11 ; Mons, 11.11.
,, 3	...	Mutiny at Kiel ; Italians land at Trieste.
,, 4	...	Hostilities between Austro-Hungary and Entente cease at noon ; revolution in Hamburg.
,, 5	...	Italians enter Pola. Marshal Foch in supreme strategical direction.
,, 8	...	Marshal Foch receives German delegates ; numerous German Princes abdicate, including King of Württemberg ; Bavaria a Republic.
,, 9	...	Kaiser decides to abdicate. Revolution in Berlin.
,, 10	...	Kaiser and Crown Prince flee to Holland. Allies enter Rumania.
,, 11	...	Mons captured. Armistice signed at 5 a.m. HOSTILITIES CEASE AT 11 A.M. Great rejoicings.
,, 13	...	Allied Fleet at Constantinople. Abdication of Emperor Karl.
,, 14	...	Von Lettow-Vorbeck surrenders in Rhodesia.
,, 15	...	Adm. Beatty receives Rear Adm. von Meurer in Firth of Forth.

Nov. 16 ... ... Allied troops begin to move towards Germany. Poland proclaimed an Independent and Sovereign State.

,, 19 ... ... King and Queen of Belgians enter Antwerp. French troops enter Metz. Surrender of German submarines.

,, 21 ... ... Surrender of German Fleet off Firth of Forth.

,, 22 ... ... King and Queen of Belgians re-enter Brussels.

,, 23 ... ... Yugo-Slav State proclaimed.

,, 25 ... ... Marshal Foch enters Strasbourg.

,, 26 ... ... Last Germans evacuate Belgium; Entente squadron at Odessa.

,, 28 ... ... British patrols reach German frontier.

Dec. 1 ... ... British and American Armies enter Germany. Bukarest re-occupied.

,, 2 ... ... Belgian troops enter Germany.

,, 6 ... ... British troops enter Cologne.

,, 9 ... ... American troops reach the Rhine.

,, 14 ... ... General Election in the United Kingdom.

,, 26 ... ... President Wilson arrives in London.

,, 28 ... ... Result of General Election: Coalition Unionists sweep the board.

APPENDICES, 1918.

(¹) *Jan.* 1.—Petrograd reports that German Peace Note declares occupation of Poland, Courland, Lithuania and Esthonia to be an indispensable condition of peace. News of departure of British and French ships from Archangel creates deep impression and is considered premature by friends of Western Powers.

(²) *Jan.* 1.—" All-Indian Moslem Association," under Prince of Arcot, formed in Calcutta to oppose Home Rule doctrines of " Indian National Congress " and " All India Moslem League."

(³) *Jan.* 2.—Air Council established by Order in Council. Lord Rothermere is President and Secretary of State, and Major-General Trenchard, Chief of Air Staff.

(⁴) *Jan.* 2.—Principal recommendations made by American delegates to Paris Conference are : (1) Constant and speedy despatch of American troops to Europe. (2) Speeding up of merchant ship building. (3) Close co-operation with other belligerents.

(⁵) *Jan.* 3.—At Man-Power Conference between Government and Trade Unions Sir A. Geddes states the position is now completely altered by Russian situation. It will be ultimately redressed by American Armies, but meanwhile great strain will be thrown on this country.

(⁶) *Jan.* 5.—Turkish peace terms to Russia include total demobilisation and disarmament for Russia while Turkey remains armed ; also annulment of treaties referring to Persia.

(⁷) *Jan.* 5.—Mr. Lloyd George, addressing Man-Power Conference, says we have no desire to destroy Germany or any other nation, but we must have restoration, reparation, freedom for nations now enslaved and settlement of Asiatic and African problems. He also hopes for an international organisation to reduce chances of war and to limit armaments. The speech is well received in Allied countries.

(⁸) *Jan.* 7.—Russo-German peace negotiations at Brest-Litovsk. Trotski is defiant and demands free, independent Russia, and threatens general rising of the people if it is not granted. Germans consent to continue negotiations.

(⁹) *Jan.* 7.—The Earl of Reading appointed British High Commissioner and Ambassador Extraordinary and Plenipotentiary on Special Mission ; to have full authority over all British Missions in U.S.A. in connection with the War. Lord Northcliffe remains in London as Chairman of London Headquarters of British Mission to U.S.

(¹⁰) *Jan.* 8.—Sir D. Haig's Despatch describes Battles of Arras, Lens, Messines and Ypres in the summer of 1917, resulting in defeat of 131 German divisions. It mentions changes made necessary by Russian revolution and refers to training and supply of men.

(¹¹) *Jan.* 8.—Mr. Wilson in address on peace programme demands open diplomacy, freedom of seas, removal of economic barriers and reduction of armaments. He also emphasises necessity of complete restoration and suggests an Association of Nations. He lays down 14 points :

1. Open diplomacy.
2. Freedom of navigation.
3. Removal of economic barriers.
4. Reduction of armaments.
5. Colonial claims dependent on interest of populations concerned.
6. Evacuation of Russian territory and assistance in unhampered development.
7. Evacuation and restoration of Belgium.
8. French territory evacuated and the Alsace Lorraine wrong to be righted.
9. Italian frontiers readjusted nationally.
10. Austro-Hungarian people to be allowed autonomous development.
11. Rumania, Serbia and Montenegro evacuated and Balkan questions settled.
12. Turkish non-Ottoman nationalities to have free autonomous development and Dardanelles opened.
13. Independent Polish State.
14. General Association of Nations with mutual guarantees of independence and integrity.

(¹²) *Jan.* 9.—Russo-German negotiations. Germany definitely refuses to change meeting-place to neutral country. Russian delegates agree.

(¹³) *Jan.* 10.—General Maude's Despatch dated October 15th, 1917, deals with operations in Mesopotamia from April 1st to September 30th, and includes operations on Tigris, Diala and Euphrates fronts.

(¹⁴) *Jan.* 10.—Mr. Balfour at Edinburgh says : " We did not go into this War for selfish objects, we did not stay in for selfish objects, and we are not going to fight to a finish for selfish objects." But though " the horrors of war are great, they are nothing to the horrors which would come from a German peace."

(¹⁵) *Jan.* 14.—Sir A. Geddes, in his survey of man-power problem says it is necessary to raise immediately 420,000 to 450,000 men ; the secession of Russia has added a possible 1,600,000 men to enemy strength ; the resources of Allies and America are sufficient for victory, but till full American force is felt everything depends on British man-power. Government does not propose to alter military age nor to introduce Conscription in Ireland, but women's service will be developed under Lady Mackworth.

(¹⁶) *Jan.* 15.—Cambrai enquiry : War Cabinet is of opinion that High Command was not surprised by attack of Nov. 30th ; that all proper dispositions were made to meet it, and that public discussion of the affair is detrimental to national interests.

(¹⁷) *Jan.* 15.—Following arrest of Rumanian minister Bolshevik ultimatum to Rumania states that Rumania is engaged in hostile acts against Russian soldiers, and threatens war if arrested soldiers are not released and guarantees given that acts will not be repeated.

(¹⁸) *Jan.* 17.—East Africa : On January 7th and 8th a German force operating 90 miles N.E. of Fort Johnston on Lake Nyassa was driven northwards. 40 miles further north, near Mwembe, appreciable losses have been inflicted on enemy in patrol actions. Rains have commenced and rivers are rising rapidly.

(¹⁹) *Jan.* 18.—Mr. Lloyd George says there are no alternatives to Government's scheme but raising the military age or sending back wounded men time after time. Men would not be withdrawn from industries unless necessity was urgent ; resolutions cannot win the war ; but men and guns can.

(²⁰) *Jan.* 20.—Naval action : " Goeben " and " Breslau " with Turkish destroyers attacked British naval forces N. of Imbros. H.M. monitor " Raglan " and a smaller monitor, M28, were sunk. " Goeben " and " Breslau " then steamed to S. of Imbros, British ships then forced " Breslau " into a mine field, causing her to sink. " Goeben " then steamed towards Dardanelles and also struck a mine, being finally beached near Nagara Point under continuous bombing by British naval aircraft.

(²¹) *Jan.* 21.—Agreement between Central Powers and Ukraine includes : (1) Declaration that state of war is at an end. (2) Troops on both sides to be withdrawn on conclusion of peace. (3) Arrangements to be made for immediate resumption of commercial and diplomatic intercourse.

(²²) *Jan.* 21.—Portuguese East Africa : 50 miles S.W. of Port Amelia British troops have been in contact with the enemy. Lorembula Boma, 90 miles N.E. of Fort Johnston, has been occupied. Floods have destroyed bridges on enemy line of retreat.

(²³) *Jan.* 21.—Sir E. Carson resigns from War Cabinet on Irish question, feeling that in any further decisions to be taken on this question he cannot vote as a member of the War Cabinet and at the same time leader of Ulster Unionists.

(²⁴) *Jan.* 22.—First meeting of Allied Naval Council, consisting of Vice-Admiral F. J. de Bon (France), Sir E. Geddes and Admiral Sir R. Wemyss (England), Vice-Admiral Count T. de Revel (Italy), Rear-Admiral Funakoshi (Japan), Vice-Admiral W. Sims (U.S.A.).

(²⁵) *Jan.* 23.—General Staff Appointments : Lt.-General Sir H. Lawrence, Chief of General Staff ; Colonel E. W. Cox, Chief of Intelligence ; Lt.-General Travers Clark, Q.M.G. at British H.Q.

(²⁶) *Jan.* 23.—At Labour Party Conference at Nottingham, the chairman challenges Germany to declare her war aims ; Conference adopts resolution calling for a joint statement of Allied war aims and suggesting an international Labour Peace Conference in Switzerland.

(²⁷) *Jan.* 24.—Count Hertling, in Reichstag, says he hopes Russian negotiations will soon reach good conclusion ; then, referring to British and American declarations, says he " cannot discern a friendly spirit " in Mr. Lloyd George's speech, but rather one of "sitting in judgment on Germany." He lays blame for War on England, France and Russia in turn. He discusses Mr. Wilson's 14 points, the principle of which he professes to admit. He then draws attention to the favourable war situation of Central Powers and invites Britain and America to reconsider their proposals. Count Czernin, in Vienna, also discusses Mr. Wilson's proposals individually, but evades a direct answer to essential points.

(²⁸) *Jan.* 25.—Portuguese East Africa : British column from Port Amelia has reached Nahuya, 50 miles from coast. In Western area (Mwembe district) considerable losses have been inflicted on enemy. Heavy rains continue.

(²⁹) *Jan.* 25.—Mr. Lloyd George, in a letter to the chairman of Irish Convention, says that before the Convention comes to a decision on certain issues the War Cabinet would be ready to confer with leading members representing different sections. The Convention authorises chairman to arrange such a meeting.

(³⁰) *Jan.* 25.—General Allenby's despatch deals with operations in Palestine since June 28th, 1917, and includes period from capture of Beersheba to fall of Jerusalem.

(³¹) *Jan.* 28.—During last ten days extensive raids have been made by Hejaz troops on the railway 70 miles N.W. of Medina and 60 miles S. of Maan, in which the track has been severely damaged and heavy losses inflicted on the Turks.

(³²) *Jan.* 28.—Mr. Baker, Secretary of War, says that U.S.A. will have 500,000 men in France early this year, and 1½ million more ready to go in 1918.

(³³) *Jan.* 29.—General Diaz's army, aided by Allied artillery and airmen, wins back important heights between Asiago Plateau and Brenta. Battle begins on 28th ; 1,500 prisoners captured. Next day Monte di Val Bella and Col di Rosso are captured and prisoners increased to 2,600, with much war material. Two enemy divisions practically destroyed.

(³⁴) *Jan.* 30.—German strikes : German papers estimate number affected to have been from 300,000 to 500,000 on 28th, since when strike has spread to dockyards at Kiel and Hamburg. " Vorwärts " considers that international movement is aimed at. Meeting in Berlin demands peace, food and franchise.

(³⁵) *Feb.* 10.—The Peace Treaty between the Central Powers and the Ukraine declares that the frontier of the new Ukrainian Republic shall on the S.W. follow the frontier of Galicia—to the north of which an area of territory, at present occupied by the enemy, in the Governments of Volhynia, Lyublin, Siedlce, Grodno and Minsk is to become part of the new Ukrainian State, and is to be immediately evacuated. Both parties renounce the reinbursement of their war costs. Provision for exchange of agricultural and industrial products.

(³⁶) *Feb.* 16.—Sir W. Robertson found himself unable to agree to the changes introduced by the formation of the Versailles Council regarding relations between the C.I.G.S. and the Allied High Command, and declined to be the British Representative on the Versailles Council.

(³⁷) *Feb.* 19.—By these conditions Russia renounces all claim to Finland, Baltic provinces, Lithuania, Poland and the Ukraine. Russia is to conclude peace with Ukrainian People's Republic ; Ukraine and Finland to be immediately evacuated by Russian troops and Red Guards. Russia will secure for Turkey the return of its Eastern Anatolian frontiers and recognises the annulment of the Turkish " Capitulations " ; Russia to demobilise her army completely ; Russian warships to be sent to and kept in Russian harbours till conclusion of general peace (Entente warships in sphere of Russian authorities are included) ; Russia to give guarantees of free untarified export of ores, and her propaganda against Quadruple Alliance to cease. Russian-German Commercial Treaty of 1904 to come into force with certain exceptions.

(³⁸) *Feb.* 23.—Statement of war aims by Inter-Allied Labour and Socialist Conference: " Liberation and reparation for Belgium; Alsace-Lorraine, Serbia, Montenegro, Rumania, Albania to dispose of their own destinies. Claims of Italians outside Italy to be united with Italy supported, also legitimate interests of Italy in the adjacent seas recognised. Poland reconstituted in independence with free access to sea. German annexation of Baltic Provinces inadmissible. Dardanelles permanently neutralised under control of League of Nations. Palestine to be a free State. Armenia, Mesopotamia and Arabia, if unable to settle own destinies, to be under administration of International Commission. Czecho-Slovaks and Yugo-Slavs' claim to independence to be recognised. Natives of Colonies to be protected against capitalist exploitation. Administrative autonomy to be granted to groups sufficiently civilised ; to others a progressive participation in local government. No economic boycott. The opinion is expressed that an International Conference of Labour and Socialist organisations would help to remove obstacles to peace ; all organisations represented publicly to declare their peace terms in conformity with the principles of "No annexations or punitive indemnities, and the right of all peoples to self-determination."

(³⁹) *March* 3.—The principal terms of the Treaty may be summarised as follows :— (*a*) Russia renounces all rights West of an agreed line so drawn as to deprive her of Riga, Courland, the province of Kovno, about half of the provinces of Vilna and Grodno, and the whole of Poland. Germany and Austria are " to decide the fate of these territories in agreement with their populations." (*b*) German and Austrian troops are to evacuate all territory east of the line when a general peace has been concluded and the demobilisation of the Russian army completed, but a German " police force " shall occupy Esthonia and Livonia " until their security is guaranteed by their own national institutions and until their own state organisation is restored." (*c*) Russia is to conclude peace with the Ukraine, to accept the terms agreed upon as between the Ukraine and Germany and her Allies, and to withdraw all military forces from Ukrainian territories ; to evacuate Livonia, Esthonia, the Aaland Islands and Finland, and to abstain from all propaganda against the Finnish Government, while the fortifications on the Aaland Islands are to be removed " with all possible despatch," and an agreement is to be made between Germany, Russia, Sweden and Finland for the " permanent non-fortification " of the islands. (*d*) Russia is to withdraw her troops from the districts of Ardahan, Kars, and Batum, and is not to interfere in their reorganisation, which shall be carried out by the inhabitants "in agreement with the neighbouring States, particularly Turkey." (*e*) The Russian army is at once to be completely demobilised, and Russian warships shall be kept in Russian harbours until a general peace is concluded, or else disarmed. (*f*) Prisoners of war on both sides shall be sent home. (*g*) The contracting parties renounce the indemnification of war costs and war damages. (*h*) The economic relations of the parties are to be settled according to the terms of the recent German ultimatum.

(⁴⁰) *March* 5.—The following were the main conditions :—(*a*) Rumania cedes to Germany and her Allies the Dóbruja as far as the Danube, but provision is to be made for the maintenance of a trade-route for Rumania to Constanza. (*b*) The Rumano-Hungarian frontier is to be " rectified." (*c*) Rumania concedes in principle the economic measures "corresponding to the situation." (*d*) Eight divisions of the Rumanian army are to be demobilised at once, and the rest as soon as peace is made between Rumania and Russia, except for a guard on the Russian frontier. (*e*) The Rumanian Government is to assist the transport of troops of Germany and her Allies through Moldavia and Bessarabia to Odessa.

(⁴¹) *March* 5.—The First Lord reviewed the naval situation as a whole, but dealt particularly with the decline in the output of British shipping and with the submarine campaign. The former he ascribed partly to labour unrest, partly to lack of zeal on the part of employers. The submarine menace, he said, was " held, but not yet mastered." The losses in the current quarter were much lower than in the early months of 1917, and it was believed that the British and the Americans were together sinking German submarines as fast as they were being built.

(⁴²) *March* 6.—The figures given by Sir E. Geddes on March 5 were repeated and supplemented in a statement issued next day by the War Cabinet, from which the following tables are extracted :—

1.—*Losses and Gains of Allied and Neutral Shipping to the end of* 1917.

	British shipping.	Allied and Neutral shipping.	Total.
	Gross tons.	Gross tons.	Gross tons.
Losses	7,079,492	4,748,080	11,827,572
Gains :—			
New construction	3,031,555	3,574,720	6,606,275
Enemy tonnage captured ...	780,000	1,809,000	2,589,000
Total gains	3,811,555	5,383,720	9,195,275
Net loss (−) or gain (+) ...	−3,267,937	+635,640	−2,632,297

2.—*Merchant Tonnage Lost in* 1917.

Period.	British shipping.	Allied and Neutral shipping.	Total.
	Gross tons.	Gross tons.	Gross tons.
1st Quarter	911,840	707,533	1,619,373
2nd Quarter	1,361,870	875,064	2,236,934
3rd Quarter	952,938	541,535	1,494,473
4th Quarter	782,889	489,954	1,272,843
Totals	4,009,537	2,614,086	6,623,623

3.—*Output of Merchant Shipping in* 1917.

Period.	United Kingdom	Allied and Neutral countries.	Total.
	Gross tons.	Gross tons.	Gross tons.
1st Quarter	246,239	282,200	528,439
2nd Quarter	249,331	377,109	626,440
3rd Quarter	248,283	368,170	616,453
4th Quarter	419,621	512,402	932,023
Totals	1,163,474	1,539,881	2,703,355

Sir E. Geddes admitted the gravity of the situation disclosed by these figures, and deplored the unsatisfactory output of British shipping since the beginning of 1918— 58,000 tons in January and 100,000 tons in February. He urged as a partial excuse that the energies of the shipyards had of late been largely devoted to the repair of damaged vessels—a double-edged argument—and predicted a speedy increase in new construction. One of the most encouraging features of the general situation, he said, was the remarkable success of the convoy system.

(¹³) *March* 7.—Germany undertakes to exert herself to secure general recognition of Finland's independence, and Finland promises to cede no territory, or grant any easement on her territory, to a foreign Power without Germany's consent. Each party renounces indemnification for war costs or damages. Other clauses refer to future diplomatic and commercial relations, and the question of the Aaland Islands is dealt with as in the treaty of Brest-Litovsk.

(⁴⁴) *March* 7.—The history of the negotiations regarding Dutch ships lying idle in ports of the Allies was sketched by President Wilson in a statement published on March 21, and by Lord Robert Cecil in a speech in the House of Commons on the same day. The German submarine warfare being directed against neutral as well as belligerent vessels, the Allied Governments had consistently striven to induce neutrals to make the fullest possible use of their shipping. In pursuance of this policy, negotiations were opened with the Dutch Government, whose representatives, on January 4, 1918, agreed to permit Dutch ships to be chartered by the Allies, provided that Holland might retain enough for her essential needs, and that the ships chartered should not be required to enter the so-called "danger zone." As the ratification of this agreement by the Dutch Government was delayed, a *modus vivendi* was arranged whereby, among other provisions, Dutch vessels were to be chartered for the shipment from America of supplies destined for Switzerland and Belgium, while for every ship that reached a Dutch port under this scheme another was to be allowed to sail from Holland. The Dutch Government, however, informed the Allies that the German Government had declared that it would use force to prevent ships sailing from Dutch ports in exchange for vessels arriving there from America, and that in consequence Holland could not comply with this part of the arrangement. At the same time the Dutch Government repeatedly showed its reluctance to carry out the other stipulations, and it remained completely silent as to its intentions regarding the ratification of the agreement of January 4. Meanwhile, the Allies had been compelled to make arrangements for the use of their own shipping, which rendered it impossible to guarantee that Dutch ships chartered by them would not be required to enter the danger zone. Accordingly, on March 7 they demanded the unconditional use of the Dutch shipping in their ports, promising, however, to replace at the end of the war any Dutch ship sunk by the enemy in the danger zone. The Dutch Government replied that it could not consent, except on certain conditions—the chief of which was that no Dutch ships should carry war materials, a limitation which would have rendered them practically useless. The Allied Governments, thereupon, decided to terminate the negotiations and to requisition the shipping in question. They undertook that private owners should suffer no loss, repeated their offer to replace ships sunk by the enemy, and promised to allow the shipment of 100,000 tons of wheat from American ports to Holland. Lord Robert Cecil justified the action of the Allies by the " right of angary," and President Wilson on the ground that Holland was not a free agent, but was deterred from doing as she wished by German threats.

(⁴⁵) *March* 26.—The Conference at Doullens (17 miles N. of Amiens) was attended by President Poincaré, M. Clémenceau, M. Loucheur (Minister of Munitions), Lord Milner (representing British Government), Sir Douglas Haig, Generals Plumer, Horne, Rawlinson, Byng and Wilson (C.I.G.S.), General Pétain and General Foch. It was agreed that the Executive Council of Generals had proved to be too slow to deal with the real emergency that had arisen, and that it should be replaced by true unity of command. Political difficulties vanished, and General Foch was given authority to co-ordinate the action of the Allied armies on the Western Front. General Pershing was too far away to attend the Conference, but sent a hearty letter of agreement to General Foch, two days later. General Foch was formally appointed Commander-in-Chief of the Allied Armies in France on April 14.

(⁴⁵ᵃ) *March* 28.—General Pershing wrote to General Foch :—" America would feel greatly honoured if its troops were engaged in the present battle. I ask that it should be so in its behalf as well as in my own . . . everything we have is yours, dispose of us as you wish . . . ." In America the notification of the offer meets with warm approval.

(⁴⁶) *March* 30.—Mr. Lloyd George, in his statement, says that since the present battle began, the decision has been taken to appoint General Foch to " co-ordinate the action of Allies on Western Front." This appointment has cordial co-operation of British and French Commanders in Chief. " The country must be prepared for further sacrifices . . . " " Necessary plans . . . will be announced when Parliament meets."

(⁴⁷) *March* 31.—Comparative statement of bombs dropped by British and German aircraft in March.

	British.	German.
By day.	23,099	517
By night.	13,080	1,948
	36,179	2,465

(⁴⁸) *March* 31.—In Mesopotamia the Turkish force defeated at Khan Baghdadie has been pursued to beyond Ana (83 miles N.W. of Hit). British troops were in Ana on 28th and captured large depots of munitions and increased number of prisoners to 5,000.

(⁴⁹) *March* 31.—In Palestine operations continued E. of Jordan on 28th and 29th. Several miles of Hejaz railway have been destroyed. W. of Jordan British advanced on 28th on an 8 mile front to a depth of 2 miles and occupied places on the plain W. of Shechem road and N. of Wadi Dir Ballut.

(⁵⁰) *March* 31.—*Hejaz.* On March 16 Turkish Camel Corps is dispersed by Hejaz troops N.W. of Medina: on 19 railway near Bowat (N. Medina) is raided and much damage done: on 20 a train is derailed and on 23 and 24 ports in Medina area are raided.

(⁵¹) *March* 31.—*Arbeiter Zeitung* (Vienna) article on sea power says " the greatest victory on land cannot force England and America to a peace by compulsion " and . . . " can still cut off our supplies."

(⁵²) *Apr.* 3.—Baltic Submarines.—These submarines were the last of the British naval contingent in the Baltic which for the first three years of the war had co-operated with the Russian navy and had done brilliant work in waylaying and destroying German battleships and merchant vessels operating in the Baltic.   After the defection of Russia from the Allies and on the approach of the German naval forces to Hangö (S.W. Finland), these seven ships were taken outside the harbour and blown up in Helsingfors Bay, together with one or two barges containing some hundreds of mines and torpedo war heads.   They sank in 17 fathoms of water and their crews were transferred to Petrograd.

(⁵³) *Apr.* 3.—Count Czernin in Vienna details terms of peace with Rumania which involve "slight frontier rectification," and suggests compensation to Rumania in Bessarabia.   He lays blame for continuance of war on Western powers : confesses that supplies from the Ukraine are unsatisfactory and denies that President Wilson desires to separate Austria from Germany.   As to Serbia he says "the best state egoism is to come to terms with a beaten neighbour."

(⁵⁴) *Apr.* 4.—Estimated that Germans have here used 20 divisions.   They have gained some ground on a front of about 4 miles, and claim 90,000 prisoners and 1,300 guns since March 21.

(⁵⁵) *Apr.* 4.—Germans in Marocco are reported to have made following arrangements with Raisuli and others :—In the event of a German victory a revolution is to break out and all Allied subjects are to be massacred : Spain will then be forced to cede sovereignty to Germany.   Raisuli to be Sultan of Northern province and another selected by Germany of Southern : Sus district to be ceded to German syndicate : civil and military administration to be in German hands.

(⁵⁶) *Apr.* 5.—Germans appear to have arrived in Finland by invitation of the White Guards, who seized the ice-breaker "Volinets" to pilot German ships from Reval. Besides Hangö Germans have occupied two railway stations towards Helsingfors. Germans say operations will be confined to Finland and will not extend to Russia. The Russian warships at Helsingfors have left for Kronstadt.

(⁵⁷) *Apr.* 5.—East African despatch dated 21.1.18 deals with events from 30 May to 31 Dec., 1917.   In May the Germans were in two main parties : one of 4 to 5,000 under von Lettow-Vorbeck in Kilwa and Lindi region ; the other based on Mahenge.   A smaller detachment was raiding in Portuguese E.A. and another the central railway district in German E.A.   This latter force was rounded up.   In November von Lettow escaped into Portuguese East Africa, and the campaign in German East Africa came to an end for the time being on Nov. 28 with the capture of the last remaining detachment.

(⁵⁸) *Apr.* 6.—President Wilson at Baltimore, says, "the reasons for the war . . . are more clearly disclosed than ever before" and "we know what the war must cost . . . if need be all that we possess."   He calls his countrymen to witness that he did not rush into war 'intemperately' ; and has asked Germany to say plainly what she seeks.   Germany has acknowledged 'that it was not justice but dominion and the unhindered execution of her will.'   This answer is 'from her military leaders who are her real rulers.'   Her statesmen give lip service to peace ; the 'real test of their justice and fair play' appears in their action in Russia and Rumania.   The German idea is a world empire of 'gain and commercial supremacy.'   He does not wish at 'that moment of utter disillusionment' to judge harshly and is still ready to discuss an honest peace.   But German proceedings in Russia have given him his answer and he 'accepts the challenge.'   Only one answer is possible and that is 'force . . . force without limit.'"

(⁵⁹) *Apr.* 8.—The Emperor of Austria's letter, dated March, 1917. and forwarded through Prince Sixte of Bourbon, records his adhesion to "the just French claims in regard to Alsace-Lorraine" and states that he is in agreement with his government.

(⁶⁰) *Apr.* 8.—Speaking on conditions in Quebec, Sir Sam Hughes says their recruits could not be obtained in the French province owing to the opposition of the priests : and that there is evidence that some of these are in collusion with German agents in the States.

(⁶¹) *Apr.* 9.—Man Power Bill provides for comb-out among munition-workers ; call-up of more miners, transport workers and civil servants : cancelling of certain exemptions : shortening period of calling up notice : raising of military age to 50 : extension of Military Service Acts to Ireland.

(⁶²) *Apr.* 9.—In his review of the battle situation, Mr. Lloyd George makes the following points :—(1) At beginning of battle German strength less than that of Allies. (2) At one period position was very critical. (3) War Cabinet have called for report on retirement of 5th Army. (4) Position now appears to be stabilised, but further attacks must be expected. (5) More reinforcements have lately been sent to France than in any similar period before. (6) Captures of prisoners, guns and machine guns greatly exaggerated by enemy.

([63]) *Apr.* 9.—Speaking on Irish question, Mr. Lloyd George says Government proposes to extend Military Service Act to Ireland and meanwhile " to invite Parliament to pass a measure for self-government for Ireland." " The report of the remarkable Convention which has just brought its proceedings to a termination affords the British Parliament another opportunity of approaching this vexed question with more hope of success."

([64]) *Apr.* 11.—Report shows :—(1) That British prisoners have long been employed close to the firing line and treated with utmost brutality. (2) That they are still being so employed in spite of agreement of April, 1917. (3) That they are still treated with extreme brutality and forced to do work barred by Hague Convention till they become useless owing to weakness.

([65]) *Apr.* 12.—Sir H. Plumer's despatch, dated 9 March, 1918, dealt with affairs from 10 Nov., 1917. On that date the stability of Piave line being doubtful the two British divisions were stationed in Vicenza district with the French. On Dec. 4, the British took over Montello section of front, a hinge to the whole Italian line. In December local Austrian attacks were severe and a break through was possible till, towards the end of the month, the Italian and French captures of Monte Asolone and Monte Tomba improved the situation, British artillery taking part. On January 28, 1918, the British took over a further section of line to the right, and the artillery co-operated with Italians in the attack on Monte Val Bella. Work of R.F.C. has been quite brilliant—64 enemy machines having been destroyed against a loss of 12. Artillery work excellent, Austrian batteries having been pushed back on the whole British line.

([66]) *Apr.* 13.—Irish Convention report, dated 5 Apr. Summary—An Irish Parliament to be formed : Government to be through Lord Lieutenant, representing the King, with advice of Irish Executive Committee : supreme power of Parliament of United Kingdom to remain : taxation other than customs and excise to be under control of Irish Parliament : principle of Imperial contribution is recognised : provisions for land purchase are recommended.

([67]) *Apr.* 13.—Sir D. Haig, in his special order of the day, refers briefly to enemy attacks on 50-mile front with object of separating British and French armies and destroying the former. In spite of enormous sacrifices, enemy has so far failed, thanks to splendid resistance offered. " Many amongst us are now tired . . . Victory will belong to the side which holds out longest . . . " " There is no other course than to fight it out . . . with our backs to the wall . . . each one of us must fight on to the end."

([68]) *Apr.* 17.—Portuguese East Africa.—From Apr. 1 to 12 British columns from coast (General Edwards) and Lake Nyassa (General Northey) have been converging on German forces in Lurio R. region (100 miles S. of G.E.A. border), on 5, 11, and 12 enemy were engaged and suffered severe losses and were driven S.W.

([69]) *Apr.* 17.—Canadian Government asks Parliamentary approval of an order giving authority to Military Department to call to the colours any class and abolishing exemption of such class.

([70]) *Apr.* 18.—Third Military Service Bill receives Royal Assent within ten days of its introduction. This is intended to be the last man-power measure of the war. Chief provisions are :—Military age raised to 50 and if necessary to 55. Returned prisoners of war and time-expired men are liable to further service. The Act may be extended to Ireland. A " national emergency " may be declared and exemptions withdrawn.

([71]) *Apr.* 20.—It is reported in Stockholm that Finnish " White Party " intends :—(1) To defend the Reds or Socialists. (2) To establish a Monarchy on the German pattern. (3) To control the Murman railway and have an ice-free port on the Atlantic. (4) To make Finland a part of a confederacy reaching from the North Cape to Baghdad.

([72]) *Apr.* 21.—Versailles Council consists of :—

France ...	...	General Belin (President)
England	...	General Sackville-West.
Italy ...	...	General Di Robilant.
U.S.A. ...	...	General Bliss.

(73) *Apr.* 22-23.—Zeebrugge and Ostend raid.—Admiralty report says " . . . a naval raid was made on Ostend and Zeebrugge . . . with exception of covering ships the force employed consisted of auxiliary vessels and six obsolete cruisers. Five of these, filled with concrete, were used as blockships . . . and, in accordance with orders, were blown up and abandoned by their crews." Two blockships were sunk in the entrance to the Bruges Canal at Zeebrugge and a third ship grounded on the way in : storming parties landed on the Mole, which was much damaged by the blowing up of a submarine laden with explosives. A German destroyer was torpedoed and other craft damaged. One British destroyer and two motor boats were lost. At Ostend two blockships were run ashore and blown up. Vice-Admiral Roger Keyes was in command of operations from destroyer "Warwick" and Captain Carpenter commanded " Vindictive," which ran alongside the Mole and landed storming parties. Casualties (circâ.) : 16 officers, 86 men killed ; 5 officers, 121 men wounded.

(74) *Apr.* 22.—Cabinet Council held at the Hague to consider German demands as to transport of sand and gravel for which Germany demands unlimited transport. Situation regarded with misgivings.

(75) *Apr.* 22.—Budget proposals :—Income tax to be raised to 6s. : new allowances for wives : Farmers' tax doubled : Super-tax up to 4s. 6d. : Twopenny cheque stamp : Beer and Spirits duty doubled : Tobacco and Match duty raised : Sugar duty raised : Luxury tax : Letter rate raised. Expenditure, £2,972,197,000 ; Revenue, £842,050,000; Deficit, £2,130,147,000.

(76) *Apr.* 23.—Special despatch from G.H.Q. says that since March 21 Germans have used 102 divisions against British alone ; many of these twice and three times. Following British divisions are specially "mentioned": Guards, 31st, 3rd, 4th, 21st, 25th, 34th, 42nd(T), 62nd(T), 50th, 3rd, 4th and 5th Australians and New Zealand divisions.

(77) *Apr.* 23.—*Hejaz.* From April 11 to 17 Arab troops have continually raided the Hejaz railway and caused much damage to line N. and S. of Maan. Between 14th and 17th Maan was attacked and entered : the Hejaz troops then withdrew to outer defences which they still hold.

(78) *Apr.* 23.—Dr. Wekerle, Hungarian Premier, says " By a personal examination of this letter (Emperor to Prince Sixte) . . . I ascertained that it contained nothing but peace efforts made in agreement with German Empire . . . We shall continue to act in full harmony with our Allies . . . " (Dr. Wekerle resigned on 16th, but had been asked to carry on the Government).

(79) *Apr.* 24.—Naval raid. Observation by aircraft was difficult owing to clouds, and machines descended to 50 ft. A clear break 20 yards wide appears at inner end of Zeebrugge Mole. At Ostend a sunken object lies between the piers and blocks greater part of the fairway.

(80) *Apr.* 25.—Mr. Churchill, in his speech on the work of the Ministry of Munitions, shows that the supply of munitions is sufficient to carry on fighting at high pressure throughout the year. We had lost nearly 1,000 guns and between 4 and 5,000 machine guns—also much ammunition in dumps : these losses had been made good, and we had actually more serviceable guns in France than before the battle. German claims to guns were double of what was really lost : supply of aeroplanes is in advance of that of pilots : lost tanks are replaced by newer and better ones : since last May 100,000 men had been released from munition work : 750,000 women are working on munitions, and nine-tenths of the whole manufacture of shells is due to their labours.

(81) *April* 28.—Polish Government addresses Note to the Central Powers offering alliance on condition that integrity of Russian Poland is respected (but certain frontier rectifications in Suvalki and Grodno are proposed), that Poland's economic access to the sea is safeguarded, and that administration of the country is immediately handed over to the Poles.

(82) *May* 7.—This Treaty between Germany, Austria, Bulgaria and Turkey on the one hand, and Rumania on the other, is comprised in eight paragraphs and contains the following main provisions :—

The immediate demobilisation of the Rumanian army.
The cession to Bulgaria of all territory she lost by the Treaty of 1913.
The cession to the Central Powers of a strip of territory which would give them complete control over the mouths of the Danube.
An army of occupation to remain indefinitely in Rumania and to be maintained at her expense.

The final ratification of this Treaty was always postponed by Rumania.

(⁸³) *May* 10.—The sinking of the " Vindictive " (filled with concrete) at the entrance of Ostend harbour was a sequel to the attack made against Zeebrugge and Ostend on April 23rd, when the " Brilliant " and " Sirius " failed to block the harbour mouth. Leaving Dover at midnight the " Vindictive " set out in favourable weather, escorted by monitors, destroyers, motor launches and coastal boats ; a destroyer went on ahead to lay the light-buoy which was to guide her when she reached her destination. The main element of success being to secure a surprise attack, no preliminary bombardment was made, and, undetected by the enemy, the monitors were able to anchor in their firing positions out to sea. When the " Vindictive " arrived the motor launches built a smoke screen round her ; destroyers patrolled to seaward of the small craft to keep off enemy destroyers known to be about ; airmen above waited the given signal to bomb the town, and the great siege batteries of the Royal Marine Artillery in Flanders stood by to neutralise the big German artillery along the coast. Fifteen minutes before the " Vindictive " was due to arrive at the harbour mouth, two motor-boats dashed in towards the ends of the high wooden piers and torpedoed them, destroying a machine gun on the end of one of them. This was the signal for attack ; the marines, monitors and aeroplanes opened fire, the enemy batteries replied, while the " Vindictive," escorted by motor-boats, approached the harbour mouth. Unfortunately a sea fog drifting down at the moment obscured everything, and the " Vindictive " was obliged to put her helm over and cruise about for twenty minutes searching for the entrance. Twice she passed it ; the third time the fog lifted and she steamed in. Under a hail of fire her Commander put her stem against the eastern pier and swung her stern so that her full length lay across the channel ; then, by the explosion of magazines which tore her bottom plates out, she sank about 200 yards inside the entrance. During these operations she was hit every few seconds by enemy fire ; the after-control was demolished and the conning-tower struck by a shell from the shore batteries, causing several casualties, among others that of the Commander. Having accomplished their object the crew abandoned ship and were removed with their wounded by two motor-boats ; it was during this work of rescue that the majority of the casualties occurred. Other motor-boats also searched the shores under very heavy fire. At 2.30 a.m. recall-rockets were sent up and gradually the launches and motor-boats returned and transferred their wounded to the destroyers, one motor-boat only having to be destroyed, being too badly damaged to be brought home. The result of this brilliant operation was to prevent the use of the harbour for cruisers and greatly impede its use for destroyers and submarines. Casualties : 4 officers, 16 men killed ; 4 officers, 8 men wounded.

(⁸⁴) *May* 11.—In 1917 it was known to the British Admiralty that Germany was building submarine cruisers of a larger type than the earlier U-boats. The special characteristics of these boats were a greater displacement, much heavier armament, increased deck space and height, and better accommodation for a more numerous crew. They were also able to descend to greater depths than formerly with the object of carrying them under mine-fields. On the other hand they offered a larger target and needed greater depth of water in which to manœuvre.

(⁸⁵) *May* 12.—Colonel Semenov, the organiser of the Siberian Cossacks against the Bolsheviks, is a Cossack officer who under the Kerenski "régime" raised part of a Mongol regiment for service in Mesopotamia and Persia. This force was used later for maintaining order on the Manchurian frontier when Bolshevik disorders broke out in Eastern Siberia, and became a rallying point for the Cossack communities in Trans-Baikalia.

(⁸⁶) *May* 13.—In the House of Commons Mr. Bonar Law, in outlining the economic policy of Great Britain and the Allies, said that the French Government had denounced all commercial conventions containing a general clause regarding " most favoured nations " ; and that in view of the probable scarcity of raw material after the war and the necessity of providing for the needs of the British Empire and the Allies, the British Government intended to adopt a similar course.

(⁸⁷) *May* 16.—This Convention between China and Japan was a purely military one, having for its object the effective co-ordination of their military forces to combat the German menace in the Far East. China agreed to facilitate the transport of Japanese troops through her territories, and moreover to supply war material and munitions as well as engineers and a medical staff. Japan in return undertook to respect Chinese sovereignty and local customs, and to evacuate Chinese territory as soon as the operations were terminated. The agreement to cease automatically at the end of the War.

(⁸⁸) *May* 24.—This official statement, based upon intercepted documents in possession of the British Government, shows conclusively that negotiations between the Sinn Fein leaders and Germany had been virtually continuous for three-and-a-half years. At first the Irish-Americans, with the help of Count Bernstorff in Washington and the German Legation in Norway, were intermediaries for most of the discussions; but since America's entrance into the war, communications with the enemy tended to be more direct. There were, moreover, numerous private wireless receiving-stations in Ireland, which are mentioned by Bernstorff in one of his messages to Berlin. The intercepted messages and correspondence show how Germany was sending over money to the rebels—£1,000 being provided for the defence of Casement—how the rebels pressed for German troops and munitions to aid in their several risings, offering as an inducement the advantage to Germany of having submarine and Zeppelin bases in the West of Ireland to " menace the shipping of all nations." Three separate risings were attempted : (1) the Easter rising of 1916 ; (2) another in February, 1917 ; (3) and lastly one in May, 1918. For this rising the evidence shows that German munitions were actually shipped on submarines at Cuxhaven at the beginning of May. The second rising only broke down because Germany was unable to send troops ; the last rising was prevented by the arrest of the leaders.

(⁸⁹) *May* 30.—The Notes were :—

March 25.—Exchange of Notes : " Matters to be arranged are to be put into execution as the Government may decide."

May 16.—Agreement signed *re* the Army, embodying arrangements as to co-operation not made public.

May 19.—Similar agreement *re* the Navy; with a supplementary Note that any Japanese troops stationed in Chinese territory are to be withdrawn at the end of the war.

(⁹⁰) *June* 2.—Secret convention between Germany and Finland published in " Politiken " (Swedish Socialist paper). Finnish Government to carry through Diet establishment of Monarchy under German dynasty; to place Finnish army under German leadership; to grant use of Aaland Islands or part of coast opposite as naval base, and use of Finnish outlet in Arctic as commercial and shipping harbour to Germany ; to take measures to combat anarchism. Germany to have right to maintain army in Finland till these conditions fulfilled.

(⁹¹) *June* 3.—Formal recognition by British Government of Czecho-Slovak aims. National Council of Czecho-Slovaks recognised as supreme organ of the movement by Allied countries. Great Britain prepared to recognise Czecho-Slovak army as organised unit in Allied cause.

(⁹²) *June* 3.—Declaration at Versailles by Premiers of Great Britain, France and Italy :—(1) Creation of independent united Polish State with free access to sea as a condition of peace. (2) Sympathy expressed for nationalistic aims of Czecho-Slovaks and Yugo-Slavs.

(⁹³) *June* 3.—Proclamation of Lord French asking for 50,000 volunteers from Ireland before October 1, and after October 1 2,000 to 3,000 recruits per month. Farming and food production not to be interfered with. Age limit, 18 to 27. Land to be given to soldiers.

(⁹⁴) *June* 4.—Continental Idea : Expansion of Mittel-Europa (all Europe to be bound together by economic reciprocity against British Empire and U.S.A.) ; explained by Ludwig Quessel (Imperial Socialist) in " Sozialistische Monatshefte " of 4.6.18.

(⁹⁵) *June* 5.—Count Tisza describes value of Dual Alliance shown in war, waged to repel enemies' attacks ; its strengthening will increase military capacities of both ; main importance of new Alliance is economic. Agrarian duties must be revived after war. Hungary to have right of veto against including new comrades in Alliance.

(⁹⁶) *June* 9.—Hague Conference *re* Prisoners of War opens. Sir G. Cave, Lord Newton, Lieut. Gen. Sir H. Belfield, Capt. Kitson, R.N., British delegates. General Friedrichs, Von Hatzfeld-Willenburg, Councillor of Legation Eckhardt, Dr. Krauss, Major Draudt, Naval Capt. von Müller, German delegates.

(⁹⁷) *June* 9.—Mr. Wilson stated that the aims of the U.S.A. in war were disinterested. U.S.A. would stand by Russia as by other Allies. Suggested Pan-American Agreement for preservation of independence and territorial integrity of American States ; similar Agreement meant the foundation of the future life of nations of the world : " Peace can only come by trust."

(⁹⁸) *June* 11.—(1) Finland to be a Constitutional Monarchy ; hereditary sovereign, evangelical faith. (2) King to decide foreign policy ; treaties to be ratified by Diet ;

no offensive war without Diet's consent.   (3) Executive power is the King's ; legislative power is that of the King and Riksdag together ; judicial power is that of independent law courts.   (4) The King cannot be sovereign of another state ; members of State Council to be Finnish citizens chosen by King.   (5) Before law courts Swedish and Finnish languages can be used ; State to provide education for Swedish and Finnish population.   (6) Riksdag represents Finnish people.   (7) King has absolute veto on legislation ; Acts vetoed become law if approved by Riksdag after new elections by majority of two-thirds members sitting.   (8) Administrative districts to be divided as far as possible according as inhabitants speak Swedish or Finnish.   (9) Foreigners may be employed in military service.

(⁹⁹) *June* 11.—Speech of von Stein (German War Minister) : The victory of May 27 is a great defeat for Entente.   Americans on the Western Front are few.   The liberation of Finland has been accomplished by German troops.   In the Ukraine negotiations *re* frontier are proceeding.   The British are unable to maintain successes in Palestine and Mesopotamia.   In Transcaucasia Turks are in region of Batum, Erivan and Kars, etc., etc.

(¹⁰⁰) *June* 12.—Imperial War Conference Members :—

Sir R. Borden	...	Premier ... ... ⎫
Mr. A. Meighen	...	Minister of Interior ... ... ⎪
Mr. J. A. Calder	...	Minister of Immigration and Colonisation... ⎪
Mr. N. W. Rowell	...	President of Privy Council ... ... ⎬ Canada.
Mr. T. C. Norris	...	Premier of Manitoba... ... ... ⎪
Mr. C. Stewart	...	Premier of Alberta ... ... ⎪
Mr. W. M. Martin	...	Premier of Saskatchewan ... ... ⎭
Mr. W. F. Lloyd, K.C.		Premier ... ... Newfoundland.
Lieut. Gen. J. C. Smuts	...	... ... ⎫ Union of
Mr. H. Burton, K.C. ...		Minister of Railways and Harbours ⎬ S. Africa.
Mr. W. M. Hughes	...	Premier ... ... ⎫
Mr. Joseph Cook	...	Minister of Navy ... ... ⎬ Australia.
Mr. W. F. Massey	...	Premier ... ... ⎫
Sir J. Ward ...	...	Minister of Finance ... ... ⎬ New Zealand.
Mr. E. S. Montagu	...	Secretary of State for India ... ... ⎫
Sir Satyendra P. Sinha		Nominee of Viceroy ... ... ⎬ India.
Maharaja of Patiala ...		Representative of Indian States ... ⎭

(¹⁰¹) *June* 14.—The Provisional Treaty between Russia and the Ukraine provided for the cessation of hostilities and expressed the willingness of the two parties to enter into final peace negotiations.

(¹⁰²) *June* 18.—Secret Treaty of Brest-Litovsk *re* Poland between Bolsheviks and Germans published in " Nation's Voice " of Cracow.   (1) Polish policy to be conducted by Germany.   (2) Russian Government not to interfere in organisation of Poland. (3) Bolshevik Government to remain in touch with democratic and revolutionary clubs in Poland ; names of agitators sent there to be on lists of German Information Bureaux at Petrograd and Warsaw.   (4) Bolsheviks not to send agitators to Germany and Austria.   (5) Bolshevik Government to prevent enlistment of Polish national groups in Russian Territorial Army.   (6) Violation of frontiers of Lithuania and Ukraine by Poles to be considered a declaration of war on Germany and Austria ; Russia to help in crushing Poles.   (7) Bolshevik Government to prevent Russians investing capital in Polish industries.   (8) Bolshevik Government to recognise new state of things in Poland and to defend it against Entente.

(¹⁰³) *June* 18.—Agreement between Allies and Sweden : Allies to have services of 400,000 tons of Swedish shipping.   Sweden to receive stipulated quantities of food-stuffs on guarantee against re-export.   Export of Swedish iron ore regulated.

(¹⁰⁴) *June* 19.—Report of Sub-Committee of Reconstruction Committee *re* increase of home-grown food.   Recommendations : — (1) Country to be made independent of overseas supplies of corn, potatoes and dairy produce.   (2) Principles to be embodied in agricultural legislation : (a) guaranteed price of wheat ; (b) minimum wage ; (c) power of State to enforce proper cultivation.   (3) Reorganisation of agricultural administration by establishment of National Agricultural Councils for England, Wales, Scotland, Ireland ; Statutory County Agricultural Committees ; Agricultural Minister for Scotland.   (4) Encouragement of education and research ; Board of Agriculture (not County Councils) to be responsible for agricultural education ; improved curriculum for schools ; better prospects for rural teachers ; establishment of demonstration and illustration farms; better opportunities for agricultural education of women, and of studying rural economy at public schools and universities. Research work to be developed. (5) Land for soldiers. (6) National policy of afforestation. (7) Transport improvement; discarded army motors to be used. (8) Dublin Wage Board to be permanent with power to create local wage boards.

(¹⁰⁵) *June* 20.—" League of Nations" by Viscount Grey: The conditions of effectiveness are that (1) The idea of the League must be adopted by executive heads of States; (2) Recognition by peoples and governments of the limitations that the League imposes on the national action of each. The alternative to regulation of relations of States to each other must result in anarchy and more terrible wars.

(¹⁰⁶) *June* 20.—Report of Shipping Committee:—(1) Repudiation of State ownership in shipping and shipbuilding after war. (2) Surrender of enemy's shipping after war as punishment for crimes. (3) Prosecution of energetic shipbuilding during and after war. (4) British trade with S. America and Far East essential to British ascendency in world's carrying trade. (5) German competition to be met by greater co-operation between British shipping members and by steps to counteract unfair competition. (6) Freedom of seas, *i.e.*, equal treatment of all flags in all ports to be our post-war policy.

(¹⁰⁷) *June* 20.—Speech of Earl Curzon in Lords *re* Irish policy; Conscription for Ireland justified by German advance on Western Front; no connection with Home Rule policy; abandonment of Home Rule due to discovery of Sinn Fein conspiracy and policy of R.C. clergy in resisting conscription; scheme of voluntary enlistment introduced to prevent strife; land for soldiers no new policy; internment of Sinn Feiners without trial legal for sake of realm.

(¹⁰⁸) *June* 20.—Speech of Mr. Balfour in Commons *re* Peace: No serious peace offers from Central Powers; the "Secret Treaties" published form no obstacle to reasonable peace nor ground for discord between us and Italy. Our immediate task is resistance to German effort in the West and help to Russia. Future peace to be guaranteed by rearrangement of territory or constitution, supplemented by League of Nations. Present importance of realising German ambition.

(¹⁰⁹) *June* 21.—Speech of von Kühlmann (German Imperial Secretary for Foreign Affairs) *re* Balkans: Northern Dobruja to be united to Bulgaria; Bulgaria not to be favoured at the expense of Turkey. Future relations of Germany to Bulgaria hopeful.

(¹¹⁰) *June* 21.—Labour Ministers' Manifesto: "Incessant sniping" by anti-national factionalists denounced; appeal for national unity during war and Labour unity after.

(¹¹¹) *June* 22.—Turkish war aims (in "Vorwärts," 22.6.18): (1) Surrender of occupied territories of Irak, Palestine, Jezireh. (2) Restoration of Turkish domination in Egypt. (3) Independence of Persia; ousting of British influence. (4) Domination of Turkey over Black Sea and placing all states bordering on that sea under Turkish Protectorate; Ottoman prince in Crimea, German prince in Georgia, Austrian archduke in Armenia as regents. (5) Bulgaria to have North Dobruja, to surrender Cherna basin; Constanza and Dedeagach to be free ports. (6) Austria not to evacuate North Italy till Tripoli, Cyrenaica and Dodekanese are in Turks' hands. (7) Crete to be returned to Turkey. (8) Victualling of Turkey to be guaranteed.

(¹¹²) *June* 24.—Speech of Mr. Lloyd George in Commons *re* war: Americans in great numbers in France since March 21. "We are on the eve of great events." Allies never better prepared. Recent Italian victory one of the most disastrous defeats of Central Powers. Italian difficulties greater than ours.

(¹¹³) *June* 24.—Speech of von Kühlmann *re* war: Relations with Austria, Bulgaria, Turkey satisfactory. Russia in state of ferment and partition. Finnish independence achieved with help of German troops. Courland and Lithuania separated from Russia. Position of other Baltic provinces to be discussed with Bolsheviks. Polish question unsettled. Caucasian affairs to be settled at Conference at Constantinople. Initiative of war in German hands. Duration of war uncertain. No desire for peace among enemies. Germany does not desire world domination. Russia planned the war; France desired it; Great Britain "unchained" Russia. Germany aims at (1) Independence within her historic boundaries. (2) Overseas possessions corresponding to German greatness. (3) Freedom to carry trade on free sea to all countries. A purely military decision not to be expected. Germany ready to receive peace proposals.

(¹¹⁴) *June* 25.—Speech of Mr. Shortt (Irish Secretary) *re* Irish situation : (1) Two sources of information *re* German plot : (*a*) inside Ireland, from literature and posters ; (*b*) outside Ireland, information that Germany in spring was trying to get in touch with Ireland. German agent landed in West Ireland April 12. Two German submarines off West coast, where destruction of shipping impossible. (2) Justification of Government policy. Voluntary recruiting proclamation essential before conscription ; promise of land to soldiers made to English, Scottish and Welsh soldiers. Central Recruiting Council set up. Propaganda for Ireland being attended to.

(¹¹⁵) *June* 26-28.—Labour Conference in London resolves : Political truce no longer to be recognised. Appearance and speech of Kerenski : " Russia will shortly join in fight for freedom."

(¹¹⁶) *June* 27.—450 Bolsheviks, 75 Revolutionary Socialists, 30 Mensheviks. M. Zinoviev president.

(¹¹⁷) *June* 27.—Yugo-Slav deputation at Rome. Signor Orlando declares Italy upholds principle of nationality ; will not leave other nationalities in lurch.

(¹¹⁸) *July* 1.—Mr. Lloyd George replied to Federalist Deputation that Federalism was a rational solution of the Home Rule problem. No change possible during war without general assent. This not yet given.

(¹¹⁹) *July* 2.—General Botha (Premier of South African Union) stated at Pretoria tdat military and police measures were necessitated by discovery of movement for subversion of Constitution by violence. " Demon of intrigue " at work.

(¹²⁰) *July* 2.—Austrian Socialists' Declaration *re* Peace : (1) League of Nations to be established. (2) No annexations : disputed territorial problems to be settled by self-determination of Nations. (3) Equal freedom of economic development and avoidance of economic war. (4) Peace not to be based on victory. (5) Austria-Hungary to be federation of autonomous nations. (6) Creation of free Balkan peoples. (7) Treaties of Brest-Litovsk and Bukarest to be annulled. (8) Restoration and indemnification of Belgium.

(¹²¹) *July* 3.—Programme of new Provisional Government at Vladivostok : Liberation of Siberia from Bolshevists ; avoidance of foreign interference ; summons of a constituent assembly ; universal suffrage.

(¹²²) *July* 4.—Conditions on which British Government waived right of search *re* Dutch convoy to East Indies : (1) List of passengers to be furnished ; only Dutch Government officials and families allowed. (2) Full particulars of cargo to be furnished. (3) Guarantee from Dutch Government that goods not of enemy origin. (4) Ships under Dutch naval flag to furnish complete lists of civilians and goods, other than warlike stores, for colonies.

(¹²³) *July* 4.—American Independence Day Celebrations : Speech of President Wilson at Washington :—Four great aims of Allies : (1) Destruction of arbitrary power (2) Self-determination of peoples. (3) National morality to be same as individual morality. (4) A peace organisation to prevent war. 100 ships launched. Speech of M. Poincaré at Paris : Tribute to President Wilson ; power of New World placed at service of ideals of liberty, loyalty, justice. Speech of Mr. Churchill in London Reconciliation between U.S. and Britain complete. Future for world bright. War is conflict between Christian civilisation and scientific barbarism. No compromise possible.

(¹²⁴) *July* 6.—Montagu-Chelmsford Report *re* Indian Constitutional Reforms I.—Historical Survey. II.—Proposals : (1) *Parliament and India Office :* Salary of Secretary of State for India to be defrayed from Home revenues, voted annually by Parliament. A Select Committee to be appointed at beginning of every session to report to Commons on Indian affairs. (2) *Government of India :* To be kept responsible to Parliament alone. *Viceregal Legislature :* (i) Legislative Assembly of 100 members, two-thirds elected, one third nominated by Governor-General. (ii) Council of State of 50 members, 29 nominated, 21 elected. A Privy Council for India and a Council of Princes. *Provinces :* First steps towards responsible government to be taken in Provinces. In each province (*a*) *Legislative Council* with large elected majority (*b*) *Executive Government :* (i) Governor and Executive Council of two members to be in charge of reserved subjects ; (ii) Minister or Ministers chosen by Governor from elected Members of Legislative Council to be in charge of transferred subjects ; (c) *Grand Committees* chosen partly by election, partly by nomination, to legislate on reserved subjects. *Local Self-Government* to be made independent of official control

Commissions of Inquiry : Working of system to be reviewed by tribunal appointed by Parliament every 10 or 12 years.

([125]) *July* 10.—New Siberian Government : General Horvath, Premier, issues programme, *viz.*, abolition of Bolshevik rule, fidelity to Allies, autonomy for Siberia as part of Russia ; religious toleration.

([126]) *July* 11.—Speech of Count Hertling *re* Foreign Policy. Resignation of von Kühlmann denotes no change in policy. Germany ready to consider honourable peace. Treaty of Brest-Litovsk to be maintained. Murder of Count Mirbach probably instigated by Allies. Kühlmann's retirement due to lack of confidence between him and others. Adm. Hintze to carry out Hertling's policy.

([127]) *July* 12.—Speech of Rt. Hon. W. M. Hughes (Australian Premier) *re* Pacific Islands. Australia will not consent to return to Germany captured Pacific Islands.

([128]) *July* 14.—Hague Conference *re* Prisoners of war : Combatants to be exchanged man for man, rank for rank. Better treatment of prisoners on line of Franco-German agreement of April, 1918.

([130]) *July* 18.—Debate in Reichsrat : von Seidler declares Germans in Austria to be backbone of State. Czernin declares Austria destined to mediate in duel between Germany and England ; Austria's interests are those of Germany. Treaties of Brest and Bukarest necessitated by military and food reasons.

([131]) *July* 19.—Lord R. Cecil, Assistant Foreign Secretary ; Brig.-Gen. Seely, Parliamentary Secretary of Munitions ; Sir L. W. Evans, Minister of Blockage.

([132]) *July* 19.—Statement of Lord R. Cecil *re* Allies' trade policy : Paris Resolutions represent narrow defensive alliance ; capable of expansion ; change of German mind necessary before Germany be admitted to Economic Association of Nations ; no selfish policy to be pursued by U.S. or British Empire.

([133]) *July* 23.—Siberian Government Council proclaims independence of Siberia, annuls Bolshevist decrees, re-establishes Siberian Duma, restores land owners.

([134]) *July* 27.—Speech of Mr. Montagu, Secretary of State for India, at Cambridge : Home Rule for India not yet possible. Progressive realisation of responsible government in the principle of British rule. Proposals of Reform Scheme : (1) In local self-government official interference to cease. (2) In provincial government partial responsibility. (3) In Imperial Affairs of India greater powers of criticism to be given to Indians.

([135]) *July* 31.—Unification of Foreign Office and Diplomatic Service. Re-organisation of work in embassies and legations : sufficient salaries ; diplomacy to concern itself with commerce and all national interests.

([136]) *July* 31.—Economic policy of Great Britain : Must be in accord with Dominions and Allies. Opinion of U.S. *re* Paris resolutions not yet expressed. Prospect of agreement with Great Britain hopeful. British essential industries must never be let down. Government control of trade to remain to certain extent after war till transition period over. Partnership with Dominions and Allies to be maintained.

([137]) *August* 6.—Speech of Rt. Hon. E. S. Montagu, Secretary of State for India. House of Commons on Indian Constitutional Reform : Explanation of Chelmsford-Montagu Scheme : not to be translated unaltered into Act of Parliament. Government assent given to appointment of two Committees to consider questions of electorate, "reserved" and "transferred" subjects, Government of India and Provincial Governments. Limitations in Reform Scheme based not on distrust but on facts and time. Present time opportune for starting building of self-governing India as integral part of Empire.

([138]) *August* 7.—Speech of Rt. Hon. D. Lloyd George in House of Commons on war position. (i) *Navy and Army :* Navy, now of 8,000,000 tons, has destroyed 150 submarines in past year, patrols every trade route, blockades Germany. *Army :* Number of men raised from Great Britain amounts to 6,250,000, from Dominions 1,000,000, from India 1,250,000. (ii) *Western Front :* Britain faced on March 21 by flower of German army. In one fortnight 268,000 men, in one month 355,000 crossed Channel. Germans, repulsed by British, attack the French. Foch's brilliant counter-stroke. Elements of Allied success are rapid repair of British losses, arrival of Americans, and unity of command. (iii) *Position of Enemy :* German effort not exhausted, but their high-water-mark has been reached. Economic position of Central Powers desperate. (iv) *Allies and Russia :* Russia seeking help from Allies. Czecho-Slovaks were at their own request sent in British ships to Vladivostok. (v) *Peace :* impossible till the supremacy of the German military party at an end.

(¹³⁹) *Aug.* 8.—Reply of Rt. Hon. A. Balfour to pacifists in House of Commons: German militarism is the real obstacle to peace. German guilt *re* Belgium not yet confessed. From Finland to Black Sea German military and economic dominion being forced on peoples. British and German methods of conquest contrasted: Palestine and Mesopotamia more prosperous. Belgium, Poland, Ukraine ravaged. Negotiation between Central Powers and Allies not possible. The return to Germany of her African Colonies would mean German submarine bases on trade routes, and the tyrannical government of Africans. German policy *re* Russia amounts to Russian disintegration. A pacifist peace means a set-back to civilisation.

(¹⁴⁰) *Aug.* 9.—Declaration of British Government to peoples of Russia issued at Vladivostok, Murmansk and Archangel, giving assurance of help and goodwill, and repudiating desire for Russian territory or of imposing any political system on Russia.

(¹⁴¹) *Aug.* 15.—Spanish Note to Germany *re* shipping losses. In future Spain will replace Spanish tonnage sunk by that of German tonnage in Spanish harbours.

(¹⁴²) *Aug,* 18.—British Government announcement *re* representation of Dominions in Imperial War Cabinet. Premiers of Dominions to have right to communicate on matters of Cabinet importance direct with Premier of U.K. Each Dominion to have right to nominate visiting or resident Minister in London to be member of Imperial War Cabinet at other meetings than those attended by Premiers. Meetings to be held at regular intervals. Arrangements to be made for representation of India.

(¹⁴³) *Aug.* 20.—Speech of Dr. Solf, German Colonial Secretary, in reply to Mr. Balfour's speech of August 8.18. Pan-Germans only a minority. Allies care not for Belgium, but for destruction of Germany's Brest Treaty made by agreement. Germans to protect border peoples in transition from oppression to freedom. Colonial questions should be settled on principle of correspondence to economic strength of European nations and merits shown in care of coloured peoples. The " knock-out " policy must be abandoned. War-waging nations must awaken to knowledge of common tasks.

(¹⁴⁴) *Aug.* 20.—Publication of names of Committee of Representatives established by Inter-Allied Food Council:—

Chairman	...	Sir John Beale, K.B.E.
U.K. ...	...	Major Hon. W. Astor, M.P., Mr. W. H. Beveridge, Captain Brooke (additional).
U.S.A. ...	...	Mr. J. P. Cotton, Mr. L. P. Sheldon, Mr. G. S. Jackson (additional).
France ...	...	Major R. Fillioux, M. Genestal, M. Destombes (additional).
Italy ...	...	Commendatore Prof. Attolico, C.B., Signor Nimmo, Lieut. Amadio (additional).
Secretary	...	Mr. Franklyn L. Turner, C.B.

(¹⁴⁵) *Aug.* 21.—Speech of Lord Reading, British Ambassador to U.S.A., *re* U.S.A. and War to American Club in London. During March a great awakening in U.S.A. America—nation of idealists. Redoubled effort needed to secure Allied aims. War drawing Great Britain and America nearer each other: both will emerge stronger.

(¹⁴⁶) *Aug.* 22.—Statement of Allies at Archangel of aims. Allies called in by legitimate representative of Murman Government to expel Germans and annul Brest Treaty: guaranteed there would be no interference in internal affairs of Russia.

(¹⁴⁷) *Aug.* 23.—Statement of Lord Robert Cecil, Assistant Foreign Secretary, *re* Dr. Solf's speech of August 20.18. Pan-Germans still influential, as Kühlmann's fall shows. Statement *re* Belgium unsatisfactory. Dr. Solf's view of Brest Treaty as temporary is new. Border States so constituted as to have little independence. German Colonial policy brutal. No possibility of League of Nations till Germany acknowledges militarism a crime.

(¹⁴⁸) *Aug.* 25.—Coup d'état of General Horvath, Cossack leader. Proclamation declaring Russian military forces in Far East to be under his command, and depriving Colonel Tolstov of command of Russian volunteer force organized by Vladivostok Zemstvo.

(¹⁴⁹) *Aug.* 26.—Letter of Lord Hugh Cecil (M.P. for Oxford University) on Lord Lansdowne's policy. War is one for civilisation and not merely of one group of nations against another. Alliance against Germany is a rudimentary form of the League of Nations. Submission, not destruction, of Germany is the aim of the Allies. Moloch must be humiliated before its votaries accept purer faith. Terms of peace must include beginning of League of Nations. To make League effective centre of human allegiance must be shifted from nationality to something higher.

(¹⁵⁰) *Aug.* 27.—*Supplements to Brest-Litovsk Treaty*:—The main features of this supplementary Treaty were as follows :—

1. Russia promised to fight against the troops of the Entente Powers in Northern Russia.
2. Russia accepted the situation as regards Esthonia and Livonia and renounced sovereignty over them ; their destiny to be settled in accordance with the wishes of the population.
3. The boundary line of all fronts to be defined. Germany to evacuate the whole of the occupied territories east of Livonia and Esthonia as soon as the frontiers had been established, and all the Black Sea regions outside the Caucasus.
4. Germany promised that Finland would not attack Russia.
5. Russia was to pay Germany £300,000,000 for war damages ; damages caused by annulment of loans and industrial losses.

(¹⁵¹) *Aug.* 30.—London Police Strike. Demands were for increased war bonus, reinstatement of a dismissed constable, official recognition of Police Union.

(¹⁵²) *Sept.* 14.—Towards the end of July, 1918, at the urgent request of the Armenian population, General Marshall despatched a small British force from Mesopotamia, across the Caspian Sea from Enzeli to Baku, to stiffen the local forces against the Turks. Unfortunately the Armenian troops from the first proved unreliable and failed to co-operate with the British against repeated Turkish attacks ; while our lack of control over the shipping on the Caspian created another danger to our force. Owing to superior communications the Turks were able to increase their forces, and eventually on the 14th September made a determined attack. After a fight lasting 16 hours, the brunt of which was borne by the British, our troops evacuated Baku, the Russians supplying the necessary shipping.

(¹⁵³) *Sept.* 29.—The **Allied terms** laid down by General Franchet d'Esperey and **accepted by Bulgarian envoys** at Salonika were :—

Immediate suspension of hostilities.

Immediate demobilisation of the Bulgarian Army (except three Divisions of Infantry and four regiments of Cavalry).

The handing over of all stores and equipment.

Immediate Bulgarian evacuation of Serbia and Greek territory.

All Bulgarian means of transport, including Danube transport, to be placed at the disposal of the Allies.

Bulgarian territory to be available for Allied operations against the enemy.

Bulgaria to cease to be a belligerent, except with Allied consent.

Departure within four weeks of all Germans and Austro-Hungarians.

It followed that the German route to the East was cut and placed under Allied control, and that the whole centre of military gravity in S.E. Europe was shifted ; the Armistice was in fact the beginning of the end of German domination.

(¹⁵⁴) *Sept.* 30.—Mr. Bonar Law stated that 1,120 millions had been subscribed to War Bonds in the past year, and appealed for 25 millions a week. He reviewed the situation and the past "wonderful week." Since July 18, British forces have recovered 1,000 square miles of French territory and 250 villages, and taken more than 120,000 prisoners ; three Turkish Armies destroyed, 60,000 prisoners captured. Announces Bulgaro-Allied Convention, hostilities ending at noon. German Middle East dream gone for ever. More than 1,600 millions of pounds lent to the Allies. Mr. Balfour welcomed the League of Nations idea and sketched the broad lines of conditions of peace necessary.

(¹⁵⁵) *Sept.* 30.—The Kaiser's "decree," forming part of his letter accepting Count Hertling's resignation, states: "I desire that the German people shall co-operate more effectively than hitherto in deciding the fate of the Fatherland. It is therefore my will that men who are sustained by the people's trust shall to a wide extent co-operate in the rights and duties of Government. I beg you to terminate your work by continuing the conduct of business and preparing the way for the measures desired by me," etc., etc.

(¹⁵⁶) *Oct.* 1.—The Majority Party's programme was reported by the *Tageblatt* to be an absolute endorsement of the Reichstag resolution of July 19.17. It professed readiness to join the League of Nations, and proposed the restoration of Belgium, autonomy for Alsace-Lorraine, abolition of Article 9 (paragraph 2) of Constitution, and equal suffrage in Prussia.

(¹⁵⁷) *Oct.* 3.—The following order from German Head Quarters (vouched for by a French Deputy and a member of the Army Committee) was found on a German officer : " You are requested, in the case of French prisoners newly captured, to carry out in future, as expedient, the following instructions :—

1. The cantonment of all prisoners, including deserters, for several days, as far as possible in the open air, surrounded by barbed wire, with as little food as possible.
2. The methodical seizure of all articles of value belonging to the captured prisoners . . . (as a guarantee).
3. Set them to do the severest labour, with an extension of the hours of work."

(¹⁵⁸) *Oct.* 4.—On October 4 it was announced that the following have been captured by the Allied Armies on the Western Front between the 15th July and the 30th September, 1918 :—

Officers	...	...	...	5,518
Men	...	...	...	248,494
Guns	...	...	...	3,669
Machine-guns	...	...	...	23,000

besides 25,000 prisoners in Macedonia and 70,000 in Palestine.

(¹⁵⁹) *Oct.* 4.—The **German Note to President Wilson,** forwarded through Switzerland, was as follows :—

" The German Government requests the President of the United States of America to take in hand the restoration of peace, acquaint all belligerent States with this request, and invite them to send plenipotentiaries for the purpose of opening negotiations. It accepts the programme set forth by the President of the United States in his message to Congress of January 8, 1918, and in his later pronouncements, especially his speech of September 27, as a basis for peace negotiations.

" With a view to avoiding further bloodshed, the German Government requests the immediate conclusion of an armistice on land and water and in the air.

" (Signed) MAX, PRINCE OF BADEN, Imperial Chancellor."

(¹⁶⁰) *Oct.* 4.—The **Austro-Hungarian Note to President Wilson,** forwarded through Sweden, was as follows :—

" The Austro-Hungarian Monarchy, which has always waged the war solely as a defensive war, and has repeatedly announced its readiness to put an end to the bloodshed and to attain a just and honourable peace, approaches herewith the President of the United States of America with a proposal to conclude with him and his Allies an immediate armistice on land and sea and in the air, and immediately, therefore, to enter into negotiations for the conclusion of peace, for which the Fourteen Points of President Wilson's Message to Congress of January 8, 1918, and the Four Points in his speech of February 12, 1918, should serve as a basis, whereby attention will be paid to the declarations by President Wilson on September 27, 1918.

(¹⁶¹) *Oct.* 5.—Prince Max took his stand on the programme of the Majority parties, which included the resolution of 19.7.17, adhered to the German answer to the Pope's Note of 1.8.17, declared his acceptance of the League of Nations idea, and agreed to the complete restoration of Belgium and representative bodies in the Baltic Provinces ; his new Government was for a just peace, regardless of the war situation, and intended so bring the co-operation of the Reichstag into the Imperial leadership. Civilians were to have executive authority in all civilian matters, especially including censorship and the right of assemblage, and labour questions were to be brought forward at the Peace Conference. He had therefore furthered the question of peace by sending the plea of October 4 to President Wilson, with the object of saving suffering humanity, etc., etc. An honourable and enduring Peace was his aim, and he hoped the President would receive his offer as it was intended. The Reichstag was adjourned in order to allow members to exchange views.

(¹⁶²) *Oct.* 5.—During September, 311,219 U.S.A. troops arrived in Europe : of these there were 153,246 in France and 157,973 in England. British ships carried 59%, American 37%, and French 4%. The grand total of U.S.A. troops brought to Europe amounted to 1,766,160, of which nearly 950,000 had been brought in British ships, the largest convoy carrying 31,108. The British Fleet provided 70% of the convoying forces, the American 27% and the French 3%

(¹⁶³) *Oct.* 6.—This private letter, written to Prince Alexander of Hohenlohe in Switzerland (text in *Times*, 16.10.) was meant to explain his speech of December 14, 1917, at Baden, which had been "misunderstood." He abuses the *Frankfurter Zeitung* as well as the Pan Germans ; jeers at the judicial attitude and the " democratic war-cry " of the Western Powers, and calls the Peace resolution of 19.7.17 (on which he now affects to take his stand) a " disgusting child born of fear and the Berlin dog-days." The whole tone is strongly against allowing the people a real voice in Government. Prince Max was called on later in the Reichstag, on 14.10, for an explanation of these sentiments, and produced but very lame excuses.

(¹⁶⁴) *Oct.* 8.—Text of President Wilson's reply (through the Swiss Chargé d' Affairs) to the German Peace Note of 4.10 :—

THE DEPARTMENT OF STATE,
OCTOBER 8, 1918.

" Sir,—I have the honour to acknowledge, on behalf of the President, your Note of October 6, enclosing a communication from the German Government to the President ; and I am instructed by the President to request you to make the following communication to the Imperial German Chancellor :—

" Before making a reply to the request of the Imperial German Government, and in order that the reply shall be as candid and straightforward as the momentous interests involved require, the President of the United States deems it necessary to assure himself of the exact meaning of the Note of the Imperial Chancellor.

" Does the Imperial Chancellor mean that the Imperial German Government accepts the terms laid down by the President in his address to the Congress of the United States on January 8 last and in subsequent addresses, and that its object in entering into discussions would be only to agree upon the practical details of their application ?

" The President feels bound to say, with regard to the suggestion of an armistice, that he would not feel at liberty to propose a cessation of arms to the Governments with which the Government of the United States is associated against the Central Powers so long as the Armies of those Powers are upon their soil.

" The good faith of any discussion would manifestly depend upon the consent of the Central Powers immediately to withdraw their forces everywhere from invaded territory.

" The President also feels that he is justified in asking whether the Imperial Chancellor is speaking merely for the constituted authorities of the Empire who have so far conducted the war.

" He deems the answer to these questions vital from every point of view. "Accept, Sir, the renewed assurances of my high consideration.—ROBERT LANSING."

It was officially announced that no answer to the Austrian peace proposals was contemplated for the present.

(¹⁶⁵) *Oct.* 10.—Lord Grey said that peace was within sight but not yet within reach ; it was time to work out the scheme and machinery of a League of Nations, which must not be a substitute for the termination of the war, but must arise out of it. Germany must enter the League, but this latter must be a working proposition and not a sham, and must keep the weapon of economic boycott held in reserve.

(¹⁶⁶) *Oct.* 12.—The German reply reached Washington 14.10 and was as follows :—

" Die Deutsche Regierung hat die Sätze angenommen, die Präsident Wilson in seiner Ansprache vom 8ten Januar und in seinen späteren Ansprachen als Grundloge eines dauernden Rechtsfriedens niedergelegt hat. Der Zweck der einzuleitenden Besprechungen wäre also lediglich sich über praktische Einzelheiten ihrer Anwendung zu verständigen. Die Deutsche Regierung nimmt an, dass auch die Regierungen der mit den Vereinigten Staaten verbündeten Mächte sich auf den Boden der Kundgebungen des Präsidenten Wilson stellen.

" Die Deutsche Regierung erklärt sich, in Einvernehmen mit der Oesterreichisch-Ungarischen Regierung, bereit, zur Herbeiführung eines Waffenstillstandes (some words omitted in transmission) zu entsprechen. Sie stellt dem Präsidenten anheim, den Zusammentritt einer gemischten Kommission zu veranlassen, der es obliegen würde, die zur Räumung erforderlichen Vereinbarungen zu treffen.

" Die jetzige Deutsche Regierung, die die Verantwortung für den Friedensschritt trägt, ist gebildet durch Verhandlungen und in Uebereinstimmung mit der grossen Mehrheit des Reichstages. In jeder seiner Handlungen gestützt auf dem Willen dieser

Mehrheit, spricht der Reichskanzler im Namen der Deutschen Regierung und des Deutschen Volkes."

The following is a literal translation of the German text :—

" The German Government has accepted the theses (*Sätze*) which President Wilson, in his address of January 8 and in his later addresses laid down as the basis of a lasting peace of Right. The purpose, therefore, of the discussions to be initiated would be solely to agree about practical details of the application of those theses. The German Government assumes that the Governments of the Powers which are allied with the United States place themselves also upon the basis of the pronouncements of President Wilson.

" The German Government, in agreement with the Austro-Hungarian Government, declares itself ready for the bringing about of an armistice to comply with [? the proposals of the President]. It submits that the President should arrange for the meeting of a Mixed Commission, whose business it would be to arrive at the agreements necessary for the evacuation.

" The present German Government, which bears the responsibility for the peace step, is formed by negotiations and in agreement with the great majority of the Reichstag. Sustained in all his actions by the will of this majority, the Imperial Chancellor speaks in the name of the German Government and of the German people."

(167) *Oct.* 14.—Germany is called upon by the British Government to redress grievances *re* British prisoners. Unless this is done satisfactorily within four weeks, reprisals will be taken.

(168) *Oct.* 14.—In answer to the German notes of October 4 and 12, President Wilson wrote October 14 that the process of evacuation and conditions of an Armistice must be left to the Allied military advisers. He (and no doubt also the Allies) could not consent to consider an armistice so long as the German illegal and inhumane practices are persisted in. He also pointed out that the Germans had by their previous Note, accepted the principle in his Mount Vernon speech of 4.7.18., *i.e.* the destruction or reduction to impotence of every arbitrary power which aimed at disturbing the peace of the world ; such evil tendencies must be curtailed. The whole process of peace will depend on satisfactory guarantees in this matter—(meaning that the militarist Government must be deposed and a constitutional Government take its place, before the Allies could deal with Germany).

(169) *Oct.* 14.—The report of Mr. Justice Younger's Committee (Cd. 9106) " on the treatment by the Germans of Prisoners of War taken during the spring offensives of 1918," dated August 29, reveals further the grossest brutality on the part of the Germans, who not only starved and ill-treated our men, but kept them hard at work close up to their lines—in defiance of their own signed agreement—and under British fire, by which many were killed and wounded.

(170) *Oct.* 14.—In exchange for Spanish ships sunk by German submarines. The seven ships only aggregated 21,000 tons.

(171) *Oct.* 16.—The Emperor Karl's manifesto states his desire to accomplish the reconstruction of the Fatherland, and proclaims that in accordance with the will of her people Austria will become a Federal State in which each race, within its natural domain, shall form its own national State. " The reconstruction will guarantee the independence of each national State."

(172) *Oct.* 21.—The despatch covers the operations on the Western Front from the end of the first week in December, 1917 (fighting near Cambrai), to the 30th April, 1918, when the French re-took Locre. It mentions the extension by 28 miles of the British Front, that front by the end of January comprising 125 miles ; the organisation and training of British units, preparations for defence, indications of approaching German attack (192 divisions), and describes in detail, giving the numbers and commanders of the British divisions engaged, the ensuing operations. 64 German divisions on the first day attacked 32 British, and shortly afterwards there were 73 in the field against 35. The 3rd and 5th and part of the 1st British Armies engaged and were pressed back. The French came to the rescue south of Péronne ; our troops were driven back across the Ancre and Somme battlefields. General Foch assumed supreme control on March 26 ; enemy in Albert 26.3 ; fighting in Avre and Luce valleys 29.3 to 2.4 ; final German effort 4, 5.4 ; Lys battle opens 7.4 ; Portuguese and British driven back, but hold retired positions and south flank ; loss of Merville 11.4 ; of Bailleul 15.4 ; withdrawal from Passchendaele 12.4 ; attacks on Kemmel 16.4 ; Kemmel

Hill taken 25.4 ; enemy attack stayed 28.4. British fought magnificently, but enormously outnumbered.

(**¹⁷³**) *Oct.* 21.—The Note dated October 20 stated that Germany denied all illegal and inhuman practices, and denied that in sinking ships the German Navy had destroyed lifeboats and their occupants. Orders sent out to stop torpedoing passenger vessels. Hitherto Parliament has had no effect on the formation of the Government ; in future this will be altered. The Constitution is now being amended. " The Government is now free from all arbitrariness and irresponsible influence, and is supported by the approval of the overwhelming majority of the German people."

(**¹⁷⁴**) *Oct.* 22.—Lord Cavan's despatch describes British operations on the Italian Front since 10.3, including raids. Austrian attack June 15, 16, etc.

(**¹⁷⁵**) *Oct.* 22.—Prince Max expected Germany not to submit to a " peace of violence " without a fight ; announced electoral reform in Prussia, an Alsatian Governor for Alsace-Lorraine, a bill for the people's representatives to take more share in the Government, more political liberty, civil control over censorship, rights of meeting, pardon of labour-crimes, etc.

(**¹⁷⁶**) *Oct.* 23.—The main points of Mr. Balfour's speech at an Australian and New Zealand luncheon were that " I am convinced that in no circumstances is it consistent with the safety or unity of the British Empire that the German Colonies should be returned to Germany " ; that our aims were Imperialist and not Imperialistic ; and that our communications should never be at the mercy of any unscrupulous Power.

(**¹⁷⁷**) *Oct.* 23.—The President considers the only Armistice possible is one which renders a renewal of hostilities on the part of Germany impossible. He has therefore transmitted the correspondence to the Allies, suggesting that the military advisers should draw up proper terms. Extraordinary safeguards must be demanded, as it does not appear that the principle of a German Government responsible to the people has yet been worked out. " The nations of the world do not and cannot trust the word of those hitherto the masters of German policy." If the United States of America must deal with the military masters of Germany they must demand, not peace conditions, but surrender.

(**¹⁷⁸**) *Oct.* 23.—Grossly impudent German reply, arguing that the delay in the agreement *re* the prisoners is because Great Britain refuses to protect German prisoners in China. It states that Germany has much more reason to complain of the bad treatment of her prisoners than Great Britain of hers. Threatens reprisals if Great Britain does not treat prisoners better.

(**¹⁷⁹**) *Oct.* 27.—The German Note stated that the negotiations will be conducted by a people's Government, to which the Military authorities are also subject. " The German Government now awaits proposals for an Armistice which shall be a first step towards a just peace."

The Austro-Hungarian Note adheres to President Wilson's point of view " *re* the rights of the people of Austria-Hungary." Consequently nothing stands in the way of the commencement of pourparlers and an immediate armistice, and it begs President Wilson to make overtures on the subject.

(**¹⁸⁰**) *Oct.* 27.—The Austro-Hungarian Note was as follows :—

" In reply to the Note which President Wilson on October 18 addressed to the Austro-Hungarian Government, and in the sense of the decision of the President to deal in particular with Austria-Hungary in regard to the question of an armistice and peace, the Austro-Hungarian Government has the honour to declare that, as in the case of the preceding statements of the President, it also adheres to his point of view, as laid down in his last Note, in regard to the rights of the peoples of Austria-Hungary, particularly those of the Czecho-Slovaks and the Yugo-Slavs.

" Consequently, as Austria-Hungary accepts all the conditions upon which the President makes an entry into negotiations with regard to an armistice and peace dependent, nothing now stands in the way, in the opinion of the Austro-Hungarian Government, of the commencement of pourparlers.

" The Austro-Hungarian Government declares itself in consequence prepared, without awaiting the result of other negotiations, to enter into pourparlers in regard to peace between Austria-Hungary and the States of the opposing party and in regard to an immediate armistice on all the fronts of Austria-Hungary.

" It begs President Wilson to be good enough to make overtures on this subject."

([181]) *Nov. 2.*—**Terms of Armistice with Turkey :**—

1. Opening of Dardanelles and Bosporus and access to the Black Sea. Allied occupation of Dardanelles and Bosporus forts.

2. Positions of all minefields, torpedo-tubes, and other obstructions in Turkish waters to be indicated, and assistance given to sweep or remove them as may be required.

3. All available information as to mines in the Black Sea to be communicated.

4. All Allied prisoners of war and Armenian interned persons and prisoners to be collected in Constantinople and handed over unconditionally to the Allies.

5. Immediate demobilisation of the Turkish Army, except for such troops as are required for the surveillance of the frontiers and for the maintenance of internal order. Number of effectives and their disposition to be determined later by the Allies after consultation with the Turkish Government.

6. Surrender of all war vessels in Turkish waters, or in waters occupied by Turkey. These ships to be interned at such Turkish port or ports as may be directed, except such small vessels as are required for police or similar purposes in Turkish territorial waters.

7. The Allies to have the right to occupy any strategic points in the event of any situation arising which threatens the security of the Allies.

8. Free use by Allied ships of all ports and anchorages now in Turkish occupation and denial of their use by enemy. Similar conditions to apply to Turkish mercantile shipping in Turkish waters for purpose of trade and demobilisation of the Army.

9. Use of all ship repair facilities at all Turkish ports and arsenals.

10. Allied occupation of the Taurus tunnel system.

11. Immediate withdrawal of Turkish troops from North-west Persia to behind the pre-war frontier has already been ordered, and will be carried out. Part of Trans-caucasia has already been ordered to be evacuated by Turkish troops, the remainder to be evacuated if required by the Allies after they have studied the situation there.

12. Wireless telegraph and cable stations to be controlled by the Allies, Turkish Government messages excepted.

13. Prohibition to destroy any naval, military, or commercial material.

14. Facilities to be given for the purchase of coal, oil-fuel, and naval material from Turkish sources, after the requirements of the country have been met. None of the above material to be exported.

15. Allied Control Officers to be placed on all railways, including such portions of the Transcaucasian railways now under Turkish control, which must be placed at the free and complete disposal of the Allied authorities, due consideration being given to the needs of the population. This clause to include Allied occupation of Batum. Turkey will raise no objection to the occupation of Baku by the Allies.

16. The surrender of all garrisons in the Hejaz, Asir, Yemen, Syria, and Mesopotamia to the nearest Allied Commander and the withdrawal of troops from Cilicia, except those necessary to maintain order, as will be determined under Clause 5.

17. The surrender of all Turkish officers in Tripolitania and Cyrenaica to the nearest Italian garrison. Turkey guarantees to stop supplies and communication with these officers if they do not obey the order to surrender.

18. The surrender of all ports occupied in Tripolitania and Cyrenaica, including Misurata, to the nearest Allied garrison.

19. All Germans and Austrians, naval, military, and civilian, to be evacuated within one month from Turkish dominions. Those in remote districts as soon after as may be possible.

20. Compliance with such orders as may be conveyed for the disposal of the equipment, arms, and ammunition, including transport of that portion of the Turkish Army which is demobilised under Clause 5.

21. An Allied representative to be attached to the Turkish Ministry of Supplies in order to safeguard Allied interests. This representative to be furnished with all necessary for this purpose.

22. Turkish prisoners to be kept at the disposal of the Allied Powers. The release of Turkish civilian prisoners and prisoners over military age to be considered.

23. Obligation on the part of Turkey to cease all relations with the Central Powers.

24. In case of disorder in the six Armenian vilayets the Allies reserve to themselves the right to occupy any part of them.

25. Hostilities between the Allies and Turkey shall cease from noon, local time, on Thursday, October 31, 1918.

(¹⁸²) *Nov.* 4.—Demands of German sailors at Kiel:—Recognition of Soldiers' Council; better treatment of crews; exemption from duty to salute; liberation of imprisoned sailors; immunity from punishment of mutinying crews.

(¹⁸³) *Nov.* 5.—Announcement in Commons by Mr. Lloyd George *re* Armistice :— (1) Versailles Conference in complete agreement *re* terms. (2) President Wilson requested to inform German Government that application for terms must be made to Marshal Foch. (3) If Germany applies for armistice British naval representative must be associated with Marshal Foch.

(¹⁸⁴) *Nov.* 6.—German Armistice delegates : General von Gündell, State-Secretary Erzberger, Count Oberndorff (ex Minister in Sofia), General Von Winterfeld, Naval Captain von Selow.

(¹⁸⁵) *Nov.* 6.—**Terms of Armistice with Austria-Hungary :—**

I.—MILITARY CLAUSES.

1. The immediate cessation of hostilities by land, sea, and air.

2. Total demobilisation of the Austro-Hungarian Army, and immediate withdrawal of all Austro-Hungarian forces operating on the front from the North Sea to Switzerland.

Within Austro-Hungarian territory, limited as in Clause 3 below, there shall only be maintained as an organized military force a maximum of 20 Divisions, reduced to pre-war peace effectives.

Half the Divisional, Corps, and Army artillery and equipment shall be collected at points to be indicated by the Allies and United States of America for delivery to them, beginning with all such material as exists in the territories to be evacuated by the Austro-Hungarian forces.

3. Evacuation of all territories invaded by Austria-Hungary since the beginning of the war. Withdrawal within such periods as shall be determined by the Commander-in-Chief of the Allied forces on each front of the Austro-Hungarian Armies behind a line fixed as follows :—

From Piz Umbrail to the north of the Stelvio it will follow the crest of the Rhætian Alps up to the sources of the Adige and the Eisach, passing thence by Mounts Reschen and Brenner and the heights of Oetz and Ziller ; the line thence turns south, crossing Mount Toblach, and meeting the present frontier of the Carnic Alps. It follows this frontier up to Mount Tarvis, and after Mount Tarvis the watershed of the Julian Alps by the Col of Predil, Mount Mangart, the Tricorno (Terglou), and the watershed of the Cols di Podberdo, Podlaniscam, and Idria. From this point the line turns south-east towards the Schneeberg, excluding the whole basin of the Save and its tributaries ; from the Schneeberg it goes down towards the coast in such a way as to include Castua, Mattuglia, and Volosca in the evacuated territories.

It will also follow the administrative limits of the present province of Dalmatia, including to the north Licarica and Trivania, and to the south territory limited by a line from the shore of Cape Planca to the summits of the watershed eastwards, so as to include in the evacuated area all the valleys and watercourses flowing towards Sebenico, such as the Cicola, Kerka, Butisnica, and their tributaries. It will also include all the islands in the north and west of Dalmatia, from Premuda, Selve, Ulbo, Scherda, Maon, Pago, and Puntadura in the north up to Meleda in the south, embracing Sant' Andrea, Busi, Lissa, Lesina, Tercola, Curzola, Cazza, and Lagosta, as well as the neighbouring rocks and islets and Pelagosa, only excepting the islands of Great and Small Zirona, Bua, Solta, and Brazza.

All territories thus evacuated will be occupied by the troops of the Allies and of the United States of America.

All military and railway equipment of all kinds (including coal), belonging to or within these territories, to be left *in situ*, and surrendered to the Allies according to special orders given by the Commanders-in-Chief of the forces of the Associated Powers on the different fronts. No new destruction, pillage, or requisition to be done by enemy troops in the territories to be evacuated by them and occupied by the forces of the Associated Powers.

4. The Allies shall have the right of free movement over all road and rail and waterways in Austro-Hungarian territory and of the use of the necessary Austrian and Hungarian means of transportation.

The Armies of the Associated Powers shall occupy such strategic points in Austria-Hungary at such times as they may deem necessary to enable them to conduct military operations or to maintain order.

They shall have the right of requisition on payment for the troops of the Associated Powers wherever they may be.

5. Complete evacuation of all German troops within 15 days, not only from the Italian and Balkan fronts, but from all Austro-Hungarian territory.

Internment of all German troops which have not left Austria-Hungary within that date.

6. The administration of the evacuated territories of Austria-Hungary will be entrusted to the local authorities under the control of the Allied and Associated Armies of Occupation.

7. The immediate repatriation without reciprocity of all Allied prisoners of war and interned subjects, and of civil populations evacuated from their homes, on conditions to be laid down by the Commanders-in-Chief of the forces of the Associated Powers on the various fronts.

8. Sick and wounded who cannot be removed from evacuated territory will be cared for by Austro-Hungarian *personnel*, who will be left on the spot with the medical material required.

II.—NAVAL CONDITIONS.

1. Immediate cessation of all hostilities at sea, and definite information to be given as to the location and movements of all Austro-Hungarian ships.

Notification to be made to neutrals that freedom of navigation in all territorial waters is given to the naval and mercantile marines of the Allied and Associated Powers, all questions of neutrality being waived.

2. Surrender to the Allies and United States of America of 15 Austro-Hungarian submarines, completed between the years 1910 and 1918, and of all German submarines which are in or may hereafter enter Austro-Hungarian territorial waters. All other Austro-Hungarian submarines to be paid off and completely disarmed, and to remain under the supervision of the Allies and United States of America.

3. Surrender to the Allies and United States of America, with their complete armament and equipment, of :—

> Three battleships,
> Three light cruisers,
> Nine destroyers,
> Twelve torpedo-boats,
> One minelayer,
> Six Danube monitors,

to be designated by the Allies and the United States of America. All other surface warships (including river craft) are to be concentrated in Austro-Hungarian naval bases to be designated by the Allies and the United States of America, and are to be paid off and completely disarmed and placed under the supervision of the Allies and United States of America.

4. Freedom of navigation to all warships and merchant ships of the Allied and Associated Powers to be given in the Adriatic and up the River Danube and its tributaries in the territorial waters and territory of Austria-Hungary.

The Allies and Associated Powers shall have the right to sweep up all minefields and obstructions, and the positions of these are to be indicated.

In order to ensure the freedom of navigation on the Danube, the Allies and the United States of America shall be empowered to occupy or to dismantle all fortifications or defence works.

5. The existing blockade conditions set up by the Allied and Associated Powers are to remain unchanged, and all Austro-Hungarian merchant ships found at sea are to remain liable to capture, save exceptions which may be made by a Commission nominated by the Allies and United States of America.

6. All naval air craft are to be concentrated and immobilised in Austro-Hungarian bases to be designated by the Allies and United States of America.

7. Evacuation of all the Italian coasts and of all ports occupied by Austria-Hungary outside their national territory, and the abandonment of all floating craft, naval materials, equipment, and materials for inland navigation of all kinds.

8. Occupation by the Allies and the United States of America of the land and sea fortifications and the islands which form the defences and of the dockyards and arsenal at Pola.

9. All merchant vessels held by Austria-Hungary belonging to the Allies and Associated Powers to be returned.

10. No destruction of ships or of materials to be permitted before evacuation, surrender, or restoration.

11. All naval and mercantile marine prisoners of war of the Allied and Associated Powers in Austro-Hungarian hands to be returned without reciprocity.

([186]) *Nov.* 6.—President Wilson's **Reply to Germany** *re* **Armistice.** (1) Allies ready to make peace on terms laid down by him with qualifications : (*a*) Freedom of seas being ambiguous term, Allies reserve to themselves freedom on subject. (*b*) Compensation must be made by Germans for damage to civilians. (2) German Government must apply to Marshal Foch for conditions of armistice.

([187]) *Nov.* 7.—Health Ministry Bill. (1) Health duties of Local Government Board, Insurance Commission, Board of Education, Privy Council, Home Office, brought under one Minister. (2) Power to add other health duties, *e.g.*, medical inspection and treatment of school children, sick soldiers, mental deficiency. (3) Provision of Advisory or Consultative Council.

([188]) *Nov.* 8.—Approximate number of Germans taken prisoner since January 1, 1918 :—By British, 200,000 ; by French, 140,000 ; by Americans, 50,000 ; by Belgians, 15,000.

([189]) *Nov.* 8.—Proclamation of Prince Max to Germans living abroad :—Germans abroad not to abandon trust in German people. Soldiers fought heroically, unheard-of endurance shown by people in Homeland. Germans, deserted by allies, unable to carry on war. Hope for victory not granted, greater one won in conquest by Germany of her former belief in justice of might. Equal care to be shown by German Government and people to mitigate for Germans abroad and in Homeland sufferings due to war.

([190]) *Nov.* 9.—A speech of Mr. Lloyd George at Guildhall, London :—The most dramatic change in history ; a dramatic judgement in abdication of Kaiser and Crown Prince, both latter being condemned by Germans. Choice before Germany is immediate surrender or a worse fate. Justice must be satisfied. India and the Dominions to have a voice in determining peace terms. Next few years fateful for British Empire. Unity as necessary now as during war.

([191]) *Nov.* 11.—Message of King George to British Empire :—Pledge made to fight till end achieved now redeemed. Empire, one at beginning is more united now. Hour one of thanksgiving and gratitude.

([192]) *Nov.* 11.—Speech of President Wilson at Washington announcing armistice terms :—Nations associated to destroy armed Imperialism now united to establish peace, securing rights of weak and of strong. Versailles War Council taking steps to relieve food scarcity in Central Europe. Hunger breeds madness. Central Europe in revolution. Nations disciplined by freedom must help peoples just freed from arbitrary rule. Liberty not to be found in fratricidal strife. Peace must define place of Germany and enable Germans to live in security and contentment.

([193]) *Nov.* 12.—**Terms of Armistice with Germany :—**
The following is the full text of the Terms of Armistice between the Associated Powers and Germany which were accepted and signed November 11 by the German Plenipotentiaries :—

A.—CLAUSES RELATING TO WESTERN FRONT.

I.—Cessation of operations by land and in the air six hours after the signature of the Armistice.

II.—Immediate evacuation of invaded countries—Belgium, France, Alsace-Lorraine, Luxemburg—so ordered as to be completed within 14 days from the signature of the Armistice.

German troops which have not left the above-mentioned territories within the period fixed will become prisoners of war.

Occupation by the Allies and the United States Forces jointly will keep pace with evacuation in these areas.

All movements of evacuation and occupation will be regulated in accordance with a Note (Annexure 1).

III.—Repatriation, beginning at once, to be completed within 14 days, of all inhabitants of the countries above enumerated (including hostages, persons under trial, or convicted).

IV.—Surrender in good condition by the German Armies of the following equip-

5,000 guns (2,500 heavy, 2,500 field).

30,000 machine guns.

3,000 *Minenwerfer*.

2,000 aeroplanes (fighters, bombers—firstly D.7's—and night-bombing machines).

The above to be delivered *in situ* to the Allied and United States troops in accordance with the detailed conditions laid down in the Note (Annexure 1).

V.—Evacuation by the German Armies of the countries on the left bank of the Rhine. These countries on the left bank of the Rhine shall be administered by the local authorities under the control of the Allied and United States Armies of occupation.

The occupation of these territories will be carried out by Allied and United States garrisons holding the principal crossings of the Rhine (Mayence, Coblenz, Cologne) together with bridgeheads at these points of a 30 kilometre [about 19 miles] radius on the right bank, and by garrisons similarly holding the strategic points of the regions.

A neutral zone shall be set up on the right bank of the Rhine between the river and a line drawn 10 kilometres [6¼ miles] distant, starting from the Dutch frontier to the Swiss frontier. In the case of inhabitants, no person shall be prosecuted for having taken part in any military measures previous to the signing of the Armistice.

No measure of a general or official character shall be taken which would have, as a consequence, the depreciation of industrial establishments or a reduction of their *personnel*.

Evacuation by the enemy of the Rhinelands shall be so ordered as to be completed within a further period of 16 days, in all 31 days after the signature of the Armistice.

All movements of evacuation and occupation will be regulated according to the Note (Annexure 1).

VI.—In all territory evacuated by the enemy there shall be no evacuation tants, no damage or harm shall be done to the persons or property of the inhabitants.

No destruction of any kind to be committed.

Military establishments of all kinds shall be delivered intact, as well as military stores of food, munitions, equipment not removed during the periods fixed for evacuation.

Stores of food of all kinds for the civil population, cattle, etc., shall be left *in situ*.

Industrial establishments shall not be impaired in any way, and their *personnel* shall not be moved.

VII.—Roads and means of communication of every kind, railroads, waterways, main roads, bridges, telegraphs, telephones shall be in no manner impaired.

All civil and military *personnel* at present employed on them shall remain.

5,000 locomotives, 150,000 wagons, and 5,000 motor lorries in good working order, with all necessary spare parts and fittings, shall be delivered to the Associated Powers within the period fixed for the evacuation of Belgium and Luxemburg.

The railways of Alsace-Lorraine shall be handed over within the same period, together with all pre-war *personnel* and material.

Further, material necessary for the working of railways in the country on the left bank of the Rhine shall be left *in situ*.

All stores of coal and material for upkeep of permanent way, signals, and repair shops shall be left *in situ* and kept in an efficient state by Germany, as far as the means of communication are concerned, during the whole period of the Armistice.

All barges taken from the Allies shall be restored to them. The Note appended as Annexure 2 regulates the detail of these measures.

VIII.—The German Command shall be responsible for revealing all mines or delay-action fuses disposed on territory evacuated by the German troops and shall assist in their discovery and destruction.

The German Command shall also reveal all destructive measures that may have have been taken (such as poisoning or pollution of springs, wells, etc.), under penalty of reprisals.

IX.—The right of requisition shall be exercised by the Allied and United States Armies in all occupied territory, save for settlement of accounts with authorised persons.

The upkeep of the troops of occupation in the Rhineland (excluding Alsace-Lorraine) shall be charged to the German Government.

X.—The immediate repatriation, without reciprocity, according to detailed conditions which shall be fixed, of all Allied and United States prisoners of war ; the Allied Powers and the United States of America shall be able to dispose of these prisoners as they wish. However, the return of German prisoners of war interned in Holland and Switzerland shall continue as heretofore. The return of German prisoners of war shall be settled at peace preliminaries.

XI.—Sick and wounded who cannot be removed from evacuated territory will be cared for by the German *personnel*, who will be left on the spot, with the medical material required.

B.—CLAUSES RELATING TO THE EASTERN FRONTIERS OF GERMANY.

XII.—All German troops at present in any territory which before the war belonged to Russia, Rumania, or Turkey shall withdraw within the frontiers of Germany as they existed on August 1, 1914, and all German troops at present in territories which before the war formed part of Russia must likewise return to within the frontiers of Germany as above defined as soon as the Allies shall think the moment suitable, having regard to the internal situation of these territories.

XIII.—Evacuation by German troops to begin at once ; and all German instructors, prisoners, and civilian as well as military agents now on the territory of Russia (as defined on August 1, 1914) to be recalled.

XIV.—German troops to cease at once all requisitions and seizures, and any other undertaking with a view to obtaining supplies intended for Germany in Rumania and Russia, as defined on August 1, 1914.

XV.—Abandonment of the Treaties of Bukarest and Brest-Litovsk and of the Supplementary Treaties.

XVI.—The Allies shall have free access to the territories evacuated by the Germans on their Eastern frontier, either through Danzig or by the Vistula, in order to convey supplies to the populations of these territories or for the purpose of maintaining order.

C.—CLAUSE RELATING TO EAST AFRICA.

XVII.—Unconditional evacuation of all German forces operating in East Africa within one month.

D.—GENERAL CLAUSES.

XVIII.—Repatriation, without reciprocity, within a maximum period of one month, in accordance with detailed conditions hereafter to be fixed, of all civilians interned or deported who may be citizens of other Allied or Associated States than those mentioned in Clause III.

XIX.—With the reservation that any future claims and demands of the Allies and United States of America remain unaffected, the following financial conditions are required :—

Reparation for damage done.

While the Armistice lasts no public securities shall be removed by the enemy which can serve as a pledge to the Allies for the recovery or reparation for war losses.

Immediate restitution of the cash deposit in the National Bank of Belgium and, in general, immediate return of all documents, specie, stock, shares, paper money, together with plant for the issue thereof, touching public or private interests in the invaded countries.

Restitution of the Russian and Rumanian gold yielded to Germany or taken by that Power.

This gold to be delivered in trust to the Allies until the signature of peace.

E.—NAVAL CONDITIONS.

XX.—Immediate cessation of all hostilities at sea, and definite information to be given as to the location and movements of all German ships.

Notification to be given to neutrals that freedom of navigation in all territorial waters is given to the Naval and Mercantile Marines of the Allied and Associated Powers, all question of neutrality being waived.

XXI.—All Naval and Mercantile Marine prisoners of war of the Allied and Associated Powers in German hands to be returned, without reciprocity.

XXII.—Handing over to the Allies and the United States of all submarines (including all submarine cruisers and minelayers) which are present at the moment with full complement in the ports specified by the Allies and the United States. Those that cannot put to sea to be deprived of crews and supplies, and shall remain under the supervision of the Allies and the United States. Submarines ready to put to sea shall be prepared to leave German ports immediately on receipt of wireless order to sail to the port of surrender, the remainder to follow as early as possible. The conditions of this Article shall be carried [out] within 14 days after the signing of the Armistice.

XXIII.—The following German surface warships, which shall be designated by the Allies and the United States of America, shall forthwith be disarmed and thereafter interned in neutral ports, or, failing them, Allied ports, to be designated by the Allies and the United States of America, and placed under the surveillance of the Allies and the United States of America, only caretakers being left on board, namely :—

    6 Battle Cruisers.
    10 Battle Ships.
    8 Light Cruisers, including two minelayers.
    50 Destroyers of the most modern types.

All other surface warships (including river craft) are to be concentrated in German Naval bases to be designated by the Allies and the United States of America, and are to be paid off and completely disarmed and placed under the supervision of the Allies and the United States of America. All vessels of the auxiliary fleet (trawlers, motor-vessels, etc.) are to be disarmed. All vessels specified for internment shall be ready to leave German ports seven days after the signing of the Armistice. Directions of the voyage will be given by wireless.

NOTE :—A declaration has been signed by the Allied Delegates and handed to the German Delegates to the effect that, in the event of ships not being handed over owing to the mutinous state of the Fleet, the Allies reserve the right to occupy Heligoland as an advanced base to enable them to enforce the terms of the Armistice. The German Delegates have on their part signed a Declaration that they will recommend the Chancellor to accept this.

XXIV.—The Allies and the United States of America shall have the right to sweep up all minefields and obstructions laid by Germany outside German territorial waters, and the positions of these are to be indicated.

XXV.—Freedom of access to and from the Baltic to be given to the Naval and Mercantile Marines of the Allied and Associated Powers. To secure this, the Allies and the United States of America shall be empowered to occupy all German forts, fortifications, batteries, and defence works of all kinds in all the entrances from the Kattegat into the Baltic, and to sweep up all mines and obstructions within and without German territorial waters without any questions of neutrality being raised, and the positions of all such mines and obstructions are to be indicated.

XXVI.—The existing blockade conditions set up by the Allied and Associated Powers are to remain unchanged, and all German merchant ships found at sea are to remain liable to capture. The Allies and United States contemplate the provisioning of Germany during the Armistice as shall be found necessary.

XXVII.—All Naval aircraft are to be concentrated and immobilized in German bases to be specified by the Allies and the United States of America.

XXVIII.—In evacuating the Belgian coasts and forts Germany shall abandon all merchant ships, tugs, lighters, cranes, and all other harbour materials, and all materials for inland navigation, all aircraft and air materials and stores, all arms and armaments, and all stores and apparatus of all kinds.

XXIX.—All Black Sea ports are to be evacuated by Germany ; all Russian warships of all descriptions seized by Germany in the Black Sea are to be handed over to the Allies and the United States of America ; all neutral merchant ships seized are to be released ; all warlike and other materials of all kinds seized in those ports are to be returned, and German materials as specified in Clause XXVIII. are to be abandoned.

XXX.—All merchant ships in German hands belonging to the Allied and Associated Powers are to be restored in ports to be specified by the Allies and the United States of America without reciprocity.

XXXI.—No destruction of ships or of materials to be permitted before evacuation, surrender, or restoration.

XXXII.—The German Government shall formally notify the neutral Governments of the world, and particularly the Governments of Norway, Sweden, Denmark, and Holland, that all restrictions placed on the trading of their vessels with the Allied and

Associated countries, whether by the German Government or by private German interests, and whether in return for specific concessions, such as the export of ship-building materials or not, are immediately cancelled.

XXXIII.—No transfers of German merchant shipping of any description to any neutral flag are to take place after signature of the Armistice.

F.—DURATION OF ARMISTICE.

XXXIV.—The duration of the Armistice is to be 36 days, with option to extend. During this period, on failure of execution of any of the above clauses, the Armistice may be denounced by one of the contracting parties on 48 hours' previous notice.

G.—TIME LIMIT FOR REPLY.

XXXV.—This Armistice to be accepted or refused by Germany within 72 hours of notification. -

[194] *Nov.* 12.—A new Parliament necessary to settle problems ahead. Peace to be permanent must not contravene justice. League of Nations more necessary than ever to protect small nations reborn during war, for reduction of armaments and abolition of conscription. Reaction and disunion rather than Revolution and Bolshevism to be feared. Watchword to be wise progress. Support of British Liberalism needed.

[195] *Nov.* 12.—Letter of Mr. Lloyd George : (1) *Economic Policy :* Prevention of dumping, protection of key industries, Imperial preference, no food taxes. (2) *Welsh Disestablishment :* Reconsideration of financial provisions of Act. (3) *Irish Question :* Home Rule : no coercion for Ulster. (4) *Social Reform :* Housing and land schemes to be carried.

[196] *Nov.* 12.—Statement of Dr. Addison : Unemployment to be met by Out-of-work Donations for 6 months for civil workers, 12 months for soldiers ; soldiers with places waiting them to be demobilised first, and according to importance of industry. Permanent appointments in Civil Service for ex-officers and ex-soldiers. Ex-service men to have facilities *re* land settlement. Supply of materials for industry adequate in case of most essentials.

[197] *Nov.* 13.—Plenipotentiaries of Workmen's and Soldiers' Council of German Fleet : Rear Admiral Hugo von Meurer, Korvetten-Kapitän Hintzmann, Kapitän-leutnant Saalwächter, Kapitän-leutnant von Preudenreuch, Leutnant-zur-See Braurack.

[197a] *Nov.* 13.—Assignment of Offices in new German Government :—

Herr Ebert (Socialist Majority) ...	... Minister of Interior and Military Affairs.
Herr Haase (Socialist Minority) ...	... Foreign Affairs.
Herr Scheidemann (Socialist Majority)	... Finance and Colonies.
Herr Dittmann (Socialist Minority)	... Demobilisation,Transport, Justice, Health.
Herr Landsberg (Socialist Majority)	... Publicity, Art, Literature.
Herr Barek (Socialist Minority) ...	... Social Policy.

[198] *Nov.* 13.—Message of President Wilson to Germany promising food and asking for assurance for maintenance of public order and equitable distribution of food.

[199] *Nov.* 13.—Meeting asked to appoint joint Committee to advise Government *re* (1) redemption of Government pledge of 1915 for restoration of Trade Union privileges. War not yet over. (2) Wages : cost of living high. Government rate of wages to be maintained for present. Appeal for continued unity between classes. Victory not an end, but a beginning.

[200] *Nov.* 14.—Labour Programme :—(i) *International.* (1) Labour to have representation at Peace Conference ; (2) World Labour Conference to be held at same time and place as Peace Conference. (ii) *National Reconstruction.* (1) Provision for discharged soldiers and civil workers ; (2) Restoration of Trade Unions, freedom of speech, travel, occupation, abolition of Conscription ; (3) Adult suffrage, abolition of 2nd Chamber ; (4) Home Rule for Ireland, England, Wales, Scotland ; (5) State ownership of railways, coal and iron mines, Government supervision of electrical super-power stations ; (6) Amendment and extension of Factory, Mines, Board of Trade Acts, revision of Rates, abolition of Poor Law ; (7) Extension of powers of County, Borough and Parish Councils ; (8) Housing measures to be promptly carried ; (9) Reorganisation of Agriculture by State ownership of land ; (10) National education

free from nursery to University; (11) Nationalisation of Life Assurance; (12) Development of Post Office Savings Banks; (13) No food taxes, increase of super-tax and death duties, graduated capital tax, taxation of land values.

(201) *Nov.* 15.—Appeal of Dr. Solf (German Foreign Secretary) to convene a Conference at the Hague of U.S.A. and German plenipotentiaries to discuss how " to save Germany from the worst."

(202) *Nov.* 15.—New German Ministry appointed by Council of National Plenipotentiaries (" The Ministry of the six Socialists ")—Dr. Solf, Foreign Affairs; Herr Erzberger, State Secretary, to conduct preliminaries of peace negotiations with Dr. Solf; and four others.

(203) *Nov.* 16.—Dr. Solf appeals further to President Wilson to allow German Commissioners to leave for America to lay condition of Germany before U.S.A. Government.

(204) *Nov.* 16.—Government election campaign opens. Speech by Mr. Lloyd George:—New Parliament necessary for task of re-construction. Higher percentage of " unfits " in Britain than in France and Germany. Housing a national task. Industrial reform needed. Best traditions of every Party necessary.

(205) *Nov.* 17.—Serb Coalition Ministry :—

M. Pashich	...	Premier.
M. Trifkovich (Independent Radical)	...	Interior.
M. Protich (Old Radical)	...	Finance.
M. Gavritovich (Non-Party) ...	...	Foreign Affairs.
M. Marinkivich (Progressive) ...	...	Commerce.
M. Davidovich (Young Radical)	...	Public Instruction.
General Rachich (Non-Party) ...	...	War.
M. Jurichich (Old Radical) ...	...	Agriculture.

(206) *Nov.* 18.—" Election, a blunder and a calamity."

(207) *Nov.* 21.—Resignation of Lord Robert Cecil on account of Government's Welsh Church policy. Resignation of Mr. Clynes on ground of Labour Party's policy.

(208) *Nov.* 22.—Unity of Nation must not be relaxed. Tasks of new Parliament are : Conclusion of peace, reduction of armaments, formation of League of Nations, land for soldiers, promotion of scientific farming, improvement of village life, housing scheme, larger educational opportunities, drink traffic regulations, preference to Colonial trade, encouragement of key industries, no dumping, removal of Government control from industries, development of means of communication, improved consular service, removal of sex inequalities, reform of the House of Lords, gradual responsible Government for India, Home Rule for Ireland without forcible submission of Ulster.

(209) *Nov.* 24.—Despatches proving guilt of Germany in declaring war : *e.g.*, Absence of Kaiser, Chief of General Staff and Prussian War Minister from Berlin, July, 1914, intended as blind to Foreign Powers. On August 4 Prussian Staff, confident of overthrow of France in four weeks, decided to violate Belgium's neutrality.

(210) *Nov.* 27.—Labour Election Manifesto declaring against secret diplomacy and economic war, and demanding International Labour Charter; withdrawal of Allied forces from Russia; freedom for Ireland and India; no conscription; land for workers; improved houses; Free Trade; levy on capital; nationalisation of mines, shipping, armaments and electric power; minimum wage; right to work; limitation of hours of labour; amendment of Factory Acts and Workmen's Compensation; adult suffrage for men and women; equal pay for men and women.

(211) *Nov.* 27.—Address of Mr. Asquith : No tampering with Free Trade; Home Rule for Ireland; removal of restrictions on personal liberty; strengthening of ties with Dominions; redemption of pledges to India; life to be made worth living.

(212) *Nov.* 28.—According to Reuter the Kaiser renounced " for all the future " his rights to the Crown of Prussia and to the German Imperial Crown, released all officials of the German Empire and of Prussia, and all non-commissioned officers and men of the Prussian army and the federal contingents, from their oath of fealty, and declared that he expected them to support those " who have been entrusted with the duty of protecting the nation against the threatening danger of anarchy, famine and foreign rule."

(²¹³) *Dec.* 1.—The British portion of the German Rhine provinces to be occupied being too narrow to admit of more than one Army being employed, the 2nd Army was selected, under General Plumer, consisting of :—

1st Cavalry Division.

II. Corps	:	9th, 29th and New Zealand Divisions.
VI. Corps	:	Guards, 2nd and 3rd Divisions.
IX. Corps	:	1st, 6th and 62nd Divisions.
Canadian	:	1st and 2nd Canadian Divisions.

(²¹⁴) *Dec.* 4.—The following tables are extracted from the statement.—

(a) *Losses and gains of shipping of Associated Powers and Neutrals from beginning of war to October* 31, 1918.

		Gross Tons.
Losses		15,053,786
Gains :		
New construction ...	10,849,527	
Enemy tonnage captured	2,392,675	
		13,242,202
Net Loss		1,811,534

(b) *Losses and gains of British shipping in the same period.*

		Gross Tons.
Losses		9,031,828
Gains :		
New construction in		
United Kingdom ...	4,342,296	
Purchases abroad ...	530,000	
Enemy tonnage captured	716,520	
		5,588,816
Net Loss		3,443,012

(c) *Losses of shipping of Associated Powers and Neutrals in* 1918.

	British. Gross tons.	Foreign. Gross tons.	Total. Gross tons.
1st Quarter ...	697,668	445,668	1,143,336
2nd ,, ...	630,862	331,145	962,007
3rd ,, ...	512,030	403,483	915,513
October ...	83,952	93,582	177,534

From October 31 to the date of the statement, British losses by enemy action amounted to 11,916 tons, foreign losses to 2,159 tons.

(d) *Output of shipping by Associated Powers and Neutrals in* 1918.

	United Kingdom	Other Countries	Total.
1st Quarter ...	320,280	550,037	870,317
2nd ,, ...	442,966	800,308	1,243,274
3rd ,, ...	411,395	972,735*	1,384,130
October ...	136,100	375,000*	511,100

(²¹⁵) *Dec.* 5.—The statement is couched in a hortatory style, and while it holds up to admiration a number of ideals, it does not always make clear what means the Government proposes to adopt for their attainment. The salient features of the paragraphs relating to the terms of peace may be gathered from the following excerpts :—

" The Kaiser must be prosecuted . . . The British Government referred the question of the criminal culpability of the Kaiser and his accomplices to their Law officers some weeks ago. They invited a body of jurists in England to investigate

---

* Provisional figures.

the matter, and they have unanimously come to the conclusion that the Kaiser and his accomplices in the making of this war ought to be tried by an International Court.

" There were other matters, such as murder on the high seas and the abominable maltreatment of prisoners, also referred to the Law officers . . . the same Legal Committee reported strongly in favour of the punishment of those who were guilty of these offences, and the British Government will certainly use its influence in the Peace Conference to see that justice is executed.

" After what has happened . . . it is quite impossible to entertain in our midst a population of which a considerable portion has . . . abused our hospitality . . . They have forfeited any claim to remain.

" All the European Allies have accepted the principle that the Central Powers must pay the cost of the war up to the limit of their capacity."

The rest of the announcement deals with domestic policy, and is concerned especially with the Government's intentions regarding the support of dependents of the fallen, the provision of employment or land for returned soldiers and sailors, the re-organisation of British industry, transport, and education, the improvement of the relations between capital and labour, and the amelioration of social conditions.

(²¹⁶) *Dec.* 6.—The Government conceded the principle of an 8-hour day for all members of the wages staff; this was to come into operation on February 1, 1919. Existing conditions of service were to be reviewed by a Committee, pending whose decisions they were to remain unaltered.

(²¹⁷) *Dec.* 10.—The six " points " were:—" Trial of the Kaiser; punishment of those responsible for atrocities; fullest indemnities from Germany; Britain for the British, socially and industrially; rehabilitation of those broken in the war; a happier country for all."

(²¹⁸) *Dec.* 11.—Mr. Lloyd George said that it was not true that the Government meant to keep up a great conscript army in this country. " The Military Service Act was passed in order to meet a great emergency. When the emergency is past, the need is past; the Act will lapse, and there is no intention to renew it . . . Whether you will require conscription in the future . . . will depend entirely upon the terms of peace . . . The real guarantee against conscription in this country, and in every other country, is to put an end by the terms of the Peace Conference to the great conscript armies of the enemy states." Regarding indemnities Mr. Lloyd George said that Germany ought in justice to pay the full cost of the war, but added that it was not yet certain how far she was able to do so. The Government, he said, proposed to demand the whole cost, and to insist that Germany should satisfy the claims of her enemies before paying off her own war debt.

The Kaiser, according to the Premier, had committed a crime against national right. " As far as the European Allies are concerned—and I hope that America will take the same view—there is no doubt at all as to the demand which will be put forward on the part of all the European Allies to make the Kaiser and his accomplices responsible for this terrible crime."

(²¹⁹) *Dec.* 13.—The agreement stipulated that the carrying out of the conditions of the armistice of November 11 must be continued and completed within the period of extension. The following condition was added to the terms of the original armistice : " The Supreme Command of the Allies henceforth reserves the right, should it consider this advisable, and in order to obtain fresh guarantees, to occupy the neutral zone on the right bank of the Rhine, north of the Cologne bridgehead and as far as the Dutch frontier. Notice of this occupation will be given six days previously by the Supreme Command of the Allies."

The Germans also agreed to the demand, made on behalf of Mr. Hoover, that the 2,500,000 tons of cargo space lying in German ports should be placed under the control of the Allies to supply Germany with food-stuffs. The ships, it was stated by the delegation of the Allies, would under this arrangement remain German property and might be provided with German crews.

(²²⁰) *Dec.* 13.—The statement was made to the Press. Mr. Lloyd George said " I wish to make it clear beyond all doubt that I stand for the abolition of conscript armies in all lands. Without that . . . the Peace Conference would be a failure and a sham . . . Any delegate that represents Great Britain at the Conference must labour to the end I have stated."

(²²¹) *Dec.* 18.—The Conference resolved that the People's Commissaries (*i.e.* the Ebert Government) should hold legislative and executive powers until the meeting of the National Assembly, and appointed a Central Council of Workers' and Soldiers' Councils to exercise parliamentary supervision over the German and Prussian cabinets, with the right to appoint and depose the Commissaries of the Empire and of Prussia. As regards Prussia, the powers of the Council were to continue until the settlement of the permanent constitution of that state.

([222]) *Dec.* 19.—The statement was in the form of a reply to a letter received from a correspondent. " The reason," Lord Milner wrote, " why Allied . . . forces . . . were sent to Russia is that the Bolshevists . . . were . . . assisting our enemies in every possible way . . . The Allies, every one of them, were most anxious to avoid interference in Russia. But it was an obligation of honour to save the Czecho-Slovaks, and it was a military necessity . . . to prevent those vast portions of Russia which were struggling to escape the tyranny of the Bolshevists from being overrun by them, and so thrown open as a source of supply to the enemy . . " And this intervention was successful . . . The Czecho-Slovaks were saved from destruction. The resources of Siberia and south-eastern Russia were denied to the enemy. The northern ports of European Russia were prevented from becoming bases for German submarines . . . These were important achievements and contributed materially to the defeat of Germany . . .

" But thousands of Russians have taken up arms and fought on the side of the Allies. How can we . . . come away and leave them to the tender mercies of their and our enemies before they have had time to arm, train, and organise so as to be strong enough to defend themselves ? . . .

" The last thing the Government desires is to leave any British soldiers in Russia a day longer than is necessary to discharge the moral obligations we have incurred. And that, I believe, is the guiding principle of all the Allies. Nor do I myself think that the time when we can withdraw without disastrous consequences is necessarily distant. But . . . if the Allies were all to scramble out of Russia at once, the result would almost certainly be that the barbarism which at present reigns in a part only of that country would spread over the whole of it. . . The ultimate consequences of such a disaster . . . would assuredly involve a far greater strain on the resources of the British Empire than our present commitments."

([223]) *Dec.* 28.—The results, including unopposed returns and University polls, were as follows :—

Coalition	Unionists	...	...	...	...	...	338
	Liberals	...	......	...	...	137	485
	National Democratic Party (Labour)	...				10	

Non-Coalition	Sinn Fein	...	...	...	...	73	
	Labour	...	...	...	...	59	
	Unionists	...	...	...	...	48	
	Liberals	...	...	...	...	26	222
	Irish Nationalists	...	...	...	7	
	National Party	...	...	...	...	2	
	Independents, etc.	...	...	...	7	

Mr. Asquith failed to be returned.

([224]) *Dec.* 28.—In his speech President Wilson discussed the general features which, he said, should mark the Peace Treaty. The kernel of the speech lies in the following passages :—" As I have conversed with the soldiers I have been more and more aware that they fought . . . to do away with the old order and establish a new one. And the centre and characteristic of the old order was that unstable thing which we used to call the Balance of Power . . . It is very interesting to me to observe how from every quarter, from every sort of mind, from every sort of counsel, there comes the suggestion that there must be, not one powerful group of nations set off against another, but a single, overwhelming, powerful group of nations, which shall be the trustee of the peace of the world."

([225]) *Dec.* 29.—After a brief allusion to President Wilson's arrival from America " with high ideals," M. Clémenceau said that France, as the country nearest Germany, was in a particularly difficult position. " There is an old system which appears to be discredited to-day, but to which I am not afraid of saying I am still faithful. Countries have organised solidly defended frontiers, with the necessary armaments and the balance of Powers. This system seems to be condemned by a few high authorities ; but . . . if we had had such a balance of Powers before the war, if the United States,

Great Britain, France, and Italy had declared that whoever attacked one of them would have to expect the other three to assume the task of common defence, this atrocious war would not have taken place.

" This system of alliance, which I do not renounce, shall be my guiding thought at the Conference ... There must be nothing which can separate in the period after the war the four Great Powers whom the war has united. I shall make every sacrifice to maintain that Entente. . .

" As to international guarantees, I say that if France is left free to organise her own military defence ... if she is mistress of her own military organisations, I shall accept any supplementary guarantee which may be given me. I go further, and say that if those guarantees are such as will demand sacrifices in the way of military preparation, I shall accept those sacrifices with joy."

Later, in reference to the freedom of the seas, M. Clémenceau stated that President Wilson had assured him that each Power should maintain its liberty.

M. Pichon dwelt more upon points of detail. He said that a policy of annexation was far from the Government's thoughts, but that it reserved full freedom to discuss the frontier of Alsace-Lorraine—a question which was " not one of annexation, but involved principles of justice and matters essential to the safety of France." M. Pichon said that in no way, territorially or otherwise, could Germany be allowed to remain as she had been. " We will limit the German strength," he added, " to what it ought to be, by removing the possibility of Germany finding in those Austrian populations who have remained outside Bohemia and Hungary compensation for what she has lost to us ... Victory gives us rights over the vanquished." Referring to French claims in Syria, M. Pichon said that while recognising that the Franco-British agreement regarding Turkish territories must be submitted to the judgment of the Peace Conference, the French Government considered that it remained binding on the signatories. With regard to Russia he asserted that Allied intervention there was directed against Germany and did not constitute interference in Russia's internal affairs. He however added that the Allies had cleared the Trans-Siberian Railway in order to preserve for themselves the means of intervening if it became necessary to protect their own subjects in Russia. Nevertheless, M. Clémenceau had given strict orders that any efforts to crush Bolshevism should be made by Russian forces. If these had received material support from the Allies, it was merely with the object of effecting the economic encirclement of Bolshevism. At the same time any peace which allowed Russia to continue in a state of civil war, " with her present hateful and abominable Government," would not be a peace of justice.

(226) *Dec.* 30.—One of the speeches contained the following notable passages :— " Heretofore the world has been governed . . . by partnerships of interest, and they have broken down. Interest does not bind men together ... There is only one thing that can bind people together, and that is a common devotion to right . . . The United States has always felt . . . that she must keep herself separate from any kind of connection with European politics, and . . . she is not now interested in European politics. But she is interested in the partnership of right between America and Europe. If the future had nothing for us but a new attempt to keep the world at a right poise by a balance of power, the United States would take no interest, because she will join no combination or Power which is not a combination of all of us. She is not interested merely in the Peace of Europe, but in the peace of the world."

(227) *March* 15.—Much excitement was caused both in Germany and England by the publication of a memorandum by Prince Lichnowsky, who had been the German Ambassador in London up to the beginning of the war. The Memorandum dealt chiefly with the negotiations immediately before the declaration of war, and completely vindicated Sir E. Grey's course of action which had been so ridiculously attacked in Germany. It proved conclusively that Great Britain had been working for peace all along, and that the provocation was in no sense caused by any action on the part of the Allies. Herr v. Jagow, German Foreign Minister, issued a very lame statement in reply. Prince Lichnowsky was deprived of his seat in the Prussian Herrenhaus and sent into retirement.

(228) *May* 7.—General Maurice, recently Director of Military Operations on the Headquarters Staff in London, challenged, in his letter to the *Times*, the veracity of certain Ministerial statements in the House of Commons which, he alleged, gave a totally misleading impression of what had occurred. He disputed a statement by Mr. Bonar Law that the extension of the British line in France was not settled by the

Versailles Council ; he challenged as "incorrect" an implication in the Premier's statement that the British Army was stronger on January 1.18 than on January 1.17 ; and he contradicted Mr. Lloyd George's estimate of white troops in the Eastern theatres of war.   In the subsequent debate in the House of Commons (9.5), Mr. Lloyd George upheld all the Ministerial statements, and the House defeated a motion by Mr. Asquith for a Select Committee.   General Maurice was subsequently placed on retired pay.

BRITISH MERCHANT VESSELS LOST BY ENEMY ACTION.

	By Cruisers, T.B.D's., etc.		By Submarines.		By Mines.		Total.		
	No.	Lives.	No.	Lives.	No.	Lives.	No.	Lives.	Gross Tonnage.
1918.									
January ...	—	—	57	291	—	—	57	291	179,973
February ...	—	—	68	697	1	—	69	697	226,896
March	—	—	79	490	3	20	82	510	199,458
April	3	—	67	488	2	1	72	489	215 543
May	—	—	59	407	1	—	60	407	192,436
June	—	—	49	453	2	16	51	469	162,990
July	—	—	37	202	—	—	37	202	165,449
August ...	—	—	41	217	—	—	41	217	145,721
September ...	—	—	48	521	—	—	48	521	136,859
October	1	—	23	318	1	—	25	318	59,229
To November 11	—	—	2	1	—	—	2	1	10,195
1918 Total ...	4	—	530	4,085	10	37	544	4,122	1,694,749
Total during the years 1914 to 1918 (inclusive)							2,479	14,287	7,759,090

NUMBERS OF SICK ARRIVING IN ENGLAND FROM FRANCE DURING THE YEARS 1914-15-16-17-18.

	Officers.	Other Ranks.
1914	892	25,013
1915	5,558	121,006
1916	12,818	219,539
1917	15,311	321,628
1918	14,805	265,735
Total ...	49,384	952,921

Figures relating to admissions to hospitals in France are not available.

NUMBERS OF ADMISSIONS OF SICK TO HOSPITALS IN THE FOLLOWING COUNTRIES.

				All Ranks.
ITALY	British and Colonials for year 1918	...	42,770
EGYPT	,, ,, ,, 1916	...	136,110
	1917	...	138,821
SALONIKA	,, ,, ,, 1916	...	128,630
	1917	...	170,900
MESOPOTAMIA	,, ,, ,, 1916 (last 22 weeks)		32,813
	1917 (for year)		110,613
E. AFRICA	,, ,, ,, 1917 Aug.-Dec.		24,706

(Before this date the figures are not complete).

Figures for British and Colonials in Egypt, Salonika, Mesopotamia and East Africa for the year 1918 not yet available.

This does not include sick in the Native Indian Forces.

AIR RAIDS ON GREAT BRITAIN, 1918.

AIR RAIDS ON

(Zeppelin [italic];

Date.			Locality.	Civilian Killed.			
				Men.	Women.	Children.	Total.
Jan.	28/29	... ...	Kent, Essex and London	22	26	17	65
,,	29/30	... ...	Kent, Essex and London	2	3	5	10
Feb.	16/17	... ...	Kent, Essex and London	1	5	3	9
Feb.	17/18	... ...	Kent, Essex and London	16	4	—	20
Feb.	18/19	... ...	Kent, Essex and London	—	—	—	—
March	7/8	... ...	Kent, Essex, Herts, Beds, London ...	8	9	4	21
March	*12/13*	... ...	*East Riding*	—	*1*	—	*1*
March	*13/14*	... ...	*Durham*...	*2*	*2*	*4*	*8*
Apr.	*12/13*	... ...	*Lincoln, Lancs. and Warwick* ...	*2*	*4*	*1*	*7*
May	19/20	... ...	Kent, Essex and London	17	20	6	43
June	17...	... ...	Kent	—	—	—	—
July	18...	... ...	Kent	—	—	—	—
July	20...	... ...	Kent	—	—	—	—
Aug.	*5* ...	... ...	*Off the Wash*	—	—	—	—
			TOTALS	70	74	40	184

GREAT BRITAIN, 1918.
Aeroplane.)

Casualties.				Sailors and Soldiers.		Grand Total.		Remarks.
Injured								
Men.	Women.	Children.	Total.	Killed.	Injured.	Killed.	Injured.	
79	50	31	160	2	6	67	166	One aeroplane downed.
7	2	1	10	—	—	10	10	
3	—	3	6	3	—	12	6	One aeroplane downed.
17	9	—	26	1	6	21	32	
—	—	—	—	—	—	—	—	Fail to penetrate London defences.
9	28	2	39	2	—	23	39	One Gotha downed.
—	—	—	—	—	—	1	—	*Hull bombed.*
11	19	9	39	—	—	8	39	*Hartlepool bombed.*
10	6	4	20	—	—	7	20	
57	67	26	150	6	27	49	177	Considerable damage; 5 raiders downed.
—	—	—	—	—	—	—	—	
—	—	—	—	—	—	—	—	
—	—	—	—	—	—	—	—	*5 attack; one downed 40 miles from land.*
193	181	76	450	14	39	198	489	

APPROXIMATE NUMBER OF BRITISH ARMY CASUALTIES IN THE FOLLOWING THEATRES OF WAR FOR THE YEARS 1914-15-16-17 and 18. (War Office figures.)
ALL FORCES.*

	Killed (including Died of Wounds and Died other causes).		Wounded.		Missing (including Prisoners).		Total.		Prisoners.	
	Officers.	Other Ranks.	Officers.	Other Ranks.	Officers.	Other Ranks.	Officers.	Other Ranks.	Officers.	Other Ranks.
1914—										
France	1,278	15,896	2,209	48,760	783	25,728	4,270	90,384	540	19,050
Egypt	2	30	—	3	—	—	2	33	—	—
East Africa	36	431	48	368	3	101	87	900	—	—
Mesopotamia	7	105	35	644	—	18	42	767	—	—
Other Theatres	26	238	46	656	40	558	112	1,452	—	—
Total	1,349	16,700	2,338	50,431	826	26,405	4,513	93,536	540	19,050
1915—										
France	3,887	62,528	7,908	197,205	802	23,754	12,597	283,487	400	7,895
Egypt	18	278	18	206	—	2	36	486	—	—
Dardanelles	1,752	29,880	3,056	75,380	283	8,621	5,091	113,881	27	415
Salonika	8	184	19	416	11	705	38	1,305	7	477
East Africa	22	412	22	316	15	282	59	1,010	5	94
Mesopotamia	201	2,199	457	8,994	18	812	676	12,005	6	400
Other Theatres	91	319	72	510	9	349	172	1,178	—	—
Total	5,979	95,800	11,552	283,027	1,138	34,525	18,669	413,352	445	9,281
1916—										
France	8,549	141,582	19,352	427,535	1,628	42,047	29,529	611,164	770	14,430
Egypt	131	1,345	141	1,484	31	372	303	3,201	27	277
Dardanelles	17	837	19	510	—	1	36	1,348	—	—
Salonika	94	2,074	228	3,733	10	288	332	6,095	3	96
East Africa	92	1,785	112	1,791	3	93	207	3,669	—	31
Mesopotamia	523	10,233	1,005	18,714	511	11,119	2,039	40,066	470	10,441
Other Theatres	13	29	20	120	2	1	35	150	—	—
Total	9,419	157,885	20,877	453,887	2,185	53,921	32,481	665,693	1,270	25,275

	Killed (including Died of Wounds and Died other causes).		Wounded.		Missing (including Prisoners).		Total.		Prisoners.	
	Officers.	Other Ranks.	Officers.	Other Ranks.	Officers.	Other Ranks.	Officers.	Other Ranks.	Officers.	Other Ranks.
1917—										
France ...	10,557	179,458	26,038	510,466	2,634	51,160	39,229	771,084	1,249	21,662
Egypt ...	634	7,978	1,425	23,797	136	3,391	2,195	35,166	41	802
Salonika ...	107	2,663	321	7,390	67	982	495	11,035	18	291
East Africa.	177	4,056	248	3,956	20	421	445	8,433	14	120
Mesopotamia	529	8,912	832	19,221	43	2,023	1,404	30,156	31	352
Italy ...	10	67	22	251	2	1	34	319	31	—
Other Theatres...	10	131	14	236	1	12	25	379	—	—
Total ...	12,024	203,265	28,900	595,317	2,903	57,990	43,827	856,572	1,353	23,227
1918—										
France ...	8,790	132,190	27,168	542,644	5,066	166,222	41,024	841,056	3,787	103,562
Egypt ...	441	8,569	946	15,062	26	661	1,413	24,292	20	452
Salonika ...	89	3,290	245	4,628	39	894	373	8,812	15	584
East Africa	92	3,715	57	965	11	164	160	4,844	3	46
Mesopotamia	132	9,603	152	1,616	3	50	287	11,269	—	15
Italy ...	128	1,007	368	4,313	44	710	540	6,030	20	167
North Russia and Vladivostok ...	6	75	7	97	2	74	15	246	1	30
Other Theatres...	26	95	29	107	—	—	55	202	—	—
Total ...	9,704	158,544	28,972	569,132	5,191	168,775	43,867	896,751	3,846	104,856
Totals ...	38,475	632,194	92,639	1,953,094	12,243	341,616	143,357	2,925,904	7,454	181,689

*"All Forces" does not include Royal Navy or Mercantile Marine, but includes Colonials. The figures given include Regular and Territorial Force, Royal Flying Corps to 31st March, 1918, Royal Naval Division, all Colonials, Indian and African natives with the exception of Indian and African Followers attached to the East African Expeditionary Force. The Royal Air Force (i.e., since 1st April, 1918) is not included.

APPROXIMATE NUMBER OF BRITISH ARMY DEATHS ON SERVICE FROM ALL CAUSES IN THE FOLLOWING THEATRES OF WAR DURING THE YEARS 1914-15-16-17 and 18. (War Office figures.) ALL FORCES.*

	Killed and Died from Wounds.		Died from Other Causes.		Total Deaths.	
	Officers.	Other Ranks.	Officers.	Other Ranks.	Officers.	Other Ranks.
1914—						
France	1,263	15,317	15	579	1,278	15,896
Egypt	1	21	1	9	2	30
East Africa	36	415	—	16	36	431
Mesopotamia	7	102	—	3	7	105
Other Theatres	21	180	5	58	26	238
Total	1,328	16,035	21	665	1,349	16,700
1915—						
France	3,785	59,484	102	3,044	3,887	62,528
Egypt	10	60	8	218	18	278
Dardanelles	1,646	26,400	106	3,480	1,752	29,880
Salonika	6	96	2	88	8	184
East Africa	19	181	3	231	22	412
Mesopotamia	192	1,799	9	400	201	2,199
Other Theatres	34	157	57	162	91	319
Total	5,692	88,177	287	7,623	5,979	95,800
1916—						
France	8,320	135,970	229	5,612	8,549	141,582
Egypt	73	536	58	809	131	1,345
Dardanelles	10	379	7	458	17	837
Salonika	74	1,204	20	870	94	2,074
East Africa	64	709	28	1,076	92	1,785
Mesopotamia	453	5,980	70	4,253	523	10,233
Other Theatres	5	26	8	3	13	729
Total	8,999	144,804	420	13,081	9,419	157,885

	Killed and Died from Wounds.		Died from Other Causes.		Total Deaths.	
	Officers.	Other Ranks.	Officers.	Other Ranks.	Officers.	Other Ranks.
1917—						
France	10,286	171,307	271	8,151	10,557	179,458
Egypt	554	6,686	80	1,292	634	7,978
Salonika	82	1,619	25	1,044	107	2,663
East Africa	136	1,527	41	2,529	177	4,056
Mesopotamia	431	6,285	98	2,627	529	8,912
Italy	10	67	—	—	10	67
Other Theatres	9	124	1	7	10	131
Total	11,508	187,615	516	15,650	12,024	203,265
1918—						
France	8,155	118,405	635	13,785	8,790	132,190
Egypt	335	5,772	106	2,797	441	8,569
Salonika	63	1,626	26	1,664	89	3,290
East Africa	65	1,685	27	2,030	92	3,715
Mesopotamia	55	5,859	77	3,744	132	9,603
Italy	118	652	10	355	128	1,007
North Russia and Vladivostok	6	53	—	22	6	75
Other Theatres	4	20	22	75	26	95
Total	8,801	134,072	903	24,472	9,704	158,544
Totals	36,328	570,703	2,147	61,491	38,475	632,194

Total Loss to Strength:—	Officers.	Other Ranks.	Total heads.
Killed and Died	38,475	632,194	670,669
Missing (including Prisoners) ...	12,243	341,616	353,859
Total	50,718	973,810	1,024,528

* v. Footnote on p. 193.

MISCELLANEOUS LOSSES TABLES.

A.—LOSSES OF ALL COUNTRIES TO NOVEMBER 11, 1918.

Owing to the different bases on which these tables of losses have been drawn up by the different countries, it is impossible to obtain an accurate comparison. The figures are, broadly, official, and were published as such during the spring of 1919; but no responsibility can be accepted for their accuracy.*

MILITARY.

Austria (not including Hungary) :—

Killed	...	...	...	800,000
Wounded	...	...	...	3,200,000

Austro-Hungarian losses to the end of Sept., 1918, were officially given as :—

Killed	...	...	...	687,534
Missing	...	...	...	855,283
Prisoners	...	...	...	1,229,289
				2,772,106

No figures for wounded.

British :—
(but v. pp. 192-195)

Killed	...	...	...	658,704
Wounded	...	...	...	2,032,142
Missing and prisoners		...	...	359,145
				3,049,991

New Zealand :—

Killed	...	...	...	16,302
Wounded	...	...	...	25,133

South Africa :— Total war losses : 7,089 white and 1,105 coloured.

France :—

Dead	...	...	...	1,071,300
Missing	...	...	...	314,000
Prisoners	...	...	...	446,300
				1,831,600

No figures for wounded.

Germany:—

Killed and died	...	...	1,600,000
Wounded	...	...	...	4,064,000
Missing	...	...	...	103,000
Prisoners	...	...	...	618,000
				6,385,000

Germany—Württemberg :—

Killed	...	...	...	59,000
Wounded	...	...	...	158,000
Missing	...	...	...	17,000

Italy :—

	Army.		Navy.	
Killed	... 462,391	...	Killed ...	3,169
Wounded	... 953,886	...	Wounded ...	5,252
Total	...	...	1,424,698	

* In several cases they do not agree with other " official " figures given elsewhere in this volume.

Rumania :—

Killed	85,000
Died in hospital	155,000
Died in captivity... ...	60,000
Total	300,000

Besides 450,000 civilians.

Russia :—

Killed	1,700,000
Wounded	4,950,000
Prisoners	2,500,000
	9,150,000

Turkey :—

Killed	436,974
Wounded	407,772
Prisoners	103,731
	948,477

U.S.A. :—

Killed	51,036
Wounded	208,223
Prisoners	4,534
Missing	2,293
	263,793

B.—BRITISH NAVAL CASUALTIES.

Casualties to Royal Navy and Reserves (including Mercantile Marine Reserve while serving in H.M. Ships and Merchant Ships* :—

	Officers.	Men.
Killed in action or died of wounds ...	2,074	20,735
Died otherwise	400	11,433
Wounded in action	549	3,961
Injured, not in action	256	392
Missing	—	2
Prisoners of War	211	824
Interned	51	170
Total Casualties	3,541	37,517

* Not including Royal Naval Division nor British Mercantile Marine.

C.—GENERAL NAVAL LOSSES.
From an " authoritative " (Paris) source :—

	Great Britain	France	Italy	Japan	U.S.A.	Germany	Austro-Hungary
Battleships	13	4	3	1	—	1	3
Battle Cruisers	3	—	—	—	—	1	—
Cruisers	25	5	2	4	1	24	2
Monitors	6	—	1	—	—	—	3
Destroyers	64	14	10	3	2	72	5
Torpedo Boats	10	8	5	1	—	51	4
Submarines	50*	14	8	—	1	205†	8
Small Craft	27	9	—	—	—	—	—
Thousands of tons ...	550	110	76	50	17	350	65

* An earlier official list gives 59. † An earlier official list gives 216.

Total Allied loss	803,000 tons.
Total Enemy loss	415,000 tons.

BRITISH WARSHIP LOSSES (ADMIRALTY):—

Class.	1914.	1915.	1916.	1917.	1918.	Total.	Tonnage.
Battleships	2	6	2	2	1	13	200,735
Battle Cruisers	—	—	3	—	—	3	63,000
Cruisers	6	2	4	1	—	13	158,300
Light Cruisers	3	—	3	—	6	12	46,255
Monitors	—	—	1	1	3	5	8,125
Destroyers	1	8	14	23	18	64	52,045
Torpedo Boats	—	5	3	2	1	11	2,230
Submarines	4	10	12	7	21*	54*	43,649
Merchant Cruisers	1	4	1	6	5	17	179,169
Boarding Steamers	—	2	3	4	4	13	23,779
Other Small Craft	3	3	6	17	20	49	83,568
TOTAL	20	40	52	63	79	254	860,855

Besides 815 Auxiliary Vessels, of 1,129,733 tonnage, including 244 colliers, 246 Trawlers, and 130 Drifters.

* 7 of these purposely sunk in the Baltic.

D.—GERMAN NAVAL LOSSES.

The total German losses to the end of 1918 are given (Berlin) as:—

Ship of the line	1
Battle cruiser	1
Old armoured cruisers	6
Modern cruisers	3
Old small cruisers	10
Gunboats	7
River gunboats	3
Destroyers	39
Large torpedo-boats	21
Small torpedo-boats	41
Mine-sweepers	28
Auxiliary cruisers	9
Fishing vessels, luggers, etc.	122
"U" boats	199

Eighty-two submarines went down in the North Sea and the Atlantic; three in the Baltic; 72 off Flanders; 16 in the Mediterranean; and five in the Black Sea. Fourteen were blown up by their own crews and seven were interned in neutral ports.

The losses of men killed in the naval services are given as:—

Fleet:—946 officers, 5,222 deck officers and non-commissioned officers, and 12,686 men.

Marine Corps:—328 officers, 1,488 deck officers and non-commissioned officers, and 8,809 men.

There fell in Tsingtau 10 officers, 33 non-commissioned officers, and 163 men.

The losses at Jutland are given officially as:—Officers killed, 172; wounded, 41; Men killed, 2,414; wounded, 449.

During the Battle of Jutland (31 May-1 June, 1916) the following enemy vessels were destroyed (official):—

"Pommern" (battleship); "Lützow" (battle-cruiser); "Wiesbaden," "Rostock," "Elbing," "Frauenlob" (cruisers); 5 destroyers (V.4, V.27, V.29, V.48, and S.35).

There were total crews of 4,537 on board these ships at the beginning of the action.

E—BRITISH AIR LOSSES.

British Flying Forces:—Killed, 6,166; other casualties, 10,457.

INDEX.

Figures in black type represent the month: *e.g.*, 4.1=4th Jan.; 23.11
=23rd Nov.; etc.

N.B.—In the following index a number of items are included which, by
reason of their uncertainty or for some other cause, it has not been
found easy or convenient to place in the Chronological Tables.
Dates which can at present be only approximately given are
indicated thus :—" *c.* 25.8."

Queen, enters Ostend, 17.10; Flies to Bruges, 23.10; Enters Antwerp, 19.11; Enters Brussels, 22.11.

ALEPPO.
British advanced troops occupy, 26.10.

ALEXANDRETTA (N. Syria).
French occupy, 9.11.

ALEXANDROPOL (Transcauc.)
Severe fighting near, 28.5.

ALEXEIEV, GENERAL.
Advances with 30,000 men towards Moscow *v.* Bolsheviks. 4.2; Death of, 10.10.

ALIENS, LEGISLATION *re.*
Committee to investigate, appointed, 1.7; Report recommending stricter treatment, 8.7; Government proclamation 11.7; British Nationality and Aliens Bill passed in Commons, 12.7, 19.7.

ALLEMANT (N. of River Aisne).
French capture, 14.9.

ALLENBY, GENERAL SIR E. (v. Palestine).
Palestine Despatches of 16.12.17, published 25.1; of 18.9.18, published 6.11; of 31.10.18; published 18.12.

ALLIED NAVAL COUNCIL.
Meets in London, 22.1.

ALLIED WAR COUNCIL.
Meets at Versailles, 30.1.

ALLIED PURCHASE COMMITTEE.
Meets in Paris, 1.1.

ALLOWANCES.
Higher, to dependents of combatants, given 18.10.

ALSACE.
French repulse fierce attack at Anspach 3.1; Fierce fighting round Hartmannsweilerkopf 28.1 to 7.2 and 23.3; Do. in Upper, 11.2 to 14.3, 5.4, 15.8.

ALTO MULOCUE (Port. E. Africa, 225 miles S. by W. from Mozambique).
Germans in retreat, 15.6.

ALTON KEUPRI (Mes.).
Turks defeated at, 11.5.

AMIENS.
Violent German attack in, section, 24.4: " 2nd Battle of Amiens " 8 to 13.8.

AMMAN (on Hejaz R'y, E. of R. Jordan).
British advance on, 26.3; British air raids on, 31.5; 3, 4, 11.6; 18.8; Turks retreat to, 23.9; British seize, 25.9.

ANCONA (Italy).
Some Austrian sailors land at, and are captured, 5.4.

ANCRE, RIVER.
Enemy concentration dispersed, 22.4; German retreat from, begins, 14.8; British cross Ancre to Thiepval Wood, 15.8; British attack on 10-m. front, between Beaucourt and Moyenneville, 21.8.

" ANDANIA " s.s. (Cunard liner).
Sunk by submarine, 27.1.

ANDRASSY, COUNT JULIUS.
Resigns position of Austrian Foreign Minister, 3.11.

ANKWALIE (E. Africa.)
Occupation of, by British, 28.1.

ANTHEUIL (N. of Compiègne).
Germans reach, 10.6; are expelled, 11.6.

ANTIVARI (Port of Montenegro).
Italian navy occupies, 4.11.

ANTWERP.
Re-entered by Belgian troops, 18.11; by King and Queen, 19.11.

APILLY (Oise).
French reach, 4.9.

APREMONT, FOREST OF, (Argonne).
Continued attacks on French and Americans fail, 12.4.

ARABS.
Raid Hejaz railway perpetually, notably in Jan.; Capture convoy E. of Medina, 18.1; Large force advances E. of British Army, May to Sept.; Occupy Damascus, 1.10; Status of their forces recognised by Allies, 2.10.

" ARBUTUS " H.M.S.
(British mine-sweeping sloop) torpedoed, 1.1.

ARCHANGEL.
Allied forces land, 2.8; Government statement *re* their status, 22.8; Allied success near, 31.8; U.S.A. troops arrive, 11.9; British repel Bolsheviks, 160 miles S. of, 18.10; British occupy Kadish, 19.10; Bolshevik attack on River Dvina, position repulsed, 23.10; General Manishevski C.i.C. loyal Russians, 20.11.

ARDENNES CANAL.
French occupy S. bank between Semuy and Le Chesne, 4.11; and cross, 5.11.

ARDRE, RIVER (S. trib. of Vesle).
British, Italians and French win ground in valley, 20.7; Allied advance continued, 21.7.

ARGENTINA.
Allied Wheat Convention with, signed, 14.1; " Ministro Iriondo " torpedoed off Toulon, 27.1.

ARGONNE.
French raids in, 11, 21.1; Franco-American attack begins, 27.9; Allies advance on N. of forest, 1.11; Germans retreat clear of, 2 3.11.

ARMAGEDDON, FIELD OF.
British cross, 20.9.

ARMANCOURT (S.W. of Roye).
Allies capture, 11.8.

ARMENIA.
Russians evacuate, 18.2; Declaration of independence, 27.6; General Andranik harasses Turks near Erivan, 16.10.

BELLEAU WOOD (N.W. of Château-Thierry, Marne).
Capture by Americans, 11.6; Conquest completed, 12.6; French counterattack from, 18.7.

BELLUNO (Venetia, Italy).
Allies enter, 2.11.

BELVAL (1½ miles S. of Lassigny).
French capture, 13.8.

BERAT (S. Albania).
Italians threaten, 8, 9.7; Italians capture, 10.7; Austrians re-capture, 25.8; Italians re-enter, 3.10.

BERLIN.
Strike declared at Munich and Hamburg, state of siege in Berlin and other towns, 30.1; Strike Council dissolved and Martial Law proclaimed in, 31.1; Fighting in, 6, 12, 18, 24.12; Soviet Councils in, 16, 18, 20.12.

BERRY AU BAC (Aisne R.).
Germans take, 28.5; French re-take, 7.10.

BERTIGO (Mt. on Asiago Plateau).
French capture, 19.6.

BETHUNE.
Heavy bombardment of, 14.5; Successful British midnight attack along La Bassée Canal, E. of, 14.6.

BIEFVILLERS (N. of Bapaume).
British capture, 24.8.

BISSOLATI, SIGNOR.
Resigns from Italian Government, 28.12.

BLACK SEA.
British Fleet enters, 15.11; Surrender of German-controlled ships at Odessa, etc. 26.11; Surrender of Bolshevik naval forces in, c. 5.12; Batum occupied by British, 27.12.

BLAGOVESHCHENSK (Siberia).
Japanese take, 18.9.

BLIGNY (S.W. of Reims).
Germans capture village and height, height recovered by British, 6.6; Village recaptured by British, 7.6.

BLIGNY, MONTAGNE DE (Ardre Valley).
British retake, 28. 7.

BLOCKADE.
Sir L. W. Evans appointed Minister of, 19.7.

BOIS DE COURTON (S.W. of Reims).
Severe fighting, Allies win ground, 20.7; and capture, 21.7.

BOIS LE CHÂTELET (between Ourcy and Marne Rivers).
French and Americans occupy, 23.7

BOIS DU SART (between Rivers Scarpe and Sensée).
British capture, 27.8.

BOLO PASHA.
Trial commences, 4.2; Condemned to death, 14.2; Executed, 17.4.

BOLSHEVIKS (v. Russia).

BONAR LAW, RT. HON. A.
Speeches on "Man power Bill," 11.4; Introduces the Budget, 22.4; On Trade Policy, 31.7.

"BONNET ROUGE."
Treason trial regarding the, 29.4 to 15.5; Duval sentenced to death, 15.5.

BORDEN, SIR R. (Premier, Canada).
Represents Canada in Imperial War Conference, 12.6; Speech at Empire gathering, 21.6.

BORIS, TSAR OF BULGARIA.
Succeeds to the throne, 4.10; abdicates, 1.11.

BOTHA, GENERAL L.
Statement at Pretoria re Military and police measures, 2.7.

BOULOGNE.
Serious German air-raid on, 26.1.

BOURBON, PRINCE SIXTE OF.
Emperor Charles' letter through, disclosed, 8.4.

BOURESCHES (Château-Thierry).
To S.E., German attack repulsed by French, 2.6; Captured by French and Americans, 7.6.

BOURLON WOOD (Cambrai).
Canadians take, 27.9.

BOYELLES (S. of Arras).
German attacks defeated in Boiry and Boyelles region, 30.3; Heavy fighting in district, 16.4.

"BOXER," H.M.S.
Destroyer, sunk in English Channel, 8.2.

BRATIANU, M.
Rumanian Cabinet resigns, 6.2.

BRAY (Somme).
Captured by Germans, 26.3; Road to Albert seized by British, 22.8; British recapture, 24.8.

BRAZIL.
Decides to send naval squadron to co-operate with Allied Fleets in European waters, 30.1.

"BRESLAU," GERMAN CRUISER.
Sunk in action, 20.1.

BREST-LITOVSK, TREATY OF.
Bolsheviks formally agree to conditions, 19.2; Resume negotiations for, 28.2; Signed, 3.3 (v. App. 39); Ratified by Congress of Soviets, 14.3; Entente Governments refuse to recognise, 18.3; Denounced by Mr. A. Henderson in name of British Labour, 20.3; Publication of, 18.6; Supplementary agreements signed, 27.8.

BRIEULLES (on Meuse, between Stenay and Verdun).
Americans capture, 28.9; Americans cross Meuse near, 5.11.

BRIEY (Coal and Iron District _.raine)
Americans enter, 18.11.

"BRITANNIA," H.M.S.
Sunk off Gibraltar, 9.11.

BRUGES.
Stormed by Belgians, 19.10.

BRUNSWICK, DUKE ERNST AUGUST OF.
Abdicates, 8.11.

BRUSSELS.
Re-entered by Belgian troops, 18.11; King Albert makes formal entry, 22.11.

"BRUSSELS," S.S.
Torpedoed at Zeebrugge, 14.10.

BRUYÈRES (Fère-en-Tardenois).
French line reaches, 27.7.

BUCHANAN, Sir G.
Granted leave of absence from Petrograd, 3.1.

BUCHAREST v. Bukarest.

BUCQUOY (S. Arras).
Germans repulsed at, 27.3; Considerable artillery activity at, 4.4; Germans attack from Somme to, 5.4; Two German attacks fail, 7.4; Captured by Germans, c. 15.4; Germans evacuate, 14.8.

BUDGET (British).
Introduced, 22.4; passed Commons, 21.6.

BUKAREST.
Re-occupied by Rumanian and Allied troops, 1.12.

BUKAREST, TREATY OF.
Signed, 7.5; Passed by Reichstag, 5.7.

BUKOVINA.
Deputation to Jassy announces desire of union with Rumania, 24.11.

BULGARIA.
Malinov Government suceeds Radoslavov, 21.6; Asks for Armistice, 26.9; Signed at Salonika, 28.9; Accepts Allied terms, hostilities cease at noon, opening of Sobranyé and King's speech, 30.9; King Ferdinand abdicates, succeeded by Prince Boris, 4.10; Demobilisation of Army Order signed 4.10; 65,000 troops surrendered to date, 6.10; Peaceful Manifesto by King, 6.10; Cleared of Germans, 18.10; Abdication of King Boris and establishment of Peasant Government under M. Stambuliski, 1.11.

BULLECOURT (Cambrai).
Strong German attacks repulsed, 5, 8.1; British raid, 29.1; Captured by Germans, c. 23.3; Violent struggle for, 30.31.8.

BUNSEN, Sir MAURICE DE.
Sent on South American Mission, 21.4 to 21.9.

BURES (Lorraine).
Successful extensive French raid N. of, 500 prisoners, 20.2.

BURIAN, BARON.
Succeeds Count Czernin as A.-H. Foreign Minister, 15.4; Resigns c. 2.11.

BUTTE DU MESNIL.
French win salient between Tahure and, 13.2.

BUZANCY (N. of Argonne Forest).
Americans capture, 2.11.

BUZANCY (S. of Soissons).
Capture by French and British, 29.7.

CADY, MOUNT (N. of Tonale Pass).
Austrian attack defeated, 13.6.

CAESAR'S CAMP (W. of Roye).
Trenches captured by French, 17.8.

CAGNICOURT (W.N.W. of Cambrai).
British capture, 2.9.

CAILLAUX, M.
Arrested in Paris, 14.1; U.S.A. publish documents referring to case of, 16.1; Indicted in French Senate, 29.10.

CALAIS.
Numerous German air raids on, during year, especially 26.1.

CALCUTTA.
All-Indian Moslem Association formed, 1.1.

"CALGARIAN," H.M.S.
Sunk, 1.3.

"CALYPSO," H.M.S.
Captures of Bolshevist destroyers by, announced, 27.12.

CAMBRAI.
German raid near Flesquières, 7.1; Raids and counter raids in district, 19.1; British raids near Harrincourt and Bullecourt, 29.1; Fighting in region of, 16.2; N. suburbs captured by Canadians, 29.9; Set on fire by Germans, 30.9; British take, 9.10.

CAMBRAI ENQUIRY.
Result of, published, 15.1.

CAMBRONNE (near junction of rivers Matz and Oise).
French capture, 11.8.

CAMPAGNE (N. of Noyon).
French take, 31.8.

CANADA.
Anti-conscription riots, 1.4; Statement by Prime Minister, 2.4; Quebec reported quiet, 3.4; Appropriation for war expenditure introduced, 10.4; Increase of man power proposed, 17.4.

CANAL DES ARDENNES.
Between Semuy and Neuville, captured by French, 2.11.

CHURCHILL RT. HON. W.
Reviews work of Ministry of Munitions, 25.4; Vigorous speech on situation, 4.7.
CLEMENCEAU, M. (French Premier).
Denies receipt of peace offer from Austrians, 3.4; Discloses Emperor's letter 8.4; Declines to recognise Russian Government, 14.4; Fine speech, 4.6; In London, 1-3.12; Speech of, on conditions of peace, 29.12.
CLÉRY (N.W. of Péronne).
British capture, 30.8.
CLYNES, RT. HON. J.R.
Appointed Food Controller, 9.7; Resigns, on grounds of Labour policy. 21.11.
COBLENZ,
British air-raids on, 12.3, 20.5; Occupied by Americans, 11.12; Americans occupy bridgehead of, 13.12.
COL DEL ROSSO (Asiago Plateau).
Italians capture, 30.6.
COLOGNE.
British air raid on, 24.3; British daylight air raid, 18.5; Entered by British 6.12; British occupy bridgehead of, 12-13.12.
CONDÉ (W. of Mons).
British capture, 8.11.
CONSTANTINOPLE.
Great fire at, 31.5 and 1.6; Bombed by British, 27.8, 20.9; Allied Fleet reaches, 13.11; French troops land at, 21.11.
COPENHAGEN.
British Squadron (30 ships) anchors off, 28.11.
"CORK," s.s.
Sunk by submarine, 26.1.
"CORRINGTON " (U.S. Transport).
Torpedoed and sunk, 1.7.
CORTELAZZO (at mouth of Piave).
Austrian line broken, 20.6.
COSSACKS (Don).
Independence of, declared, 28.5; Loyal agreement with Kuban Cossacks to combat anarchy, etc, 14.6.
COSTALUNGA, MOUNT (Asiago Plateau).
Italians capture, 19.6.
COSTA RICA.
Declares war on Germany, 25.5.
COURCELLES (Soissons).
German attack fails, 9.6; Captured by Germans, re-captured by French, 10.6.
COURTRAI.
Bombed by British airmen, 10, 22, 23, 24, 25.1.
CREFELD.
Occupied by Belgians, 6.12.
CROATIA.
Croats seize Fiume, 23.10; National Council meets, 24.10; Independence

(with Yugo-Slavia) proclaimed at Agram, 29.10.
CROMIE, CAPT., R.N.
Killed at British Embassy, Petrograd, 29.8.
CROWN PRINCE (Germany).
Flight to Holland, 9.11.
CROZAT CANAL.
French cross, 7, 9.9.
CUBA.
Troops offered to U.S.A., 10.10.
CUISLES (N. of Châtillon-sur-Marne).
French line reaches, 27.7.
CURFEW ORDER.
Comes into force, 2.4.
CURZOLA (island off Dalmatia).
Italians occupy, 4.11.
CUTRY PLATEAU (Villers Cotterets).
German advance on, 12.6; French capture, 28.6.
CAVILLY (S.E. of Montdidier).
Capture by Germans, 9.6.
CZECHO-SLOVAKS.
Vote against Austrian budget, 6.8; Great Britain recognises as Allied Nation, 13.8; Recognised by U.S.A., 3.9; Receive set-back on Volga, 20.9; Pushed back in E. Russia, 18.10; Proclamation of Czech Republic in Prague, 17.10; Paris Council declares independence, 18.10; With French, push enemy back on the Serre river, 22.10; National Council takes over administration in Prague, 28.10.
CZERNIN, COUNT O.
Replies to war aims speeches, 24.1; Resigns on Emperor's letter question, 15.4; Defends "German course" in Austrian policy, 18.7.

DAMASCUS.
Turks flee towards, 25.9; British cavalry reach El Kuneitra, 40 miles from, 28.9; British approach, 29.9; And enter at night, 30.9; Occupied by British and Arabs, 1.10.
DAMASCUS RAILWAY.
Arabs cut, 21.9.
DAMERY (N.W. of Roye).
British repulse German attack, 16.8.
DANUBE, RIVER.
French reach, at Vidin (Bulg.), 19.10; French capture convoy at Lom Palanka, 21.10; Serbs reach, E. of Semendria, 30.10; Flotilla handed over to Yugo-Slavs, 1.11.
DARDANELLES.
Naval action near, 20.1; Allied fleet passes through, 12.11.
DEAD SEA.
Turkish forces defeated S. of (Kerak-Tafile Road), 26.1.

DVINA, RIVER (Southern).
German army crosses, and marches on Dvinsk and Lutsk, 18.2.

DVINSK.
Germans occupy, and Lutsk, 19.2; Bolshevist troops capture, 26.11.

EAST AFRICA.
Three columns pursue Germans in Mozambique, 11.1; British column disembarks at Port Amelia, 12.1; Fighting in Portuguese East Africa, 7, 17, 21, 25.1; 22.2; 12, 21.3; General van Deventer's despatch published, 5.4; further fighting in April; Action at Nhamacurra, 25 miles N. of Quilimane, c. 4 to 7.7; Germans moving towards Lake Nyasa, 10.10; General v. Lettow-Vorbeck surrenders on Chambezi river, N. Rhodesia, 14.11.

EAST ANGLIA.
Five German airships attack, one downed at sea, 5.8.

EBERT, HERR.
Becomes Chancellor in Germany, 9.11; Opens Federal States Meeting at Berlin to consider future German Government, 25.11.

EDUCATION ACT.
Receives Royal assent, 8.8.

EICHHORN, FIELD MARSHAL von.
German Military Dictator in the Ukraine, 1.5; Assassinated at Kiev, 31.7.

EISNER, HERR KURT.
Assumes Premiership and Ministry of Foreign Affairs of Bavarian Republic, 9.11; Threatens to break off relations with Berlin, 26.11.

EKATERINBURG.
Bolsheviks defeated near, 16.12.

ELIOT, SIR CHARLES.
(Principal of Hong Kong University), Appointed British High Commissioner in Siberia, 16.8.

EPÉHY (S.W. of Cambrai).
British advance round, 25.9.

ERZERUM.
Re-captured by Turks, 12.3.

ES SALT (Palestine).
British advance on, 24.3; And capture, 25.3; British troops again advance, 30.4; Capture, 1.5; Fighting for, 2.5; British withdraw from, 3.5; British again reach, 23.9.

ESSEX.
Aeroplane raids on (v. Table of Air Raids, pp. 190, 191).

ESTAIRES (River Lys).
British and Portuguese fall back to, 9.4; From, to Givenchy German attacks fail : Brilliant defence by Guards Division, etc, 10.4.

ESTHONIA.
Invaded by Bolsheviks, 8, 16, 26.12; British share in defence of, 12, 28.12.

EVANS, SIR L. WORTHINGTON, BT.
Appointed Minister of Blockade, 19.7.

FATHA (Tigris).
British take, 17.5; British bomb Turkish camp near, 30.5; Turks held by British at, 18.10; Turks retire from 23.10; Successful British pursuit, 24.10.

FAVEROLLES (N. of River Ourcq).
Capture by Germans, re-taken by French, and re-taken by Germans, 2.6; Re-capture by French, 3.6.

FAVREUIL (N. of Bapaume).
British capture, 25.8.

FÈRE-EN-TARDENOIS (River Ourcq).
Germans take, 30.5; French and Americans advance towards, 24.7; And occupy, 28.7.

FESTUBERT (La Bassée).
Continuous fighting at, British hold line, 13.4.

FEUILLÈRES (W. of Péronne).
British cross Somme at, 30.8.

FIELDING, SIR CHARLES W.
Appointment as Director-General of Food production, 31.7.

FIERI (S. Albania).
Italians occupy, 8.7; Austrians re-capture, 25.8.

FIFE (Frontier post between Rhodesia and German E. Africa).
German attack repulsed at, 2.11.

FISHER, RT. HON. W. HAYES.
Resigns Presidency of Local Government Board, 5.11.

FINLAND.
Republic recognised by Sweden, 5.1; By France and Germany, 6.1; Civil war, Helsingfors captured by socialists, 28.1; General Mannerheim gathers together White Army in the N., c. 15.2; reinforced by Germans, 20.2; Independence recognised by Russia, 3.3; Makes peace with Germany, 7.3; German ultimatum to Russia re, 1.4; 40,000 German troops land at Hangö, 2.4; Destruction of Russian warships in, waters, 4.4; Germans occupy Helsingfors, 14.4; White Army reaches Russian frontier, 23.4; Viborg taken by Whites, 29.4; Question of German King, May; Secret convention with Germany published in *Politiken*, 2.6; Bill for new Constitution, 11.6; Postponed, 19.6; Repudiates German Murman expedition, 26.8; Adolf Friedrich, Duke of Mecklenburg Schwerin, resigns candidature for Finnish throne, 26.8; Pr. Fried. Karl of Hesse candidate as King, 11.9; Elected formally, 9.10;

14.1; Issues orders for "thinning out," 10.4; President of Local Government Board, 5.11.

GEDDES, RT. HON. SIR E. (First Lord of Admiralty).
Reviews shipping situation, 5.3 (v. App. 42); Gives statistics regarding submarine warfare and shipbuilding, 20.3 Appointed Co-ordinator of demobilisation, 19.12.

GEORGE V., H.M. KING.
Returns from visit to front, 30.3; Greetings to U.S.A., 6.4; Message to munition workmen, 21.4; Presents £10,000 to Red Cross, 14.10; Receives Inter-Parliamentary delegates, 21.10; Message to British Empire, 11.11; Visits Paris with Prince of Wales and Prince Albert, 27.11.

GEORGE, RT. HON. D. LLOYD.
Addresses Man-power Conference, 5, 13.1; Confers with Sig. Orlando, 24.1; Agrees to Gen. Foch's appointment, 29.3; Message to Dominions, 31.3; Returns from front, 4.4; Introduces Man-power Bill, 9.4; At War Council, 1.5; In Edinburgh, 24.5; Speech at Empire Gathering, 21.6; In H. of C. re war, 24.6; Reply to Federalists published, 1.7; Speech to Allied Food Controllers, 25.7; To Manufacturers, 31.7; "Hold fast" message, 5.8; Reviews the War, 7.8; Guildhall speech, announces Emperor's abdication, 9.11; Letter on his Domestic Policy, 12.11; Speech to Employers and Trades Unions, 13.11;At Central Hall, opens Election campaign, 16.11; Election Manifesto, 22.11; At Newcastle, 29.11; Aims and Policy, 5.12; Election programme, 10.12; At Bristol, 11.12; Policy re Conscription, 13.12.

GEORGIA.
Trans - Caucasian independence declared by Diet of Trans-Caucasia, 27.4; Georgia proclaims its own independence, 23.5; Diet dissolves itself, 26.5.

GERMANY.
Chancellor replies to war aim speeches and the 14 points, 24.1; v. Kühlmann on situation, 25.1; Great strikes in Berlin, spreading to Kiel and Hamburg, 30.1; Kühlmann on German Ukrainian treaty, 20.2; Hertling on Foreign Affairs, 25.2 and 18.3; Eighth War Loan, 18.3 to 18.4, produces £750,071,000; Lichnowsky's Memorandum published by Swedish "Politiken," 15.3; Russian and Rumanian Treaties adopted by Reichstag, 23.3; Budget of £366,600,000, 24.3; Food Dictator on economic situation, 12.4; Estimates of German losses to July, 1917, published, 22.4; State grain-bureau formed in Ukraine, 29.4; Kühlmann on political and military situation, 24.6;

Great sensation, Kühlmann resigns, 9.7; Succeeded by Admiral v. Hintze, 10.7; Severe food privations from March onwards; Vote of Credit £750,000,000, 12.7; More speeches by Hertling and Hintze, 24.9; They both resign, 30.9; Situation impossible; All Secretaries of State resign, 1.10; Conference in Berlin, 2.10; Prince Max of Baden appointed Chancellor, New Socialist Cabinet formed, 4.10; Addresses plea for Armistice to President Wilson, 4.10; Prince Max on situation, 5.10; New Secretaries, 5, 7, 10.10; Prince Max's letter of 12.1.18 revealed 6.10; President Wilson's answer, 8.10; Militarism dead (?), 11.10; Reply to President Wilson, 12.10; Latter's answer, 14.10; Spain takes 7 ships, 14.10; Peace demonstrations and riots in Berlin, 16.10; Reply to U.S., 21.10; Hindenburg order re Peace steps captured, 22.10; Programme of reforms announced by Chancellor, 22.10; K. Liebknecht released, 22.10; Dr. Solf on situation, 23.10; Growing desire for Kaiser to abdicate, 24.10; Mark drops, 24.10; German reply to U.S.A. Note of 23.10, 27.10; Note awaiting Armistice terms sent to U.S.A., 28.10; Mutiny at Kiel, 3.11; Majority Socialists demand abdication of Kaiser and Crown Prince, 7.11; Prince Max resigns, 8.11; Abdication of Kaiser announced, 9.11 (formal signature, 28.11)); Kaiser and Crown Prince flee to Holland, 10.11; Ebert succeeds as Chancellor, 9.11; Socialist Coalition Ministry formed, 11.11; Members announced, 13.11; Approved by Council of National Plenipotentiaries, 15.11; Dr. Solf succeeded as Foreign Minister by Count Rantzau, 15.12; Date of elections for National Assembly fixed, 20.12; draft of German Constitution published by *Vorwärts*, 31.12.

GERMANY (Naval).
Destruction of 150 submarines announced in H. of C., 7.8; Squadron appears off Frisian Coast after aircraft action, 11.8; Submarines ordered to base, 19.10; Mutiny at Kiel, 3.11; R. Admiral v. Meurer received by Admiral Beatty, 15.11; Surrender of German Navy in Firth of Forth, 21.11; Surrender of submarines off Harwich, 19.11 to 1.12.

GHENT.
British bomb aerodrome, 23, 25.1; Allies reach approaches to, 3.11; Belgians enter suburbs, 4.11.

GIOLITTI, SIGNOR (former Italian Premier).
Speech on reconstruction after war, 12.8.

"GIRALDA," (Spanish s.s.).
Sunk by submarine, 26.1.

GREECE.
Mutiny of Greek troops at Lamia, arrest of MM. Skouloudhis and Lambros, 1.2 ; More evidence of ex-King's treachery published, 18.4 ; Greek troops take strong Bulgarian position at Srka di Legen, 30.5 ; Greek troops fight gallantly in last advance ; occupy Seres and Demir Hissar, 4.10, and Drama, 8.10, and Kavalla, 9.10 ; Cleared of Bulgars, 16.10 ; Announces decision to strengthen union with Serbia and Rumania, 21.11 ; Germans refuse to allow interned Greek soldiers to quit Germany, many escape, Dec.

GREY, VISCOUNT.
Publication of "The League of Nations," 20.6.

" GRIVE," H.M.S.
(British armed boarding steamer.) Torpedoed, 1.1.

GRIVESNES (Noyon).
French heavily attacked, 1.4 ; French counter-attack between Grivesnes and Noyon, 4.4 ; French success at, 9.5.

GUATEMALA.
Declares war on Germany, 23.4.

" GUILDFORD CASTLE " (Hospital Ship)
Torpedoed, 10.3.

GUISCARD (Noyon).
Captured by Germans, 24.3 ; French recover, 4.9.

GUISE (River Oise).
British and French advance from Scheldt to Oise begins, 4.11 ; French capture, 5.11.

HAGUE, THE.
Conference re Prisoners of War opens, 9.6.

HAIFA (Palestine).
British take, 23.9.

HAIG, F.M. SIR D.
Despatches on 3rd Battle of Ypres published, 8.1 ; Despatch on Battle of Cambrai, 20.2 ; Special order of the day issued, 13.4 ; Issues special despatch for 55th Division, 16.4, and for 14 other divisions, 23.4 ; Despatch of 20.7, on March and April fighting, published, 21.10 ; Welcomed in London, 19.12.

HAITI.
Declares war on Germany, 15.7.

HAM (Somme).
Captured by Germans, 23.3 ; Allies approach, 5.9 ; French retake, 6.9.

HAMBURG.
Strike declared at, 30.1 ; Martial Law proclaimed in, 31.1 ; Revolutionary outbreaks in, 5.11 ; Soviets formed, 6.11.

HAMEL (Somme).
Taken by Germans, 28, 29.3 ; British forced back near 4.4 ; Recaptured by

Australians and Americans, 4.7 ; Germans retreat from neighbourhood, 3.8.

HAPPENCOURT (Somme).
French take, 8.9.

HARDECOURT (E. of Albert).
British capture, 28.8.

HARINGTON, MAJOR GENERAL C.
Appointed Deputy Chief of Imperial General Staff, 30.4.

HARTLEPOOL.
Bombed by Zeppelin, 13.3.

HAUMONT (Verdun).
American actions near, 23.9.

HAVRINCOURT (Cambrai).
British take, 12, 14.9.

HAVRINCOURT WOOD (Cambrai).
British reach, 4 and 5.9.

" HAZARD," H.M.S.
Sunk in collision, 28.1.

HEALTH MINISTRY BILL.
Introduced into Commons, 7.11.

HÉBUTERNE (N. of Albert).
Heavy fighting at, 1, 5, 6, 20.4.

HEJAZ RAILWAY (v. also Maan, Amman, etc.).
Jericho taken, Hejaz Railway threatened by British new line, 21.2 ; Frequent attacks by Arabs on, specially 12, 17.5, 20.8, 20.9 ; Retreat of Turks along, 23.9.

HELFFERICH, HERR.
Appointed German Ambassador at Moscow, 23.7 ; Moves Embassy to Pskov, 11.8.

HELIGOLAND BIGHT.
Destroyer action in, 30.4 ; British squadron attacked by German seaplanes, 19.6.

HELSINGFORS (Finland).
Bolsheviks evacuate, 7.4 ; Occupied by Germans, 15.4.

HENDECOURT (S. of Arras-Cambrai Road).
British attack and take, 30.8.

HENDERSON, RT. HON. A.
Denounces Brest-Litovsk Treaty in name of British Labour, 20.3 ; On Labour policy, 14.11.

HERTFORDSHIRE.
Aeroplane raid on, 7.3.

HERTLING, COUNT.
Replies to War Aims speech, 24.1 ; Speech replying to Entente and Wilson, 25.2 ; On Russian situation, 18.3 ; On foreign policy, 11.7 ; On Belgium, 12.7 ; Final speeches, 24.9 ; Resigns Chancellorship, 30.9.

HESSE, GRAND DUKE OF.
Abdication of, 11.11.

HESSE, PRINCE FREDERICK CHARLES OF.
Chosen King of Finland, 11.9 ; Formally elected, 9.10, but does not take over.

18.4; Nationalist M.P.'s oppose conscription, 20.4. Proclamation of Lord French asking for 50,000 volunteers, 3.6; Appeal of Recruiting Council to all Irishmen to enlist, 24.6.

IRISH CONVENTION.
Adopts draft report, 5.4; Report published, 13.4.

IRKUTSK.
Czecho-Slovaks occupy, 8.7; And recapture, 17.8.

ISHTIP (Serbia).
Serbians capture, 25, 26.9.

ITALIAN FRONT (v. also Piave, Grappa, Asiago, etc.)
British line extended, 12.2; Sir H.. Plumer's despatch published, 12.4; Austrian attack on Piave, etc., 15 to 24.6; General advance, 26.10 to 3.11.

ITALY.
Important speeches by Orlando, 12.2; and Sonnino, 23.2; Roman Conference on Yugo-Slav question, 8 to 10.4; Socialist Conference, c. 4.9; Agitation in favour of annexationist policy, Nov.; Resignation of Bissolati and other Ministers, 29.12.

JAPAN.
Despatches warship to Vladivostok, 13.1; Marshal Terauchi, Prime Minister warns Russia of possible intervention, 22.1 and 24.2; Mr. Balfour defends proposed intervention, 14.3; Prime Minister on Siberian situation, 26.3; Baron Goto succeeds Viscount Motono as Foreign Minister, 23.4; Agreement with China signed, 16.5; Military agreement signed, 30.5; Prince Arthur of Connaught arrives on Mission, 18.6; Japanese Diplomatic Council approves U.S.'s proposal for intervention in Siberia, 18.7; Official announcement of U.S.'s proposal for intervention in Siberia, 26.7; Rice-riots, 29.7. Government decides to act with U.S. in sending troops to Vladivostok, 2.8; New Cabinet under Mr. Kei Hara, 29.9; Viscount Uchida Foreign Minister, Troops join Semenov, 3.10; Prince Yorikito arrives in London, 28.10.

JAULGONNE (River Marne).
French and American troops force Germans back over Marne, 3.6.

JENIN (Palestine).
British at, 21.9.

JERICHO.
British within 8 miles of, 19.2; Allenby occupies, 21.2; Turkish attack 7 miles N. of, defeated, 14.7.

JERUSALEM.
Lieut.-Col. R. Storrs made Governor, 5.1; British gain all objectives in attack

E. of, 19.2; and advance on Shechem Road, 20.2.

JISR ED DAMIEH (Palestine).
Slight British reverse at, 1.5; Turks cross Jordan at, 2.5.

JISR BENAT YAKUB (Palestine).
British at, 28.9.

JORDAN, RIVER.
Jericho occupied, British established on line of Jordan to E., 21.2; British patrols reach Rujm el Bahr, 2 miles E. of mouth, 26,2; British advance in valley, 9 and 14.3; Cross river, 22.3; Turks attack British positions on passages of, 13.7; but fail, 14.7; British cross, 28.9.

JUGO-SLAVS v. YUGO-SLAVS.

JÜLICH (N.E. of Aix-la-Chapelle).
Occupied by Belgians, 2.12.

"JUSTICIAR" (White Star Liner).
Torpedoed at 2.30 p.m. off N. Irish coast, 19.7; sunk at 12.40 p.m., 20.7.

KAISER, WILLIAM II., The
Meets Emperor Charles at Main Head Quarters, 15.8; Visits Tsar Ferdinand of Bulgaria at Nauheim, 29.8; Issues Imperial Decree on popular Government, 30.9; Decree stating his office is one of service to his people, 28.10; Abdicates and flees to Holland, 9.11; Signs formal abdication re Germany and Prussia, 28.11.

KAISERSLAUTERN.
British air raid on, 17.3.

KALÉDIN, GENERAL
Reported to have relinquished leadership of Cossacks to General Alexeiev, 4.2; Commits suicide (reported), 13.2.

KAMNA, MOUNT (S.W. of Lake Ochrida, Macedonia.)
Carried by French, 10.6.

KARLSRUHE.
Bombed by British, 14.1, 25.6, 11.8, 15.9.

KAROLYI, COUNT M.
Becomes Premier in Hungary, 1.11; Resigns Presidency of National Council, 3.11.

KATTEGAT.
British naval forces sink German trawlers in, 15.4.

KAVADAR (Serbia).
The Allies reach, 21.9.

"KAWACHI" (Japanese battleship).
Blown up and sunk in Tokuyama Bay, 500 casualties, 12.7.

KAZAN (River Volga).
Czecho-Slovaks capture, 12.7; Re-occupied by Czecho-Slovaks, 25.8; Fighting for, 10, 20.9.

" MARNE," H.M.S. (Destroyer).
Sinks German submarine off N. coast of Ireland, 20.7.

MARNE, RIVER.
Germans reach, near Jaulgonne, 30.5, and from Château Thierry to Dormans, 31.5; Second battle of the, Germans begin offensive, cross river, 15.7; Germans driven back, recross, 20.7; Cleared of enemy by Americans, 23.7.

MAROCCO.
German intrigues in, Spring and Summer; French defeat Abdul Malek, c. July.

MARSHALL, GENERAL SIR W. R. (C.i.C. Mesopotamia).
Publication of 1st Despatch for 6 months ending March 31 re Mesopotamia operations, 30.8.

MASARYK, PROFESSOR THOMAS G.
Elected 1st President of Czecho-Slovak Republic, 15.11.

MASSEY, RT. HON. W. F. (Premier of New Zealand).
Representing N.Z. at Imperial War Conference, 12.6; Speech at Empire Gathering, 21.6.

MASSIGES, MAIN DE (S.E. of Reims).
German offensive E. of Reims opens, 15.7; French retake whole of, 25.7.

MAUBEUGE.
British advancing towards, 6.11; British capture, 8.11; British enter, 9.11.

MAUDE, GENERAL SIR S. (late).
Last despatch published, 10.1.

MAURICE, MAJOR-GENERAL SIR F.
Letter re 5th Army, controverting Government Statements in H. of C., published, 7.5; Debate in Commons on, 9.5; Placed on retired pay, c. 20.5.

MAX, PRINCE OF BADEN.
Succeeds Count Hertling as Chancellor, 4.10; Addresses plea for Armistice, 4.10; Speaks on the situation, 5.10; Awkward letter of 12.1 to Prince A. Hohenlohe revealed, 6.10; Resigns, 8.11; Proclamation to Germans abroad declaring Germany beaten, issued, 9.11.

" MECHANICIAN," H.M.S.
Torpedoed, 20.1.

MECKLENBURG-SCHWERIN.
Abdication of Grand Duke, 11.11.

MEDINA (Arabia).
Turks attacked by Arabs near, 5.9.

MELEDA (off Dalmatian coast).
Italians occupy, 4.11.

MENIN.
British bomb aerodrome, 22.1; British enter, 29.9.

MERRIS (N. of River Lys).
German attack on British repulsed, 30.6; Successful Australian raid, 11.7; Australians capture, 29.7.

MERVILLE (River Lys).
Captured by Germans, 11.4; Germans make 7 attacks in Merville sector, 14.4; British capture prisoners W. of, 25.4; British success at, 20, 21.5; British enter 19.8.

MESNIL, BUTTE DE (Champagne).
Local fighting near, 1, 3, 14.3; Retaker by French, 27.9.

MESOPOTAMIA.
General Maude's last despatch published, 10.1; Hit taken by British, 9.3; Ana captured, 28.3; Progress beyond Ana, 1.4; Sir W. Marshall's 1st despatch (1.10.17 to 31.3.18) pub., 15.4; Sinjabis defeated, 28.4; Turks driven from Kifri, 28.4; Kirkuk captured, 7.5; Detachments sent to Persia and Caspian, end of May; Relief of Urmia, end of July; British cross Lesser Zab River, attack Turks W. of Tigris River, 25.10; Turks retreat to hills covering Shergat, 27.10; British attack successfully at Shergat, 28.10; Entire Turkish army surrenders, 30.10.

MESSINES.
British line forced back to Messines Ridge, 10.4; German attacks on repulsed, 11.4; Germans occupy, 12.4; Allies retake Ridge, 29.9.

METEREN (Bailleul).
Continuous fighting round, 13.4; Lost and retaken, 16.4; Again taken by Germans, 17.4; Heavy bombardment and infantry attack between Meteren and Voormezeele, 29.4; British line advanced v. salient S.W. of, 23.6; Captured by British, 19.7.

METZ.
Allied air-raids in district, 3, 4, 14, 16, 21, 27.1; 12, 17.2; 12.4; 17, 22, 29.5; Americans approach, 15.9; French enter, 19.11.

MEURER, REAR ADMIRAL von.
Plenipotentiary of German Naval High Command received by Sir David Beatty on board H.M.S. " Queen Elizabeth " in Firth of Forth, 15.11.

MEUSE, RIVER.
Enemy attempt at Bethincourt repulsed, 7.1; French repel attack on Chaume Wood, 12, 14.1; French and German raids, 3.4; Strong German attacks near Beaumont, 6.4; Americans attacked N.W. Toul, 13.4; Heavy fighting on both banks by American and French throughout October; Pershing attacks, 4.10; Americans cross S. of Stenay, 5.11; Cleared of Germans by French and Americans by 8.11.

MUKHMAS (N.E. of Jerusalem).
British line advanced 2 miles on 6-mile front, 14.2.

MÜNCHEN-GLADBACH.
Occupied by Belgians, 5.12.

MUNICH.
Strike declared at Hamburg and, 30.1; Bavarian Republic declared at, 7.11; Government formed under Kurt Eisner, 9.11.

MUNITION WORKERS.
Appeal of Ministry of Munitions to workers not to strike during critical battle, 21.7; Workers strike at Coventry, 23.7; Workers strike at Birmingham, 24.7; National Engineering and Allied Trades' Council decides for general strike, 25.7; Government warning : after 29.7 alternative is return to work or military service, 26.7; Strike ended, 29.7.

MURMAN.
Agreement for safeguarding railway reported, 3.4; Bolshevik agreement with Finland regarding coast, 2.6; Germans prepare to advance on railway, 3.7; Agreement between Allies and Council, 7.7; Allied forces arrive on coast, 12.7; Push on to Soroka (White Sea), 18.10; Karelia cleared of Bolsheviks and Germans, 19.10.

MUSLIMIA (Baghdad Railway).
British cavalry seize, 27.10.

MWEMBE (E. Africa).
British occupy, 24.1.

NABLUS (Shechem).
British advance towards, 2 to 11.8; Captured by Allied cavalry, 21.9.

NAMPULA (Portuguese E. Africa).
Report of occupation by British, 21.3.

NAMUR.
British enter, 21.11.

NANUNGU (Portuguese E. Africa).
Fighting and German defeat at, 1, 5, 19, 22.5.

NAPLES.
Raided by sea-planes, 11.3.

NARVA (Gulf of Finland).
Bolshevist troops capture, 26.11.

NARVA (S. Albania).
French capture, 14.7.

NAZARETH.
British cavalry reach, Liman von Sanders bolts, 20.9.

NEBI MUSA (Palestine).
British attack and capture, 20.2.

NEGOTIN (Serbia).
Allies reach, 21.9.

NERVESA (River Piave).
Austrians cross Piave at, 15.6; Recaptured by Italians, 20.6.

NESLE (Somme-Oise).
Captured by Germans, 24.8; Recaptured by French, 28.8.

NEUILLY ST. FRONT (River Ourcq).
Reached by Germans, 1.6; Captured by French, 19.7.

NEUSS (Düsseldorf).
Entered by Belgians, 4.12.

NEUVE ÉGLISE (Bailleul).
Penetrated by Germans, 12.4; And re-occupied by British, 13.4; Taken by Germans, 14.4; Recaptured by British, 1.9.

NEWFOUNDLAND.
Sir E. Morris, Prime Minister, resigns, 2.1; New Cabinet formed by Mr. W. F. Lloyd, 5.1; Conscription Bill introduced, 23.4, and passed, c. 6.5.

NEW JERSEY COAST (U.S.A.).
Vessels sunk by German submarines, 3.6.

NHAMACURRA (Portuguese E. Africa).
Germans under Lettow-Vorbeck fight British and Portuguese, 1.7; Retreat of Germans, 3.7.

NICARAGUA.
Declares war on Germany, 7.5.

NICHOLAS II. (Ex-Tsar).
Removed to the Urals, 2.5; Shot with his family at Ekaterinburg, capital of Red Ural, by order of Ural Regional Council, 16.7.

NIEPPE FOREST (N. W. of Armentières).
British success to E. (420 prisoners, etc.), 28.6.

NIEUPORT (Belgian coast).
A German attack on, 23.1; Further attacks repulsed, 30.3.

NIKOLAIEV (Black Sea).
Occupied by Germans, 18.3.

NIKOLAIEVSK (N. of Vladivostok).
Czecho-Slovaks defeat Bolsheviks and occupy town, 4.7; Japanese advancing beyond, 20.8.

NIKOLSK (N. of Vladivostok).
Cossacks fight Bolsheviks to N.W. of, 6.7; Czecho-Slovaks capture, 6.7.

NISH.
Serbs capture, 12.10; Drive enemy back N. of, 13.10.

NIZHNE-UDINSK (Siberia).
Anti-Bolshevik Government established, 19.6.

NORTHEY, MAJOR-GENERAL E.
Appointed Governor and Commander-in-Chief of East Africa Protectorate and High Commissioner for Zanzibar Protectorate, 20.6.

NORTH SEA.
Admiralty announce further prohibited area for May 15, 30.4.

30.10, in force, **31.10**; 75,000 prisoners, including 46,000 by Mounted Corps, and including 200 German and Austrian officers and 3,500 men, 360 guns, 800 machine guns, etc., etc., captured between **19.9** and **26.10**.

PARIS.
14 tons of bombs dropped on, **30.1**; Air raids on, **8**, **11.3**, **12**, **23.4**, **21**, **22.5**, **6**, **15**, **26**, **27.6**, **15.8**, **16.9**; Bombardment by long-range gun begins, **23.3**; Church hit and many killed, **29.3** (Good Friday); Enthusiastic demonstration, **11.11**.

PARLIAMENT (British).
Dissolved, **25.11**.

PASSCHENDAELE.
Fighting in region of, **12.2**; British forced back from, **16.4**; Belgians repulse attacks N.W. of, **18.4**; Allies take, **29.9**.

PASSY (N.E. of Dormans, River Marne).
Allies cross Marne, **22.7**; French line reaches, **27.7**.

"PATIA" (British armed Mercantile Cruiser).
Torpedoed and sunk by German submarine, **13.6**.

PEACE NOTES.
From Austria (to all Powers) and Germany (to Belgium), **14.9** (v. also Armistice, Austria, Germany, U.S.A., etc.).

PERM.
Loss of, by Bolsheviks, announced **29.12**.

PERNANT (W. of Soissons).
Capture by Germans, **3.6**.

PÉRONNE.
Captured by Germans, **23.3**; Recaptured by Australians, **1.9**.

PERSHING, GENERAL (v. also U.S.A. Troops.)
Asks that American troops should be employed, **28.3**; Takes St. Mihiel salient, **12.9**; Attacks between Meuse and Argonne, **26.9**.

PERSIA.
Declares recent agreements null and void, *c.* **2.5**; Small British force enters, from Mesopotamia, *c.* **15.5**; Two Turkish forces enter, towards Urmia and towards Azerbaijan, *c.* **26.5**; General Dunsterville's Mission reaches Kazvin, **1.6**; Small British detachment moves with Russians to Enzeli, **8.6**, and attacks Jangalis at Manjil, **11.6**; Turks take Tabriz, **14.6**; Jangalis repulsed at Resht, **20.7**; Small British Mission sent to Baku, **30.7**; Turks attack Assyrians near Urmia, July, and take it, **2.8**; British assistance rendered, **4.8**; Turks attack small British post near Miane, **5.9**, and occupy it, **9.9**.

PETROGRAD.
Germans advance via Esthonia towards, **19.2**; British Embassy raided by Bolsheviks, Captain Cromie, R.N., killed, **29.8**.

PIAVE, RIVER.
British raid across, **1.1**; Italians advance in, Delta and in Asolone region, **14.1**; and repulse enemy attacks, **15.16.1**; Crossed by Austrians in Nervesa area and between Fagare and Musile, **15.6**; Italians repulse Austrian attempts to cross opposite Maserada and Candelu, **17.6**; Further Austrian attempts to cross between S. Andrea and Candelu repulsed, Piave in flood, **18.6**; Austrian retreat begins, **22.6**; Right bank (portion opposite San Dona excepted) in Italian hands, **23.6**; Right bank cleared of Austrians, **24.6**; Successful Italian attack on Austrians in Delta begins, **2.7**; Italian advance continued, **4.7**; Delta cleared of Austrians, **6.7**; British and Italians force passage, **26.10**.

PICHON, M. (French Foreign Minister).
Speech of, on terms of peace, **29.12**.

"PINAR DEL RIO" (American s.s.).
Sunk by U-boat off Maryland, **8.6**.

PIRRIE, LORD.
Appointment as Controller-General of Merchant Shipbuilding announced, **20.3**.

PLOEGSTEERT.
British line forced back to, **10.4**; and beyond, **11.4**; British attack and capture, **4.9**.

PLUMER, SIR H.
Italian despatch published, **12.4**; Drives across Messines Ridge and clears Lys Valley, **1.10**; Crosses the Lys at Menin and Courtrai, **16.10**.

POINCARÉ, M. (President of French Republic).
Great speech at Paris, **4.7**; Enters Metz, **8.12**; and Strasbourg, **9.12**.

POLA (Austria).
Daring motor-boat raid on, by Commander Pellegrini, **13.5**; Major Rossetti and Surgeon-Lieut. Paolucci enter and blow up "Viribus Unitis" battleship with floating mine, **31.10**, **1.11**; Entered by Italian warships under Vice-Admiral Cagni, **5.11**.

POLAND.
Cabinet resigns as protest against Ukraine treaty, **11.2**; New Cabinet formed, **2.4**; Publication of Brest-Litovsk treaty, **18.6**; M. Kucharzewski, Prime Minister, **2.10**; Polish manifesto, **8.10**; National Army recognised by Allied Powers, **12.10**, **17.10** and **4.11**.

French advance N. of Montagne, etc.,
22.7; Heavy German counter-attacks,
30.7; Germans fall back from plateaux
of, to Aisne, 1.10; Stiff fighting N.W. of,
3.10; Moronvilliers Massif occupied by
French, 5.10.

RETHEL (on River Aisne).
French capture, 6.11.

RETHONDES (4 miles from Compiègne
on Soissons Railway).
Marshal Foch receives German Armistice delegation, 8.11.

REVAL.
Germans enter Esthonia and press
towards Petrograd and, 19.2; Germans
within 60 miles of, 21.2; Germans
occupy, 25.2; British Naval forces at,
12.12.

" REWA," (Hospital ship).
Torpedoed in Bristol Channel, 4.1;
Spanish guarantee that conditions were
observed published, 16.1.

RHINE, RIVER.
Allied Armies begin march to the,
17.11; Reached by Belgians, 4.12;
by British, 6.12; by Americans, 9.12;
Crossed by British, 12.12; by Americans,
13.12.

RHONDDA, LORD (Food Controller).
Death of, 4.7.

RIBECOURT (River Oise).
French retreat on, 10.6; French
recapture, 14.8.

RICHTHOFEN, CAPTAIN BARON VON.
(German airman), killed, 21.4;

ROBERTSON, GENERAL SIR Wm.
Succeeded by Sir H. Wilson as Chief
of Imperial Staff, 16.2; Appointed to
command of Home Forces, 5.6.

ROEUX (River Scarpe).
Held by British during German
offensive, 26.3; British reach outskirts
of, 26.8; and capture, 27.8.

ROSTOV (S. Russia).
Germans occupy, 8.5.

ROULERS.
British bomb aerodrome, 22, 28.1;
Allies reach, 29.9.

ROVIGNO (town on Istrian Coast).
Italians occupy, 4.11.

ROYAL AIR FORCE.
Formed, 1.4; Sir D. Henderson
resigns from Air Board, 18.4; Lord
Rothermere resigns, 25.4; Sir W. Weir
appointed Secretary of State, 27.4; Debate on resignation of Major-General
Trenchard, 29.4.

ROYE.
Captured by Germans, 26.3; French
re-occupy, 27.8.

RUJM EL BAHR (N. end of Dead Sea).
British patrols reach, 26.2.

RUMANIA.
Minister in Petrograd arrested by
Bolsheviks, 12.1; Bolsheviks issue ultimatum to, 15.1; Release of Minister, 15.1;
Arrest of King of, ordered by Bolsheviks,
15.1; Further Bolshevik ultimatum to,
18.1; Fighting between, and Bolsheviks
at Galatz, 25.1; Legation ordered by
Bolsheviks to leave Petrograd, 28.1;
German ultimatum to, Bratianu Cabinet
resigns, 6.2; General Averescu forms
Cabinet, 9.2; First meeting of German,
Austrian and Rumanian peace delegates,
25.2; Agrees to negotiate for peace, 2.3;
Marghiloman succeeds Averescu, 4.3;
Signs preliminary peace treaty, 5.3;
Treaty refused recognition by Allies,
18.3; Peace of Bukarest signed, 7.5;
Promise of U.S.A. to exercise influence to
secure for Rumania political and territorial
rights, 6.11; Recognition of Marghiloman
Cabinet, 9.11; General Coanda forms a
new Cabinet, 9.11; Ultimatum to Marshal
v. Mackensen, German troops to leave
within 24 hours, 9.11.

RUSSIA.
Reported German peace terms cause
consternation, 1.1; Central Committee
of Soviets meets, 2.1; Peace negotiations
at Brest-Litovsk, 7, 9.1; Bolshevik
excesses, 11.1; Peace Conference adjourns
12.1; Attempted assassination of Lenin
at Petrograd, 14.1; German warning
to, as to peace terms, 14.1; Germany
refuses to withdraw troops from, 18.1;
Bolsheviks forcibly dissolve Constituent
assembly, 19.1; Protests against German
omissions in peace proceedings, 22.1;
Trotski declares German policy a " monstrous annexation "; Rioting in Moscow;
Soviets meet in Petrograd, 23.1; Trotski
states, no longer at war with Quadruple
Alliance, 10.2; Demobilisation order
given, 10.2; Campaign v. Orthodox
Church, rouses opposition, 11.2; Bolsheviks defeat General Alexeiev, 13.2; End
of Armistice, 18.2; Declares willingness
to sign peace on German conditions,
19.2; Accepts German terms of Peace,
24.2; Japan proposes military action
in Siberia, 27.2; Makes peace at Brest-Litovsk, 3.3; Congress of Soviets ratifies
treaty, 14.3; Entente Governments refuse recognition and denounce German
policy towards Russia, 18.3; Berlin
reports ratification of Brest-Litovsk
Treaty, 29.3; Bessarabian agreement
between, and Rumania completed, 31.3;
Protests against landings in Finland
and Vladivostok, 7.4; Germany demands
disarmament of Russian fleet, 8.4;
Recognition of Ukraine Government by
Central Powers, 4.6; Allied Forces

SEMENOV (Captain, pr. " Semyónov ").
Fights Bolsheviks in E. Siberia, 12 to 24.5; Defeats Bolsheviks, N. of Manchuria Station, 11.8; Joined by Japanese detachment, 22.8; Captures Matsyerskaya, 23.8; Advances, 28.8, 2.9; Joined by Japanese at Ruchlevo, 3.10.

SENSÉE, RIVER (Douai).
Germans retreat from. 11.10.

SERBIA.
Resignation of M. Pashich and Cabinet, 28.2; Allied advance into, begins, 15.9; French cavalry enter Üsküb, 29.9; Serbs take Gradishte, and carry Premys (Ochrida), 30.9; Allied forces in touch with Austro-Germans, 3.10; Serbs and French move victoriously through, driving back Austro-Germans throughout Oct., Knyazhevats and Krushevats occupied, 17.10; Over half cleared of enemy, 17.10; Serbs occupy Zayechar, 19.10; drive enemy back along Morava, 24.10; Reach Kraguyevats, 25.10; Formation of Serb Coalition Ministry at Paris, under M. Pashich, 17.11.

SERINGES (Fère-en-Tardenois).
Americans capture, 28.7; Severe fighting, 31.7.

SERRE (N.W. of River Ancre).
Germans evacuate, 14.8.

SHECHEM v. NABLUS.

SHIPPING.
First monthly statement issued, 3.4, Report of Committee on, 20.6; Losses (v. table, p. 188).

SHORTT, RT. HON. EDWARD.
Becomes Chief Secretary for Ireland. 6.5; Speech in House of Commons on, 25.6.

SIBERIA.
Japanese and British troops land in Vladivostok, 5.4; Disorders in Vladivostok, 6.4; Japanese troops fired on by Bolsheviks, 10.4; Defeat of Bolsheviks by Semenov in E., 2.6; Retreat of Semenov on Borsia, 3.6; Retreat of Semenov into Chinese territory, 10.6; Czecho-Slovaks control railway between Cheliabinsk and Nizhne-Udinsk (W. ½ of railway); former evacuated by Bolsheviks; Czechs threaten Samara, 11.6; Fighting at Irkutsk between Red and White Guards, 13.6; Anti-Bolshevik Government set up at Nizhne-Udinsk; capture of Tomsk, 19.6; New provisional Government established at Vladivostok, 3.7; General Horvath establishes Government at Gvodekovo, 10.7; Government at Vladivostok resigns, 23.7; Siberian Government Council proclaims independence of Siberia, annuls Bolshevist decrees, re-establishes Siberian Duma,

restores landowners, 23.7; Bolsheviks blow up railway tunnel E. of Lake Baikal, 24.8; French, British and Japanese troops enter, proper, 13.10; Bolsheviks try to stop British at Zema, 16.10; Coalition Ministry formed under Admiral Kolchak, 28.10; Resignation of Government in favour of " All-Russian " Government at Ufa (Russia), 5.11; Admiral Kolchak becomes Dictator, 18.11.

SIDON (Palestine).
Occupied by British, 7.10.

SIMBIRSK (130 miles N.W. of Samara).
Czecho-Slovaks capture, 25.7.

SINN FEIN.
German plot by, 17, 24.5; Officially proclaimed a dangerous organisation, 3.7.

SLATUST (on Trans-Siberian Railway).
Defeat of Czecho-Slovaks by Bolsheviks, 11.6.

SMUTS, GENERAL J. C.
Speech in London re future of South Africa, 24.7.

SOCIALISTS.
French, pass Bolshevist resolutuon, 10.10.

SOISSONS.
Heavy fighting round, 28.5; Fall of, 29, 30.5; French hold out to W. and S.W. of, 30.5 to 15.7; Allies enter, 2.8.

SOLDIERS' AND WORKERS' COUNCILS, GERMAN.
Imperial Conference of, at Berlin, 16 to 20.12.

SOLF, Dr. (German Colonial Secretary).
Reply to Mr. Balfour's speech of 8.8, 20.8; Appointed Foreign Minister, 1.10; Appeals to President Wilson for mitigation of armistice terms, 11.11; Appeals to President Wilson for immediate peace negotiations, 12.11; Appeals to President Wilson to convene Conference at Hague of U.S. and German plenipotentiaries, 15.11; Appeals to President Wilson to allow German Commissioners to leave for America, 16.11; Appeals to Allied Governments to mitigate armistice conditions, 18.11.

SOMME CANAL.
Allies cross, 5.9.

SOMME, RIVER.
Reached by Germans, 23.3; Crossed, 24.3; German advance down, 25 to 29.3; Heavy fighting in district, 1 to 7, 21.4; Allies improve position and advance, 30.6 to 7.8; Great Allied advance, 30,000 prisoners taken, 8 to 15.8; Further British advance, 21 to 29.8; Allies cross, S. of Péronne, 5.9.

SONNINO, BARON (Italian Foreign Minister).
In London, 1-3.12.

TIGRIS, RIVER (v. also Mesopotamia).
British capture Kifri, 27.4; Reach
Ak Su river, 28.4; Capture Tuz Khur-
mati, 29.4; Turks held at Fatha, 18.10;
Retire thence, 23.10; British turn Turkish
position on Lower Zab River, 25.10;
British cavalry occupy Kirkuk, 25.10;
Turks retreat to Kalaat Shergat, 26.10;
British beat Turks on, 27 to 29.10.

"TICONDEROGA" (U.S. Transport).
Torpedoed, 30.9.

TISZA, COUNT.
Speech on extension of Dual Alliance,
5.6; Mission to Bosnia a failure, 26.9;
Assassinated, 31.10.

"TITHONUS," H.M.S. (Boarding
Steamer).
Torpedoed, 28.3.

TOMASEK, FRANZ.
Elected 1st President of Czecho-
Slovak National Assembly, 15.11.

TOMSK (Siberia).
Taken by Anti-Bolsheviks, 19.6.

TOURNAI.
British bomb aerodrome, 25.1; British
occupy W. part of, 8.11; and capture,
9.11.

TRANSCASPIA.
Fighting at Bairam Ali, 15.8; at
Kaakha, 25-31.8; Heavy fighting;
Dushak taken by British, 14, 17.10.

TRANSYLVANIA.
Rumanians of, and Banat vote for
union with Rumania, 4.12.

TRAWLERS.
British drifters and, sunk by German
destroyers in Straits of Dover, 15.2.

TREATIES, COMMERCIAL.
Denunciation of certain, by British
Government, 13.5.

TREBIZOND (Black Sea).
Turks within 8 miles of, 18.2; Turks
re-occupy, 24.2.

TRENT.
Italians occupy, 3.11.

TRESCAULT (S.W. of Cambrai).
British take, 12.9.

TRÈVES (TRIER).
Bombed by British, 24, 27.1; Occupied by Americans, 1.12.

TREVISA.
Bombed by Austrian airmen, 1, 3,
26.1.

TRIESTE.
Administration taken over by Italians
and Slovenes, 31.10; Italian troops
land at, 3.11.

TRIPOLI (Syria).
British enter, 13.10.

TROELSTRA, M. (Dutch Socialist Leader).
Passport to visit England refused,
20.6.

TRÔNES WOOD (E. of Albert).
British capture, 27.8.

TURKEY.
Communicates peace terms to Russia,
5.1; Ratifies peace with Ukraine and
Russia, 29.3; Turkish war aims published
in "Vorwärts," 22.6; Death of Sultan
Mohammed V., succeeded by his brother
Vahid ed Din, 3.7; Changes in Cabinet,
fall of Talaat and Enver Pashas, 9.10;
Peace Note received in U.S.A., 14.10;
Izzet P. Grand Vizir and War Minister,
14.10; Armistice signed with, 30.10;
Comes into force at noon, 31.10; Terms
published, 2.11; Tewfik P. forms Pro-
Entente Government, 10.11; Complete
surrender of navy announced, 5.12.

"TUSCANIA," ss.
American troopship, torpedoed off
Irish coast, 166 lost, 5.2.

UDINE (Venetia).
Italians enter, 3.11.

UKHTINSKAYA (Karelia).
German-led Finns defeated by Kare-
lians at, 18.9.

UKRAINE.
Recognised as separate State by
Germany and Bolsheviks, 10.1; Settlement in principle between, and Central
Powers, 16.1; Germany announces agreement with, 21.1; Declares its complete
independence, 26.1; Fighting between,
and Bolsheviks at Lutsk, 28.1; Central
Powers formally recognise Ukraine Republic as Independent State, 1.2; Peace
Treaty signed between Central Powers
and Ukraine Rada, 9.2; Publication of
same, 10.2; German army advances
into Ukraine against Bolsheviks, 18.2;
Austria-Hungary and Ukraine sign
agreement by which Kholm district of
Poland will not necessarily be included
in Republic, 19.2; German Reichstag
adopts peace treaty with, 21.2; Germans
reach Zhitómir, temporary capital of,
25.2; Ukraine Soviet accepts Rada
Treaty, 27.2; German invasion of,
begins, 28.2; Germans approach Odessa,
6.4; and Sevastopol, 25.4; German
dictatorship in, 1.5; Congress of Peasants,
11.5; Signs provisional treaty with
Russia, 14.6; National Council in Paris
appeals to Allied Peoples against Germany,
26.8; assumes administration of E.
Galicia, 1.11; Fighting between Poles
and Ukrainians, 3.11, etc.

UNITED STATES OF AMERICA.
Results of American War Mission
published, 2.1; Supreme Court upholds
right of Congress to decree compulsory
military service, 5.1; President Wilson

defines war-aims in message to Congress, giving 14 points, 8.1; Labour party supports war-aims, 11.1; War labour administrator appointed, 15.1; Mr. Baker makes statement on strength of army, 28.1; President Wilson asks for new powers to re-organise Government and War-machine, 6.2; Lord Reading arrives as British Ambassador and High Commissioner; President Wilson re-states war-aims, 11.2; Government takes over control of foreign trade, 15.2; Agreement between Capital and Labour announced, 31.3; 513,000 Regulars, 450,000 National Guard, 645,000 Conscripts announced by 1.4; President Wilson speaks at Baltimore, 6.4; Mr. Taft on the war, 12.4; Mr. Schwab appointed Director-General of Shipbuilding, 16.4; Report on Ukraine issued, 18.4; Statement on landing at Vladivostok issued, 19.4; 3rd Liberty Loan, resulting in £835,303,370, issued, 30.4; Further increase of Army sanctioned, 1.5; First million tons of shipping on the seas, 14.5; Delegates in London received by King and Queen, 16.5; Sedition Bill passed, 22.5; King Albert thanks U.S.A., 25.5; Arbitration Treaty renewed, 4.6; Anglo-American Union proposed by Lord Reading, 23.6; Total expenditure for previous twelve months, £2,716,360,494, 30.6; Man-Power Bill (18 to 45) introduced, 5.8, passed, 24.8; Relations with Bolsheviks severed, 15.8; Registration of 13,000,000 more citizens for military service, 12.9; President Wilson receives, 15.9, and rejects, 18.9, Austro-Hungarian proposal for unofficial Peace Conference; Mr. J. Davis appointed Ambassador to Great Britain, 19.9; President Wilson speaks on Peace Terms (5 conditions), 27.9; Fourth Liberty Loan, resulting in over 1,200 million £, issued, 27.9; German Note to President Wilson, asking for Armistice, 4.10; Solid U.S.A. views on, 7.10; British Naval Mission arrives, 7.10; President Wilson answers German Note, 8.10; Luxemburg asks for protection of rights, 12.10; German reply to President, 12.10; President replies, 14.10; German Note, 21.10; President replies, 23.10; Colonel House in Paris, 27.10; German reply, 27.10; German Note awaiting Armistice Terms received, 30.10; Elections for Congress, Republican majority, 5.11; Intimation to German Government re communications on Armistice, 16.11; Ships built, three million tons by 25.12; President Wilson arrives in London, 26.12; a Big Navy urged in Congress, 31.12.

UNITED STATES OF AMERICA (AIR SERVICE).
First aerial "super - Dreadnought" launched near New York, 6.7.

UNITED STATES OF AMERICA (ARMY IN EUROPE).
American troops in front line, 4.2; Troops to be brigaded with British and French, 2.4; Entry of troops under French command announced, 28.4; Over 1,000,000 troops embarked for Europe by 2.7; General Pershing made G.C.B., 17.7; 311,000 troops in fighting line in France by 1.9; Americans attack and take St. Mihiel salient, 12, 13.9; 1,766,160 troops in Europe, of which 59 per cent. carried in British ships, and 3 millions volunteered or conscripted, by 30.9; Heavy fighting N. of Verdun, both banks of Meuse, and in the Argonne throughout October; Figures re troops in Europe published, 5.10; Troops heavily engaged between the Oise and Le Cateau, etc., 19.10, etc.; Last drive towards Sedan, 1 to 10.11; Final Franco-American drive begins, 1.11; Americans reach Sedan, 6.11; Total losses (k. 36,154, d. 17,015, w. 179,625, m. and p. 3,323, total 236,117) published, 30.11.

UNITED STATES OF AMERICA (NAVY).
Reaches over 300,000 men by 6.4; Engaged in transport, convoy and guard duties, all the year; Admiral Sims made G.C.M.G., 19.7.

URDINGEN (Rhine).
Occupied by Belgians, 8.12.

URMIA (N.W. Persia).
Turks occupy, 2.8.

USHNU (Persia).
Turks capture, 11.5.

ÜSKÜB (Serbia).
Serbians approach, 25, 26.9; French cavalry enter, 29.9.

USSURI, RIVER (S. tributary of Amur).
Bolsheviks defeated by Czecho-Slovaks, 17.8; Bolshevist successful attack on Allies, 19.8; Successful Allied attack, 24.8; Retreat of Bolsheviks to, 28.8.

VAHID ED-DIN, SULTAN OF TURKEY.
Proclaimed Sultan at Constantinople, 4.7.

VAILLY (River Aisne).
French take, 16.9.

VALENCIENNES.
Region above, flooded by Germans, 30.10; British attack S. of, and reach S. outskirts, 1.11; British enter, 2.11; Formal British entry, 7.11.

Q

VARDAR, RIVER (Macedonia).
British airmen in valley of, 1.5; Allies reach, 21.9; Serbians cross, 23.9; Allies move N. along, 24.9, etc.

VAUX (River Marne, W. of Château Thierry).
Captured by Americans, 1.7; Americans repulse Germans, 15.7.

VAUX (Somme).
French take, 8.9.

VELES (or Küprülü) (Serbia).
Bulgarian retreat to, 23.9; Serbians capture, 25.9; Serbians storm Bulgarian position 11 miles N.E. of, 29.9.

VENICE.
Bombed, 3 to 20.2.

VENIZELOS, M.
Arrives in London, 13.10.

VERDUN.
French repulse raids at Beaumont, near, 1.1; Successful French raid S.E. of, 16.1; Local fighting near, 1, 16, 17, 20.3; German attacks fail, 8.4; Enemy driven back N. of, 8, 9.10; Heavy fighting by French and Americans N. of, throughout October.

VERSAILLES.
Supreme War Council meets at, 30.1 to 2.2; Mr. Asquith asks for explanation of extension of its powers, 12.2; Declaration of Premiers *re* Habsburg subject races at, 3.6; Conference at, 1.11.

VESLE, RIVER (Aisne).
Germans cross, 28, 29.5; Germans retreat to, 2.8; Allies cross, 4.8.

VIBORG (Finland).
Capture of, by White Guards, 29.4.

VIENNA.
Disturbance *re* reduced bread ration, 17.6; Food crisis eased, 21.6; Italian propaganda air-raid, 9.8; Revolution in, National Council takes over, 31.10.

VIEUX-BERQUIN (Armentières).
Heavy German attacks develop, 16.4; British take strong point to W. of, 26.6; British establish posts S. and S.E. of, 14.8.

VILLERS-BRETONNEUX.
British forced back between, and Hamel, 4.4; Local fighting near, 21.4; Enemy concentrations dispersed, 22.4; Captured by Germans, 24.4; Re-captured by Allies, 25.4; Heavy fighting round, May; Australians advance at, 5.7.

"VINDICTIVE," H.M.S.
Sunk at Ostend, 10.5.

"VIRIBUS UNITIS."
Austrian flagship, sunk by Italians, 1.11.

VLADIVOSTOK (v. Siberia).
British force lands, 3.8; First Japanese troops arrive, 11.8; General Otani arrives, 16.8; U.S. troops arrive, 17.8.

VOJUSA, RIVER (S. Albania).
Successful Italian attack on Lower and Middle, 7.7; Italians win passage of, 8.7.

VOORMEZEELE (Ypres).
Heavy fighting for, 26.4; Twice attacked by Germans, 27.4; Further fighting at, 29.4; 8-27.5.

VORBECK, GENERAL von LETTOW-.
Surrenders on Chambezi River, 14.11.

VOSGES.
French and German raids, Jan. to March; Strong German attempt fails, 8.4.

VOUZIERS (Upper Aisne River).
French take, 12.10; Heavy fighting near, 18, 23, etc., 10.

VRANYA (Serbia).
Franco-Serbs take, 5.10.

VREGNY (River Aisne).
French driven off the plateau, 28, 29.5.

VRIGNY (7 miles W. of Reims).
German attack from, to Sillery repulsed by French. 18.6.

WAGES COMMITTEE
(Men and Women's wages) started, 1.10.

WALK (Livonia).
Occupation by Bolsheviks reported, 18.12.

WARDROP, MR. (British Consul at Moscow).
Arrested by Bolsheviks, 9.8; Released, 13.8.

"WARILDA" (Ambulance Transport, British).
Torpedoed and sunk, homeward bound, 100 lost, 3.8.

WAR INDEMNITY, RUSSIAN.
Sent to Germany, 7.9.

WEMYSS, ADMIRAL SIR ROSSLYN.
Appointed British Naval Representative with Marshal Foch to receive German delegates, 7.11.

"WESTOVER" (U.S. Supply-Ship).
Torpedoed and sunk in European waters, 11.7.

WILSON, LIEUT.-GEN. SIR HENRY.
Succeeds Sir Wm. Robertson as Chief of Imperial Staff, 16.2.

WILSON, PRESIDENT (v. also U.S.A.).
Addresses Congress on Peace programme (14 Points), 8.1; Asks for new powers, 6.2; Speech to Mexican Mission, 9.6; Speech at Washington (4 Great Aims), 4.7; Message *re* food position, 23.7; On Peace Terms (5 Conditions), 27.9; Correspondence with German and Austro-Hungarian Governments, 8.10 to 16.11; Message to Germany *re* food, 13.11; Sails for Europe, 4.12; lands at Brest, 13.12; arrives in Paris, 14.12; Arrives in London, 26.12; Confers with British

1919

1919.

CHRONOLOGICAL TABLES.

January.

2. Bolshevist forces advancing on Riga and Reval ; fighting in the Ukraine.
2. Fighting between Czechs and Magyars at Pressburg.
2. Sir H. Trenchard's despatch on Independent Air Force published.
2. Brigadier-General Cockerill's message on Special Intelligence work published.
3. President Wilson arrives in Rome.
3. Protest of soldiers at Folkestone, *re* demobilisation.
3. Food Council to feed enemy appointed under Mr. Hoover in Paris.
4. President Wilson, acclaimed in Rome, asks for £20 million for food for Central Europe.
4. Bolsheviks take Riga.
4. Death of Count Hertling, German Ex-Chancellor, aged 76.
5. Troubles in Warsaw ; *coup d'état* under Prince Sapieha crushed.
5. President Wilson arrives at Milan.
6-9. Fighting in Berlin between Government party and Spartacists.
7. British squadron leaves the Baltic ; British force sent to Caucasus.
7. President Wilson arrives in Paris.
7. Herr Noske appointed Governor of Berlin.
8. Sir D. Haig's despatch of 21.12.18 published (May-Nov., 1918).
8. Turks completely evacuate the Caucasus.
9. Martial law in Berlin ; Spartacist movement spreads to Westphalia.
10. British take over administration of Baghdad, and French of European Turkish railways.
10. New Government appointments published ([1]).
11. Poles relieve Lemberg.
11. British Ministers arrive in Paris for Peace Conference.
11. Republic of Luxemburg proclaimed by small party (v. 14th).
12. Large anti-Bolshevik forces in the field in the South.
12. Supreme War Council sits *re* renewal of Armistice.
12. Chief Representatives consider procedure for Peace Conference.
13. Bolsheviks moving on Poland ; Kolchak remains C.i.C. in Siberia, French General Janin in direction of operations.
13. Air-raids on Great Britain ; tables published (v. p. 190-191).
13. Medina capitulates to the King of the Hejaz.
13. Government troops defeat Spartacists in Berlin.
14. Princess Charlotte Adelgonde succeeds her sister as Grand Duchess of Luxemburg.
15. Herr Karl Liebknecht and Frau Rosa Luxemburg shot dead in Berlin.
16. Allies defeat Bolsheviks in fight for Merv.
17. M. Paderewski Prime Minister of Poland.
17. Germany signs new Armistice Terms ([2]). Armistice extended.
18. British National War Bonds subscribed to date £1,645,337,734.
18. First Peace Conference Meeting ; M. Clémenceau elected President.
19-25. Bolsheviks attack Archangel front at Shenkursk, 180 miles S. of Archangel ; Allies withdraw.
19. Polling in Germany for National Assembly.
22. Prinkipo proposal approved by Peace Conference ([3]).
22. Civil and Military Allied Mission announced to be sent to Poland.
23. Split between MM. Lenin and Trotski.
23. General Milne's despatch of 1.12.18 on final Balkan operations published ([4]).
23. Result of German Elections declared ([5]).
24. Greeks fight Turks at Smyrna.
24-28. Czecho-Slovaks beat Poles in Galicia.

January.
25. League of Nations officially recognised as part of Treaty.
26. Memo. issued by War Office *re* Army in Transition period.
26-30. Fighting at Wilhelmshaven.
27. General Russki and hostages murdered at Piatigorsk.
29. Bonus to British Forces announced ; Army Order *re* Transition period.
29. Allies again withdraw on Archangel front.
30. South African War losses published (v. p. 196).
31. Three British gunboats arrive at Strasbourg.

February.
1. New issue of British 5% National War Bonds commences.
1. Total casualties in British Flying Service announced (v. p. 198).
3-9. General Denikin routs Bolsheviks in N. Caucasus, 31,000 prisoners.
5. Guards' Memorial Service held at St. Paul's Cathedral.
6. National German Assembly opens at Weimar.
7. Military protest in London (men from Folkestone) *re* demobilisation.
8. More fighting in Berlin.
10. More fighting in Archangel region.
11. Provisional German Constitution published. Herr Ebert elected President of German Republic.
12. Renewal of Armistice conditions settled by Allies.
12. Allied Mission arrives at Warsaw.
12. Ukrainians defeat Bolsheviks near Kiev.
12. U.S.A. passes 3 years' Naval Programme.
14. Bolsheviks invade Esthonia.
14. League of Nations Covenant approved ; published following day.
15. President Wilson leaves France for U.S.A.
16. Elections held in Austria for National Assembly.
17. Extension of Armistice ; Terms signed.
19. Attempted assassination of M. Clémenceau by Cottin.
20. Emir of Afghanistan (Habibullah Khan) assassinated.
20. Allies beat Bolsheviks on Murman front.
20. Zeebrugge despatch of 9.5.18 published.
21. Herr Kurt Eisner (Bavarian Premier) assassinated by Count Arco Valley ; Herr Auer and two others killed, and three wounded, in Munich Diet ; Riots in Munich for two days.
21. Sir W. Marshall's despatch of 1.10.18 (1.4-30.9.18) published.
23. Fighting in Posen and at Lemberg (Galicia).
24. President Wilson arrives in New York.
25. Guards' Division returns to England.
26. More strikes in Central Germany.
28. Italian War losses published (v. p. 196).
28. Senator Lodge speaks against League of Nations.
28. Lord Reading arrives in New York.

March.
1. Austrian losses published (v. p. 196).
1. British losses published (v. p. 196).
1. French losses published (v. p. 196).
1. German losses published (v. p. 196).
1. British Army Estimates published ; 2,500,000 men, to be reduced to 952,000 ; cost for year, £287 million.
1-9. Fighting 140 miles S.E. of Archangel ; Allies withdraw a mile.
1. Ukraine Commander denounces truce with Poles.
1. American losses published (v. p. 197).
3. More fighting in Berlin, 3 to 14 March, and general strike, 3 to 6 March.
3. Rushdi Pasha, Prime Minister of Egypt, resigns.
3. Damad Ferid Pasha succeeds Tewfik Pasha as Grand Vizier.
4. Mr. Justice Sankey's Coal Commission begins sittings.
4. Canadian riot at Rhyl.
4. Estimate of total losses during the War given by C. of S., U.S.A.
4. Confident speech by President Wilson.

March.
5. President Wilson sails for Paris.
6. Naval Estimates (£149,200,000) published.
6. Rumanian losses published (v. p. 197).
8. Zaghlul Pasha, Ismail P. Sidki, Mohd. P. Mahmud and Hamed P. Basil deported from Egypt.
9. Riots in Cairo, 9 to 11 March.
9. Attempted assassination of M. Trotski.
10. Germany's Army to be limited to 100,000, voluntary engagements, etc.
10. Return of reductions of armies since Armistice given in House of Commons.
10. General Plumer's telegram on food situation (very bad) to Peace Conference.
10. Statement issued *re* U.S.A. shipping (*).
11. Riots in Egypt for ten days.
13. Armistice negotiations renewed at Brussels.
13. Sir W. Robertson appointed C.i.C., Rhine.
13. Sir D. Haig to command Forces in Great Britain.
13. President Wilson arrives back in France.
15. Bolshevik reverses reported in the Urals, Esthonia and Kurland.
15. Fighting at Nikolaiev, near Odessa.
16. Germany accepts food terms (300,000 tons cereals and 70,000 tons fats per month) handing over 32 million tons of merchant marine.
17. French and Allies evacuating Odessa ; Bolsheviks advancing.
18. 3 British officers and 5 other ranks murdered in train at Deirut, Upper Egypt.
19. Germany's Navy to be limited to 36 ships (Order by Peace Conference).
21. Soviet Government in Hungary ; Count M. Karolyi resigns.
21. General Allenby appointed Special High Commissioner of Egypt.
21. Navigation of the Danube thrown open.
22. March of Guards' Division through London.
22. General Bulfin C.i.C. in Egypt.
24. Rumanians defeat Bolsheviks on the Dniester River.
25. General Allenby arrives in Egypt.
26. Allied Missions leave Buda Pest.
29. Adalia (Asia Minor) occupied by Italians ; two companies bluejackets landed.
30. Summer time begins (till 28 September).
30. Lenin offers alliance to Germany with Hungary against Entente and Poland.
30. Press Bureau closes.
31. Bolsheviks attack Archangel front ; repulsed.
31. General Maynard represses Bolshevist revolt at Murmansk.

April.
2. Admirals Jellicoe and Beatty promoted Admirals of the Fleet.
2. General Smuts' Mission to Buda Pest a failure (2 to 6 April).
4. British nervousness *re* positions in Archangel and Murman regions.
4. Soviet Republic in Bavaria.
5. Bolsheviks again attack Archangel front and are repulsed.
7. Grand Fleet goes out of being.
7. Zaghlul Pasha, etc., released ; more troubles in Egypt.
8. Odessa evacuated by Allies (announced).
8. Bolsheviks enter the Crimea.
9. Voluntary British relief force being despatched to Archangel.
9. Rushdi Pasha returns as Egyptian Prime Minister.
10. Rioting at Amritsar ; 3 Europeans killed.
10-15. Bolsheviks retire on Ural front.
11. Bavarian Soviet Republic overthrown.
11. Sir D. Haig's final despatch of 21.3.19 (11 Nov.–31 Dec., 1918) published.
11. Rumanians withdraw temporarily from Hungarian territory.
12. Rioting at Kasur (India).
12. Sir W. Marshall's final despatch on Mesopotamia published (1.10–31.12.18).
12. Bolsheviks occupy Yalta (Crimea).
13. Over 2 millions British demobilised by this date.
13. Bavarian Soviet Government gains upper hand again.
14. Rioting in the Punjab for 5 days.
14. Siberians under General Kolchak advancing W.

April.

15. General outline of Peace conditions drawn up by this date.
15. Sir D. Haig takes over command of Forces in Great Britain.
15. Set-back to Allies in S. Russia.
17. Allies refuse to consider Dr. Nansen's offer of food to Russia unless hostilities cease.
17. Russian troops, under General Maynard, rout Bolshevik troops at Lake Vigo.
18-22. British Naval squadron entertained for 5 days in France.
18. Rioting at Delhi.
19. General Robertson arrives at Cologne.
19. Zaghlul Pasha, etc., arrive in Paris.
19. British forces reported to have evacuated Transcaspian territory (except Krasnovodsk).
20. Allies refuse to receive German " messengers " and insist on plenipotentiaries.
20. Allies intend to extend zone of occupation and to occupy German ports if Germans refuse to accept Peace Terms. Reparation Commission accepts Sub-Commission's report.
20. The Skupshtina of Montenegro pronounces King Nicholas dethroned.
21. Rioting in Vienna.
21. Rumanians advancing in Hungary.
21. Siberians reach point 100 miles E. of Kazan and drive back Bolsheviks.
22. General Robertson relieves General Plumer as C.i.C. Rhine.
22. Egyptian Government employees ordered to return to work.
23. Rushdi Cabinet resigns in Egypt.
23. Successful Allied work on Archangel front reported.
23. Bolsheviks invade Bessarabia.
24. Italian delegates refuse to modify Adriatic claims ; Signor Orlando leaves Paris.
24. President Wilson appeals to Italy *re* Adriatic.
24. Plundering in Hamburg.
25. Anzac Day ; Australians and New Zealanders march through London.
26. General van Deventer's last despatch (German E. Africa, 20.1.19) published.
26. Rumanians reach the Theiss River.
28. Report of Commission on Responsibility for War submitted to Peace Conference.
28. League of Nations comes into being.
28. German delegates arrive in Paris, 28 and 29 : Count Brockdorff-Rantzau in charge.
28. Lord Milner's Mission proposed.
29. Further advance of Rumanians in Hungary.
30. President Wilson's Memo. of 14.4, on Adriatic published in Rome.
30. Description of Deirut (Egypt) murders of March 18 published.
30. British Budget introduced (£1,434,910,000 expenditure, £1,201,100,000 revenue).

May.

1. Civilian flying allowed in Great Britain.
1. Munich taken by Government troops.
1. British Budget discussed (⁷). Lord French's " 1914 " appears.
2. Settled that Buda Pest be occupied by Allied troops.
2. Bolsheviks repulsed in Archangel region.
2. Admiralty publishes Dardanelles despatches *re* March, 1915.
3. Oversea troops march through London.
4. Belgium decides to sign Treaty.
5. Rumanian Terms presented to Hungary.
5. Public feeling in U.S.A. running against President Wilson.
6. Peace Treaty approved by private plenary session ; Marshal Foch dissatisfied with security for France.
6. Italian delegates return to Paris.
6. Afghans cross N.W. Frontier and occupy hills.
6. Great Britain recognises independence of Finland.
7. Disposal of German Colonies settled by Peace Conference.
7. Peace Terms communicated to German delegates and published.
7. U.S.A. recognise independence of Finland.
8. Germany protests against Peace Terms.
8. Rumanian advance stopped by Allies.

May.

8-15. Successes by General Denikin in S. Russia.
8. Numbers killed and wounded in Egyptian rioting published (*).
9. Afghans repulsed by our troops.
10. Bolsheviks again repulsed in Archangel region.
11. German delegates protest against Terms officially.
12. National Assembly meets in Berlin.
13. Greek troops landed at Smyrna.
13. Esthonian army moves on Petrograd.
14. Austrian delegates arrive in Paris.
14. German protest-Note against economic terms received.
14. Nurse Cavell's body brought to England ; and buried after services in London, etc., 15th.
14. Afghans falsely sue for Peace.
15. Committee sits on Cippenham scheme.
15. British enter Afghanistan.
15. General Kolchak's army falls back.
16. Mr. Asquith answers Lord French (*re* supersession by Lord Kitchener).
16. British drive back Afghans.
17. British Naval force defeats Bolshevik warships near Kronstadt.
18. M. Paderewski resigns Premiership of Poland.
19. General Pilsudski (Pole) prepares to attack the Ukraine.
20. Rhine Army ready to march into Germany in case of refusal of Peace Terms.
20. German troops again occupy Riga.
22. Allies stern reply to German protest.
23. Esthonians within 30 miles of Petrograd.
25. Rising in Kurdistan ; British officers captured.
25. Conditional recognition of General Kolchak's Government by Allies.
26. Demonstration by ex-Service Men in London.
26. Afghan counter-offensive.
27. Draft Treaty presented by Peace Conference to Poland.
27. Mohammed Said Pasha becomes Prime Minister of Egypt.
28. Counter proposals by German Government, published 15 June.
28. Emir of Afghanistan (Amanullah Khan) proposes Peace.
28. General Yudénich and Esthonians closing on Petrograd.
29. German Naval losses in the War given (v. p. 198).
31. Allies present Note to Germany *re* troops in Baltic Provinces.
31. British warships again defeat Bolsheviks near Kronstadt.
31. Bolsheviks withdraw from Gulf of Riga.

June.

2. New Loan of £250 millions proposed in House of Commons.
2. British Government recognises Yugo-Slavia as kingdom of the Serbs, Croats and Slovenes.
2. Terms of Peace presented to Austrian delegates.
3. Austrian Peace Terms published.
3. Mr. Asquith answers Lord French on the shells question.
3. British reinforcements reach Archangel.
5. 104,743 officers and 2,725,403 other ranks demobilised to date.
6. Finland declares war on Bolshevist Russia.
8. Denikin's army advances successfully in S. Russia.
10. Austrian delegates protest against Peace Terms.
10. Agitation in China against Shantung decision of Peace Conference.
10. Senator Knox's resolution (asking separation of League of Nations Covenant from Peace Treaty).
13. Terms of New Victory Loan issued.
16. Allies reply to German counter proposals presented and published.
17. Bela Kun agrees to peaceable action in Hungary.
18. British prisoners in Kurdistan rescued.
19. Allies ready to occupy German territory if Peace not signed.
20. Report of Coal Commission presented ; published 23 June.
20. Signor Orlando resigns ; Signor Nitti forms fresh Cabinet.
20. German (Scheidemann) Cabinet decides against signing Peace Treaty, and falls.

June.
21. Turkish army advancing on Greeks in Asia Minor (Aidin).
21. Germans scuttle their Fleet at Scapa Flow.
22. Herr Bauer forms German Ministry.
22. Denikin's army 24 miles from Kharkov.
23. Germany announces readiness to sign.
23. Allied advance on N. Dvina River (Archangel front).
24. Truce between Hungarian and Czecho-Slovakian armies.
25. Bolsheviks 20 miles from Perm, and advancing E. of Ufa.
26. Fighting at Berlin and Hamburg.
27. Turkey's case and Allied Reply published.
27. Bolsheviks abandon Kharkov.
28. President Wilson signs Treaty by which U.S.A. will assist France in case of unprovoked German attack.
28. PEACE TREATY SIGNED AND PUBLISHED ([9]).

July.
5. London troops reviewed by the King.
7. Peace Treaty ratified by the German Government.
8. President Wilson returns to the United States.
19. Peace celebrations in the United Kingdom.
24. General Sir H. H. Wilson promoted to Field-Marshal.
31. Generals Sir H. Plumer and Sir E. Allenby promoted to Field Marshals ; General Sir H. Rawlinson sent to N. Russia to co-ordinate withdrawal.
31. German Constitution Bill passed by National Assembly.

August.
1. Bela Kun's Government overthrown at Buda Pest.
4. Rumanian troops enter Buda Pest.
6. Peerages, etc., awarded to high Naval and Military Commanders ([10]).
8. Afghan War ends.
10. Anglo-Russians defeat Bolsheviks on N. Dvina River (Archangel).
18. British Naval success in Gulf of Finland ; 2 Bolshevik battleships sunk.
30, etc. Series of Anglo-Russian successes in N. Russia.

September.
10. Austria signs Peace Treaty in Paris ([11]).
14. G. d'Annunzio occupies Fiume.
16. Sir E. Allenby arrives in England.
27. British troops withdrawn from Archangel.
28. Referendum taken in Luxemburg.

October.
7. King of Italy signs and ratifies Peace Treaty.
10. King George signs and ratifies Peace Treaty.
10. British troops withdrawn from Murmansk region.
10. Result of Luxemburg Referendum published : for Grand Duchy.
13. President Poincaré signs and ratifies Peace Treaty.
13. Lord Beatty succeeds Admiral Sir R. Wemyss as First Sea Lord.
14. Ali Riza Pasha appointed Grand Vizir, Ottoman Empire.
18. Austrian Government ratifies Peace Treaty. Lord Allenby appointed High Commissioner in Egypt.

November
3. Sir R. Wemyss created Baron.
10. President and Madame Poincaré arrive in England.
14. Rumanian troops evacuate Buda Pest.
19. U.S. Senate defeats motion of Ratification (with 15 reservations) of Peace Treaty by 51 to 41. Treaty shelved.
27. Peace Treaty with Bulgaria signed at Neuilly ([12]).
28. Yusef Wahba Pasha succeeds Mohammed Said Pasha as Premier of Egypt.

December.
3. Lord Milner's Mission arrives in Egypt.
15. M. Paderewski succeeded as Prime Minister by M. Skulski.
18. Announced that coal export would be permitted from 1.1.20.
20. Appointment of British Chargé d'Affaires (Lord Kilmarnock) at Berlin.
24. Command of British troops in France reduced to a Brigadier-General's.
30. Acute food distress in Austria : Bread ration in Vienna 4 oz. per week.

RÉSUMÉ OF MAIN EVENTS IN 1919.

Jan. 3 ... ... Food Council to feed enemy appointed in Paris.

„ 17 ... ... Germany signs new Armistice Terms.

„ 18 ... ... Peace Conference opens at Versailles.

„ 25 ... ... League of Nations Covenant recognised as part of Peace Treaty.

Feb. 6 ... ... German National Assembly opens at Weimar.

„ 11 ... ... Provisional German Constitution published.

„ 14 ... ... League of Nations Covenant approved.

Mar. 9 to 20 ... ... Disturbances in Egypt.

„ 15 to Apr. 20 ... Bolshevist advance in S. Russia.

Apr. 9 ... ... British relief force sent to N. Russia.

„ 10 to 18 ... ... Riots in India.

„ 21 to May 8 ... Rumanian advance in Hungary.

„ 24 ... ... Trouble over Adriatic claims.

„ 28 ... ... League of Nations comes into being; German delegates arrive in Paris.

May 6 to Aug. 8 ... Afghan campaign.

„ 7 ... ... German Peace Terms published.

„ 14 ... ... Austrian delegates arrive in Paris.

„ 25 ... ... Rising in Kurdistan.

June 3 ... ... Austrian Peace Terms published.

„ 20 ... ... German Cabinet decides against signing Peace Terms.

„ 21 ... ... Germans scuttle their fleet at Scapa Flow.

„ 23 ... ... Germany announces readiness to sign.

„ 28 ... ... PEACE TREATY SIGNED AND PUBLISHED.

July 7 ... ... Peace Treaty ratified by Germany.

Aug. 4 to Nov. 14 ... Rumanians in Buda Pest.

Sept. 10 ... ... Austria signs Peace Treaty.

„ 14 ... ... D'Annunzio occupies Fiume.

„ 27 ... ... British troops withdrawn from Archangel.

Oct. 7 ... ... King of Italy ratifies Peace Treaty.

„ 10 ... ... King George ratifies Peace Treaty. British troops withdrawn from Murmansk region.

„ 13 ... ... President Poincaré ratifies Peace Treaty.

„ 18 ... ... Austria ratifies Peace Treaty.

Nov. 19 ... ... U.S. Senate refuses ratification.

„ 27 ... ... Bulgaria signs Peace Treaty.

APPENDICES FOR 1919.

(¹) *Jan.* 10.—

Mr. D. Lloyd George	Prime Minister and First Lord of the Treasury.
Mr. A. Chamberlain	Chancellor of Exchequer.
Mr. A. J. Balfour	Foreign Office.
Mr. W. Churchill	War Office and Air Ministry.
Mr. W. Long	Admiralty.
Lord Milner	Colonial Office.
Mr. E. S. Montagu	India Office.
Mr. E. Shortt	Home Office.
Lord Birkenhead	Lord Chancellor.
Mr. I. Macpherson	Chief Secretary for Ireland.
Mr. R. Prothero	Board of Agriculture.
Sir A. Stanley	Board of Trade.
Mr. C. Addison	Local Government Board.
etc.	etc.

(²) *Jan.* 17.—Terms :—

Armistice extended to Feb. 17.
Germany to furnish large quantities of agricultural implements.
Remaining submarines to be handed over or destroyed.
Germany to put her merchant fleet under Allied control.
Allies reserve the right to occupy sector of Strasbourg fortifications on right bank of Rhine.

(³) *Jan.* 22.—The " Prinkipo Proposal " was that three representatives from each Russian party should meet Allied representatives at Prinkipo Island (Sea of Marmora) on Feb. 15, in order to come to some arrangement regarding Russia. The respectable Russian parties refused to attend, and the whole proposal was received with such scorn and contumely by Europe in general that it quickly fell through

(⁴) *Jan.* 23.—The despatch covers the period from Oct. 1, 1917, to Nov. 11, 1918, including the final advance of the Allies on Sofia.

(⁵) *Jan.* 23.—The result of the German elections was :—

Majority Socialists 165	
Democratic Party 75	(Radicals.)
Independent Socialists 22	(" Minority Socialists. ")
German People's Party 22	(late " National Liberals.")
National People's Party 38	(late "Conservatives.")
Centre 91	(or " Christian People's Party.")
Various 8	
Total 421	

(⁶) *Mar.* 10.—45 per cent. of U.S.A. cargoes now carried in U.S.A. ships, vice 9.7 per cent. before the War ; tonnage of U.S. merchant ships raised from 1,196,237 tons before the War to 3,834,760 tons after it.

(⁷) *May* 1.—Budget :

Revenue	£1,201,100,000
Expenditure	£1,434,910,000
Deficit	£233,810,000

No change in the Income Tax ; duties on spirits and beer increased ; Excess Profits Duty decreased from 80 to 40 per cent.

(**) *May* 8.—Casualties in March and April rioting :—
   Killed   ... 5 officers, 18 British and 6 Indian other ranks.
   Wounded... 6 ,,   50 ,,   ,, 25 ,,   ,,   ,,

(**) *June* 28.—The Treaty was signed in the Galerie des Glaces at Versailles by representatives of all the combatants except China—which Power refused to sign on account of the Shantung clauses. For Germany it was signed by Herren H. Müller and Bell. The news was received with great rejoicings in London and Paris. Owing to its great length, the text of the Treaty cannot here be reproduced : but the reader is referred to an excellent summary on pp. 80 to 108 of the *Annual Register* for 1919.

(**) *Aug.* 6.—Honours awarded : Haig and Beatty created Earls ; Allenby, Viscount ; Plumer, Rawlinson, Byng and Horne, Barons ; Madden, Keyes, de Robeck, Tyrwhitt, Wilson, Robertson, Birdwood and Trenchard, Baronets.

(**) *Sept.* 10.—Summary given in *Annual Register*, 1919, pp. 109 to 125.

(**) *Nov.* 27.—Summary given in *Annual Register*, 1919, pp. 125 to 131.

MISCELLANEOUS ITEMS.

Progress of Demobilisation :—

1919.
Jan. 14—472,383 officers and men demobilised or discharged.

,, 16—538,912 officers and men demobilised or discharged.

Mar. 4.—46,430 officers and 1,783,278 other ranks.

,, 13—Over 2 millions.

Apr. 25—83,275 officers and 2,453,591 other ranks.

June 5—104,743 officers and 2,725,403 other ranks.

Number of U.S.A. troops transported to Europe before 11 November, 1918— 2,500,000.

New Zealand mobilised 124,211 during the war—over 11 per cent. of her population. Of these just over 100,000 (including 92,000 volunteers) were sent overseas and suffered a loss of 16,302 killed and 25,133 wounded—total 41,435.

EXPENDITURE 1913–1914 and 1918–1919.

The following table was given in an abstract issued by the Treasury on 5 July, 1920:—

	1913–14. Audited Expenditure. £	1918–19. Audited Expenditure. £
National Debt Services	24,500,000	269,964,650
Road Improvement Fund	1,394,951	—
Payments to Local Taxation Accounts ...	9,734,128	9,680,811
Land Settlements	—	—
Other Consolidated Fund Services	1,693,890	1,699,406
Total Consolidated Fund Services ...	37,322,969	281,344,867
Army	35,208,842	974,033,762
Navy	50,819,150	356,044,688
Air Force	—	85,445,084
Total Fighting Services	86,027,992	1,415,523,534
War Pensions	—	50,634,470
Loans to Dominions and Allies	—	264,575,684
Railway Agreements	—	48,610,564
Miscellaneous War Services, Foreign Office..	—	12,082,230
Ministry of Munitions	—	562,227,196
Ministry of Shipping	—	285,466,121
Ministry of Food	—	4,281,680
War Graves Commission	—	8,000
Old-Age Pensions	12,425,821	17,776,900
Public Education	19,169,647	25,719,344
Boards of Agriculture	850,072	1,184,500
Ministry of Health and Health Insurance ...	5,341,163	9,286,977
Ministry of Labour and Unemployment Grants	1,161,712	20,549,739
Police	1,681,583	3,500,482
Foreign and Colonial Services	1,669,463	2,269,637
Works and Public Buildings	3,621,378	8,319,431
Stationery Office	1,232,735	8,366,693
Legal and Judicial Departments	2,661,627	2,904,034
Other Civil Services	5,190,521	13,509,288
Miscellaneous Vote of Credit Services ..	—	58,279,235
Total Civil Services	55,005,722	1,399,552,205
Customs and Inland Revenue	4,578,227	6,817,049
Post Office	24,882,527	43,237,913
Total Revenue Departments	29,460,754	50,054,962
Total Supply Services	170,494,468	2,865,130,701
Total Gross Expenditure	207,817,437	3,146,475,568

The following is an abstract of the expenditure for 1913–1914, as compared with that for 1920–1921 :—

1913–1914. Actual Expenditure. £		1920–1921. Estimated Expenditure. £	
National Debt ...	24,500,000	National Debt ...	345,000,000
Fighting Services ...	86,027,992	Fighting Services ...	269,170,000
Civil Services ...	55,005,722	Civil Services ...	555,626,000
Revenue Departments	29,460,754	Revenue Departments	61,280,000
Total	194,994,468		1,231,076,000

Increase : about 1,036 million £ : almost septupled.

INDEX.

Figures in black type represent the month : *e.g.*, 4.1 = 4th Jan.; 23.11 = 23rd Nov.; etc.

N.B.—In the following index a number of items are included which, by reason of their uncertainty or for some other cause, it has not been found easy or convenient to place in the Chronological Tables. Dates which can at present be only approximately given are indicated thus :—" c. 23.8."

of Armistice, 12.1; Peace Conference procedure considered, 12.1; Princess Charlotte Adelgonde succeeds as Grand Duchess of Luxemburg, 15.1; Germany signs new Armistice Terms, 17.1; First P.C. meeting : M. Clémenceau President, 18.1; P.C. approves Prinkipo proposal, 22.1; League of Nations recognised as part of Treaty, 25.1; Renewal of Armistice conditions settled, 12.2; League of Nations Covenant approved, 14.2; and published, 15.2; Extension of armistice terms signed, 17.2; Germany's army to be limited to 100,000, voluntary, 12 years, etc., 10.3, 11.3; Return of reductions of armies since Armistice, given in House of Commons, 10.3; General Plumer's telegram on food situation to P.C., 10.3; Armistice negotiations resumed at Brussels, 13.3; Germany's navy to be limited to 36 ships, 19.3; Navigation of the Danube thrown open, 21.3; General outline of peace drawn by, 15.4; Allies refuse to receive German "messengers"—insist on Plenipotentiaries, 20.4; Italian delegates refuse to modify Adriatic claims, 24.8; Sr. Orlando leaves Paris, 24.4; Pres. Wilson appeals to Italy re Adriatic, 24.4; Report of Commission on responsibility for War submitted to Paris Conference, 28.4; League of Nations comes into being, 28.4; German delegates arrive, 28-29.4; President Wilson's memo. of 14.4 on Adriatic, published in Rome, 30.4; Belgium decides to sign Treaty, 4.5; Treaty approved by private plenary session; Marshal Foch dissatisfied with security for France, 6.5; Italian delegates return to Paris, 6.5; Peace Terms communicated to German delegates and published, 7.5; Disposal of German colonies settled, 7.5; German delegates protest against terms. 11.5; Austrian delegates arrive in Paris, 14.5; German protest-note against economic terms, 14.5; Rhine Army ready to march into Germany in case of German refusal of peace terms, 20.5; Allies' stern reply to German protest, 22.5; Draft treaty presented to Poland, 27.5; Counterproposals from German Government, 28.5, published 15.6; Allies present Note to Germany concerning troops in Baltic Provinces, 31.5; Terms of Peace presented to Austrian delegates, 2.6; Austrian Peace Terms published, 3.6; Austrian delegates' protest, 10.6; Allies reply to German counter-proposals, presented and published, 16.6; Allied Armies ready to occupy German territory if Treaty not signed, 19.6; Germany announces readiness to sign, 23.6; President Wilson signs Treaty for U.S.A.

with France, 28.6; Peace Treaty signed and published, 28.6.

GERMAN EAST AFRICA.
General van Deventer's last despatch of 20.1.19, published 26.4.

GERMANY (v. under **General** for negotiations with Allies, etc.).
Death of Count Hertling. 4.1; Fighting in Berlin between Spartacists and Government Party, 6, 7, 8, 9.1; Herr Noske Governor of Berlin, 7.1; Martial Law; Spartacist movement spreads to Westphalia, 9.1; Government defeat Spartacists in Berlin, 13.1; Liebknecht and Rosa Luxemburg shot dead, 15.1; Polling for National Assembly, 19.1; Returns published, 23.1; Fighting at Wilhelmshaven, 26-30.1; Three British gunboats arrive at Strasbourg, 31.1; Württemberg losses published, 30.1; National Assembly opens at Weimar, 6.2; More fighting in Berlin, 8.2; Herr Ebert elected President of German Republic, Provisional Constitution published, 11.2; Herr K. Eisner assassinated by Count Arco Valley, Herr Auer and two others killed and several wounded in Munich Diet, 21.2; Riots in Munich, 21-22.2; Losses at battle of Jutland published, 22.2; More strikes in Central, 26.2;- Casualties (total 6,385,000), published, 1.3; More fighting in Berlin, 3, 4, 6 to 14.3; and general strike, 3-6.3; General Robertson to be G.O.C.-i.-C.Rhine, 13.3; arrives, 19.4; vice Gen. Plumer, takes on, 22.4; Accepts food terms, handing over merchant navy (3½ million tons) 16.3; Soviet Representatives in Bavaria, 4.4; overthrown 11.4; upper hand again, 13.4; Plundering in Hamburg, 27.4; Munich taken by Government troops, 1.5; Protests against Treaty terms, 8.5; National Assembly meets in Berlin, 12.5; Naval losses published, 29.5; Fall of German (Scheidemann's) Cabinet, after deciding against signing Peace Treaty, 20.6; Germans scuttle their fleet at Scapa Flow, 21.6; Herr Bauer forms Ministry, 22.6; Germany ready to sign Peace Treaty, 23.6; Fighting at Hamburg and Berlin, 26.6; Signs Peace Treaty, 28.6; Ratifies Peace Treaty, 7.7.

GREAT BRITAIN.
Sir H. M. Trenchard's despatch on work of Independent Air Force, 5.7 to 11.11.18, published, 2.1; Brig-Gen. Cockerill's message on Special Intelligence Directorate work published, 2.1; Protest of soldiers at Folkestone re demobilisation, 3.1; Sir D. Haig's despatch (May to Nov., 1918) of 21.12.18, published, 8.1; New Government appointments published, 10.1; Air raids table

published, 13.1; Announcement of total National War Bonds subscribed, 18.1; Memo. on Army in Transition period published, 26.1; Army Order *re* Transition period published, 29.1; Gratuity to Forces announced, 29.1; New issue of 5 per cent. National War Bonds commences, 1.2; Total casualties in Flying Services published, 1.2; Guards' memorial service held, 5.2; Soldiers' protest *re* demobilisation, 7.2; Zeebrugge despatch (dated 9.5.18) published, 20.2; Guards Division begins to arrive, 25.2; Summer time begins, 30.3 (to 28.9); "British" losses to 10.11.18 published, 1.3; Army estimates published, 1.3; Sankey Coal Commission, 4.3 to 20.6; Canadian riot at Rhyl, 4, 5.3; Navy estimates published, 6.3; Sir D. Haig C.i.C. forces in Great Britain, 13.3; takes up, 15.4; Sir W. Robertson to command on Rhine, 13.3; takes up, 18.4; 2,000,000 demobilised by, 13.3; Guards' march, 22.3; Press Bureau closes, 30.3; Admirals Jellicoe and Beatty promoted Admirals of the Fleet, 2.4; Grand Fleet ceases, 7.4; Sir D. Haig's final despatch (21.3.19) published, 11.4; He takes up command, 15.4; Sir W. Robertson to Cologne, 18.4; British Naval squadrons entertained in France, 18-23.4; Australians march through London, 25.4; Budget introduced, 30.4; Civilian flying permitted, 1.5; Lord French's "1914" appears, 1.5; Nurse Cavell's body brought to England, 14.5; Service in London and buried at Norwich, 15.5; Committee sits on Cippenham scheme, 15.5; Mr. Asquith answers Lord French *re* Lord Kitchener, 16.5; Demonstration by ex-Service men, 26.5; New Loan of 250 millions proposed, 2.6; Mr. Asquith answers Lord French on the shells question, 3.6; Terms of new Victory Loan issued, 13.6; Report of Coal Commission presented, 20.6, published, 23.6; Rejoicings on signature of Peace Treaty, 28.6; London troops reviewed by the King, 5.7; Peace celebrations in the United Kingdom, 19.7; Generals promoted to Field Marshals, 24, 31.7; Honours awarded to high Naval and Military Commanders, 6.8; Sir E. Allenby arrives, 16.9; King George signs Peace Treaty, 10.10; Lord Beatty appointed First Sea Lord, 13.10; Sir R. Wemyss created Baron, 3.11.

HAIG, F.-MARSHAL SIR D.
Despatch of 21.12.18 (May to Nov. 1918) published, 8.1; To command forces at home, 13.3; takes up, 15.4; Despatch

of 21.3.19 (11.11-31.12.18) published, 11.4; Made an Earl, 6.8.
HERTLING, COUNT.
Death of Ex-Chancellor, 4.1.
HUNGARY.
Fighting with Czecho-Slovaks at Pressburg, 2.1; Soviet Government, Count M. Karolyi resigns, 21.3; Allied Missions leave Buda Pest, 26.3; General Smuts' mission a failure, 2-6.4; Rumanians advancing in, 21,4; Reach the Theiss, 26, 29.4; Buda Pest to be occupied by Allied troops, 2.5; Rumanian terms presented, 5.5; Rumanian advance stopped by Allies, 8.5; Bela Kun agrees to take no violent action, 17.6; Truce between Czecho-Slovak and Hungarian armies, 24.6; Bela Kun overthrown, 1.8; Rumanians enter Buda Pest, 4.8; and evacuate it, 14.11.

INDIA.
Emir of Afghanistan assassinated, 20.2; Rioting at Amritsar, 10-13.4, at Kasur, 12.4, in the Punjab, 14-18.4, at Delhi, 18.4; Afghans cross frontier and occupy hills, 6.5; engaged by our troops and repulsed, 9.5; Afghans falsely sue for peace, 14.5; British enter Afghanistan, 15.5; and drive back enemy, 16.5; Afghan counter-offensive, 26.5; Emir proposes peace, 28.5; end of war, 8.8.
ITALY.
President and Mrs. Wilson in Rome, 3.1, 4.1; arrive in Milan, 5.1 Paris, 7.1; Italian delegates refuse to modify Adriatic claims; Sig. Orlando, etc., leave Paris, 24.4; return to Paris, 6.5; Italian War losses published, 28.2; Signor Orlando resigns; and Signor Nitti forms new Cabinet, 20.6; King signs and ratifies Peace Treaty, 7.10.

LEAGUE OF NATIONS.
Recognised as part of Treaty, 25.1; Covenant approved, 14.2; published, 15.2; Comes into being, 28.4; Senator Knox's resolution re, 10.6.
LIEBKNECHT, HERR KARL.
Shot dead, 15.1.
LUXEMBURG, GRAND DUCHY.
Proclaimed a Republic, 11.1; New Grand Duchess succeeds, 14.1; Referendum taken, 28.9; in favour of Grand Duchy, 10.10.
LUXEMBURG, FRÄULEIN ROSA.
Shot dead, 15.1.

MARSHALL, LIEUT.-GENERAL SIR W. (Mesopotamia).
Despatch of 1.10.18 (1.4.-30.9.18) published, 21.2; Despatch of 1.2.19 (1.10-31.12.18) published 12.4.

MILNE, LIEUT.-GENERAL SIR G.
Final despatch (Macedonia—1.10.17-11.11.18) published, 23.1.

MILNER, VISCOUNT.
Mission to Egypt proposed, 28.4; Arrives in Egypt, 3.12.

MONTENEGRO.
Skupshtina deposes King Nicholas, 20.4.

MURMAN EXPEDITION (v. Russian Territories).

ORLANDO, SIGNOR (v. Italy).

OTTOMAN TERRITORIES.
Medina capitulates to King of Hejaz, 13.1; British administer Baghdad railway, French the European Turkish railways, 10.1; Turks completely evacuate the Caucasus, 8.1; Greeks fight Turks at Smyrna, 24.1; Sir W. Marshall's despatch of 1.10.18 published, 21.2; Damad Ferid Pasha Grand Vizir, 3.3; Adalia occupied by Italians, 29.3; Sir W. Marshall's final despatch of 1.2.19, published, 12.4; Greek troops landed at Smyrna, 13.5; Rising in Kurdistan: British officers captured, 25.5; British troops rescued, 18.6; Turkish Army advancing on Greeks in Asia Minor (Aidin), 21.5; Turkey's case and Allies' reply published, 27,6; Ali Riza Pasha Grand Vizir, 14.10.

PEACE CONFERENCE (v. General).
Commenced, 12.1; Treaty signed, 28.6.

PEACE TREATY (v. also General).
Of Versailles, terms presented to Germans and published, 7.5; Signed, 28.6; Ratified by Germany, 7.7; By Italy, 7.10; By Great Britain, 10.10; By France, 13.10; With Austria, signed, 10.9; Ratified by Austria, 18.10; With Bulgaria, signed, 27.11.

POLAND.
Troubles in Warsaw, coup d'état under Prince Sapieha crushed, 5.1; M. Paderewski Prime Minister, 17.1; Civil and Military Allied Mission to be sent to, 22.1; Arrives, 12.2; Fighting in Posen and Lemberg, 23.2; M. Paderewski resigns, 18.5; Gen. Pilsudski prepares to attack Ukrainians, 19.5; Allies present Draft Treaty to, 27.5.

PRINKIPO PROPOSAL.
Approved by Peace Conference, 22.1; Falls to the ground, c. 1.2.

ROBERTSON, GENERAL SIR W.
Appointed G.O.C.i.C. Rhine, 13.3; Arrives Cologne, 19.4; Takes over from General Plumer, 22.4.

RUMANIA.
Losses in the War published, 1.3; Rumanians beat Bolsheviks on River Dniester, c. 24.3; Rumanians advancing in Hungary, 21.4; Reach the Theiss River, 26, 29.4; Offer terms, 5.5; Rumanian advance stopped by Allies, 8.5.

RUSHDI PASHA (v. Egypt).

RUSSIAN TERRITORIES.
Bolshevist forces advancing on Riga and Reval, fighting in the Ukraine, 2.1; Bolsheviks take Riga, 4.1; British squadron leaves the Baltic, 7.1; British force sent to Caucasus, 7.1; Large anti-Bolshevik armies in field in S., 12.1; Bolsheviks moving on Poland, 13.1; Admiral Kolchak remains C.-i.-C. in Siberia, French General Janin in direction of operations, 13.1; Split between MM. Lenin and Trotski, 23.1; Bolsheviks attack Archangel front, 19 to 25.1, Allies withdraw; Allies again retreat, 29, 30.1; Allies defeat Bolsheviks in fight for Merv, 16.1; General Russki and hostages murdered at Piatigorsk, c. 27.1; More fighting at Archangel, 10, 11.2; General Denikin routs Bolsheviks in N. Caucasus, 3 to 9.2; Bolsheviks invade Esthonia, 14.2; Ukrainians beat Bolsheviks near Kiev, 12.2; Allies beat Bolsheviks 60 miles S. of Murman, c. 20.2; Russian War losses published, 1.3; Fighting 140 miles S.E. of Archangel, Allies withdraw a mile, 1 to 9.3; Attempt on Trotski's life, 9.3; Bolshevik reverses in Urals, Esthonia and Kurland, c. 15.3; French and Allies evacuating Odessa, c. 17.3; Fighting at Nikolaiev (near Odessa), c. 15.3; Kolchak advances in Urals, 15.3; Rumanians beat Bolsheviks on Dniester, c. 24.3; British nervousness re Archangel and Murman fronts, 4.4; Bolsheviks attack Archangel front, 31.3, 1.4, 5.4, repulsed; General Maynard at Murman stops Bolshevik revolt, 31.3; British voluntary relief force being sent to Archangel, 9.4, etc.; Odessa evacuated by Allies, announced, 8.4; Bolsheviks enter Crimea, c. 8.4; Lenin offers alliance to Germany with Hungary v. Entente and Poland, c. 30.3; Bolsheviks occupy Yalta (Crimea), 12.4; Bolsheviks retire on Ural front, 10 to 15.4; repulsed; Siberians under Kolchak advancing W., 14.4; Allied set-back in S. Russia, 15.4; Russian troops under Maynard rout Bolsheviks at Lake Vigo, 17.4; Dr. Nansen's offer of food, 17.4; British forces have evacuated Transcaspia (except Krasnovodsk) reported, 19.4; Siberians reach 100 miles E. of Kazan and drive back Bolsheviks, 21.4; Successful work on Archangel front reported, 23.4; Bolsheviks attack Arch-

1920.

1. Peace with Germany was finally ratified on January 10.
2. The Turkish Treaty was handed to the Ottoman representatives at the French Foreign Office on May 11. Its main provisions are as follows :—

Turkey cedes Thrace (except a small portion just outside Constantinople), Tenedos, Imbros, and other islands then occupied by Greece, to Greece ; and also cedes to her the administration of a considerable area in Asia Minor, including Smyrna, Ak Hissar, Aivali, etc., etc. This territory to have a parliament, and may annex itself after five years by plebiscite to Greece.

Turkey recognises the independence of Armenia, Mesopotamia, Syria, and the Hejaz, and confers autonomy on Kurdistan. The President of U.S.A. to fix the Western boundaries of Armenia, whilst Syria, Mesopotamia and Palestine are to be assisted by Mandatory Powers (names not mentioned in the Treaty).

Turkey recognises British, French and Italian Protectorate in Egypt and the Sudan, Tunisia and Marocco, and Libya, the Dodecanese* and Castellorizo respectively.

Commissions to control the Dardanelles, Marmora and Bosporus.
Army to be limited to 50,000 men.
Turkish finances to be controlled by Allied Commission.
Capitulations to be replaced by new legal system.
The Treaty was signed by Turkey at Sèvres on August 10.
3. The Hungarian Treaty was handed to the Hungarian representatives at Versailles on June 4.
4. Peace with Austria was finally ratified on July 16.
5. Peace with Bulgaria was finally ratified on August 9.
An Order in Council defining the Termination of the War cannot be issued until all the above Treaties have been ratified.

---

* Italy subsequently handed over the Dodecanese to Greece.

"BLOOD AND TREASURE."*

In some quarters the belief still lingers that Britain did not do her share in the Great War as a member of the Alliance. This belief is obviously due to ignorance of the facts, and the following brief summary, compiled from official sources, should help to remove it. Many of the figures, necessarily withheld during the continuance of hostilities, are now brought together for the first time.

THE NAVY. In July, 1914, the personnel of the Royal Navy numbered 146,047 officers and men; on November 11th, 1918 (the date of the Armistice), the number stood at 408,316.

In August, 1914, the total tonnage of the Fleet employed in naval services was 4,000,000 tons. During the war some 2,300,000 tons have been built for the Navy at an approximate cost of £300,000,000 sterling, besides a large number of vessels chartered and acquired from private and other sources.

In 1914 mine-sweepers and patrol boats numbered 12; by the end of 1918 they numbered 3,714. There are now 235 dry docks in the British Isles, exclusive of Royal Naval Docks, which have handled 90 per cent. of the maximum tonnage within their capacity. In one month 1,200 warships and auxiliaries completed repairs and refits, and since August, 1915, 47,000 ships have been slipped and docked, exclusive of vessels belonging to Allied nations.

From the outbreak of war until March 12th, 1919, the Navy has been instrumental in transporting overseas for the British and Allied Armies 23,388,228 effectives and 3,336,241 non-effectives with a loss by enemy action of only 4,394†; 192,899 prisoners (including sick and wounded); 2,264,134 animals; 512,400 vehicles; 47,992,839 tons of British military stores; 4,964,811 tons of Allied stores and over 60,000,000 tons of oil and fuel. In addition, 130,000,000 tons of food and other material have been conveyed to this country in British ships, diverted for this purpose from their own trade routes.

The British Fleet was mobilised and ready for action on the first day of the war. From that day until the signature of peace it maintained the blockade of the enemy, without which the war could not have been won, and protected the communications of the Allies. It patrolled incessantly, and in all weathers, the 140,000 square miles of the North Sea, and was in the main responsible for the protection of the entire coast of Europe from Archangel to Alexandria—a distance of 5,000 miles.

In one month British warships proper travelled 1,000,000 sea miles in home waters alone, while auxiliary vessels, including mine-sweepers and patrol boats, covered 6,000,000 sea miles or 250 times the circuit of the globe.

The increasing effectiveness of our blockade is shown by the fact that in 1915 during two months, 256 out of 1,400 ships eluded the patrol squadrons; in the latter half of the following year only 60 out of 3,000 escaped interception. In one month of 1917 not a single vessel trading with neutral countries crossed the North Atlantic and Arctic oceans without being held up and examined.

Before the entry of America it fell to the British Navy to deal single-handed with the enemy's submarine campaign—undoubtedly the most serious menace of the war, directed indiscriminately against the Allies and neutrals. Out of some 200 enemy submarines accounted for, about 150 were destroyed by British effort. The number of British submarines lost was 54.

* Acknowledgments to Mr. R. Sheridan, (late of the Ministry of Information).
† Including those drowned in Hospital Ships.

The British Fleet was not, as has sometimes been suggested, content with a passive rôle. It lost no opportunity of attacking the enemy's naval forces wherever they were found at large. On December 8, 1914, a squadron under von Spee was destroyed at the Falkland Islands. Two months later the *Blücher* and other ships were encountered by Beatty and sunk off the Dogger Bank. The enemy did not again expose his main Fleet until May 31, 1916, when it was engaged by the Grand Fleet off Jutland Bank. The losses on both sides were considerable, but the conditions were unfavourable to pursuit and the German Fleet was only saved by mist and darkness from annihilation. The decisive character of the British victory is shown by the fact that the command of the sea remained with the Allies, and since the action the German surface ships never left their harbours until after the Armistice, when practically the entire navy surrendered for internment without striking a blow.

British naval casualties* reported for the period August 4, 1914—May 31, 1919, are as follows :—

	Officers.	Men.	Total.
Killed in action and died of wounds ...	2,498	27,446	29,944
Died from other causes	406	11,382	11,788
Wounded	1,582	23,758	25,340

The estimated losses of merchant and fishing tonnage during the war are as follows :—

	Number of vessels.	Gross tonnage.
British	3,154	7,830,855
Allied	1,824	2,699,921
Neutral	1,463	2,320,000

The number of British lives lost in merchant and fishing vessels was 15,313.

THE ARMY. In August, 1914, the British Land Forces comprised :—

Regulars (U.K. and Channel Islands)...	253,045
Reserves	211,362
Territorials (partly trained)	269,107
Total	733,514

The first Expeditionary Force of 160,000 men arrived in France in mid-August, 1914, and took part with decisive effect in the famous retreat and subsequent battle of the Marne.

On August 8 (four days after the declaration of war) Lord Kitchener opened his recruiting campaign. In October, 1915, Lord Derby's scheme of recruiting was started and met with such success that within two months 2,521,661 attested for immediate or deferred enlistment. By March 2, 1916, when compulsory service became law, the number of men voluntarily enlisted was 5,041,000.

The general effect of the various Acts passed from 1916 to 1918 was to make military service compulsory on all unmarried and subsequently on all married men in Great Britain, between the ages of 18 and 41, unless exempted for medical or other special reasons. The significance of this achievement will be better appreciated when it is remembered that compulsory service was an innovation in the life of the British people, who have always been opposed to it on principle and relied on voluntary forces for the defence of their Empire.

The high-water mark of the British effort was reached in the spring of 1918, when to meet the grave situation created by the German offensive an Act was passed raising the age limit to 50 and cancelling previous exemptions. A number of units were transferred from other theatres to the Western front, and within a month from March 21 no fewer than 355,000 were sent across the Channel. The maximum feeding strength of the British Army in France at any one time is estimated at 2,700,000 men.

The total number of enlistments in the British Empire, including the strength existing in 1914, amounts to 7,165,280, to which must be added 1,524,187 Indian and other coloured troops, making a grand total of 8,689,467.

---

* Including Marines and Royal Naval Division, and Royal Naval Air Service up to April 1st, 1918.

The following tables show (a) the total forces of the United Kingdom existing in August, 1914, and subsequently recruited, (b) enlistments for the British Dominions,* (c) the distribution of the British Forces in the various theatres of war :—

(a)

Country.	Existing in August, 1914.	Since recruited.	Total.
United Kingdom ...	733,514	—	733,514
England	—	4,006,158	
Scotland	—	557,618	
Wales and Monmouth	—	272,924	
Ireland	—	134,202	
			4,970,902
			5,704,416

(b)

Country.	Total in arms.	Sent overseas.
Canada	628,964	418,035
Australia and Tasmania	416,809	330,000
New Zealand	220,099	100,471
South Africa	136,070	74,196
Newfoundland	11,922	10,610
West Indies (to end of 1917)	16,000	—
Other Dominions	31,000	—
	1,460,864	—

(c)

	Maximum strength.	Total employed.
Western Front (France and Belgium) ...	2,046,901	5,399,563
Italy	132,667	145,764
Salonika	285,021	404,207
Gallipoli (Dardanelles)	127,737	468,987
Egypt and Palestine	432,857	1,192,511
Mesopotamia	447,531	889,702
Other Theatres	293,095	475,210

Casualties in the British Forces reported up to July 13, 1919, are as follows :—

Theatre of operations.	Killed (including died of wounds and other causes).	Wounded.	Missing (including prisoners).	Total.
France	616,552	1,869,279	239,480	2,725,411
Italy	1,639	4,237	316	6,192
Dardanelles ...	31,035	73,381	7,624	112,040
Salonika ...	9,714	16,923	2,576	29,213
Mesopotamia ...	34,643	52,568	14,728	101,939
Egypt	18,588	37,973	3,643	60,204
East Africa ...	11,078	7,928	575	19,581
Afghanistan ...	120	383	2	505
N. Russia and Vladivostok ...	215	264	114	603
Other Theatres ...	823	1,515	959	3,297
	724,407	2,064,451	270,117	3,058,985

* These figures include certain forms of auxiliary service not included in the figures for the United Kingdom.

THE AIR SERVICES. The following tables show (a) the growth of personnel, (b) the output of machines and engines at different stages of the war.

(a)

	Period.	Officers.	Other Ranks.	Total.
R.F.C. and R.N.A.S.	August, 1914 ...	285	1,835	2,120
	December, 1915	2,904	24,794	27,698
	December, 1916	9,318	74,306	83,624
	December, 1917	20,287	147,289	167,576
R.A.F.	October, 1918 ...	27,906	263,842	291,748

(b)

Period.		Aeroplanes.	Seaplanes.	Engines.
August-December, 1914 ...	...	193	52	99
January-December, 1915 ...	...	1,680	252	1,721
January-December, 1916 ...	...	5,716	433	5,363
January-December, 1917 ...	...	13,554	867	11,536
January-October, 1918 ...	...	27,282	1,139	19,180

Since July, 1916, on the Western front and January, 1918, on all other fronts* 4,849 enemy machines were destroyed and 2,428 brought down out of control by British airmen, in addition to 631 unanalysed ; the loss of British machines was only 2,782. 7,965 tons of bombs were dropped, slightly under 12 million rounds were fired at ground targets and slightly under half a million photographs were taken from the air.†

Though spared the calamity of invasion, Great Britain has been 12 times bombarded from the sea and 108 times attacked from the air—51 times by airships and 57 times by aeroplanes. By these raids 1,260 persons have been killed and 3,490 injured, and the estimated damage to civilian property exceeds £3,000,000.

MUNITIONS. The Ministry of Munitions was formed in June, 1915, to stimulate and control production of war material, which was then very far below the requirements of the Army. In September, 1915, the headquarters staff numbered 1,700 ; on the date of the armistice the number employed was 25,000, of whom 60 per cent. were men. The number of persons engaged on munition work prior to the war is estimated at 50,000 ; about the date of the armistice the numbers so employed were 2,300,000 men and 900,000 women.

Such was the stimulus given to the production of war material that by the time of the German offensive of April, 1918, practically every loss was replaced within a fortnight. In August, when the British offensive began, the expenditure of gun ammunition was 2,900,000 rounds a week, while at the culmination of the fighting in October the maximum expenditure for one week was 3,500,000 rounds. On the day the British Army broke the Hindenburg line they fired 943,837 shells—a weight of 40,000 tons. This was a greater quantity than was fired throughout the whole 2½ years of the South African war.

The following table illustrates the growth of output following on the establishment of the Ministry :—

Guns—				1915 (3rd quarter).	1918 (3rd quarter).
Light ...	...	...	...	903	1,949
Medium	...	...	...	195	437
Heavy	...	...	...	20	678
Machine Guns	...	...	...	1,719	33,507
Rifles	...	...	...	176,239	287,755
Aeroplanes ...	...	...	...	707	8,503
Aeroplane engines ...	...	...	458	7,628
Ammunition (artillery, rounds) ...				2,083,000	15,780,000
Ammunition (small arms, rounds)				368,500,000	746,000,000
Propellants (tons) ...	...	...		10,470	43,601
High Explosives (tons)	...	...		3,309	15,816

---

* No records are available of results obtained prior to these dates.
† For further details of the work of the Air Force see the White Paper " Synopsis of British Air Effort during the War " (Cmd. 100).

Total production during the war :—

		Rifles	...	...	...	3,954,200
Guns (new)	 25,430	Aeroplanes	...	...		52,000
Guns (repaired) ...	... 9,170	Ammunition (gun-r'ds)				162,553,800
Machine Guns ...	... 239,850					

The following table shows the supply of railway material furnished by the British Government —

Theatre	Miles of track laid.		Locomotives supplied.	Wagons supplied.
	Broad gauge	Narrow gauge		
France	3,019	1,904	2,938	68,493
Italy	...	80	31	240
Salonika	30	140	173	5,031
Mesopotamia	155	621	191	3,960
Egypt and Palestine	420	...	...	...
German South-West Africa ...	430	...	...	...
German East Africa	80	...	...	...
Total	4,134	2,745	3,333	77,724

MEDICAL SERVICES. The rapid growth of the army called for a corresponding expansion of the medical services. The elaborate British system for the evacuation of the wounded and their treatment in progressive stages from the clearing stations in the field to the base hospitals, and their transport overseas to hospitals at home, was perfected during the war and has generally been adopted as the standard method of dealing with casualties. The regular military services have been reinforced by large numbers of civilian doctors, trained nurses, and voluntary helpers of both sexes working under the Joint Committee of the two principal British Societies, the British Red Cross and the Order of St. John of Jerusalem. The efficiency of their labours is proved by the fact that the British Army in France lost only 3,000 men by disease in three years, as compared with 50,000 deaths from disease during the South African war.

The following tables illustrate (a) the growth of personnel in various branches of the medical services, (b) the material provided through the agency of the Joint Committee.

(a)

	1914.	1918.
Royal Army Medical Corps : Officers	3,168	16,330
Royal Army Medical Corps : Other ranks	13,063	131,099
Nurses, trained	2,607	13,218
Voluntary Aid Detachments (women)	—	11,601
Royal Army Veterinary Corps : Officers	197	1,356
Royal Army Veterinary Corps : Other ranks ...	332	27,861

(b)

Motor Ambulances provided	3,415
Motor Ambulances sent overseas	2,750
Hospitals and convalescent homes maintained abroad ...	24
Hospital beds found in United Kingdom	91,650
Trained nurses employed	1,638
Articles of clothing, bedding, etc., sent out	10,940,950
Spent on surgical dressings, appliances, etc.	£2,883,790
Spent on transport of wounded	£1,735,400
Spent on parcels of food for British prisoners ...(a week)	£50,000
Total spent on Red Cross work to October, 1918	£14,500,000

WOMEN'S WORK. Before the war Great Britain had approximately 200,000 female workers, mostly employed in the textile industries. By the end of the war over 5,000,000 British women were engaged in 1,701 different kinds of work previously done by men. In no other country was the experiment of enrolling women for non-combatant services made on so extensive a scale and with such successful results.

The following table shows the numbers engaged in various forms of national service (other than nursing and munitions) at the date of the Armistice :—

	Officers.	Other ranks.
Army (Queen Mary's Army Auxiliary Corps) ...	1,077	39,565
Navy (Women's Royal Naval Service)	450	5,578
Air Force (Women's Royal Air Force)	532	23,483
Land Army	180	14,754
Government Service	—	220,000

SUPPLIES TO THE ALLIES. The following table shows the value (in pounds sterling) of the commodities shipped from the United Kingdom to the Allies during the war. It does not include shipments from other parts of the British Empire nor goods supplied by credits in Allied and neutral countries :—

	FRANCE. £	ITALY. £	RUSSIA. £
Armaments	14,637,427	11,815,737	51,709,804
Explosives and Chemicals	12,476,763	9,385,271	6,398,331
Naval Supplies	13,152,692	3,152,229	4,677,095
Aviation Material	3,033,291	610,603	1,404,233
Mechanical Transport	3,072,620	817,247	5,809,020
Metals	74,724,750	14,723,254	14,711,541
Leather	10,909,470	3,345,769	17,822,869
Cotton, Linen, Wool	27,223,816	12,957,555	12,909,134
Machinery	8,770,861	3,099,219	2,240,621
Medical Supplies	881,764	1,012,550	2,418,622
Oils, Fats, Paints	1,482,032	1,715,511	612,348
Rubber	5,216,348	1,496,355	8,944,548
Foodstuffs and Beverages	25,923,387	3,135,105	96,103
Coal and Coke	104,454,942	31,450,464	5,638,038
Miscellaneous	16,337,855	1,335,688	1,471,889
	322,298,018	100,052,557	136,864,196

	BELGIUM. £	PORTUGAL. £	JAPAN. £
Armaments	7,085,442	239,820	26,650
Explosives and Chemicals	2,741,789	91,756	9,913
Naval Supplies	211,133	80,027	381,120
Aviation Material	100,433	4,950	173,961
Mechanical Transport	1,952,389	368,394	39,663
Metals	2,008,546	978,858	1,734,848
Leather	2,951,179	53,486	2,581
Cotton, Linen, Wool	5,696,403	616,555	21,922
Machinery	2,080,319	215,903	958,219
Medical Supplies	338,384	65,415	79,428
Oils, Fats, Paints	750,711	45,021	9,713
Rubber	59,861	6,387	22,204
Foodstuffs and Beverages	17,285,615	3,184,259	—
Coal and Coke	545,666	2,094,336	—
Miscellaneous	3,113,745	1,342,302	193,189
	46,921,605	9,387,469	3,653,411

	SERBIA. £	RUMANIA. £	GREECE. £
Armaments	667,231	685,980	834,000
Explosives and Chemicals	156,739	111,019	132,003
Naval Supplies	50,072	2,565	172,379
Aviation Material	—	29,125	33,287
Mechanical Transport	31,197	77,038	577,596

	SERBIA.	RUMANIA.	GREECE.
	£	£	£
Metals	32,128	7,769	4,233
Leather	948,790	759,154	70,788
Cotton, Linen, Wool	811,992	293,113	1,774,112
Machinery	29,554	5,171	7,018
Medical Supplies	300,095	20,318	141,075
Oils, Fats, Paints	4,603	40,442	10,770
Rubber	1,997	—	1,173
Foodstuffs and Beverages	5,694,795	13,081	1,829,657
Coal and Coke	—	—	98,985
Miscellaneous	74,847	19,591	359,284
	8,804,040	2,064,366	6,046,360

	U.S.A.	BRAZIL.	TOTAL.*
	£	£	£
Armaments	32,858	—	89,372,385
Explosives and Chemicals	79,926	1,841	31,585,351
Naval Supplies	1,771,685	120,860	23,807,398
Aviation Material	1,906,296	6,020	7,702,199
Mechanical Transport	1,498,954	—	14,294,118
Metals	1,842,848	223	110,768,998
Leather	.116,380	221	36,980,797
Cotton, Linen, Wool	1,434,526	80,152	63,858,704
Machinery	401,742	755	17,809,777
Medical Supplies	424,515	12	5,730,178
Oils, Fats, Paints	212,794	16,985	4,900,930
Rubber	8,683	140	15,757,696
Foodstuffs and Beverages	2,722,916	—	59,884,918
Coal and Coke	945,281	263,458	145,491,170
Miscellaneous	19,514,106	3,846	44,376,342
	32,913,510	494,573	672,320,961

Throughout the war Great Britain has been the principal clearing-house for the supply of war material to the Alliance. By a system of inter-Allied Commissions sitting in London, supplies and tonnage were allotted to each country in proportion to its needs, and wasteful overlapping eliminated. In particular, coal, for which the Allies were almost wholly dependent on Great Britain, was supplied to them at fixed prices, which excluded the possibility of any private profits being made at their expense.

FINANCE†. The direct cost of the war to the belligerents (i.e., the excess over normal peace expenditure) has been estimated at £40,000,000,000. Of this gigantic burden Great Britain has borne, and continues to bear, an incomparably larger part than any other of her allies. Some details of the British expenditure are illustrated by the tables which follow.

Daily average pre-war expenditure on public services :—

		£
April, 1913—March, 1914		541,000
April 1st—November 9th, 1918		7,442,000
Total expenditure August, 1914, to March 31st, 1919		9,531,000,000
Raised by revenue (28.1%)		2,678,000,000
Raised by borrowing (71.9%)		6,853,000,000
Votes of Credit, 1914–1915 (eight months)		362,000,000
„ „ 1915–1916		1,420,000,000
„ „ 1916–1917		2,010,000,000
„ „ 1917–1918		2,450,000,000
„ „ 1918–1919		2,550,000,000
Total Votes of Credit		8,792,000,000

* These totals include small quantities supplied to other Allies.
† See also p. 242.

Loans to Allies :—

									£
France	...	...	...	...	...	...	...	...	434,000,000
Italy	...	...	...	...	...	...	...	...	413,000,000
Russia	...	...	...	...	...	...	...	...	568,000,000
Other Allies	...	...	...	...	...	...	...	...	153,000,000

Total £1,568,000,000

Loans to Dominions £171,000,000

Direct taxation of Incomes :—

	1913.	1919.
Income Tax	1s. 2d. in the £	6s. in the £
Super Tax	6d. in the £	up to 4s. 6d. in the £
Excess Profits Duty	None	40 per cent.
		(reduced from 80 per cent. 1st Jan., 1919.)
Total yield	£47,250,000	£654,000,000

The effect of the war on the taxpayer may be illustrated by the subjoined table relating to the Income Tax (and Super Tax) :—

Earned Income.	Tax before War.			Tax 1919.			Unearned Income.	Tax before War.			Tax 1919.		
£	£	s.	d.	£	s.	d.	£	£	s.	d.	£	s.	d.
161			9	4	12	3	161		1	2	6	3	0
200	1	10	0	9	0	0	200	2	6	8	12	0	0
300	5	5	0	20	5	0	300	8	3	4	27	0	0
400	9	0	0	31	10	0	400	14	0	0	42	0	0
500	13	2	6	45	0	0	500	20	8	4	60	0	0
800	30	0	0	120	0	0	800	46	13	4	150	0	0
1,000	37	10	0	150	0	0	1,000	58	6	8	187	10	0
2,000	75	0	0	450	0	0	2,000	116	13	4	525	0	0
5,000	291	13	4	1,787	10	0	5,000	291	13	4	1,787	10	0
50,000	4,091	13	4	25,187	10	0	50,000	4,091	13	4	25,187	10	0
100,000	8,258	6	8	51,437	10	0	100,000	8,258	6	8	51,437	10	0

In the year 1919–1920 it was estimated that :—

Income Tax (including Super Tax) would yield £354,000,000

Excess Profits Duty (and Munitions Levy) would yield £300,000,000

£654,000,000

and that £547,100,000 would be derived from other sources, which include indirect taxation, making a total revenue of £1,201,100,000.

Indirect taxation :—

				1914.	1919.
Tea (lb.)				5d.	1s.*
Cocoa (raw, cwt.)				9s. 4d.	42s.*
Coffee (raw, cwt.)				14s.	42s.*
Chicory (raw, cwt.)				12s. 1d. and 13s. 3d.	38s. 6d. and 39s. 8d.*
Sugar (cwt.)				10d.—1s. 10d.	11s. 2d.—25s. 8d.*
Motor Spirit (gallon)				1½d. and 3d.	3d. and 6d.*
Beer (standard barrel, 36 gall.) ...				7s. 9d.	70s.
Spirits (gallon)				14s. 9d.—25s. 1d.	50s.—87s. 7d.*
Tobacco (raw, imported, lb.) ...				3s. 8d.—4s. 1½d.	8s. 2d.—9s. 1d.*
Tobacco (manuf., imported, lb.) ...				4s. 5d.—7s.	9s. 9½d.—15s. 7d.*
Clocks, watches, motor cars and cycles, musical instruments (ad valorem)					33⅓ per cent.*
Cinema Films (linear foot) ...					½d.—5d.*
Matches (ten thousand)					3s. 4d.—5s. 2d.
Table Waters and Cider (gallon) ...					2d.—8d.

* These duties are to be reduced when the goods are consigned from, and grown, produced or manufactured in the British Empire.

Railway fares and postal charges have been increased by 50 per cent. or more, and a tax of 1½d. to 4d. in the shilling is levied on all tickets for entertainments. Along with the increase in taxation, the prices of all necessaries of life have risen, while the purchasing power of money, as elsewhere, has declined. Moreover, certain trade restrictions, imposed by the events of war, have added to the burdens of the tax-payer. The sum due to be spent on war pensions alone is estimated at £100,000,000 a year.

"Before America entered the war," said the Chancellor of the Exchequer in 1918, "we had to mortgage every security we possessed. We had risked our credit to the last shilling to finance not ourselves, but our Allies."

The price paid in Blood and Treasure has been heavy, but if it has helped to lay the foundations of a better world order in which the security of a League of Nations has replaced the menace of German militarism, the sacrifice of Britain and her Allies will not have been made in vain.